The Natural Law Reader

The Natural Law Reader

Edited by

Jacqueline A. Laing
and Russell Wilcox

WILEY Blackwell

This edition first published 2014
© 2014 Blackwell Publishing Ltd

Blackwell Publishing was acquired by John Wiley & Sons in February 2007. Blackwell's publishing program has been merged with Wiley's global Scientific, Technical, and Medical business to form Wiley-Blackwell.

Registered Office
John Wiley & Sons, Ltd, The Atrium, Southern Gate, Chichester, West Sussex, PO19 8SQ, UK

Editorial Offices
350 Main Street, Malden, MA 02148-5020, USA
9600 Garsington Road, Oxford, OX4 2DQ, UK
The Atrium, Southern Gate, Chichester, West Sussex, PO19 8SQ, UK

For details of our global editorial offices, for customer services, and for information about how to apply for permission to reuse the copyright material in this book please see our website at www.wiley.com/wiley-blackwell.

The right of Jacqueline A Laing and Russell Wilcox to be identified as the authors of the editorial material in this work has been asserted in accordance with the UK Copyright, Designs and Patents Act 1988.

Library of Congress Cataloguing-in-Publication Data is available upon request

A catalogue record for this book is available from the British Library.

Cover image: Justice by Raphael, detail from ceiling, Stanza della Segnatura, Vatican.
Photo © 2013 Scala, Florence
Cover design by www.simonlevy.co.uk

Set in 10/12pt Minion by SPi Publisher Services, Pondicherry, India
Printed in Malaysia by Ho Printing (M) Sdn Bhd

1   2014

Jacqueline Laing dedicates this volume to her husband, Paul, and her parents.
Russell Wilcox dedicates this volume to his parents and the memory of his grandfather.

Contents

Acknowledgements

The editors would like to thank their families for all their patience and support that they have shown over the years. Dr Paul M. King read much of the present manuscript at the typesetting stage and is owed a considerable debt of thanks. Dr Jeff Dean and the staff at Wiley-Blackwell have displayed professionalism throughout the project. Finally, Russell Wilcox wishes also, and in particular, to acknowledge the support of Dr Denis Chang CBE SC, JP, through whose kind generosity his work on this project was made possible.

1

General Introduction

The purpose of the present volume is to collect together a representative and wide-ranging series of readings that demonstrates the intellectual wealth of natural law thinking in the Western world. The tradition has animated Western ethical, political, and jurisprudential development since the time of ancient Greece. In *Antigone*, Sophocles refers to that immutable unwritten law which, like justice, was neither born today nor yesterday and springs from the creator of all things.[1] In the *Apology*, a dialogue concerning the death of his beloved teacher, Socrates, Plato tells us that Socrates was expected by the corrupt leaders of his time, the Thirty Tyrants, to collaborate in the arrest and wrongful execution of the innocent Leon of Salamis. Socrates regards this as not merely unjust but as a threat to his own soul. "The difficulty, my friends," he says, "is not in avoiding death, but in avoiding unrighteousness; for that runs faster than death…. I depart hence condemned by you to suffer the penalty of death, and [my accusers], too, go their ways condemned by the truth to suffer the penalty of villainy and wrong; and I must abide by my award – let them abide by theirs."[2]

For Socrates it is better to suffer than to do evil. Because the body is transient and truth is eternal, it is literally ill-judged to live for transient verities and short-lived satisfactions. This is one of the foundations on which the central tradition of natural law thinking in ethics is based. At the core of that tradition lies a vision of human nature, both as individual and social, which irreducibly manifests the material and immaterial aspects of the human being, giving due proportion to each. The ancients and the medievals see the natural law as both objective and universal owing to the fact that it partakes in a timeless, eternal law that finds expression in the very structure of the knowable universe. To regard the cosmos thus, as having a moral as well as a physical order that can be put out of balance by wrongdoing, is not,

[1] Sophocles, *Antigone*, tr. F. Storr (London: William Heinemann, 1912).
[2] Plato, *Apology*, in *The Dialogues of Plato*, Volume 2, tr. Benjamin Jowett, 3rd edition (Oxford: Oxford University Press, 1892).

The Natural Law Reader, First Edition. Edited by Jacqueline A. Laing and Russell Wilcox.
© 2014 Blackwell Publishing Ltd. Published 2014 by Blackwell Publishing Ltd.

of course, a new idea. It has echoes throughout the many traditional religious and cosmological systems of the world. The claims of the central tradition have the potential to resonate, therefore, far more broadly than the selections brought together in the present reader might, at first sight, suggest. Indeed, if space permitted, and its central claims were vindicated, the vision it embodies would naturally provide us with a way into the metaphysics, ethics, politics, and jurisprudence of many of the great sacred traditions of the world. As all selections must by their very nature have a focus, however, ours is limited in scope to presenting some of the more important mainstays of the tradition as it originally, and explicitly, unfolded in Western thought, along with instances of its continued survival among more recent and contemporary thinkers.

Although the natural law tradition has been at the heart of Western philosophical thinking, it has not been without its detractors. Utilitarians, like Jeremy Bentham, distrust it and liberals revile it. Empiricists, like David Hume, reject it outright, regarding it an illicit attempt to derive an 'ought' from an 'is', while many, though by no means all,[3] Marxist or Marxist-inspired thinkers regard it as much an opiate and instrument of oppression as any religion. Thus it is sometimes complained that the natural law tradition appears to afford a moral justification for existing social and economic structures and their legal systems.[4] This need not be so. The tale of the death of Socrates and many of the readings contained herein suggest that the tradition involves a critical approach to the conduct of philosophy, law, ethics, and politics. This is precisely because it is rooted in metaphysics. Its general insistence that there are objective, universal, timeless, and eternal verities stands in stark contrast to the schools of thought that doubt that this could ever be so. Amongst the common characteristics of the central tradition, then, are at least four commitments within ethical and jurisprudential discourse, those to: intelligibility, immutability, universality, and objectivity. Our readings in the classical, early Christian, medieval, early modern, and modern sections of the present volume serve to draw out the continued emphasis of the tradition upon these features.

For later thinkers, like Thomas Hobbes and John Locke, the term 'natural law', in contrast, is principally allied to the idea of the social contract and so, for us, their versions mark a move away from the core tradition. Accordingly, our selection of texts contains little of the social contractarian understanding of ethics, politics, and law. Although certain aspects of human law do derive from a social contract or may be thought to be essentially conventional, contracts and constructs by no means exhaust the natural law. Indeed, the social contractarian account leaves us at a loss as to how to explain and reject some of the injustices into which we have been given insight throughout history and perhaps most starkly in the twentieth century. Because the paradigmatic tradition has a discrete integrity all of its own and because there has been a revival of interest in it since World War II, we are concerned to look at contemporary and historical explorations within this tradition. We do not deny that there is a series of fundamentally different philosophical formulations in Western legal thought often falling under the title of "natural law." It is not, however, our purpose in the current volume to cover each of these conflicting versions. Instead, we concentrate on

---

[3] See, for example, E. Bloch, *Natural Law and Human Dignity* (Cambridge, MA: MIT Press, 1986). More recently, see also T. Burns, *Aristotle and Natural Law* (London: Continuum, 2011).

[4] K. Marx and F. Engels, *The German Ideology* ed. C. J. Arthur, (NY: International Publishers 1947 2005 ed.) p. 65 (Part I B) "The ideas of the ruling class are in every epoch the ruling ideas" often presented by the elite as an "eternal law".

[handwritten marginalia: "introduction"; "Eastern traditions"; "Joys into Rel text classification etc"; "can be understood, unchanging, universal, objective"; "this deals specifically with rules of law"]

[handwritten note at bottom:] Why don't people believe in natural law? - Science, differentiation between moral + material world, plural world   - thre bk of thre in power

what we regard as the most enduring of these traditions, those that can make claim to falling within what we call the paradigmatic or central natural law tradition. As such, we postulate a departure in the history of the use of the term 'natural law' and only touch upon these alternative traditions of usage insofar as they help to explain movement away from the central tradition.

In characterizing the focus of the present reader as the central natural law tradition, then, we mean to refer to that body of thinking which takes as its standard of reference the moral, legal, and political theorizing of Thomas Aquinas. In part this is because of the truism, baldly stated by Mark Murphy, that "if any moral theory is a theory of natural law it is Aquinas,"[5] but it is also because of the coherence such a focus gives to a selection that, even under present limitations, threatened constantly to expand to unmanageable proportions. Yet neither conventional usage nor editorial expediency exhausts the deeper rationale of our chosen agenda. For that, it is necessary to come to an appreciation of the uniquely summative nature of Aquinas' mind. Owing as much to fortuity as to undoubted native genius, Aquinas represents a confluence of the three great currents of antiquity, flowing respectively through Athens, Rome, and Jerusalem, whose animating spirit it was his peculiar achievement to express in a synthesis of astonishing scope, complexity, and rigor. We have confined our selection almost exclusively to thinkers who have either anticipated that synthesis or who continue, more or less, to accept the theoretical and metaphysical foundations upon which it is based.

Ours is not, then, a neutral selection. Rather, it is one situated within, and guided by a broader understanding of, the tradition we find useful and persuasive. That understanding finds expression in a growing body of work making with renewed vigor the argument, always present but previously somewhat marginalized, that it is only as a series of challenges (more or less stable) to the bases of the medieval synthesis, embodied in Aquinas, that the subsequent development of Western intellectual history can be accurately understood.[6] Although it would be wrong to suggest that all the authors of the selections we include here would agree with the wider perspective we adopt, it would be equally disingenuous not to acknowledge that they have, at least in part, been selected

---

[5] M. Murphy, "The Natural Law Tradition in Ethics," *Stanford Encyclopedia of Philosophy (Winter 2011 Edition)*, ed. Edward N. Zalta, http://plato.stanford.edu/archives/win2011/entries/natural-law-ethics/, accessed March 13, 2013.

[6] The most recent work to make such an argument is M.A. Gillespie, *The Theological Origins of Modernity* (Chicago: Chicago University Press, 2008). Amongst other works, see L. Dupre, *The Passage to Modernity* (Yale: Yale University Press, 1993); K. Lowith, *Meaning in History: The Theological Presuppositions of the Philosophy of History* (Chicago: University of Chicago Press, 1949); E. Voeglin, *The New Science of Politics* (Chicago: University of Chicago Press, 1952); E. Voeglin, *From Enlightenment to Revolution* (Durham, NC: Duke University Press, 1975); E. Tiryankian, "The Metacultures of Modernity: Christian, Gnostic, Chthonic," *Theory, Culture and Society* 13, 1 (1996), pp. 99–118; H. De Lubac, *The Drama of Atheist Humanism* (San Francisco: Ignatius Press, 1995); M. Buckley, *At the Origins of Modern Atheism* (Yale: Yale University Press, 1987); W. Cavanaugh, *Theopolitical Imagination* (Edinburgh: T&T Clark, 2003); M. Hanby, *Augustine and Modernity* (London: Routledge, 2003); J. Milbank, *Theology and Social Theory: Beyond Secular Reason* (Oxford: Wiley-Blackwell, 2006); and O. O'Donovan, *The Desire of Nations: Rediscovering the Roots of Political Theology* (Cambridge: Cambridge University Press, 1996). In a related vein, see also E. Gilson, *The Unity of Philosophical Experience* (London: Charles Scribner's Sons, 1937). See also Y. Simon, *The Great Dialogue of Nature and Space* (Carthage Reprint) (South Bend, IN: St. Augustine's Press, 2001); J. Pieper, *The End of Time: A Meditation on the Philosophy of History* (South Bend, IN: St. Augustine's Press, 1998). Less theoretically, see M. Burleigh, *Earthly Powers: The Conflict between Religion and Politics from the French Revolution to the Great War* (London: Harper Perennial, 2006).

Idea logy - something that prevents people from living a human life - the powerful force those) Marxist less powerful to obey

on that basis. At the same time, we have sought to ensure that the inclusion of each selection can be justified on less ambitious grounds as in some way or other simply illuminating or contributing to the central tradition.

With respect especially to the contemporary selections, it is now far less difficult to find suitable material than it once was. Indeed, although the central tradition was viewed, until relatively recently, as something of a Cinderella figure in ethical and jurisprudential circles, over the past thirty years it has undergone a significant revival of interest, mirroring, and drawing upon, a similar revival of interest in the tradition of virtue ethics. It now grounds renewed critical reflection on a wide number of specific policy issues as well as being the subject of intense internal debate on issues of a more profound and abstract nature. It is, in part, in this upsurge of interest that the present volume finds its justification: as the record of a rich vein of enquiry even its most hardened critics can no longer dismiss as a mere historical irrelevance.

In order to emphasize all of this as well as to draw out both the historical significance and the contemporary relevance of the central natural law tradition, we have chosen to organize the following sets of extracts into three broad sections. The first section comprises readings that show the historical continuity and endurance of the central natural law tradition. The second section comprises selections from contemporary or near contemporary debates that seek to re-establish and/or vindicate the central tradition's relevance to current ethical, political, and jurisprudential discourse. Finally, the third section comprises selections that address specific areas of public policy.

2
Historical Readings

2.1 Ancient

[handwritten: Hume: "is does not imply "ought?"]

[handwritten: Natural law issues — power — science — plural]

Introduction

The basic precepts of the natural law tradition find expression, in one form or another, in the conceptions of almost all peoples at all times. The search for truth, both scientific and moral, and the reality of injustice are its fuel. It would be wrong to regard the natural law tradition as one which concerned itself only with jurisprudential and moral questions. Its foundations are in metaphysics and logic as well as in epistemology, ethics, and jurisprudence. The natural law tradition encompasses the eternal law that directs not only the natural physical laws which govern the universe but also the natural moral law which governs men. *[handwritten: - Both physical + spiritual]*

For Sophocles (*c.* 497–406 BC), it refers to that immutable unwritten law which, like justice, was born neither today nor yesterday and springs from the author of all things. Cicero (106–43 BC) regarded it as the highest reason, inherent in nature, which enjoins what ought to be done and forbids the opposite. Regarding law as a force of nature, the intelligence and reason of the wise, Cicero says in *The Laws*:

> The moral power of law, is not only far more ancient than … legal institutions of states and peoples, but it is coeval with God himself, who beholds and governs both heaven and earth. For it is impossible that the divine mind should exist without reason; and divine reason must necessarily be possessed of a power to determine what is virtuous and what is vicious.[1]

For Cicero, the natural law is bound up with right reason. It is "right reason conformable with nature."[2] As such it does not fluctuate with time or public opinion. Whilst attitudes might change, the natural law does not. It is "unchangeable, eternal, whose commands urge us to duty, and whose prohibitions restrain us from evil … This law cannot be

---

[1] Marcus Tullius Cicero, *The Political Works of Marcus Tullius Cicero: Comprising his Treatise on the Commonwealth; and his Treatise on the Laws*, tr. Francis Barham, Esq. (London: Edmund Spettigue, 1841–1842), Volume 1, *The Laws*, Book I, 19.

[2] Ibid., *The Republic*, Book III.

The Natural Law Reader, First Edition. Edited by Jacqueline A. Laing and Russell Wilcox.
© 2014 Blackwell Publishing Ltd. Published 2014 by Blackwell Publishing Ltd.

contradicted by any other law, and is not liable either to derogation or abrogation." This law cannot be altered by the will of any ruling elite or by any public consensus. It does not change depending on where you find yourself.

> Neither the senate nor the people can give us any dispensation for not obeying this universal law of justice.... It is not one thing at Rome and another at Athens; one thing today and another tomorrow; but in all times and nations this universal law must forever reign, eternal and imperishable. It is the sovereign master and emperor of all beings. God himself is its author – its promulgator – its enforcer. He who obeys it not, flies from himself, and does violence to the very nature of man. For his crime he must endure the severest penalties hereafter, even if he avoid the usual misfortunes of the present life.[3]

Heraclitus (c. 535–c. 475 BC), now principally remembered for his thesis that "All is flux," is often thought to reside outside the central natural law tradition. Despite appearances, his insistence that a fundamental and everlasting logos which it is wisdom to comprehend captures an essential aspect of natural law thinking and, for that reason, we have included some of his *Fragments* here. Rejecting hedonism and consensus as the hallmark of true wisdom, he urges us to the eternal law for "all human laws are fed by one divine law, which prevaileth as far as it listeth and suffices for all things and excels all things."[4]

Plato (429–347 BC) and Aristotle (384–322 BC) have a well-established place in the central natural law tradition. Both introduce in their thinking many of the essential components necessary for the development of a natural law account. Plato, like Heraclitus, discusses the transience of bodily existence and the nature of the soul. Dialogues describing the death of Socrates (c. 469–399 BC) (*Apology*, *Crito*, *Phaedo*) highlight the futility of living entirely for the flesh rather than the soul given the transient nature of the former. Reality is superior to appearance, the universal to the particular, form to matter, and the soul to the body. These dialogues involve, however, a close analysis not only of the idea of injustice but also of law, of the soul, and of the good. When asked why he does not escape unjust detention by his persecutors, Socrates refers back to his love of his homeland, the good of law, and the futility of escape. "It is better to suffer than to do evil," says Socrates.

> The difficulty, my friends, is not in avoiding death, but in avoiding unrighteousness; for that runs faster than death. I am old and move slowly, and the slower runner has overtaken me, and my accusers are keen and quick, and the faster runner, who is unrighteousness, has overtaken them. And now I depart hence condemned by you to suffer the penalty of death, and they, too, go their ways condemned by the truth to suffer the penalty of villainy and wrong; and I must abide by my award – let them abide by theirs. I suppose that these things may be regarded as fated, – and I think that they are well.[5]

Socrates' crime consists in "nothing but ... persuading ... old and young alike, not to take thought for [their] persons and properties, but first and chiefly to care about the greatest improvement of the soul.... [V]irtue is not given by money, but that from virtue come money and every other good of man, public as well as private." [6]

---

[3] Ibid.
[4] Heraclitus, *Fragments* (sixth century BC), in Charles M. Bakewell, *Sourcebook of Ancient Philosophy* (New York: Charles Scribner's Sons, 1907), Fragment 113–114.
[5] Plato, *Apology*, in *The Dialogues of Plato*, Volume 2, tr. Benjamin Jowett, 3rd edition (Oxford: Oxford University Press, 1892).
[6] Ibid.

Socrates is an embarrassment to the prevailing corrupt elite of his time. He highlights their misdeeds and urges them to self-reflection. Fearing neither for his income nor for his station, he refuses to collaborate with evildoers in persecuting and executing the innocent Leon of Salamis. Nor does he cease from teaching philosophy and stirring people to consider the effects of their choices upon their souls. The idea he articulates, that it is better to suffer than to do evil, is fundamental to the central natural law tradition. It lies behind the related principle that the end does not justify the means, a principle that is directly at odds with what is known in contemporary philosophy as utilitarianism. He rejects hedonism or the view that happiness is to be found in the maximization of pleasure. Plato, like his teacher, encourages his listeners to the life of the soul, the contemplation of the eternal and the preference for truth.

In the *Republic*, Plato challenges timocracy and oligarchy, the shifting sands of misinformed and often disinformed opinion, so often the touchstone of (what he characterizes as) democracy, and the grotesqueness of tyranny. Genially, he recommends that his listeners dialogue with kindness and good humor. A debate still burns as to whether the *Republic* is regarded by Plato as a paradigm of good governance. Karl Popper in *The Open Society and Its Enemies*,[7] for example, is noted for disliking it as an illiberal and totalitarian state not unlike the tyranny or timocracy Plato himself rejects. Popper's literalist interpretation of the *Republic*, aside from being at odds with Plato's own rejection of four forms of bad government, is also at variance with the dialogic and exploratory character of the text. The literalist interpretation contradicts Plato's profound discussion of the soul and is blind to his metaphor of the Sun, which urges us as individuals out of the world of opinion, shadows, and transient half-truth. Further, if injustice and evil are *not* dwelt upon by philosophers, their reality is likely to intrude into individual and political life as a rank reminder. To complain that Plato describes a class system that is best downplayed as a marketing strategy for the free and open society suggests a false understanding of human vice, injustice, and temptation. When Thrasymachus proclaims that justice is nothing else but the interest of the stronger, he describes a familiar sophistical strategy, one that is far removed from the City of God described by Augustine and an idea that would undermine the City of Man. For Plato, justice is most certainly not merely a reflection of the interests of the ruling power. To understand why justice is not Thrasymachean in character, it is necessary to identify Thrasymachus' error. If one cannot perceive a hole into which one might fall, one is likely to collapse right into it. Accordingly, we do well to meditate upon the dialogues of the *Republic* as a source of truth and a path to the good.

Aristotle's metaphysics and his ethics supply a foundation for the universality and timelessness of the natural law. His teleological approach holds things to be designed for or directed toward an end or purpose. This end or purpose is sometimes referred to as a thing's "final cause." For Aristotle, the highest good for man, his *summum bonum* in the words of Aquinas, is happiness, flourishing, or *eudaimonea*; but not just any happiness. True happiness, or blessedness, consists in virtue. It is this account that has allowed others, such as Aquinas and many contemporary neo-Aristotelians, to develop his natural law theory to supply an account of the basic human goods or good of man. Aristotle expands upon the virtues as understood as a kind of mean between extremes. He gives an analysis of the place of the virtues in the polis. In this way, his alternative

---

[7] Karl Popper, *The Open Society and Its Enemies, Volume 1: The Spell of Plato* (London: Routledge, 1945).

metaphysics can be used to examine the concept of a law which is both objective and universal. If positive law is true law only when it is just, then some standard should be forthcoming for determining this justice. Aristotle's teleological theory allows precisely this fuller account. His description is crucial because his metaphysics has been applied by his disciples down the millennia to give a sophisticated analysis of the natural law. Again, Aristotle's *Politics* discusses the nature of tyranny, oligarchy, and democracy and compares this with constitutional monarchy. As always, he starts with general observations:

> Every state is a community of some kind, and every community is established with a view to some good; for mankind always acts in order to obtain that which they think good. But, if all communities aim at some good, the state or political community, which is the highest of all, and which embraces all the rest, aims at good in a greater degree than any other, and at the highest good.[8]

Aristotle speaks freely of slave and master, which to modern ears will simultaneously disgust and perplex. The reader is invited to consider the significance of this given the collapse of the Roman Empire and its excesses. Given what civilization became in Rome, the actual content of the natural law needs continual consideration when its exponents have such diverse views.

Cicero and Marcus Aurelius (121–180 BC) are included in our selections to remind the reader that the Romans, and in particular the Stoics, had their own natural law theorists. Among the thinkers of ancient Rome are those who insist that there is an eternal and universal law, a higher law that governs man, one that is neither purely hedonistic nor based on transient opinion, consensus, or contract. These writers speak eloquently of this law and give us reason to believe that it is understood well by many and assumed into their very reasoning, even if there are divergences as to the precise ethical content of the law itself.

[8]   Aristotle, *Politics*, tr. Benjamin Jowett (Oxford: Clarendon Press, 1885), Book I, Part I.

2.1.1 Heraclitus
Fragments

[handwritten: ~ 500 bc: - Jewish + Greeks are starting to emerge as monotheistic - Wider, more diverse world]

[handwritten: Logos - objective, reason   Wisdom - subjective]

[handwritten: logic   words   power]

1. This Word [*logos*] is everlasting, but men are unable to comprehend it before they have heard it or even after they have heard it for the first time. Although everything happens in accordance with this Word, they behave like inexperienced men whenever they make trial of words and deeds such as I declare as I analyze each thing according to its nature and show what it is. But other men have no idea what they are doing when awake, just as they forget what they do when they are asleep.

2. One ought to follow the lead of that which is common to all men. But although the Word [*logos*] is common to all, yet most men live as if each had a private wisdom of his own. *[handwritten: - subjective reality]*

4. If happiness consisted in the pleasures of the body, we should call cattle happy when they find grass to eat.

17. Most men have no comprehension even of such things as they meet with, nor do they understand what they experience though they themselves think they do.

23. Were there no injustice men would never have known the name of justice. *[handwritten: - Knowledge of good + evil - bible?]*

27. There await men after death things they do not expect nor dream of.

28. Even he who is most highly esteemed knows and cherishes nothing but opinions. And yet justice shall surely overcome forgers of lies and false witnesses.

29. There is one thing that the best men prize above all – eternal glory above all perishable things. Most men, however, stuff themselves with food like cattle.

32. Wisdom is one and one only. It is both willing and unwilling to be called by the name of Zeus. *[handwritten: - coming from a higher power - or, it is itself a higher power]*

34. Fools even when they hear the truth are like deaf men. Of them the proverb holds true, 'being present they are absent.'

35. Right many things must men know who are lovers of wisdom.

40. Much learning does not teach wisdom, […]

41. Wisdom is one thing. It is to know the thought by which all things through all are guided. *[handwritten: ↳ the Word]*

43. It is more necessary to extinguish wantonness than a conflagration.

[handwritten: where does moral law come from? - Tree of change - all tribes/societies are human beings]

[handwritten: big ass fire]

Charles M. Bakewell, Sourcebook of Ancient Philosophy (New York: Charles Scribner' Sons, 1907).

44. The people ought to fight in defense of the law as they do of their city wall.
45. You could not discover the boundaries of the soul though you tried every path, so deep does its reason [*logos*] reach down.
47. Let us not make random conjectures about the weightiest matters.
49. One to me is as good as ten thousand if he be but the best.
50. It is wise to hearken not to me, but to the Word, and to confess that all things are one.
72. From reason [*logos*], the guide of all things, with which they are most continually associated they are become estranged; and things they meet with every day appear to them unfamiliar.
73. We ought not to act and speak like men asleep.
77. Man is kindled and put out like a light in the night time.
85. It is hard to contend against the heart; for it is ready to sell the soul to purchase its desires.
86. For the most part the knowledge of things divine escapes us because of our unbelief.
90. All things flow; nothing abides.
91. One cannot step twice into the same river.
95. It is best to hide one's folly, but it is hard when relaxed over the wine cups.
102. To god all things are beautiful and good and right; men deem some things wrong and some right.
103. In the circumference of a circle beginning and end coincide.
104. What wisdom, what understanding is theirs? They put their trust in bards and take the mob for their teacher, not knowing that many are bad and few good.
107. Eyes and ears are bad witnesses to men who have not an understanding heart.
108. No one of all the men whose words I have heard has arrived at the knowledge that wisdom is something apart from all other things.
110. It were not good for men that all their wishes should be fulfilled.
111. It is disease that makes health pleasant; evil, good; hunger, plenty; weariness, rest.
112. Wisdom is the foremost virtue, and wisdom consists in speaking the truth, and in lending an ear to nature and acting according to her.
113–
114. Wisdom is common to all […] They who would speak with intelligence must hold fast to the [wisdom that is] common to all, as a city holds fast to its law, and even more strongly. For all human laws are fed by one divine law, which prevaileth as far as it listeth and suffices for all things and excels all things.
116. It is in the power of all men to know themselves and to practice temperance.

✗ Wisdom is part of all things

2.1.2 Sophocles
Antigone

The brothers of Ismene and Antigone battle for control of Thebes. Both die. One brother is buried a hero, while the other is deemed a traitor. King Creon issues an edict requiring that traitors such as he be left to rot. No one is to give him a burial. King Creon has just learned that Antigone has defied his laws by providing a proper burial for her disgraced brother.

ANTIGONE:
Yea, for these laws were not ordained of Zeus,
And she who sits enthroned with gods below,
Justice, enacted not these human laws.
Nor did I deem that thou, a mortal man,
Could'st by a breath annul and override
The immutable unwritten laws of Heaven.
They were not born today nor yesterday;
They die not; and none knoweth whence they sprang.
I was not like, who feared no mortal's frown,
To disobey these laws and so provoke
The wrath of Heaven. I knew that I must die,
E'en hadst thou not proclaimed it; and if death
Is thereby hastened, I shall count it gain.
For death is gain to him whose life, like mine,
Is full of misery. Thus my lot appears
Not sad, but blissful; for had I endured
To leave my mother's son unburied there,
I should have grieved with reason, but not now.
And if in this thou judgest me a fool,
Methinks the judge of folly's not acquit.

[handwritten margin notes: "Do the gods have to follow natural law?"; "— mortal vs divine"; "Going against men's law to abide by natural law?"]

Tr. F. Storr (Cambridge, MA: Harvard University Press, 1912).

2.1.3 The Hippocratic Oath

I swear by Apollo Physician and Asclepius and Hygieia and Panaceia and all the gods and goddesses, making them my witnesses, that I will fulfill according to my ability and judgment this oath and this covenant:

To hold him who has taught me this art as equal to my parents and to live my life in partnership with him, and if he is in need of money to give him a share of mine, and to regard his offspring as equal to my brothers in male lineage and to teach them this art – if they desire to learn it – without fee and covenant; to give a share of precepts and oral instruction and all the other learning to my sons and to the sons of him who has instructed me and to pupils who have signed the covenant and have taken an oath according to the medical law, but no one else.

I will apply dietetic measures for the benefit of the sick according to my ability and judgment; I will keep them from harm and injustice.

I will neither give a deadly drug to anybody who asked for it, nor will I make a suggestion to this effect. Similarly I will not give to a woman an abortive remedy. In purity and holiness I will guard my life and my art.

I will not use the knife, not even on sufferers from stone, but will withdraw in favor of such men as are engaged in this work.

Whatever houses I may visit, I will come for the benefit of the sick, remaining free of all intentional injustice, of all mischief and in particular of sexual relations with both female and male persons, be they free or slaves.

What I may see or hear in the course of the treatment or even outside of the treatment in regard to the life of men, which on no account one must spread abroad, I will keep to myself, holding such things shameful to be spoken about.

If I fulfill this oath and do not violate it, may it be granted to me to enjoy life and art, being honored with fame among all men for all time to come; if I transgress it and swear falsely, may the opposite of all this be my lot.

Translation by Ludwig Edelstein. From *The Hippocratic Oath: Text, Translation, and Interpretation* by Ludwig Edelstein (Baltimore: Johns Hopkins University Press, 1943). Reprinted with permission of The Johns Hopkins University Press.

2.1.4 Plato
Apology

Socrates' Defense

How you have felt, O men of Athens, at hearing the speeches of my accusers, I cannot tell; but I know that their persuasive words almost made me forget who I was – such was the effect of them; and yet they have hardly spoken a word of truth […] Well, then, I will make my defence, and I will endeavor in the short time which is allowed to do away with this evil opinion of me which you have held for such a long time; and I hope I may succeed, if this be well for you and me, and that my words may find favor with you. But I know that to accomplish this is not easy – I quite see the nature of the task. Let the event be as God wills: in obedience to the law I make my defence. — natural or man law?

I will begin at the beginning, and ask what the accusation is which has given rise to this slander of me, […] What do the slanderers say? They shall be my prosecutors, and I will sum up their words in an affidavit. "Socrates is an evil-doer, and a curious person, who searches into things under the earth and in heaven, and he makes the worse appear the better cause; and he teaches the aforesaid doctrines to others." […] After this I went to one man after another, being not unconscious of the enmity which I provoked, and I lamented and feared this: but necessity was laid upon me – the word of God, I thought, ought to be considered first. […]

[Socrates visits the politicians, the poets and the artisans and finds that their ignorance overshadows their understanding so that they may not be said to possess wisdom.]

This investigation has led to my having many enemies of the worst and most dangerous kind, and has given occasion also to many calumnies, and I am called wise, for my hearers always imagine that I myself possess the wisdom which I find wanting in others: but the truth is, O men of Athens, that God only is wise; and in this oracle he means to say that the wisdom of men is little or nothing; he is not speaking of Socrates, he is only using my name as an illustration, as if he said, He, O men, is the wisest, who, like Socrates, knows that his wisdom is in truth worth nothing. And so I go my way, obedient to the god, and make inquisition into the wisdom of anyone, whether citizen or stranger, who appears to be wise; and if he is not wise, then in vindication of the oracle I show him that he is not wise; and this occupation quite absorbs me, and I have no time to give either to

The Dialogues of Plato, Volume 2, tr. Benjamin Jowett, 3rd edition (Oxford: Oxford University Press, 1892).

any public matter of interest or to any concern of my own, but I am in utter poverty by reason of my devotion to the god.

[…] And this, O men of Athens, is the truth and the whole truth; I have concealed nothing, I have dissembled nothing. And yet I know that this plainness of speech makes them hate me, and what is their hatred but a proof that I am speaking the truth? […]

I have said enough in my defence against the first class of my accusers; I turn to the second class, […]: these new accusers must also have their affidavit read. What do they say? Something of this sort: – That Socrates is a doer of evil, and corrupter of the youth, and he does not believe in the gods of the state, and has other new divinities of his own. That is the sort of charge; and now let us examine the particular counts. He says that I am a doer of evil, who corrupt the youth; but I say, O men of Athens, that Meletus is a doer of evil, and the evil is that he makes a joke of a serious matter, and is too ready at bringing other men to trial from a pretended zeal and interest about matters in which he really never had the smallest interest. And the truth of this I will endeavor to prove.

[…]

Then, by the gods, Meletus, of whom we are speaking, tell me and the court, in somewhat plainer terms, what you mean! […] do you mean to say that I am an atheist simply, and a teacher of atheism?

I mean the latter – that you are a complete atheist.

That is an extraordinary statement, Meletus. […] And so, Meletus, you really think that I do not believe in any god? _Socrates is monotheistic?

I swear by Zeus that you believe absolutely in none at all.

You are a liar, Meletus, not believed even by yourself. For I cannot help thinking, O men of Athens, that Meletus is reckless and impudent, and that he has written this indictment in a spirit of mere wantonness and youthful bravado. […]

Did ever man, Meletus, believe in the existence of human things, and not of human beings? […] I wish, men of Athens, that he would answer, […] the next question: Can a man believe in spiritual and divine agencies, and not in spirits or demigods?

He cannot.

I am glad that I have extracted that answer, by the assistance of the court; nevertheless you swear in the indictment that I teach and believe in divine or spiritual agencies (new or old, no matter for that); at any rate, I believe in spiritual agencies, as you say and swear in the affidavit; but if I believe in divine beings, I must believe in spirits or demigods; – is not that true? Yes, that is true, for I may assume that your silence gives assent to that. Now what are spirits or demigods? are they not either gods or the sons of gods? Is that true? Yes, that is true.

But this is just the ingenious riddle of which I was speaking: the demigods or spirits are gods, and you say first that I don't believe in gods, and then again that I do believe in gods; that is, if I believe in demigods. For if the demigods are the illegitimate sons of gods, whether by the Nymphs or by any other mothers, as is thought, that, as all men will allow, necessarily implies the existence of their parents. You might as well affirm the existence of mules, and deny that of horses and asses. Such nonsense, Meletus, could only have been intended by you as a trial of me. You have put this into the indictment because you had nothing real of which to accuse me. But no one who has a particle of understanding will ever be convinced by you that the same man can believe in divine and superhuman things, and yet not believe that there are gods and demigods and heroes.

[...]

Someone will say: And are you not ashamed, Socrates, of a course of life which is likely to bring you to an untimely end? To him I may fairly answer: There you are mistaken: a man who is good for anything ought not to calculate the chance of living or dying; he ought only to consider whether in doing anything he is doing right or wrong – acting the part of a good man or of a bad. [...]

For this is the command of God, as I would have you know; and I believe that to this day no greater good has ever happened in the state than my service to the God. For I do nothing but go about persuading you all, old and young alike, not to take thought for your persons and your properties, *but first and chiefly to care about the greatest improvement of the soul. I tell you that virtue is not given by money, but that from virtue come money and every other good of man, public as well as private.* This is my teaching, and if this is the doctrine which corrupts the youth, my influence is ruinous indeed. But if anyone says that this is not my teaching, he is speaking an untruth. Wherefore, O men of Athens, I say to you, [...] either acquit me or not; but whatever you do, know that I shall never alter my ways, not even if I have to die many times.

Men of Athens, do not interrupt, but hear me; there was an agreement between us that you should hear me out. And I think that what I am going to say will do you good: for [...] if you kill such a one as I am, you will injure yourselves more than you will injure me. Meletus and Anytus will not injure me: they cannot; for it is not in the nature of things that a bad man should injure a better than himself. I do not deny that he may, perhaps, kill him, or drive him into exile, or deprive him of civil rights; and he may imagine, and others may imagine, that he is doing him a great injury: but in that I do not agree with him; for the evil of doing as Anytus is doing – of unjustly taking away another man's life – is greater far. And now, Athenians, I am not going to argue for my own sake, as you may think, but for yours, that you may not sin against the God, or lightly reject his boon by condemning me. For if you kill me you will not easily find another like me, who, if I may use such a ludicrous figure of speech, am a sort of gadfly, given to the state by the God; and the state is like a great and noble steed who is tardy in his motions owing to his very size, and requires to be stirred into life. I am that gadfly which God has given the state and all day long and in all places am always fastening upon you, arousing and persuading and reproaching you. And as you will not easily find another like me, I would advise you to spare me. I dare say that you may feel irritated at being suddenly awakened when you are caught napping; and you may think that if you were to strike me dead, as Anytus advises, which you easily might, then you would sleep on for the remainder of your lives, unless God in his care of you gives you another gadfly. And that I am given to you by God is proved by this: – that if I had been like other men, I should not have neglected all my own concerns, or patiently seen the neglect of them during all these years, and have been doing yours, coming to you individually, like a father or elder brother, exhorting you to regard virtue; this I say, would not be like human nature. And had I gained anything, or if my exhortations had been paid, there would have been some sense in that: but now, as you will perceive, not even the impudence of my accusers dares to say that I have ever exacted or sought pay of anyone; they have no witness of that. And I have a witness of the truth of what I say; my poverty is a sufficient witness.

Someone may wonder why I go about in private, giving advice and busying myself with the concerns of others, but do not venture to come forward in public and advise the state. I will tell you the reason of this. You have often heard me speak of an oracle or sign which comes to me, and is the divinity which Meletus ridicules in the indictment. This sign I have had ever since I was a child. The sign is a voice which comes to me and always forbids me to do something which I am going to do, but never commands me to do anything, and this is what stands in the way of my being a politician. And rightly, as I think. For I am certain, O men of Athens, that if I had engaged in politics, I should have perished long ago and done no good either to you or to myself. And don't be offended at my telling you the truth: for the truth is that no man who goes to war with you or any other multitude, honestly struggling against the commission of unrighteousness and wrong in the state, will save his life; he who will really fight for the right, if he would live even for a little while, must have a private station and not a public one.

I can give you as proofs of this, not words only, but deeds, which you value more than words. Let me tell you a passage of my own life, which will prove to you that I should never have yielded to injustice from any fear of death, and that if I had not yielded I should have died at once. I will tell you a story – tasteless, perhaps, and commonplace, but nevertheless true. The only office of state which I ever held, O men of Athens, was that of senator [...] [W]hen the oligarchy of the Thirty was in power, they sent for me and four others into the rotunda, and bade us bring Leon the Salaminian from Salamis, as they wanted to execute him. This was a specimen of the sort of commands which they were always giving with the view of implicating as many as possible in their crimes; and then I showed, not in words only, but in deed, that, if I may be allowed to use such an expression, I cared not a straw for death, and that my only fear was the fear of doing an unrighteous or unholy thing. For the strong arm of that oppressive power did not frighten me into doing wrong; and when we came out of the rotunda the other four went to Salamis and fetched Leon, but I went quietly home. For which I might have lost my life, had not the power of the Thirty shortly afterwards come to an end. And to this many will witness.

Now do you really imagine that I could have survived all these years, if I had led a public life, supposing that like a good man I had always supported the right and had made justice, as I ought, the first thing? No, indeed, men of Athens, neither I nor any other. But I have been always the same in all my actions, public as well as private, and never have I yielded any base compliance to those who are slanderously termed my disciples or to any other. For the truth is that I have no regular disciples: but if anyone likes to come and hear me while I am pursuing my mission, whether he be young or old, he may freely come. Nor do I converse with those who pay only, and not with those who do not pay; but anyone, whether he be rich or poor, may ask and answer me and listen to my words; and whether he turns out to be a bad man or a good one, that cannot be justly laid to my charge, as I never taught him anything. And if anyone says that he has ever learned or heard anything from me in private which all the world has not heard, I should like you to know that he is speaking an untruth. [...]

[...] For if, O men of Athens, by force of persuasion and entreaty, I could overpower your oaths, then I should be teaching you to believe that there are no gods, and convict myself, in my own defence, of not believing in them. But that is not the case; for I do believe that there are gods, and in a far higher sense than that in which any of my accusers believe in them. And to you and to God I commit my cause, to be determined by you as is best for you and me.

The jury finds Socrates guilty.

Socrates' Proposal for his Sentence

There are many reasons why I am not grieved, O men of Athens, at the vote of condemnation. I expected it, and am only surprised that the votes are so nearly equal; for I had thought that the majority against me would have been far larger; but now, had thirty votes gone over to the other side, I should have been acquitted. And I may say that I have escaped Meletus. And I may say more; for without the assistance of Anytus and Lycon, he would not have had a fifth part of the votes, as the law requires, in which case he would have incurred a fine of a thousand drachmae, as is evident.

And so he proposes death as the penalty. And what shall I propose on my part, O men of Athens? Clearly that which is my due. And what is that which I ought to pay or to receive? What shall be done to the man who has never had the wit to be idle during his whole life; but has been careless of what the many care about – wealth, and family interests, and military offices, and speaking in the assembly, and magistracies, and plots, and parties. […]

There is the same objection. I should have to lie in prison, for money I have none, and I cannot pay. And if I say exile (and this may possibly be the penalty which you will affix), I must indeed be blinded by the love of life if I were to consider that when you, who are my own citizens, cannot endure my discourses and words, and have found them so grievous and odious that you would fain have done with them, others are likely to endure me. No, indeed, men of Athens, that is not very likely. And what a life should I lead, at my age, wandering from city to city, living in ever-changing exile, and always being driven out! For I am quite sure that into whatever place I go, as here so also there, the young men will come to me; and if I drive them away, their elders will drive me out at their desire: and if I let them come, their fathers and friends will drive me out for their sakes.

Someone will say: Yes, Socrates, but cannot you hold your tongue, and then you may go into a foreign city, and no one will interfere with you? Now I have great difficulty in making you understand my answer to this. For if I tell you that this would be a disobedience to a divine command, and therefore that I cannot hold my tongue, you will not believe that I am serious; and if I say again that the greatest good of man is daily to converse about virtue, and all that concerning which you hear me examining myself and others, and that the life which is unexamined is not worth living – that you are still less likely to believe. […]

The jury condemns Socrates to death.

Socrates' Comments on his Sentence

Not much time will be gained, O Athenians, in return for the evil name which you will get from the detractors of the city, who will say that you killed Socrates, a wise man; for they will call me wise even although I am not wise when they want to reproach you. If you had waited a little while, your desire would have been fulfilled in the course of nature. For I am far advanced in years, as you may perceive, and not far from death. I am speaking now only to those of you who have condemned me to death. And I have another thing to say to them: You think that I was convicted through deficiency of words – I mean, that if I had thought fit to leave nothing undone, nothing unsaid, I might have gained an acquittal. Not so; the deficiency which led to my conviction was not of words – certainly not. But I had not the boldness or impudence or inclination to address you as you would have liked me to address you, weeping and wailing and lamenting, and saying and doing many things which you have been accustomed to hear from others, and which, as I say, are unworthy of me. But I thought that I ought not to do anything common or mean in the hour of danger: nor do I now repent of the manner of my defence, and I would rather die having spoken after my manner, than speak in your manner and live. For neither in war nor yet at law ought any man to use every way of escaping death. For often in battle there is no doubt that if a man will throw away his arms, and fall on his knees before his pursuers, he may escape death; and in other dangers there are other ways of escaping death, if a man is willing to say and do anything. *The difficulty, my friends, is not in avoiding death, but in avoiding unrighteousness; for that runs faster than death.* I am old and move slowly, and the slower runner has overtaken me, and my accusers are keen and quick, and the faster runner, who is unrighteousness, has overtaken them. And now I depart hence condemned by you to suffer the penalty of death, and they, too, go their ways condemned by the truth to suffer the penalty of villainy and wrong; and I must abide by my award – let them abide by theirs. I suppose that these things may be regarded as fated, – and I think that they are well.

And now, O men who have condemned me, I would fain prophesy to you; for I am about to die, and that is the hour in which men are gifted with prophetic power. And *I prophesy to you who are my murderers, that immediately after my death punishment far heavier than you have inflicted on me will surely await you. Me you have killed because you wanted to escape the accuser, and not to give an account of your lives. But that will not be as you suppose: far otherwise. For I say that there will be more accusers of you than there are now; accusers whom hitherto I have restrained: and as they are younger they will be more severe with you, and you will be more offended at them. For if you think that by killing men you can avoid the accuser censuring your lives, you are mistaken; that is not a way of escape which is either possible or honorable; the easiest and noblest way is not to be crushing others, but to be improving yourselves.* This is the prophecy which I utter before my departure, to the judges who have condemned me.

[…]

Let us reflect in another way, and we shall see that there is great reason to hope that death is a good, for one of two things: – either death is a state of nothingness and utter unconsciousness, or, as men say, there is a change and migration of the soul from this world to another. Now if you suppose that there is no consciousness, but a sleep like the sleep of him who is undisturbed even by the sight of dreams, death will be an unspeakable gain. For if a person were to select the night in which his sleep was undisturbed even by dreams, and were to compare with this the other days and nights of his life, and then were to tell us how many days and nights he had passed in the course of his life better and more pleasantly than this one, I think that any man, I will not say a private man, but even the great king, will not find many such days or nights, when compared with the others. Now if death is like this, I say that to die is gain; for eternity is then only a single night. But if death is the journey to another place, and there, as men say, all the dead are, what good, O my friends and judges, can be greater than this? If indeed when the pilgrim arrives in the world below, he is delivered from the professors of justice in this world, and finds the true judges who are said to give judgment there, [...] that pilgrimage will be worth making. [...] For in that world they do not put a man to death for this; certainly not. For besides being happier in that world than in this, they will be immortal, if what is said is true.

Wherefore, O judges, be of good cheer about death, and know this of a truth – that no evil can happen to a good man, either in life or after death. He and his are not neglected by the gods; nor has my own approaching end happened by mere chance. But I see clearly that to die and be released was better for me; and therefore the oracle gave no sign. For which reason also, I am not angry with my accusers, or my condemners; they have done me no harm, although neither of them meant to do me any good; and for this I may gently blame them.

Still I have a favor to ask of them. When my sons are grown up, I would ask you, O my friends, to punish them; and I would have you trouble them, as I have troubled you, if they seem to care about riches, or anything, more than about virtue; or if they pretend to be something when they are really nothing, – then reprove them, as I have reproved you, for not caring about that for which they ought to care, and thinking that they are something when they are really nothing. And if you do this, I and my sons will have received justice at your hands.

The hour of departure has arrived, and we go our ways – I to die, and you to live. Which is better God only knows.

THE END

2.1.5 Plato
Crito

From *Crito* (*c.* 360 BC)

Persons of the Dialogue: Socrates, Crito
Scene: The Prison of Socrates

SOCRATES	Why have you come at this hour, Crito? it must be quite early.
CRITO	Yes, certainly.
SOCRATES	What is the exact time?
CRITO	The dawn is breaking.
SOCRATES	I wonder the keeper of the prison would let you in.
CRITO	He knows me because I often come, Socrates; moreover, I have done him a kindness.
SOCRATES	And are you only just come?
CRITO	No, I came some time ago.
SOCRATES	Then why did you sit and say nothing, instead of awakening me at once?
CRITO	Why, indeed, Socrates, I myself would rather not have all this sleeplessness and sorrow. But I have been wondering at your peaceful slumbers, and that was the reason why I did not awaken you, because I wanted you to be out of pain. I have always thought you happy in the calmness of your temperament; but never did I see the like of the easy, cheerful way in which you bear this calamity.
SOCRATES	Why, Crito, when a man has reached my age he ought not to be repining at the prospect of death. [...]
CRITO	[...] But, O! my beloved Socrates, let me entreat you once more to take my advice and escape. For if you die I shall not only lose a friend who can never be replaced, but there is another evil: people who do not know you and me will believe that I might have saved you if I had been willing to give money, but that I did not care. Now, can there be a worse disgrace than this – that I should be thought to value money more than the life of a friend? For the many will not be persuaded that I wanted you to escape, and that you refused.

The Dialogues of Plato, Volume 2, tr. Benjamin Jowett, 3rd edition (Oxford: Oxford University Press, 1892).

SOCRATES	But why, my dear Crito, should we care about the opinion of the many? Good men, and they are the only persons who are worth considering, will think of these things truly as they happened.
CRITO	But do you see, Socrates, that the opinion of the many must be regarded, as is evident in your own case, because they can do the very greatest evil to anyone who has lost their good opinion?
SOCRATES	I only wish, Crito, that they could; for then they could also do the greatest good, and that would be well. But the truth is, that they can do neither good nor evil: they cannot make a man wise or make him foolish; and whatever they do is the result of chance.
CRITO	Well, I will not dispute about that; but please do tell me, Socrates, whether you are not acting out of regard to me and your other friends: are you not afraid that if you escape hence we may get into trouble with the informers for having stolen you away, and lose either the whole or a great part of our property; or that even a worse evil may happen to us? Now, if this is your fear, be at ease for in order to save you, we ought surely to run this or even a greater risk; be persuaded, then, and do as I say.
SOCRATES	Yes, Crito, that is one fear which you mention, but by no means the only one. [...] Now you, Crito, are a disinterested person who are not going to die to-morrow. [...] Tell me, then, whether I am right in saying that some opinions, and the opinions of some men only, are to be valued, and other opinions, and the opinions of other men, are not to be valued. I ask you whether I was right in maintaining this?
CRITO	Certainly.
SOCRATES	The good are to be regarded, and not the bad?
CRITO	Yes.
SOCRATES	And the opinions of the wise are good, and the opinions of the unwise are evil?
CRITO	Certainly.
SOCRATES	And what was said about another matter? Was the disciple in gymnastics supposed to attend to the praise and blame and opinion of every man, or of one man only – his physician or trainer, whoever that was?
CRITO	Of one man only.
SOCRATES	And he ought to fear the censure and welcome the praise of that one only, and not of the many?
CRITO	That is clear.
SOCRATES	And he ought to live and train, and eat and drink in the way which seems good to his single master who has understanding, rather than according to the opinion of all other men put together?
CRITO	True.
SOCRATES	And if he disobeys and disregards the opinion and approval of the one, and regards the opinion of the many who have no understanding, will he not suffer evil?
CRITO	Certainly he will.
SOCRATES	And what will the evil be, whither tending and what affecting, in the disobedient person?
CRITO	Clearly, affecting the body; that is what is destroyed by the evil.
SOCRATES	Very good; and is not this true, Crito, of other things which we need not separately enumerate? In the matter of just and unjust, fair and foul, good and evil, which are the subjects of our present consultation, ought we to follow the opinion of the many and to fear them; or the opinion of the one man

who has understanding, and whom we ought to fear and reverence more than all the rest of the world: and whom deserting we shall destroy and injure that principle in us which may be assumed to be improved by justice and deteriorated by injustice; is there not such a principle?

CRITO   Certainly there is, Socrates [...]

SOCRATES   Then, my friend, we must not regard what the many say of us: but what he, the one man who has understanding of just and unjust, will say, and what the truth will say. And therefore you begin in error when you suggest that we should regard the opinion of the many about just and unjust, good and evil, honorable and dishonorable. Well, someone will say, "But the many can kill us."

CRITO   Yes, Socrates; that will clearly be the answer.

SOCRATES   That is true; but still I find with surprise that the old argument is, as I conceive, unshaken as ever. And I should like to know whether I may say the same of another proposition – that not life, but a good life, is to be chiefly valued?

CRITO   Yes, that also remains.

SOCRATES   And a good life is equivalent to a just and honorable one – that holds also?

CRITO   Yes, that holds.

SOCRATES   From these premises I proceed to argue the question whether I ought or ought not to try to escape without the consent of the Athenians: and if I am clearly right in escaping, then I will make the attempt; but if not, I will abstain [...] But now, since the argument has thus far prevailed, the only question which remains to be considered is, whether we shall do rightly either in escaping or in suffering others to aid in our escape and paying them in money and thanks, or whether we shall not do rightly; and if the latter, then death or any other calamity which may ensue on my remaining here must not be allowed to enter into the calculation.

CRITO   I think that you are right, Socrates; how then shall we proceed?

SOCRATES   Let us consider the matter together, and do you either refute me if you can, and I will be convinced; or else cease, my dear friend, from repeating to me that I ought to escape against the wishes of the Athenians: for I am extremely desirous to be persuaded by you, but not against my own better judgment. And now please to consider my first position, and do your best to answer me.

CRITO   I will do my best. [...]

SOCRATES   Then I will proceed to the next step, which may be put in the form of a question: Ought a man to do what he admits to be right, or ought he to betray the right?

CRITO   He ought to do what he thinks right.

SOCRATES   But if this is true, what is the application? In leaving the prison against the will of the Athenians, do I wrong any? or rather do I not wrong those whom I ought least to wrong? Do I not desert the principles which were acknowledged by us to be just? What do you say?

CRITO   I cannot tell, Socrates, for I do not know.

SOCRATES   Then consider the matter in this way: Imagine that I am about to play truant (you may call the proceeding by any name which you like), and the laws and the government come and interrogate me: "Tell us, Socrates," they say; "what are you about? are you going by an act of yours to overturn us – the laws and the whole State, as far as in you lies? Do you imagine that a State can subsist and not be overthrown, in which the decisions of law have no power, but are set aside and overthrown by individuals?" What will be our answer, Crito, to these and the like words? Anyone, and especially a clever rhetorician, will have a good deal to urge about the evil of setting aside the law which requires a sentence to be carried out; and we might reply, "Yes; but the State has injured us and given an unjust sentence." Suppose I say that?

CRITO   Very good, Socrates.

SOCRATES   "And was that our agreement with you?" the law would say, "or were you to abide by the sentence of the State?" And if I were to express astonishment at their saying this, the law would probably add: "Answer, Socrates, instead of opening your eyes: you are in the habit of asking and answering questions. Tell us what complaint you have to make against us which justifies you in attempting to destroy us and the State? In the first place did we not bring you into existence? Your father married your mother by our aid and begat you. Say whether you have any objection to urge against those of us who regulate marriage?" None, I should reply. "Or against those of us who regulate the system of nurture and education of children in which you were trained? Were not the laws, who have the charge of this, right in commanding your father to train you in music and gymnastic?" Right, I should reply. "Well, then, since you were brought into the world and nurtured and educated by us, can you deny in the first place that you are our child and slave, as your fathers were before you? And if this is true you are not on equal terms with us; nor can you think that you have a right to do to us what we are doing to you. Would you have any right to strike or revile or do any other evil to a father or to your master, if you had one, when you have been struck or reviled by him, or received some other evil at his hands? – you would not say this? And because we think right to destroy you, do you think that you have any right to destroy us in return, and your country as far as in you lies? And will you, O professor of true virtue, say that you are justified in this? Has a philosopher like you failed to discover that our country is more to be valued and higher and holier far than mother or father or any ancestor, and more to be regarded in the eyes of the gods and of men of understanding? also to be soothed, and gently and reverently entreated when angry, even more than a father, and if not persuaded, obeyed? And when we are punished by her, whether with imprisonment or stripes, the punishment is to be endured in silence; and if she leads us to wounds or death in battle, thither we follow as is right; neither may anyone yield or retreat or leave his rank, but whether in battle or in a court of law, or in any other place, he must do what his city and his country order him; or he must change their view of what is just: and if he may do no violence to his father or mother, much less may he do violence to his country." What answer shall we make to this, Crito? Do the laws speak truly, or do they not?

CRITO   I think that they do.

SOCRATES   Then the laws will say: "Consider, Socrates, if this is true, that in your present attempt you are going to do us wrong. For, after having brought you into the world, and nurtured and educated you, and given you and every other citizen a share in every good that we had to give, we further proclaim and give the right to every Athenian, that if he does not like us when he has come of age and has seen the ways of the city, and made our acquaintance, he may go where he pleases and take his goods with him; and none of us laws will forbid him or interfere with him. Any of you who does not like us and the city, and who wants to go to a colony or to any other city, may go where he likes, and take his goods with him. But he who has experience of the manner in which we order justice and administer the State, and still remains, has entered into an implied contract that he will do as we command him. And he who disobeys us is, as we maintain, thrice wrong: first, because in disobeying us he is disobeying his parents; secondly, because we are the authors of his education; thirdly, because he has made an agreement with us that he will duly obey our commands; and he neither obeys them nor convinces us that our commands are wrong; and we do not rudely impose them, but give him the alternative of obeying or convincing us; that is what we offer and he does neither. These are the sort of accusations to which, as we were saying, you, Socrates, will be exposed if you accomplish your intentions; you, above all other Athenians." Suppose I ask, why is this? they will justly retort upon me that I above all other men have acknowledged the agreement. "There is clear proof," they will say, "Socrates, that we and the city were not displeasing to you. Of all Athenians you have been the most constant resident in the city, which, as you never leave, you may be supposed to love. For you never went out of the city either to see the games, except once when you went to the Isthmus, or to any other place unless when you were on military service; nor did you travel as other men do. Nor had you any curiosity to know other States; or their laws: your affections did not go beyond us and our State we were your especial favorites, and you acquiesced in our government of you; and this is the State in which you begat your children, which is a proof of your satisfaction. Moreover, you might, if you had liked, have fixed the penalty at banishment in the course of the trial – the State which refuses to let you go now would have let you go then. But you pretended that you preferred death to exile, and that you were not grieved at death. And now you have forgotten these fine sentiments, and pay no respect to us, the laws, of whom you are the destroyer; and are doing what only a miserable slave would do, running away and turning your back upon the compacts and agreements which you made as a citizen. And first of all answer this very question: Are we right in saying that you agreed to be governed according to us in deed, and not in word only? Is that true or not?" How shall we answer that, Crito? Must we not agree?

CRITO   There is no help, Socrates.

SOCRATES   Then will they not say: "You, Socrates, are breaking the covenants and agreements which you made with us at your leisure, not in any haste or under any compulsion or deception, but having had seventy years to think of them, during which time you were at liberty to leave the city, if we were not to your mind, or if our covenants appeared to you to be unfair. You had your choice, and might have gone either to Lacedaemon or Crete, which you often praise for their good government, or to some other Hellenic or foreign State. Whereas you, above all other Athenians, seemed to be so fond of the State, or, in other words, of us her laws (for who would like a State that has no laws?), that you never stirred out of her: the halt, the blind, the maimed, were not more stationary in her than you were. And now you run away and forsake your agreements. Not so, Socrates, if you will take our advice; do not make yourself ridiculous by escaping out of the city". For just consider, if you transgress and err in this sort of way, what good will you do, either to yourself or to your friends? that your friends will be driven into exile and deprived of citizenship, or will lose their property, is tolerably certain; and you yourself, if you fly to one of the neighboring cities, as, for example, Thebes or Megara, both of which are well-governed cities, will come to them as an enemy, Socrates, and their government will be against you, and all patriotic citizens will cast an evil eye upon you as a subverter of the laws, and you will confirm in the minds of the judges the justice of their own condemnation of you. For he who is a corrupter of the laws is more than likely to be corrupter of the young and foolish portion of mankind. Will you then flee from well-ordered cities and virtuous men? and is existence worth having on these terms? Or will you go to them without shame, and talk to them, Socrates? And what will you say to them? What you say here about virtue and justice and institutions and laws being the best things among men? Would that be decent of you? Surely not. But if you go away from well-governed States to Crito's; friends in Thessaly, where there is great disorder and license, they will be charmed to have the tale of your escape from prison, set off with ludicrous particulars of the manner in which you were wrapped in a goatskin or some other disguise, and metamorphosed as the fashion of runaways is – that is very likely; but will there be no one to remind you that in your old age you violated the most sacred laws from a miserable desire of a little more life? Perhaps not, if you keep them in a good temper; but if they are out of temper you will hear many degrading things; you will live, but how? – as the flatterer of all men, and the servant of all men; and doing what? – eating and drinking in Thessaly, having gone abroad in order that you may get a dinner. And where will be your fine sentiments about justice and virtue then? Say that you wish to live for the sake of your children, that you may bring them up and educate them – will you take them into Thessaly and deprive them of Athenian citizenship? Is that the benefit which you would confer upon them? Or are you under the impression that they will be better cared for and educated here if you are still alive, although absent from them; for that your friends will take care of them? Do you fancy that if you are an inhabitant of Thessaly they will take care of them, and if you are an inhabitant of the other world they will not take care of them? Nay; but if they who call themselves friends are truly friends, they surely will. "Listen, then, Socrates, to us who have brought you up. Think not of life and children first, and of justice afterwards, but of justice first, that you may be justified before the princes of the world below. For neither will you nor any that belong to you be happier or holier or juster in this life, or happier in another, if you do as Crito bids. Now you depart in innocence, a sufferer and not a doer of evil a victim, not of the laws, but of men. But if you go forth, returning evil for evil, and injury for injury, breaking the covenants and agreements which you have made with us, and wronging those whom you ought least to wrong, that is to say, yourself, your friends, your country, and us, we shall be angry with you while you live, and our brethren, the laws in the world below, will receive you as an enemy for they will know that you have done your best to destroy us. Listen, then, to us and not to Crito." This is the voice which I seem to hear murmuring in my ears, like the sound of the flute in the ears of the mystic that voice, I say, is humming in my ears, and prevents me from hearing any other. And I know that anything more which you will say will be in vain. Yet speak, if you have anything to say.

CRITO   I have nothing to say, Socrates.

SOCRATES Then let me follow the intimations of the will of God.

2.1.6 Plato
Phaedo

And these you can touch and see and perceive with the senses, but the unchanging things you can only perceive with the mind – they are invisible and are not seen?

That is very true, he said.

Well, then, he added, let us suppose that there are two sorts of existences, one seen, the other unseen.

Let us suppose them.

The seen is the changing, and the unseen is the unchanging.

That may be also supposed.

And, further, is not one part of us body, and the rest of us soul?

To be sure.

And to which class may we say that the body is more alike and akin?

Clearly to the seen: no one can doubt that.

And is the soul seen or not seen?

Not by man, Socrates.

And by "seen" and "not seen" is meant by us that which is or is not visible to the eye of man?

Yes, to the eye of man.

And what do we say of the soul? is that seen or not seen?

Not seen.

Unseen then?

Yes.

Then the soul is more like to the unseen, and the body to the seen?

That is most certain, Socrates.

And were we not saying long ago that the soul when using the body as an instrument of perception, that is to say, when using the sense of sight or hearing or some other sense (for the meaning of perceiving through the body is perceiving through the senses) – were we not saying that the soul too is then dragged by the body into the region of the changeable, and wanders and is confused; the world spins round her, and she is like a drunkard when under their influence?

Very true.

Tr. Benjamin Jowett (New York: C. Scribner's Sons, 1871).

But when returning into herself she reflects; then she passes into the realm of purity, and eternity, and immortality, and unchangeableness, which are her kindred, and with them she ever lives, when she is by herself and is not let or hindered; then she ceases from her erring ways, and being in communion with the unchanging is unchanging. And this state of the soul is called wisdom?

That is well and truly said, Socrates, he replied.

And to which class is the soul more nearly alike and akin, as far as may be inferred from this argument, as well as from the preceding one?

I think, Socrates, that, in the opinion of everyone who follows the argument, the soul will be infinitely more like the unchangeable – even the most stupid person will not deny that.

And the body is more like the changing?

Yes.

Yet once more consider the matter in this light: When the soul and the body are united, then nature orders the soul to rule and govern, and the body to obey and serve. Now which of these two functions is akin to the divine? and which to the mortal? Does not the divine appear to you to be that which naturally orders and rules, and the mortal that which is subject and servant?

True.

And which does the soul resemble?

The soul resembles the divine and the body the mortal – there can be no doubt of that, Socrates.

Then reflect, Cebes: is not the conclusion of the whole matter this? – that the soul is in the very likeness of the divine, and immortal, and intelligible, and uniform, and indissoluble, and unchangeable; and the body is in the very likeness of the human, and mortal, and unintelligible, and multiform, and dissoluble, and changeable. Can this, my dear Cebes, be denied?

No, indeed.

But if this is true, then is not the body liable to speedy dissolution? and is not the soul almost or altogether indissoluble?

Certainly.

And do you further observe, that after a man is dead, the body, which is the visible part of man, and has a visible framework, which is called a corpse, and which would naturally be dissolved and decomposed and dissipated, is not dissolved or decomposed at once, but may remain for a good while, if the constitution be sound at the time of death, and the season of the year favorable? For the body when shrunk and embalmed, as is the custom in Egypt, may remain almost entire through infinite ages; and even in decay, still there are some portions, such as the bones and ligaments, which are practically indestructible. You allow that?

Yes.

And are we to suppose that the soul, which is invisible, in passing to the true Hades, which like her is invisible, and pure, and noble, and on her way to the good and wise God, whither, if God will, my soul is also soon to go – that the soul, I repeat, if this be her nature and origin, is blown away and perishes immediately on quitting the body as the many say? That can never be, dear Simmias and Cebes. The truth rather is that the soul which is pure at departing draws after her no bodily taint, having never voluntarily had connection with the body, which she is ever avoiding, herself gathered into herself (for such abstraction has been the study of her life). And what does this mean but that she has been a true disciple of philosophy and has practised how to die easily? And is not philosophy the practice of death?

Certainly.

That soul, I say, herself invisible, departs to the invisible world to the divine and immortal and rational: thither arriving, she lives in bliss and is released from the error and folly of men, their fears and wild passions and all other human ills, and forever dwells, as they say of the initiated, in company with the gods. Is not this true, Cebes?

Yes, said Cebes, beyond a doubt.

But the soul which has been polluted, and is impure at the time of her departure, and is the companion and servant of the body always, and is in love with and fascinated by the body and by the desires and pleasures of the body, until she is led to believe that the truth only exists in a bodily form, which a man may touch and see and taste and use for the purposes of his lusts – the soul, I mean, accustomed to hate and fear and avoid the intellectual principle, which to the bodily eye is dark and invisible, and can be attained only by philosophy – do you suppose that such a soul as this will depart pure and unalloyed?

That is impossible, he replied.

She is engrossed by the corporeal, which the continual association and constant care of the body have made natural to her.

Very true.

And this, my friend, may be conceived to be that heavy, weighty, earthy element of sight by which such a soul is depressed and dragged down again into the visible world, because she is afraid of the invisible and of the world below – prowling about tombs and sepulchres, in the neighborhood of which, as they tell us, are seen certain ghostly apparitions of souls which have not departed pure, but are cloyed with sight and therefore visible.

That is very likely, Socrates.

Yes, that is very likely, Cebes; and these must be the souls, not of the good, but of the evil, who are compelled to wander about such places in payment of the penalty of their former evil way of life; and they continue to wander until the desire which haunts them is satisfied and they are imprisoned in another body. And they may be supposed to be fixed in the same natures which they had in their former life.

What natures do you mean, Socrates?

I mean to say that men who have followed after gluttony, and wantonness, and drunkenness, and have had no thought of avoiding them, would pass into asses and animals of that sort. What do you think?

I think that exceedingly probable.

And those who have chosen the portion of injustice, and tyranny, and violence, will pass into wolves, or into hawks and kites; whither else can we suppose them to go?

Yes, said Cebes; that is doubtless the place of natures such as theirs. And there is no difficulty, he said, in assigning to all of them places answering to their several natures and propensities?

There is not, he said.

Even among them some are happier than others; and the happiest both in themselves and their place of abode are those who have practised the civil and social virtues which are called temperance and justice, and are acquired by habit and attention without philosophy and mind.

Why are they the happiest?

Because they may be expected to pass into some gentle, social nature which is like their own, such as that of bees or ants, or even back again into the form of man, and just and moderate men spring from them.

That is not impossible.

But he who is a philosopher or lover of learning, and is entirely pure at departing, is alone permitted to reach the gods. And this is the reason, Simmias and Cebes, why the true votaries of philosophy abstain from all fleshly lusts, and endure and refuse to give themselves up to them – not because they fear poverty or the ruin of their families, like the lovers of money, and the world in general; nor like the lovers of power and honor, because they dread the dishonor or disgrace of evil deeds.

No, Socrates, that would not become them, said Cebes.

No, indeed, he replied; and therefore they who have a care of their souls, and do not merely live in the fashions of the body, say farewell to all this; they will not walk in the ways of the blind: and when philosophy offers them purification and release from evil, they feel that they ought not to resist her influence, and to her they incline, and whither she leads they follow her.

What do you mean, Socrates?

I will tell you, he said. The lovers of knowledge are conscious that their souls, when philosophy receives them, are simply fastened and glued to their bodies: the soul is only able to view existence through the bars of a prison, and not in her own nature; she is wallowing in the mire of all ignorance; and philosophy, seeing the terrible nature of her confinement, and that the captive through desire is led to conspire in her own captivity (for the lovers of knowledge are aware that this was the original state of the soul, and that when she was in this state philosophy received and gently counseled her, and wanted to release her, pointing out to her that the eye is full of deceit, and also the ear and other senses, and persuading her to retire from them in all but the necessary use of them and to be gathered up and collected into herself, and to trust only to herself and her own intuitions of absolute existence, and mistrust that which comes to her through others and is subject to vicissitude) – philosophy shows her that this is visible and tangible, but that what she sees in her own nature is intellectual and invisible. And the soul of the true philosopher thinks that she ought not to resist this deliverance, and therefore abstains from pleasures and desires and pains and fears, as far as she is able; reflecting that when a man has great joys or sorrows or fears or desires he suffers from them, not the sort of evil which might be anticipated – as, for example, the loss of his health or property, which he has sacrificed to his lusts – but he has suffered an evil greater far, which is the greatest and worst of all evils, and one of which he never thinks.

And what is that, Socrates? said Cebes.

Why, this: When the feeling of pleasure or pain in the soul is most intense, all of us naturally suppose that the object of this intense feeling is then plainest and truest: but this is not the case.

Very true.

And this is the state in which the soul is most enthralled by the body.

How is that?

Why, because each pleasure and pain is a sort of nail which nails and rivets the soul to the body, and engrosses her and makes her believe that to be true which the body affirms to be true; and from agreeing with the body and having the same delights she is obliged to have the same habits and ways, and is not likely ever to be pure at her departure to the world below, but is always saturated with the body; so that she soon sinks into another body and there germinates and grows, and has therefore no part in the communion of the divine and pure and simple.

That is most true, Socrates, answered Cebes.

And this, Cebes, is the reason why the true lovers of knowledge are temperate and brave; and not for the reason which the world gives.

Certainly not.

Certainly not! For not in that way does the soul of a philosopher reason; she will not ask philosophy to release her in order that when released she may deliver herself up again to the thraldom of pleasures and pains, doing a work only to be undone again, weaving instead of unweaving her Penelope's web. But she will make herself a calm of passion and follow Reason, and dwell in her, beholding the true and divine (which is not matter of opinion), and thence derive nourishment. Thus she seeks to live while she lives, and after death she hopes to go to her own kindred and to be freed from human ills. Never fear, Simmias and Cebes, that a soul which has been thus nurtured and has had these pursuits, will at her departure from the body be scattered and blown away by the winds and be nowhere and nothing.

When Socrates had done speaking, for a considerable time there was silence; he himself and most of us appeared to be meditating on what had been said; only Cebes and Simmias spoke a few words to one another. And Socrates observing this asked them what they thought of the argument, and whether there was anything wanting? For, said he, much is still open to suspicion and attack, if anyone were disposed to sift the matter thoroughly. If you are talking of something else I would rather not interrupt you, but if you are still doubtful about the argument do not hesitate to say exactly what you think, and let us have anything better which you can suggest; and if I am likely to be of any use, allow me to help you.

Simmias said: I must confess, Socrates, that doubts did arise in our minds, and each of us was urging and inciting the other to put the question which he wanted to have answered and which neither of us liked to ask, fearing that our importunity might be troublesome under present circumstances.

Socrates smiled and said: O Simmias, how strange that is; I am not very likely to persuade other men that I do not regard my present situation as a misfortune, if I am unable to persuade you, and you will keep fancying that I am at all more troubled now than at any other time. Will you not allow that I have as much of the spirit of prophecy in me as the swans? For they, when they perceive that they must die, having sung all their life long, do then sing more than ever, rejoicing in the thought that they are about to go away to the god whose ministers they are. But men, because they are themselves afraid of death, slanderously affirm of the swans that they sing a lament at the last, not considering that no bird sings when cold, or hungry, or in pain, not even the nightingale, nor the swallow, nor yet the hoopoe; which are said indeed to tune a lay of sorrow, although I do not believe this to be true of them any more than of the swans. But because they are sacred to Apollo and have the gift of prophecy and anticipate the good things of another world, therefore they sing and rejoice in that day more than they ever did before. And I, too, believing myself to be the consecrated servant of the same God, and the fellow servant of the swans, and thinking that I have received from my master gifts of prophecy which are not inferior to theirs, would not go out of life less merrily than the swans. Cease to mind then about this, but speak and ask anything which you like, while the eleven magistrates of Athens allow.

2.1.7 Plato
Laws

Persons of the Dialogue: An ATHENIAN STRANGER; CLEINIAS, a Cretan; MEGILLUS, a Lacedaemonian

Book IV

ATHENIAN STRANGER	Then let us invoke God at the settlement of our state may he hear and be propitious to us, and come and set in order the State and the laws!
CLEINIAS	May he come!
ATHENIAN STRANGER	But what form of polity are we going to give the city?
CLEINIAS	Tell us what you mean a little more clearly. Do you mean some form of democracy, or oligarchy, or aristocracy, or monarchy? For we cannot suppose that you would include tyranny.
ATHENIAN STRANGER	Which of you will first tell me to which of these classes his own government is to be referred?
MEGILLUS	Ought I to answer first, since I am the elder?
CLEINIAS	Perhaps you should.
MEGILLUS	And yet, Stranger, I perceive that I cannot say, without more thought, what I should call the government of Lacedaemon, for it seems to me to be like a tyranny – the power of our Ephors is marvellously tyrannical; and sometimes it appears to me to be of all cities the most democratical; and who can reasonably deny that it is an aristocracy? We have also a monarchy which is held for life, and is said by all mankind, and not by ourselves only, to be the most ancient of all monarchies; and, therefore, when asked on a sudden, I cannot precisely say which form of government the Spartan is.
CLEINIAS	I am in the same difficulty, Megillus; for I do not feel confident that the polity of Cnosus is any of these.
ATHENIAN STRANGER	The reason is, my excellent friends, that you really have polities, but the states of which we were just now speaking are merely

Tr. Benjamin Jowett (New York: C. Scribner's Sons, 1871).

aggregations of men dwelling in cities who are the subjects and servants of a part of their own state, and each of them is named after the dominant power; they are not polities at all. But if states are to be named after their rulers, the true state ought to be called by the name of the God who rules over wise men.

CLEINIAS And who is this God?

ATHENIAN STRANGER May I still make use of fable to some extent, in the hope that I may be better able to answer your question: shall I?

CLEINIAS By all means.

ATHENIAN STRANGER In the primeval world, and a long while before the cities came into being whose settlements we have described, there is said to have been in the time of Cronos a blessed rule and life, of which the best-ordered of existing states is a copy.

CLEINIAS It will be very necessary to hear about that.

ATHENIAN STRANGER I quite agree with you; and therefore I have introduced the subject.

CLEINIAS Most appropriately; and since the tale is to the point, you will do well in giving us the whole story.

ATHENIAN STRANGER I will do as you suggest. There is a tradition of the happy life of mankind in days when all things were spontaneous and abundant. And of this the reason is said to have been as follows: – Cronos knew what we ourselves were declaring, that no human nature invested with supreme power is able to order human affairs and not overflow with insolence and wrong. Which reflection led him to appoint not men but demigods, who are of a higher and more divine race, to be the kings and rulers of our cities; he did as we do with flocks of sheep and other tame animals. For we do not appoint oxen to be the lords of oxen, or goats of goats; but we ourselves are a superior race, and rule over them. In like manner God, in his love of mankind, placed over us the demons, who are a superior race, and they with great case and pleasure to themselves, and no less to us, taking care of us and giving us peace and reverence and order and justice never failing, made the tribes of men happy and united. And this tradition, which is true, declares that cities of which some mortal man and not God is the ruler, have no escape from evils and toils. Still we must do all that we can to imitate the life which is said to have existed in the days of Cronos, and, as far as the principle of immortality dwells in us, to that we must hearken, both in private and public life, and regulate our cities and houses according to law, meaning by the very term "law," the distribution of mind. But if either a single person or an oligarchy or a democracy has a soul eager after pleasures and desires – wanting to be filled with them, yet retaining none of them, and perpetually afflicted with an endless and insatiable disorder; and this evil spirit, having first trampled the laws under foot, becomes the master either of a state or of an individual – then, as I was saying, salvation is hopeless. And now, Cleinias, we have to consider whether you will or will not accept this tale of mine.

CLEINIAS Certainly we will.

ATHENIAN STRANGER	You are aware – are you not? – that there are said to be as many forms of laws as there are of governments, and of the latter we have already mentioned all those which are commonly recognized. Now you must regard this as a matter of first-rate importance. For what is to be the standard of just and unjust, is once more the point at issue. Men say that the law ought not to regard either military virtue, or virtue in general, but only the interests and power and preservation of the established form of government this is thought by them to be the best way of expressing the natural definition of justice.
CLEINIAS	How?
ATHENIAN STRANGER	Justice is said by them to be the interest of the stronger.
CLEINIAS	Speak plainer.
ATHENIAN STRANGER	I will:– "Surely," they say, "the governing power makes whatever laws have authority in any state?"
CLEINIAS	True.
ATHENIAN STRANGER	"Well," they would add, "and do you suppose that tyranny or democracy, or any other conquering power, does not make the continuance of the power which is possessed by them the first or principal object of their laws?"
CLEINIAS	How can they have any other?
ATHENIAN STRANGER	"And whoever transgresses these laws is punished as an evil-doer by the legislator, who calls the laws just?"
CLEINIAS	Naturally.
ATHENIAN STRANGER	"This, then, is always the mode and fashion in which justice exists."
CLEINIAS	Certainly, if they are correct in their view.
ATHENIAN STRANGER	Why, yes, this is one of those false principles of government to which we were referring.
CLEINIAS	Which do you mean?
ATHENIAN STRANGER	Those which we were examining when we spoke of who ought to govern whom. Did we not arrive at the conclusion that parents ought to govern their children, and the elder the younger, and the noble the ignoble? And there were many other principles, if you remember, and they were not always consistent. One principle was this very principle of might, and we said that Pindar considered violence natural and justified it.
CLEINIAS	Yes; I remember.
ATHENIAN STRANGER	Consider, then, to whom our state is to be entrusted. For there is a thing which has occurred times without number in states –
CLEINIAS	What thing?
ATHENIAN STRANGER	That when there has been a contest for power, those who gain the upper hand so entirely monopolize the government, as to refuse all share to the defeated party and their descendants – they live watching one another, the ruling class being in perpetual fear that some one who has a recollection of former wrongs will come into power and rise up against them. Now, according to our view, such governments are not polities at all, nor are laws right which are passed for the good of particular classes and not for the good of the whole state. States which

have such laws are not polities but parties, and their notions of justice are simply unmeaning. I say this, because I am going to assert that we must not entrust the government in your state to any one because he is rich, or because he possesses any other advantage, such as strength, or stature, or again birth: but he who is most obedient to the laws of the state, he shall win the palm and to him who is victorious in the first degree shall be given the highest office and chief ministry of the gods and the second to him who bears the second palm; and on a similar principle shall all the other be assigned to those who come next in order. And when I call the rulers servants or ministers of the law, I give them this name not for the sake of novelty, but because I certainly believe that upon such service or ministry depends the well- or ill-being of the state. For that state in which the law is subject and has no authority, I perceive to be on the highway to ruin but I see that the state in which the law is above the rulers, and the rulers are the inferiors of the law, has salvation, and every blessing which the Gods can confer.

CLEINIAS   Truly, Stranger, you see with the keen vision of age.

ATHENIAN STRANGER   Why, yes; every man when he is young has that sort of vision dullest, and when he is old keenest.

CLEINIAS   Very true.

ATHENIAN STRANGER   And now, what is to be the next step? May we not suppose the colonists to have arrived, and proceed to make our speech to them?

CLEINIAS   Certainly.

ATHENIAN STRANGER   "Friends," we say to them, – "God, as the old tradition declares, holding in his hand the beginning, middle, and end of all that is, travels according to his nature in a straight line towards the accomplishment of his end. Justice always accompanies him, and is the punisher of those who fall short of the divine law. To justice, he who would be happy holds fast, and follows in her company with all humility and order; but he who is lifted up with pride, or elated by wealth or rank, or beauty, who is young and foolish, and has a soul hot with insolence, and thinks that he has no need of any guide or ruler, but is able himself to be the guide of others, he, I say, is left deserted of God; and being thus deserted, he takes to him others who are like himself, and dances about, throwing all things into confusion, and many think that he is a great man, but in a short time he pays a penalty which justice cannot but approve, and is utterly destroyed, and his family and city with him. Wherefore, seeing that human things are thus ordered, what should a wise man do or think, or not do or think?

CLEINIAS   Every man ought to make up his mind that he will be one of the followers of God; there can be no doubt of that.

ATHENIAN STRANGER   Then what life is agreeable to God, and becoming in his followers? One only, expressed once for all in the old saying that "like agrees with like, with measure measure," but things which have no measure agree neither with themselves nor with the things which have. Now God ought to be to us the measure of all things, and not man, as men commonly say (Protagoras): the words are far more true of him. And he who would be dear to God must, as far as is possible, be like him; and such as he is. Wherefore the temperate man is the friend of God, for he is like him and the intemperate man is unlike him, and different from him, and unjust. And the same applies to other things; and this is the conclusion, which is also the noblest and truest of all sayings – that for the good man to offer sacrifice to the Gods, and hold converse with them by means of prayers and offerings and every kind of service, is the noblest and best of all things, and also the most conducive to a happy life, and very fit and meet. But with the bad man, the opposite of this is true: for the bad man has an impure soul, whereas the good is pure; and from one who is polluted, neither good man nor God can without impropriety receive gifts. Wherefore the unholy do only waste their much service upon the Gods, but when offered by any holy man, such service is most acceptable to them. This is the mark at which we ought to aim. But what weapons shall we use, and how shall we direct them? In the first place, we affirm that next after the Olympian Gods and the Gods of the State, honour should be given to the Gods below; they should receive everything in even and of the second choice, and ill omen, while the odd numbers, and the first choice, and the things of lucky omen, are given to the Gods above, by him who would rightly hit the mark of piety. Next to these Gods, a wise man will do service to the demons or spirits, and then to the heroes, and after them will follow the private and ancestral Gods, who are worshipped as the law prescribes in the places which are sacred to them. Next comes the honour of living parents, to whom, as is meet, we have to pay the first and greatest and oldest of all debts, considering that all which a man has belongs to those who gave him birth and brought him up, and that he must do all that he can to minister to them, first, in his property, secondly, in his person, and thirdly, in his soul, in return for the endless care and travail which they bestowed upon him of old, in the days of his infancy, and which he is now to pay back to them when they are old and in the extremity of their need. And all his life long he ought never to utter, or to have uttered, an unbecoming word to them; for of light and fleeting words the penalty is most severe; Nemesis, the messenger of justice, is appointed to watch over all such matters. When they are angry and want to satisfy their feelings in word or deed, he should give way to them; for a father who thinks that he has been wronged by his son may be reasonably expected to be very angry. At their death, the most moderate funeral is best, neither exceeding the customary expense, nor yet falling short of the honour which has been usually shown by the former generation to their parents. And let a man not forget to pay the yearly tribute of respect to the dead, honouring them chiefly by omitting nothing that conduces to a perpetual remembrance of them, and giving a reasonable portion of his fortune to the dead. Doing this, and living after this manner, we shall receive our reward from the Gods and those who are above us [i.e., the demons]; and we shall spend our days for the most part in good hope. And how a man ought to order what relates to his descendants and his kindred and friends and fellow-citizens, and the rites of hospitality taught by Heaven, and the intercourse which arises out of all these duties, with a view to the embellishment and orderly regulation of his own life – these things, I say, the laws, as we proceed with them, will accomplish, partly persuading, and partly when natures do not yield to the persuasion of custom, chastising them by might and right, and will thus render our state, if the Gods co-operate with us, prosperous and happy. But of what has to be said, and must be said by the legislator who is of my way of thinking, and yet, if said in the form of law, would be out of place – of this I think that he may give a sample for the instruction of himself and of those for whom he is legislating; and then when, as far as he is able, he has gone through all the preliminaries, he may proceed to the work of legislation. Now, what will be the form of such prefaces? There may be a difficulty in including or describing them all under a single form, but I think that we may get some notion of them if we can guarantee one thing.

CLEINIAS   What is that?

ATHENIAN STRANGER   I should wish the citizens to be as readily persuaded to virtue as possible; this will surely be the aim of the legislator in all his laws.

CLEINIAS   Certainly.

ATHENIAN STRANGER   The proposal appears to me to be of some value; and I think that a person will listen with more gentleness and good-will to the precepts addressed to him by the legislator, when his soul is not altogether unprepared to receive them. Even a little done in the way of conciliation gains his ear, and is always worth having. For there is no great inclination or readiness on the part of mankind to be made as good, or as quickly good, as possible. The case of the many proves the wisdom of Hesiod, who says that the road to wickedness is smooth and can be travelled without perspiring, because it is so very short: But before virtue the immortal Gods have placed the sweat of labour, and long and steep is the way thither, and rugged at first; but when you have reached the top, although difficult before, it is then easy.

CLEINIAS   Yes; and he certainly speaks well.

2.1.8 Plato
Republic

Book VII

The allegory of the cave highlights the illusory and transient nature of material existence and establishes the importance of Forms, which we apprehend only through reason, over mere opinions, which are derived from our fleeting experience of the physical world.

Socrates – GLAUCON

And now, I said, let me show in a figure how far our nature is enlightened or unenlightened: – Behold! human beings living in an underground den, which has a mouth open towards the light and reaching all along the den; here they have been from their childhood, and have their legs and necks chained so that they cannot move, and can only see before them, being prevented by the chains from turning round their heads. Above and behind them a fire is blazing at a distance, and between the fire and the prisoners there is a raised way; and you will see, if you look, a low wall built along the way, like the screen which marionette players have in front of them, over which they show the puppets.

I see.

And do you see, I said, men passing along the wall carrying all sorts of vessels, and statues and figures of animals made of wood and stone and various materials, which appear over the wall? Some of them are talking, others silent.

You have shown me a strange image, and they are strange prisoners.

Like ourselves, I replied; and they see only their own shadows, or the shadows of one another, which the fire throws on the opposite wall of the cave?

True, he said; how could they see anything but the shadows if they were never allowed to move their heads?

And of the objects which are being carried in like manner they would only see the shadows?

Yes, he said.

And if they were able to converse with one another, would they not suppose that they were naming what was actually before them?

Tr. Benjamin Jowett (New York: C. Scribner's Sons, 1871).

Very true.

And suppose further that the prison had an echo which came from the other side, would they not be sure to fancy when one of the passers-by spoke that the voice which they heard came from the passing shadow?

No question, he replied.

To them, I said, the truth would be literally nothing but the shadows of the images.

That is certain.

And now look again, and see what will naturally follow if the prisoners are released and disabused of their error. At first, when any of them is liberated and compelled suddenly to stand up and turn his neck round and walk and look towards the light, he will suffer sharp pains; the glare will distress him, and he will be unable to see the realities of which in his former state he had seen the shadows; and then conceive some one saying to him, that what he saw before was an illusion, but that now, when he is approaching nearer to being and his eye is turned towards more real existence, he has a clearer vision, – what will be his reply? And you may further imagine that his instructor is pointing to the objects as they pass and requiring him to name them, – will he not be perplexed? Will he not fancy that the shadows which he formerly saw are truer than the objects which are now shown to him?

Far truer.

And if he is compelled to look straight at the light, will he not have a pain in his eyes which will make him turn away to take refuge in the objects of vision which he can see, and which he will conceive to be in reality clearer than the things which are now being shown to him?

True, he said.

And suppose once more, that he is reluctantly dragged up a steep and rugged ascent, and held fast until he's forced into the presence of the sun himself, is he not likely to be pained and irritated? When he approaches the light his eyes will be dazzled, and he will not be able to see anything at all of what are now called realities.

Not all in a moment, he said.

He will require to grow accustomed to the sight of the upper world. And first he will see the shadows best, next the reflections of men and other objects in the water, and then the objects themselves; then he will gaze upon the light of the moon and the stars and the spangled heaven; and he will see the sky and the stars by night better than the sun or the light of the sun by day?

Certainly.

Last of all he will be able to see the sun, and not mere reflections of him in the water, but he will see him in his own proper place, and not in another; and he will contemplate him as he is.

Certainly.

He will then proceed to argue that this is he who gives the season and the years, and is the guardian of all that is in the visible world, and in a certain way the cause of all things which he and his fellows have been accustomed to behold?

Clearly, he said, he would first see the sun and then reason about him.

And when he remembered his old habitation, and the wisdom of the den and his fellow-prisoners, do you not suppose that he would felicitate himself on the change, and pity them?

Certainly, he would.

And if they were in the habit of conferring honours among themselves on those who were quickest to observe the passing shadows and to remark which of them went before, and which followed after, and which were together; and who were therefore best able to draw conclusions as to the future, do you think that he would care for such honours and glories, or envy the possessors of them? Would he not say with Homer,

Better to be the poor servant of a poor master, and to endure anything, rather than think as they do and live after their manner?

Yes, he said, I think that he would rather suffer anything than entertain these false notions and live in this miserable manner.

Imagine once more, I said, such an one coming suddenly out of the sun to be replaced in his old situation; would he not be certain to have his eyes full of darkness?

To be sure, he said.

And if there were a contest, and he had to compete in measuring the shadows with the prisoners who had never moved out of the den, while his sight was still weak, and before his eyes had become steady (and the time which would be needed to acquire this new habit of sight might be very considerable) would he not be ridiculous? Men would say of him that up he went and down he came without his eyes; and that it was better not even to think of ascending; and if any one tried to loose another and lead him up to the light, let them only catch the offender, and they would put him to death.

No question, he said.

This entire allegory, I said, you may now append, dear Glaucon, to the previous argument; the prison-house is the world of sight, the light of the fire is the sun, and you will not misapprehend me if you interpret the journey upwards to be the ascent of the soul into the intellectual world according to my poor belief, which, at your desire, I have expressed whether rightly or wrongly God knows. But, whether true or false, my opinion is that in the world of knowledge the idea of good appears last of all, and is seen only with an effort; and, when seen, is also inferred to be the universal author of all things beautiful and right, parent of light and of the lord of light in this visible world, and the immediate source of reason and truth in the intellectual; and that this is the power upon which he who would act rationally, either in public or private life must have his eye fixed.

I agree, he said, as far as I am able to understand you.

Moreover, I said, you must not wonder that those who attain to this beatific vision are unwilling to descend to human affairs; for their souls are ever hastening into the upper world where they desire to dwell; which desire of theirs is very natural, if our allegory may be trusted.

Yes, very natural.

Book VIII

[*Plato, having described aristocracy, famously goes on to consider oligarchy, democracy, and tyranny. Government by the wise, rulers trained in philosophy and lovers of wisdom, is the highest form of government.*]

[…] Then let us now proceed to describe the inferior sort of natures, being the contentious and ambitious, who answer to the Spartan polity; also the oligarchical, democratical, and tyrannical. Let us place the most just by the side of the most unjust, and when we see them we shall be able to compare the relative happiness or unhappiness of him who leads a life of pure justice or pure injustice. The enquiry will then be completed. And we shall know whether we ought to pursue injustice, as Thrasymachus advises, or in accordance with the conclusions of the argument to prefer justice.

Certainly, he replied, we must do as you say.

Shall we follow our old plan, which we adopted with a view to clearness, of taking the State first and then proceeding to the individual, and begin with the government of honour? – I know of no name for such a government other than timocracy, or perhaps timarchy. We will compare with this the like character in the individual; and, after that, consider oligarchical man; and then again we will turn our attention to democracy and the democratical man; and lastly, we will go and view the city of tyranny, and once more take a look into the tyrant's soul, and try to arrive at a satisfactory decision.

That way of viewing and judging of the matter will be very suitable.

[*Plato considers oligarchy or rule by the wealthiest individuals as a group and considers the effects of oligarchy upon the souls of its practioners.*]

The new government which thus arises will be of a form intermediate between oligarchy and aristocracy?

Very true.

Such will be the change, and after the change has been made, how will they proceed? Clearly, the new State, being in a mean between oligarchy and the perfect State, will partly follow one and partly the other, and will also have some peculiarities.

True, he said.

In the honour given to rulers, in the abstinence of the warrior class from agriculture, handicrafts, and trade in general, in the institution of common meals, and in the attention paid to gymnastics and military training – in all these respects this State will resemble the former.

True.

But in the fear of admitting philosophers to power, because they are no longer to be had simple and earnest, but are made up of mixed elements; and in turning from them to passionate and less complex characters, who are by nature fitted for war rather than peace; and in the value set by them upon military stratagems and contrivances, and in the waging of everlasting wars – this State will be for the most part peculiar.

Yes.

Yes, I said; and men of this stamp will be covetous of money, like those who live in oligarchies; they will have a fierce secret longing after gold and silver, which they will hoard in dark places, having magazines and treasuries of their own for the deposit and concealment of them; also castles which are just nests for their eggs, and in which they will spend large sums on their wives, or on any others whom they please.

That is most true, he said.

And they are miserly because they have no means of openly acquiring the money which they prize; they will spend that which is another man's on the gratification of their desires, stealing their pleasures and running away like children from the law, their father.

[…]

[…] Let us next proceed to consider the nature and origin of the individual who answers to this State. […] Does not the timocratical man change into the oligarchical on this wise?

How?

A time arrives when the representative of timocracy has a son: at first he begins by emulating his father and walking in his footsteps, but presently he sees him of a sudden foundering against the State as upon a sunken reef, and he and all that he has is lost; he may have been a general or some other high officer who is brought to trial under a prejudice raised by informers, and either put to death, or exiled, or deprived of the privileges of a citizen, and all his property taken from him.

Nothing more likely.

And the son has seen and known all this – he is a ruined man, and his fear has taught him to knock ambition and passion head-foremost from his bosom's throne; humbled by poverty he takes to money-making and by mean and miserly savings and hard work gets a fortune together. Is not such an one likely to seat the concupiscent and covetous element on the vacant throne and to suffer it to play the great king within him, girt with tiara and chain and scimitar?

Most true, he replied.

And when he has made reason and spirit sit down on the ground obediently on either side of their sovereign, and taught them to know their place, he compels the one to think only of how lesser sums may be turned into larger ones, and will not allow the other to worship and admire anything but riches and rich men, or to be ambitious of anything so much as the acquisition of wealth and the means of acquiring it.

[*Plato discusses the democratic state.*]

And then democracy comes into being after the poor have conquered their opponents, slaughtering some and banishing some, while to the remainder they give an equal share of freedom and power; and this is the form of government in which the magistrates are commonly elected by lot.

Yes, he said, that is the nature of democracy, whether the revolution has been effected by arms, or whether fear has caused the opposite party to withdraw.

And now what is their manner of life, and what sort of a government have they? for as the government is, such will be the man.

Clearly, he said.

In the first place, are they not free; and is not the city full of freedom and frankness – a man may say and do what he likes? […] And where freedom is, the individual is clearly able to order for himself his own life as he pleases?

Clearly.

Then in this kind of State there will be the greatest variety of human natures?

There will.

This, then, seems likely to be the fairest of States, being an embroidered robe which is spangled with every sort of flower. And just as women and children think a variety of colours to be of all things most charming, so there are many men to whom this State, which is spangled with the manners and characters of mankind, will appear to be the fairest of States. […] Yes, my good Sir, and there will be no better in which to look for a government.

Why?

Because of the liberty which reigns there – they have a complete assortment of constitutions; and he who has a mind to establish a State, as we have been doing, must go to a democracy as he would to a bazaar at which they sell them, and pick out the one that suits him; then, when he has made his choice, he may found his State.

He will be sure to have patterns enough.

And there being no necessity, I said, for you to govern in this State, even if you have the capacity, or to be governed, unless you like, or go to war when the rest go to war, or to be at peace when others are at peace, unless you are so disposed – there being no necessity also, because some law forbids you to hold office or be a dicast, that you should not hold office or be a dicast, if you have a fancy – is not this a way of life which for the moment is supremely delightful?

For the moment, yes.

And is not their humanity to the condemned in some cases quite charming? Have you not observed how, in a democracy, many persons, although they have been sentenced to death or exile, just stay where they are and walk about the world – the gentleman parades like a hero, and nobody sees or cares?

Yes, he replied, many and many a one.

See too, I said, the forgiving spirit of democracy, and the "don't care" about trifles, and the disregard which she shows of all the fine principles which we solemnly laid down at the foundation of the city – as when we said that, except in the case of some rarely gifted nature, there never will be a good man who has not from his childhood been used to play amid things of beauty and make of them a joy and a study – how grandly does she trample all these fine notions of ours under her feet, never giving a thought to the pursuits which make a statesman, and promoting to honour any one who professes to be the people's friend.

Yes, she is of a noble spirit.

These and other kindred characteristics are proper to democracy, which is a charming form of government, full of variety and disorder, and dispensing a sort of equality to equals and unequals alike. [...]

Book IX

[*The tyrannical are made up of lusts and ambitions while the philosopher king has the virtues: wisdom, courage, temperance, and justice.*]

Last of all comes the tyrannical man; about whom we have once more to ask, how is he formed out of the democratical? and how does he live, in happiness or in misery? [...]

[...] [W]hen a man's pulse is healthy and temperate, and when before going to sleep he has awakened his rational powers, and fed them on noble thoughts and enquiries, collecting himself in meditation; after having first indulged his appetites neither too much nor too little, but just enough to lay them to sleep, and prevent them and their enjoyments and pains from interfering with the higher principle – which he leaves in the solitude of pure abstraction, free to contemplate and aspire to the knowledge of the unknown, whether in past, present, or future: when again he has allayed the passionate element, if he has a quarrel against any one – I say, when, after pacifying the two irrational principles, he rouses up the third, which is reason, before he takes his rest, then, as you know, he attains truth most nearly, and is least likely to be the sport of fantastic and lawless visions.

[...]

[*Glaucon on the nature of justice and injustice.*]

[...]

Then if the man is like the State, I said, must not the same rule prevail? his soul is full of meanness and vulgarity – the best elements in him are enslaved; and there is a small ruling part, which is also the worst and maddest.

Inevitably.

And would you say that the soul of such an one is the soul of a freeman, or of a slave?

He has the soul of a slave, in my opinion.

And the State which is enslaved under a tyrant is utterly incapable of acting voluntarily?

Utterly incapable.

[*The wise man will strive to harmonize the nobler elements of his nature and control his bodily habits. His principal ambition is not health but harmony of soul. He will scorn the pursuit of wealth as such and accept honours that will not imperil his character. He possesses a city of his own whose ideal pattern will be the law of his life.*]

From what point of view, then, and on what ground can we say that a man is profited by injustice or intemperance or other baseness, which will make him a worse man, even though he acquire money or power by his wickedness?

From no point of view at all.

What shall he profit, if his injustice be undetected and unpunished? He who is undetected only gets worse, whereas he who is detected and punished has the brutal part of his nature silenced and humanized; the gentler element in him is liberated, and his whole soul is perfected and ennobled by the acquirement of justice and temperance and wisdom, more than the body ever is by receiving gifts of beauty, strength and health, in proportion as the soul is more honourable than the body.

Certainly, he said.

To this nobler purpose the man of understanding will devote the energies of his life. And in the first place, he will honour studies which impress these qualities on his soul, and will disregard others?

Clearly, he said.

In the next place, he will regulate his bodily habit and training, and so far will he be from yielding to brutal and irrational pleasures, that he will regard even health as quite a secondary matter; his first object will be not that he may be fair or strong or well, unless he is likely thereby to gain temperance, but he will always desire so to attemper the body as to preserve the harmony of the soul?

Certainly he will, if he has true music in him.

And in the acquisition of wealth there is a principle of order and harmony which he will also observe; he will not allow himself to be dazzled by the foolish applause of the world, and heap up riches to his own infinite harm?

Certainly not, he said.

He will look at the city which is within him, and take heed that no disorder occur in it, such as might arise either from superfluity or from want; and upon this principle he will regulate his property and gain or spend according to his means.

Very true.

And, for the same reason, he will gladly accept and enjoy such honours as he deems likely to make him a better man; but those, whether private or public, which are likely to disorder his life, he will avoid? and he will only accept such political honours as will not deteriorate his character.

Then, if that is his motive, he will not be a statesman.

By the dog of Egypt, he will! in the city which is his own he certainly will, though in the land of his birth perhaps not, unless he have a divine call.

He has a city of his own, and the ideal pattern of this will be the law of his life.

I understand; you mean that he will be a ruler in the city of which we are the founders, and which exists in idea only; for I do not believe that there is such an one anywhere on earth?

In heaven, I replied, there is laid up a pattern of it, methinks, which he who desires may behold, and beholding, may set his own house in order. But whether such an one exists, or ever will exist in fact, is no matter; for he will live after the manner of that city, having nothing to do with any other.

I think so, he said.

2.1.9 Aristotle
Rhetoric and *Nicomachean Ethics*

Rhetoric

Book I, Chapter 13

[**1373b**] It will now be well to make a complete classification of just and unjust actions. We may begin by observing that they have been defined relatively to two kinds of law, and also relatively to two classes of persons. By the two kinds of law I mean particular law and universal law. Particular law is that which each community lays down and applies to its own members: this is partly written and partly unwritten. Universal law is the law of Nature. For there really is, as every one to some extent divines, a natural justice and injustice that is binding on all men, even on those who have no association or covenant with each other. It is this that Sophocles' Antigone clearly means when she says that the burial of Polyneices was a just act in spite of the prohibition: she means that it was just by nature.

> Not of to-day or yesterday it is,
> But lives eternal: none can date its birth.

And so Empedocles, when he bids us kill no living creature, says that doing this is not just for some people while unjust for others,

> Nay, but, an all-embracing law, through the realms of the sky
> Unbroken it stretcheth, and over the earth's immensity.

Tr. W. Rhys Roberts (London: Oxford University Press, 1924).
From *Ethica Nicomachea*, tr. W.D. Ross, from *Ethics* from *The Oxford Translation of Aristotle*, ed. W.D. Ross, Volume 9 (Oxford: Clarendon Press, 1925). Reprinted with permission of Oxford University Press.

*[handwritten: * teles - end, aim, desired outcome]*

Nicomachean Ethics

Book 1

Chapter 1

EVERY art and every inquiry, and similarly every action and pursuit, is thought to aim at some good; and for this reason the good has rightly been declared to be that at which all things aim. But a certain difference is found among ends; some are activities, others are products apart from the activities that produce them. Where there are ends apart from the actions, it is the nature of the products to be better than the activities. Now, as there are many actions, arts, and sciences, their ends also are many; the end of the medical art is health, that of shipbuilding a vessel, that of strategy victory, that of economics wealth. But where such arts fall under a single capacity – as bridle-making and the other arts concerned with the equipment of horses fall under the art of riding, and this and every military action under strategy, in the same way other arts fall under yet others – in all of these the ends of the master arts are to be preferred to all the subordinate ends; for it is for the sake of the former that the latter are pursued. It makes no difference whether the activities themselves are the ends of the actions, or something else apart from the activities, as in the case of the sciences just mentioned. *[handwritten: Aristotle sees the pluralism in natural law – each art has a particular 'small' good, but each is interconnected]*

[handwritten: →desire points us to an ultimate thing – ultimate object of desire]

Chapter 2

If, then, there is some end of the things we do, which we desire for its own sake (everything else being desired for the sake of this), and if we do not choose everything for the sake of something else (for at that rate the process would go on to infinity, so that our desire would be empty and vain), clearly this must be the good and the chief good. Will not the knowledge of it, then, have a great influence on life? Shall we not, like archers who have a mark to aim at, be more likely to hit upon what is right? If so, we must try, in outline at least, to determine what it is, and of which of the sciences or capacities it is the object. It would seem to belong to the most authoritative art and that which is most truly the master art. And politics appears to be of this nature; for it is this that ordains which of the sciences should be studied in a state, and which each class of citizens should learn and up to what point they should learn them; and we see even the most highly esteemed of capacities to fall under this, e.g. strategy, economics, rhetoric; now, since politics uses the rest of the sciences, and since, again, it legislates as to what we are to do and what we are to abstain from, the end of this science must include those of the others, so that this end must be the good for man. For even if the end is the same for a single man and for a state, that of the state seems at all events something greater and more complete whether to attain or to preserve; though it is worth while to attain the end merely for one man, it is finer and more godlike to attain it for a nation or for city-states. These, then, are the ends at which our inquiry aims, since it is political science, in one sense of that term.

[handwritten: Politics is most art – highest good?]

Chapter 4

Verbally there is very general agreement; for both the general run of men and people of superior refinement say that it is happiness, and identify living well and doing well with being happy; but with regard to what happiness is they differ, and the many do not give the same account as the wise. For the former think it is some plain and obvious thing, like pleasure, wealth, or honour; they differ, however, from one another and often even the same man identifies it with different things, with health when he is ill, with wealth when he is poor; but, conscious of their ignorance, they admire those who proclaim some great ideal that is above their comprehension. Now some thought that apart from these many goods there is another which is self-subsistent and causes the goodness of all these as well. [...]

What is the ultimate desire?

Chapter 7

Now we call that which is in itself worthy of pursuit more final than that which is worthy of pursuit for the sake of something else, and that which is never desirable for the sake of something else more final than the things that are desirable both in themselves and for the sake of that other thing, and therefore we call final without qualification that which is always desirable in itself and never for the sake of something else.

Now such a thing happiness, above all else, is held to be; for this we choose always for self and never for the sake of something else, but honour, pleasure, reason, and every virtue we choose indeed for themselves (for if nothing resulted from them we should still choose each of them), but we choose them also for the sake of happiness, judging that by means of them we shall be happy. Happiness, on the other hand, no one chooses for the sake of these, nor, in general, for anything other than itself [...]

From the point of view of self-sufficiency the same result seems to follow; for the final good is thought to be self-sufficient. Now by self-sufficient we do not mean that which is sufficient for a man by himself, for one who lives a solitary life, but also for parents, children, wife, and in general for his friends and fellow citizens, since man is born for citizenship. But some limit must be set to this; for if we extend our requirement to ancestors and descendants and friends' friends we are in for an infinite series. Let us examine this question, however, on another occasion; the self-sufficient we now define as that which when isolated makes life desirable and lacking in nothing; and such we think happiness to be; and further we think it most desirable of all things, without being counted as one good thing among others – if it were so counted it would clearly be made more desirable by the addition of even the least of goods; for that which is added becomes an excess of goods, and of goods the greater is always more desirable. Happiness, then, is something final and self-sufficient, and is the end of action.

Presumably, however, to say that happiness is the chief good seems a platitude, and a clearer account of what it is still desired. This might perhaps be given, if we could first ascertain the function of man. For just as for a flute-player, a sculptor, or an artist, and, in general, for all things that have a function or activity, the good and the 'well' is thought to reside in the function, so would it seem to be for man, if he has a function. Have the carpenter, then, and the tanner certain functions or activities, and has man none? Is he born without a function? Or as eye, hand, foot, and in general each of the parts evidently has a function, may one lay it down that man similarly has a function apart from all these? What then can this be? Life seems to be common even to plants, but we are seeking what is peculiar to man. Let us exclude, therefore, the life of nutrition and growth. Next there would be a life of perception, but it also seems to be common even to the horse, the ox, and every animal. There remains, then, an active life of the element that has a rational principle; of this, one part has such a principle in the sense of being

the human is his purpose

obedient to one, the other in the sense of possessing one and exercising thought. And, as 'life of the rational element' also has two meanings, we must state that life in the sense of activity is what we mean; for this seems to be the more proper sense of the term. Now if the function of man is an activity of soul which follows or implies a rational principle, and if we say 'so-and-so' and 'a good so-and-so' have a function which is the same in kind, e.g. a lyre, and a good lyre-player, and so without qualification in all cases, eminence in respect of goodness being added to the name of the function (for the function of a lyre-player is to play the lyre, and that of a good lyre-player is to do so well): if this is the case, and we state the function of man to be a certain kind of life, and this to be an activity or actions of the soul implying a rational principle, and the function of a good man to be the good and noble performance of these, and if any action is well performed when it is performed in accordance with the appropriate excellence: if this is the case, human good turns out to be activity of soul in accordance with virtue, and if there are more than one virtue, in accordance with the best and most complete.

But we must add 'in a complete life.' For one swallow does not make a summer, nor does one day; and so too one day, or a short time, does not make a man blessed and happy […]

Chapter 13

Since happiness is an activity of soul in accordance with perfect virtue, we must consider the nature of virtue; for perhaps we shall thus see better the nature of happiness. The true student of politics, too, is thought to have studied virtue above all things; for he wishes to make his fellow citizens good and obedient to the laws. As an example of this we have the lawgivers of the Cretans and the Spartans, and any others of the kind that there may have been. And if this inquiry belongs to political science, clearly the pursuit of it will be in accordance with our original plan. But clearly the virtue we must study is human virtue; for the good we were seeking was human good and the happiness human happiness. By human virtue we mean not that of the body but that of the soul; and happiness also we call an activity of soul. But if this is so, clearly the student of politics must know somehow the facts about soul, as the man who is to heal the eyes or the body as a whole must know about the eyes or the body; and all the more since politics is more prized and better than medicine; but even among doctors the best educated spend much labour on acquiring knowledge of the body. The student of politics, then, must study the soul, and must study it with these objects in view, and do so just to the extent which is sufficient for the questions we are discussing; for further precision is perhaps something more laborious than our purposes require […]

Book 2

Chapter 1

VIRTUE, then, being of two kinds, intellectual and moral, intellectual virtue in the main owes both its birth and its growth to teaching (for which reason it requires experience and time), while moral virtue comes about as a result of habit, whence also its name (ethike) is one that is formed by a slight variation from the word ethos (habit). From this it is also plain that none of the moral virtues arises in us by nature; for nothing that exists by nature can form a habit contrary to its nature. For instance the stone which by nature moves downwards cannot be habituated to move upwards, not even if one tries to train it by throwing it up ten thousand times; nor can fire be habituated to move downwards, nor can anything else that by nature behaves in one way be trained to behave in another. Neither by nature, then, nor contrary to nature do the virtues arise in us; rather we are adapted by nature to receive them, and are made perfect by habit.

Again, of all the things that come to us by nature we first acquire the potentiality and later exhibit the activity (this is plain in the case of the senses; for it was not by often seeing or often hearing that we got these senses, but on the contrary we had them before we used them, and did not come to have them by using them); but the virtues we get by first exercising them, as also happens in the case of the arts as well. For the things we have to learn before we can do them, we learn by doing them, e.g. men become builders by building and lyre-players by playing the lyre; so too we become just by doing just acts, temperate by doing temperate acts, brave by doing brave acts. [...]

Thus, in one word, states of character arise out of like activities. This is why the activities we exhibit must be of a certain kind; it is because the states of character correspond to the differences between these. It makes no small difference, then, whether we form habits of one kind or of another from our very youth; it makes a very great difference, or rather all the difference. [...]

Chapter 6

We must, however, not only describe virtue as a state of character, but also say what sort of state it is. We may remark, then, that every virtue or excellence both brings into good condition the thing of which it is the excellence and makes the work of that thing be done well; e.g. the excellence of the eye makes both the eye and its work good; for it is by the excellence of the eye that we see well. Similarly the excellence of the horse makes a horse both good in itself and good at running and at carrying its rider and at awaiting the attack of the enemy. Therefore, if this is true in every case, the virtue of man also will be the state of character which makes a man good and which makes him do his own work well. [...]

Virtue, then, is a state of character concerned with choice, lying in a mean, i.e. the mean relative to us, this being determined by a rational principle, and by that principle by which the man of practical wisdom would determine it. Now it is a mean between two vices, that which depends on excess and that which depends on defect; and again it is a mean because the vices respectively fall short of or exceed what is right in both passions and actions, while virtue both finds and chooses that which is intermediate. Hence in respect of its substance and the definition which states its essence virtue is a mean, with regard to what is best and right an extreme.

Book 3

Chapter 1

SINCE virtue is concerned with passions and actions, and on voluntary passions and actions praise and blame are bestowed, on those that are involuntary pardon, and sometimes also pity, to distinguish the voluntary and the involuntary is presumably necessary for those who are studying the nature of virtue, and useful also for legislators with a view to the assigning both of honours and of punishments. Those things, then, are thought involuntary, which take place under compulsion or owing to ignorance; and that is compulsory of which the moving principle is outside, being a principle in which nothing is contributed by the person who is acting or is feeling the passion, e.g. if he were to be carried somewhere by a wind, or by men who had him in their power [...]

The compulsory, then, seems to be that whose moving principle is outside, the person compelled contributing nothing. [...]

Since that which is done under compulsion or by reason of ignorance is involuntary, the voluntary would seem to be that of which the moving principle is in the agent himself, he being aware of the particular circumstances of the action. Presumably acts done by reason of anger or appetite are not rightly called involuntary. For in the first place, on that showing none of the other animals will act voluntarily, nor will children; and secondly, is it meant that we do not do voluntarily any of the acts that are due to appetite or anger, or that we do the noble acts voluntarily and the base acts involuntarily? Is not this absurd, when one and the same thing is the cause? [...]

– Humans are rational
– Humans are social

Chapter 3

Do we deliberate about everything, and is everything a possible subject of deliberation, or is deliberation impossible about some things? We ought presumably to call not what a fool or a madman would deliberate about, but what a sensible man would deliberate about, a subject of deliberation. Now about eternal things no one deliberates, e.g. about the material universe or the incommensurability of the diagonal and the side of a square. But no more do we deliberate about the things that involve movement but always happen in the same way, whether of necessity or by nature or from any other cause, e.g. the solstices and the risings of the stars; nor about things that happen now in one way, now in another, e.g. droughts and rains; nor about chance events, like the finding of treasure. But we do not deliberate even about all human affairs; for instance, no Spartan deliberates about the best constitution for the Scythians. For none of these things can be brought about by our own efforts.

We deliberate about things that are in our power and can be done; and these are in fact what is left. For nature, necessity, and chance are thought to be causes, and also reason and everything that depends on man. Now every class of men deliberates about the things that can be done by their own efforts. And in the case of exact and self-contained sciences there is no deliberation, e.g. about the letters of the alphabet (for we have no doubt how they should be written); but the things that are brought about by our own efforts, but not always in the same way, are the things about which we deliberate, e.g. questions of medical treatment or of money-making. [...]

We deliberate not about ends but about means. For a doctor does not deliberate whether he shall heal, nor an orator whether he shall persuade, nor a statesman whether he shall produce law and order, nor does any one else deliberate about his end. They assume the end and consider how and by what means it is to be attained; and if it seems to be produced by several means they consider by which it is most easily and best produced, while if it is achieved by one only they consider how it will be achieved by this and by what means this will be achieved, till they come to the first cause, which in the order of discovery is last. For the person who deliberates seems to investigate and analyse in the way described as though he were analysing a geometrical construction (not all investigation appears to be deliberation – for instance mathematical investigations – but all deliberation is investigation), and what is last in the order of analysis seems to be first in the order of becoming. [...]

The same thing is deliberated upon and is chosen, except that the object of choice is already determinate, since it is that which has been decided upon as a result of deliberation that is the object of choice. For every one ceases to inquire how he is to act when he has brought the moving principle back to himself and to the ruling part of himself; for this is what chooses. This is plain also from the ancient constitutions, which Homer represented; for the kings announced their choices to the people. The object of choice being one of the things in our own power which is desired after deliberation, choice will be deliberate desire of things in our own power; for when we have decided as a result of deliberation, we desire in accordance with our deliberation.

Chapter 5

The end, then, being what we wish for, the means what we deliberate about and choose, actions concerning means must be according to choice and voluntary. Now the exercise of the virtues is concerned with means. Therefore virtue also is in our own power, and so too vice. For where it is in our power to act it is also in our power not to act, and vice versa; so that, if to act, where this is noble, is in our power, not to act, which will be base, will also be in our power, and if not to act, where this is noble, is in our power, to act, which will be base, will also be in our power. Now if it is in our power to do noble or base acts, and likewise in our power not to do them, and this was what being good or bad meant, then it is in our power to be virtuous or vicious. [...]

Witness seems to be borne to this both by individuals in their private capacity and by legislators themselves; for these punish and take vengeance on those who do wicked acts (unless they have acted under compulsion or as a result of ignorance for which they are not themselves responsible), while they honour those who do noble acts, as though they meant to encourage the latter and deter the former. But no one is encouraged to do the things that are neither in our power nor voluntary; it is assumed that there is no gain in being persuaded not to be hot or in pain or hungry or the like, since we shall experience these feelings none the less. Indeed, we punish a man for his very ignorance, if he is thought responsible for the ignorance, as when penalties are doubled in the case of drunkenness; for the moving principle is in the man himself, since he had the power of not getting drunk and his getting drunk was the cause of his ignorance. And we punish those who are ignorant of anything in the laws that they ought to know and that is not difficult, and so too in the case of anything else that they are thought to be ignorant of through carelessness; we assume that it is in their power not to be ignorant, since they have the power of taking care [...]

We may take it, then, that we have described choice in outline, and stated the nature of its objects and the fact that it is concerned with means.

BOOK 5

Chapter 1

With regards to justice and injustice we must (1) consider what kind of actions they are concerned with, (2) what sort of mean justice is, and (3) between what extremes the just act is intermediate. Our investigation shall follow the same course as the preceding discussions.

We see that all men mean by justice that kind of state of character which makes people disposed to do what is just and makes them act justly and wish for what is just; and similarly by injustice that state which makes them act unjustly and wish for what is unjust. Let us too, then, lay this down as a general basis. For the same is not true of the sciences and the faculties as of states of character. A faculty or a science which is one and the same is held to relate to contrary objects, but a state of character which is one of two contraries does not produce the contrary results; e.g. as a result of health we do not do what is the opposite of healthy, but only what is healthy; for we say a man walks healthily, when he walks as a healthy man would.

Now often one contrary state is recognized from its contrary, and often states are recognized from the subjects that exhibit them; for (A) if good condition is known, bad condition also becomes known, and (B) good condition is known from the things that are in good condition, and they from it. If good condition is firmness of flesh, it is necessary both that bad condition should be flabbiness of flesh and that the wholesome should be that which causes firmness in flesh. And it follows for the most part that if one contrary is ambiguous the other also will be ambiguous; e.g. if 'just' is so, that 'unjust' will be so too.

Now 'justice' and 'injustice' seem to be ambiguous, but because their different meanings approach near to one another the ambiguity escapes notice and is not obvious as it is, comparatively, when the meanings are far apart, e.g. (for here the difference in outward form is great) as the ambiguity in the use of *kleis* for the collar-bone of an animal and for that with which we lock a door. Let us take as a starting-point, then, the various meanings of 'an unjust man'. Both the lawless man and the grasping and unfair man are thought to be unjust, so that evidently both the law-abiding and the fair man will be just. The just, then, is the lawful and the fair, the unjust the unlawful and the unfair.

Since the unjust man is grasping, he must be concerned with goods – not all goods, but those with which prosperity and adversity have to do, which taken absolutely are always good, but for a particular person are not always good. Now men pray for and pursue these things; but they should not, but should pray that the things that are good absolutely may also be good for them, and should choose the things that are good for them. The unjust man does not always choose the greater, but also the less – in the case of things bad absolutely; but because the lesser evil is itself thought to be in a sense good, and graspingness is directed at the good, therefore he is thought to be grasping. And he is unfair; for this contains and is common to both.

Since the lawless man was seen to be unjust and the law-abiding man just, evidently all lawful acts are in a sense just acts; for the acts laid down by the legislative art are lawful, and each of these, we say, is just. Now the laws in their enactments on all subjects aim at the common advantage either of all or of the best or of those who hold power, or something of the sort; so that in one sense we call those acts just that tend to produce and preserve happiness and its components for the political society. And the law bids us do both the acts of a brave man (e.g. not to desert our post nor take to flight nor throw away our arms), and those of a temperate man (e.g. not to commit adultery nor to gratify one's lust), and those of a good-tempered man (e.g. not to strike another nor to speak evil), and similarly with regard to the other virtues and forms of wickedness, commanding some acts and forbidding others; and the rightly-framed law does this rightly, and the hastily conceived one less well. This form of justice, then, is complete virtue, but not absolutely, but in relation to our neighbour. And therefore justice is often thought to be the greatest of virtues, and 'neither evening nor morning star' is so wonderful; and pro-verbially 'in justice is every virtue comprehended'. And it is complete virtue in its fullest sense, because it is the actual exercise of complete virtue. It is complete because he who possesses it can exercise his virtue not only in himself but towards his neighbour also; for many men can exercise virtue in their own affairs, but not in their relations to their neighbour. This is why the saying of Bias is thought to be true, that 'rule will show the man'; for a ruler is necessarily in relation to other men and a member of a society. For this same reason justice, alone of the virtues, is thought to be 'another's good', because it is related to our neighbour; for it does what is advantageous to another, either a ruler or a copartner. Now the worst man is he who exercises his wickedness both towards himself and towards his friends, and the best man is not he who exercises his virtue towards him-self but he who exercises it towards another; for this is a difficult task. Justice in this sense, then, is not part of virtue but virtue entire, nor is the contrary injustice a part of vice but vice entire. What the difference is between virtue and justice in this sense is plain from what we have said; they are the same but their essence is not the same; what, as a relation to one's neighbour, is justice is, as a certain kind of state without qualification, virtue.

Chapter 2

But at all events what we are investigating is the justice which is a part of virtue; for there is a justice of this kind, as we maintain. Similarly it is with injustice in the particular sense that we are concerned.

That there is such a thing is indicated by the fact that while the man who exhibits in action the other forms of wickedness acts wrongly indeed, but not graspingly (e.g. the man who throws away his shield through cowardice or speaks harshly through bad temper or fails to help a friend with money through meanness), when a man acts grasp-ingly he often exhibits none of these vices, – no, nor all together, but certainly wicked-ness of some kind (for we blame him) and injustice. There is, then, another kind of injustice which is a part of injustice in the wide sense, and a use of the word 'unjust' which answers to a part of what is unjust in the wide sense of 'contrary to the law'. Again if one man commits adultery for the sake of gain and makes money by it, while another does so at the bidding of appetite though he loses money and is penalized for it, the latter would be held to be self-indulgent rather than grasping, but the former is unjust, but not self-indulgent; evidently, therefore, he is unjust by reason of his making gain by his act. Again, all other unjust acts are ascribed invariably to some particular kind of wicked-ness, e.g. adultery to self-indulgence, the desertion of a comrade in battle to cowardice, physical violence to anger; but if a man makes gain, his action is ascribed to no form of wickedness but injustice. Evidently, therefore, there is apart from injustice in the wide sense another, 'particular', injustice which shares the name and nature of the first, because its definition falls within the same genus; for the significance of both consists in a rela-tion to one's neighbour, but the one is concerned with honour or money or safety [...] and its motive is the pleasure that arises from gain [...]

The unjust has been divided into the unlawful and the unfair [...] unfair and the unlawful are not the same, but are different as a part is from its whole (for all that is unfair is unlawful, but not all that is unlawful is unfair) [...] for practically the majority of the acts commanded by the law are those which are prescribed from the point of view of virtue taken as a whole; for the law bids us practise every virtue and forbids us to practise any vice. And the things that tend to produce virtue taken as a whole are those of the acts prescribed by the law which have been prescribed with a view to education for the common good. [...]

Of particular justice and that which is just in the corresponding sense, (A) one kind is that which is manifested in distributions of honour or money or the other things that fall to be divided among those who have a share in the constitution (for in these it is possible for one man to have a share either unequal or equal to that of another), and (B) one is that which plays a rectifying part in transactions between man and man [...]

Chapter 3

(A) We have shown that both the unjust man and the unjust act are unfair or unequal [...] but this is the origin of quarrels and complaints – when either equals have and are awarded unequal shares, or unequals equal shares. Further, this is plain from the fact that awards should be 'according to merit'; for all men agree that what is just in distribution must be according to merit in some sense, though they do not all specify the same sort of merit, but democrats identify it with the status of freeman, supporters of oligarchy with wealth (or with noble birth), and supporters of aristocracy with excellence.

This, then, is what the just is – the proportional; the unjust is what violates the proportion. Hence one term becomes too great, the other too small, as indeed happens in practice; for the man who acts unjustly has too much, and the man who is unjustly treated too little, of what is good. [...]

This, then, is one species of the just.

Chapter 4

(B) The remaining one is the rectificatory, which arises in connexion with transactions both voluntary and involuntary. This form of the just has a different specific character from the former. For the justice which distributes common possessions is always in accordance with the kind of proportion mentioned above (for in the case also in which the distribution is made from the common funds of a partnership it will be according to the same ratio which the funds put into the business by the partners bear to one another); and the injustice opposed to this kind of justice is that which violates the proportion. But the justice in transactions between man and man is a sort of equality indeed, and the injustice a sort of inequality; not according to that kind of proportion, however, but according to arithmetical proportion. For it makes no difference whether a good man has defrauded a bad man or a bad man a good one, nor whether it is a good or a bad man that has committed adultery; the law looks only to the distinctive character of the injury, and treats the parties as equal, if one is in the wrong and the other is being wronged, and if one inflicted injury and the other has received it. Therefore, this kind of injustice being an inequality, the judge tries to equalize it; for in the case also in which one has received and the other has inflicted a wound, or one has slain and the other been slain, the suffering and the action have been unequally distributed; but the judge tries to equalize by means of the penalty, taking away from the gain of the assailant. [...] This is why, when people dispute, they take refuge in the judge; and to go to the judge is to go to justice; for the nature of the judge is to be a sort of animate justice; and they seek the judge as an intermediate, and in some states they call judges mediators, on the assumption that if they get what is intermediate they will get what is just. [...]

Chapter 5

Some think that reciprocity is without qualification just, as the Pythagoreans said; for they defined justice without qualification as reciprocity. Now 'reciprocity' fits neither distributive nor rectificatory justice – yet people want even the justice of Rhadamanthus to mean this:

Should a man suffer what he did, right justice would be done – for in many cases reciprocity and rectificatory justice are not in accord; e.g. (1) if an official has inflicted a wound, he should not be wounded in return, and if some one has wounded an official, he ought not to be wounded only but punished in addition. Further (2) there is a great difference between a voluntary and an involuntary act. But in associations for exchange this sort of justice does hold men together – reciprocity in accordance with a proportion and not on the basis of precisely equal return. For it is by proportionate requital that the city holds together. Men seek to return either evil for evil – and if they cannot do so, think their position mere slavery – or good for good – and if they cannot do so there is no exchange, but it is by exchange that they hold together [...] *- outside the household - forms of exchange*
- inside is fundamentally different

Chapter 6

Now we have previously stated how the reciprocal is related to the just; but we must not forget that what we are looking for is not only what is just without qualification but also political justice. This is found among men who share their life with a view to self sufficiency, men who are free and either proportionately or arithmetically equal, so that between those who do not fulfil this condition there is no political justice but justice in a special sense and by analogy. For justice exists only between men whose mutual relations are governed by law; and law exists for men between whom there is injustice; for legal justice is the discrimination of the just and the unjust. And between men between whom there is injustice there is also unjust action (though there is not injustice between all between whom there is unjust action), and this is assigning too much to oneself of things good in themselves and too little of things evil in themselves. This is why we do not allow a man to rule, but rational principle, because a man behaves thus in his own interests and becomes a tyrant. The magistrate on the other hand is the guardian of justice, and, if of justice, then of equality also. And since he is assumed to have no more than his share, if he is just (for he does not assign to himself more of what is good in itself, unless such a share is proportional to his merits – so that it is for others that he labours, and it is for this reason that men, as we stated previously, say that justice is 'another's good'), therefore a reward must be given him, and this is honour and privilege; but those for whom such things are not enough become tyrants.

The justice of a master and that of a father are not the same as the justice of citizens, though they are like it; for there can be no injustice in the unqualified sense towards thing that are one's own, but a man's chattel, and his child until it reaches a certain age and sets up for itself, are as it were part of himself, and no one chooses to hurt himself (for which reason there can be no injustice towards oneself). Therefore the justice or injustice of citizens is not manifested in these relations; for it was as we saw according to law, and between people naturally subject to law, and these [...] are people who have an equal share in ruling and being ruled [...]

Community - man is the head - household is the body

Chapter 7

Of political justice part is natural, part legal, natural, that which everywhere has the same force and does not exist by people's thinking this or that; legal, that which is originally indifferent, but when it has been laid down is not indifferent, e.g. that a prisoner's ransom shall be a mina, or that a goat and not two sheep shall be sacrificed, and again all the laws that are passed for particular cases, e.g. that sacrifice shall be made in honour of Brasidas, and the provisions of decrees. Now some think that all justice is of this sort, because that which is by nature is unchangeable and has everywhere the same force (as fire burns both here and in Persia), while they see change in the things recognized as just. This, however, is not true in this unqualified way, but is true in a sense; or rather, with the gods it is perhaps not true at all, while with us there is something that is just even by nature, yet all of it is changeable; but still some is by nature, some not by nature. It is evident which sort of thing, among things capable of being otherwise, is by nature, and which is not but is legal and conventional, assuming that both are equally changeable. And in all other things the same distinction will apply; by nature the right hand is stronger, yet it is possible that all men should come to be ambidextrous. The things which are just by virtue of convention and expediency are like measures; for wine and corn measures are not everywhere equal, but larger in wholesale and smaller in retail markets. Similarly, the things which are just not by nature but by human enactment are not everywhere the same, since constitutions also are not the same, though there is but one which is everywhere by nature the best. Of things just and lawful each is related as the universal to its particulars; for the things that are done are many, but of them each is one, since it is universal.

There is a difference between the act of injustice and what is unjust, and between the act of justice and what is just; for a thing is unjust by nature or by enactment; and this very thing, when it has been done, is an act of injustice, but before it is done is not yet that but is unjust. So, too, with an act of justice (though the general term is rather 'just action', and 'act of justice' is applied to the correction of the act of injustice).

Each of these must later be examined separately with regard to the nature and number of its species and the nature of the things with which it is concerned.

BOOK 10

Chapter 7

If happiness is activity in accordance with virtue, it is reasonable that it should be in accordance with the highest virtue; and this will be that of the best thing in us. Whether it be reason or something else that is this element which is thought to be our natural ruler and guide and to take thought of things noble and divine, whether it be itself also divine or only the most divine element in us, the activity of this in accordance with its proper virtue will be perfect happiness. That this activity is contemplative we have already said.

Now this would seem to be in agreement both with what we said before and with the truth. For, firstly, this activity is the best (since not only is reason the best thing in us, but the objects of reason are the best of knowable objects); and secondly, it is the most continuous, since we can contemplate truth more continuously than we can do anything. And we think happiness has pleasure mingled with it, but the activity of philosophic wisdom is admittedly the pleasantest of virtuous activities; at all events the pursuit of it is thought to offer pleasures marvellous for their purity and their enduringness, and it is to be expected that those who know will pass their time more pleasantly than those who inquire. And the self-sufficiency that is spoken of must belong most to the contemplative activity. For while a philosopher, as well as a just man or one possessing any other virtue, needs the necessaries of life, when they are sufficiently equipped with things of that sort the just man needs people towards whom and with whom he shall act justly, and the temperate man, the brave man, and each of the others is in the same case, but the philosopher, even when by himself, can contemplate truth, and the better the wiser he is; he can perhaps do so better if he has fellow-workers, but still he is the most self-sufficient. And this activity alone would seem to be loved for its own sake; for nothing arises from it apart from the contemplating, while from practical activities we gain more or less apart from the action. And happiness is thought to depend on leisure; for we are busy that we may have leisure, and make war that we may live in peace [...] but the activity of reason, which is contemplative, seems both to be superior in serious worth and to aim at no end beyond itself, and to have its pleasure proper to itself (and this augments the activity), and the self-sufficiency, leisureliness, unweariedness (so far as this is possible for man), and all the other attributes ascribed to the supremely happy man are evidently those connected with this activity, it follows that this will be the complete happiness of man [...]

But such a life would be too high for man; for it is not in so far as he is man that he will live so, but in so far as something divine is present in him; and by so much as this is superior to our composite nature is its activity superior to that which is the exercise of the other kind of virtue. If reason is divine, then, in comparison with man, the life according to it is divine in comparison with human life. But we must not follow those who advise us, being men, to think of human things, and, being mortal, of mortal things, but must, so far as we can, make ourselves immortal, and strain every nerve to live in accordance with the best thing in us; for even if it be small in bulk, much more does it in power and worth surpass everything. This would seem, too, to be each man himself, since it is the authoritative and better part of him. It would be strange, then, if he were to choose not the life of his self but that of something else. And what we said before will apply now; that which is proper to each thing is by nature best and most pleasant for each thing; for man, therefore, the life according to reason is best and pleasantest, since reason more than anything else is man. This life therefore is also the happiest. [...]

Chapter 9
[...] Now if arguments were in themselves enough to make men good, they would justly, as Theognis says, have won very great rewards, and such rewards should have been provided; but as things are, while they seem to have power to encourage and stimulate the generous-minded among our youth, and to make a character which is gently born, and a true lover of what is noble, ready to be possessed by virtue, they are not able to encourage the many to nobility and goodness. For these do not by nature obey the sense of shame, but only fear, and do not abstain from bad acts because of their baseness but through fear of punishment; living by passion they pursue their own pleasures and the means to them, and the opposite pains, and have not even a conception of what is

noble and truly pleasant, since they have never tasted it. What argument would remould such people? It is hard, if not impossible, to remove by argument the traits that have long since been incorporated in the character; and perhaps we must be content if, when all the influences by which we are thought to become good are present, we get some tincture of virtue.

Now some think that we are made good by nature, others by habituation, others by teaching. Nature's part evidently does not depend on us, but as a result of some divine causes is present in those who are truly fortunate; while argument and teaching, we may suspect, are not powerful with all men, but the soul of the student must first have been cultivated by means of habits for noble joy and noble hatred, like earth which is to nourish the seed. For he who lives as passion directs will not hear argument that dissuades him, nor understand it if he does; and how can we persuade one in such a state to change his ways? And in general passion seems to yield not to argument but to force. The character, then, must somehow be there already with a kinship to virtue, loving what is noble and hating what is base.

But it is difficult to get from youth up a right training for virtue if one has not been brought up under right laws; for to live temperately and hardily is not pleasant to most people, especially when they are young. For this reason their nurture and occupations should be fixed by law; for they will not be painful when they have become customary. But it is surely not enough that when they are young they should get the right nurture and attention; since they must, even when they are grown up, practise and be habituated to them, we shall need laws for this as well, and generally speaking to cover the whole of life; for most people obey necessity rather than argument, and punishments rather than the sense of what is noble.

This is why some think that legislators ought to stimulate men to virtue and urge them forward by the motive of the noble, on the assumption that those who have been well advanced by the formation of habits will attend to such influences; and that punishments and penalties should be imposed on those who disobey and are of inferior nature, while the incurably bad should be completely banished. A good man (they think), since he lives with his mind fixed on what is noble, will submit to argument, while a bad man, whose desire is for pleasure, is corrected by pain like a beast of burden. This is, too, why they say the pains inflicted should be those that are most opposed to the pleasures such men love […]

And surely he who wants to make men, whether many or few, better by his care must try to become capable of legislating, if it is through laws that we can become good. For to get any one whatever – any one who is put before us – into the right condition is not for the first chance comer; if any one can do it, it is the man who knows, just as in medicine and all other matters which give scope for care and prudence.

Must we not, then, next examine whence or how one can learn how to legislate? Is it, as in all other cases, from statesmen? Certainly it was thought to be a part of statesmanship. Or is a difference apparent between statesmanship and the other sciences and arts? In the others the same people are found offering to teach the arts and practising them, e.g. doctors or painters; but while the sophists profess to teach politics, it is practised not by any of them but by the politicians, who would seem to do so by dint of a certain skill and experience rather than of thought; for they are not found either writing or speaking about such matters (though it were a nobler occupation perhaps than composing speeches for the law-courts and the assembly), nor again are they found to have made statesmen of their own sons or any other of their friends. But it was to be expected that they should if they could; for there is nothing better than such a skill that they could have left to their cities, or could prefer to have for themselves, or, therefore, for those dearest to them. Still, experience seems to contribute not a little; else they could not have become politicians by familiarity with politics; and so it seems that those who aim at knowing about the art of politics need experience as well. [...]

Now our predecessors have left the subject of legislation to us unexamined; it is perhaps best, therefore, that we should ourselves study it, and in general study the question of the constitution, in order to complete to the best of our ability our philosophy of human nature [...]

2.1.10 Aristotle
Politics

BOOK 1

Part I

EVERY STATE is a community of some kind, and every community is established with a view to some good; for mankind always act in order to obtain that which they think good. But, if all communities aim at some good, the state or political community, which is the highest of all, and which embraces all the rest, aims at good in a greater degree than any other, and at the highest good.

Some people think that the qualifications of a statesman, king, householder, and master are the same, and that they differ, not in kind, but only in the number of their subjects. For example, the ruler over a few is called a master; over more, the manager of a household; over a still larger number, a statesman or king, as if there were no difference between a great household and a small state. The distinction which is made between the king and the statesman is as follows: When the government is personal, the ruler is a king; when, according to the rules of the political science, the citizens rule and are ruled in turn, then he is called a statesman.

But all this is a mistake; for governments differ in kind, as will be evident to any one who considers the matter according to the method which has hitherto guided us. As in other departments of science, so in politics, the compound should always be resolved into the simple elements or least parts of the whole. We must therefore look at the elements of which the state is composed, in order that we may see in what the different kinds of rule differ from one another, and whether any scientific result can be attained about each one of them.

Part II

He who thus considers things in their first growth and origin, whether a state or anything else, will obtain the clearest view of them. In the first place there must be a union of those who cannot exist without each other; namely, of male and female, that the race may continue (and this is a union which is formed, not of deliberate purpose, but because, in

From *Politica*, tr. B. Jowett, from *Politics and Economics* from *The Oxford Translation of Aristotle*, ed. W.D. Ross, Volume 10 (Oxford: Clarendon Press, 1921). Reprinted with permission of Oxford University Press.

common with other animals and with plants, mankind have a natural desire to leave behind them an image of themselves), and of natural ruler and subject, that both may be preserved. For that which can foresee by the exercise of mind is by nature intended to be lord and master, and that which can with its body give effect to such foresight is a subject, and by nature a slave; hence master and slave have the same interest. [...]

Out of these two relationships between man and woman, master and slave, the first thing to arise is the family, and Hesiod is right when he says, First house and wife and an ox for the plough, for the ox is the poor man's slave. The family is the association established by nature for the supply of men's everyday wants, and the members of it are called by Charondas 'companions of the cupboard', and by Epimenides the Cretan, 'companions of the manger'. But when several families are united, and the association aims at something more than the supply of daily needs, the first society to be formed is the village. And the most natural form of the village appears to be that of a colony from the family, composed of the children and grandchildren, who are said to be suckled 'with the same milk'. And this is the reason why Hellenic states were originally governed by kings; because the Hellenes were under royal rule before they came together, as the barbarians still are. Every family is ruled by the eldest, and therefore in the colonies of the family the kingly form of government prevailed because they were of the same blood. As Homer says: Each one gives law to his children and to his wives. For they lived dispersedly, as was the manner in ancient times. Wherefore men say that the Gods have a king, because they themselves either are or were in ancient times under the rule of a king. For they imagine, not only the forms of the Gods, but their ways of life to be like their own.

When several villages are united in a single complete community, large enough to be nearly or quite self-sufficing, the state comes into existence, originating in the bare needs of life, and continuing in existence for the sake of a good life. And therefore, if the earlier forms of society are natural, so is the state, for it is the end of them, and the nature of a thing is its end. For what each thing is when fully developed, we call its nature, whether we are speaking of a man, a horse, or a family. Besides, the final cause and end of a thing is the best, and to be self-sufficing is the end and the best.

Hence it is evident that the state is a creation of nature, and that man is by nature a political animal. And he who by nature and not by mere accident is without a state, is either a bad man or above humanity; he is like the tribeless, lawless, hearthless one, whom Homer denounces – the natural outcast is forthwith a lover of war; he may be compared to an isolated piece at draughts.

Now, that man is more of a political animal than bees or any other gregarious animals is evident. Nature, as we often say, makes nothing in vain, and man is the only animal whom she has endowed with the gift of speech. And whereas mere voice is but an indication of pleasure or pain, and is therefore found in other animals (for their nature attains to the perception of pleasure and pain and the intimation of them to one another, and no further), the power of speech is intended to set forth the expedient and inexpedient, and therefore likewise the just and the unjust. And it is a characteristic of man that he alone has any sense of good and evil, of just and unjust, and the like, and the association of living beings who have this sense makes a family and a state.

Further, the state is by nature clearly prior to the family and to the individual, since the whole is of necessity prior to the part; for example, if the whole body be destroyed, there will be no foot or hand, except in an equivocal sense, as we might speak of a stone hand;

almost Marxist

for when destroyed the hand will be no better than that. But things are defined by their working and power; and we ought not to say that they are the same when they no longer have their proper quality, but only that they have the same name. The proof that the state is a creation of nature and prior to the individual is that the individual, when isolated, is not self-sufficing; and therefore he is like a part in relation to the whole. But he who is unable to live in society, or who has no need because he is sufficient for himself, must be either a beast or a god: he is no part of a state. A social instinct is implanted in all men by nature, and yet he who first founded the state was the greatest of benefactors. For man, when perfected, is the best of animals, but, when separated from law and justice, he is the worst of all; since armed injustice is the more dangerous, and he is equipped at birth with arms, meant to be used by intelligence and virtue, which he may use for the worst ends. Wherefore, if he have not virtue, he is the most unholy and the most savage of animals, and the most full of lust and gluttony. But justice is the bond of men in states, for the administration of justice, which is the determination of what is just, is the principle of order in political society.

household – village – state

2.1.11 Marcus Aurelius
The Meditations

Book Three

We ought to consider not only that our life is daily wasting away and a smaller part of it is left, but another thing also must be taken into the account, that if a man should live longer, it is quite uncertain whether the understanding will still continue sufficient for the comprehension of things, and retain the power of contemplation which strives to acquire the knowledge of the divine and the human. For if he shall begin to fall into dotage, perspiration and nutrition and imagination and appetite, and whatever else there is of the kind, will not fail; but the power of making use of ourselves, and filling up the measure of our duty, and clearly separating all appearances, and considering whether a man should now depart from life, and whatever else of the kind absolutely requires a disciplined reason, all this is already extinguished. We must make haste then, not only because we are daily nearer to death, but also because the conception of things and the understanding of them cease first […]

Body, soul, intelligence: to the body belong sensations, to the soul appetites, to the intelligence principles. To receive the impressions of forms by means of appearances belongs even to animals; to be pulled by the strings of desire belongs both to wild beasts and to men who have made themselves into women, and to a Phalaris and a Nero: and to have the intelligence that guides to the things which appear suitable belongs also to those who do not believe in the gods, and who betray their country, and do their impure deeds when they have shut the doors. If then everything else is common to all that I have mentioned, there remains that which is peculiar to the good man, to be pleased and content with what happens, and with the thread which is spun for him; and not to defile the divinity which is planted in his breast, nor disturb it by a crowd of images, but to preserve it tranquil, following it obediently as a god, neither saying anything contrary to the truth, nor doing anything contrary to justice. And if all men refuse to believe that he lives a simple, modest, and contented life, he is neither angry with any of them, nor does he deviate from the way which leads to the end of life, to which a man ought to come pure, tranquil, ready to depart, and without any compulsion perfectly reconciled to his lot.

Tr. George Long.

✥ Book Four ✥

If our intellectual part is common, the reason also, in respect of which we are rational beings, is common: if this is so, common also is the reason which commands us what to do, and what not to do; if this is so, there is a common law also; if this is so, we are fellow-citizens; if this is so, we are members of some political community; if this is so, the world is in a manner a state. For of what other common political community will any one say that the whole human race are members? And from thence, from this common political community comes also our very intellectual faculty and reasoning faculty and our capacity for law; or whence do they come? For as my earthly part is a portion given to me from certain earth, and that which is watery from another element, and that which is hot and fiery from some peculiar source (for nothing comes out of that which is nothing, as nothing also returns to non-existence), so also the intellectual part comes from some source.

Death is such as generation is, a mystery of nature; a composition out of the same elements, and a decomposition into the same; and altogether not a thing of which any man should be ashamed, for it is not contrary to the nature of a reasonable animal, and not contrary to the reason of our constitution.

It is natural that these things should be done by such persons, it is a matter of necessity; and if a man will not have it so, he will not allow the fig-tree to have juice. But by all means bear this in mind, that within a very short time both thou and he will be dead; and soon not even your names will be left behind.

Take away thy opinion, and then there is taken away the complaint, "I have been harmed." Take away the complaint, "I have been harmed," and the harm is taken away.

That which does not make a man worse than he was, also does not make his life worse, nor does it harm him either from without or from within.

The nature of that which is universally useful has been compelled to do this.

Consider that everything which happens, happens justly, and if thou observest carefully, thou wilt find it to be so. I do not say only with respect to the continuity of the series of things, but with respect to what is just, and as if it were done by one who assigns to each thing its value. Observe then as thou hast begun; and whatever thou doest, do it in conjunction with this, the being good, and in the sense in which a man is properly understood to be good. Keep to this in every action.

Do not have such an opinion of things as he has who does thee wrong, or such as he wishes thee to have, but look at them as they are in truth.

A man should always have these two rules in readiness; the one, to do only whatever the reason of the ruling and legislating faculty may suggest for the use of men; the other, to change thy opinion, if there is any one at hand who sets thee right and moves thee from any opinion. But this change of opinion must proceed only from a certain persuasion, as of what is just or of common advantage, and the like, not because it appears pleasant or brings reputation.

Hast thou reason? I have. – Why then dost not thou use it? For if this does its own work, what else dost thou wish?

Thou hast existed as a part. Thou shalt disappear in that which produced thee; but rather thou shalt be received back into its seminal principle by transmutation.

Many grains of frankincense on the same altar: one falls before, another falls after; but it makes no difference.

Within ten days thou wilt seem a god to those to whom thou art now a beast and an ape, if thou wilt return to thy principles and the worship of reason.

Do not act as if thou wert going to live ten thousand years. Death hangs over thee. While thou livest, while it is in thy power, be good.

How much trouble he avoids who does not look to see what his neighbour says or does or thinks, but only to what he does himself, that it may be just and pure; or as Agathon says, look not round at the depraved morals of others, but run straight along the line without deviating from it.

He who has a vehement desire for posthumous fame does not consider that every one of those who remember him will himself also die very soon; then again also they who have succeeded them, until the whole remembrance shall have been extinguished as it is transmitted through men who foolishly admire and perish. But suppose that those who will remember are even immortal, and that the remembrance will be immortal, what then is this to thee? And I say not what is it to the dead, but what is it to the living? What is praise except indeed so far as it has a certain utility? For thou now rejectest unseasonably the gift of nature, clinging to something else [...]

Everything which is in any way beautiful is beautiful in itself, and terminates in itself, not having praise as part of itself. Neither worse then nor better is a thing made by being praised. I affirm this also of the things which are called beautiful by the vulgar, for example, material things and works of art. That which is really beautiful has no need of anything; not more than law, not more than truth, not more than benevolence or modesty. Which of these things is beautiful because it is praised, or spoiled by being blamed? Is such a thing as an emerald made worse than it was, if it is not praised? Or gold, ivory, purple, a lyre, a little knife, a flower, a shrub?

If souls continue to exist, how does the air contain them from eternity? – But how does the earth contain the bodies of those who have been buried from time so remote? For as here the mutation of these bodies after a certain continuance, whatever it may be, and their dissolution make room for other dead bodies; so the souls which are removed into the air after subsisting for some time are transmuted and diffused, and assume a fiery nature by being received into the seminal intelligence of the universe, and in this way make room for the fresh souls which come to dwell there. And this is the answer which a man might give on the hypothesis of souls continuing to exist. But we must not only think of the number of bodies which are thus buried, but also of the number of animals which are daily eaten by us and the other animals. For what a number is consumed, and thus in a manner buried in the bodies of those who feed on them! And nevertheless this earth receives them by reason of the changes of these bodies into blood, and the transformations into the aerial or the fiery element.

What is the investigation into the truth in this matter? The division into that which is material and that which is the cause of form, the formal.

Do not be whirled about, but in every movement have respect to justice, and on the occasion of every impression maintain the faculty of comprehension or understanding.

Everything harmonizes with me, which is harmonious to thee, O Universe. Nothing for me is too early nor too late, which is in due time for thee. Everything is fruit to me which thy seasons bring, O Nature: from thee are all things, in thee are all things, to thee all things return. The poet says, Dear city of Cecrops; and wilt not thou say, Dear city of Zeus?

2.1.12 Cicero
The Republic, Book III

There is a true law, a right reason, conformable to nature, universal, unchangeable, eternal, whose commands urge us to duty, and whose prohibitions restrain us from evil. Whether it enjoins or forbids, the good respect its injunctions, and the wicked treat them with indifference. This law cannot be contradicted by any other law, and is not liable either to derogation or abrogation. Neither the senate nor the people can give us any dispensation for not obeying this universal law of justice. It needs no other expositor and interpreter than our own conscience. It is not one thing at Rome and another at Athens; one thing to-day and another to-morrow; but in all times and nations this universal law must for ever reign, eternal and imperishable. It is the sovereign master and emperor of all beings. God himself is its author, – its promulgator, – its enforcer. He who obeys it not, flies from himself, and does violence to the very nature of man. For his crime he must endure the severest penalties hereafter, even if he avoid the usual misfortunes of the present life.

The virtue which obeys this law, nobly aspires to glory, which is virtue's sure and appropriate reward, – a prize she can accept without insolence, or forego without repining. When a man is inspired by virtue such as this, what bribes can you offer him, – what treasures, – what thrones, – what empires? He considers these but mortal goods, and esteems his own, divine. And if the ingratitude of the people, and the envy of his competitors, or the violence of powerful enemies, despoil his virtue of its earthly recompense, he still enjoys a thousand consolations in the approbation of conscience, and sustains himself by contemplating the beauty of moral rectitude.

This virtue, in order to be true, must be universal. Tiberius Gracchus continued faithful to his fellow-citizens, but he violated the rights and treaties guaranteed to our allies and the Latin peoples. If this habit of arbitrary violence extends and associates our authority, not with equity, but force, so that those who had voluntarily obeyed us, are only restrained by fear; then, although we, during our days, may escape the peril, yet am I solicitous respecting the safety of our posterity, and the immortality of the Commonwealth itself, which, doubtless, might become perpetual and invincible, if our people would maintain their ancient institutions and manners.

Marcus Tullius Cicero, *The Political Works of Marcus Tullius Cicero: Comprising his Treatise on the Commonwealth; and his Treatise on the Laws*. Translated from the original, with Dissertations and Notes in Two Volumes. By Francis Barham, Esq. (London: Edmund Spettigue, 1841–1842). Volume 1.

When Lælius had ceased to speak, all those that were present expressed the extreme pleasure they found in his discourse. But Scipio, more affected than the rest, and ravished with the delight of sympathy, exclaimed: – You have pleaded, my Lælius, many causes with an eloquence superior to that of Servius Galba, our colleague, whom you used, during his life, to prefer to all others, even the Attic orators; and never did I hear you speak with more energy than to-day, while pleading the cause of justice.

This justice (continued Scipio) is the very foundation of lawful government in political constitutions. Can we call the state of Agrigentum a Commonwealth, where all men are oppressed by the cruelty of a single tyrant? – where there is no universal bond of right, nor social consent and fellowship, which should belong to every people, properly so named. It is the same in Syracuse, – that illustrious city which Timæus calls the greatest of the Grecian towns. It was indeed a most beautiful city; and its admirable citadel, its canals distributed through all its districts, its broad streets, its porticoes, its temples, and its walls, gave Syracuse the appearance of a most flourishing state. But while Dionysus its tyrant reigned there, nothing of all its wealth belonged to the people, and the people were nothing better than the slaves of an impious despot. Thus wherever I behold a tyrant, I know that the social constitution must be, not merely vicious and corrupt, as I stated yesterday, but in strict truth, no social constitution at all.

2.1.13 Cicero
The Laws

Book I

Marcus.

– This human animal – prescient, sagacious, complex, acute, full of memory, reason and counsel, which we call man, – is generated by the supreme God in a more transcendent condition than most of his fellow-creatures. For he is the only creature among the earthly races of animated beings endued with superior reason and thought, in which the rest are deficient. And what is there, I do not say in man alone, but in all heaven and earth, more divine than reason, which, when it becomes ripe and perfect, is justly termed wisdom?

There exists, therefore, since nothing is better than reason, and since this is the common property of God and man, a certain aboriginal rational intercourse between divine and human natures. This reason, which is common to both, therefore, can be none other than right reason; and since this *right reason* is what we call *Law*, God and men are said by Law to be consociated. Between whom, since there is a communion of law, there must be also a communication of Justice.

Law and Justice being thus the common rule of immortals and mortals, it follows that they are both the fellow-citizens of one city and commonwealth. And if they are obedient to the same rule, the same authority and denomination, they may with still closer propriety be termed fellow-citizens, since one celestial regency, one divine mind, one omnipotent Deity then regulates all their thoughts and actions.

This universe, therefore, forms one immeasurable Commonwealth and city, common alike to gods and mortals. And as in earthly states, certain particular laws, which we shall hereafter describe, govern the particular relationships of kindred tribes; so in the nature of things doth an universal law, far more magnificent and resplendent, regulate the affairs of that universal city where gods and men compose one vast association.

When we thus reason on universal nature, we are accustomed to reason after this method. We believe that in the long course of ages and the uninterrupted succession of celestial revolutions, the seed of the human race was sown on our planet, and being

Marcus Tullius Cicero, *The Political Works of Marcus Tullius Cicero: Comprising his Treatise on the Commonwealth; and his Treatise on the Laws*. Translated from the original, with Dissertations and Notes in Two Volumes. By Francis Barham, Esq. (London: Edmund Spettigue, 1841–1842). Volume 2.

scattered over the earth, was animated by the divine gift of souls. Thus men retained from their terrestrial origin, their perishable and mortal bodies, while their immortal spirits were ingenerated by Deity. From which consideration we are bold to say that we possess a certain consanguinity and kindred fellowship with the celestials. And so far as we know, among all the varieties of animals, man alone retains the idea of the Divinity. And among men there is no nation so savage and ferocious as to deny the necessity of worshipping God, however ignorant it may be respecting the nature of his attributes. From whence we conclude that every man must recognize a Deity, who considers the origin of his nature and the progress of his life.

Now the law of virtue is the same in God and man, and cannot possibly be diverse. This virtue is nothing else than a nature perfect in itself, and developed in all its excellence. There exists therefore a similitude between God and man; nor can any knowledge be more appropriate and sterling than what relates to this divine similitude.

[...]

Marcus.

– [...] For of all the questions on which our philosophers argue, there is none which it is more important thoroughly to understand than this, *that man is born for justice, and that law and equity are not a mere establishment of opinion, but an institution of nature*. This truth will become still more apparent if we investigate the nature of human association and society.

There is no one thing more like to another, more homogeneous and analogous, than man is to man. And if the corruption of customs, and the variation of opinions, had not induced an imbecility of minds, and turned them aside from the course of nature, no one would more nearly resemble himself than all men would resemble all men. Therefore whatever definition we give of man, it must include the whole human race. And this is a good argument, that no portion of mankind can be heterogeneous or dissimilar from the rest; because, if this were the case, one definition could not include all men.

In fact, reason, which alone gives us so many advantages over beasts, by means of which we conjecture, argue, refute, discourse, and accomplish and conclude our designs, is assuredly common to all men; for the faculty of acquiring knowledge is similar in all human minds, though the knowledge itself may be endlessly diversified. By the same senses we all perceive the same objects, and that which strikes the sensibilities of the few, cannot be indifferent to those of the many. Those first rude elements of intelligence which, as I before observed, are the earliest developments of thought, are similarly exhibited by all men; and that faculty of speech which is the soul's interpreter, agrees in the ideas it conveys, though it may differ in the syllables that express them. And therefore there exists not a man in any nation, who, adopting his true nature for his true guide, may not improve in virtue.

Nor is this resemblance which all men bear to each other remarkable in those things only which accord to right reason. For it is scarcely less conspicuous in those corrupt practices by which right reason is most cruelly violated. For all men alike are captivated by voluptuousness, which is in reality no better than disgraceful vice, though it may seem to bear some natural relations to goodness; for by its delicious delicacy and luxury it insinuates error into the mind, and leads us to cultivate it as something salutary, forgetful of its poisonous qualities.

An error, scarcely less universal, induces us to shun death, as if it were annihilation; and to cling to life, because it keeps us in our present stage of existence, which is perhaps rather a misfortune than a desideratum. Thus, likewise, we erroneously consider pain as one of the greatest evils, not only on account of its present asperity, but also because it seems the precursor of mortality. Another common delusion obtains, which induces all mankind to associate renown with honesty, as if we are necessarily happy when we are renowned, and miserable when we happen to be inglorious.

In short, our minds are all similarly susceptible of inquietudes, joys, desires and fears; and if opinions are not the same in all men, it does not follow, for example, that the people of Egypt who deify dogs and cats, do not labour under superstition in the same way as other nations, though they may differ from them in the forms of its manifestation.

But in nothing is the uniformity of human nature more conspicuous than in its respect for virtue. What nation is there, in which kindness, benignity, gratitude, and mindfulness of benefits are not recommended? What nation in which arrogance, malice, cruelty, and unthankfulness, are not reprobated and detested! This uniformity of opinions, invincibly demonstrates that mankind was intended to compose one fraternal association. And to affect this, the faculty of reason must be improved till it instructs us in all the arts of well-living. If what I have said meets your approbation, I will proceed; or if any of my argument appears defective, I will endeavour to explain it.

Atticus.
– We see nothing to object to, if I may reply for both of us.

Marcus.
– It follows, then, in the line of our argument, *that nature made us just that we might participate our goods with each other, and supply each others' wants*. You observe in this discussion whenever I speak of nature, I mean *nature in its genuine purity*, and not in the corrupt state which is displayed by the depravity of evil custom, which is so great, that the natural and innate flame of virtue is often almost extinguished and stifled by the antagonist vices, which are accumulated around it.

But if our true nature would assert her rights, and teach men the noble lesson of the poet, who says, "I am a man, therefore no human interest can be indifferent to me," – then would justice be administered equally by all and to all. For nature hath not merely given us reason, but right reason, and consequently that law, which is nothing else than right reason enjoining what is good, and forbidding what is evil.

Now if nature hath given us law, she hath also given us justice, – for as she has bestowed reason on all, she has equally bestowed the sense of justice on all. And therefore did Socrates deservedly execrate the man who first drew a distinction between the law of nature and the law of morals, for he justly conceived that this error is the source of most human vices.

It is to this essential union between the naturally honorable, and the politically expedient, that this sentence of Pythagoras refers: – "Love is universal: let its benefits be universal likewise." From whence it appears that when a wise man is attached to a good man by that friendship whose rights are so extensive, that phenomenon takes place which is altogether incredible to worldlings, and yet it is a necessary consequence, that he loves himself not more dearly than he loves his friend. For how can a difference of interests arise where all interests are similar? If there could be such a difference of interests, however minute, it would be no longer a true friendship, which vanishes immediately when, for the sake of our own benefit, we would sacrifice that of our friend.

I have made these preliminary remarks, to prepare you the better for the main subject ,of our discourse, in order that you may more easily understand the principle, that nature herself is the foundation of justice. When I have explained this a little more at large, I shall come to the consideration of that civil law to which all my arguments refer.

[…]

Marcus.

[…] [I]f we are determined to the practice of goodness, not by its own intrinsic excellence, but for the sake of some private advantage, we are cunning, rather than good men. What will not that man do in the dark who fears nothing but a witness and a judge? Should he meet a solitary individual in a desert place, with a large sum of money about him, and altogether unable to defend himself from being robbed, how would he behave? In such a case the man whom we have represented to be honest from principle, and the nature of the thing itself, would converse with the stranger, assist him, and show him the way. But as to the man who does nothing for the sake of another, and measures every thing by the advantage it brings to himself, it is obvious, I suppose, how such a one would act; and should he deny that he would kill the man or rob him of his treasure, his reason for this cannot be that he apprehends there is any moral turpitude in such actions, but only because he is afraid of a discovery, and the bad consequences that would thence ensue. A sentiment this, at which not only learned men, but even clowns must blush.

It is therefore an absurd extravagance in some philosophers to assert that all things are necessarily just, which are established by the civil laws and the institutions of the people. Are then the laws of tyrants just, simply because they are laws? If the thirty tyrants of Athens imposed certain laws on the Athenians, and if these Athenians were delighted with these tyrannical laws, are we therefore bound to consider these laws as just? For my own part, I do not think such laws deserve any greater estimation than that past during our own interregnum, which ordained, that the dictator should be empowered to put to death with impunity, whatever citizens he pleased, without hearing them in their own defence.

There can be but one essential justice, which cements society, and one law which establishes this justice. This law is right reason, which is the true rule of all commandments and prohibitions. Whoever neglects this law, whether written or unwritten, is necessarily unjust and wicked.

But if justice consists in submission to written laws and national customs, and if, as the Epicureans persist in affirming, every thing must be measured by utility alone, he who wishes to find an occasion of breaking such laws and customs, will be sure to discover it. So that real justice remains powerless if not supported by nature, and this pretended justice is overturned by that very utility which they call its foundation.

But this is not all. If nature does not ratify law, all the virtues lose their sway. What becomes of generosity, patriotism, or friendship? Where should we find the desire of benefitting our neighbours, or the gratitude that acknowledges kindness? For all these virtues proceed from our natural inclination to love and cherish our associates. This is the true basis of justice, and without this, not only the mutual charities of men, but the religious services of the gods, would become obsolete; for these are preserved, as I imagine, rather by the natural sympathy which subsists between divine and human beings, than by mere fear and timidity.

If the will of the people, the decrees of the senate, the adjudications of magistrates, were sufficient to establish justice, the only question would be how to gain suffrages, and to win over the votes of the majority, in order that corruption and spoliation, and the falsification of wills, should become lawful. But if the opinions and suffrages of foolish men had sufficient weight to outbalance the nature of things, might they not determine among them, that what is essentially bad and pernicious should henceforth pass for good and beneficial? Or why should not a law able to enforce injustice, take the place of equity? Would not this same law be able to change evil into good, and good into evil?

As far as we are concerned, we have no other rule capable of distinguishing between a good or a bad law, than our natural conscience and reason. These, however, enable us to separate justice from injustice, and to discriminate between the honest and the scandalous. For common sense has impressed in our minds the first principles of things, and has given us a general acquaintance with them, by which we connect with Virtue every honourable and excellent quality, and with Vice all that is abominable and disgraceful.

Now we must entirely take leave of our senses, ere we can suppose that law and justice have no foundation in nature, and rely merely on the transient opinions of men. We should not venture to praise the virtue of a tree or a horse, in which expression there is an abuse of terms, were we not convinced that this virtue was in their nature, rather than in our opinion. For a stronger reason, it is mainly with respect to the moral nature of things, that we ought to speak of honour and shame among men.

If opinion could determine respecting the character of universal virtue, it might also decide respecting particular or partial virtues. But who will dare to determine that a man is prudent and cautious in his moral disposition, from any external appearances. For virtue evidently lies in perfect rationality, and this resides in the inmost depths of our nature. The same remark applies to all honour and honesty, for we judge of true and false, creditable and discreditable, rather by their essential qualities, than their external relations. Thus we judge according to their intrinsic nature, that rationality of life, which is virtue, must be ever constant and perpetual, and that inconstancy must necessarily be vicious.

We form an estimate of the opinions of youths, but not by their opinions. Those virtues and vices which reside in their moral natures, must not be measured by opinions. And so of all moral qualities, we must discriminate between honourable and dishonourable by reference to the essential nature of the things themselves.

The good we commend, must needs contain in itself something commendable. For as I before stated, goodness is not a mode of opinion: it is what it is, by the force of its very essence. If it were otherwise, opinion alone might constitute virtue and happiness, which is the most absurd of suppositions. And since we judge of good and evil by their nature, and since good and evil are the true constituents of honour and shame, we should judge in the same manner all honourable and all shameful qualities, testing them by the law of nature, without prejudice or passion. But our steady attention to this moral law of nature is often too much disturbed by the dissention of men and the variation of opinions. We might perhaps obey this law of nature more exactly, if we attended more accurately to the evidence of our senses, which being absolutely natural, are less likely to be deceived by artificial objects. Those objects, indeed, which sometimes present to us one appearance, sometimes another, we term fictions of the senses; but it is far otherwise. For neither parent, nor nurse, nor master, nor poet, nor drama, deceive our senses; nor do popular prejudices seduce them. But our delusions are connected with corruption of our mental opinions. And this corruption is either superinduced by those causes of error I have enumerated, which, taking possession of the young and uneducated, betray them into a thousand perversities, or by that voluptuousness which is the mimic of goodness, implicated and interfused through all our senses – the prolific mother of all human disasters. For she so corrupts us by her bewitching blandishments that we no longer perceive that things may be essentially excellent, though they have none of this deliciousness and pruriency. (Quæ natura bona sunt quia, dulcedine hac et scabie carent.)

From what I have said on this subject, it may then easily be concluded, that Justice and Equity are desirable for their own sake. For all virtuous men love Justice and Equity, for what they are in themselves; and we cannot believe that such virtuous men should delude themselves by loving something which does not deserve their affection. Justice and Right are therefore desirable and amiable in themselves; and if this is true of Right, it must be true of all the moral virtues with which it is connected. What then shall we say of liberality? Is it to be exercised gratuitously, or does it covet some reward and recompense? If a man does good without expecting any recompense for his kindness, then it is gratuitous: if he does expect compensation, it is a mere matter of traffic. Doubtless, he who truly deserves the reputation of a generous and good-natured man, performs his philanthropical duties without consulting his secular interests. In the same way the virtue of justice demands neither emolument nor salary, and therefore we desire it for its own sake, because it is its own reward. And for this reason we should entertain the same estimate of all moral virtues.

Besides this, if we weigh virtue by the mere utility and profit that attend it, and not by its own merit, the virtue which results will be in fact a species of vice (malitia rectissime decitur.) For the more a man's views are self-interested, the further he recedes from probity. It therefore necessarily happens, that those who measure virtue by profit, acknowledge no other virtue than this usurious vice. For who could he called benevolent, if none endeavoured to do good for the love of others? Where could we find the grateful person, if those who are disposed to gratitude could meet no benefactor disinterested enough to deserve it? What would become of sacred friendship, if we were not to love our friends for their own sake with all our heart and soul? In pursuance of this pseudo-benovelence, we must desert our friend, as soon as we can derive no further assistance from him. What can be more inhuman! But if friendship ought rather to be cultivated on its own account, for the same reason are society, equality, and justice, desirable for themselves. If this were not so, there could be no justice at all, since nothing is more opposite to the very essence of virtue than selfish interest.

What then shall we say of temperance, sobriety, continence, modesty, bashfulness, and chastity? Is it the fear of laws, or the dread of judgments and penalties, which restrain intemperance and dissoluteness? Do we then live in innocence and moderation, only to acquire a certain secular reputation? And when we blush at licentious discourse, is it only through a squeamish prudery, lest our reputation should be stained? How I am ashamed at those philosophers, who assert that there are no vices to be avoided but those which the laws have branded with infamy. Can it be said that those are truly chaste, who abstain from adultery, merely for the fear of public exposure, and that disgrace which is only one of its many evil consequences? Indeed, my dear Atticus, what can you praise or blame with reason, if you depart from that great law and rule of nature, which makes the difference between right and wrong? Shall corporal defects, if they are remarkable, shock our sensibilities, and shall those of the soul make no impression on us? – Of the soul, I say, whose turpitude is so evidently proved by its vices. For what is there more hideous than avarice, more ferocious than lust, more contemptible than cowardice, more base than stupidity and folly? Well, therefore, may we style unhappy, those persons in whom any one of these vices is conspicuous, not on account of the disgraces or losses to which they are exposed, but on account of the moral baseness of their sins.

We may apply the same ethical test to those who are distinguished for their virtue. For if virtue be not the highest excellence to which we aspire, it necessarily follows that there is something better than virtue. Is it money, fame, beauty, health? All these appear of little value to us when we possess them, especially when we consider that the duration of their enjoyment is altogether uncertain. Is it that basest of all things, voluptuousness? Certainly not; for nothing gives so much dignity to virtue, as its capacity of overruling and despising all the gratifications of secular and sensual life.

You see the long series of facts and arguments I have brought forward. Such is the connection between one doctrine of truth and another, – I should have proceeded further still, if I had not kept myself in check.

Quintus.

– To what point do your arguments tend, my brother? – for I would willingly go hand in hand with you through this discussion.

Marcus.

– The point they bear on, is the *moral end* of our actions, (ad finem bonorum) to which all things are to be referred, and for the sake of which all things are to be undertaken. This subject is, however, one of great controversy, and full of debate among the learned; yet I shall some day venture to publish my opinions respecting it.

Book II

Marcus.

– Let us, then, once more examine, before we descend to particulars, what is the essence and moral obligation of law; lest, when we come to apply it to its subordinate relations, we should not exactly understand each other for want of explanation; and lest we should be ignorant of the force of those terms which are usually employed in jurisprudence.

Quintus.

– This is a very necessary caution, and the proper method of seeking truth.

Marcus.

– This, then, as it appears to me, hath been the decision of the wisest philosophers; that law, was neither excogitated by the genius of men, nor is it any thing discovered in the progress of society; but a certain eternal principle, which governs the entire universe; wisely commanding what is right, and prohibiting what is wrong. Therefore, that aboriginal and supreme law is the Spirit of God himself; enjoining virtue, and restraining vice. For this reason it is, that this law, which the gods have bestowed on the human race, is so justly applauded. For it is the reason and mind of Wisdom, urging us to good, and deterring us from evil.

Quintus.

– You have already touched on this topic. But before you come to treat of civil laws, endeavour to explain the force and power of this divine and celestial law, lest the torrent of custom should overwhelm our understanding, and betray us into the vulgar method of expression.

Marcus.

– From little children have we learned, my Quintus, such phrases as this, "that a man appeals to justice, and goes to law;" and a great many municipal laws have we heard mentioned; but we should not understand that such commandments and prohibitions have sufficient moral power to make us practise virtue and avoid vice.

The moral power of law, is not only far more ancient than these legal institutions of states and peoples, but it is coeval with God himself, who beholds and governs both heaven and earth. For it is impossible that the divine mind should exist without reason; and divine reason must necessarily be possessed of a power to determine what is virtuous and what is vicious. Nor, because it was no where written, that one man should maintain the pass of a bridge against the enemy's whole army, and that he should order the bridge behind him to be cut down, are we therefore to imagine that the valiant Cocles did not perform this great exploit, agreeably to the laws of nature and the dictates of true bravery. Again, though in the reign of Tarquin there was no written law concerning adultery, it does not therefore follow that Sextus Tarquinius did not offend against the eternal law when he committed a rape on Lucretia, daughter of Tucipitinus. For, even then he had the light of reason deduced from the nature of things, that incites to good actions and dissuades from evil ones. And this has the force of a law, not from the time it was written, but from the first moment it began to exist. Now, this existence of moral obligation is coeternal with that of the divine mind. Therefore the true and supreme law, whose commands and prohibitions are equally infallible, is the right reason of the Sovereign Deity.

Quintus.

– I grant you, my brother, that whatever is the just is always the true law; nor can this true law either be originated or abrogated by any written enactments.

Marcus.

– Therefore, as the Divine Mind, or reason, is the supreme law, so it exists in the mind of the sage, so far as it can be perfected in man. With respect to civil laws, which differ in all ages and nations, the name of law belongs to them not so much by right as by the favour of the people. For every law which deserves the name of a law ought to be morally good and laudable, as we might demonstrate by the following arguments. It is clear, that laws were originally made for the security of the people, for the preservation of cities, for the peace and benefit of society. Doubtless, the first legislators persuaded the people that they would write and publish such laws only as should conduce to the general morality and happiness, if they would receive and obey them. Such were the regulations, which being settled and sanctioned, they justly entitled *Laws*. From which we may reasonably conclude, that those who made unjustifiable and pernicious enactments for the people, counteracted their own promises and professions; and established any thing rather than *laws*, properly so called, since it is evident that the very signification of the word *law*, comprehends the essence and energy of justice and equity.

[…]

Marcus.

– Now a state which has no law, is it not for that reason to be reckoned no state?

Quintus.

– We must needs say so.

Marcus.

– We must therefore reckon law among the very best things.

Quintus.

– I entirely agree with you.

Marcus.

– If then in the majority of nations, many pernicious and mischievous enactments are made, as far removed from the law of justice we have defined as the mutual engagements of robbers, are we bound to call them laws? For as we cannot call the recipes of ignorant empirics, who give poisons instead of medicines, the prescriptions of a physician, we cannot call that the true law of the people, whatever be its name, if it enjoins what is injurious, let the people receive it as they will. For law is the just distinction between right and wrong, conformable to nature, the original and principal regulator of all things, by which the laws of men should be measured, whether they punish the guilty or protect the innocent.

Quintus.

– I quite agree with you, and think that no law but that of justice should either be proclaimed as a law or enforced as a law.

2.1.14 The Holy Bible, Romans 2: 1–16

1 Wherefore thou art inexcusable, O man, whosoever thou art that judgest. For wherein thou judgest another, thou condemnest thyself. For thou dost the same things which thou judgest. 2 For we know that the judgment of God is, according to truth, against them that do such things. 3 And thinkest thou this, O man, that judgest them who do such things and dost the same, that thou shalt escape the judgment of God? 4 Or despisest thou the riches of his goodness and patience and longsuffering? Knowest thou not that the benignity of God leadeth thee to penance? 5 But according to thy hardness and impenitent heart, thou treasurest up to thyself wrath, against the day of wrath and revelation of the just judgment of God: 6 Who will render to every man according to his works. 7 To them indeed who, according to patience in good work, seek glory and honour and incorruption, eternal life: 8 But to them that are contentious and who obey not the truth but give credit to iniquity, wrath and indignation. 9 Tribulation and anguish upon every soul of man that worketh evil: of the Jew first, and also of the Greek. 10 But glory and honour and peace to every one that worketh good: to the Jew first, and also to the Greek. 11 For there is no respect of persons with God. 12 For whosoever have sinned without the law shall perish without the law: and whosoever have sinned in the law shall be judged by the law. 13 For not the hearers of the law are just before God: but the doers of the law shall be justified. 14 For when the Gentiles, who have not the law, do by nature those things that are of the law; these, having not the law, are a law to themselves. 15 Who shew the work of the law written in their hearts, their conscience bearing witness to them: and their thoughts between themselves accusing or also defending one another, 16 In the day when God shall judge the secrets of men by Jesus Christ, according to my gospel.

The Holy Bible (Douay–Rheims translation). Reprinted with permisson of Saint Benedict Press/TAN Books.

2.2 Early Christian and Medieval

Introduction

St. Paul (*c.* 5–67 AD), in his letter to the Romans, writes: "For when the Gentiles, who have not the law, do by nature those things that are of the law; these, having not the law, are a law to themselves. Who shew the work of the law written in their hearts, their conscience bearing witness to them: and their thoughts between themselves accusing or also defending one another, in the day when God shall judge the secrets of men by Jesus Christ, according to my gospel" (Romans 2: 14–16). Here we see how the impersonal reason of Aurelius and Cicero, and the external and deistic cause of Aristotle, is replaced, in the hands of St. Paul, by a personal creator God. This highlights the fact that although Stoic conceptions of natural law were important precursors to their medieval successors, they were also subject to significant revision. In the first instance, then, they underwent revision as to the account they gave of the ultimate origins and source of natural law. With the introduction of a creator God, the universal cosmic order, with which natural law was, by the Stoics, identified, could no longer be treated as self-sufficient and wholly immanent. Instead, it had now to be understood as an order pre-existing in the mind of God: its expression in creation being merely a reflection or embodiment of that higher order, one that was continuously dependent upon the divine creative sanction. In the second place, there began to emerge a much clearer distinction between the 'eternal law', that is, the divinely rooted normative order as it applied to and governed the entirety of creation, and the 'natural law' properly so called, or that part of the divinely rooted normative order which applied specifically to the human person. This gradually came to be couched in participatory terms so that the natural law was seen as pertaining to the peculiar way in which the human being freely and actively engaged in the created order. It was, in part, linked to the manner in which, at least in Judeo-Christian teaching, man was taken to be made in the image of God such as to set him quite apart in dignity from the rest of creation. This had the longer-term consequence of placing much greater emphasis on the worth and dignity of each human person and of emphasizing the need for that dignity to be respected if the natural, created, order was to be kept in proper harmony.

This growing sensitivity to the special importance of the human person was seen nowhere more clearly than in the growing value placed upon human life itself. Of course, the destruction of the innocent was regarded as unjust even in the earliest stages of the central tradition, but for patristic writers, like Tertullian (*c.* 160–220 AD), such prohibitions seemed to take on an altogether heightened significance, being extended even to innocent human life growing in the womb:

> But to us, to whom homicide has been once for all forbidden, it is not permitted to break up even what has been conceived in the womb, while as yet the blood is being drawn (from the parent body) for a human life. Prevention of birth is premature murder, and it makes no difference whether it is a life already born that one snatches away, or a life in the act of being born that one destroys; that which is to be a human-being is also human; the whole fruit is already actually present in the seed.[1]

With St. Augustine (354–430), these developments are given early and important expression. Of course, he was quick to treat eternal law as one and the same with supreme reason and eternal truth: God's law governing the ontological order, such that the eternal law is taken, in important respects, to be identical with the immutable nature of God. But he also speaks, in his *De libero arbitrio*, of the moral law as being the distinctive impression of the eternal law in the heart of man. From this base, he elsewhere goes on to consider the place of states without justice and regards them as colossal robberies: "Justice being taken away, then, what are kingdoms but great robberies?"[2] Similarly, it is to Augustine that we owe the memorable expression "Lex iniusta non est lex." Later, in *The City of God*, he reminds us that "no one lives as he wishes but the blessed, and that no one is blessed but the righteous." But even the "righteous himself does not live as he wishes, until he has arrived where he cannot die, be deceived, or injured, and until he is assured that this shall be his eternal condition." Thus: "For this nature demands; and nature is not fully and perfectly blessed till it attains what it seeks."[3]

Justinian the Great (483–565) was Eastern Roman (Byzantine) emperor from 527 to 565. His *Institutes*, a rewriting of Roman law, constitute the foundation of civil law in many modern European states. They begin by stating that: "Justice is the constant and perpetual wish to render every one his due. Jurisprudence is the knowledge of things divine and human; the science of the just and the unjust."[4] Justinian outlines the law of nature for all peoples and of the state. For him the law of nature is that law instilled by nature in all creation. The law which natural reason makes for all mankind is applied the same universally: "the law which natural reason appoints for all mankind obtains equally among all nations, because all nations make use of it."[5] Accordingly, the "people of Rome … are governed partly by their own laws, and partly by the laws which are common to all mankind."[6] There is, then, express recognition of the natural law as the foundation for jurisprudence in both the study and practice of law.

---

[1] Tertullian, *Apologeticus: Defence of the Christians Against the Heathen*, tr. Alexander Souter (1917). This was not so common in antiquity. Famous for his rhetorical swipe "What has Athens to do with Jerusalem or the academy with the church?" implying a dissonance between faith and reason, Tertullian is wrongly regarded as rejecting reason. As Marcia Colish, among others, points out: "By natural law, [Tertullian] means both the order of the universe and the moral bonds that unite all men, as well as man's natural capacity to know them." Marcia L. Colish, The Stoic Tradition from Antiquity to the Early Middle Ages (Leiden: E. J. Brill, 1985), 1617. Tertullian is, however, condemned by the Roman Catholic Church as a Montanist and it is true that some of his writings have a feverish quality to them.

[2] Augustine, *The City of God*, tr. Marcus Dods. From *Nicene and Post-Nicene Fathers*, First Series, Volume 2, ed. Philip Schaff (Buffalo, NY: Christian Literature Publishing Co., 1887), Book IV, Chapter 4.

[3] Ibid., Book XIV, Chapter 25.

[4] Justinian, *The Institutes of Justinian*, tr. J.B. Moyle, 5th edition (Oxford: Clarendon Press, 1913), Book I, Part I, paragraph 1.

[5] Ibid., Book I, Part I, paragraph 2.

[6] Ibid.

The medieval natural law tradition sees divine revelation as an important, even indispensable, adjunct to principles that may be gleaned using reason. Judaic, Christian, and Islamic accounts of the natural law often refer to identical precepts reflecting a common belief in an objective and universal order, though their reasons and methodologies for so doing are often importantly different. This commitment highlights the rich possibilities of engagement between the central natural law tradition and many of the diverse sacred traditions of the world. For present purposes, it should come as no surprise that Thomas Aquinas (1225–1274) – the paradigmatic natural law thinker – drew extensively upon the works of Jewish and Islamic philosophers – Maimonides (1135–1204), Averroes (1126–1198), and Avicenna (980–1037) – in the course of forging his own theological and philosophical synthesis. It is worth noting that Aquinas respectfully calls Maimonides "Rabbi Moses" and Averroes "the Commentator" (i.e. commentator on Aristotle to whom Aquinas, in turn, refers as "the Philosopher"). In discussing "Rabbi Moses'" *Guide of the Perplexed*, for example, Aquinas engages in a profound exploration of Maimonides' renowned proofs for the existence of God. In relation to the thought of Avicenna, he analyzes the distinction between essence and existence, developing it into the foundation for his own metaphysical thought. Likewise, he draws dialectically upon certain of Averroes' epistemological principles to develop an account of human nature and the unity of the human person as both body and soul, though this ultimately leads to his rejection of Averroeanism as incompatible with Christian orthodoxy.

Aquinas is rightly considered one of the greatest philosophers and theologians of all time. His influence on medieval and much modern Western thought is beyond question. At the age of 19 he resolved to become a Dominican despite the protestations of his family. Luckily, he was able to shake off his mother's worldly ambitions for him[7] and, in 1245, became a student of the University of Paris, where he met Albert the Great. Thereafter he took up a Chair in Theology at the College of St. James in Paris, taught at Cologne, the University of Paris as Regent Master, and set up a Studium Generale in Naples. His *Summa Theologica* is a masterpiece of metaphysics, epistemology, ethics, jurisprudence, and theology. His collected work is vast, comprehensive, intelligible, and perennially relevant. We reproduce his section on the natural law from the *Summa Theologica* and include parts of the *Summa Contra Gentiles*. For Aquinas the eternal law is the source of all law, both physical and moral. Not only are there human agents, there are angelic ones. Not only are there general physical laws, there is the possibility of miracles and thus exceptions to natural physical laws by way of an eternal source of all law. The eternal source can reveal itself in time and space, by way of miracles. Thus divine revelation can inform human understanding and human society. In this way, ecclesiastical law will be of relevance within a Christian state, for example, having implications for the institution of marriage, enjoining monogamy over polygamy, establishing certain holy days, and institutionalizing liturgical, sacramental, and educational practice. Thus Aquinas distinguishes between eternal law, divine law, human law, and natural law.

Maimonides' *Eight Chapters* is an introduction to his commentary on the *Pirkei Avot* and part of his *Commentary on the Mishnah*. Like Plato and Aristotle, he regards the soul as capable of being diseased or healthy. Those who are diseased in the soul need the wise as their physicians. His understanding of the soul and the conditions needed for its flourishing or perfection are illustrated via the Judaic law. Chief among these conditions is the realization

---

[7]   It should be added that her ambitions for him were not so worldly that they did not involve a desire that he would join the Benedictines and advance socially in that capacity.

of the golden mean, a place between extremes. In *Eight Chapters* IV.55, he writes: "Virtues are psychic conditions and dispositions which are mid-way between two reprehensible extremes, one of which is characterized by an exaggeration, the other by a deficiency." Like Aristotle, he stresses that virtue is a habit that can only be developed by practice. A wise ruler will therefore prescribe actions and moral habits that must be repeated until they are no longer burdensome and become part of a person's character. If a person develops the wrong habits and goes to excess, the ruler is required to promote equilibrium.

Maimonides points to Psalm 19: 8, "The law of the Lord is perfect, restoring the soul; the testimony of the Lord is sure, making wise the simple," as evidence that scripture recognizes the idea of disease of the soul. He also connects adherence to the mean with the doctrine of the imitation of God, by arguing that: "The works of the deity are most perfect, and with regard to them there is no possibility of an excess or a deficiency."[8] Commenting on Maimonides and Aquinas on the natural law, David Novak remarks that "To discover natural law is to discover what is divine within the universe, especially as it pertains to the human condition."[9] Perhaps that is why so many of the scholars of the great sacred traditions and so many more generally find intellectual succor in it. These similarities notwithstanding, there are undoubtedly variations and divergences between the Abrahamic and other religions more generally.[10]

It is often said that works of the ancient Greeks only survived because of Arabic translations. But this would be to overstate the matter. Part of the reason it is thought that Aristotle was handed on to the West by Islam is because the major works of Aristotle, such as the *Organon*, had been translated into Latin but were lost in Western Roman lands before the Middle Ages. But these writings were never lost to Byzantium in their Greek translation. So it was from Byzantium that the Islamic philosophers discovered Aristotle and Plato, not vice versa. It is true, however, that some medieval Christian thinkers in relation to certain texts were first reintroduced to Plato and Aristotle by reading Arabic translations of the Greek, but it would be an exaggeration to assert that the Greeks were passed on to the West via Islam.[11]

Nonetheless, what is often called the Golden Age of Islam, from 750 to 1250 CE, saw a flowering of intellectual thought, both in the sciences and in the arts. Perhaps most spectacular were the architectural achievements of the age. Avicenna, or Ibn Sina, was a philosopher, physicist, and poet living between 980 and 1037 CE. His Canon of Medicine is a tract on the same subject not unlike that of Galen and Hippocrates. In his thesis "On Love," part of which we have here reproduced, he affirms that: "Every being which is determined by a design strives by nature toward its perfection, i.e. that goodness of

---

[8]   Maimonides, *Guide of the Perplexed* 2.28.

[9]   David Novak, "Maimonides and Aquinas on Natural Law," in *St. Thomas Aquinas and the Natural Law Tradition: Contemporary Perspectives*, ed. John Goyette, Mark Latkovic, and Richard S. Myers (Washington, DC: Catholic University of America, 2004), p. 46. See also Mercedes Rubio, *Aquinas and Maimonides on the Possibility of the Knowledge of God* (Dordrecht, Netherlands: Springer, 2006).

[10]   While the Noahide Laws, for example, prohibit idolatry, murder, theft, forbidden relations, blasphemy, and consumption of the flesh of live animals while enjoining the establishment of a legal system and courts of law (Talmud Sanhedrin 56a), they are arguably at odds with mainstream Christian teaching on the Trinity, Incarnation, marriage, and apposite temporal punishment of transgressors, for example. There is nonetheless continuing discussion of how the laws are to be interpreted. Cf David Novak, *The Image of the Non-Jew in Judaism: An Historical and Constructive Study of the Noahide Laws* (New York: Edwin Mellen Press, 1983).

[11]   F. Klein-Frank, "Al-Kindi," in O. Leaman and H. Nasr, *History of Islamic Philosophy* (London: Routledge, 2001), p. 165. Charles Burnett, "The Coherence of the Arabic–Latin Translation Program in Toledo in the Twelfth Century," *Science in Context* 14 (2001), pp. 249–288.

reality which ultimately flows from the reality of the Pure Good, and by nature it shies away from its specific defect which is the evil in it, i.e. materiality and non-being, for every evil results from attachment to matter and non-being."[12] Although he is ordinarily regarded as a neo-Platonist, in this we hear echoes of Aristotle's theory of the good, of the mean, and of human flourishing. Part V of the tract, which is included and which deserves further investigation, however, proceeds on the assumption that conjugal relations between a man and his wives and *female slaves* are ennobling and refined.[13]

Averroes, addressed by Aquinas as "the Commentator" such was his respect for his work, in *On the Harmony of Religions and Philosophy*, supplies a poetic account of the argument from design. To observe the points of convergence between the central natural law tradition and the great sacred traditions is not to suggest that there are no differences between them. Manifestly there are. Teachings in relation to marriage, family, divorce, liturgical practice, and ritual can all depend upon the perceived place of revelation. However, that there are points of commonality is also clear. For Averroes there is no contradiction between the aims of religion and philosophy. Renowned for his translations and commentaries on the works of Aristotle, he challenges Al Ghazali's critique of Avicenna. Further he rejects Al Ghazali's conclusion that philosophy has the propensity to undermine religion and Islamic teaching in particular. Averroes sees this view as not merely mistaken but misplaced in its interpretation of Avicenna. He regards religion and philosophy as occupying two separate but not mutually exclusive spheres. Religion he sees as teaching by way of symbols and allegories, while philosophy he thought of as imparting knowledge of truth itself. However, a more Platonic and esoteric direction, no part of the Thomistic vision, emerges when he suggests that philosophical truth is higher than the symbolic ideas perceived by the multitude.

The teachings of Avicenna and Averroes on the intellect and the soul are unalike. Whereas Avicenna taught that the active intellect is universal and separate and the passive intellect is individual and inherent in the soul, Averroes holds that both the active and the passive intellect are separate from the individual soul and are universal, that is, one and the same in all individuals. One of the implications of this, for Aquinas at least, is that it seems to make impossible any immortality of the individual soul, a matter that would conflict with Christian scriptural, magisterial, and traditional teaching. Aquinas' account of the soul is developed as in contrast to Averroes' monopsychism, or view that there is just one mind. Aquinas stresses the immortality of the individual soul. Whereas Averroes permits a concept of an individual mind communicating with an Active Intellect who is One and then appears to conflate this concept of the mind with the soul, Aquinas resists this move separating the universal mind from that of the soul which, for him, is multiple and distinct again from the body. Despite these differences, there can be no denying that Aquinas holds Avicenna and Averroes in such high esteem that he presents a metaphysic which in certain ways is best understood as a response to their accounts. The dialogue demonstrates the wealth of shared philosophical understanding that there is between the great monotheistic religions.

---

[12]   Avicenna, *On Love*, Emil L. Fackenheim, "A Treatise of Love by Ibn Sina," *Medieval Studies* 7 (1945), pp. 208–228.

[13]   "Rational love can, therefore, not be pure except when the animal faculty is altogether subdued. With respect to the desire for conjugal union, … it is permissible and may find approval only in the case of a man with either his wife *or female slave*," ibid., p. 222. This, however, is consistent with Islamic doctrine on the keeping of concubines and the recognition of polygamy.

2.2.1 Tertullian
Against Marcion and *Apologeticus*

Against Marcion

Book II

Chapter II

We have now, then, cleared our way to the contemplation of the Almighty God, the Lord and Maker of the universe. His greatness, as I think, is shown in this, that from the beginning He made Himself known: He never hid Himself, but always shone out brightly, even before the time of Romulus, to say nothing of that of Tiberius; with the exception indeed that the heretics, and they alone, know Him not, although they take such pains about Him. They on this account suppose that another god must be assumed to exist, because they are more able to censure than deny Him whose existence is so evident, deriving all their thoughts about God from the deductions of sense; just as if some blind man, or a man of imperfect vision, chose to assume some other sun of milder and healthier ray, because he sees not that which is the object of sight. There is, O man, but one sun which rules this world and even when you think otherwise of him, he is best and useful; and although to you he may seem too fierce and baneful, or else, it may be, too sordid and corrupt, he yet is true to the laws of his own existence. Unable as you are to see through those laws, you would be equally impotent to bear the rays of any other sun, were there one, however great and good. Now, you whose sight is defective in respect of the inferior god, what is your view of the sublimer One? Really you are too lenient to your weakness; and set not yourself to the proof of things, holding God to be certainly, undoubtedly, and therefore sufficiently known, the very moment you have discovered Him to exist, though you know Him not except on the side where He has willed His proofs to lie. But you do not even deny God intelligently, you treat of Him ignorantly; nay, you accuse Him with a semblance of intelligence, whom if you did but know Him, you would never accuse, nay, never treat of. You give Him His name indeed, but you deny the essential truth of that name, that is, the greatness which is called

From *The Ante-Nicene Fathers: Translations of the Writings of the Fathers down to* A.D. *325*, ed. Rev. Alexander Roberts, D.D., and James Donaldson, LL.D. American reprint of the Edinburgh edition. Revised and chronologically arranged, with brief prefaces and occasional notes, by A. Cleveland Coxe, D.D. (Buffalo, NY: The Christian Literature Publishing Company, 1885–1896), 10 volumes.

God; not acknowledging it to be such as, were it possible for it to have been known to man in every respect, would not be greatness. Isaiah even so early, with the clearness of an apostle, foreseeing the thoughts of heretical hearts, asked, "Who hath known the mind of the Lord? For who hath been His counsellor? With whom took He counsel? […] or who taught Him knowledge, and showed to Him the way of understanding?" With whom the apostle agreeing exclaims, "Oh the depth of the riches both of the wisdom and knowledge of God! how unsearchable are His judgments, and His ways past finding out!" "His judgments unsearchable," as being those of God the Judge; and "His ways past finding out," as comprising an understanding and knowledge which no man has ever shown to Him, except it may be those critics of the Divine Being, who say, God ought not to have been this, and He ought rather to have been that; as if any one knew what is in God, except the Spirit of God. Moreover, having the spirit of the world, and "in the wisdom of God by wisdom knowing not God," they seem to themselves to be wiser than God; because, as the wisdom of the world is foolishness with God, so also the wisdom of God is folly in the world's esteem. We, however, know that "the foolishness of God is wiser than men, and the weakness of God is stronger than men." Accordingly, God is then especially great, when He is small to man; then especially good, when not good in man's judgment; then especially unique, when He seems to man to be two or more. Now, if from the very first "the natural man, not receiving the things of the Spirit of God," has deemed God's law to be foolishness, and has therefore neglected to observe it; and as a further consequence, by his not having faith, "even that which he seemeth to have hath been taken from him" – such as the grace of paradise and the friendship of God, by means of which he might have known all things of God, if he had continued in his obedience – what wonder is it, if he, reduced to his material nature, and banished to the toil of tilling the ground, has in his very labour, downcast and earth–gravitating as it was, handed on that earth-derived spirit of the world to his entire race, wholly natural and heretical as it is, and not receiving the things which belong to God? Or who will hesitate to declare the great sin of Adam to have been heresy, when he committed it by the choice of his own will rather than of God's? Except that Adam never said to his fig-tree, Why hast thou made me thus? He confessed that he was led astray; and he did not conceal the seducer. He was a very rude heretic. He was disobedient; but yet he did not blaspheme his Creator, nor blame that Author of his being, Whom from the beginning of his life he had found to be so good and excellent, and Whom he had perhaps made his own judge from the very first.

Chapter III– God Known by His Works. His Goodness Shown in His Creative Energy; But Everlasting in Its Nature; Inherent in God, Previous to All Exhibition of It. The First Stage of This Goodness Prior to Man.

It will therefore be right for us, as we enter on the examination of the known God, when the question arises, in what condition He is known to us, to begin with His works, which are prior to man; so that His goodness, being discovered immediately along with Himself, and then constituted and prescriptively settled, may suggest to us some sense whereby we may understand how the subsequent order of things came about. The disciples of Marcion, moreover, may possibly be able, while recognising the goodness of our God, to learn how worthy it is likewise of the Divine Being, on those very grounds whereby we have proved it to be unworthy in the case of their god. Now this very point, which is a material one in their scheme, *Marcion* did not find in any other god, but eliminated it for himself out of his own god. The first goodness, then, was that of the Creator, whereby God was unwilling to remain hidden for ever; in other words, (unwilling) that there should not be a something by which God should become known. For what, indeed, is so good as the knowledge and fruition of God? Now, although it did not transpire that this was good, because as yet there existed nothing to which it could transpire, yet God foreknew what good would eventually transpire, and therefore He set Himself about developing His own perfect goodness, for the accomplishment of the good which was to transpire; not, indeed, a sudden goodness issuing in some accidental boon or in some excited impulse, such as must be dated simply from the moment when it began to operate. For if it did itself produce its own beginning when it began to operate, it had not, in fact, a beginning itself when it acted. When, however, an initial act had been once done by it, the scheme of temporal seasons began, for distinguishing and noting which, the stars and luminaries of heaven were arranged in their order. "Let them be," says God, "for seasons, and for days, and years." Previous, then, to this temporal course, (the goodness) which created time had not time; nor before that beginning which the same goodness originated, had it a beginning. Being therefore without all order of a beginning, and all mode of time, it will be reckoned to possess an age, measureless in extent and endless in duration; nor will it be possible to regard it as a sudden or adventitious or impulsive emotion, because it has nothing to occasion such an estimate of itself; in other words, no sort of temporal sequence. It must therefore be accounted an eternal attribute, inbred in God, and everlasting, and on this account worthy of the Divine Being, putting to shame for ever the benevolence of Marcion's god, subsequent as he is to (I will not say) all beginnings and times, but to the very malignity of the Creator, if indeed malignity could possibly have been found in goodness.

Chapter IV– The Next Stage Occurs in the Creation of Man by the Eternal Word.
Spiritual as Well as Physical Gifts to Man. The Blessings of Man's Free-Will.
The goodness of God having, therefore, provided man for the pursuit of the knowledge of Himself, added this to its original notification, that it first prepared a habitation for him, the vast fabric (of the world) to begin with, and then afterwards the vaster one (of a higher world,) that he might on a great as well as on a smaller stage practise and advance in his probation, and so be promoted from the *good* which God had given him, that is, from his high position, to God's *best*; that is, to some higher abode. In this good work *God* employs a most excellent minister, even His own Word. "My heart" He says, "hath emitted my most excellent Word." Let Marcion take hence his first lesson on the noble fruit of this truly most excellent tree. But, like a most clumsy clown, he has grafted a good branch on a bad stock. The sapling, however, of his blasphemy shall be never strong: it shall wither with its planter, and thus shall be manifested the nature of the good tree. Look at the total result: how fruitful was the Word! God issued His *fiat*, and it was done: God also saw that it was good; not as if He were ignorant of the good until He saw it; but because it was good, He therefore saw it, and honoured it, and set His seal upon it; and consummated the goodness of His works by His vouchsafing to them that contemplation. Thus God blessed what He made good, in order that He might commend Himself to you as whole and perfect, good both in word and act. As yet the Word knew no malediction, because He was a stranger to malefaction. We shall see what reasons required *this* also of God. Meanwhile the world consisted of all things good, plainly foreshowing how much good was preparing for him for whom all this was provided. Who indeed was so worthy of dwelling amongst

the works of God, as he who was His own image and likeness? That image was wrought out by a goodness even more operative than its wont, with no imperious word, but with friendly hand preceded by an almost affable utterance: "Let us make man in our image, after our likeness." Goodness spake the word; Goodness formed man of the dust of the ground into so great a substance of the flesh, built up out of one material with so many qualities; Goodness breathed into him a soul, not dead but living. Goodness gave him dominion over all things, which he was to enjoy and rule over, and even give names to. In addition to this, Goodness annexed pleasures to man so that, while master of the whole world, he might tarry among higher delights, being translated into paradise, out of the world into the Church. The self-same Goodness provided also a help meet for him, that there might be nothing in his lot that was not good.

Apologeticus (Defence of the Christians against the Heathen)

How many of those standing around and panting for the blood of the Christians, aye even of yourselves, magistrates most just and severe against us, should I prick in their consciences, for putting to death the children born to them? Since there is a difference also in the manner of the death, it is assuredly more cruel to suffocate them by drowning or to expose them to cold and starvation and the dogs; for even an older person would prefer to die by the sword. But to us, to whom homicide has been once for all forbidden, it is not permitted to break up even what has been conceived in the womb, while as yet the blood is being drawn (from the parent body) for a human life. Prevention of birth is premature murder, and it makes no difference whether it is a life already born that one snatches away, or a life in the act of being born that one destroys; that which is to be a human-being is also human; the whole fruit is already actually present in the seed.

Tr. Alexander Souter (1917).
Famous for his rhetorical swipe "What has Athens to do with Jerusalem or the academy with the church?" implying a dissonance between faith and reason, Tertullian is wrongly regarded as rejecting reason. As Marcia Colish, among others, points out: "By natural law, [Tertullian] means both the order of the universe and the moral bonds that unite all men, as well as man's natural capacity to know them." Marcia L. Colish, *The Stoic Tradition from Antiquity to the Early Middle Ages* (Leiden: E. J. Brill, 1985), 16–17. Tertullian is, however, condemned by the Roman Catholic Church as a Montanist and it is true that some of his writings have a feverish quality to them.

2.2.2 Justinian
The Institutes

Book I. Of Persons

I. Justice and Law.

JUSTICE is the constant and perpetual wish to render every one his due.

1. Jurisprudence is the knowledge of things divine and human; the science of the just and the unjust.
2. Having explained these general terms, we think we shall commence our exposition of the law of the Roman people most advantageously, if we pursue at first a plain and easy path, and then proceed to explain particular details with the utmost care and exactness. For, if at the outset we overload the mind of the student, while yet new to the subject and unable to bear much, with a multitude and variety of topics, one of two things will happen – we shall either cause him wholly to abandon his studies, or, after great toil, and often after great distrust to himself (the most frequent stumbling block in the way of youth), we shall at last conduct him to the point, to which, if he had been led by an easier road, he might, without great labor, and without any distrust of his own powers, have been sooner conducted.
3. The maxims of law are these: to live honestly, to hurt no one, to give every one his due.
4. The study of law is divided into two branches; that of public and that of private law. Public law regards the government of the Roman empire; private law, the interest of the individuals. We are now to treat of the latter, which is composed of three elements, and consists of precepts belonging to the natural law, to the law of nations, and to the civil law.

Oliver J. Thatcher, ed., *The Library of Original Sources* (Milwaukee: University Research Extension Co., 1907), Vol. III: The Roman World, pp. 100–166.

II. Natural, Common, and Civil Law.

The law of nature is that law which nature teaches to all animals. For this law does not belong exclusively to the human race, but belongs to all animals, whether of the earth, the air, or the water. Hence comes the union of the male and female, which we term matrimony; hence the procreation and bringing up of children. We see, indeed, that all the other animals besides men are considered as having knowledge of this law.

1. Civil law is thus distinguished from the law of nations. Every community governed by laws and customs uses partly its own law, partly laws common to all mankind. The law which a people makes for its own government belongs exclusively to that state and is called the civil law, as being the law of the particular state. But the law which natural reason appoints for all mankind obtains equally among all nations, because all nations make use of it. The people of Rome, then, are governed partly by their own laws, and partly by the laws which are common to all mankind. We will take notice of this distinction as occasion may arise.
2. Civil law takes its name from the state which it governs, as, for instance, from Athens; for it would be very proper to speak of the laws of Solon or Draco as the civil law of Athens. And thus the law which the Roman people make use of is called the civil law of the Romans, or that of the Quirites; for the Romans are called Quirites from Quirinum. But whenever we speak of civil law, without adding the name of any state, we mean our own law; just as the Greeks, when "the poet" is spoken of without any name being expressed, mean the great Homer, and we Romans mean Virgil.

The law of the nations is common to all mankind, for nations have established certain laws, as occasion and the necessities of human life required. Wars arose, and in their train followed captivity and then slavery, which is contrary to the law of nature; for by that law all men are originally born free. Further, by the law of nations almost all contracts were at first introduced, as, for instance, buying and selling, letting and hiring, partnership, deposits, loans returnable in kind, and very many others.

3. Our law is written and unwritten, just as among the Greeks some of their laws were written and others were not written. The written part consists of *leges* (*lex*), *plebiscita*, *senatusconsulta*, *constitutiones* of emperors, *edicta* of magistrates, and *responsa* of jurisprudents [i.e., jurists].
4. A *lex* is that which was enacted by the Roman people on its being proposed by a senatorian magistrate, as a consul. A *plebiscitum* is that which was enacted by the plebs on its being proposed by a plebeian magistrate, as a tribune. The plebs differ from the people as a species from its genus, for all the citizens, including patricians and senators, are comprehended in the *populi* (people); but the plebs only included citizens [who were] not patricians or senators. *Plebiscita*, after the Hortensian law had been passed, began to have the same force as *leges*.
5. A *senatusconsultum* is that which the senate commands or appoints: for, when the Roman people was so increased that it was difficult to assemble it together to pass laws, it seemed right that the senate should be consulted in place of the people.

6.　That which seems good to the emperor has also the force of law; for the people, by the *Lex Regia*, which is passed to confer on him his power, make over to him their whole power and authority. Therefore whatever the emperor ordains by *rescript*, or decides in adjudging a cause, or lays down by edict, is unquestionably law; and it is these enactments of the emperor that are called *constitutiones*. Of these, some are personal, and are not to be drawn into precedent, such not being the intention of the emperor. Supposing the emperor has granted a favor to any man on account of his merit, or inflicted some punishment, or granted some extraordinary relief, the application of these acts does not extend beyond the particular individual. But the other *constitutiones*, being general, are undoubtedly binding on all.

7.　The edicts of the praetors are also of great authority. These edicts are called the *ius honorarium*, because those who bear honors [i.e., offices] in the state, that is, the magistrates, have given them their sanction. The curule aediles also used to publish an edict relative to certain subjects, which edict also became a part of the *ius honorarium*.

8.　The answers of the *jurisprudenti* are the decisions and opinions of persons who were authorized to determine the law. For anciently it was provided that there should be persons to interpret publicly the law, who were permitted by the emperor to give answers on questions of law. They were called *jurisconsulti*; and the authority of their decision and opinions, when they were all unanimous, was such, that the judge could not, according to the constitutiones, refuse to be guided by their answers.

9.　The unwritten law is that which usage has established; for ancient customs, being sanctioned by the consent of those who adopt them, are like laws.

10.　The civil law is not improperly divided into two kinds, for the division seems to have had its origin in the customs of the two states, Athens and Lacedaemon. For in these states it used to be the case, that the Lacedaemonians rather committed to memory what they observed as law, while the Athenians rather observed as law what they had consigned to writing, and included in the body of their laws.

11.　The laws of nature, which all nations observe alike, being established by a divine providence, remain ever fixed and immutable. But the laws which every state has enacted, undergo frequent changes, either by the tacit consent of the people, or by a new law being subsequently passed.

III. The Law of Persons.

All our law relates either to persons, or to things, or to actions. Let us first speak of persons; as it is of little purpose to know the law, if we do not know the persons for whose sake the law was made. The chief division in the rights of persons is this: men are all either free or slaves.

1.　Freedom, from which men are said to be free, is the natural power of doing what we each please, unless prevented by force or by law.

2.　Slavery is an institution of the law of nations, by which one man is made the property of another, contrary to natural right.

3.　Slaves are denominated *servi*, because generals order their captives to be sold, and thus preserve them, and do not put them to death. Slaves are also called *mancipia*, because they are taken from the enemy by the strong hand.

2.2.3 St. Augustine, various extracts

Confessions

3.7.13

Nor had I knowledge of that true inner righteousness, which does not judge according to custom, but out of the most perfect law of God Almighty, by which the manners of places and times were adapted to those places and times – being itself the while the same always and everywhere, not one thing in one place, and another in another; according to which Abraham, and Isaac, and Jacob, and Moses, and David, and all those commended by the mouth of God were righteous, Hebrews 11:8–40 but were judged unrighteous by foolish men, judging out of man's judgment, 1 Corinthians 4:3 and gauging by the petty standard of their own manners the manners of the whole human race.

4.9.14

This is it that is loved in friends; and so loved that a man's conscience accuses itself if he love not him by whom he is beloved, or love not again him that loves him, expecting nothing from him but indications of his love. Hence that mourning if one die, and gloom of sorrow, that steeping of the heart in tears, all sweetness turned into bitterness, and upon the loss of the life of the dying, the death of the living. Blessed be he who loves You, and his friend in You, and his enemy for Your sake. For he alone loses none dear to him to whom all are dear in Him who cannot be lost. And who is this but our God, the God that created heaven and earth, Genesis 1:1 and fills them, Jeremiah 23:24 because by filling them He created them? None loses You but he who leaves You. And he who leaves You, whither goes he, or whither flees he, but from You well pleased to You angry? For where does not he find Your law in his own punishment? "*And Your law is the truth*," and truth Thou.

Confessions, tr. J.G. Pilkington, from *Nicene and Post-Nicene Fathers*, First Series, Volume 1, ed. Philip Schaff (Buffalo, NY: Christian Literature Publishing Co., 1887).

5.8.14

At Carthage, on the contrary, there was among the scholars a shameful and intemperate license. They burst in rudely, and, with almost furious gesticulations, interrupt the system which any one may have instituted for the good of his pupils. Many outrages they perpetrate with astounding phlegm, which would be punishable by law were they not sustained by custom; that custom showing them to be the more worthless, in that they now do, as according to law, what by Your unchangeable law will never be lawful. And they fancy they do it with impunity, whereas the very blindness whereby they do it is their punishment, and they suffer far greater things than they do.

On Eighty Three *Diverse Questions*

De div. quest., 53(2)

From this ineffable and sublime arrangement of affairs, then, which is accomplished by divine providence, a natural law [*naturalis lex*] is, so to speak, inscribed upon the rational soul, so that in the very living out of this life and in their earthly activities people might hold to the tenor of such dispensations.

Commentary on the Sermon on the Mount

De Serm. Dom. in Mont., 2.9.32

For who but God has written the law of nature in the hearts of men? – that law concerning which the apostle says: "*For when the Gentiles, which have not the law, do by nature the things contained in the law, these, having not the law, are a law unto themselves: which show the work of the law written in their hearts, their conscience also bearing them witness, and their thoughts the meanwhile accusing or else excusing one another, in the day when the Lord shall judge the secrets of men.*" And therefore, as in the case of every rational soul, which thinks and reasons, even though blinded by passion, we attribute whatever in its reasoning is true, not to itself but to the very light of truth by which, however faintly, it is according to its capacity illuminated, so as to perceive some measure of truth by its reasoning.

On Eighty Three *Diverse Questions,* tr. Boniface Ramsey (New York: New York City Press, 2008), Augustinian Heritage Institute.
Commentary on the Sermon on the Mount, tr. William Findlay, from *Nicene and Post-Nicene Fathers*, First Series, Volume 6, ed. Philip Schaff (Buffalo, NY: Christian Literature Publishing Co., 1888).

De libero arbitrio (The Free Choice of the Will)

De lib. arb. I.5.11

A soldier is even ordered by law to kill the enemy and if he hangs back from the slaughter, he is punished by his commander. Shall we dare to say that those laws are unjust – or, rather, no laws at all? For that which is not just does not seem to me to be a law.

De lib. arb. I.6.15

Therefore, let me explain briefly, as well as I can put it in words, the notion of that eternal law which is impressed upon our nature: 'It is that law in virtue of which it is just that all things exist in perfect order.'

De lib. arb. I.8.18

Whatever sets man above the beast, whether we call it 'mind' [*mens*] or 'spirit' [*spiritus*] or, more correctly, both since we find both terms in Scriptures, if this rules over and commands the other parts that make up man, then man's life is in perfect order [*tunc esse hominem ordinatissimum*]. […] We are to think of a man well-ordered, therefore, when his reason rules over these movements of the soul, for we must not speak of right order, of or order at all, when the more perfect is made subject to the less perfect. […] It follows, therefore, that when reason [*ratio*], or mind [*mens*], or spirit [*spiritus*], rules over the irrational movements of the soul, then that is in control in man which ought to be, by virtue of the law which we found to be eternal.

De Trinitate

De Trin., 14.15.21

For hence it is that even the ungodly think of eternity, and rightly blame and rightly praise many things in the morals of men. And by what rules do they thus judge, except by those wherein they see how men ought to live, even though they themselves do not so live? And where do they see these rules? For they do not see them in their own [moral] nature; since no doubt these things are to be seen by the mind, and their minds are confessedly changeable, but these rules are seen as unchangeable by him who can see them

De libero arbitrio, tr. N. Kretzmann, in his article "Lex Iniusta Non Est Lex: Laws on Trial in Aquinas' Court of Conscience," *American Journal of Jurisprudence* 33 (1988), pp. 100–101; and tr. Robert P. Russell, O.S.A., in *St. Augustine, The Teacher; The Free Choice of the Will; Grace and Free Will* (Washington, DC: Catholic University of America Press, 1968).

De Trinitate, tr. Arthur West Haddan, from *Nicene and Post-Nicene Fathers*, First Series, Volume 3, ed. Philip Schaff (Buffalo, NY: Christian Literature Publishing Co., 1887).

at all; nor yet in the character of their own mind, since these rules are rules of righteousness, and their minds are confessedly unrighteous. Where indeed are these rules written, wherein even the unrighteous recognizes what is righteous, wherein he discerns that he ought to have what he himself has not? Where, then, are they written, unless in the book of that Light which is called Truth? Whence every righteous law is copied and transferred (not by migrating to it, but by being as it were impressed upon it) to the heart of the man that works righteousness; as the impression from a ring passes into the wax, yet does not leave the ring.

25th Sermon on Psalm 118

Exposition 25 of Psalm 118 (*Enarr. Psal.*, 118), 25.4

 No one injures another without at the same time hoping the same will not be done to himself, and in this respect he transgresses the law of nature; the very fact that he does not want to suffer the fate he inflicts on someone else means that he cannot plead ignorance of the natural law. Was this natural law not present in the people of Israel? Certainly it was, for they too were human. They could no more have been without the natural law than they could have been alien to the human condition itself.

Letter 157 (*Epist.*, 157)

Hence, since there is also a law in the reason of a human being who already uses free choice, a law naturally written in his heart, by which he is warned that he should not do anything to anyone else that he himself does not want to suffer, all are transgressors according to this law, even those who have not received the law given through Moses.

25th Sermon on Psalm 118, tr. Maria Boulding, in *Exposition of the Psalms 99–120* (New York: New York City Press, 2003).
Letter 157, tr. Roland Teske, S.J., in *Letters 156–210* (New York: New York City Press, 2004).

2.2.4 St. Augustine
The City of God

Book IV

[handwritten: there is some form of justice/order, even among thieves]

Chapter 4.– How Like Kingdoms Without Justice are to Robberies.

Justice being taken away, then, what are kingdoms but great robberies? For what are robberies themselves, but little kingdoms? The band itself is made up of men; it is ruled by the authority of a prince, it is knit together by the pact of the confederacy; the booty is divided by the law agreed on. If, by the admittance of abandoned men, this evil increases to such a degree that it holds places, fixes abodes, takes possession of cities, and subdues peoples, it assumes the more plainly the name of a kingdom, because the reality is now manifestly conferred on it, not by the removal of covetousness, but by the addition of impunity. Indeed, that was an apt and true reply which was given to Alexander the Great by a pirate who had been seized. For when that king had asked the man what he meant by keeping hostile possession of the sea, he answered with bold pride, What you mean by seizing the whole earth; but because I do it with a petty ship, I am called a robber, while you who does it with a great fleet are styled emperor.

Book XIV

[handwritten: whatever you do do it in the name of god]

Chapter 28.– Of the Nature of the Two Cities, the Earthly and the Heavenly.

Accordingly, two cities have been formed by two loves: the earthly by the love of self, even to the contempt of God; the heavenly by the love of God, even to the contempt of self. The former, in a word, glories in itself, the latter in the Lord. For the one seeks glory from men; but the greatest glory of the other is God, the witness of conscience. The one lifts up its head in its own glory; the other says to its God, You are my glory, and the lifter

Tr. Marcus Dods, from *Nicene and Post-Nicene Fathers*, First Series, Volume 2, ed. Philip Schaff (Buffalo, NY: Christian Literature Publishing Co., 1887), revised and edited for New Advent by Kevin Knight, http://www.newadvent.org/fathers/1201.htm.

up of mine head. In the one, the princes and the nations it subdues are ruled by the love of ruling; in the other, the princes and the subjects serve one another in love, the latter obeying, while the former take thought for all. The one delights in its own strength, represented in the persons of its rulers; the other says to its God, I will love You, O Lord, my strength. And therefore the wise men of the one city, living according to man, have sought for profit to their own bodies or souls, or both, and those who have known God glorified Him not as God, neither were thankful, but became vain in their imaginations, and their foolish heart was darkened; professing themselves to be wise, – that is, glorying in their own wisdom, and being possessed by pride – they became fools, and changed the glory of the incorruptible God into an image made like to corruptible man, and to birds, and four-footed beasts, and creeping things. For they were either leaders or followers of the people in adoring images, and worshipped and served the creature more than the Creator, who is blessed for ever. Romans 1:21–25 But in the other city there is no human wisdom, but only godliness, which offers due worship to the true God, and looks for its reward in the society of the saints, of holy angels as well as holy men, that God may be all in all. 1 Corinthians 15:28

Book XIX

Chapter 12.– That Even the Fierceness of War and All the Disquietude of Men Make Towards This One End of Peace, Which Every Nature Desires.

[…] He, then, who prefers what is right to what is wrong, and what is well-ordered to what is perverted, sees that the peace of unjust men is not worthy to be called peace in comparison with the peace of the just. And yet even what is perverted must of necessity be in harmony with, and in dependence on, and in some part of the order of things, for otherwise it would have no existence at all. Suppose a man hangs with his head downwards, this is certainly a perverted attitude of body and arrangement of its members; for that which nature requires to be above is beneath, and *vice versâ*. This perversity disturbs the peace of the body, and is therefore painful. Nevertheless the spirit is at peace with its body, and labors for its preservation, and hence the suffering; but if it is banished from the body by its pains, then, so long as the bodily framework holds together, there is in the remains a kind of peace among the members, and hence the body remains suspended. And inasmuch as the earthly body tends towards the earth, and rests on the bond by which it is suspended, it tends thus to its natural peace, and the voice of its own weight demands a place for it to rest; and though now lifeless and without feeling, it does not fall from the peace that is natural to its place in creation, whether it already has it, or is tending towards it. For if you apply embalming preparations to prevent the bodily frame from mouldering and dissolving, a kind of peace still unites part to part, and keeps the whole body in a suitable place on the earth – in other words, in a place that is at peace with the body. If, on the other hand, the body receive no such care, but be left to the natural course, it is disturbed by exhalations that do not harmonize with one another, and that offend our senses; for it is this which is perceived in putrefaction until it is assimilated to the elements of the world, and particle by particle enters into peace with them. Yet throughout this process the laws of the most high Creator and Governor are strictly observed, for it is by Him the peace of the universe is administered. For although minute animals are produced from the carcass of a larger animal, all these little atoms, by the law of the same Creator, serve the animals they belong to in peace. And although the flesh of dead animals be eaten by others, no matter where it be carried, nor what it be brought into contact with, nor what it be converted and changed into, it still is ruled by the same laws which pervade all things for the conservation of every mortal race, and which bring things that fit one another into harmony.

Chapter 13.– Of the Universal Peace Which the Law of Nature Preserves Through All Disturbances, and by Which Every One Reaches His Desert in a Way Regulated by the Just Judge.

The peace of the body then consists in the duly proportioned arrangement of its parts. The peace of the irrational soul is the harmonious repose of the appetites, and that of the rational soul the harmony of knowledge and action. The peace of body and soul is the well-ordered and harmonious life and health of the living creature. Peace between man and God is the well-ordered obedience of faith to eternal law. Peace between man and man is well-ordered concord. Domestic peace is the well-ordered concord between those of the family who rule and those who obey. Civil peace is a similar concord among the citizens. The peace of the celestial city is the perfectly ordered and harmonious enjoyment of God, and of one another in God. The peace of all things is the tranquillity of order. Order is the distribution which allots things equal and unequal, each to its own place. And hence, though the miserable, in so far as they are such, do certainly not enjoy peace, but are severed from that tranquillity of order in which there is no disturbance, nevertheless, inasmuch as they are deservedly and justly miserable, they are by their very misery connected with order. They are not, indeed, conjoined with the blessed, but they are disjoined from them by the law of order. And though they are disquieted, their circumstances are notwithstanding adjusted to them, and consequently they have some tranquillity of order, and therefore some peace. But they are wretched because, although not wholly miserable, they are not in that place where any mixture of misery is impossible. They would, however, be more wretched if they had not that peace which arises from being in harmony with the natural order of things. When they suffer, their peace is in so far disturbed; but their peace continues in so far as they do not suffer, and in so far as their nature continues to exist. As, then, there may be life without pain, while there cannot be pain without some kind of life, so there may be peace without war, but there cannot be war without some kind of peace, because war supposes the existence of some natures to wage it, and these natures cannot exist without peace of one kind or other.

And therefore there is a nature in which evil does not or even cannot exist; but there cannot be a nature in which there is no good. Hence not even the nature of the devil himself is evil, in so far as it is nature, but it was made evil by being perverted. Thus he did not abide in the truth, John 8:44 but could not escape the judgment of the Truth; he did not abide in the tranquillity of order, but did not therefore escape the power of the Ordainer. The good imparted by God to his nature did not screen him from the justice of God by which order was preserved in his punishment; neither did God punish the good which He had created, but the evil which the devil had committed. God did not take back all He had imparted to his nature, but something He took and something He left, that there might remain enough to be sensible of the loss of what was taken. And this very sensibility to pain is evidence of the good which has been taken away and the good which has been left. For, were nothing good left, there could be no pain on account of the good which had been lost. For he who sins is still worse if he rejoices in his loss of righteousness. But he who is in pain, if he derives no benefit from it, mourns at least the loss of health. And as righteousness and health are both good things, and as the loss of any good thing is matter of grief, not of joy – if, at least, there is no compensation, as spiritual righteousness may compensate for the loss of bodily health – certainly it is more suitable for a wicked man to grieve in punishment than to rejoice in his fault. As, then, the joy of a sinner who has abandoned what is good is evidence of a bad will, so his grief for the good he has lost when he is punished is evidence of a good nature. For he who laments the peace his nature has lost is stirred to do so by some relics of peace which make his nature friendly to itself. And it is very just that in the final punishment the wicked and godless should in anguish bewail the loss of the natural advantages they enjoyed, and should perceive that they were most justly taken from them by that God whose benign liberality they had despised. God, then, the most wise Creator and most just Ordainer of all natures, who placed the human race upon earth as its greatest orna-ment, imparted to men some good things adapted to this life, to wit, temporal peace, such as we can enjoy in this life from health and safety and human fellowship, and all things needful for the preservation and recovery of this peace, such as the objects which are accommodated to our outward senses, light, night, the air, and waters suitable for us, and everything the body requires to sustain, shelter, heal, or beautify it: and all under this most equitable condition, that every man who made a good use of these advantages suited to the peace of this mortal condition, should receive ampler and better blessings, namely, the peace of immortality, accompanied by glory and honor in an endless life made fit for the enjoyment of God and of one another in God; but that he who used the present blessings badly should both lose them and should not receive the others.

Chapter 14. – Of the Order and Law Which Obtain in Heaven and Earth, Whereby It Comes to Pass that Human Society Is Served by Those Who Rule It.

The whole use, then, of things temporal has a reference to this result of earthly peace in the earthly community, while in the city of God it is connected with eternal peace. And therefore, if we were irrational animals, we should desire nothing beyond the proper arrangement of the parts of the body and the satisfaction of the appetites, – nothing, therefore, but bodily comfort and abundance of pleasures, that the peace of the body might contribute to the peace of the soul. For if bodily peace be awanting, a bar is put to the peace even of the irrational soul, since it cannot obtain the gratification of its appe-tites. And these two together help out the mutual peace of soul and body, the peace of harmonious life and health. For as animals, by shunning pain, show that they love bodily peace, and, by pursuing pleasure to gratify their appetites, show that they love peace of soul, so their shrinking from death is a sufficient indication of their intense love of that peace which binds soul and body in close alliance. But, as man has a rational soul, he subordinates all this which he has in common with the beasts to the peace of his rational soul, that his intellect may have free play and may regulate his actions, and that he may thus enjoy the well-ordered harmony of knowledge and action which constitutes, as we have said, the peace of the rational soul. And for this purpose he must desire to be neither molested by pain, nor disturbed by desire, nor extinguished by death, that he may arrive at some useful knowledge by which he may regulate his life and manners. But, owing to the liability of the human mind to fall into mistakes, this very pursuit of knowledge may be a snare to him unless he has a divine Master, whom he may obey without misgiving, and who may at the same time give him such help as to preserve his own freedom. And because, so long as he is in this mortal body, he is a stranger to God, he walks by faith, not by sight; and he therefore refers all peace, bodily or spiritual or both, to that peace which mortal man has with the immortal God, so that he exhibits the well-ordered obedience of faith to eternal law. But as this divine Master inculcates two precepts, – the love of God and the love of our neighbor – and as in these precepts a man finds three things he has to love – God, himself, and his neighbor – and that he who loves God loves himself thereby, it follows that he must endeavor to get his neighbor to love God, since he is ordered to love his neighbor as himself. He ought to make this endeavor in behalf of his wife, his children, his household, all within his reach, even as he would wish his neighbor to do the same for him if he needed it; and consequently he will be at peace, or in well-ordered concord, with all men, as far as in him lies. And this is the order of this concord, that a man, in the first place, injure no one, and, in the second, do good to every one he can reach. Primarily, therefore, his own household are his care, for the law of nature and of society gives him readier access to them and greater opportunity of serving them. And hence the apostle says, Now, if any provide not for his own, and specially for those of his own house, he has denied the faith, and is worse than an infidel. 1 Timothy 5:8 This is the origin of domestic peace, or the well-ordered concord of those in the family who rule and those who obey. For they who care for the rest rule – the husband the wife, the parents the children, the masters the servants; and they who are cared for obey – the women their husbands, the children their parents, the servants their masters. But in the family of the just man who lives by faith and is as yet a pilgrim journeying on to the celestial city, even those who rule serve those whom they seem to command; for they rule not from a love of power, but from a sense of the duty they owe to others – not because they are proud of authority, but because they love mercy.

Chapter 15.– Of the Liberty Proper to Man's Nature, and the Servitude Introduced by Sin – A Servitude in Which the Man Whose Will is Wicked is the Slave of His Own Lust, Though He is Free So Far as Regards Other Men.

This is prescribed by the order of nature: it is thus that God has created man. For let them, He says, have dominion over the fish of the sea, and over the fowl of the air, and over every creeping thing which creeps on the earth. Genesis 1:26 He did not intend that His rational creature, who was made in His image, should have dominion over anything but the irrational creation, – not man over man, but man over the beasts. And hence the righteous men in primitive times were made shepherds of cattle rather than kings of men, God intending thus to teach us what the relative position of the creatures is, and what the desert of sin; for it is with justice, we believe, that the condition of slavery is the result of sin. And this is why we do not find the word slave in any part of Scripture until righteous Noah branded the sin of his son with this name. It is a name, therefore, introduced by sin and not by nature. The origin of the Latin word for slave is supposed to be found in the circumstance that those who by the law of war were liable to be killed were sometimes preserved by their victors, and were hence called servants. And these circumstances could never have arisen save through sin. For even when we wage a just war, our adversaries must be sinning; and every victory, even though gained by wicked men, is a result of the first judgment of God, who humbles the vanquished either for the sake of removing or of punishing their sins. Witness that man of God, Daniel, who, when he was in captivity, confessed to God his own sins and the sins of his people, and declares with pious grief that these were the cause of the captivity. Daniel ix The prime cause, then, of slavery is sin, which brings man under the dominion of his fellow – that which does not happen save by the judgment of God, with whom is no unrighteousness, and who knows how to award fit punishments to every variety of offense. But our Master in heaven says, Every one who does sin is the servant of sin. John 8:34 And thus there are many wicked masters who have religious men as their slaves, and who are yet themselves in bondage; for of whom a man is overcome, of the same is he brought in bondage. 2 Peter 2:19 And beyond question it is a happier thing to be the slave of a man than of a lust; for even this very lust of ruling, to mention no others, lays waste men's hearts with the most ruthless dominion. Moreover, when men are subjected to one another in a peaceful order, the lowly position does as much good to the servant as the proud position does harm to the master. But by nature, as God first created us, no one is the slave either of man or of sin. This servitude is, however, penal, and is appointed by that law which enjoins the preservation of the natural order and forbids its disturbance; for if nothing had been done in violation of that law, there would have been nothing to restrain by penal servitude. And therefore the apostle admonishes slaves to be subject to their masters, and to serve them heartily and with good-will, so that, if they cannot be freed by their masters, they may themselves make their slavery in some sort free, by serving not in crafty fear, but in faithful love, until all unrighteousness pass away, and all principality and every human power be brought to nothing, and God be all in all.

Chapter 16.– Of Equitable Rule.

And therefore, although our righteous fathers had slaves, and administered their domestic affairs so as to distinguish between the condition of slaves and the heirship of sons in regard to the blessings of this life, yet in regard to the worship of God, in whom we hope for eternal blessings, they took an equally loving oversight of all the members of their household. And this is so much in accordance with the natural order, that the head of the household was called *paterfamilias*; and this name has been so generally accepted, that even those whose rule is unrighteous are glad to apply it to themselves. But those who are true fathers of their households desire and endeavor that all the members of their household, equally with their own children, should worship and win God, and should come to that heavenly home in which the duty of ruling men is no longer

Ancient
~~Early Modern~~ Medieval - individual
human rights aren't as important, →
you look for a communal good

Modern - early modern
individual good

necessary, because the duty of caring for their everlasting happiness has also ceased; but, until they reach that home, masters ought to feel their position of authority a greater burden than servants their service. And if any member of the family interrupts the domestic peace by disobedience, he is corrected either by word or blow, or some kind of just and legitimate punishment, such as society permits, that he may himself be the better for it, and be readjusted to the family harmony from which he had dislocated himself. For as it is not benevolent to give a man help at the expense of some greater benefit he might receive, so it is not innocent to spare a man at the risk of his falling into graver sin. To be innocent, we must not only do harm to no man, but also restrain him from sin or punish his sin, so that either the man himself who is punished may profit by his experience, or others be warned by his example. Since, then, the house ought to be the beginning or element of the city, and every beginning bears reference to some end of its own kind, and every element to the integrity of the whole of which it is an element, it follows plainly enough that domestic peace has a relation to civic peace – in other words, that the well-ordered concord of domestic obedience and domestic rule has a relation to the well-ordered concord of civic obedience and civic rule. And therefore it follows, further, that the father of the family ought to frame his domestic rule in accordance with the law of the city, so that the household may be in harmony with the civic order.

Chapter 17.– What Produces Peace, and What Discord, Between the Heavenly and Earthly Cities.

But the families which do not live by faith seek their peace in the earthly advantages of this life; while the families which live by faith look for those eternal blessings which are promised, and use as pilgrims such advantages of time and of earth as do not fascinate and divert them from God, but rather aid them to endure with greater ease, and to keep down the number of those burdens of the corruptible body which weigh upon the soul. Thus the things necessary for this mortal life are used by both kinds of men and families alike, but each has its own peculiar and widely different aim in using them. The earthly city, which does not live by faith, seeks an earthly peace, and the end it proposes, in the well-ordered concord of civic obedience and rule, is the combination of men's wills to attain the things which are helpful to this life. The heavenly city, or rather the part of it which sojourns on earth and lives by faith, makes use of this peace only because it must, until this mortal condition which necessitates it shall pass away. Consequently, so long as it lives like a captive and a stranger in the earthly city, though it has already received the promise of redemption, and the gift of the Spirit as the earnest of it, it makes no scruple to obey the laws of the earthly city, whereby the things necessary for the maintenance of this mortal life are administered; and thus, as this life is common to both cities, so there is a harmony between them in regard to what belongs to it. But, as the earthly city has had some philosophers whose doctrine is condemned by the divine teaching, and who, being deceived either by their own conjectures or by demons, supposed that many gods must be invited to take an interest in human affairs, and assigned to each a separate function and a separate department – to one the body, to another the soul; and in the body itself, to one the head, to another the neck, and each of the other members to one of the gods; and in like manner, in the soul, to one god the natural capacity was assigned, to another education, to another anger, to another lust; and so the various affairs of life were assigned – cattle to one, grain to another, wine to another, oil to another, the woods to another, money to another, navigation to another, wars and victories to another, marriages to another, births and fecundity to another, and other things to other gods: and as the celestial city, on the other hand, knew that one God only was to be worshipped, and that to Him alone was due that service which the Greeks call λατρεία, and which can be given only to a god, it has come to pass that the two cities could not have common laws of religion, and that the heavenly city has been compelled in this matter to dissent, and to become obnoxious to those who think differently, and to stand the brunt of their anger and hatred and persecutions, except in so far as the minds of their enemies have been alarmed by the multitude of the Christians and quelled by the manifest protection of God accorded to them. This heavenly city, then, while it sojourns on earth, calls citizens out of all nations, and gathers together a society of pilgrims of all languages, not scrupling about diversities in the manners, laws, and institutions whereby earthly peace is secured and maintained, but recognizing that, however various these are, they all tend to one and the same end of earthly peace. It therefore is so far from rescinding and abolishing these diversities, that it even preserves and adopts them, so long only as no hindrance to the worship of the one supreme and true God is thus introduced. Even the heavenly city, therefore, while in its state of pilgrimage, avails itself of the peace of earth, and, so far as it can without injuring faith and godliness, desires and maintains a common agreement among men regarding the acquisition of the necessaries of life, and makes this earthly peace bear upon the peace of heaven; for this alone can be truly called and esteemed the peace of the reasonable creatures, consisting as it does in the perfectly ordered and harmonious enjoyment of God and of one another in God. When we shall have reached that peace, this mortal life shall give place to one that is eternal, and our body shall be no more this animal body which by its corruption weighs down the soul, but a spiritual body feeling no want, and in all its members subjected to the will. In its pilgrim state the heavenly city possesses this peace by faith; and by this faith it lives righteously when it refers to the attainment of that peace every good action towards God and man; for the life of the city is a social life.

Chapter 20.– That the Saints are in This Life Blessed in Hope.

Since, then, the supreme good of the city of God is perfect and eternal peace, not such as mortals pass into and out of by birth and death, but the peace of freedom from all evil, in which the immortals ever abide; who can deny that that future life is most blessed, or that, in comparison with it, this life which now we live is most wretched, be it filled with all blessings of body and soul and external things? And yet, if any man uses this life with a reference to that other which he ardently loves and confidently hopes for, he may well be called even now blessed, though not in reality so much as in hope. But the actual possession of the happiness of this life, without the hope of what is beyond, is but a false happiness and profound misery. For the true blessings of the soul are not now enjoyed; for that is no true wisdom which does not direct all its prudent observations, manly actions, virtuous self-restraint, and just arrangements, to that end in which God shall be all and all in a secure eternity and perfect peace.

Chapter 21.– Whether There Ever Was a Roman Republic Answering to the Definitions of Scipio in Cicero's Dialogue.

This, then, is the place where I should fulfill the promise gave in the second book of this work, and explain, as briefly and clearly as possible, that if we are to accept the definitions laid down by Scipio in Cicero's *De Republica*, there never was a Roman republic; for he briefly defines a republic as the good of the people. And if this definition be true, there never was a Roman republic, for the people's good was never attained among the Romans. For the people, according to his definition, is an assemblage associated by a common acknowledgment of right and by a community of interests. And what he means by a common acknowledgment of right he explains at large, showing that a republic cannot be administered without justice. Where, therefore, there is no true justice there can be no right. For that which is by right is justly done, and what is unjustly done cannot be done by right. For the unjust inventions of men are neither to be considered nor spoken of as rights; for even they themselves say that right is that which flows from the fountain of justice, and deny the definition which is commonly given by those who misconceive the matter, that right is that which is useful to the stronger party. Thus, where there is not true justice there can be no assemblage of men associated by a common acknowledgment of right, and therefore there can be no people, as defined by Scipio or Cicero; and if no people, then no good of the people, but only of some promiscuous multitude unworthy of the name of people. Consequently, if the republic is the good of the people, and there is no people if it be not associated by a common acknowledgment of right, and if there is no right where there is no justice, then most certainly it follows that there is no republic where there is no justice.

Chapter 24.– The Definition Which Must Be Given of a People and a Republic, in Order to Vindicate the Assumption of These Titles by the Romans and by Other Kingdoms.

But if we discard this definition of a people, and, assuming another, say that a people is an assemblage of reasonable beings bound together by a common agreement as to the objects of their love, then, in order to discover the character of any people, we have only to observe what they love. Yet whatever it loves, if only it is an assemblage of reasonable beings and not of beasts, and is bound together by an agreement as to the objects of love, it is reasonably called a people; and it will be a superior people in proportion as it is bound together by higher interests, inferior in proportion as it is bound together by lower. According to this definition of ours, the Roman people is a people, and its good is without doubt a commonwealth or republic. But what its tastes were in its early and subsequent days, and how it declined into sanguinary seditions and then to social and civil wars, and so burst asunder or rotted off the bond of concord in which the health of a people consists, history shows, and in the preceding books I have related at large. And yet I would not on this account say either that it was not a people, or that its administration was not a republic, so long as there remains an assemblage of reasonable beings bound together by a common agreement as to the objects of love. But what I say of this people and of this republic I must be understood to think and say of the Athenians or any Greek state, of the Egyptians, of the early Assyrian Babylon, and of every other nation, great or small, which had a public government. For, in general, the city of the ungodly, which did not obey the command of God that it should offer no sacrifice save to Him alone, and which, therefore, could not give to the soul its proper command over the body, nor to the reason its just authority over the vices, is void of true justice...

Chapter 25.– That Where There is No True Religion There are No True Virtues.

For though the soul may seem to rule the body admirably, and the reason the vices, if the soul and reason do not themselves obey God, as God has commanded them to serve Him, they have no proper authority over the body and the vices. For what kind of mistress of the body and the vices can that mind be which is ignorant of the true God, and which, instead of being subject to His authority, is prostituted to the corrupting influences of the most vicious demons? It is for this reason that the virtues which it seems to itself to possess, and by which it restrains the body and the vices that it may obtain and keep what it desires, are rather vices than virtues so long as there is no reference to God in the matter. For although some suppose that virtues which have a reference only to themselves, and are desired only on their own account, are yet true and genuine virtues, the fact is that even then they are inflated with pride, and are therefore to be reckoned vices rather than virtues. For as that which gives life to the flesh is not derived from flesh, but is above it, so that which gives blessed life to man is not derived from man, but is something above him; and what I say of man is true of every celestial power and virtue whatsoever. ⌞Aristotle + Plato

Chapter 26.– Of the Peace Which is Enjoyed by the People that are Alienated from God, and the Use Made of It by the People of God in the Time of Its Pilgrimage.

Wherefore, as the life of the flesh is the soul, so the blessed life of man is God, of whom the sacred writings of the Hebrews say, Blessed is the people whose God is the Lord. Miserable, therefore, is the people which is alienated from God. Yet even this people has a peace of its own which is not to be lightly esteemed, though, indeed, it shall not in the end enjoy it, because it makes no good use of it before the end. But it is our interest that it enjoy this peace meanwhile in this life; for as long as the two cities are commingled, we also enjoy the peace of Babylon. For from Babylon the people of God is so freed that it meanwhile sojourns in its company. And therefore the apostle also admonished the Church to pray for kings and those in authority, assigning as the reason, that we may live a quiet and tranquil life in all godliness and love. And the prophet Jeremiah, when predicting the captivity that was to befall the ancient people of God, and giving them the divine command to go obediently to Babylonia, and thus serve their God, counselled them also to pray for Babylonia, saying, In the peace thereof shall you have peace, Jeremiah 29:7 – the temporal peace which the good and the wicked together enjoy.

2.2.5 Saint Thomas Aquinas
Summa Contra Gentiles
(*Of God and His Creatures*)

[handwritten: "homage" to Aristotle]

[handwritten: — thinks he's merging the best of Aristotle + Augustine]

Book III, Chapter 2

That every Agent acts to some End

[handwritten: If people want something, they'll try to get it]

In the case of agents that manifestly act to some end, we call that the end to which the effort of the agent tends. Gaining that, he is said to gain his end; and missing that, he is said to miss his intended end. Nor on this point does it make any difference whether the end be tended to with knowledge or not: for as the target is the end of the archer, so is it also the end of the path of the arrow. The effort of every agent tends to some certain end. Not any and every action can proceed from any and every power. Action is sometimes terminated to some product, sometimes not. When action is terminated to some product, the effort of the agent tends to the same. When action is not terminated to any product, the effort of the agent tends to the action itself. Every agent therefore must intend some end in his action, sometimes the action itself, sometimes something produced by the action.

3. It is impossible for the chain of actions to extend to infinity: there must then be something, in the getting of which the effort of the agent comes to rest. Therefore every agent acts to some end.

6. Actions are open to criticism only so far as they are taken to be done as means to some end. It is not imputed as a fault to any one, if he fails in effecting that for which his work is not intended. A physician is found fault with if he fails in healing, but not a builder or a grammarian. We find fault in points of art, as when a grammarian does not speak correctly; and also in points of nature, as in monstrous births. Therefore both the natural agent, and the agent who acts according to art and with a conscious purpose, acts for an end.

7. To an agent that did not tend to any definite effect, all effects would be indifferent. But what is indifferent to many things, does not do one of them rather than another: hence from an agent open to both sides of an alternative (*a contingente ad utrumque*) there does not follow any effect, unless by some means it comes to be determined to one above the rest: otherwise it could not act at all. Every agent therefore tends to some definite effect, and that is called its end.

Tr. Joseph Rickaby, S.J. (London: Burns and Oates, 1905).

Still there are actions that do not seem to be for any end, as things done for sport, and acts of contemplation, and things done without advertence, as the stroking of the beard and the like: from which instances one may suppose that there is such a thing as an agent acting not for any end. But we must observe that though acts of contemplation are not for any other end, they are an end in themselves: as for things done in sport, sometimes they are their own end, as when one plays solely for the amusement that he finds in play; sometimes they are for an end, as when we play that afterwards we may resume work more vigorously: while things done without advertence may proceed not from the understanding, but from some phantasy or physical principle; yet even these acts tend to certain ends, though beyond the scope of the intellect of the agent.

Hereby is banished the error of certain ancient natural philosophers (Empedocles and Democritus, mentioned in Aristotle, *Physics* II, ii, 6) who supposed all things to happen by necessity of matter, and eliminated final causes from the universe.

Book III, Chapter 3

That every Agent acts to some Good

That to which an agent definitely tends must be suited to it: for it would not tend to the thing except for some suitability to itself. But what is suitable to a thing is good for it. Therefore every agent acts to some good.

6. An intellectual agent acts for an end by determining its own end. A physical agent, though acting for an end, does not determine its own end, having no idea of an end, but moves in the direction of an end determined for it by another. Now an intellectual agent does not fix for itself an end except under some aspect of good: for a term of intellect is a motive only under an aspect of good, which is the object of will. Therefore a physical agent also does not move or act to any end except inasmuch as it is good. Such an agent has its end determined by some natural appetite or tendency.

7. It is part of the same plan of action to shun evil and to seek good. But all things are found to shun evil. Intellectual agents shun a thing for this reason, that they apprehend its evil: while all physical agents, to the full extent of the power that is in them, resist destruction, because that is the evil of everything. All things therefore act to some good.

Book III, Chapter 27

That the Happiness of Man does not consist in Bodily Pleasures

ACCORDING to the order of nature, pleasure is for the sake of activity, and not the other way about. If therefore certain activities are not the final end, the pleasures ensuing upon these activities are neither the final end nor accessories of the final end. But certainly the activities on which bodily pleasures follow are not the final end: for they are directed to other obvious ends, the preservation of the body and the begetting of offspring. Therefore the aforesaid pleasures are not the final end, nor accessories of the final end, and happiness is not to be placed in them.

3. Happiness is a good proper to man: dumb animals cannot be called happy except by an abuse of language. But bodily pleasures are common to man and brute: happiness therefore cannot consist in them.
4. The final end of a thing is noblest and best of all that appertains to the thing. But bodily delights do not appertain to a man in respect of what is noblest in him.
5. The highest perfection of man cannot consist in his being conjoined with things lower than himself, but in his conjunction with something above him.
7. In all things that are said to be 'ordinarily' (*per se*), 'more' follows upon 'more,' if 'absolutely' goes with 'absolutely.' If then bodily pleasures were good in themselves, to take them to the utmost would be the best way of taking them. But this is manifestly false: for excessive use of such things is accounted a vice, injures the body, and bars further enjoyments of the same sort.
8. If human happiness consisted in bodily pleasures, it would be a more praiseworthy act of virtue to take such pleasures than to abstain from them. But this is manifestly false, for it is the special praise of the act of temperance to abstain from such pleasures.
9. The last end of everything is God (Chap. XVIII). That then must be laid down to be the last end of man, whereby he most closely approaches to God. But bodily pleasures injure a man from any close approach to God: for God is approached by contemplation, and the aforesaid pleasures are a hindrance to contemplation.

Hereby is excluded the error of the Epicureans, who placed the happiness of man in these pleasures: in whose person Solomon says: This seemed to me good, that man should eat and drink and make merry on the fruit of his toil (Eccles. V, 17). Everywhere let us leave behind us signs of mirth, for this is our portion and this our lot (Wisd. ii, 9). Also the error of the followers of Cerinthus is excluded, who spread the fable of a thousand years of the pleasures of the belly as an element in the kingdom of Christ after the resurrection, hence they are called Chiliasts, or Millennarians. Also the fables of the Saracens, who place the rewards of the just in the aforesaid pleasures.

Book III, Chapters 28–29

That Happiness does not consist in Honours nor in Human Glory

THE last end and happiness of man is his most perfect activity (Chap. XXVI). But the honour paid to a man does not consist in any act of his own, but in the act of another towards him.

2. That is not the last end, which is good and desirable on account of something else. But such is honour: for a man is not rightly honoured except for some other good thing existing in him.
4. Even bad men may be honoured. It is better then to become worthy of honour than to be honoured. Therefore honour is not the highest good of man.

Hence it appears that neither does man's chief good consist in glory, or celebrity of fame. For glory, according to Cicero, is "a frequent mention of a man with praise"; or according to St Augustine, "brilliant notoriety with praise" (*clara notitia cum laude*). So then men wish for notoriety, attended with praise and a certain brilliance, that they may be honoured by those to whom they become known. Glory then is sought for the sake of honour. If then honour is not the highest good, much less is glory.

Book III, Chapter 30

That Man's Happiness does not consist in Riches

RICHES are not desired except for the sake of something else: for of themselves they do no good, but only as we use them. But the highest good is desired for its own sake, and not for the sake of something else.

2. The possession or preservation of those things cannot be the highest good, which benefit man most in being parted with. But such is the use of riches, to spend.
3. The act of liberality and munificence, the virtues that deal with money, is more praiseworthy, in that money is parted with, than that money is got. Man's happiness therefore does not consist in the possession of riches.
4. That in the gaining of which man's chief good lies must be some thing better than man. But man is better than his riches, which are things ordained to his use.
5. The highest good of man is not subject to fortune: for fortuitous events happen without effort of reason, whereas man must gain his proper end by reason. But fortune has great place in the gaining of riches.

Book III, Chapter 31

That Happiness does not consist in Worldly Power

MAN is called good inasmuch as he attains to the sovereign good. But inasmuch as he has power he is not called either good or evil: for he is not good who can do good things, nor is a man evil of being able to do evil things. Therefore the highest good does not consist in being powerful. [...]

3. All power is over another (*ad alterum*). But the highest good is not over another.

Book III, Chapter 32

That Happiness does not consist in the Goods of the Body

THE soul is better than the body. Therefore the good of the soul, as understanding and the like, is better than the good of the body. The good of the body therefore is not the highest good of man [...]

3. These goods are common to man and other animals: but happiness is the proper good of man alone.
4. For goods of the body, many animals are better off than man: some are swifter, some are stronger, and so of the rest. If in these things the highest good consisted, man would not be the most excellent of animals.

Book III, Chapter 34

That the Final Happiness Man does not consist in Acts of the Moral Virtues

HUMAN happiness, if it is final, is not referable to any further end. But all moral acts are referable to something further: thus acts of fortitude in war are directed to securing victory and peace: acts of justice to the preservation of peace amongst men by every one remaining in quiet possession of his own.

2. Moral virtues aim at the observance of the golden mean in passions and in the disposal of external things. But the moderation of the passions or of external things cannot possibly be the final end of human life, since these very passions and external things are referable to something else.
3. Man is man by the possession of reason; and therefore happiness, his proper good, must regard what is proper to reason. But that is more proper to reason which reason has in itself than what it does in another. Since then the good of moral virtue is something which reason establishes in things other than itself, moral virtue cannot be the best thing in man, which is happiness.

Book III, Chapter 34

That the Final Happiness of Man consists in the Contemplation of God

IF then the final happiness of man does not consist in those exterior advantages which are called goods of fortune, nor in goods of the body, nor in goods of the soul in its sentient part, nor in the intellectual part in respect of the moral virtues, nor in the virtues of the practical intellect, called art and prudence, it remains that the final happiness of man consists in the contemplation of truth. This act alone in man is proper to him, and is in no way shared by any other being in this world. This is sought for its own sake, and is directed to no other end beyond itself. By this act man is united in likeness with pure spirits, and even comes to know them in a certain way. For this act also man is more self-sufficient, having less need of external things. Likewise to this act all other human activities seem to be directed as to their end. For to the perfection of contemplation there is requisite health of body; and all artificial necessaries of life are means to health. Another requisite is rest from the disturbing forces of passion: that is attained by means of the moral virtues and prudence. Likewise rest from exterior troubles, which is the whole aim of civil life and government. Thus, if we look at things rightly, we may see that all human occupations seem to be ministerial to the service of the contemplators of truth.

Now it is impossible for human happiness to consist in that contemplation which is by intuition of first principles, – a very imperfect study of things, as being the most general, and not amounting to more than a potential knowledge: it is in fact not the end but the beginning of human study: it is supplied to us by nature, and not by any close investigation of truth. Nor can happiness consist in the sciences, the object-matter of which is the meanest things, whereas happiness should be an activity of intellect dealing with the noblest objects of intelligence. Therefore the conclusion remains that the final happiness of man consists in contemplation guided by wisdom to the study of the things of God. Thus we have reached by way of induction the same conclusion that was formerly established by deductive reasoning, that the final happiness of man does not consist in anything short of the contemplation of God.

2.2.6 St. Thomas Aquinas
Summa Theologica

First Part of the Second Part (*Prima Secundæ Partis*)

Book II, Part I, 55–56, 90–97

Question 55. The virtues, as to their essence

Article 1. Whether human virtue is a habit?   The Philosopher says (Categor. vi) that science and virtue are habits.

Virtue denotes a certain perfection of a power. Now a thing's perfection is considered chiefly in regard to its end. But the end of power is act. Wherefore power is said to be perfect, according as it is determinate to its act.

Now there are some powers which of themselves are determinate to their acts; for instance, the active natural powers. And therefore these natural powers are in themselves called virtues. But the rational powers, which are proper to man, are not determinate to one particular action, but are inclined indifferently to many: and they are determinate to acts by means of habits, as is clear from what we have said above (Question 49, Article 4). Therefore human virtues are habits.

Article 2. Whether human virtue is an operative habit?   The Philosopher (Ethic. ii, 6) says that "virtue of a thing is that which makes its work good."

Virtue, from the very nature of the word, implies some perfection of power, as we have said above (Article 1). Wherefore, since power [the one Latin word *potentia* is rendered 'potentiality' in the first case, and 'power' in the second] is of two kinds, namely, power in reference to being, and power in reference to act; the perfection of each of these is called virtue. But power in reference to being is on the part of matter, which is potential being, whereas power in reference to act, is on the part of the form, which is the principle of action, since everything acts in so far as it is in act.

Now man is so constituted that the body holds the place of matter, the soul that of form. The body, indeed, man has in common with other animals; and the same is to be said of the forces which are common to the soul and body: and only those forces which are

From *The Summa Theologica of St. Thomas Aquinas*, second and revised edition (1920), literally translated by Fathers of the English Dominican Province. Online edition copyright © 2008 by Kevin Knight.

proper to the soul, namely, the rational forces, belong to man alone. And therefore, human virtue, of which we are speaking now, cannot belong to the body, but belongs only to that which is proper to the soul. Wherefore human virtue does not imply reference to being, but rather to act. Consequently it is essential to human virtue to be an operative habit.

Article 3. Whether human virtue is a good habit?   Augustine says (De Moribus Eccl. vi): "No one can doubt that virtue makes the soul exceeding good": and the Philosopher says (Ethic. ii, 6): "Virtue is that which makes its possessor good, and his work good likewise."

[V]irtue implies a perfection of power: wherefore the virtue of a thing is fixed by the limit of its power (De Coelo i). Now the limit of any power must needs be good: for all evil implies defect; wherefore Dionysius says (Div. Hom. ii) that every evil is a weakness. And for this reason the virtue of a thing must be regarded in reference to good. Therefore human virtue which is an operative habit, is a good habit, productive of good works.

Article 4. Whether virtue is suitably defined?   We have the authority of Augustine from whose words this definition is gathered, and principally in De Libero Arbitrio ii, 19.

This definition comprises perfectly the whole essential notion of virtue. For the perfect essential notion of anything is gathered from all its causes. Now the above definition comprises all the causes of virtue. For the formal cause of virtue, as of everything, is gathered from its genus and difference, when it is defined as "a good quality": for "quality" is the genus of virtue, and the difference, "good." But the definition would be more suitable if for "quality" we substitute "habit," which is the proximate genus.

Now virtue has no matter "out of which" it is formed, as neither has any other accident; but it has matter "about which" it is concerned, and matter "in which" it exits, namely, the subject. The matter about which virtue is concerned is its object, and this could not be included in the above definition, because the object fixes the virtue to a certain species, and here we are giving the definition of virtue in general. And so for material cause we have the subject, which is mentioned when we say that virtue is a good quality "of the mind."

The end of virtue, since it is an operative habit, is operation. But it must be observed that some operative habits are always referred to evil, as vicious habits: others are sometimes referred to good, sometimes to evil; for instance, opinion is referred both to the true and to the untrue: whereas virtue is a habit which is always referred to good: and so the distinction of virtue from those habits which are always referred to evil, is expressed in the words "by which we live righteously": and its distinction from those habits which are sometimes directed unto good, sometimes unto evil, in the words, "of which no one makes bad use."

Lastly, God is the efficient cause of infused virtue, to which this definition applies; and this is expressed in the words "which God works in us without us." If we omit this phrase, the remainder of the definition will apply to all virtues in general, whether acquired or infused.

Question 56. The subject of virtue
Article 1. Whether the subject of virtue is a power of the soul?   "Virtue is the limit of power" (De Coelo ii). But the limit is in that of which it is the limit. Therefore virtue is in a power of the soul.

It can be proved in three ways that virtue belongs to a power of the soul. First, from the notion of the very essence of virtue, which implies perfection of a power; for perfection is in that which it perfects. Secondly, from the fact that virtue is an operative habit, as we have said above (Question 55, Article 2): for all operation proceeds from the soul through a power. Thirdly, from the fact that virtue disposes to that which is best: for the best is the end, which is either a thing's operation, or something acquired by an operation proceeding from the thing's power. Therefore a power of the soul is the subject of virtue.

Article 2. Whether one virtue can be in several powers?　　The subject of virtue is a power of the soul. But the same accident cannot be in several subjects. Therefore one virtue cannot be in several powers of the soul.

I answer that, It happens in two ways that one thing is subjected in two. First, so that it is in both on an equal footing. In this way it is impossible for one virtue to be in two powers: since diversity of powers follows the generic conditions of the objects, while diversity of habits follows the specific conditions thereof: and so wherever there is diversity of powers, there is diversity of habits; but not vice versa. In another way one thing can be subjected in two or more, not on an equal footing, but in a certain order. And thus one virtue can belong to several powers, so that it is in one chiefly, while it extends to others by a kind of diffusion, or by way of a disposition, in so far as one power is moved by another, and one power receives from another.

Article 3. Whether the intellect can be the subject of virtue?　　The mind is chiefly called the intellect. But the subject of virtue is the mind, as is clear from the definition, above given, of virtue (55, 4). Therefore the intellect is the subject of virtue.

As we have said above (Question 55, Article 3), a virtue is a habit by which we work well. Now a habit may be directed to a good act in two ways. First, in so far as by the habit a man acquires an aptness to a good act; for instance, by the habit of grammar man has the aptness to speak correctly. But grammar does not make a man always speak correctly: for a grammarian may be guilty of a barbarism or make a solecism: and the case is the same with other sciences and arts. Secondly, a habit may confer not only aptness to act, but also the right use of that aptness: for instance, justice not only gives man the prompt will to do just actions, but also makes him act justly.

And since good, and, in like manner, being, is said of a thing simply, in respect, not of what it is potentially, but of what it is actually: therefore from having habits of the latter sort, man is said simply to do good, and to be good; for instance, because he is just, or temperate; and in like manner as regards other such virtues. And since virtue is that "which makes its possessor good, and his work good likewise," these latter habits are called virtuous simply: because they make the work to be actually good, and the subject good simply. But the first kind of habits are not called virtues simply: because they do not make the work good except in regard to a certain aptness, nor do they make their possessor good simply. For through being gifted in science or art, a man is said to be good, not simply, but relatively; for instance, a good grammarian or a good smith. And for this reason science and art are often divided against virtue; while at other times they are called virtues (Ethic. vi, 2).

Hence the subject of a habit which is called a virtue in a relative sense, can be the intellect, and not only the practical intellect, but also the speculative, without any reference to the will: for thus the Philosopher (Ethic. vi, 3) holds that science, wisdom and understanding, and also art, are intellectual virtues. But the subject of a habit which is called a virtue simply, can only be the will, or some power in so far as it is moved by the will. And the reason of this is, that the will moves to their acts all those other powers that are in some way rational, as we have said above (9, 1; 17, A1,5; I, 82, 4): and therefore if man do well actually, this is because he has a good will. Therefore the virtue which makes a man to do well actually, and not merely to have the aptness to do well, must be either in the will itself; or in some power as moved by the will.

Now it happens that the intellect is moved by the will, just as are the other powers: for a man considers something actually, because he wills to do so. And therefore the intellect, in so far as it is subordinate to the will, can be the subject of virtue absolutely so called. And in this way the speculative intellect, or the reason, is the subject of Faith: for the intellect is moved by the command of the will to assent to what is of faith: for "no man believeth, unless he will" [Augustine: Tract. xxvi in Joan.]. But the practical intellect is the subject of prudence. For since prudence is the right reason of things to be done, it is a condition thereof that man be rightly disposed in regard to the principles of this reason of things to be done, that is in regard to their ends, to which man is rightly disposed by the rectitude of the will, just as to the principles of speculative truth he is rightly disposed by the natural light of the active intellect. And therefore as the subject of science, which is the right reason of speculative truths, is the speculative intellect in its relation to the active intellect, so the subject of prudence is the practical intellect in its relation to the right will.

Article 4. Whether the irascible and concupiscible powers are the subject of virtue?   Fortitude is assigned to the irascible power, and temperance to the concupiscible power. Whence the Philosopher (Ethic. iii, 10) says that "these virtues belong to the irrational part of the soul."

The irascible and concupiscible powers can be considered in two ways. First, in themselves, in so far as they are parts of the sensitive appetite: and in this way they are not competent to be the subject of virtue. Secondly, they can be considered as participating in the reason, from the fact that they have a natural aptitude to obey reason. And thus the irascible or concupiscible power can be the subject of human virtue: for, in so far as it participates in the reason, it is the principle of a human act. And to these powers we must needs assign virtues.

For it is clear that there are some virtues in the irascible and concupiscible powers. Because an act, which proceeds from one power according as it is moved by another power, cannot be perfect, unless both powers be well disposed to the act: for instance, the act of a craftsman cannot be successful unless both the craftsman and his instrument be well disposed to act. Therefore in the matter of the operations of the irascible and concupiscible powers, according as they are moved by reason, there must needs be some habit perfecting in respect of acting well, not only the reason, but also the irascible and concupiscible powers. And since the good disposition of the power which moves through being moved, depends on its conformity with the power that moves it: therefore the virtue which is in the irascible and concupiscible powers is nothing else but a certain habitual conformity of these powers to reason.

Article 5. Whether the sensitive powers of apprehension are the subject of virtue? All virtues are either intellectual or moral (Ethic. ii, 1). Now all the moral virtues are in the appetite; while the intellectual virtues are in the intellect or reason, as is clear from Ethic. vi, 1. Therefore there is no virtue in the interior sensitive powers of apprehension.

In the interior sensitive powers of apprehension there are some habits. And this is made clear principally from what the Philosopher says (De Memoria ii), that "in remembering one thing after another, we become used to it; and use is a second nature." Now a habit of use is nothing else than a habit acquired by use, which is like unto nature. Wherefore Tully says of virtue in his Rhetoric that "it is a habit like a second nature in accord with reason." Yet, in man, that which he acquires by use, in his memory and other sensitive powers of apprehension, is not a habit properly so called, but something annexed to the habits of the intellective faculty, as we have said above (50, 4, ad 3).

Nevertheless even if there be habits in such powers, they cannot be virtues. For virtue is a perfect habit, by which it never happens that anything but good is done: and so virtue must needs be in that power which consummates the good act. But the knowledge of truth is not consummated in the sensitive powers of apprehension: for such powers prepare the way to the intellective knowledge. And therefore in these powers there are none of the virtues, by which we know truth: these are rather in the intellect or reason.

Article 6. Whether the will can be the subject of virtue? Greater perfection is required in the mover than in the moved. But the will moves the irascible and concupiscible powers. Much more therefore should there be virtue in the will than in the irascible and concupiscible powers.

Since the habit perfects the power in reference to act, then does the power need a habit perfecting it unto doing well, which habit is a virtue, when the power's own proper nature does not suffice for the purpose.

Now the proper nature of a power is seen in its relation to its object. Since, therefore, as we have said above (Question 19, Article 3), the object of the will is the good of reason proportionate to the will, in respect of this the will does not need a virtue perfecting it. But if man's will is confronted with a good that exceeds its capacity, whether as regards the whole human species, such as Divine good, which transcends the limits of human nature, or as regards the individual, such as the good of one's neighbor, then does the will need virtue. And therefore such virtues as those which direct man's affections to God or to his neighbor are subjected in the will, as charity, justice, and such like.

Question 90. The essence of law

Article 1. Whether law is something pertaining to reason? Law is a rule and measure of acts, whereby man is induced to act or is restrained from acting: for "lex" [law] is derived from "ligare" [to bind], because it binds one to act. Now the rule and measure of human acts is the reason, which is the first principle of human acts, as is evident from what has been stated above (1, 1, ad 3); since it belongs to the reason to direct to the end, which is the first principle in all matters of action, according to the Philosopher (Phys. ii). Now that which is the principle in any genus, is the rule and measure of that genus: for instance, unity in the genus of numbers, and the first movement in the genus of movements. Consequently it follows that law is something pertaining to reason.

Article 2. Whether the law is always something directed to the common good?   Isidore says (Etym. v, 21) that "laws are enacted for no private profit, but for the common benefit of the citizens."

I answer that, As stated above (Article 1), the law belongs to that which is a principle of human acts, because it is their rule and measure. Now as reason is a principle of human acts, so in reason itself there is something which is the principle in respect of all the rest: wherefore to this principle chiefly and mainly law must needs be referred. Now the first principle in practical matters, which are the object of the practical reason, is the last end: and the last end of human life is bliss or happiness, as stated above (2, 7; 3, 1). Consequently the law must needs regard principally the relationship to happiness. Moreover, since every part is ordained to the whole, as imperfect to perfect; and since one man is a part of the perfect community, the law must needs regard properly the relationship to universal happiness. Wherefore the Philosopher, in the above definition of legal matters mentions both happiness and the body politic: for he says (Ethic. v, 1) that we call those legal matters "just, which are adapted to produce and preserve happiness and its parts for the body politic": since the state is a perfect community, as he says in Polit. i, 1.

Now in every genus, that which belongs to it chiefly is the principle of the others, and the others belong to that genus in subordination to that thing: thus fire, which is chief among hot things, is the cause of heat in mixed bodies, and these are said to be hot in so far as they have a share of fire. Consequently, since the law is chiefly ordained to the common good, any other precept in regard to some individual work, must needs be devoid of the nature of a law, save in so far as it regards the common good. Therefore every law is ordained to the common good.

Article 3. Whether the reason of any man is competent to make laws?   Isidore says (Etym. v. 10): "A law is an ordinance of the people, whereby something is sanctioned by the Elders together with the Commonalty."

A law, properly speaking, regards first and foremost the order to the common good. Now to order anything to the common good, belongs either to the whole people, or to someone who is the vicegerent of the whole people. And therefore the making of a law belongs either to the whole people or to a public personage who has care of the whole people: since in all other matters the directing of anything to the end concerns him to whom the end belongs.

Article 4. Whether promulgation is essential to a law?   It is laid down in the Decretals, dist. 4, that "laws are established when they are promulgated."

As stated above (Article 1), a law is imposed on others by way of a rule and measure. Now a rule or measure is imposed by being applied to those who are to be ruled and measured by it. Wherefore, in order that a law obtain the binding force which is proper to a law, it must needs be applied to the men who have to be ruled by it. Such application is made by its being notified to them by promulgation. Wherefore promulgation is necessary for the law to obtain its force.

Thus from the four preceding articles, the definition of law may be gathered; and it is nothing else than an ordinance of reason for the common good, made by him who has care of the community, and promulgated.

Question 91. The various kinds of law

Article 1. Whether there is an eternal law?   Augustine says (De Lib. Arb. i, 6): "That Law which is the Supreme Reason cannot be understood to be otherwise than unchangeable and eternal."

As stated above (90, 1, ad 2; A3,4), a law is nothing else but a dictate of practical reason emanating from the ruler who governs a perfect community. Now it is evident, granted that the world is ruled by Divine Providence, as was stated in the I, 22, A1,2, that the whole community of the universe is governed by Divine Reason. Wherefore the very Idea of the government of things in God the Ruler of the universe, has the nature of a law. And since the Divine Reason's conception of things is not subject to time but is eternal, according to Proverbs 8:23, therefore it is that this kind of law must be called eternal.

Article 2. Whether there is in us a natural law?   A gloss on Romans 2:14: "When the Gentiles, who have not the law, do by nature those things that are of the law," comments as follows: "Although they have no written law, yet they have the natural law, whereby each one knows, and is conscious of, what is good and what is evil."

As stated above (90, 1, ad 1), law, being a rule and measure, can be in a person in two ways: in one way, as in him that rules and measures; in another way, as in that which is ruled and measured, since a thing is ruled and measured, in so far as it partakes of the rule or measure. Wherefore, since all things subject to Divine providence are ruled and measured by the eternal law, as was stated above (Article 1); it is evident that all things partake somewhat of the eternal law, in so far as, namely, from its being imprinted on them, they derive their respective inclinations to their proper acts and ends. Now among all others, the rational creature is subject to Divine providence in the most excellent way, in so far as it partakes of a share of providence, by being provident both for itself and for others. Wherefore it has a share of the Eternal Reason, whereby it has a natural inclination to its proper act and end: and this participation of the eternal law in the rational creature is called the natural law. Hence the Psalmist after saying (Psalm 4:6): "Offer up the sacrifice of justice," as though someone asked what the works of justice are, adds: "Many say, Who showeth us good things?" in answer to which question he says: "The light of Thy countenance, O Lord, is signed upon us": thus implying that the light of natural reason, whereby we discern what is good and what is evil, which is the function of the natural law, is nothing else than an imprint on us of the Divine light. It is therefore evident that the natural law is nothing else than the rational creature' participation of the eternal law.

Article 3. Whether there is a human law?   Augustine (De Lib. Arb. i, 6) distinguishes two kinds of law, the one eternal, the other temporal, which he calls human.

As stated above (90, 1, ad 2), a law is a dictate of the practical reason. Now it is to be observed that the same procedure takes place in the practical and in the speculative reason: for each proceeds from principles to conclusions, as stated above (De Lib. Arb. i, 6). Accordingly we conclude that just as, in the speculative reason, from naturally known indemonstrable principles, we draw the conclusions of the various sciences, the knowledge of which is not imparted to us by nature, but acquired by the efforts of reason, so too it is from the precepts of the natural law, as from general and indemonstrable principles, that the human reason needs to proceed to the more particular determination of certain matters. These particular determinations, devised by human reason, are called human laws, provided the other essential conditions of law be observed, as stated above (90, A2,3,4). Wherefore Tully says in his Rhetoric (De Invent. Rhet. ii) that "justice has its source in nature; thence certain things came into custom by reason of their utility; afterwards these things which emanated from nature and were approved by custom, were sanctioned by fear and reverence for the law."

Article 4. Whether there was any need for a Divine law? David prayed God to set His law before him, saying (Psalm 118:33): "Set before me for a law the way of Thy justifications, O Lord."

Besides the natural and the human law it was necessary for the directing of human conduct to have a Divine law. And this for four reasons. First, because it is by law that man is directed how to perform his proper acts in view of his last end. And indeed if man were ordained to no other end than that which is proportionate to his natural faculty, there would be no need for man to have any further direction of the part of his reason, besides the natural law and human law which is derived from it. But since man is ordained to an end of eternal happiness which is inproportionate to man's natural faculty, as stated above (Question 5, Article 5), therefore it was necessary that, besides the natural and the human law, man should be directed to his end by a law given by God.

Secondly, because, on account of the uncertainty of human judgment, especially on contingent and particular matters, different people form different judgments on human acts; whence also different and contrary laws result. In order, therefore, that man may know without any doubt what he ought to do and what he ought to avoid, it was necessary for man to be directed in his proper acts by a law given by God, for it is certain that such a law cannot err.

Thirdly, because man can make laws in those matters of which he is competent to judge. But man is not competent to judge of interior movements, that are hidden, but only of exterior acts which appear: and yet for the perfection of virtue it is necessary for man to conduct himself aright in both kinds of acts. Consequently human law could not sufficiently curb and direct interior acts; and it was necessary for this purpose that a Divine law should supervene.

Fourthly, because, as Augustine says (De Lib. Arb. i, 5,6), human law cannot punish or forbid all evil deeds: since while aiming at doing away with all evils, it would do away with many good things, and would hinder the advance of the common good, which is necessary for human intercourse. In order, therefore, that no evil might remain unforbidden and unpunished, it was necessary for the Divine law to supervene, whereby all sins are forbidden.

And these four causes are touched upon in Psalm 118:8, where it is said: "The law of the Lord is unspotted," i.e. allowing no foulness of sin; "converting souls," because it directs not only exterior, but also interior acts; "the testimony of the Lord is faithful," because of the certainty of what is true and right; "giving wisdom to little ones," by directing man to an end supernatural and Divine.

Article 5. Whether there is but one Divine law?   The Apostle says (Hebrews 7:12): "The priesthood being translated, it is necessary that a translation also be made of the law." But the priesthood is twofold, as stated in the same passage, viz. the levitical priesthood, and the priesthood of Christ. Therefore the Divine law is twofold, namely the Old Law and the New Law.

As stated in the I, 30, 3, distinction is the cause of number. Now things may be distinguished in two ways. First, as those things that are altogether specifically different, e.g. a horse and an ox. Secondly, as perfect and imperfect in the same species, e.g. a boy and a man: and in this way the Divine law is divided into Old and New. Hence the Apostle (Galatians 3:24–25) compares the state of man under the Old Law to that of a child "under a pedagogue"; but the state under the New Law, to that of a full grown man, who is "no longer under a pedagogue."

Now the perfection and imperfection of these two laws is to be taken in connection with the three conditions pertaining to law, as stated above. For, in the first place, it belongs to law to be directed to the common good as to its end, as stated above (Question 90, Article 2). This good may be twofold. It may be a sensible and earthly good; and to this, man was directly ordained by the Old Law: wherefore, at the very outset of the law, the people were invited to the earthly kingdom of the Chananaeans (Exodus 3:8–17). Again it may be an intelligible and heavenly good: and to this, man is ordained by the New Law. Wherefore, at the very beginning of His preaching, Christ invited men to the kingdom of heaven, saying (Matthew 4:17): "Do penance, for the kingdom of heaven is at hand." Hence Augustine says (Contra Faust. iv) that "promises of temporal goods are contained in the Old Testament, for which reason it is called old; but the promise of eternal life belongs to the New Testament."

Secondly, it belongs to the law to direct human acts according to the order of righteousness (4): wherein also the New Law surpasses the Old Law, since it directs our internal acts, according to Matthew 5:20: "Unless your justice abound more than that of the Scribes and Pharisees, you shall not enter into the kingdom of heaven." Hence the saying that "the Old Law restrains the hand, but the New Law controls the mind" (Sentent. iii, D, xl).

Thirdly, it belongs to the law to induce men to observe its commandments. This the Old Law did by the fear of punishment: but the New Law, by love, which is poured into our hearts by the grace of Christ, bestowed in the New Law, but foreshadowed in the Old. Hence Augustine says (Contra Adimant. Manich. discip. xvii) that "there is little difference [the "little difference" refers to the Latin words *timor* and *amor* – 'fear' and 'love'] between the Law and the Gospel – fear and love."

Article 6. Whether there is a law in the fomes of sin?   The Apostle says (Romans 7:23): "I see another law in my members, fighting against the law of my mind."

The law, as to its essence, resides in him that rules and measures; but, by way of participation, in that which is ruled and measured; so that every inclination or ordination which may be found in things subject to the law, is called a law by participation, as stated above (2; 90, 1, ad 1). Now those who are subject to a law may receive a twofold inclination from the lawgiver. First, in so far as he directly inclines his subjects to something; sometimes indeed different subjects to different acts; in this way we may say that there is a military law and a mercantile law. Secondly, indirectly; thus by the very fact that a lawgiver deprives a subject of some dignity, the latter passes into another order, so as to be under another law, as it were: thus if a soldier be turned out of the army, he becomes a subject of rural or of mercantile legislation.

Accordingly under the Divine Lawgiver various creatures have various natural inclinations, so that what is, as it were, a law for one, is against the law for another: thus I might say that fierceness is, in a way, the law of a dog, but against the law of a sheep or another meek animal. And so the law of man, which, by the Divine ordinance, is allotted to him, according to his proper natural condition, is that he should act in accordance with reason: and this law was so effective in the primitive state, that nothing either beside or against reason could take man unawares. But when man turned his back on God, he fell under the influence of his sensual impulses: in fact this happens to each one individually, the more he deviates from the path of reason, so that, after a fashion, he is likened to the beasts that are led by the impulse of sensuality, according to Psalm 48:21: "Man, when he was in honor, did not understand: he hath been compared to senseless beasts, and made like to them."

So, then, this very inclination of sensuality which is called the "fomes," in other animals has simply the nature of a law (yet only in so far as a law may be said to be in such things), by reason of a direct inclination. But in man, it has not the nature of law in this way, rather is it a deviation from the law of reason. But since, by the just sentence of God, man is destitute of original justice, and his reason bereft of its vigor, this impulse of sensuality, whereby he is led, in so far as it is a penalty following from the Divine law depriving man of his proper dignity, has the nature of a law.

Question 92. The effects of law

Is an effect of law to make men good? Are the effects of law to command, to forbid, to permit, and to punish, as the Jurist states?

The Philosopher says (Ethic. ii, 1) that the "intention of every lawgiver is to make good citizens."

A law is nothing else than a dictate of reason in the ruler by whom his subjects are governed. Now the virtue of any subordinate thing consists in its being well subordinated to that by which it is regulated: thus we see that the virtue of the irascible and concupiscible faculties consists in their being obedient to reason; and accordingly "the virtue of every subject consists in his being well subjected to his ruler," as the Philosopher says (Polit. i). But every law aims at being obeyed by those who are subject to it. Consequently it is evident that the proper effect of law is to lead its subjects to their proper virtue: and since virtue is "that which makes its subject good," it follows that the proper effect of law is to make those to whom it is given, good, either simply or in some particular respect. For if the intention of the lawgiver is fixed on true good, which is the common good regulated according to Divine justice, it follows that the effect of the law is to make men good simply. If, however, the intention of the lawgiver is fixed on that which is not simply good, but useful or pleasurable to himself, or in opposition to Divine justice; then the law does not make men good simply, but in respect to that particular government. In this way good is found even in things that are bad of themselves: thus a man is called a good robber, because he works in a way that is adapted to his end.

Article 2. Whether the acts of law are suitably assigned?   Isidore says (Etym. v, 19): "Every law either permits something, as: 'A brave man may demand his reward'": or forbids something, as: "No man may ask a consecrated virgin in marriage": or punishes, as: "Let him that commits a murder be put to death."

Just as an assertion is a dictate of reason asserting something, so is a law a dictate of reason, commanding something. Now it is proper to reason to lead from one thing to another. Wherefore just as, in demonstrative sciences, the reason leads us from certain principles to assent to the conclusion, so it induces us by some means to assent to the precept of the law.

Now the precepts of law are concerned with human acts, in which the law directs, as stated above (90, A1,2; 91, 4). Again there are three kinds of human acts: for, as stated above (Question 18, Article 8), some acts are good generically, viz. acts of virtue; and in respect of these the act of the law is a precept or command, for "the law commands all acts of virtue" (Ethic. v, 1). Some acts are evil generically, viz. acts of vice, and in respect of these the law forbids. Some acts are generically indifferent, and in respect of these the law permits; and all acts that are either not distinctly good or not distinctly bad may be called indifferent. And it is the fear of punishment that law makes use of in order to ensure obedience: in which respect punishment is an effect of law.

Question 93. The eternal law

Article 1. Whether the eternal law is a sovereign type [Ratio] existing in God?   Augustine says (De Lib. Arb. i, 6) that "the eternal law is the sovereign type, to which we must always conform."

Just as in every artificer there pre-exists a type of the things that are made by his art, so too in every governor there must pre-exist the type of the order of those things that are to be done by those who are subject to his government. And just as the type of the things yet to be made by an art is called the art or exemplar of the products of that art, so too the type in him who governs the acts of his subjects, bears the character of a law, provided the other conditions be present which we have mentioned above (Article 90). Now God, by His wisdom, is the Creator of all things in relation to which He stands as the artificer to the products of his art, as stated in the I, 14, 8. Moreover He governs all the acts and movements that are to be found in each single creature, as was also stated in the I, 103, 5. Wherefore as the type of the Divine Wisdom, inasmuch as by It all things are created, has the character of art, exemplar or idea; so the type of Divine Wisdom, as moving all things to their due end, bears the character of law. Accordingly the eternal law is nothing else than the type of Divine Wisdom, as directing all actions and movements.

Article 2. Whether the eternal law is known to all?   Augustine says (De Lib. Arb. i, 6) that "knowledge of the eternal law is imprinted on us." A thing may be known in two ways: first, in itself; secondly, in its effect, wherein some likeness of that thing is found: thus someone not seeing the sun in its substance, may know it by its rays. So then no one can know the eternal law, as it is in itself, except the blessed who see God in His Essence. But every rational creature knows it in its reflection, greater or less. For every knowledge of truth is a kind of reflection and participation of the eternal law, which is the unchangeable truth, as Augustine says (De Vera Relig. xxxi). Now all men know the truth to a certain extent, at least as to the common principles of the natural law: and as to the others, they partake of the knowledge of truth, some more, some less; and in this respect are more or less cognizant of the eternal law.

Article 3. Whether every law is derived from the eternal law? Divine Wisdom says (Proverbs 8:15): "By Me kings reign, and lawgivers decree just things." But the type of Divine Wisdom is the eternal law, as stated above (Article 1). Therefore all laws proceed from the eternal law.

The law denotes a kind of plan directing acts towards an end. Now wherever there are movers ordained to one another, the power of the second mover must needs be derived from the power of the first mover; since the second mover does not move except in so far as it is moved by the first. Wherefore we observe the same in all those who govern, so that the plan of government is derived by secondary governors from the governor in chief; thus the plan of what is to be done in a state flows from the king's command to his inferior administrators: and again in things of art the plan of whatever is to be done by art flows from the chief craftsman to the under-craftsmen, who work with their hands. Since then the eternal law is the plan of government in the Chief Governor, all the plans of government in the inferior governors must be derived from the eternal law. But these plans of inferior governors are all other laws besides the eternal law. Therefore all laws, in so far as they partake of right reason, are derived from the eternal law. Hence Augustine says (De Lib. Arb. i, 6) that "in temporal law there is nothing just and lawful, but what man has drawn from the eternal law."

Article 4. Whether necessary and eternal things are subject to the eternal law? Things that are necessary cannot be otherwise, and consequently need no restraining. But laws are imposed on men, in order to restrain them from evil, as explained above (Question 92, Article 2). Therefore necessary things are not subject to the eternal law.

The eternal law is the type of the Divine government. Consequently whatever is subject to the Divine government, is subject to the eternal law: while if anything is not subject to the Divine government, neither is it subject to the eternal law. The application of this distinction may be gathered by looking around us. For those things are subject to human government, which can be done by man; but what pertains to the nature of man is not subject to human government; for instance, that he should have a soul, hands, or feet. Accordingly all that is in things created by God, whether it be contingent or necessary, is subject to the eternal law: while things pertaining to the Divine Nature or Essence are not subject to the eternal law, but are the eternal law itself.

Article 5. Whether natural contingents are subject to the eternal law? It is written (Proverbs 8:29): "When He compassed the sea with its bounds, and set a law to the waters, that they should not pass their limits."

We must speak otherwise of the law of man, than of the eternal law which is the law of God. For the law of man extends only to rational creatures subject to man. The reason of this is because law directs the actions of those that are subject to the government of someone: wherefore, properly speaking, none imposes a law on his own actions. Now whatever is done regarding the use of irrational things subject to man, is done by the act of man himself moving those things, for these irrational creatures do not move themselves, but are moved by others, as stated above (Question 1, Article 2). Consequently man cannot impose laws on irrational beings, however much they may be subject to him. But he can impose laws on rational beings subject to him, in so far as by his command or pronouncement of any kind, he imprints on their minds a rule which is a principle of action.

Now just as man, by such pronouncement, impresses a kind of inward principle of action on the man that is subject to him, so God imprints on the whole of nature the principles of its proper actions. And so, in this way, God is said to command the whole of nature, according to Psalm 148:6: "He hath made a decree, and it shall not pass away." And thus all actions and movements of the whole of nature are subject to the eternal law. Consequently irrational creatures are subject to the eternal law, through being moved by Divine providence; but not, as rational creatures are, through understanding the Divine commandment.

Article 6. Whether all human affairs are subject to the eternal law? There are two ways in which a thing is subject to the eternal law, as explained above (Article 5): first, by partaking of the eternal law by way of knowledge; secondly, by way of action and passion, i.e. by partaking of the eternal law by way of an inward motive principle: and in this second way, irrational creatures are subject to the eternal law, as stated above (Article 5). But since the rational nature, together with that which it has in common with all creatures, has something proper to itself inasmuch as it is rational, consequently it is subject to the eternal law in both ways; because while each rational creature has some knowledge of the eternal law, as stated above (Article 2), it also has a natural inclination to that which is in harmony with the eternal law; for "we are naturally adapted to the recipients of virtue" (Ethic. ii, 1).

Both ways, however, are imperfect, and to a certain extent destroyed, in the wicked; because in them the natural inclination to virtue is corrupted by vicious habits, and, moreover, the natural knowledge of good is darkened by passions and habits of sin. But in the good both ways are found more perfect: because in them, besides the natural knowledge of good, there is the added knowledge of faith and wisdom; and again, besides the natural inclination to good, there is the added motive of grace and virtue.

Accordingly, the good are perfectly subject to the eternal law, as always acting according to it: whereas the wicked are subject to the eternal law, imperfectly as to their actions, indeed, since both their knowledge of good, and their inclination thereto, are imperfect; but this imperfection on the part of action is supplied on the part of passion, in so far as they suffer what the eternal law decrees concerning them, according as they fail to act in harmony with that law. Hence Augustine says (De Lib. Arb. i, 15): "I esteem that the righteous act according to the eternal law; and (De Catech. Rud. xviii): Out of the just misery of the souls which deserted Him, God knew how to furnish the inferior parts of His creation with most suitable laws."

Question 94. The natural law

Article 1. Whether the natural law is a habit? Augustine says (De Bono Conjug. xxi) that "a habit is that whereby something is done when necessary." But such is not the natural law: since it is in infants and in the damned who cannot act by it. Therefore the natural law is not a habit.

A thing may be called a habit in two ways. First, properly and essentially: and thus the natural law is not a habit. For it has been stated above (90, 1, ad 2) that the natural law is something appointed by reason, just as a proposition is a work of reason. Now that which a man does is not the same as that whereby he does it: for he makes a becoming speech by the habit of grammar. Since then a habit is that by which we act, a law cannot be a habit properly and essentially.

Secondly, the term habit may be applied to that which we hold by a habit: thus faith may mean that which we hold by faith. And accordingly, since the precepts of the natural law are sometimes considered by reason actually, while sometimes they are in the reason only habitually, in this way the natural law may be called a habit. Thus, in speculative matters, the indemonstrable principles are not the habit itself whereby we hold those principles, but are the principles the habit of which we possess.

Article 2. Whether the natural law contains several precepts, or only one?   The precepts of the natural law in man stand in relation to practical matters, as the first principles to matters of demonstration. But there are several first indemonstrable principles. Therefore there are also several precepts of the natural law.

The precepts of the natural law are to the practical reason, what the first principles of demonstrations are to the speculative reason; because both are self-evident principles. Now a thing is said to be self-evident in two ways: first, in itself; secondly, in relation to us. Any proposition is said to be self-evident in itself, if its predicate is contained in the notion of the subject: although, to one who knows not the definition of the subject, it happens that such a proposition is not self-evident. For instance, this proposition, "Man is a rational being," is, in its very nature, self-evident, since who says "man," says "a rational being": and yet to one who knows not what a man is, this proposition is not self-evident. Hence it is that, as Boethius says (De Hebdom.), certain axioms or propositions are universally self-evident to all; and such are those propositions whose terms are known to all, as, "Every whole is greater than its part," and, "Things equal to one and the same are equal to one another." But some propositions are self-evident only to the wise, who understand the meaning of the terms of such propositions: thus to one who understands that an angel is not a body, it is self-evident that an angel is not circumscriptively in a place: but this is not evident to the unlearned, for they cannot grasp it.

Now a certain order is to be found in those things that are apprehended universally. For that which, before aught else, falls under apprehension, is "being," the notion of which is included in all things whatsoever a man apprehends. Wherefore the first indemonstrable principle is that "the same thing cannot be affirmed and denied at the same time," which is based on the notion of "being" and "not-being": and on this principle all others are based, as is stated in Metaph. iv, text. 9. Now as "being" is the first thing that falls under the apprehension simply, so "good" is the first thing that falls under the apprehension of the practical reason, which is directed to action: since every agent acts for an end under the aspect of good. Consequently the first principle of practical reason is one founded on the notion of good, viz. that "good is that which all things seek after." Hence this is the first precept of law, that "good is to be done and pursued, and evil is to be avoided." All other precepts of the natural law are based upon this: so that whatever the practical reason naturally apprehends as man's good (or evil) belongs to the precepts of the natural law as something to be done or avoided.

Since, however, good has the nature of an end, and evil, the nature of a contrary, hence it is that all those things to which man has a natural inclination, are naturally apprehended by reason as being good, and consequently as objects of pursuit, and their contraries as evil, and objects of avoidance. Wherefore according to the order of natural inclinations, is the order of the precepts of the natural law. Because in man there is first of all an inclination to good in accordance with the nature which he has in common with all substances: inasmuch as every substance seeks the preservation of its own being, according to its nature: and by reason of this inclination, whatever is a means of preserving human life, and of warding off its obstacles, belongs to the natural law. Secondly, there is in man an inclination to things that pertain to him more specially, according to that nature which he has in common with other animals: and in virtue of this inclination, those things are said to belong to the natural law, "which nature has taught to all animals" [Pandect. Just. I, tit. i], such as sexual intercourse, education of offspring and so forth. Thirdly, there is in man an inclination to good, according to the nature of his reason, which nature is proper to him: thus man has a natural inclination to know the truth about God, and to live in society: and in this respect, whatever pertains to this inclination belongs to the natural law; for instance, to shun ignorance, to avoid offending those among whom one has to live, and other such things regarding the above inclination.

Article 3. Whether all acts of virtue are prescribed by the natural law? Damascene says (De Fide Orth. iii, 4) that "virtues are natural." Therefore virtuous acts also are a subject of the natural law. We may speak of virtuous acts in two ways: first, under the aspect of virtuous; secondly, as such and such acts considered in their proper species. If then we speak of acts of virtue, considered as virtuous, thus all virtuous acts belong to the natural law. For it has been stated (2) that to the natural law belongs everything to which a man is inclined according to his nature. Now each thing is inclined naturally to an operation that is suitable to it according to its form: thus fire is inclined to give heat. Wherefore, since the rational soul is the proper form of man, there is in every man a natural inclination to act according to reason: and this is to act according to virtue. Consequently, considered thus, all acts of virtue are prescribed by the natural law: since each one's reason naturally dictates to him to act virtuously. But if we speak of virtuous acts, considered in themselves, i.e. in their proper species, thus not all virtuous acts are prescribed by the natural law: for many things are done virtuously, to which nature does not incline at first; but which, through the inquiry of reason, have been found by men to be conducive to well-living.

Article 4. Whether the natural law is the same in all men? Isidore says (Etym. v, 4): "The natural law is common to all nations."

As stated above (2,3), to the natural law belongs those things to which a man is inclined naturally: and among these it is proper to man to be inclined to act according to reason. Now the process of reason is from the common to the proper, as stated in Phys. i. The speculative reason, however, is differently situated in this matter, from the practical reason. For, since the speculative reason is busied chiefly with the necessary things, which cannot be otherwise than they are, its proper conclusions, like the universal principles, contain the truth without fail. The practical reason, on the other hand, is busied with contingent matters, about which human actions are concerned: and consequently, although there is necessity in the general principles, the more we descend to matters of detail, the more frequently we encounter defects. Accordingly then in speculative matters truth is the same in all men, both as to principles and as to conclusions: although the truth is not known to all as regards the conclusions, but only as regards the principles which are called common notions. But in matters of action, truth or practical rectitude is not the same for all, as to matters of detail, but only as to the general principles: and where there is the same rectitude in matters of detail, it is not equally known to all.

It is therefore evident that, as regards the general principles whether of speculative or of practical reason, truth or rectitude is the same for all, and is equally known by all. As to the proper conclusions of the speculative reason, the truth is the same for all, but is not equally known to all: thus it is true for all that the three angles of a triangle are together equal to two right angles, although it is not known to all. But as to the proper conclusions of the practical reason, neither is the truth or rectitude the same for all, nor, where it is the same, is it equally known by all. Thus it is right and true for all to act according to reason: and from this principle it follows as a proper conclusion, that goods entrusted to another should be restored to their owner. Now this is true for the majority of cases: but it may happen in a particular case that it would be injurious, and therefore unreasonable, to restore goods held in trust; for instance, if they are claimed for the purpose of fighting against one's country. And this principle will be found to fail the more, according as we descend further into detail, e.g. if one were to say that goods held in trust should be restored with such and such a guarantee, or in such and such a way; because the greater the number of conditions added, the greater the number of ways in which the principle may fail, so that it be not right to restore or not to restore.

Consequently we must say that the natural law, as to general principles, is the same for all, both as to rectitude and as to knowledge. But as to certain matters of detail, which are conclusions, as it were, of those general principles, it is the same for all in the majority of cases, both as to rectitude and as to knowledge; and yet in some few cases it may fail, both as to rectitude, by reason of certain obstacles (just as natures subject to generation and corruption fail in some few cases on account of some obstacle), and as to knowledge, since in some the reason is perverted by passion, or evil habit, or an evil disposition of nature; thus formerly, theft, although it is expressly contrary to the natural law, was not considered wrong among the Germans, as Julius Caesar relates (De Bello Gall. vi).

Article 5. Whether the natural law can be changed? It is said in the Decretals (Dist. v): "The natural law dates from the creation of the rational creature. It does not vary according to time, but remains unchangeable."

A change in the natural law may be understood in two ways. First, by way of addition. In this sense nothing hinders the natural law from being changed: since many things for the benefit of human life have been added over and above the natural law, both by the Divine law and by human laws.

Secondly, a change in the natural law may be understood by way of subtraction, so that what previously was according to the natural law, ceases to be so. In this sense, the natural law is altogether unchangeable in its first principles: but in its secondary principles, which, as we have said (4), are certain detailed proximate conclusions drawn from the first principles, the natural law is not changed so that what it prescribes be not right in most cases. But it may be changed in some particular cases of rare occurrence, through some special causes hindering the observance of such precepts, as stated above (Article 4).

Article 6. Whether the law of nature can be abolished from the heart of man?

Augustine says (Confess. ii): "Thy law is written in the hearts of men, which iniquity itself effaces not." But the law which is written in men's hearts is the natural law. Therefore the natural law cannot be blotted out.

There belong to the natural law, first, certain most general precepts, that are known to all; and secondly, certain secondary and more detailed precepts, which are, as it were, conclusions following closely from first principles. As to those general principles, the natural law, in the abstract, can nowise be blotted out from men's hearts. But it is blotted out in the case of a particular action, in so far as reason is hindered from applying the general principle to a particular point of practice, on account of concupiscence or some other passion, as stated above (Question 77, Article 2). But as to the other, i.e. the secondary precepts, the natural law can be blotted out from the human heart, either by evil persuasions, just as in speculative matters errors occur in respect of necessary conclusions; or by vicious customs and corrupt habits, as among some men, theft, and even unnatural vices, as the Apostle states (Romans 1), were not esteemed sinful.

Question 95. Human law

Article 1. Whether it was useful for laws to be framed by men?

Isidore says (Etym. v, 20): "Laws were made that in fear thereof human audacity might be held in check, that innocence might be safeguarded in the midst of wickedness, and that the dread of punishment might prevent the wicked from doing harm." But these things are most necessary to mankind. Therefore it was necessary that human laws should be made.

Man has a natural aptitude for virtue; but the perfection of virtue must be acquired by man by means of some kind of training. Thus we observe that man is helped by industry in his necessities, for instance, in food and clothing. Certain beginnings of these he has from nature, viz. his reason and his hands; but he has not the full complement, as other animals have, to whom nature has given sufficiency of clothing and food. Now it is difficult to see how man could suffice for himself in the matter of this training: since the perfection of virtue consists chiefly in withdrawing man from undue pleasures, to which above all man is inclined, and especially the young, who are more capable of being trained. Consequently a man needs to receive this training from another, whereby to arrive at the perfection of virtue. And as to those young people who are inclined to acts of virtue, by their good natural disposition, or by custom, or rather by the gift of God, paternal training suffices, which is by admonitions. But since some are found to be depraved, and prone to vice, and not easily amenable to words, it was necessary for such to be restrained from evil by force and fear, in order that, at least, they might desist from evil-doing, and leave others in peace, and that they themselves, by being habituated in this way, might be brought to do willingly what hitherto they did from fear, and thus become virtuous. Now this kind of training, which compels through fear of punishment, is the discipline of laws. Therefore in order that man might have peace and virtue, it was necessary for laws to be framed: for, as the Philosopher says (Polit. i, 2), "as man is the most noble of animals if he be perfect in virtue, so is he the lowest of all, if he be severed from law and righteousness"; because man can use his reason to devise means of satisfying his lusts and evil passions, which other animals are unable to do.

Article 2. Whether every human law is derived from the natural law?   Tully says (Rhet. ii): "Things which emanated from nature and were approved by custom, were sanctioned by fear and reverence for the laws."

As Augustine says (De Lib. Arb. i, 5) "that which is not just seems to be no law at all": wherefore the force of a law depends on the extent of its justice. Now in human affairs a thing is said to be just, from being right, according to the rule of reason. But the first rule of reason is the law of nature, as is clear from what has been stated above (91, 2, ad 2). Consequently every human law has just so much of the nature of law, as it is derived from the law of nature. But if in any point it deflects from the law of nature, it is no longer a law but a perversion of law.

But it must be noted that something may be derived from the natural law in two ways: first, as a conclusion from premises, secondly, by way of determination of certain generalities. The first way is like to that by which, in sciences, demonstrated conclusions are drawn from the principles: while the second mode is likened to that whereby, in the arts, general forms are particularized as to details: thus the craftsman needs to determine the general form of a house to some particular shape. Some things are therefore derived from the general principles of the natural law, by way of conclusions; e.g. that "one must not kill" may be derived as a conclusion from the principle that "one should do harm to no man": while some are derived therefrom by way of determination; e.g. the law of nature has it that the evil-doer should be punished; but that he be punished in this or that way, is a determination of the law of nature.

Accordingly both modes of derivation are found in the human law. But those things which are derived in the first way, are contained in human law not as emanating therefrom exclusively, but have some force from the natural law also. But those things which are derived in the second way, have no other force than that of human law.

Hence the Philosopher says (Ethic. vi, 11) that in such matters, "we ought to pay as much attention to the undemonstrated sayings and opinions of persons who surpass us in experience, age and prudence, as to their demonstrations."

Article 3. Whether Isidore's description of the quality of positive law is appropriate?   Whenever a thing is for an end, its form must be determined proportionately to that end; as the form of a saw is such as to be suitable for cutting (Phys. ii, text. 88). Again, everything that is ruled and measured must have a form proportionate to its rule and measure. Now both these conditions are verified of human law: since it is both something ordained to an end; and is a rule or measure ruled or measured by a higher measure. And this higher measure is twofold, viz. the Divine law and the natural law, as explained above (2; 93, 3). Now the end of human law is to be useful to man, as the jurist states [Pandect. Justin. lib. xxv, ff., tit. iii; De Leg. et Senat.]. Wherefore Isidore in determining the nature of law, lays down, at first, three conditions; viz. that it "foster religion," inasmuch as it is proportionate to the Divine law; that it be "helpful to discipline," inasmuch as it is proportionate to the nature law; and that it "further the common weal," inasmuch as it is proportionate to the utility of mankind.

All the other conditions mentioned by him are reduced to these three. For it is called virtuous because it fosters religion. And when he goes on to say that it should be "just, possible to nature, according to the customs of the country, adapted to place and time," he implies that it should be helpful to discipline. For human discipline depends on first on the order of reason, to which he refers by saying "just": secondly, it depends on the ability of the agent; because discipline should be adapted to each one according to his ability, taking also into account the ability of nature (for the same burdens should be not laid on children as adults); and should be according to human customs; since man cannot live alone in society, paying no heed to others: thirdly, it depends on certain circumstances, in respect of which he says, "adapted to place and time." The remaining words, "necessary, useful," etc. mean that law should further the common weal: so that "necessity" refers to the removal of evils; "usefulness" to the attainment of good; "clearness of expression," to the need of preventing any harm ensuing from the law itself. And since, as stated above (Question 90, Article 2), law is ordained to the common good, this is expressed in the last part of the description.

Article 4. Whether Isidore' division of human laws is appropriate?   A thing can of itself be divided in respect of something contained in the notion of that thing. Thus a soul either rational or irrational is contained in the notion of animal: and therefore animal is divided properly and of itself in respect of its being rational or irrational; but not in the point of its being white or black, which are entirely beside the notion of animal. Now, in the notion of human law, many things are contained, in respect of any of which human law can be divided properly and of itself. For in the first place it belongs to the notion of human law, to be derived from the law of nature, as explained above (Article 2). In this respect positive law is divided into the "law of nations" and "civil law," according to the two ways in which something may be derived from the law of nature, as stated above (Article 2). Because, to the law of nations belong those things which are derived from the law of nature, as conclusions from premises, e.g. just buyings and sellings, and the like, without which men cannot live together, which is a point of the law of nature, since man is by nature a social animal, as is proved in Polit. i, 2. But those things which are derived from the law of nature by way of particular determination, belong to the civil law, according as each state decides on what is best for itself.

Secondly, it belongs to the notion of human law, to be ordained to the common good of the state. In this respect human law may be divided according to the different kinds of men who work in a special way for the common good: e.g. priests, by praying to God for the people; princes, by governing the people; soldiers, by fighting for the safety of the people. Wherefore certain special kinds of law are adapted to these men.

Thirdly, it belongs to the notion of human law, to be framed by that one who governs the community of the state, as shown above (Question 90, Article 3). In this respect, there are various human laws according to the various forms of government. Of these, according to the Philosopher (Polit. iii, 10) one is "monarchy," i.e. when the state is governed by one; and then we have "Royal Ordinances." Another form is "aristocracy," i.e. government by the best men or men of highest rank; and then we have the "Authoritative legal opinions" [Responsa Prudentum] and "Decrees of the Senate" [Senatus consulta]. Another form is "oligarchy," i.e. government by a few rich and powerful men; and then we have "Praetorian," also called "Honorary," law. Another form of government is that of the people, which is called "democracy," and there we have "Decrees of the commonalty" [Plebiscita]. There is also tyrannical government, which is altogether corrupt, which, therefore, has no corresponding law. Finally, there is a form of government made up of all these, and which is the best: and in this respect we have law sanctioned by the "Lords and Commons," as stated by Isidore (Etym. v, 4, seqq.).

Fourthly, it belongs to the notion of human law to direct human actions. In this respect, according to the various matters of which the law treats, there are various kinds of laws, which are sometimes named after their authors: thus we have the "Lex Julia" about adultery, the "Lex Cornelia" concerning assassins, and so on, differentiated in this way, not on account of the authors, but on account of the matters to which they refer.

Question 96. *The power of human law*

Article 1. Whether human law should be framed for the community rather than for the individual?   The jurist says (Pandect. Justin. lib. i, tit. iii, art. ii; De legibus, etc.) that "laws should be made to suit the majority of instances; and they are not framed according to what may possibly happen in an individual case."

I answer that, Whatever is for an end should be proportionate to that end. Now the end of law is the common good; because, as Isidore says (Etym. v, 21) that "law should be framed, not for any private benefit, but for the common good of all the citizens." Hence human laws should be proportionate to the common good. Now the common good comprises many things. Wherefore law should take account of many things, as to persons, as to matters, and as to times. Because the community of the state is composed of many persons; and its good is procured by many actions; nor is it established to endure for only a short time, but to last for all time by the citizens succeeding one another, as Augustine says (De Civ. Dei ii, 21; xxii, 6).

Article 2. Whether it belongs to the human law to repress all vices?   We read in De Lib. Arb. i, 5: "It seems to me that the law which is written for the governing of the people rightly permits these things, and that Divine providence punishes them." But Divine providence punishes nothing but vices. Therefore human law rightly allows some vices, by not repressing them.

Law is framed as a rule or measure of human acts. Now a measure should be homogeneous with that which it measures, as stated in Metaph. x, text. 3,4, since different things are measured by different measures. Wherefore laws imposed on men should also be in keeping with their condition, for, as Isidore says (Etym. v, 21), law should be "possible both according to nature, and according to the customs of the country." Now possibility or faculty of action is due to an interior habit or disposition: since the same thing is not possible to one who has not a virtuous habit, as is possible to one who has. Thus the same is not possible to a child as to a full-grown man: for which reason the law for children is not the same as for adults, since many things are permitted to children, which in an adult are punished by law or at any rate are open to blame. In like manner many things are permissible to men not perfect in virtue, which would be intolerable in a virtuous man.

Now human law is framed for a number of human beings, the majority of whom are not perfect in virtue. Wherefore human laws do not forbid all vices, from which the virtuous abstain, but only the more grievous vices, from which it is possible for the majority to abstain; and chiefly those that are to the hurt of others, without the prohibition of which human society could not be maintained: thus human law prohibits murder, theft and such like.

Article 3. Whether human law prescribes acts of all the virtues?   The Philosopher says (Ethic. v, 1) that the law "prescribes the performance of the acts of a brave man [...] and the acts of the temperate man [...] and the acts of the meek man: and in like manner as regards the other virtues and vices, prescribing the former, forbidding the latter."

The species of virtues are distinguished by their objects, as explained above (54, 2; 60, 1; 62, 2). Now all the objects of virtues can be referred either to the private good of an individual, or to the common good of the multitude: thus matters of fortitude may be achieved either for the safety of the state, or for upholding the rights of a friend, and in like manner with the other virtues. But law, as stated above (Question 90, Article 2) is ordained to the common good. Wherefore there is no virtue whose acts cannot be prescribed by the law. Nevertheless human law does not prescribe concerning all the acts of every virtue: but only in regard to those that are ordainable to the common good – either immediately, as when certain things are done directly for the common good – or mediately, as when a lawgiver prescribes certain things pertaining to good order, whereby the citizens are directed in the upholding of the common good of justice and peace.

Article 4. Whether human law binds a man in conscience?   It is written (1 Peter 2:19): "This is thankworthy, if for conscience [...] a man endure sorrows, suffering wrongfully."

Laws framed by man are either just or unjust. If they be just, they have the power of binding in conscience, from the eternal law whence they are derived, according to Proverbs 8:15: "By Me kings reign, and lawgivers decree just things." Now laws are said to be just, both from the end, when, to wit, they are ordained to the common good – and from their author, that is to say, when the law that is made does not exceed the power of the lawgiver – and from their form, when, to wit, burdens are laid on the subjects, according to an equality of proportion and with a view to the common good. For, since one man is a part of the community, each man in all that he is and has, belongs to the community; just as a part, in all that it is, belongs to the whole; wherefore nature inflicts a loss on the part, in order to save the whole: so that on this account, such laws as these, which impose proportionate burdens, are just and binding in conscience, and are legal laws.

On the other hand laws may be unjust in two ways: first, by being contrary to human good, through being opposed to the things mentioned above – either in respect of the end, as when an authority imposes on his subjects burdensome laws, conducive, not to the common good, but rather to his own cupidity or vainglory – or in respect of the author, as when a man makes a law that goes beyond the power committed to him – or in respect of the form, as when burdens are imposed unequally on the community, although with a view to the common good. The like are acts of violence rather than laws; because, as Augustine says (De Lib. Arb. i, 5), "a law that is not just, seems to be no law at all." Wherefore such laws do not bind in conscience, except perhaps in order to avoid scandal or disturbance, for which cause a man should even yield his right, according to Matthew 5:40–41: "If a man [...] take away thy coat, let go thy cloak also unto him; and whosoever will force thee one mile, go with him other two."

Secondly, laws may be unjust through being opposed to the Divine good: such are the laws of tyrants inducing to idolatry, or to anything else contrary to the Divine law: and laws of this kind must nowise be observed, because, as stated in Acts 5:29, "we ought to obey God rather than man."

Article 5. Whether all are subject to the law?   The Apostle says (Romans 13:1): "Let every soul be subject to the higher powers." But subjection to a power seems to imply subjection to the laws framed by that power. Therefore all men should be subject to human law.

The notion of law contains two things: first, that it is a rule of human acts; secondly, that it has coercive power. Wherefore a man may be subject to law in two ways. First, as the regulated is subject to the regulator: and, in this way, whoever is subject to a power, is subject to the law framed by that power. But it may happen in two ways that one is not subject to a power. In one way, by being altogether free from its authority: hence the subjects of one city or kingdom are not bound by the laws of the sovereign of another city or kingdom, since they are not subject to his authority. In another way, by being under a yet higher law; thus the subject of a proconsul should be ruled by his command, but not in those matters in which the subject receives his orders from the emperor: for in these matters, he is not bound by the mandate of the lower authority, since he is directed by that of a higher. In this way, one who is simply subject to a law, may not be a subject thereto in certain matters, in respect of which he is ruled by a higher law.

Secondly, a man is said to be subject to a law as the coerced is subject to the coercer. In this way the virtuous and righteous are not subject to the law, but only the wicked. Because coercion and violence are contrary to the will: but the will of the good is in harmony with the law, whereas the will of the wicked is discordant from it. Wherefore in this sense the good are not subject to the law, but only the wicked.

Article 6. Whether he who is under a law may act beside the letter of the law?   Hilary says (De Trin. iv): "The meaning of what is said is according to the motive for saying it: because things are not subject to speech, but speech to things." Therefore we should take account of the motive of the lawgiver, rather than of his very words.

Every law is directed to the common weal of men, and derives the force and nature of law accordingly. Hence the jurist says [Pandect. Justin. lib. i, ff., tit. 3, De Leg. et Senat.]: "By no reason of law, or favor of equity, is it allowable for us to interpret harshly, and render burdensome, those useful measures which have been enacted for the welfare of man." Now it happens often that the observance of some point of law conduces to the common weal in the majority of instances, and yet, in some cases, is very hurtful. Since then the lawgiver cannot have in view every single case, he shapes the law according to what happens most frequently, by directing his attention to the common good. Wherefore if a case arise wherein the observance of that law would be hurtful to the general welfare, it should not be observed. For instance, suppose that in a besieged city it be an established law that the gates of the city are to be kept closed, this is good for public welfare as a general rule: but, it were to happen that the enemy are in pursuit of certain citizens, who are defenders of the city, it would be a great loss to the city, if the gates were not opened to them: and so in that case the gates ought to be opened, contrary to the letter of the law, in order to maintain the common weal, which the lawgiver had in view.

Nevertheless it must be noted, that if the observance of the law according to the letter does not involve any sudden risk needing instant remedy, it is not competent for everyone to expound what is useful and what is not useful to the state: those alone can do this who are in authority, and who, on account of such like cases, have the power to dispense from

the laws. If, however, the peril be so sudden as not to allow of the delay involved by referring the matter to authority, the mere necessity brings with it a dispensation, since
necessity knows no law.

Question 97. Change in laws

Article 1. Whether human law should be changed in any way?   Augustine says (De
Lib. Arb. i, 6): "A temporal law, however just, may be justly changed in course of time."

I answer that, As stated above (Question 91, Article 3), human law is a dictate of reason,
whereby human acts are directed. Thus there may be two causes for the just change of
human law: one on the part of reason; the other on the part of man whose acts are regulated by law. The cause on the part of reason is that it seems natural to human reason to
advance gradually from the imperfect to the perfect. Hence, in speculative sciences, we
see that the teaching of the early philosophers was imperfect, and that it was afterwards
perfected by those who succeeded them. So also in practical matters: for those who first
endeavored to discover something useful for the human community, not being able by
themselves to take everything into consideration, set up certain institutions which were
deficient in many ways; and these were changed by subsequent lawgivers who made institutions that might prove less frequently deficient in respect of the common weal.

On the part of man, whose acts are regulated by law, the law can be rightly changed
on account of the changed condition of man, to whom different things are expedient
according to the difference of his condition. An example is proposed by Augustine
(De Lib. Arb. i, 6): "If the people have a sense of moderation and responsibility, and
are most careful guardians of the common weal, it is right to enact a law allowing
such a people to choose their own magistrates for the government of the commonwealth. But if, as time goes on, the same people become so corrupt as to sell their
votes, and entrust the government to scoundrels and criminals; then the right of
appointing their public officials is rightly forfeit to such a people, and the choice
devolves to a few good men."

**Article 2. Whether human law should always be changed, whenever something better
occurs?**   It is stated in the Decretals (Dist. xii, 5): "It is absurd, and a detestable shame,
that we should suffer those traditions to be changed which we have received from the
fathers of old."

Human law is rightly changed, in so far as such change is conducive to the common
weal. But, to a certain extent, the mere change of law is of itself prejudicial to the common
good: because custom avails much for the observance of laws, seeing that what is done
contrary to general custom, even in slight matters, is looked upon as grave. Consequently,
when a law is changed, the binding power of the law is diminished, in so far as custom is
abolished. Wherefore human law should never be changed, unless, in some way or other,
the common weal be compensated according to the extent of the harm done in this
respect. Such compensation may arise either from some very great and every evident
benefit conferred by the new enactment; or from the extreme urgency of the case, due to
the fact that either the existing law is clearly unjust, or its observance extremely harmful.
Wherefore the jurist says [Pandect. Justin. lib. i, ff., tit. 4, De Constit. Princip.] that "in
establishing new laws, there should be evidence of the benefit to be derived, before
departing from a law which has long been considered just."

Article 3. Whether custom can obtain force of law?   Augustine says (Ep. ad Casulan. xxxvi): "The customs of God's people and the institutions of our ancestors are to be considered as laws. And those who throw contempt on the customs of the Church ought to be punished as those who disobey the law of God."

All law proceeds from the reason and will of the lawgiver; the Divine and natural laws from the reasonable will of God; the human law from the will of man, regulated by reason. Now just as human reason and will, in practical matters, may be made manifest by speech, so may they be made known by deeds: since seemingly a man chooses as good that which he carries into execution. But it is evident that by human speech, law can be both changed and expounded, in so far as it manifests the interior movement and thought of human reason. Wherefore by actions also, especially if they be repeated, so as to make a custom, law can be changed and expounded; and also something can be established which obtains force of law, in so far as by repeated external actions, the inward movement of the will, and concepts of reason are most effectually declared; for when a thing is done again and again, it seems to proceed from a deliberate judgment of reason. Accordingly, custom has the force of a law, abolishes law, and is the interpreter of law.

Article 4. Whether the rulers of the people can dispense from human laws?   The Apostle says (1 Corinthians 9:17): "A dispensation is committed to me."

Dispensation, properly speaking, denotes a measuring out to individuals of some common goods: thus the head of a household is called a dispenser, because to each member of the household he distributes work and necessaries of life in due weight and measure. Accordingly in every community a man is said to dispense, from the very fact that he directs how some general precept is to be fulfilled by each individual. Now it happens at times that a precept, which is conducive to the common weal as a general rule, is not good for a particular individual, or in some particular case, either because it would hinder some greater good, or because it would be the occasion of some evil, as explained above (Question 96, Article 6). But it would be dangerous to leave this to the discretion of each individual, except perhaps by reason of an evident and sudden emergency, as stated above (Question 96, Article 6). Consequently he who is placed over a community is empowered to dispense in a human law that rests upon his authority, so that, when the law fails in its application to persons or circumstances, he may allow the precept of the law not to be observed. If however he grant this permission without any such reason, and of his mere will, he will be an unfaithful or an imprudent dispenser: unfaithful, if he has not the common good in view; imprudent, if he ignores the reasons for granting dispensations. Hence Our Lord says (Luke 12:42): "Who, thinkest thou, is the faithful and wise dispenser [Douay: steward], whom his lord setteth over his family?"

2.2.7 Ibn Sina
A Treatise on Love

In the name of the all-merciful God: Abdullah 'l-Ma'sumi, the lawyer, you have asked me to compose for you a clear and brief treatise on love. In reply let me say that with the following treatise I have done my utmost to win your approval and to satisfy your desire. I have let it consist of the following seven chapters:

- (I) On the power of love as pervading all beings;
- (II) On the existence of love in those substances' which are simple and inanimate;
- (III) On the existence of love in those beings which have the faculty of assimilating food, insofar as they possess that faculty;
- (IV) On the existence of love in the animal substances, in respect of their possession of the animal faculty;
- (V) On the love of those who are noble-minded and young for external beauty;
- (VI) On the love of the divine souls;
- (VII) General conclusion.

I.

On the Power of Love As Pervading All Beings.

Every being which is determined by a design strives by nature toward its perfection, i.e., that goodness of reality which ultimately flows from the reality of the Pure Good, and by nature it shies away from its specific defect which is the evil in it, i.e., materiality and non-being, for every evil results from attachment to matter and non-being. Therefore, it is obvious that all beings determined by a design possess a natural desire and an inborn love, and it follows of necessity that in such beings love is the cause of their existence. For everything that can be signified as existing belongs into one of these

Ibn Sina, *A Treatise on Love*, tr. Emil L. Fackenheim, *Mediaeval Studies* 7 (1945), pp. 208–228, with cuts. © 1945 by the Pontifical Institute of Mediaeval Studies, Toronto. Reprinted with permission of Pontifical Institute of Mediaeval Studies.

three categories: (i) either it has arrived at the specific perfection, (ii) or it has reached the maximum of defect, (iii) or it vacillates between these two states with the result that it is essentially in an intermediate position between two things. Now that which has arrived at the extreme of defect has been carried to absolute non-being, and to that which has no attachments left the term "absolute non-being" is suitably applied. Thus, while that which is disposed with complete non-being may deserve to be counted among the "beings" in a classification or in thought, its "being" must not be considered as real being. And existence, in an unqualified sense, cannot appropriately be applied to it except by way of metaphor. And in a classification it must not be made to belong to the group of beings except per accident. Beings in the real sense, then, are either such as are prepared for the maximum of perfection or such as are in a position intermediate between a defect occurring by reason of some cause and a perfection existing in the nature itself. Therefore, no being is ever free from some connection with a perfection, and this connection with it is accompanied by an innate love and desire for that which may unite it with its perfection.

This becomes clear also from another aspect, that of causality and the "why": since (i) no being which is determined by a design is devoid of a perfection specific to it; since (ii) such a being is not in itself sufficient cause for the existence of its perfection, because the perfections of the beings determined by a design emanate from the *per se* Perfect; and since (iii) one must not imagine that this Principle from which perfection emanates intends to cause a loss to any one of the particular beings – as the philosophers have expounded –; since all this is so, it is a necessary outcome of His wisdom and the excellence of His governance to plant into everything the general principle of love. The effect is that He thus indirectly preserves the perfections which He gave by emanation, and that He thus expresses His desire to bring them into being when they are absent, the purpose being that the administration [of the universe] should run according to a wise order. The never-ceasing existence of this love in all beings determined by a design is, therefore, a necessity. If this were not so, another love would be necessary to preserve this general love in its existence, to guard against its non-being and to retrieve it when it has lapsed, anxious lest it might disappear. But one of these two loves would be superfluous, and the existence of something superfluous in nature – which is divinely established – is impossible. Therefore, there is no principle of love other than this absolute and general love. And we can conclude that the existence of every being determined by a design is invariably accompanied by inborn love.

Let us now in this undertaking set out from a platform higher than our previous one by proceeding to an examination of the Highest Being and the way things behave under the governance of the Governor, to the full extent of its magnitude. Here we make the statement: The good is loved in its very essence. If this were not so, why should every being set up before itself as work and aim something it desires, aims at and works for, in imagining its goodness? If goodness were not in its very essence loved, why should every type of endeavour invariably be directed toward the good, in all its free actions? Therefore the good loves the good, for love is in truth nothing but whole-hearted approval of the pleasing and suitable. And this love is the source of its yearning for it when it is absent – if it is the sort of thing which may be absent –, and of its unification with it when it is present. Therefore every being approves of what is suitable for it and yearns for it when it is not there. And the specific good is the natural propensity of a being and the recognition of the truly suitable as such. Now approval and desire, and disapproval and aversion result in a thing from the attachment to its goodness. And a thing is in itself approved of only by reason of its goodness, for if approval is due to a thing in itself, then this is on account of its rightness and goodness. It is clear, then, that the good is loved *qua* good, whether it is the specific goodness of a thing or a goodness it has in common with others. Every type of love has as object either something already attained or something which is still to be attained. Whenever the goodness of a thing increases, the merit of the object of its love increases also, and so does the love for the good.

If this is established, then let us proceed to say this: that Being which is too exalted to be subject to the governance must be the highest object of love, because It must be the maximum in goodness. And the highest subject of love is identical with the highest object of love, namely, Its high and sublime Essence. Because the good loves the good through that attainment and penetration whereby it is connected with it, and because the First Good penetrates Itself in eternal actuality, therefore Its love for Itself is the most perfect and complete. And because there is no distinction among the divine qualities of Its Essence, love is here the essence and the being purely and simply, i.e. in the case of the Pure Good.

In all beings, therefore, love is either the cause of their being, or being and love are identical in them. It is thus evident that no being is devoid of love, and this it was our intention to show.

II.

On the Existence of Love in the Simple Inanimate Entities.

Simple inanimate entities are divided into three groups: (i) matter in the real sense of the term, (ii) that type of form which cannot subsist in separation, and (iii) accidents. The difference between accidents and this type of form lies in the fact that this type of form is constitutive of the substances. Therefore earlier metaphysicians have considered it proper to classify this type of form among the substances, because it is part of the self-subsisting substances, and they did not deny to it the name of substantiality merely because it cannot exist separately by itself, – for such is the state of the material substance. In spite of this, then, it is to be counted among the substances, and this is because it is in its very essence part of such substances as exist *per se*. Furthermore, the metaphysicians assess a special value to it, i.e., to form over matter with respect to the attainment of substantiality: The reason for this is that the substance subsists as an actual substance on account of the substantiality of this type of form, and that whenever the latter exists it necessitates the actual existence of the substance.

For this reason it has been said that form is a substance in the mode of actuality.

As for matter, this is counted among those which receive substantiality potentially. For actual existence does not necessarily result from the existence of the matter of a substance. Therefore it has been said that it is a substance in the mode of potentiality.

The true nature of form has thus definitely been established, and, also, that it has nothing at all in common with the accident, because the latter is not a constituent of the substance and cannot be considered as a substance from any point of view.

If that is clear, then we proceed to say this: every one of these simple inanimate entities is accompanied by an inborn love, from which it is never free, and this love is the cause of their being. As for matter, this is not there for the time when it merely desires to have a form, and when it exists it does so on account of its yearning for form. For that reason you will find that whenever it is deprived of a form it will hurry to receive another form in its stead, being always on guard against absolute non-being. For it is an inexorable law that all beings by nature shy away from absolute non-being. But matter is the abode of non-being. Thus, whenever a form does not substantially subsist in it, this will be equivalent to relative non-being, and if matter is not connected with a form at all, there will be absolute non-being. There is no need here for a water-tank to disclose that this is water. Matter is like a low-born and blameworthy woman who tries to prevent her ugliness from becoming known/and whenever her veil is uncovered she conceals her defects with her sleeve. It is established, then, that matter possesses an inborn love.

As for the type of form which is our concern here, the existence of inborn love in it is obvious in two respects: (i) one type of evidence lies in its clinging to its subject and its rejection of those things which would remove it from that subject; (ii) the second type of evidence lies in its adherence to its perfections and natural places when it happens to be at them, and its yearning movement toward them when it is separated from them, as is the case with the forms of the five simple bodies and the things composed of the four elements. These are the only types of thing to which form ever adheres.

As for accidents, the existence of love in them is quite obvious in their adherence to the subject, and the way this works is that the subject is connected with opposites by turns.

We conclude, then, that not one of these simple entities is devoid of love which is inborn in their nature.

III.

On the Existence of Love in the Vegetative Forms, i.e., the Vegetative Souls.

Putting this matter briefly let us say: the vegetative souls are subject to a division into three parts, namely, (i) the nutritive faculty, (ii) the faculty of growth and (iii) the faculty of procreation. Correspondingly, there is a specific love in the vegetative faculty according to these three parts: (i) The first of these is specific to the nutritive faculty, and this is the source of its desire for the presence of food in accordance with the need of matter for it, and for its maintenance in the body which receives it after its assimilation to the nature of the latter. (ii) The second type of love is specific to the faculty of growth, and this is the source of its desire for the increase fitting the proportions of the body which is nourished. (iii) The third type of love is specific to the faculty of procreation and this is the source of its desire to produce a new principle similar to the one from which it derives itself.

It is clear, then, that whenever these faculties exist, these types of love are attached to them. They, too, are therefore by nature endowed with love.

V.

On the Love of Those Who Are Noble-Minded and Young for External Beauty.

[...]

For, it is an incontrovertible truth that when a man expresses animal desire, he becomes involved in vice and is harmed in his rational soul. On the other hand [this type of love] is not specific to the rational soul alone either, for the endeavor of the latter requires the intelligible and eternal universals, not sensible and perishable particulars. This [type of love], then, results from an alliance between the two.

[...] Rational love can, therefore, not be pure except when the animal faculty is altogether subdued. With respect to the desire for conjugal union, it is fitting that a lover who entices the object of his love with this purpose in mind should be suspected, except if his need has a rational purpose, i.e., if his purpose is the propagation of the species. This is impossible with a man, and with a woman who is forbidden by religious law it is abominable. It is permissible and may find approval only in the case of a man with either his wife or female slave.

[...]

VI.

The Love of the Divine Souls.

Whenever a thing which really exists penetrates or acquires some good, it loves the latter by its very nature, as for instance the animal souls love beautiful forms. Again, whenever a really existing thing penetrates with the senses or with the intellect a thing that is of advantage to its being, and whenever it is led toward it by natural instinct, then it loves that thing by its very nature, especially when the thing in question is of advantage for its specific being. Examples thereof are the love of the animal for food and that of children for the parent. Again, whenever it is evident to a being that it is conducive to an increase in excellence and rank to imitate a certain being, to come close to it and to establish a special relation with it, then the former will invariably love the latter by its very nature. An example thereof is the case of an apprentice and his master.

Thus we can say this: the divine souls, be they human or angelic, have no claim whatever to divinity if they do not acquire knowledge of the Absolute Good. For it is obvious that these souls are characterized by perfection only after they have gained knowledge of those objects of the intellect which are caused, and the only way to conceive these is to let their conception be preceded by knowledge of the true causes, The First Cause is identical with the Pure Good which is absolute in Its essence. [This is proven in the following way:] reality is absolute in It, and the reality of nothing that is is devoid of some goodness. Now goodness is either absolute and part of the essence or derived from something else. The goodness of the First Cause – which is good – will thus either be essential and absolute, or derived from something else. But if it is derived from something else it can be so only in one of two ways: either the existence of Its goodness is necessary for the existence of the First Cause, – in which case that from which the goodness derives will be the cause of the First Cause, which is absurd; or the existence of Its goodness is not necessary for Its subsistence, and this is also absurd, as we have explained above. Should we, however, not admit the absurdity of the latter alternative, then the question is still open. Namely, if we allow this goodness to be non-essential and eliminate it as such, then clearly Its essence still remains both existing and endowed with goodness. That goodness will either be necessary and essential or derived from something else. If the latter alternative is accepted, we are reduced to an infinite regress which involves an impossibility. If, on the other hand, this goodness is posited to be essential, then we have arrived at what we search for.

Again, it is impossible that the First Cause should derive from somewhere a goodness which is not part of Its essence and does not necessarily belong to It. For the First Cause necessarily achieves perfection by its very substance. For if the First Cause did not from Its own essence completely receive all those qualities which in their relation to It really merit to be classified as "goodness", and if there was some element of potency in Its goodness, the First Cause would derive this goodness from something else. But since there is nothing outside It except the sum of the things caused by It, that from which It would derive goodness would be something caused by it. Now that which is caused by it has no goodness either in its nature or in its derivations apart from that which is derived from the First Cause. Therefore, if that which is caused by It is to bestow by emanation goodness on It, it can bestow only such goodness on It as is derived from It to begin with.

But, in the case at hand, the goodness derived from the First Cause is to have its ultimate origin in something else. In that case, this goodness would have to be not in the First Cause but in something outside It from which the First Cause would derive it. But it has already been said that it must be in the First Cause. Thus the whole suggestion [that any goodness in It is non-essential] is absurd.

In the First Cause there can be no defect of any kind or in any respect. [This is proven in the following way:] a perfection which is the opposite of a defect is (i) either impossible, and in that case there can be no defect correlative to it, or (ii) it is possible. Now, to conceive the possibility of that type of thing whose existence does not rest in anything else is to conceive along with that thing itself the cause which leads to actual achievement that which in itself has merely the potency for it. But we have already made clear that the First Cause has for Its perfection no outside cause of any kind or in any respect. Thus, there is no real possibility to a "possible" perfection in It, and consequently no defect correlative to it. The First Cause achieves *per se* completely anything that may, in its relation to It, be characterized as good. Those exalted goods which are good in every respect are not relative, and this is the type of good to which the First Cause has a relation of complete possession.

It is clear, then, that the First Cause possesses *per se* the complete sum of those perfections which in relation to It deserve that name, and that there is no element of possibility in It. It is also clear that the First Cause is good not only in Its substance but also in Its relations to all other beings, because It is the First Cause of their existence and preservation, more especially, of their being and their desire for their respective perfections. Therefore, the First Cause is good, absolutely and in every respect.

The perfection of both human and angelic souls lies in two things:

(i) the conception of those intelligible beings to which they have a possible relation, – each according to its capacity; this is in an effort to become assimilated to the essence of the Absolute Good –, and (ii) in the consequent emanation from them of such actions as are in harmony with their nature, and as are just in relation to the latter. Examples of such actions are noble deeds of men, and the movements imparted to the high substances by the angelic souls whose purpose is to preserve generation and destruction, again in an effort to become assimilated to the essence of the Absolute Good. These imitations occur for no other purpose than to make possible an approximation to the Absolute Good, and in order that from this proximity excellence and perfection should result. Now this can happen only by reason of help given by It, and they conceive this as coming from It. And we have already explained that in such a situation a being loves the thing toward which it moves. According to the preceding discourse it is necessary, then, that the Absolute Good should be loved by all souls endowed with a divine nature.

This love exists in them without ever ceasing. For they are always either in the state of perfection or in that of preparation. We have already explained that love exists in them of necessity whenever they are in the state of perfection. As for the state of preparation, this is to be found only in human and not in angelic souls. For the latter possess eternally the perfection in which their existence rests. The former which can be in the state of preparation are, while they are in that state, filled with a natural desire for the knowledge of the intelligible beings which is their perfection, especially for the knowledge of that to conceive which is most effective for the acquisition of perfection. This leads to the conception of what is similar to It, and this quality of the First Object of the intellect is the cause whereby all other objects of the intellect become object of the intellection of the souls, and it is the cause of their, existence also.

It is not an absurd thing to say that these souls have a love inborn in their nature for Absolute Reality primarily and for the other objects of the intellect secondarily. If this were not so, their specific states of preparation for their respective perfections would be without effect.

Therefore, the real object of the love of both human and angelic souls is the Pure Good.

VII.

General Conclusion.

We want to show in this chapter (i) that every single being loves the Absolute Good with an inborn love, and (ii) that the Absolute Good manifests Itself to all those that love It. However, the capacity of the latter to receive this manifestation differs in degree, and so does the connection they have with It. The highest degree of approximation to It is the reception of Its manifestation in its full reality, i.e., in the most perfect way possible, and this is what the Sufis call unification (*ittihâd*). In Its excellence It desires that Its manifestation should be received, and the existence of things depends on it.

Thus we say: since every being has a natural love for its perfection, – and "perfection" means the acquisition of its goodness – it is obvious that the term by reason of which its goodness results to the thing – no matter what the situation and form of realization – should of necessity be loved as the source from which its goodness stems. But as far as this function is concerned, there is nothing more perfect than the First Cause and nothing prior to It. It follows that It is loved by all things. The fact that most things do not know It does not contradict the fact that love of It is inborn in them, a love which is in these things directed toward their perfections. As far as Its essence is concerned, It is revealed and manifest to all beings. If It were in Its nature veiled from all things and not manifested to them, It could not be known and nothing could be obtained from It. If, on the other hand, It were manifested, but only under the influence of something else, there would have to be an external influence in Its essence which is too exalted to be subjected to such an influence; and this is impossible. [The truth is this]: as far as Its essence is concerned, It manifests Itself. If it appears veiled, this is due to the impotence of some things adequately to receive Its manifestation. Thus, in truth, the veil lies in those which are veiled, and this veil consists in impotence, weakness and defect. As far as Its manifestation is concerned, this is nothing short of Its essence itself. For, as the metaphysicians have expounded, as far as It *per se* is concerned, It never manifests Itself except in Its pure unmingled essence. It is Its noble essence itself which manifests itself, and for that reason the philosophers have called It "the Form of the Intellect".

[…]

The reason why the animal, vegetative, natural and human powers resemble It in the aims of their activities but not in the origins of the latter, lies in the fact that these origins are merely preparatory and potential states, – and the Absolute Good must be declared free from any community with states of preparation and potency –, whereas their aims are actual perfections, and to the First Cause absolute actual perfection must be attributed. Thus, it is possible that they should resemble It in the perfections which are their aim, but it is impossible that they should resemble It in their incipient states of preparation.

As for the angelic souls, they acquire resemblance to It in the forms of their essence and thus possess it eternally in complete actuality. For they contemplate It eternally and love It eternally, inasmuch as they contemplate It. And they are assimilated to It eternally inasmuch as they love It. Their desire lies in their penetration and conception of It, the most excellent kind of penetration and conception. On account of these they turn away from the direct penetration of everything else and from the direct conception of what is similar to It among the other intelligible beings. However, true knowledge of It becomes indirectly also the knowledge of the rest of existence. They conceive It, as it were, purposely and with desire, and what is similar to It concomitantly.

If it could happen that the Absolute Good did not manifest Itself, nothing could be obtained from It, and if nothing were obtained from It, nothing could exist. Thus, there can be nothing if Its manifestation is not present, since it is the cause of all existence. Because It, by Its very nature, loves the being of what is caused by It, It desires to manifest Itself. And since the love of the Most Perfect for Its own perfection is the most excellent love, it has as its true object the reception by others of Its manifestation, and this is most properly its reception by those divine souls which have reached the highest degree of assimilation to It. In this way it is possible that they become the object of Its love. This is the meaning of the tradition: God hath said: the servant of such and such a quality loves Me, and I love him. Just as wisdom in general will not allow anything that is precious in some respect to be overlooked, even though it fall short of the peak of excellence, the Absolute Good desires in Its wisdom that things should obtain some of Its gifts, even though the degree in which they will be obtained will not reach perfection. Thus, the Exalted King desires that others should imitate Him, in contrast with earthly kings who become angry when someone dares to imitate them. For the Exalted King will not bid those turn back from their aim who desire to imitate Him, whereas earthly kings will.

As we have now completed the task of this treatise we conclude it at this point. God is the Lord of all the worlds, and it is with His help alone that this treatise has been completed.

2.2.8 Ibn Rushd
On the Harmony of Religions and Philosophy

The Creation of the Universe

The Law teaches that the universe was invented and created by God, and that it did not come into being by chance or by itself. The method adopted by the Law for proving this is not the one upon which the Asharites have depended. For we have already shown that those methods are not specially certain for the learned, nor common enough to satisfy all the classes of men. The methods which are really serviceable are those which have a very few premises, and the results of which fall very near to the commonly known ideas. But in instructing the common people the Law does not favor statements composed of long and complete reasoning, based upon different problems. So everyone who, in teaching them, adopts a different course, and interprets the Law according to it, has lost sight of its purpose and gone astray from the true path. And so also, the Law in giving illustrations for its reasoning uses only those which are present before us.

Whatever has been thought necessary for the common people to know, has been explained to them by the nearest available examples, as in the case of the day of Judgment. But whatever was unnecessary for them to know, they have been told that it was beyond their knowledge, as the words of God about the Soul [Qur'an 22.85]. Now that we have established this, it is necessary that the method adopted by the Law for teaching the creation of the universe to the common people be such as would be acknowledged by all. It is also necessary that since there cannot be found anything present to illustrate the creation of the universe the Law must have used the examples of the creation of things in the visible world.

So the method adopted by Law is that the universe was made by God. If we look intently into the verse pertaining to this subject we shall see that the method adopted is that of divine solicitude, which we know to be one of those which prove the existence of God. When a man sees a thing made in a certain shape, proportion and fashion, for a particular advantage is derived from it, and purpose which is to be attained, so that it becomes clear to him, that had it not been found in that shape, and proportion, then that advantage would have been wanting in it, he comes to know for certain that there is a

Tr. Mohammed Jamil-al-Rahman, retrieved from http://en.wikisource.org/wiki/On_the_Harmony_of_Religions_and_Philosophy.

maker of that thing, and that he had made it in that shape and proportion, for a set purpose. For it is not possible that all those qualities serving that purpose be collected in that thing by chance alone. For instance, if a man sees a stone on the ground in a shape fit for sitting, and finds its proportions and fashion of the same kind, then he would come to know that it was made by a maker, and that he had made it and placed it there. But when he sees nothing in it which may have made it fit for sitting then he becomes certain that its existence in the place was by chance only, without its being fashioned by any maker.

Such is also the case with the whole of the universe. For when a man sees the sun, the moon, and all the stars, which are the cause of the four seasons; of days and nights, of rain, water and winds, of the inhabitation of the parts of the earth, of the existence of man, and of the being of all the animals and the plants and of the earth being fit for the habitation of a man, and other animals living in it; and the water fit for the animals living in it; and the air fit for birds, and if there be anything amiss in this creation and edifice, the whole world would come to confusion and disorder, then he would come to know with certainty that it is not possible that this harmony in it for the different members of the universe – man, animals, and plants – be found by chance only.

He will know that there is one who determined it, and so one who made it by intention, and that is God, exalted and magnified may He be. He would know with certainty that the universe is a created thing, for he would necessarily think that it is not possible that in it should be found all this harmony, if it be not made by someone, and had come into existence by chance alone. This kind of argument, is quite definite and at the same time clear, and some have mentioned it here. It is based upon two principles which are acknowledged by all. One of them being, that the universe, with all its component parts, is found fit for the existence of man and things; secondly, that which is found suitable in all its parts, for a single purpose, leading to a single goal, is necessarily a created thing. So those two principles lead us naturally to admit that the universe is a created thing, and that there is a maker of it. Hence "the argument of analogy" leads to two things at one and the same time, and that is why it is the best argument for proving the existence of God. This kind of reasoning is also found in the Qur'n in many verses in which the creation of the universe is mentioned.

For instance, "Have We not made the earth a bed, and the mountains for shelter to fix the same? And have We not created you of two sexes; and appointed your sleep for rest and made the night a garment to cover you, and destined the day to a gaining of a livelihood; and built over you seven heavens, and placed therein a burning lamp? And do We not send down from the clouds pressing forth rain, water pouring down in abundance, that We may hereby produce corn and herbs, and gardens planted thick with trees" [Qur'an 77.3ff]. If we ponder over this verse it would be found that our attention has been called to the suitability of the different parts of the universe for the existence of man. In the very beginning we are informed of a fact well-known to all – and that is that the earth has been created in a way which has made it suitable for our existence. Had it been unstable, or of any other shape, or in any other place, or not of the present proportion, it would not have been possible to be here, or at all created on it. All this is included in the words, "Have We not made the earth a bed for you"? for in a bed are collected together all the qualities of shape, tranquility, and peace, to which may be added those of smoothness and softness.

So how strange is this wonderful work and how excellent this blessedness, and how wonderful this collection of all the qualities! This is so because in the word *mihad* (bed) are brought together all those qualities, which are found in the earth, rendering it suitable for the existence of man. It is a thing which becomes clear to the learned after much learning and a long time, "But God will appropriate His mercy unto whom He pleases [Qur'an 2.99]. Then as to the divine words, "And the mountains for stakes," – they tell us of the advantage to be found in the tranquility of the earth on account of the mountains. For had the earth been created smaller than it is now, that is, without mountains, it would have been quivered by the motion of other elements, the water and the air, and would have been shaken and thus displaced. This would naturally have been the cause of the destruction of the animal world. So when its tranquility is in harmony with those living on it, it did not come into being by chance alone, but was made by someone's intention, and determination. Certainly it was made by One who intended it, and determined it, for the sake of those living on it.

Then He calls our attention to the suitability of the existence of night and day for animals. He says "And made the night a garment to cover you; and destined the day to a gaining of your livelihood." He means to say that He has made the night like a covering and clothing for all the things, from the heat of the sun. For had there been no setting of the sun at night, all the things, whose life has been made dependent upon the sun, would have perished – that is, the animals and the plants. As clothing protects the people from the heat of the sun, in addition to its being a covering, so God likened the night to it. This is one of the most beautiful of the metaphors. There is also another advantage in the night for the animals: their sleep in it is very deep, after the setting of the sun, which keeps faculties in motion, that is, wide awake. So God has said, "And appointed your sleep for rest," on account of the darkness of the night. Then He says, "And built over you seven heavens, and placed therein a burning lamp." Here by the word building He means their creation, and their harmony with the created things, and their arrangement and system. By strength He means that power of revolution and motion which is never slackened, and never overtaken by fatigue; and they never fall like other roofs and high edifices. To this refer the words of God, "And made the heaven a roof well-supported" [Qur'an 21.33]. By all this He shows their fitness in number, shape, fashion, and movement, for the existence of those who live on the earth round it. Were one of the heavenly bodies, not to speak of all, to stop for a moment all would be chaos on the face of the earth. Some people think the blast of the last trumpet, which will be the cause of the thunderbolt, will be nothing but a stop in the revolution of the heavenly bodies.

Then He tells us of the advantage of the sun for those living on the earth and says, "And placed therein a burning lamp." He calls it a lamp because in reality it is all darkness, and light covers the darkness of the night, and if there be no lamp, man can get no advantage out of his sense of sight at nighttime; and in the same way if there were no sun the animals can have no benefit of their sense of seeing. He calls our attention to this advantage of the suns ignoring others because it is the noblest of all the advantages and the most-apparent of all. Then He tells us of His kindness in sending down rain, for the sake of the plants and the animals. The coming down of rain in an appointed proportion, and at an appointed season, for the cultivated fields cannot be by chance alone, but is the result of divine solicitude for us all. So He says, "And do We not send down from the clouds pressing forth rain, water pouring down in abundance that We may hereby produce corn and herbs, and gardens planted thick with trees."

There are many verses of the Qur'an on this subject. For instance, He says, "Do you not see how God has created the seven heavens, one above another, and has placed the moon therein for a light, and has appointed the sun for a taper? God has also provided and caused you to bring forth wheat from the earth" [Qur'an 71.14–16]. If we were to count all such verses and comment upon them showing the kindness of the Creator for the created, it would take too many volumes. We do not intend to do it in this book. If God should grant us life and leisure we shall write a book to show the kindness of God to which He has called our attention.

It should be known that this kind of argument is just contrary to that which the Asharites think leads to the knowledge of God. They think that the creation does not lead us to the knowledge of God through any of His goodness, but through possibility, that is, the possibility which is found in all things, which we can understand to be of his shape or of quite a contrary one. But if this possibility be found alike in both the cases, then there is no wisdom in the creation of the universe, and there is found no harmony between man and the parts of it. For, as they think, if it is possible for the things to have any other form than they have now, then there can exist no harmony between man and other existent things by the creation of which God has obliged man and commanded him to be thankful to Him. This opinion, by which the creation of man, as a part of the universe, is just as possible, for instance, as his creation in the void, is like the opinion of those who say that man exists but he could have been created in quite a different shape, and yet could perform actions like a man. According to them it is also possible that he may have formed the part of another universe quite different from the existing one. In that case the blessing of the universe can have no obligation for man, for they are not necessary for his purpose. Hence man is quite careless of them and they of him. So their existence is no blessing to him. This is all against the nature of man.

On the whole, a man who denies the existence of the effects arranged according to the causes in the question of arts, or whose wisdom cannot understand it, then he has no knowledge of the art of its Maker. So also a man who denies the existence of an order of effects in accordance with causes in this universe, denies the existence of the Creator altogether. Their saying that God is above these causes, and that they cannot have any bearing on the effects by His command, is very far from the true nature of philosophy, nay, it is a destroyer of it. For if it is possible to have the same effects with other than the prescribed causes just in the same degree as by them, then where is the greatness in producing the effects from the known Causes? It is so because the effects from the causes have one of the following three reasons. Either the existence of the causes will be in place of the effects by compulsion, as a man's taking his food; or their being more perfect, that is, the effect becoming better and more perfect through them, as a man's having two eyes, or they may have neither a better nor a more compulsive effect. In this case the existence of the effect and the cause would be by chance, without any intention at all; and, hence, there would be no greatness found in it.

For instance, if the shape of a human hand, the number of the fingers, and their length be neither necessary nor adding any perfection in its work in seizing things of different kind, then the actions of the hand from this shape, and number of parts, would be by chance alone. If it be so, then it makes no difference whether a man is given a hand or a hoof, or something else, like the different animals, for their particular actions. On the whole, if we ignore the causes and their effects, then there remains nothing to refute the arguments of those who believe in the creation of the universe by chance alone, that is, those who say that there is no Creator at all, and that which has come into being in this universe is the result of material causes. For taking one of the two alternatives it is not more possible that it may have happened by chance, than done by an independent Actor. So when the Asharites say that the existence of one or more possibilities shows that there is a particular Maker of these things, they can answer and say that the existence of things by one of these possibilities was by chance alone, for intention works as one of the causes, and that which happens without any means or cause is by chance. We see that many things come into being in this way. For example, the elements mix together by chance, and then by this unintentional mixing there is produced a new thing. They mix again, and this quite unintentionally produces quite a new thing. In this way every kind of creation may be said to have come into existence by chance.

We say that it is necessary that there be found order and arrangement, the more perfect and finished than what can be imagined. This mixing together of elements is limited and prearranged, and things produced by them are sure to happen, and no disorder has ever happened in them. But all this could not happen by chance alone, for that which happens in this way by chance is of the least value. It is to this that God refers, "It is the work of the Lord, who has rightly disposed all things" [Qur'an 27.90]. I would like to know what completeness can be found in things made by chance, for such things are by no means better than their opposites. To this God refers in the following words, "You cannot see in the Creation of the most Merciful any unfitness or disproportion. Lift your eyes again to heaven, and look whether you see any flaw" [Qur'an 67.3]. But what defect can be greater than that all the things can be found with any other quality than they really possess. For the non-existent quality may be better than the existing one. In this way, if one thinks that were the Eastern movement to become Western and vice-versa, there would be no difference in the universe then he has destroyed philosophy altogether. He is like a man who thinks that were the right side of the animals to become left, and vice-versa, there would be no difference at all, for one of the two alternatives is there. For as it is possible to say that it is made according to one alternative by an independent Maker, so it is possible to assert that it was all made by chance alone. For we see so many things coming into being by themselves.

It is quite clear to you that all the people see that lower kinds of creation could have been made in a different way from that in which they really are, and as they see this lower degree in many things they think that they must have been made by chance. But in the higher creation they know that it is impossible to have been made in a more perfect and excellent form than that given to it by the Creator. So this opinion, which is one of the opinions of the Mutakallimun is both against the Law and philosophy. What we say is that the opinion of possibility in creation is closer to a complete denial of God, than leading us nearer to Him. At the same time it falsifies philosophy. For if we do not understand that there is a mean between the beginnings and ends of the Creation, upon which is based the ends of things, then there can neither be any order nor any method in it. And if they be wanting then there can be no proof of the existence of an intelligent and knowing Maker; for taking them together with cause and effect we are led to the fact that they must have been created by wisdom and knowledge.

But, on the other hand, the existence of either of two possibilities shows that they may have been performed by a not-knowing Maker and by chance alone. Just as a stone falling on the earth may fall in any place, on any side, and in any form. It will show the want of the existence either of a creator at all or at least of a wise and knowing Creator. The thing which has compelled the Mutakallimun of the Asharites to adopt this opinion is a denial of the action of those natural forces which God has put in all things, as He has endowed them with life, power and so forth. They avoided the opinion that there was any other creator but God, and God forbid that there be any other, for he is the only creator of the causes and they are made effective by His command only. We will talk of this in detail when discoursing on Fate and Predestination. They were also afraid that by admitting the natural causes they might be accused of saying that the universe came into being by chance only. They would have known that a denial of it means a denial of a great part of the arguments, which can be advanced for a proof of the existence of God. One who denies any part of God's creation denies His work, which falls very near to a denial of a part of His attributes.

On the whole as their opinion is based upon hasty conclusions, which come to the mind of a man by superficial thought and as apparently it appears that the word "intention" can be applied to one who has power to do bad or otherwise, they saw that if they did not admit that all the creation is possible, they would not be able to say that it came into existence by the action of an intending creator. So they say that all the creation is possible so that they may prove that the creator is an intelligent one. They never thought of the order which is necessary in things made, and with that their coming from an intelligent creator. These people have also ignored the blame they will have to bear in thus denying wisdom to the creator; or maintaining that chance should be found governing creation. They know, as we have said, that it is necessary, on account of the order existent in nature, that it must have been brought into being by some knowing creator, otherwise the order found in it would be by chance. When they were compelled to deny the natural forces they had to deny with them a large number of those forces which God has made subservient to His command for the creation and preservation of things. For God has created some things from causes which He has produced from outside, these are the heavenly bodies; there are other things which He has made by causes placed in the things themselves, that is; the soul, and other natural forces, by which he preserves those things. So how wicked is the man who destroys philosophy, and "invented a lie about God" [Qur'an 3.88].

This is only a part of the change which has taken place in the Law, in this and other respects, which we have already mentioned, and will mention hereafter. From all this it must have become clear to you that the method which God had adopted for teaching His creatures that the universe is made and created by Him is the method of kindness and wisdom, towards all His creatures and especially towards man. It is a method which bears the same relation to our intellect, as the sun bears to our senses. The method which it has adopted towards the common people about this problem is that of illustration from things observed. But as there was nothing which could be given as an illustration, and as the common people cannot understand a thing, an illustration of which they cannot see, God tells us that the universe was created in a certain time out of a certain thing, which He made. He tells us his condition before the creation of the universe, "His throne was above the waters" [Qur'an 11.9]. He also says, "Verily your Lord is God who created the heavens and the earth in six days" [Qur'an 7.52], and "Then He set His mind to the creation of the heavens, and it was smoke" [Qur'an 12.10]. In addition to these there are other verses of the Book, pertaining to this subject. So it is incumbent that nothing out of them should be interpreted for the common people, and nothing should be presented to them in explaining it but this illustration. For one who changes it, makes the wisdom of the Law useless. If it be said that the Law teaches about the universe that it is created, and made out of nothing and in no time, then it is a thing which even the learned cannot understand, not to speak of the common people. So we should not deviate in this matter of the Law.

[…]

The Day of Judgment

Come the Day of Judgment, some believe that the body will be different from our present body. This is only transient, that will be eternal. For this also there are religious arguments. It seems that even Abdullah ben-Abbas held this view. For it is related of him that he said, "There is nought in this world of the hereafter, but names." It seems that this view is better suited to the learned men because its possibility is based upon principles, in which there is no disagreement according to all men: the one being that the soul is immortal, and the second is that the return of the souls into other bodies does not look so impossible as the return of the bodies themselves. It is so because the material of the bodies here is found following and passing from one body to another, i.e., one and the same matter is found in many people and in many different times. The example of bodies cannot be found, for their matter is the same. For instance a man dies and his body becomes dissolved into earth. The earth ultimately becomes dissolved into vegetable, which is eaten by quite a different man from whom another man comes into being. If we suppose them to be different bodies, then our aforesaid view cannot be true.

The truth about this question is that man should follow that which he himself has thought out but anyhow it should not be the view which may deny the fundamental principle altogether. For this would be denying its existence. Such a belief leads to infidelity, on account of a distinct knowledge of this condition being given to man, both by religion and by human reason, which is all based upon the eternal nature of the soul. If it be said whether there is any argument or information in the Law about this eternal nature of the soul, we would say that it is found in the Qur'an itself, where God says, "God takes unto himself the souls of men at the time of their death; and those which die not He also takes in their sleep" [Qur'an 39.43]. In this verse sleep and death have been placed upon the same level, on account of the change in its instrument, and in sleep on account of a change in itself. For had it not been so it would not have come to its former condition after awakening. By this means we know that this cession does not effect its essence, but was only attached to it on account of change in its instrument. So it does not follow that with a cessation of the work of the instrument, the soul also ceases to exist. Death is only a cessation of work, so it is clear that its condition should be like that of sleep. As someone has said that if an old man were to get the eyes of the young, he would begin to see like him.

This is all that we thought of in an exposition of the beliefs of our religion, Islam. What remains for us is to look into things of religion in which interpretation is allowed and not allowed. And if allowed, then who are the people to take advantage of it? With this thing we would finish our discourse.

The things found in the Law can be divided into five kinds. But in the first place there are only two kinds of things: indivisible and the divisible. The second one is divided into four kinds. The first kind which is mentioned in the Qur'an, is quite clear in its meanings. The second is that in which the thing mentioned is not the thing meant but is only an example of it. This is again divided into four kinds. First, the meanings which it mentions are only illustrations such that they can only be known by the far-fetched and compound analogies, which cannot be understood, but after a long time and much labor. None can accept them but perfect and excellent natures; and it cannot be known that the illustration given is not the real thing; except by this far-fetched way. The second is just the opposite of the former: they can be understood easily, and it can be known that the example is just what is meant here. Thirdly, it can be easily known that it is merely an illustration, but what it is the example of is difficult to comprehend. The fourth kind is quite opposite to the former. The thing of which it is an example, is easily understood; while it is difficult to know that it is an example at all.

The interpretation of the first kind is wrong without doubt. The kind in which both the things are far-fetched: its interpretation particularly lies with those who are well-grounded in knowledge; and an exposition of it is not fit for any but the learned. The interpretation of its opposite – that which can be understood on both the sides – is just what is wanted, and an exposition of it is necessary. The case of the third kind is like the case of the above. For in it illustration has not been mentioned because of the difficulty for the common people to understand it: it only incites the people to action. Such is the case with the hadith of the prophet, "The black stone is God's action on Earth," etc., etc. That which can be easily known that is an example, but difficult to know of which it is an example, should not be interpreted but for the sake of particular persons and learned men. Those who understand that it is only an illustration, but are not learned enough to know the thing which it illustrates, should be told either that it is allegorical and can be understood by the well-established learned men; or the illustration should be changed in a way which might be near to their understanding. This would be the best plan to dispel doubts from their minds.

The law about this should be that which has been laid down by Abu Hamid (Al Ghazzali) in his book, *Al Tafriga bainal Islam wal Zindiga*. It should be understood that one thing has five existences which he calls by the name of essential (*Zati*); sensual (*Hissi*); rational (*Agli*); imaginative (*Khayali*); and doubtful (*Shilbhi*). So at the time of doubt it should be considered which of these five kinds would better satisfy the man who has doubts. If it be that which he has called essential than an illustration would best satisfy their minds. In it is also included the following hadith of the Prophet, "Whatever the earlier prophets saw I have seen it from my place here, even heaven and hell;" "Between my cistern of water and the pulpit there is a garden of paradise;" and "The earth will eat up the whole of a man except the extremity of the tail." All these, it can easily be known are but illustrations, but what is the thing which they illustrate it is difficult to comprehend. So it is necessary in this case to give an instance to the people which they may easily understand. This kind of illustration, when used on such an occasion, is allowable; but when used irrelevantly it is wrong. Abu Hamid has not decided about the occasion when both the sides of the question – the illustration and the illustrated – be both far-fetched and difficult to understand. In this case there would apparently be a doubt, but a doubt without any foundation. What should be done is to prove that the doubt has no basis, but no interpretation should be made, as we have shown in many places in our present book against the Mutakallimun, Asharites and the Mutazilites.

The fourth kind of occasion is quite opposite to the former. In this it is very difficult to understand that it is an example, but when once understood, you can easily comprehend the thing illustrated. In the interpretation of this also, there is a consideration: about those people who know that if it is an example, it illustrates such and such a thing; but they doubt whether it is an illustration at all. If they are not learned people, the best thing to do with them is not to make any interpretation, but only to prove the fallacy of the views which they hold about its being an illustration at all. It is also possible that an interpretation may make them still distant from the truths on account of the nature of the illustration and the illustrated. For these two kinds of occasions, if an interpretation is given, they give rise to strange beliefs, far from the law which when disclosed are denied by the common people. Such has been the case with the Sufis, and those learned men who have followed them. When this work of interpretation was done by people who could not distinguish between these occasions, and made no distinction between the people for whom the interpretation is to be made, there arose differences of opinion, at last forming into sects, which ended in accusing one another with unbelief. All this is pure ignorance of the purpose of the Law.

From what we have already said the amount of mischief done by interpretation must have become clear to you. We always try to acquire our purpose by knowing what should be interpreted, and what not; and when interpreted, how it should be done; and whether all the difficult portions of the Law and Hadith are to be explained or not. These are all included in the four kinds which have already been enumerated.

2.2.9 Moses Maimonides
Guide of the Perplexed

Book III

Chapter XXVII

THE general object of the Law is twofold: the well-being of the soul, and the well-being of the body. The well-being of the soul is promoted by correct opinions communicated to the people according to their capacity. Some of these opinions are therefore imparted in a plain form, others allegorically: because certain opinions are in their plain form too strong for the capacity of the common people. The well-being of the body is established by a proper management of the relations in which we live one to another. This we can attain in two ways: first by removing all violence from our midst: that is to say, that we do not do every one as he pleases, desires, and is able to do; but every one of us does that which contributes towards the common welfare. Secondly, by teaching every one of us such good morals as must produce a good social state. Of these two objects, the one, the well-being of the soul, or the communication of correct opinions, comes undoubtedly first in rank, but the other, the well-being of the body, the government of the state, and the establishment of the best possible relations among men, is anterior in nature and time. The latter object is required first: it is also treated [in the Law] most carefully and most minutely, because the well-being of the soul can only be obtained after that of the body has been secured. For it has already been found that man has a double perfection: the first perfection is that of the body, and the second perfection is that of the soul. The first consists in the most healthy condition of his material relations, and this is only possible when man has all his wants supplied, as they arise; if he has his food, and other things needful for his body, e.g., shelter, bath, and the like. But one man alone cannot procure all this; it is impossible for a single man to obtain this comfort; it is only possible in society, since man, as is well known, is by nature social.

The second perfection of man consists in his becoming an actually intelligent being; i.e., he knows about the things in existence all that a person perfectly developed is capable of knowing. This second perfection certainly does not include any action or good conduct, but only knowledge, which is arrived at by speculation, or established by research.

Tr. Friedländer (1904).

It is clear that the second and superior kind of perfection can only be attained when the first perfection has been acquired: for a person that is suffering from great hunger, thirst, heat, or cold, cannot grasp an idea even if communicated by others, much less can he arrive at it by his own reasoning. But when a person is in possession of the first perfection, then he may possibly acquire the second perfection, which is undoubtedly of a superior kind, and is alone the source of eternal life. The true Law, which as we said is one, and beside which there is no other Law, viz., the Law of our teacher Moses, has for its purpose to give us the twofold perfection. It aims first at the establishment of good mutual relations among men by removing injustice and creating the noblest feelings. In this way the people in every land are enabled to stay and continue in one condition, and every one can acquire his first perfection. Secondly, it seeks to train us in faith, and to impart correct and true opinions when the intellect is sufficiently developed. Scripture clearly mentions the twofold perfection, and tells us that its acquisition is the object of all the divine commandments. "And the Lord commanded us to do all these statutes, to fear the Lord our God, for our good always, that he might preserve us alive as it is this day" (Deut. vi. 24). Here the second perfection is first mentioned because it is of greater importance, being, as we have shown, the ultimate aim of man's existence. This perfection is expressed in the phrase, "for our good always." You know the interpretation of our Sages, "'that it may be well with thee' (ibid. xxii. 7), namely, in the world that is all good, 'and that thou mayest prolong thy days' (ibid.), i.e., in the world that is all eternal." In the same sense I explain the words, "for our good always," to mean that we may come into the world that is all good and eternal, where we may live permanently; and the words, "that he might preserve us alive as it is this day," I explain as referring to our first and temporal existence, to that of our body, which cannot be in a perfect and good condition except by the co-operation of society, as has been shown by us.

[...]

Book III

CHAPTER VIII

TRANSIENT bodies are only subject to destruction through their substance and not through their form, nor can the essence of their form be destroyed: in this respect they are permanent. The generic forms, as you know, are all permanent and stable. Form can only be destroyed accidentally, i.e., on account of its connexion with substance, the true nature of which consists in the property of never being without a disposition to receive form. This is the reason why no form remains permanently in a substance; a constant change takes place, one form is taken off and another is put on. How wonderfully wise is the simile of King Solomon, in which he compares matter to a faithless wife: for matter is never found without form, and is therefore always like such a wife who is never without a husband, never single; and yet, though being wedded, constantly seeks another man in the place of her husband: she entices and attracts him in every possible manner till he obtains from her what her husband has obtained. The same is the case with matter. Whatever form it has, it is disposed to receive another form; it never leaves off moving and casting off the form which it has in order to receive another. The same takes place when this second form is received. It is therefore clear that all corruption, destruction, or defect comes from matter. Take, e.g., man; his deformities and unnatural shape of limbs; all weakness, interruption, or disorder of his actions, whether innate or not, originate in the transient substance, not in the form. All other living beings likewise die or become ill through the substance of the body and not through its form. Man's shortcomings and sins are all due to the substance of the body and not to its form; while all his merits are exclusively due to his form. Thus the knowledge of God, the formation of ideas, the mastery of desire and passion, the distinction between that which is to be chosen and that which is to be rejected, all these man owes to his form; but eating, drinking, sexual intercourse, excessive lust, passion, and all vices, have their origin in the substance of his body. Now it was dear that this was the case, – it was impossible, according to the wisdom of God, that substance should exist without form, or any of the forms of the bodies without substance, and it was necessary that the very noble form of man, which is the image and likeness of God, as has been shown by us, should be joined to the substance of dust and darkness, the source of all defect and loss. For these reasons the Creator gave to the form of man power, rule, and dominion over the substance; – the form can subdue the substance, refuse the fulfilment of its desires, and reduce them, as far as possible, to a just and proper measure. The station of man varies according to the exercise of this power. Some persons constantly strive to choose that which is noble, and to seek perpetuation in accordance with the direction of their nobler part, – their form: their thoughts are engaged in the formation of ideas, the acquisition of true knowledge about everything, and the union with the divine intellect which flows down upon them, and which is the source of man's form. Whenever they are led by the wants of the body to that which is low and avowedly disgraceful, they are grieved at their position, they feel ashamed and confounded at their situation. They try with all their might to diminish this disgrace, and to guard against it in every possible way. They feel like a person whom the king in his anger ordered to remove refuse from one place to another in order to put him to shame; that person tries as much as possible to hide himself during the time of his disgrace: he perhaps removes a small quantity a short distance in such a manner that his hands and garments remain clean, and he himself be unnoticed by his fellow-men. Such would be the conduct of a free man, whilst a slave would find pleasure in such work; – he would not consider it a great burden, but throw himself into the refuse, smear his face and his hands, carry the refuse openly, laughing and singing. This is exactly the difference in the conduct of different men. Some consider, as we just said, all wants of the body as shame, disgrace, and defect to which they are compelled to attend: this is chiefly the case with the sense of touch, which is a disgrace to us according to Aristotle, and which is the cause of our desire for eating, drinking, and sensuality. Intelligent persons must, as much as possible, reduce these wants, guard against them, feel grieved when satisfying them, abstain from speaking of them, discussing them, and attending to them in company with others. Man must have control over all these desires, reduce them as much as possible, and only retain of them as much as is indispensable. His aim must be the aim of man as man, viz., the formation of ideas, and nothing else. The best and sublimest among them is the idea which man forms of God, angels, and the rest of the creation according to his capacity. Such men are always with God, and of them it is said, "Ye are princes, and all of you are children of the Most High" (Ps. lxxxii. 6). This is man's task and purpose. Others, however, that are separated from God form the multitude of fools, and do just the opposite. […]

2.2.10 Moses Maimonides
The Eight Chapters of Maimonides on Ethics (Shemonah Perakim)

Chapter I

Concerning the Human Soul and its Faculties

KNOW that the human soul is one, but that it has many diversified activities. […] Thou knowest that the improvement of the moral qualities is brought about by the healing of the soul and its activities. Therefore, just as the physician, who endeavors to cure the human body, must have a perfect knowledge of it in its entirety and its individual parts, just as he must know what causes sickness that it may be avoided, and must also be acquainted with the means by which a patient may be cured, so, likewise, he who tries to cure the soul, wishing to improve the moral qualities, must have a knowledge of the soul in its totality and its parts, must know how to prevent it from becoming diseased, and how to maintain its health.

So, I say that the soul has five faculties; the nutritive [also known as the "growing" faculty], the sensitive, the imaginative, the appetitive, and the rational. We have already stated in this chapter that our words concern themselves only with the human soul; for the nutritive faculty by which man is nourished is not the same, for instance, as that of the ass or the horse. Man is sustained by the nutritive faculty of the human soul, the ass thrives by means of the nutritive faculty of its soul, and the palm-tree flourishes by the nutritive faculty peculiar to its soul. Although we apply the same term nutrition to all of them indiscriminately, nevertheless, its signification is by no means the same. In the same way, the term sensation is used homonymously for man and beast; not with the idea, however, that the sensation of one species is the same as that of another, for each species has its own characteristic soul distinct from every other, with the result that there necessarily arises from each soul activities peculiar to itself. It is possible, however, that an activity of one soul may seem to be similar to that of another, in consequence of which one might think that both belong to the same class, and thus consider them to be alike; but such is not the case. […]

Reason, that faculty peculiar to man, enables him to understand, reflect, acquire knowledge of the sciences, and to discriminate between proper and improper actions.

Tr. Joseph Gorfinkle (New York: Columbia University Press, 1912).

Its functions are partly practical and partly speculative (theoretical), the practical being, in turn, either mechanical or intellectual. By means of the speculative power, man knows things as they really are, and which, by their nature, are not subject to change. These are called the sciences in general. The mechanical power is that by which the arts, such as architecture, agriculture, medicine, and navigation are acquired. The intellectual power is that by which one, when he intends to do an act, reflects upon what he has premeditated, considers the possibility of performing it, and, if he thinks it possible, decides how it should be done.

This is all we have deemed it necessary to say in this regard concerning the soul. Know, however, that the soul, whose faculties and parts we have described above, and which is a unit, may be compared to matter in that it likewise has a form, which is reason. If the form (reason) does not communicate its impression to the soul, then the disposition existing in the soul to receive that form is of no avail, and exists to no purpose, as Solomon says, "Also in the want of knowledge in the soul there is nothing good". This means that if a soul has not attained a form but remains without intelligence, its existence is not a good one. However, this is not the place for us to discuss such problems as that of form, matter, and the number of different kinds of intelligence, and their means of acquisition; nor is it necessary for what we have to say concerning the subject of ethics, but is more appropriately to be discussed in the Book on Prophecy, which we mention (elsewhere).

Now I conclude this chapter, and begin the next.

Chapter II

Concerning the Transgressions of the Faculties of the Soul and the Designation of Those Faculties Which Are The Seat of The Virtues and the Vices

KNOW that transgressions and observances of the Law have their origin only in two of the faculties of the soul, namely, the sensitive and the appetitive, and that to these two faculties alone are to be ascribed all transgressions and observances. The faculties of nutrition and imagination do not give rise to observance or transgression, for in connection with neither is there any conscious or voluntary act. That is, man cannot consciously suspend their functions, nor can he curtail any one of their activities. The proof of this is that the functions of both these faculties, the nutritive and the imaginative, continue to be operative when one is asleep, which is not true of any other of the soul's faculties.

As regards the rational faculty, uncertainty prevails (among philosophers), but I maintain that observance and transgression may also originate in this faculty, in so far as one believes a true or a false doctrine, though no action which may be designated as an observance or a transgression results therefrom. Consequently, as I said above, these two faculties (the sensitive and the appetitive) alone really produce transgressions and observances.

Now, as for the virtues, they are of two kinds, moral and intellectual, with the corresponding two classes of vices. The intellectual virtues belong to the rational faculty. They are (1) wisdom, which is the knowledge of the direct and indirect causes of things based on a previous realization of the existence of those things, the causes of which have been investigated; (2) reason, consisting of (a) inborn, theoretical reason, that is, axioms, (b) the acquired intellect, which we need not discuss here, and (c) sagacity and intellectual cleverness, which is the ability to perceive quickly, and to grasp an idea without delay, or in a very short time. The vices of this faculty are the antitheses or the opposites of these virtues.

Moral virtues belong only to the appetitive faculty to which that of sensation in this connection is merely subservient. The virtues of this faculty are very numerous, being moderation, [i.e. fear of sin], liberality, honesty, meekness, humility, contentedness, [which the Rabbis call "wealth", when they say, "Who is truly wealthy? He who is contented with his lot"], courage, [faithfulness], and other virtues akin to these. The vices of this faculty consist of a deficiency or of an exaggeration of these qualities.

As regards the faculties of nutrition and imagination, it cannot be said that they have vices or virtues, but that the nutritive functions work properly or improperly; as, for instance, when one says that a man' digestion is good or bad, or that one's imagination is confused or clear. This does not mean, however, that they have virtues or vices.

So much we wished to discuss in this chapter.

Chapter III

Concerning the Diseases of the Soul

THE ancients maintained that the soul, like the body, is subject to good health and illness. The soul' healthful state is due to its condition, and that of its faculties, by which it constantly does what is right, and performs what is proper, while the illness of the soul is occasioned by its condition, and that of its faculties, which results in its constantly doing wrong, and performing actions that are improper. The science of medicine investigates the health of the body. Now, just as those, who are physically ill, imagine that, on account of their vitiated tastes, the sweet is bitter and the bitter is sweet and likewise fancy the wholesome to be unwholesome and just as their desire grows stronger, and their enjoyment increases for such things as dust, coal, very acidic and sour foods, and the like which the healthy loathe and refuse, as they are not only not beneficial even to the healthy, but possibly harmful so those whose souls are ill, that is the wicked and the morally perverted, imagine that the bad is good, and that the good is bad. The wicked man, moreover, continually longs for excesses which are really pernicious, but which, on account of the illness of his soul, he considers to be good. Likewise, just as when people, unacquainted with the science of medicine, realize that they are sick, and consult a physician, who tells them what they must do, forbidding them to partake of that which they imagine beneficial, and prescribing for them things which are unpleasant and bitter, in order that their bodies may become healthy, and that they may again choose the good and spurn the bad, so those whose souls become ill should consult the sages, the moral physicians, who will advise them against indulging in those evils which they (the morally ill) think are good, so that they may be healed by that art of which I shall speak in the next chapter, and through which the moral qualities are restored to their normal condition. But, if he who is morally sick be not aware of his illness, imagining that he is well, or, being aware of it, does not seek a remedy, his end will be similar to that of one, who, suffering from bodily ailment, yet continuing to indulge himself, neglects to be cured, and who in consequence surely meets an untimely death.

Those who know that they are in a diseased state, but nevertheless yield to their inordinate passions, are described in the truthful Law which quotes their own words, "Though I walk in the stubbornness of my heart, in order that the indulgence of the passions may appease the thirst for them." (Dt. XXIX, 18) This means that, intending to quench the thirst, it is, on the contrary, intensified. He who is ignorant of his illness is spoken of in many places by Solomon, who says, "The way of the fool is straight in his own eyes, but he who hearkeneth unto counsel is wise." (Prov. XII,15) This means that he who listens to the counsel of the sage is wise, for the sage teaches him the way that is actually right, and not the one that he (the morally ill) erroneously considers to be such. Solomon also says, "There is many a way which seemeth even before a man; but its ends are ways unto death." (Ibid. XIV, 12) Again, in regard to these who are morally ill, in that they do not know what is injurious from that which is beneficial, he says, "The way of the wicked is like darkness; they do not know against what they stumble." (Ibid., IV, 19)

The art of healing the diseases of the soul will, however, form the subject-matter of the fourth chapter.

Chapter IV

Concerning the Cure of the Diseases of the Soul

GOOD deeds are such as are equibalanced, maintaining the mean between two equally bad extremes, the too much and the too little. Virtues are psychic conditions and dispositions which are mid-way between two reprehensible extremes, one of which is characterized by an exaggeration, the other by a deficiency. Good deeds are the product of these dispositions. To illustrate, abstemiousness is a disposition which adopts a mid-course between inordinate passion and total insensibility to pleasure. Abstemiousness, then, is a proper rule of conduct, and the psychic disposition which gives rise to it is an ethical quality; but inordinate passion, the extreme of excess, and total insensibility to enjoyment, the extreme of deficiency, are both absolutely pernicious. The psychic dispositions, from which these two extremes, inordinate passion and insensibility, result the one being an exaggeration, the other a deficiency are alike classed among moral imperfections.

Likewise, liberality is the mean between sordidness and extravagance; courage, between recklessness and cowardice; dignity, between haughtiness and loutishness; humility, between arrogance and self-abasement; contentedness, between avarice and slothful indifference; and magnificence, between meanness and profusion. [Since definite terms do not exist in our language with which to express these latter qualities, it is necessary to explain their content, and tell what the philosophers meant by them. A man is called magnificent whose whole intention is to do good to others by personal service, by money, or advice, and with all his power, but without meanwhile bringing suffering or disgrace upon himself. That is the medium line of conduct. The mean man is one who does not want others to succeed in anything, even though he himself may not thereby suffer any loss, hardship, or injury. That is the one extreme. The profuse man, on the contrary, is one who willingly performs the above-mentioned deeds, in spite of the fact that thereby he brings upon himself great injury, or disgrace, terrible hardship, or considerable loss. That is the other extreme.] Gentleness is the mean between irascibility and insensibility to shame and disgrace; and modesty, between impudence and shamefacedness. [The explanation of these latter terms, gleaned from the sayings of our sages (may their memory be blessed!) seems to be this. In their opinion, a modest man is one who is very bashful, and therefore modesty is the mean. This we gather from their saying, "A shamefaced man cannot learn." (Abot, II, 5) They also assert, "A modest man is worthy of Paradise" (Abot, V, 20), but they do not say this of a shamefaced man. Therefore, I have thus arranged them.] So it is with the other qualities. One does not necessarily have to use conventional terms for these qualities, if only the ideas are clearly fixed in the mind.

It often happens, however, that men err as regards these qualities, imagining that one of the extremes is good, and is a virtue. Sometimes, the extreme of the too much is considered noble, as when temerity is made a virtue, and those who recklessly risk their lives are hailed as heroes. Thus, when people see a man, reckless to the highest degree, who runs deliberately into danger, intentionally tempting death, and escaping only by mere chance, they laud such a one to the skies, and say that he is a hero. At other times, the opposite extreme, the too little, is greatly esteemed, and the coward is considered a man of forbearance; the idler, as being a person of a contented disposition; and he, who by the dullness of his nature is callous to every joy, is praised as a man of moderation, [that is, one who eschews sin]. In like manner, profuse liberality and extreme lavishness are erroneously extolled as excellent characteristics. This is, however, an absolutely mistaken view, for the really praiseworthy is the medium course of action to which every one should strive to adhere, always weighing his conduct carefully, so that he may attain the proper mean.

Know, moreover, that these moral excellences or defects cannot be acquired, or implanted in the soul, except by means of the frequent repetition of acts resulting from these qualities, which, practised during a long period of time, accustoms us to them. If these acts performed are good ones, then we shall have gained a virtue; but if they are bad, we shall have acquired a vice. Since, however, no man is born with an innate virtue or vice, as we shall explain in Chapter VIII, and, as every one's conduct from childhood up is undoubtedly influenced by the manner of living of his relatives and countrymen, his conduct may be in accord with the rules of moderation; but, then again, it is possible that his acts may incline towards either extreme, as we have demonstrated, in which case, his soul becomes diseased. In such a contingency, it is proper for him to resort to a cure, exactly as he would were his body suffering from an illness. So, just as when the equilibrium of the physical health is disturbed, and we note which way it is tending in order to force it to go in exactly the opposite direction until it shall return to its proper condition, and, just as when the proper adjustment is reached, we cease this operation, and have recourse to that which will maintain the proper balance, in exactly the same way must we adjust the moral equilibrium. [...]

Chapter V

Concerning the Application of Man's Psychic Faculties Towards the Attainment of a Single Goal

As we have explained in the preceding chapter, it is the duty of man to subordinate all the faculties of his soul to his reason. He must keep his mind's eye fixed constantly upon one goal, namely, the attainment of the knowledge of God (may He be blessed!), as far as it is possible for mortal man to know Him. Consequently, one must so adjust all his actions, his whole conduct, and even his very words, that they lead to this goal, in order that none of his deeds be aimless, and thus retard the attainment of that end. So, his only design in eating, drinking, cohabiting, sleeping, waking, moving about, and resting should be the preservation of bodily health, while, in turn, the reason for the latter is that the soul and its agencies may be in sound and perfect condition, so that he may readily acquire wisdom, and gain moral and intellectual virtues, all to the end that man may reach the highest goal of his endeavors.

Accordingly, man will not direct his attention merely to obtain bodily enjoyment, choosing of food and drink and the other things of life only the agreeable, but he will seek out the most useful, being indifferent whether it be agreeable or not. There are, indeed, times when the agreeable may be used from a curative point of view, as, for instance, when one suffers from loss of appetite, it may be stirred up by highly seasoned delicacies and agreeable, palatable food. Similarly, one who suffers from melancholia may rid himself of it by listening to singing and all kinds of instrumental music, by strolling through beautiful gardens and splendid buildings, by gazing upon beautiful pictures, and other things that enliven the mind, and dissipate gloomy moods. The purpose of all this is to restore the healthful condition of the body, but the real object in maintaining the body in good health is to acquire wisdom. Likewise, in the pursuit of wealth, the main design in its acquisition should be to expend it for noble purposes, and to employ it for the maintenance of the body and the preservation of life, so that its owner may obtain a knowledge of God, in so far as that is vouchsafed unto man.

[…]

Know that to live according to this standard is to arrive at a very high degree of perfection, which, in consequence of the difficulty of attainment, only a few, after long and continuous perseverance on the paths of virtue, have succeeded in reaching. If there be found a man who has accomplished this that is one who exerts all the faculties of his soul, and directs them towards the sole ideal of comprehending God, using all his powers of mind and body, be they great or small, for the attainment of that which leads directly or indirectly to virtue I would place him in a rank not lower than that of the prophets. Such a man, before he does a single act or deed, considers and reflects whether or not it will bring him to that goal, and if it will, then, and then only, does he do it.

Such striving does the Almighty require of us, according to the words, "Thou shalt love the Lord thy God with all thy heart, and with all thy soul, and with all thy might" (Deut. VI, 5) that is, with all the faculties of thy soul, each faculty having as its sole ideal the love of God. The prophets, similarly, urge us on in saying, "In all thy ways know Him" (Prov. III, 6), in commenting upon which the sages said, "even as regards a transgression (of the ritual or ceremonial law)," (Berakot 63a) meaning thereby that thou shouldst set for every action a goal, namely, the truth, even though it be, from a certain point of view, a transgression. The sages of blessed memory, too, have summed up this idea in so few words and so concisely, at the same time elucidating the whole matter with such complete thoroughness, that when one considers the brevity with which they expressed this great and mighty thought in its entirety, about which others have written whole books and yet without adequately explaining it, one truly recognizes that the Rabbis undoubtedly spoke through divine inspiration. This saying is found among their precepts (in this tractate), and is, "Let all thy deeds be done for the sake of God." (Abot, II, 12)

This, then, is the thought we have been dwelling upon in the present chapter, and what we have said must be considered sufficient for the needs of this introduction.

Chapter VI

Concerning the Difference Between the Saintly [or Highly Ethical] Man and Him Who [Subdues His Passions and] Has Self-Restraint

PHILOSOPHERS maintain that though the man of self-restraint performs moral and praiseworthy deeds, yet he does them desiring and craving all the while for immoral deeds, but, subduing his passions and actively fighting against a longing to do those things to which his faculties, his desires, and his psychic disposition excite him, succeeds, though with constant vexation and irritation, in acting morally. The saintly man, however, is guided in his actions by that to which his inclination and disposition prompt him, in consequence of which he acts morally from innate longing and desire. Philosophers unanimously agree that the latter is superior to, and more perfect than, the one who has to curb his passions, although they add that it is possible for such a one to equal the saintly man in many regards. In general, however, he must necessarily be ranked lower in the scale of virtue, because there lurks within him the desire to do evil, and, though he does not do it, yet because his inclinations are all in that direction, it denotes the presence of an immoral psychic disposition. Solomon, also, entertained the same idea when he said, "The soul of the wicked desireth evil" (Prov. XXI, 10), and, in regard to the saintly man's rejoicing in doing good, and the discontent experienced by him, who is not innately righteous, when required to act justly, he says, "It is bliss to the righteous to do justice, but torment to the evil-doer." (Prov. XXI, 15) This is manifestly an agreement between Scripture and philosophy.

When, however, we consult the Rabbis on this subject, it would seem that they consider him who desires iniquity, and craves for it (but does not do it), more praiseworthy and perfect than the one who feels no torment at refraining from evil; and they even go so far as to maintain that the more praiseworthy and perfect a man is, the greater is his desire to commit iniquity, and the more irritation does he feel at having to desist from it. This they express by saying, "Whosoever is greater than his neighbor has likewise greater evil inclinations." (Sukkah 52a) Again, as if this were not sufficient, they even go so far as to say that the reward of him who overcomes his evil inclination is commensurate with the torture occasioned by his resistance, which thought they express by the words, "According to the labor is the reward." (Abot, V, 23) Furthermore, they command that man should conquer his desires, but they forbid one to say, "I, by my nature, do not desire to commit such and such a transgression, even though the Law does not forbid it". Rabbi Simeon ben Gamaliel summed up this thought in the words, "Man should not say, 'I do not want to eat meat together with milk; I do not want to wear clothes made of a mixture of wool and linen; I do not want to enter into an incestuous marriage', but he should say, 'I do indeed want to, yet I must not, for my father in Heaven has forbidden it'". (Sifra to Lev. XX, 26)

At first blush, by a superficial comparison of the sayings of the philosophers and the Rabbis, one might be inclined to say that they contradict one another. Such, however, is not the case. Both are correct and, moreover, are not in disagreement in the least, [...] Therefore, the Rabbis say that man should permit his soul to entertain the natural inclination for these things, but that the Law alone should restrain him from them. Ponder over the wisdom of these men of blessed memory manifest in the examples they adduce. They do not declare, "Man should not say, 'I have no desire to kill, to steal and to lie, but I have a desire for these things, yet what can I do, since my Father in heaven forbids it!'" The instances they cite are all from the ceremonial law, such as partaking of meat and milk together, wearing clothes made of wool and linen, and entering into consanguinuous marriages. These, and similar enactments are what God called "my statutes", which, as the Rabbis say are "statutes which I (God) have enacted for thee, which thou hast no right to subject to criticism, which the nations of the world attack and which Satan denounces, as for instance, the statutes concerning the red heifer, the scapegoat, and so forth". Those transgressions, however, which the later sages called rational laws are termed commandments, as the Rabbis explained.

It is now evident from all that we have said, what the transgressions are for which, if a man have no desire at all, he is on a higher plane than he who has a longing, but controls his passion for them; and it is also evident what the transgressions are of which the opposite is true. It is an astonishing fact that these two classes of expressions should be shown to be compatible with one another, but their content points to the truth of our explanation.

This ends the discussion of the subject-matter of this chapter.

[...]

Chapter VIII

Concerning the Natural Disposition of Man

IT is impossible for man to be born endowed by nature from his very birth with either virtue or vice, just as it is impossible that he should be born skilled by nature in any particular art. It is possible, however, that through natural causes he may from birth be so constituted as to have a predilection for a particular virtue or vice, so that he will more readily practise it than any other. [...]

I have entered into this subject so thou mayest not believe the absurd ideas of astrologers, who falsely assert that the constellation at the time of one's birth determines whether one is to be virtuous or vicious, the individual being thus necessarily compelled to follow out a certain line of conduct. We, on the contrary, are convinced that our Law agrees with Greek philosophy, which substantiates with convincing proofs the contention that man's conduct is entirely in his own hands, that no compulsion is exerted, and that no external influence is brought to bear upon him that constrains him to be either virtuous or vicious, except inasmuch as, according to what we have said above, he may be by nature so constituted as to find it easy or hard, as the case may be, to do a certain thing; but that he must necessarily do, or refrain from doing, a certain thing is absolutely untrue. Were a man compelled to act according to the dictates of predestination, then the commands and prohibitions of the Law would become null and void, and the Law would be completely false, since man would have no freedom of choice in what he does. Moreover, it would be useless, in fact absolutely in vain, for man to study, to instruct, or attempt to learn an art, as it would be entirely impossible for him, on account of the external force compelling him, according to the opinion of those who hold this view, to keep from doing a certain act, from gaining certain knowledge, or from acquiring a certain characteristic. Reward and punishment, too, would be pure injustice, both as regards man towards man, and as between God and man.

[...]

Since it is an essential characteristic of man's makeup that he should of his own free will act morally or immorally, doing just as he chooses, it becomes necessary to teach him the ways of righteousness, to command and exhort him, to punish and reward him according to his deserts. It behooves man also to accustom himself to the practice of good deeds, until he acquires the virtues corresponding to those good deeds; and, furthermore, to abstain from evil deeds so that he may eradicate the vices that may have taken root in him. Let him not suppose that his characteristics have reached such a state that they are no longer subject to change, for any one of them may be altered from the good to the bad, and vice versa; and, moreover, all in accordance with his own free will. To confirm this theory, we have mentioned all these facts concerning the observances and the transgressions of the Law.

It now remains for us to explain another phase of this problem, which arises from the fact that there are several Scriptural passages in which some think they find proof that God preordains and forces man to disobedience. This being an erroneous opinion, it becomes our duty to explain these passages, since so many people are confused regarding them. One of these is that in which God said to Abraham, "and they (the Egyptians) will make them (the Israelites) serve, and they will afflict them". "Is it not evident", it is claimed, "that God decreed that the Egyptians should oppress the seed of Abraham? Then, why did He punish them, since, owing to divine predestination, it was inexorably decreed that they should enslave the Israelites?" The answer to this is as follows. Suppose God had said that of those who were to be born in the future, some were to be transgressors and others observers of the Law, some pious and some wicked. Such would take place, but it would by no means follow from this divine decree that a certain individual would necessarily have to do evil, or that another pious individual would be forced to do good. On the contrary, every evil-doer would become such of his own free will; if he preferred to be a righteous man, it would be in his power, and nothing could prevent him from becoming such. Likewise, if every righteous man preferred to do evil, nothing would hinder him, for God's decree was not pronounced against any certain individual, so that he might say, "It has already been decreed that I do this or that", but [these words] applied to the race in general, at the same time allowing every individual to retain his own free will, according to the very makeup of his nature. Consequently, every Egyptian who maltreated or oppressed the Israelites had it in his own power not to do them any injury unless he wanted to, for it was not ordained that any certain individual should harm them.

[...]

God has, moreover, expressly stated through Isaiah that He punishes some transgressors by making it impossible for them to repent, which He does by the suspension of their free will. Thus, He says, "Obdurate will remain the heart of this people and their ears will be heavy and their eyes will be shut, lest [...] they be converted and healing be granted them" (Isa. VI, 10). The meaning of these words is so plain and obvious that they need no explanation. They are, however, a key to many unopened locks.

2.3 Early Modern

[Handwritten annotations in top margin:]

as western Europeans (who inherited natural law theories) do we consider native peoples human? can they use intellect + reason?

[right side:] Colonial expansion - slave trade Spain v France v England

But also - centralized monarchies - some early democratic thinking ⸜use of individual concience ⸜looking outward (native peoples) + inward (fall of monarchies)

Introduction

The early modern tradition introduces us to the writings of Vitoria, Suarez, Las Casas, Grotius, Pufendorf, and, in certain respects, Locke and Hobbes. The editors regard neither Hobbes nor Locke as indicative or core thinkers in the central natural law tradition. William Blackstone for us completes our brief tour of this era.

Any account of the central natural law tradition will at some stage need to confront the brutal reality of the slave trade that burgeoned, particularly from the fifteenth century onwards, despite the tradition's high language and lofty metaphysical ambitions. In fact, from this time onwards, we find, as an important example of its capacity for reflective development, repeated and determined condemnation of the practice from thinkers drawing on the resources of the tradition in new and creative ways. In 1435, for example, Pope Eugene IV vehemently condemned the practice of slavery that had commenced among Christians in the Canary Islands:

> And no less do we order and command all and each of the faithful of each sex, within the space of fifteen days … that they restore to their earlier liberty all and each person of either sex … made captives since the time of their capture, and who have been made subject to slavery. These people are to be totally and perpetually free, and are to be let go without the exaction or reception of money. If this is not done when the fifteen days have passed, they incur the sentence of excommunication by the act itself, from which they cannot be absolved, except at the point of death, even by the Holy See, or by any Spanish bishop, or by the aforementioned Ferdinand, unless they have first given freedom to these captive persons and restored their goods. We will that like sentence of excommunication be incurred by one and all who attempt to capture, sell, or subject to slavery, baptized residents of the Canary Islands, or those who are freely seeking Baptism, from which excommunication cannot be absolved except as was stated above.[1]

---

[1] *Sicut Dudum*, Pope Eugene IV, "Against the Enslaving of Black Natives from the Canary Islands," January 13, 1435.

The Natural Law Reader, First Edition. Edited by Jacqueline A. Laing and Russell Wilcox.
© 2014 Blackwell Publishing Ltd. Published 2014 by Blackwell Publishing Ltd.

Likewise, Pope Paul III forbade the enslavement of Indians and all other people. Pope Paul in *Sublimis Deus* in 1537 characterized enslavers as allies of the devil and declared null and void attempts to justify such slavery.

> He (Satan) has stirred up some of his allies who, desiring to satisfy their own avarice, are presuming to assert far and wide that the Indians ... be reduced to our service like brute animals, under the pretext that they are lacking the Catholic faith. And they reduce them to slavery, treating them with afflictions they would scarcely use with brute animals ... by our Apostolic Authority decree and declare by these present letters that the same Indians and all other peoples – even though they are outside the faith – ... should not be deprived of their liberty ... Rather they are to be able to use and enjoy this liberty and this ownership of property freely and licitly, and are not to be reduced to slavery ...

More famously, the Dominican monk Bartolomé de las Casas chronicled the mistreatment of the Indians in his *The Cruelties of the Spaniards Committed in America*, a text promptly seized upon by Protestant propagandists as evidence of "Popery Truly Display'd in its Bloody Colours." Las Casas wrote of an "infinite multitude of Men [who] are by the Creation of God innocently simple, altogether void of and averse to all manner of Craft, Subtlety and Malice, and most Obedient and Loyal Subjects to their Native Sovereigns; and behave themselves very patiently, submissively and quietly towards the Spaniards, to whom they are subservient and subject; so that finally they live without the least thirst after revenge, laying aside all litigiousness, Commotion and hatred."[2] He charged that "[t]he Spaniards first set Sail to America, not for the Honour of God, or as Persons moved and merited thereunto by servant Zeal to the True Faith, nor to promote the Salvation of their Neighbours, nor to serve the King, as they falsely boast and pretend to do, but in truth, only stimulated and goaded on by insatiable Avarice and Ambition, that they might for ever Domineer, Command, and Tyrannize over the West-Indians, whose Kingdoms they hoped to divide and distribute among themselves."[3]

The colonial enterprise criticized by Las Casas was a competitive exercise undertaken by powers that were supposed to be fundamentally Catholic in their orientation, and it is this which gives his protest its peculiar intensity.[4] But his objections could just as easily have been leveled against the avarice and ambition of the diverse Protestant colonialists whose persistent assaults in the East as well as the West Indies are well documented. Likewise, Indonesia, Malaysia, and much of the Far East are testimony to the success of Islamic imperialism in Hindu and Buddhist cultures. Opponents of religion might well see in these overseas expeditions the very worst of religion's aspirations but a cursory examination of the death-dealing empires of the twentieth century should remind us that Stalin, Lenin, Pol Pot, and Mao (and other oligarchic regimes existing now) appear to share certain imperialist characteristics. Only something like the objectivism of the natural law tradition is capable of accounting for the timeless and universal injustice of these practices, however well supported they were by consensus and state power.

---

[2] Bartolomé de las Casas, *A Brief Account of the Destruction of the Indies* (Project Gutenberg), http://www-personal.umich.edu/~twod/latam-s2010/read/las_casasb2032120321-8.pdf, accessed March 21, 2013.

[3] Ibid., Introduction.

[4] It would be wrong also to think that the massive number of conversions of Indians to Christianity accounting for the sizable Christian population of Mexico and South America was all won by force.

Las Casas' powerful critique of the colonial enterprise notwithstanding, theologians Francisco de Vitoria (1483/1486–1546) and Francisco Suarez (1548–1617) demonstrate an understanding of and concern for international law and the natural *rights* governing all men as members of the human family. They recognize the rights of the Indians to their own practices, to their own religion, and to enjoyment of their lands and families, free from war conducted by discoverers of whatever denomination or persuasion.

For Suarez, man's natural social nature bestowed by God includes the capacity or potential to make laws. All legislative power is derived from God and the authority of every true law derives ultimately from His. But, for Suarez, the formation of the polis is not of itself divine but of human origin.[5] The nature of the state is to some extent determined by the people, and their natural legislative power is given to the ruler. In this he is like the English social contractarians. Although he permits social revolt in the case of tyranny, his analysis is not straightforwardly social contractarian, in that his analysis of just law ultimately resides not in the social contract but in the notion of the true and the good.

While the competing interests of the colonists in resources and trade undoubtedly involved massive exploitation, the impact of colonization was far from entirely negative. It would be both anachronistic and wrong from a natural law perspective to downplay the significant injustices existing within some of the colonized societies themselves simply in order to highlight the huge injustices perpetrated by the colonizing powers. Bernal Diaz del Castillo, for example, a friend of Cortes, who set sail for Mexico speaks of the human sacrifice engaged in by the local populace, some of whose members begged his protection. Diaz explains that Cortes told them that they ought to cease sacrificing to idols. "He added that they ought to purge themselves of the shameful vices which their young men indulged in so scandalously; and that, furthermore, there was every day a sacrifice before our eyes of four or five Indians whose hearts were offered to the idols, while their blood was scattered on the walls and their legs and thighs and arms were cut up for food, just like meat coming out of our slaughterhouses (I believe, too, that they sold them retail in their markets)." He urges the people to "abandon their evil customs and practices."[6] In the context of daily human slaughter, the natural law tradition allows certain reasonable limitation on the customs and practices of the local people. The timeless, universal, and objective character of the natural law is what is necessary conceptually to avoid the implications of moral and cultural relativism in an environment of widespread injustice.

The recognition of the natural law governing all men is supplemented by an understanding that the natural law is distinct from the *ius gentium*. For Aquinas the *ius gentium* or "the law of nations is indeed in some way natural to man, in so far as he is a reasonable being, because it is derived from the natural law by way of a conclusion that is not very remote from its premises" (ST I–II, 95, a. 4 ad 1). The notion includes the doctrine of *pacta sunt servanda*, 'pacts (commitments or contracts) are to be honored', a principle of the law of nations, properly understood (ST I–II, 95, a. 4c and II–II, 57, a. 3c). Thus the law of contract, for example, is to be regarded a matter pertaining to the *ius gentium* more than it is to the natural law. For the Romans, the *ius gentium* was an aspect of the law that governed peoples within the empire and treaties and laws with those

---

[5] *De legibus*, III.ii.4.22–34, iii.2–3, 5–6.

[6] Ernest Nys, in his introduction to Vitoria, *De Indis et De Iure Belli*, ed. Ernest Nys, tr. John Pawley Bate (rpt. New York: Oceana Publications, 1964), p. 1.

nations and people outside the empire. It was distinct from the *ius civile*, which governed only the competing domestic legal systems within the empire.

Hugo Grotius (1583–1645) was a Dutch Protestant thinker whose *De jure belli ac pacis libri tres* ("On the Law of War and Peace in Three Books")[7] was first published in 1625 and dedicated to Louis XIII of France, his patron. The treatise advances an account of natural law which is argued to be binding on all people and nations regardless of local custom or convention. Grotius' arguments constitute a theory of natural law, natural right, and just war. The second book considers questions of *ius ad bellum* (justice of the war) and the third, questions of *ius in bello* (justice in the conduct of war). In this Grotius is not unlike Suarez and Francisco de Vitoria whose work preceded his. Together they supply a vital development of the natural law tradition, taking the notion of the *ius gentium*, developing it into a full-blown account of natural rights, and applying it more coherently in the realm of international law.

In 1672 Pufendorf's (1632–1694) *De jure naturae et gentium libri octo* ("On the Laws of Nature and Nations in Eight Books") appeared and in 1675 a summary of it under the title of *De officio hominis et civis* ("On the Duty of Man and Citizen"), which, inter alia, outlined his theory of just war.[8] Adopting the account of Hugo Grotius and applying the Hobbesian vision, he posits that natural law is aimed at regulating external acts and geared towards the preservation of this life rather than attaining some higher law. He disputed Hobbes' conception of the state of nature, arguing that the state of nature is not one of war but of peace. But this peace is far from assured. Law then is an aid to the preservation of mankind. Pufendorf, while recognizing in the state a moral agent, teaches that the will of the state is the sum of individual wills that make it up, and that this association explains state action. He appears to affirm the social contractarian account of the state and thus places himself squarely in an anthropocentric vision of the natural law. Pufendorf powerfully defends the idea that international law is not restricted to Christendom but constitutes a common bond between all nations because all nations form part of humanity.

In England, Thomas Hobbes' (1588–1679) and John Locke's (1632–1704) work begins the movement towards a social contractarian and self-preservationist account of moral, political, and legal discourse. In contrast to Las Casas and Vitoria we find none of the overt concern for the rights of, for example, native peoples to their own practices, religion, lands, and families in the face of aggressive colonization. The social contractarian direction of Hobbes' and Locke's thought wrenches the natural law from that metaphysical and ontological framework within which it is situated by the central tradition, and, in so doing, recasts it in an alternative, reductionist and narrowly voluntaristic, mold. Further, since a social contract can be had between the unjust and an unfair consensus arrived at, this marks an important step in the shift away from universality and objectivity. Hobbes, for example, identifies the right of nature with a type of liberty exercised solely for the purposes of *self-preservation*. "The right of nature," he says, "which writers commonly call jus naturale, is the liberty each man hath to use his own power as he will himself for the *preservation of his own nature*; that is to say, of *his own life*; and consequently, of doing anything which, in his own judgement and reason, he shall conceive to be the aptest

7   Hugo Grotius, *On the Law of War and Peace, De Jure Belli ac Pacis*, tr. A.C. Campbell (London, 1814).

8   Samuel von Pufendorf, *De Officio Hominis et Civis Juxta Legem Naturalem Libri Duo*, Volume 2: *The Translation*, tr. Frank Gardner Moore (1927; rpt. New York and London: Oceana Publications and Wildy & Sons, 1964).

means thereunto."[9] For him, the obligation of subjects to the sovereign lasts only as long as the sovereign's power to protect them. Self-preservation and physical power[10] are central to Hobbes' account in a way they could never be to, for example, Socrates, whose central concern is not so much to avoid suffering as to avoid wrong-doing.

Similarly, John Locke's account of the natural law is a far cry from the universalist and transcendental concerns of Plato as well as the teleological understanding of nature common to Aristotelian and most medieval thinking. Locke believed that "The Law of Nature" enjoined individuals not to harm one another in their lives or possessions. Without government, however, to defend against those seeking to injure or enslave them, people, he thought, would live in fear with no security in their rights. In consequence, individuals would contract to form a state in order to protect the lives, liberty, and property of those who lived within it. Locke argued that against these standards it could and should be judged. Unlike Hobbes, Locke argued for freedom under law in his *Second Treatise of Government*. The state's legitimacy was dependent on the subjects' transfer to the government of their right of "self-preservation." Importantly he adds that: "The reason why men enter into society is the preservation of their property," which for Locke was often achieved by mixing one's labor with the land (presumably 'terra nullius'). The government thus acts as an agent of self- and property-preservation, thus offering each man an alternative to acting alone in the state of nature. Accordingly, government gets its "just powers from the consent of the governed." In this again, we see the natural law grounded in a social contract. The natural law becomes centered solely on human agreement and removed from metaphysics and ontology, grounded in man's ad hoc interests in self-preservation rather than in the nature of things. Although Locke offers an account of the soul, it is one strangely separated from his politics. Thus self-preservation and the social contract become the very substance of his vision of natural law.

A reductively anthropocentric vision of the natural law, whether one grounded in a social contract, social construct, or human consensus, represents a departure from the central tradition of natural law thinking. The central tradition gives the natural law an ontological grounding and thus saves the conceptual analysis from becoming what humans, in their deficiency, might simply like it to be at any given moment. If the tradition includes both the eternal law, which underpins the physical laws of the universe, and the moral law, which govern angels and men, there is much scope for recognition and determination of its universal and eternal character. The central tradition we believe is better fitted therefore to supplying the objectivity, universality, and timelessness that are necessary to a sound ethics, politics, and jurisprudence. Because all societies are diverse and each person is different, something greater than that which is humanly constructed is required.

---

[9]   Thomas Hobbes, *Leviathan* (London: Andrew Crooke, 1651), Chapter XIV.

[10]   David Brion Davis, *The Problem of Slavery in Western Culture* (Oxford: Oxford University Press, 1966), p. 116: "For Hobbes slavery was an inevitable part of the logic of power. Hobbes felt no sense of tension between this worldly state of obedience and discipline and the ideal state of natural freedom. He also abandoned completely the Stoic and Christian distinction between external bondage of the flesh and internal liberty of the soul. Indeed for Hobbes, the slave's will was so utterly subordinated to that of his master that he could only will what his master willed. It was therefore impossible for an owner to do injury to his slave." Thomas Hobbes, *De Cive*, ed. Sterling Lamprecht (New York: Appleton-Century-Crofts, 1949), ii, viii.

Our final selection in this section is taken from William Blackstone (1723–1780), who represents the continued vigor of the central tradition even after Hobbes and Locke. In his *Commentaries on the Laws of England* Blackstone demonstrates that the idea of the natural law is significant in the development of the common law, or case law determined by judges. In the ongoing struggle between the people, as represented by parliament, and the crown, Blackstone refers to the Fundamental Laws of England, which he characterizes as natural law principles, timeless, eternal, and universal, and imposing limits on the power of the crown. The natural law for Blackstone was crucial in determining the content of the common law and in deciding cases of equity, but was not itself identical with the laws of England. In regarding the natural law as an objective, timeless, and universal guiding light of the laws that humans posit, Blackstone represents a return to at least some of the core notions of the natural law tradition. His analysis of equity is in some ways not unlike that of Aristotle (NE 5:10). Aristotle regards equity as the rectification of law where law is defective because of its generality. Likewise, Blackstone sees both the common law and equity[11] as having their roots in the natural law. Unsurprisingly, therefore, Jeremy Bentham, the renowned utilitarian, rejected the common law and with it all talk of natural law and natural rights as rhetorical nonsense, "nonsense on stilts."[12] William Blackstone too, then, is a jurisprudential representative of the natural law tradition in that he regards some aspects of human law as referring back to the objective, timeless, and universal that exists irrespective of whether man sees, articulates, or applies it.

- W/ the ancients, natural law was metaphysical
  w/ the moderns, the social contract is important.
     ↓
  everyone agreeing
  voluntarily to a
  common good

---

[11] This, if true, would imply that Ronald Dworkin whose analysis of hard cases in *Taking Rights Seriously* (Cambridge, MA: Harvard University Press, 1977) challenges H.L.A. Hart's positivism, exists, at least to this extent, in the natural law tradition.

[12] Jeremy Bentham, *Anarchical Fallacies*, in *The Works of Jeremy Bentham*, ed. John Bowring (Edinburgh: William Tait, 1838–1843), 11 vols., Volume 2.

2.3.1 Francisco de Vitoria
De Indis et De Iure Belli Relectiones

Part 2

The passage to be discussed is from St. Matthew's Gospel: "Teach all nations, baptizing them in the name of the Father and Son and Holy Spirit," last chapter.

TWENTY-THIRD. However this may be, let our fourth proposition be: The Indian aborigines are not barred on this ground from the exercise of true dominion. This is proved from the fact that the true state of the case is that they are not of unsound mind, but have, according to their kind, the use of reason. This is clear, because there is a certain method in their affairs, for they have polities which are orderly arranged and they have definite marriage and magistrates, overlords, laws, and workshops, and a system of exchange, all of which call for the use of reason; they also have a kind of religion. Further, they make no error in matters which are self-evident to others; this is witness to their use of reason. Also, God and nature are not wanting in the supply of what is necessary in great measure for the race. Now, the most conspicuous feature of man is reason, and power is useless which is not reducible to action. [...]

TWENTY-FOURTH. The upshot of all the preceding is, then, that the aborigines undoubtedly had true dominion in both public and private matters, just like Christians, and that neither their princes nor private persons could be despoiled of their property on the ground of their not being true owners [...]

Summary of The Second Section.

On the illegitimate titles for the reduction of the aborigines of the New World into the power of the Spaniards.

1. The Emperor is not the lord of the whole world.
2. Even if the Emperor were the lord of the world, that would not entitle him to seize the provinces of the Indian aborigines and to erect new lords and put down the former lords or to levy taxes.

Francisci de Victoria, De Indis et De Iure Belli Relectiones, ed. Ernest Nys, tr. John Pawley Bate (Washington, DC: Carnegie Institution, 1917; rpt. London: Wildy & Sons, 1964).

3.   The Pope is not civil or temporal lord of the whole world, in the proper sense of civil lordship and power.

4.   Even if the Supreme Pontiff had secular power over the world, he could not give that power to secular princes.

5.   The Pope has temporal power, but only so far as it subserves things spiritual.

6.   The Pope has no temporal power over the Indian aborigines or over other unbelievers.

7.   A refusal by these aborigines to recognize any dominion of the Pope is no reason for making war on them and for seizing their goods.

8.   Whether these aborigines were guilty of the sin of unbelief, in that they did not believe in Christ, before they heard anything of Christianity.

9.   What is required in order that ignorance may be imputed to a person as, and be, sin, that is, vincible ignorance. And what about invincible ignorance?

10.   Whether the aborigines are bound to hearken to the first messengers of Christianity so as to commit mortal sin in not believing Christ's Gospel merely on its simple announcement to them.

11.   If the faith were simply announced and proposed to them and they will not straightway receive it, this is no ground for the Spaniards to make war on them or to proceed against them under the law of war.

12.   How the aborigines, if they refuse when asked and counselled to hear peaceably preachers of religion, can not be excused from mortal sin.

13.   When the aborigines would be bound to receive Christianity under penalty of mortal sin.

14.   In the author's view it is not sufficiently dear whether Christianity has been so proposed and announced to these aborigines that they are bound to believe it under the penalty of fresh sin.

15.   Even when Christianity has been proposed to them with never so much sufficiency of proof and they will not accept it, this does not render it lawful to make war on them and despoil them of their possessions.

16.   Christian princes can not, even on the authority of the Pope, restrain these aborigines from sins against the law of nature or punish them therefor.

It being premised, then, that the Indian aborigines are or were true owners, it remains to inquire by what title the Spaniards could have come into possession of them and their country.

And first, I shall advert to the titles which might be alleged, but which are not adequate or legitimate.

Secondly, I shall set out the legitimate titles under which the aborigines could have come under the sway of the Spaniards.

Part 3

THE SECOND RELECTIO OF THE REVEREND
FATHER, BROTHER FRANCISCUS DE VICTORIA,
ON THE INDIANS, OR ON THE LAW OF WAR MADE
BY THE SPANIARDS ON THE BARBARIANS.

5.   Second proposition: Every State has authority to declare and to make war. In course of proof of this be it noted that the difference herein between a private person and a

State is that a private person is entitled, as said above, to defend himself and what belongs to him, but has no right to avenge a wrong done to him, nay, not even to recapt property that has been seized from him if time has been allowed to go by since the seizure. But defense can only be resorted to at the very moment of the danger, or, as the jurists say, in continenti, and so when the necessity of defense has passed there is an end to the lawfulness of war. In my view, however, one who has been contumeliously assaulted can immediately strike back, even if the assaulter was not proposing to make a further attack, for in the avoidance of shame and disgrace one who (for example) has had his ears boxed might immediately use his sword, not for the purpose of vengeance, but, as has been said, in order to avoid infamy and disgrace. But a State is within its rights not only in defending itself, but also in avenging itself and its subjects and in redressing wrongs. This is proved by what Aristotle says in the third book of his Politics, namely, that a State ought to be sufficient unto itself. But it can not adequately protect the public weal and the position of the State if it can not avenge a wrong and take measures against its enemies, for wrongdoers would become readier and bolder for wrongdoing, if they could do wrong with impunity. It is, therefore, imperative for the due ordering of human affairs that this authority be allowed to States.

6.   Third proposition: A prince has the same authority in this respect as the State has. This is the opinion of St. Augustine (Contra Faustum): "The natural order, best adapted to secure the peace of mankind, requires that the authority to make war and the advisability of it should be in the hands of the sovereign prince." Reason supports this, for the prince only holds his position by the election of the State. Therefore he is its representative and wields its authority; aye, and where there are already lawful princes in a State, all authority is in their hands and without them nothing of a public nature can be done either in war or in peace.

7.   Now, the whole difficulty is in the questions: What is a State, and who can properly be called a sovereign prince? I will briefly reply to them by saying that a State is properly called a perfect community. But the essence of the difficulty is in saying what a perfect community is. By way of solution be it noted that a thing is called perfect when it is a completed whole, for that is imperfect in which there is something wanting, and, on the other hand, that is perfect from which nothing is wanting. A perfect State or community, therefore, is one which is complete in itself, that is, which is not a part of another community, but has its own laws and its own council and its own magistrates, such as is the Kingdom of Castile and Aragon and the Republic of Venice and other the like. For there is no obstacle to many principalities and perfect States being under one prince. Such a State, then, or the prince thereof, has authority to declare war, and no one else.

8.   Here, however, a doubt may well arise whether, when a number of States of this kind or a number of princes have one common lord or prince, they can make war of themselves and without the authorization of their superior lord. My answer is that they can do so undoubtedly, just as the kings who are subordinate to the Emperor can make war on one another without waiting for the Emperor's authorization, for (as has been said) a State ought to be self-sufficient, and this it would not be, if it had not the faculty in question.

[...]

10. Third question: What may be a reason and cause of just war? It is particularly necessary to ask this in connection with the case of the Indian aborigines, which is now before us. Here my first proposition is: Difference of religion is not a cause of just war. This was shown at length in the preceding Relectio, when we demolished the fourth alleged title for taking possession of the Indians, namely, their refusal to accept Christianity. And it is the opinion of St. Thomas (Secunda Secundae, qu. 66, art. 8), and the common opinion of the doctors – indeed, I know of no one of the opposite way of thinking.

11. Second proposition: Extension of empire is not a just cause of war. This is too well known to need proof, for otherwise each of the two belligerents might have an equally just cause and so both would be innocent. This in its turn would involve the consequence that it would not be lawful to kill them and so imply a contradiction, because it would be a just war.

12. Third proposition: Neither the personal glory of the prince nor any other advantage to him is a just cause of war. This, too, is notorious. For a prince ought to subordinate both peace and war to the common weal of his State and not spend public revenues in quest of his own glory or gain, much less expose his subjects to danger on that account. Herein, indeed, is the difference between a lawful king and a tyrant, that the latter directs his government towards his individual profit and advantage, but a king to the public welfare, as Aristotle says (Politics, bk. 4, ch. 10). Also, the prince derives his authority from the State. Therefore he ought to use it for the good of the State. Also, laws ought "not to be enacted for the private good of any individual, but in the common interest of all the citizens," as is ruled in can. 2, Dist. 4, a citation from Isadore. Therefore the rules relating to war ought to be for the common good of all and not for the private good of the prince. Again, this is the difference between freemen and slaves, as Aristotle says (Politics, bk. I, ch. 3 and 4) that masters exploit slaves for their own good and not for the good of the slaves, while freemen do not exist in the interest of others, but in their own interest. And so, were a prince to misuse his subjects by compelling them to go soldiering and to contribute money for his campaigns, not for the public good, but for his own private gain, this would be to make slaves of them.

13. Fourth proposition: There is a single and only just cause for commencing a war, namely, a wrong received. The proof of this rests in the first place on the authority of St. Augustine (Liber 83 Quaestionum* "Those wars are described as just wars," etc., as above), and it is the conclusion arrived at by St. Thomas (Secunda Secundae, qu. 40, art. 1) and the opinion of all the doctors. Also, an offensive war is for the purpose of avenging a wrong and of taking measures against an enemy, as said above. But there can be no vengeance where there is no preceding fault and wrong. Therefore. Also, a prince has no greater authority over foreigners than over his own subjects. But he may not draw his sword against his own subjects, unless they have done some wrong. Therefore not against foreigners either. This is confirmed by the text already cited from St. Paul (Romans, ch. 13) about a prince: "He beareth not the sword in vain: for he is the minister of God, a revenger to execute wrath upon him that doeth evil." Hence it is clear that we may not turn our sword against those who do us no harm, the killing of the innocent being forbidden by natural law. I omit here any injunctions inconsistent herewith which God has given in

special cases, for He is the Lord of life and death and it is within His competence to vary His dispositions.

14. Fifth proposition: Not every kind and degree of wrong can suffice for commencing a war. The proof of this is that not even upon one's own fellow-countrymen is it lawful for every offense to exact atrocious punishments, such as death or banishment or confiscation of property. As, then, the evils inflicted in war are all of a severe and atrocious character, such as slaughter and fire and devastation, it is not lawful for slight wrongs to pursue the authors of the wrongs with war, seeing that the degree of the punishment ought to correspond to the measure of the offence (Deuteronomy, ch. 25).

15. The fourth question is about the law of war, namely, what kind and degree of stress is lawful in a just war. Here let my first proposition be: In war everything is lawful which the defense of the common weal requires. This is notorious, for the end and aim of war is the defense and preservation of the State. Also, a private person may do this in self-defense, as has been proved. Therefore much more may a State and a prince.

16. Second proposition: It is permissible to recapt everything that has been lost and any part of the same. This is too notorious to need proof. For war is begun or undertaken with this object.

17. Third proposition: It is lawful to make good out of enemy property the expenses of the war and all damages wrongfully caused by the enemy. This is clear, for the enemy who has done the wrong is bound to give all this redress. Therefore the prince can claim it all and exact it all by war. Also, as before, there is the argument that, when no other way lies open, a private creditor can seize the amount of his debt from the debtor. Also, if there were any competent judge over the two belligerents, he would have to condemn the unjust aggressors and authors of wrong, not only to make restitution of what they have carried off, but also to make good the expenses of the war to the other side, and also all damages. But a prince who is carrying on a just war is as it were his own judge in matters touching the war, as we shall forthwith show. Therefore he can enforce all these claims upon his enemy.

18. Fourth proposition: Not only are the things just named allowable, but a prince may go even further in a just war and do whatever is necessary in order to obtain peace and security from the enemy; for example, destroy an enemy's fortress and even build one on enemy soil, if this be necessary in order to avert a dangerous attack of the enemy. This is proved by the fact that, as said above, the end and aim of war is peace and security. Therefore a belligerent may do everything requisite to obtain peace and security. Further, tranquillity and peace are reckoned among the desirable things of mankind and so the utmost material prosperity does not produce a state of happiness if there be no security there. Therefore it is lawful to employ all appropriate measures against enemies who are plundering and disturbing the tranquillity of the State. Also, all measures of this kind may be taken against internal foes, that is, against bad citizens. Therefore they are lawful against external foes. The antecedent is clear, for if one citizen does a wrong to a fellow citizen, the magistrate not only compels the wrongdoer to make amends to the injured party, but, if the former is a source of fear to the latter, he is compelled to give bond or quit the city, so as to remove the danger of which he is the cause. This shows that even when

victory has been won and redress obtained, the enemy may be made to give hostages, ships, arms, and other things, when this is genuinely necessary for keeping the enemy in his duty and preventing him from becoming dangerous again.

19. Fifth proposition: Not only is all this permissible, but even after victory has been won and redress obtained and peace and safety been secured, it is lawful to avenge the wrong received from the enemy and to take measures against him and exact punishment from him for the wrongs he has done. In proof of this be it observed that princes have authority not only over their own subjects, but also over foreigners, so far as to prevent them from committing wrongs, and this is by the law of nations and by the authority of the whole world. Nay, it seems to be by natural law also, seeing that otherwise society could not hold together unless there was somewhere a power and authority to deter wrongdoers and prevent them from injuring the good and innocent. Now, everything needed for the government and preservation of society exists by natural law, and in no other way can we show that a State has by natural law authority to inflict pains and penalties on its citizens who are dangerous to it. But if a State can do this to its own citizens, society at large no doubt can do it to all wicked and dangerous folk, and this can only be through the instrumentality of princes. It is, therefore, certain that princes can punish enemies who have done a wrong to their State and that after a war has been duly and justly undertaken the enemy are just as much within the jurisdiction of the prince who undertakes it as if he were their proper judge. Confirmation hereof is furnished by the fact that in reality peace and tranquillity, which are the end and aim of war, can not be had unless evils and damages be visited on the enemy in order to deter them from the like conduct in the future. All this is also proved and confirmed by the authority and examples of good men. For, as said above, the Maccabees made war not only to recover the things which they had lost, but also to avenge their wrongs. And some most Christian princes and most religious Emperors have done the same thing. Moreover, shame and disgrace are not wiped away from a State merely by its rout of Its enemies, but also by its visiting severe punishment and castigation on them. Now, among the things which a prince is bound to defend and preserve for his State are its honor and authority.

20. Many doubts are suggested by what has just been said. In the first place, there is a doubtful point in connection with the justice of a war, whether it be enough for a just war that the prince believes himself to have a just cause. On this point let my first proposition be: This belief is not always enough. And for proof I rely, first, on the fact that in some matters of less moment it is not enough either for a prince or for private persons to believe that they are acting justly. This is notorious, for their error may be vincible and deliberate, and the opinion of the individual is not enough to render an act good, but it must come up to the standard of a wise man's judgment, as appears from Ethics, bk. 2. Also the result would otherwise be that very many wars would be just on both sides, for although it is not a common occurrence for princes to wage war in bad faith, they nearly always think theirs is a just cause. In this way all belligerents would be innocent and it would not be lawful to kill them. Also, were it otherwise, even Turks and Saracens might wage just wars against Christians, for they think they are thus rendering God service.

21. Second proposition: It is essential for a just war that an exceedingly careful examination be made of the justice and causes of the war and that the reasons of those

who on grounds of equity oppose it be listened to. For (as the comic poet says) "A wise man must make trial of everything by words before resorting to force," and he ought to consult the good and wise and those who speak with freedom and without anger or bitterness or greed, seeing that (as Sallust says) "where these vices hold sway, truth is not easily distinguished." This is self-evident. For truth and justice in moral questions are hard of attainment and so any careless treatment of them easily leads to error, an error which will be inexcusable, especially in a concern of great moment, involving danger and calamity to many, and they our neighbors, too, whom we are bound to love as ourselves.

22. Second doubt: Whether subjects are bound to examine the cause of a war or whether they may serve in the war without any careful scrutiny thereof, just as the lictors had to enforce the praetor's decree without questioning. On this doubt let my first proposition be: If a subject is convinced of the injustice of a war, he ought not to serve in it, even on the command of his prince. This is clear, for no one can authorize the killing of an innocent person. But in the case before us the enemy are innocent. Therefore they may not be killed. Again, a prince sins when he commences a war in such a case. But "not only are they who commit such things worthy of death, but they, too, who consent to the doing thereof" (Romans, ch. 1). Therefore soldiers also are not excused when they fight in bad faith. Again, it is not lawful to kill innocent citizens at the prince's command. Therefore not aliens either.

23. Hence flows the corollary that subjects whose conscience is against the justice of a war may not engage in it whether they be right or wrong. This is clear, for "whatever is not of faith is sin" (Romans, ch. 14).

[…]

34. With regard to another question, namely, what degree of stress is lawful in a just war, there are also many doubts. The first is: Whether it is lawful in war to kill the innocent. It seems that it is; because, in the first place, the Sons of Israel slew children at Jericho, as appears from Joshua, ch. 6, and afterwards Saul slew children in Amalek (I Samuel, ch. 15), and in both these cases it was by the authority and at the bidding of God. "Now, whatever is written is written for our instruction," as appears from Romans, ch. 15. Therefore, if a war of the present day be just, it will be lawful to kill the innocent.

35. With regard to this doubt, let my first proposition be: The deliberate slaughter of the innocent is never lawful in itself. This is proved, firstly, by Exodus, ch. 23: "The innocent and righteous slay thou not." Secondly, the basis of a just war is a wrong done, as has been shown above. But wrong is not done by an innocent person. Therefore war may not be employed against him. Thirdly, it is not lawful within a State to punish the innocent for the wrongdoing of the guilty. Therefore this is not lawful among enemies. Fourthly, were this not so, a war would be just on both sides, although there was no ignorance, a thing which, as has been shown, is impossible. And the consequence is manifest, because it is certain that innocent folk may defend themselves against any who try to kill them. And all this is confirmed by Deuteronomy, ch. 20, where the Sons of Israel were ordered to take a certain city by force and to slay every one except women and little ones.

36. Hence it follows that even in war with the Turks it is not allowable to kill children. This is clear, because they are innocent. Aye, and the same holds with regard to the

women of unbelievers. This is clear, because so far as the war is concerned, they are presumed innocent; but it does not hold in the case of any individual woman who is certainly guilty. Aye, and this same pronouncement must be made among Christians with regard to harmless agricultural folk, and also with regard to the rest of the peaceable civilian population, for all these are presumed innocent until the contrary is shown. On this principle it follows that it is not lawful to slay either foreigners or guests who are sojourning among the enemy, for they are presumed innocent, and in truth they are not enemies. The same principle applies to clerics and members of a religious order, for they in war are presumed innocent unless the contrary be shown, as when they engage in actual fighting.

37.   Second proposition: Sometimes it is right, in virtue of collateral circumstances, to slay the innocent even knowingly, as when a fortress or city is stormed in a just war, although it is known that there are a number of innocent people in it and although cannon and other engines of war can not be discharged or fire applied to buildings without destroying innocent together with guilty. The proof is that war could not otherwise be waged against even the guilty and the justice of belligerents would be balked. In the same way, conversely, if a town be wrongfully besieged and rightfully defended, it is lawful to fire cannon-shot and other missiles on the besiegers and into the hostile camp, even though we assume that there are some children and innocent people there.

Great attention, however, must be paid to the point already taken, namely, the obligation to see that greater evils do not arise out of the war than the war would avert. For if little effect upon the ultimate issue of the war is to be expected from the storming of a fortress or fortified town wherein are many innocent folk, it would not be right, for the purpose of assailing a few guilty, to slay the many innocent by use of fire or engines of war or other means likely to overwhelm indifferently both innocent and guilty. In sum, it is never right to slay the guiltless, even as an indirect and unintended result, except when there is no other means of carrying on the operations of a just war, according to the passage (St. Matthew, ch. 13) "Let the tares grow, lest while ye gather up the tares ye root up also the wheat with them." […]

60.   All this can be summarized in a few canons or rules of warfare. First canon: Assuming that a prince has authority to make war, he should first of all not go seeking occasions and causes of war, but should, if possible, live in peace with all men, as St. Paul enjoins on us (Romans, ch. 12). Moreover, he should reflect that others are his neighbors, whom we are bound to love as ourselves, and that we all have one common Lord, before whose tribunal we shall have to render our account. For it is the extreme of savagery to seek for and rejoice in grounds for killing and destroying men whom God has created and for whom Christ died. But only under compulsion and reluctantly should he come to the necessity of war.

Second canon: When war for a just cause has broken out, it must not be waged so as to ruin the people against whom it is directed, but only so as to obtain one's rights and the defense of one's country and in order that from that war peace and security may in time result.

Third canon: When victory has been won and the war is over, the victory should be utilized with moderation and Christian humility, and the victor ought to deem that he is sitting as judge between two States, the one which has been wronged and the one which has done the wrong, so that it will be as judge and not as accuser that he will deliver the judgment whereby the injured state can obtain satisfaction, and this, so far as possible should involve the offending state in the least degree of calamity and misfortune, the offending individuals being chastised within lawful limits; and an especial reason for this is that in general among Christians all the fault is to be laid at the door of their princes, for subjects when fighting for their princes act in good faith and it is thoroughly unjust, in the words of the poet, that Quidquid delirant reges, plectantur Achivi, (For every folly their Kings commit the punishment should fall upon the Greeks.) Ps. 81, in Vulgate. In A. V. Ps. 82.

2.3.2 Francisco Suarez
De Legibus

Book 2, chap. 6

Is the natural law truly a preceptive divine law?

1. *The statement of the problem.* The problem posed by this question arises from the foundation of a previous position laid out in the preceding chapter. The problem was posed there and has not yet been resolved. For as was shown in book 1, there is no proper and preceptive law without an act of will on the part of some lawgiver; but the natural law does not depend on the will of any lawgiver; therefore, it is not properly speaking a law.

The minor premise is proved from what was adduced in chapter 5, namely, that the dictates of natural reason, in which the natural law consists, are intrinsically necessary and independent of any act of will – even a divine and conceptually prior act of will by which that will freely wills something such as that God ought to be worshipped, that parents ought to be honored, that lying is bad and ought to be avoided, etc; therefore, the natural law cannot be called a true law.

This is confirmed as follows: The natural law is not a true precept; therefore, it is not a true law. The antecedent is clear from the fact that the natural law either (a) is a precept that a man gives to himself, and this is not so, because such a precept would be either (i) nothing but a judgment that exhibits the truth regarding some matter or (ii), if it does involve an act of will (that is, a choice) that has already been made, then it is not *per se* necessary for the operation [of the will] and does not induce an obligation, but instead induces the execution [of the choice], and so it is not sufficient for, and does not contribute to, either the truth of a law or its proper force, or else (b) it is the precept of some superior, and this likewise cannot be said in light of the argument already given; for even if every act of will on the part of a superior has been ruled out, the natural law still dictates what is good or bad.

Tr. Alfred J. Freddoso, University of Notre Dame, http://www3.nd.edu/~afreddos/courses/301/suarezdelegii6.htm. © Alfred J. Freddoso. Reprinted with permission.

2. And from this it likewise seems to follow that the natural law cannot be properly called a *divine* law, that is, it cannot be said to be given by God as a lawgiver.

I say "as a lawgiver" because it is clear that natural reason and its dictates are a divine gift that comes down to us from the Father of Lights. However, it is one thing for this natural law to be from God as a *first efficient cause*, and another thing for it to be from God as a *lawgiver* who prescribes and obligates. For the first of these is absolutely certain and part of the Faith – both because (a) God is the first cause of all natural goods, among which a great good is the use and light of natural reason, and also because (b) it is in this way that every manifestation of truth is from God, according to Romans 1:18: "God's wrath is being revealed from heaven against all the wickedness and perversity of men, who in their perversity hinder God's truth." And explaining why he calls it "God's truth," Paul adds, "For what is known of God is manifest to them, because God has manifested it to them" – namely, through the natural light of reason and through visible creatures, through whom the invisible things of God can be known. Thus, it is in this sense – that is, in the sense of efficient causality and majesty (as I will put it) – that Chrysostom interprets this passage from Paul in homily 3 [on Romans] and, more fully, in *Ad populos*, homilies 12 and 13. The same holds true for Theophylactus in his commentary on this same passage from Paul; Ambrose (in the same place); Cyril in *Contra Julianum*, near the end in the paragraph beginning "For the whole …"; and especially Augustine in *De verbo Domini*, sermon 55 and in *De sermone Domini in monte* 2, chap. 9, where he says, "Who but God writes the natural law in the hearts of men?"

So there is no doubt that God is the efficient cause and, as it were, the *teacher* of the natural law. But it does not follow from this that he is the *lawgiver*. For the natural law does not involve God as lawgiver, but rather indicates what is good or bad in itself, just as an act of vision directed at a given object indicates that it is white or black, and just as an effect of God's points to God as its *author*, though not as its *lawgiver*. This is the way, then, that one should think of the natural law.

3. *The first position, which affirms that the natural law is not a properly preceptive law.* On this question, the first position is that the natural law is not a properly *prescriptive* law, because it is not a sign of the will of any superior, but is instead a law that *indicates* what ought to be done or avoided – that is, what *by its own nature* is intrinsically good and required or intrinsically bad.

Accordingly, many authors distinguish two sorts of law: one that [merely] *indicates* and another that *prescribes*. And they claim that the natural law is a law in the first sense, but not in the second. Thus, in *Sentences* 2, dist. 34, q. 1, a. 2, Gregory [of Rimini], a little after the beginning of the second corollary, cites Hugo of St. Victor, *De sacramentis*, lect. 1, pt. 6, chaps. 6 and 7. In this he is followed by Gabriel Biel, *Sentences* 2, dist. 35, q. 1, a. 1, by Almain in *Morales* 3, and by Corduba in *De conscientia* 3, q. 10, ad 2.

As a result, these authors will, it seems, concede that the natural law is not from God as a lawgiver, since it does not depend on God's will; and so with respect to the natural law God does not behave as a superior who prescribes or prohibits. Indeed, Gregory claims – and the others follow him – that even if God did not exist or did not use his reason or did not judge correctly concerning things, nonetheless, if there existed in man the same dictate of right reason – dictating, say, that it is bad to lie – then that dictate would embody the same type of law that it now does. For it would [still] be a law indicating the badness that exists intrinsically in the object.

4. *The second position, which affirms that natural law is truly divine and preceptive.* The second position, completely contrary to the first, is that the natural law is found entirely in a divine command or prohibition that proceeds from God's will as the author and governor of nature, and that, consequently, (a) this law, *as it exists in God*, is nothing other than the eternal law insofar as it prescribes or prohibits in the relevant matters, whereas (b) this same natural law, *as it exists in us*, is the judgment of reason insofar as that judgment signifies to us the will of God concerning what should be done and avoided with respect to those things that are consonant with natural reason.

This position is taken from Ockham in *Sentences* 2, q. 19, ad 3 and 4, given his claim that (a) no act is bad except insofar as it is prohibited by God and that (b) there is no bad act that could not become good if it were prescribed by God, and vice versa. Hence, he presupposes that the entire natural law consists in divine precepts issued by God – precepts that God himself could abolish and change. And if someone objected that such a law is not a *natural* law but is instead a *positive* law, he would reply that it is called a natural law because it is proportioned to the nature of things and not because it is not imposed extrinsically by God.

[...]

The basis for this position seems to be that actions are not good or bad except because they are prescribed or prohibited by God. For it is not the case that God himself wills to prescribe or forbid such-and-such an act for a creature because the act is good or bad; rather, the act is just or unjust because God wills that it be just or that it not be just – this in keeping with what Anselm says in *Proslogion*, chap. 11. Hugo of St. Victor is also of this opinion in *De sacramentis*, pt. 4, chap. 1, as is Cyprian in the book *De singularitate clericorum*, which is attributed to him.

5. *First assertion: The natural law is not just indicative of good and evil, but also contains the prescription and prohibition of them.* Neither of these positions is satisfactory to my mind, and so I believe that we must hold to a middle way, which I take to be the position of St. Thomas as well as the common position of theologians.

I assert, first, that the natural law is not only indicative of bad and good, but also contains its own proper prohibition of what is bad and prescription of what is good.

I take this from St. Thomas, *Summa Theologiae* 1–2, q. 71, a. 6, ad 4, where he says that if we are thinking of *human* law, then it is not the case that every sin [with respect to that law] is bad because it is prohibited, whereas if we are thinking of *natural* law, which is contained primarily in the eternal law and secondarily in the indication of natural reason, then every sin [with respect to that law] is evil because it is prohibited. And in *Summa Theologiae* 1–2, q. 100, a. 8, ad 2 he says that God cannot deny himself and so cannot abolish the order of his own justice – meaning that God is unable not to prohibit those things that are bad and contrary to natural reason. Bonaventure is of the same opinion in *Sentences* 2, d. 35, dub. 4, *circa litteram*, and so, explicitly, is Gerson in *De vita spirituali*, the whole of lect. 2, where he defines natural law as follows: "The preceptive natural law is a sign given to every man who is not impeded in the due use of reason, and it makes known the divine will insofar as it wants the rational human creature to be bound to do something or not to do something in pursuit of his natural end." This definition may include more than is necessary, but for now we are using it just to the extent that it serves our present purpose. The [first] assertion is likewise assumed by the authors of the second position and is defended at length by Vittoria in *De pervenientibus ad usum rationis*, nn. 8ff.

6. *The first assertion is confirmed by arguments.* This assertion is proved, first, from the properties of law. For the natural law is a law properly speaking – this is what all the Fathers, theologians, and philosophers think and say about it. In contrast, the mere cognition or proposal of an object that exists in the mind cannot be called a law, as is obvious in itself and from the definition of law given above. Therefore, etc.

Second, this point is clear in the case of acts that are bad because they are prohibited by human law. For with regard to such acts, in order for a man to sin, there must be a prior judgment of the mind that indicates that the object in question is bad. And yet this judgment does not have the character of a law or prohibition, since it only manifests what is contained in the object, wherever it might come from. Similarly, then, even if, in order for one to act well or badly in matters that pertain to the natural law, there must be a prior judgment indicating the goodness or badness of the object or act, this judgment does not have the character of a law or prohibition. Rather, it is merely a *cognition* of what is taken to be already such-and-such. Hence, the act in question, which is known to be evil through a judgment of the sort in question, is not evil because it is judged to be evil, but is instead truly judged to be evil because it is evil. Therefore, this judgment is not a standard of badness or goodness; therefore, neither is it a law or prohibition.

Third, if this were not so, then even God would have a law that is natural to him with respect to his own will. For in God, too, the judgment of the mind conceptually precedes the act of will and indicates that lying is bad and that keeping one's promises is altogether right and necessary; therefore, if this is sufficient for the notion of law, then even in God there will be a true natural law. For it will not be problematic that God has no superior, given that a natural law is not imposed by any superior. Nor will the identity [of God's intellect with his will] be a problem, since a conceptual distinction between them is sufficient for God's will to be truly said to be carried toward that which is made manifest by his intellect, and since that is in fact the way things stand. Therefore, this will suffice for there to be a law, since, after all, [the proponents of the first position] claim that this is sufficient for the notion of law.

Then, too, a judgment that indicates the nature of an act is not itself the act of a superior, but instead can exist in an equal or in an inferior who has no power to obligate; therefore, this judgment cannot have the character of a law or prohibition. Otherwise, a teacher who pointed out what is bad or good would be imposing a law – which cannot be claimed. A law, then, is a command that can induce an obligation, whereas the sort of judgment in question does not induce an obligation but instead makes manifest an obligation that has to be presupposed. Therefore, in order to have the character of a law, the judgment must indicate some *command* from which the relevant obligation might emanate.

[...]

10.   The assertion is thus confirmed by the fact that sins against the natural law are said
      in Sacred Scripture to be contrary to God's will. Thus in *De voluntate Dei* Anselm
      says, "Whoever violates the natural law is disobeying God's will." A manifest sign
      of this is that one who transgresses the natural law is in God's judgment worthy of
      punishment; therefore, he is a transgressor of God's will. For as is said in Luke 12,
      the servant who does not do his master's will will be flogged with many stripes.
      Therefore, the natural law includes God's will.

Conversely, In Matthew 6 and 1 John 2 the kingdom of heaven is promised to him who
does the will of God. This has to be interpreted as God's *preceptive* will, since it says: "If
you wish to enter into life, obey my commandments." Therefore, whoever obeys the
natural law is doing God's will; therefore, the natural law includes God's will as lawgiver.

This is further confirmed by the fact that the *signed* will that theologians posit in God
likewise extends to things that fall under the natural law, as one may infer from St.
Thomas, *Summa Theologiae* 1, q. 19, last article, along with the Master [of the *Sentences*]
and others in *Sentences* 1, dist. 45, and as is known *per se*. For whoever violates the natural
law turns away from the will of God, and when we say "Thy will be done" in the Our
Father, we are likewise asking that God's will be done in obedience to the natural law.
Therefore, the natural law as it exists in us is a sign of some volition on God's part.
Therefore, it is a sign especially of that volition by which God wills to obligate us to obey
that law. Therefore, the natural law includes this sort of will on God's part.

This is confirmed, third, by the fact that a sin against the natural law is offensive to
God and because of this has a certain infinity; therefore, this is an indication that it is
opposed to God as lawgiver. For it contains a virtual contempt for him. Therefore, the
natural law includes God's will, because without his will there is no legislation.

Then, too, the obligation that pertains to the natural law is a true obligation. But this
obligation is a certain good that exists in reality in its own way. Therefore, it must be that
this very obligation is from God's will insofar as it wills that men be bound to obey what
right reason dictates.

11.   *Second assertion: The prohibition or precept is not the whole reason for the goodness
      or badness found in obeying or transgressing the natural law.* Second, I assert that (a)
      this will – that is, prohibition or prescription – on God's part is not the whole reason
      for the goodness and badness that is found in obeying or transgressing the natural
      law, but that (b) the natural law presupposes in the acts themselves a certain
      necessary uprightness or evil, and (c) it adjoins to these a special obligation of
      divine law.

This assertion is taken from St. Thomas in the places cited above. The first part of it is
taken from the common axiom of theologians that certain bad things are prohibited
because they are bad. For if they are forbidden because they are bad, then they cannot
have the primary reason for their badness from the prohibition. For an effect is not a
reason for its cause.

This axiom has a basis in Augustine, *De sermone Domini in monte* 2, chap. 18, where
he says that certain acts such as promiscuousness and adultery cannot be done with an
upright intention, and more clearly in *De Libero Arbitrii* 1, chaps. 2 and 3, where Evodius
claims that it is not the case that adultery is bad because it is prohibited by law, but just

the opposite – a point that Augustine tacitly approves of. The same view is affirmed by the scholastics: by Durandus in *Sentences* 2, dist. 47, q. 4, nn. 7 and 8; by Scotus, Gabriel and others in *Sentences* 3, dist. 37; by Cajetan in *Summa Theologiae* 1–2, q. 100, art. 5; by Soto in *De justitia* 2, q. 3, art. 2; and by the other theologians cited above. This is the explicit view of Aristotle in *Ethics* 2, chap. 6, where he says, "There are some passions that by their very names are connected with depravity, such as malevolence, impudence, and envy, and a number of acts, such as adultery, theft, and murder. For all of these and others are so called because they themselves are evil."

The assertion can be founded on the metaphysical principle that the natures of things are immutable with respect to their essences, and, as a result, they are also immutable with respect to what is consonant with and dissonant with their natural properties. For even if a thing is capable of being deprived of a natural property or of taking on a contrary property, it nonetheless cannot be such that this status is connatural to it – as Vittoria explains at length in *Relectiones de homicidio*, dist. 4ff, and as Soto notes in the place just cited, and as we ourselves have explained concerning created essences in *Disputationes Metaphysicae*, disp. 31, at the beginning, and in *De Trinitate* 9, chap. 6.

This is confirmed *a posteriori* by the fact that if, say, an act of hating God did not have an intrinsic type of badness prior to its being prohibited, it would be able not to be prohibited. For why should this not be possible, if the act is not evil of itself? Therefore, it is able to be permissible or even righteous – which is plainly absurd.

Next, the second part of the assertion has a sufficient proof in the posing of the problem at the beginning of the chapter, along with the foundations for the first position that were put forth in the last chapter. And we will say more in discussing the impossibility of a dispensation from the natural law.

12. The last part of the assertion is taken from what was said in defense of the [first assertion]. For the natural law prohibits things that are bad in themselves; but this law is a true divine law and a true prohibition; therefore, it must add some obligation to refrain from a bad act that is bad of itself and by its nature.

Likewise, there is nothing absurd about adding to an act that is upright in itself an obligation to do it, nor about adding to an act that is evil an obligation to refrain from it. In fact, given one obligation, another can be added, especially if it has a different rationale, as is obvious with vows, with human law, and with similar things. Therefore, it is also possible for the natural law, insofar as it is a true divine law, to add a proper moral obligation that arises from a precept over and above the natural (as I will put it) badness or uprightness that the matter of the precept has in itself. In a moment this will be explained more clearly in the replies to the contrary arguments.

13. *Third assertion: The natural law is a true and proper law, with God as its lawgiver.* From what has been said I conclude and assert, third, that the natural law is a true and proper divine law whose lawgiver is God.

This assertion clearly follows from what has been said and is drawn from the Fathers already alluded to, from Epiphanius and Tertullian in the places to be cited below, and from Plutarch in his commentary *In principe requiri doctrinam*, near the beginning.

And it is made clear by the fact that the natural law can be considered either as it exists in God or as it exists in us. In God, according to the order of reason, the natural law presupposes the judgment of God himself concerning the propriety or impropriety of various acts, and it adds to this God's will to obligate men to follow what right reason dictates. All of this has already been sufficiently explained. Perhaps this is what Augustine meant to intimate in *Contra Faustum* 22, chap. 27, when he said that "the eternal law is God's reason and [*vel*] will commanding that the natural order be conserved and forbidding that it be disturbed." [...]

And thus it is, finally, that the natural law, insofar as it exists in us, not only *indicates* the evil but also *obligates* us to avoid it. And hence the natural law does not just represent the natural dissonance of such an act or object with a rational nature, but is also a sign of God's willing to forbid it.

[...]

17.   *The correct reply to the problem*. My own reply is that in a human act there is a type of goodness or badness by dint of the object, considered just by itself, insofar as it is consonant or dissonant with right reason. And, accordingly, the act can be denominated as bad and as a sin and as a fault in the senses noted above – even excluding any relation to a proper law. Beyond this, however, human acts have a special sort of goodness and badness in relation to God, given the addition of a divine law that prescribes or prohibits them. And, accordingly, a human act is denominated as a sin or fault in a special way, with respect to God, by reason of the transgression of God's own proper law. This special badness seems to be what Paul meant by the term 'transgression' when he said, "Where there is no law, there is no transgression." Hence, a human act that is contrary to a rational nature would not have this type of deformity if we posited the hypothesis that God does not prohibit it. For in that case it would not embody the sort of virtual contempt for God that the transgression of a law has with respect to the lawgiver.

Basil testifies to this in his commentary on Psalm 28, "Give glory and honor to the Lord," and it is consonant with what Paul says in Romans 2: "By transgressing the law you dishonor God." That explains why in *De vera religione*, chap. 26, Augustine said, "A prohibitive law redoubles all the sins committed." He clarifies this by adding, "For it is not just a mere sin, not just something bad, but also something forbidden."

18.   And it is in this way that St. Thomas, *Summa Theologiae* 1–2, q. 71, art. 6, ad 5, seems to distinguish sin insofar as it is contrary to reason from sin insofar as it is an offense against God, where sin in the first sense is considered by moral philosophy and in the second sense by theology. So in the case under discussion a bad act would be a sin and a fault morally speaking, but not theologically speaking, that is, with respect to God. It is in this same way, it seems, that we should understand what St. Thomas says in his reply to the fourth objection, namely, that in relation to the eternal law such sins are bad because they are prohibited, that is, they are bad with a theological badness (as I will call it) that an act would not have unless it were prohibited.

This, too, is apparently the way to understand the argument he then adds – an argument that could otherwise seem obscure. For after having claimed that in relation to the eternal law every sin is bad because it is prohibited, he adds, "By the very fact that such an act is disordered, it is contrary to the natural law." For this argument seems to prove that the act is prohibited because it is bad rather than the other way around. This is true, as long as we are speaking of the badness of being morally disordered; yet it is by reason of this disorder that the eternal law is added, along with the divine prohibition to which such a sin has a special repugnance. And from this it follows that the sin has a special disorder that it would not have were the divine prohibition not in place – a disorder by reason of which the notion of a sin, taken theologically, is satisfied, along with the notion of a fault, absolutely speaking, before God. This seems to be the way to interpret what Vittoria and several other theologians say, and this is why the replies made above do not work if they have more than merely verbal import.

19. Therefore, from the [original] hypothesis, thus explained and conceded, nothing can be inferred against our position or against the arguments by which we have proved it. For even if we concede the conditional in the sense explained, it is still the case that the natural law in fact truly and properly prohibits whatever in human acts is bad or disordered in itself. And without such a prohibition an act would not have (as I will put it) the full and complete character of a fault and offense against God – a character that cannot be denied in acts which are contrary to natural law in the precise sense.

2.3.3 Thomas Hobbes
Leviathan

Chapter XIII of the Natural Condition
of Mankind as Concerning Their Felicity
and Misery

NATURE hath made men so equal in the faculties of body and mind as that, though there be found one man sometimes manifestly stronger in body or of quicker mind than another, yet when all is reckoned together the difference between man and man is not so considerable as that one man can thereupon claim to himself any benefit to which another may not pretend as well as he. For as to the strength of body, the weakest has strength enough to kill the strongest, either by secret machination or by confederacy with others that are in the same danger with himself. […]

So that in the nature of man, we find three principal causes of quarrel. First, competition; secondly, diffidence; thirdly, glory.

The first maketh men invade for gain; the second, for safety; and the third, for reputation. The first use violence, to make themselves masters of other men's persons, wives, children, and cattle; the second, to defend them; the third, for trifles, as a word, a smile, a different opinion, and any other sign of undervalue, either direct in their persons or by reflection in their kindred, their friends, their nation, their profession, or their name.

Hereby it is manifest that during the time men live without a common power to keep them all in awe, they are in that condition which is called war; and such a war as is of every man against every man. For war consisteth not in battle only, or the act of fighting, but in a tract of time, wherein the will to contend by battle is sufficiently known: and therefore the notion of time is to be considered in the nature of war, as it is in the nature of weather. For as the nature of foul weather lieth not in a shower or two of rain, but in an inclination thereto of many days together: so the nature of war consisteth not in actual fighting, but in the known disposition thereto during all the time there is no assurance to the contrary. All other time is peace.

Whatsoever therefore is consequent to a time of war, where every man is enemy to every man, the same consequent to the time wherein men live without other security

Thomas Hobbes, *Of Man, Being the First Part of Leviathan*. Vol. XXXIV, Part 5. The Harvard Classics (New York: P.F. Collier & Son, 1909–14; Bartleby.com, 2001). www.bartleby.com/34/5/.

than what their own strength and their own invention shall furnish them withal. In such condition there is no place for industry, because the fruit thereof is uncertain: and consequently no culture of the earth; no navigation, nor use of the commodities that may be imported by sea; no commodious building; no instruments of moving and removing such things as require much force; no knowledge of the face of the earth; no account of time; no arts; no letters; no society; and which is worst of all, continual fear, and danger of violent death; and the life of man, solitary, poor, nasty, brutish, and short.

Chapter XIV of the First and Second Natural Laws, and of Contracts

THE right of nature, which writers commonly call jus naturale, is the liberty each man hath to use his own power as he will himself for the preservation of his own nature; that is to say, of his own life; and consequently, of doing anything which, in his own judgement and reason, he shall conceive to be the aptest means thereunto.

By liberty is understood, according to the proper signification of the word, the absence of external impediments; which impediments may oft take away part of a man's power to do what he would, but cannot hinder him from using the power left him according as his judgement and reason shall dictate to him.

A law of nature, lex naturalis, is a precept, or general rule, found out by reason, by which a man is forbidden to do that which is destructive of his life, or taketh away the means of preserving the same, and to omit that by which he thinketh it may be best preserved. For though they that speak of this subject use to confound jus and lex, right and law, yet they ought to be distinguished, because right consisteth in liberty to do, or to forbear; whereas law determineth and bindeth to one of them: so that law and right differ as much as obligation and liberty, which in one and the same matter are inconsistent.

And because the condition of man (as hath been declared in the precedent chapter) is a condition of war of every one against every one, in which case every one is governed by his own reason, and there is nothing he can make use of that may not be a help unto him in preserving his life against his enemies; it followeth that in such a condition every man has a right to every thing, even to one another's body. And therefore, as long as this natural right of every man to every thing endureth, there can be no security to any man, how strong or wise soever he be, of living out the time which nature ordinarily alloweth men to live. And consequently it is a precept, or general rule of reason: that every man ought to endeavour peace, as far as he has hope of obtaining it; and when he cannot obtain it, that he may seek and use all helps and advantages of war. The first branch of which rule containeth the first and fundamental law of nature, which is: to seek peace and follow it. The second, the sum of the right of nature, which is: by all means we can to defend ourselves.

From this fundamental law of nature, by which men are commanded to endeavour peace, is derived this second law: that a man be willing, when others are so too, as far forth as for peace and defence of himself he shall think it necessary, to lay down this right to all things; and be contented with so much liberty against other men as he would allow other men against himself. For as long as every man holdeth this right, of doing anything he liketh; so long are all men in the condition of war. But if other men will not lay down their right, as well as he, then there is no reason for anyone to divest himself of his: for that were to expose himself to prey, which no man is bound to, rather than to dispose himself to peace. This is that law of the gospel: Whatsoever you require that others should do to you, that do ye to them. And that law of all men, quod tibi fieri non vis, alteri ne feceris.

To lay down a man's right to anything is to divest himself of the liberty of hindering another of the benefit of his own right to the same. For he that renounceth or passeth away his right giveth not to any other man a right which he had not before, because there is nothing to which every man had not right by nature, but only standeth out of his way that he may enjoy his own original right without hindrance from him, not without hindrance from another. So that the effect which redoundeth to one man by another man's defect of right is but so much diminution of impediments to the use of his own right original.

Right is laid aside, either by simply renouncing it, or by transferring it to another. By simply renouncing, when he cares not to whom the benefit thereof redoundeth. By transferring, when he intendeth the benefit thereof to some certain person or persons. And when a man hath in either manner abandoned or granted away his right, then is he said to be obliged, or bound, not to hinder those to whom such right is granted, or abandoned, from the benefit of it: and that he ought, and it is duty, not to make void that voluntary act of his own: and that such hindrance is injustice, and injury, as being sine jure; the right being before renounced or transferred. So that injury or injustice, in the controversies of the world, is somewhat like to that which in the disputations of scholars is called absurdity. For as it is there called an absurdity to contradict what one maintained in the beginning; so in the world it is called injustice, and injury voluntarily to undo that which from the beginning he had voluntarily done. The way by which a man either simply renounceth or transferreth his right is a declaration, or signification, by some voluntary and sufficient sign, or signs, that he doth so renounce or transfer, or hath so renounced or transferred the same, to him that accepteth it. And these signs are either words only, or actions only; or, as it happeneth most often, both words and actions. And the same are the bonds, by which men are bound and obliged: bonds that have their strength, not from their own nature (for nothing is more easily broken than a man's word), but from fear of some evil consequence upon the rupture.

Whensoever a man transferreth his right, or renounceth it, it is either in consideration of some right reciprocally transferred to himself, or for some other good he hopeth for thereby. For it is a voluntary act: and of the voluntary acts of every man, the object is some good to himself. And therefore there be some rights which no man can be understood by any words, or other signs, to have abandoned or transferred. As first a man cannot lay down the right of resisting them that assault him by force to take away his life, because he cannot be understood to aim thereby at any good to himself. The same may be said of wounds, and chains, and imprisonment, both because there is no benefit consequent to such patience, as there is to the patience of suffering another to be wounded or imprisoned, as also because a man cannot tell when he seeth men proceed against him by violence whether they intend his death or not. And lastly the motive and end for which this renouncing and transferring of right is introduced is nothing else but the security of a man's person, in his life, and in the means of so preserving life as not to be weary of it. And therefore if a man by words, or other signs, seem to despoil himself of

Thomas Hobbes, *Leviathan*

the end for which those signs were intended, he is not to be understood as if he me
or that it was his will, but that he was ignorant of how such words and actions were to be
interpreted.

The mutual transferring of right is that which men call contract. […]

[…]

He that transferreth any right transferreth the means of enjoying it, as far as lieth in
his power. As he that selleth land is understood to transfer the herbage and whatsoever
grows upon it; nor can he that sells a mill turn away the stream that drives it. And they
that give to a man the right of government in sovereignty are understood to give him the
right of levying money to maintain soldiers, and of appointing magistrates for the
administration of justice.

To make covenants with brute beasts is impossible, because not understanding our
speech, they understand not, nor accept of any translation of right, nor can translate any
right to another: and without mutual acceptation, there is no covenant.

To make covenant with God is impossible but by mediation of such as God speaketh
to, either by revelation supernatural or by His lieutenants that govern under Him and in
His name: for otherwise we know not whether our covenants be accepted or not. And
therefore they that vow anything contrary to any law of nature, vow in vain, as being a
thing unjust to pay such vow. And if it be a thing commanded by the law of nature, it is
not the vow, but the law that binds them.

The matter or subject of a covenant is always something that falleth under deliberation, for to covenant is an act of the will; that is to say, an act, and the last act, of deliberation; and is therefore always understood to be something to come, and which judged
possible for him that covenanteth to perform.

And therefore, to promise that which is known to be impossible is no covenant. But if
that prove impossible afterwards, which before was thought possible, the covenant is
valid and bindeth, though not to the thing itself, yet to the value; or, if that also be impossible, to the unfeigned endeavour of performing as much as is possible, for to more no
man can be obliged.

Men are freed of their covenants two ways; by performing, or by being forgiven. For
performance is the natural end of obligation, and forgiveness the restitution of liberty, as
being a retransferring of that right in which the obligation consisted.

[…]

The force of words being (as I have formerly noted) too weak to hold men to the
performance of their covenants, there are in man's nature but two imaginable helps to
strengthen it. And those are either a fear of the consequence of breaking their word, or a
glory or pride in appearing not to need to break it. This latter is a generosity too rarely
found to be presumed on, especially in the pursuers of wealth, command, or sensual
pleasure, which are the greatest part of mankind. The passion to be reckoned upon is
fear; whereof there be two very general objects: one, the power of spirits invisible; the
other, the power of those men they shall therein offend. Of these two, though the former
be the greater power, yet the fear of the latter is commonly the greater fear. The fear of
the former is in every man his own religion, which hath place in the nature of man before
civil society. The latter hath not so; at least not place enough to keep men to their promises, because in the condition of mere nature, the inequality of power is not discerned,
but by the event of battle. So that before the time of civil society, or in the interruption

thereof by war, there is nothing can strengthen a covenant of peace agreed on against the temptations of avarice, ambition, lust, or other strong desire, but the fear of that invisible power which they every one worship as God, and fear as a revenger of their perfidy. All therefore that can be done between two men not subject to civil power is to put one another to swear by the God he feareth: which swearing, or oath, is a form of speech, added to a promise, by which he that promiseth signifieth that unless he perform he renounceth the mercy of his God, or calleth to him for vengeance on himself. Such was the heathen form, Let Jupiter kill me else, as I kill this beast. So is our form, I shall do thus, and thus, so help me God. And this, with the rites and ceremonies which every one useth in his own religion, that the fear of breaking faith might be the greater.

By this it appears that an oath taken according to any other form, or rite, than his that sweareth is in vain and no oath, and that there is no swearing by anything which the swearer thinks not God. For though men have sometimes used to swear by their kings, for fear, or flattery; yet they would have it thereby understood they attributed to them divine honour. And that swearing unnecessarily by God is but profaning of his name: and swearing by other things, as men do in common discourse, is not swearing, but an impious custom, gotten by too much vehemence of talking.

It appears also that the oath adds nothing to the obligation. For a covenant, if lawful, binds in the sight of God, without the oath, as much as with it; if unlawful, bindeth not at all, though it be confirmed with an oath.

God = civil power / state power

2.3.4 Hugo Grotius
On the Law of War and Peace
(*De Jure Belli ac Pacis*)

Book I

CHAPTER 1: On War and Right

Of War – Definition of War – Right, of Governors and of the governed, and of equals – Right as a Quality divided into Faculty and Fitness – Faculty denoting Power, Property, and Credit – Divided into Private and Superior – Right as a Rule, natural and voluntary – Law of Nature divided – Proofs of the Law of Nature – Division of Rights into human and divine – Human explained – Divine stated – Mosaic Law not binding upon Christians.

I. THE disputes arising among those who are held together by no common bond of civil laws to decide their dissensions, like the ancient Patriarchs, who formed no national community, or the numerous, unconnected communities, whether under the direction of individuals, or kings, or persons invested with Sovereign power, as the leading men in an aristocracy, and the body of the people in a republican government; the disputes, arising among any of these, all bear a relation to the circumstances of war or peace. But because war is undertaken for the sake of peace, and there is no dispute, which may not give rise to war, it will be proper to treat all such quarrels, as commonly happen, between nations, as an article in the rights of war: and then war itself will lead us to peace, as to its proper end.

II. In treating of the rights of war, the first point, that we have to consider, is, what is war, which is the subject of our inquiry, and what is the right, which we seek to establish. Cicero styled war a contention by force. But the practice has prevailed to indicate by that name, not an immediate action, but a state of affairs; so that war is the state of contending parties, considered as such. This definition, by its general extent, comprises those wars of every description, that will form the subject of the present treatise. Nor are single combats excluded from this definition. For, as they are in reality more ancient than public wars, and undoubtedly, of the same nature, they may therefore properly be comprehended under one and the same name. This agrees very well with the true derivation of the word. For the Latin word, *Bellum*, WAR, comes from the old word, *Duellum*, a DUEL, as *Bonus* from *Duonus*, and *Bis* from *Duis*. Now *Duellum* was derived from *Duo*;

Tr. A.C. Campbell (London, 1814).

and thereby implied a difference between two persons, in the same sense as we term peace, UNITY, from *Unitas*, for a contrary reason. So the Greek word, πολεμος, commonly used to signify war, expresses in its original, an idea of multitude. The ancient Greeks likewise called it λυη, which imports a DISUNION of minds; just as by the term δυη, they meant the DISSOLUTION of the parts of the body. Nor does the use of the word, WAR, contradict this larger acceptation of it. For though some times it is only applied to the quarrels of states, yet that is no objection, as it is evident that a general name is often applied to some particular object, entitled to peculiar distinction. Justice is not included in the definition of war, because the very point to be decided is, whether any war be just, and what war may be so called. Therefore we must make a distinction between war itself, and the justice of it.

III. As the Rights of War is the title, by which this treatise is distinguished, the first inquiry, as it has been already observed, is, whether any war be just, and, in the next place, what constitutes the justice of that war. For, in this place, right signifies nothing more than what is just, and that, more in a negative than a positive sense; so that RIGHT is that, which is not unjust. Now any thing is unjust, which is repugnant to the nature of society, established among rational creatures. Thus for instance, to deprive another of what belongs to him, merely for one's own advantage, is repugnant to the law of nature, as Cicero observes in the fifth Chapter of his third book of offices; and, by way of proof, he says that, if the practice were general, all society and intercourse among men must be overturned. Florentinus, the Lawyer, maintains that is impious for one man to form designs against another, as nature has established a degree of kindred amongst us. On this subject, Seneca remarks that, as all the members of the human body agree among themselves, because the preservation of each conduces to the welfare of the whole, so men should forbear from mutual injuries, as they were born for society, which cannot subsist unless all the parts of it are defended by mutual forbearance and good will. But as there is one kind of social tie founded upon an equality, for instance, among brothers, citizens, friends, allies, and another on pre-eminence, as Aristotle styles it, subsisting between parents and children, masters and servants, sovereigns and subjects, God and men. So justice takes place either amongst equals, or between the governing and the governed parties, notwithstanding their difference of rank. The former of these, if I am not mistaken, may be called the right of equality, and the latter the right of superiority.

IV. There is another signification of the word RIGHT, different from this, but yet arising from it, which relates directly to the person. In which sense, RIGHT is a moral quality annexed to the person, justly entitling him to possess some particular privilege, or to perform some particular act. This right is annexed to the person, although it sometimes follows the things, as the services of lands, which are called REAL RIGHTS, in opposition to those merely PERSONAL. Not because these rights are not annexed to persons, but the distinction is made, because they belong to the persons only who possess some particular things. This moral quality, when perfect is called a FACULTY; when imperfect, an APTITUDE. The former answers to the ACT, and the latter to the POWER, when we speak of natural things.

V. Civilians call a faculty that Right, which every man has to his own; but we shall hereafter, taking it in its strict and proper sense, call it a right. This right comprehends the power, that we have over ourselves, which is called liberty, and the power, that we have over others, as that of a father over his children, and of a master over his slaves.

It likewise comprehends property, which is either complete or imperfect; of the latter kind is the use or possession of any thing without the property, or power of alienating it, or pledges detained by the creditors till payment be made. There is a third signification which implies the power of demanding what is due, to which the obligation upon the party indebted, to discharge what is owing, corresponds.

VI. Right, strictly taken, is again twofold, the one PRIVATE, established for the advantage of each individual, the other, SUPERIOR, as involving the claims, which the state has upon individuals, and their property, for the public good. Thus the Regal authority is above that of a father and a master, and the Sovereign has a greater right over the property of his subjects, where the public good is concerned, than the owners themselves have. And when the exigencies of the state require a supply, every man is more obliged to contribute towards it, than to satisfy his creditors.

VII. Aristotle distinguishes aptitude or capacity, by the name of worth or merit, and Michael of Ephesus, gives the epithet of SUITABLE or BECOMING to the equality established by this rule of merit.

VII. [**Translator's note**: The eighth Section is omitted, the greater part of it consisting of verbal criticism upon Aristotle's notions of geometrical and arithmetical justice; a discussion no way conducive to that clearness and simplicity, so necessary to every didactic treatise.]

IX. There is also a third signification of the word Right, which has the same meaning as Law, taken in its most extensive sense, to denote a rule of moral action, obliging us to do what is proper. We say OBLIGING us. For the best counsels or precepts, if they lay us under no obligation to obey them, cannot come under the denomination of law or right. Now as to permission, it is no act of the law, but only the silence of the law it however prohibits any one from impeding another in doing what the law permits. But we have said, the law obliges us to do what is proper, not simply what is just; because, under this notion, right belongs to the substance not only of justice, as we have explained it, but of all other virtues. Yet from giving the name of a RIGHT to that, which is PROPER, a more general acceptation of the word justice has been derived. The best division of right, in this general meaning, is to be found in Aristotle, who, defining one kind to be natural, and the other voluntary, calls it a LAWFUL RIGHT in the strictest sense of the word law; and some times an instituted right. The same difference is found among the Hebrews, who, by way of distinction, in speaking, call that natural right, PRECEPTS, and the voluntary right, STATUTES: the former of which the Septuagint call δικαιώματα, and the latter ἐντολὰς.

X. Natural right is the dictate of right reason, shewing the moral turpidude, or moral necessity, of any act from its agreement or disagreement with a rational nature, and consequently that such an act is either forbidden or commanded by God, the author of nature. The actions, upon which such a dictate is given, are either binding or unlawful in themselves, and therefore necessarily understood to be commanded or forbidden by God. This mark distinguishes natural right, not only from human law, but from the law, which God himself has been pleased to reveal, called, by some, the voluntary divine right, which does not command or forbid things in themselves either binding or unlawful, but makes them unlawful by its prohibition, and binding by its command. But, to understand natural right, we must observe that some things are said to belong to that right, not properly, but, as the schoolmen say, by way of accommodation. These are not repugnant to natural right, as we have already observed that those things are called JUST, in which there is no injustice. Some times also, by a wrong use of the word, those things which reason shews to be proper, or better than things of an opposite kind, although not binding, are said to belong to natural right.

We must farther remark, that natural right relates not only to those things that exist independent of the human will, but to many things, which necessarily follow the exercise of that will. Thus property, as now in use, was at first a creature of the human will. But, after it was established, one man was prohibited by the law of nature from seizing the property of another against his will. Wherefore, Paulus the Lawyer said, that theft is expressly forbidden by the law of nature. Ulpian condemns it as infamous in its own nature; to whose authority that of Euripides may be added, as may be seen in the verse of Helena:

"For God himself hates violence, and will not have us to grow rich by rapine, but by lawful gains. That abundance, which is the fruit of unrighteousness, is an abomination. The air is common to men, the earth also where every man, in the ample enjoyment of his possession, must refrain from doing violence or injury to that of another."

Now the Law of Nature is so unalterable, that it cannot be changed even by God himself. For although the power of God is infinite, yet there are some things, to which it does not extend. Because the things so expressed would have no true meaning, but imply a contradiction. Thus two and two must make four, nor is it possible to be otherwise; nor, again, can what is really evil not be evil. And this is Aristotle's meaning, when he says, that some things are no sooner named, than we discover their evil nature. For as the substance of things in their nature and existence depends upon nothing but themselves; so there are qualities inseparably connected with their being and essence. Of this kind is the evil of certain actions, compared with the nature of a reasonable being. Therefore God himself suffers his actions to be judged by this rule, as may be seen in the xviiith chap. of Gen. 25. Isa. v. 3. Ezek. xviii. 25. Jer. ii. 9. Mich. vi. 2. From. ii. 6., iii. 6. Yet it sometimes happens that, in those cases, which are decided by the law of nature, the undiscerning are imposed upon by an appearance of change. Whereas in reality there is no change in the unalterable law of nature, but only in the things appointed by it, and which are liable to variation. For example, if a creditor forgive me the debt, which I owe him, I am no longer bound to pay it, not because the law of nature has ceased to command the payment of a just debt, but because my debt, by a release, has ceased to be a debt. On this topic, Arrian in Epictetus argues rightly, that the borrowing of money is not the only requisite to make a debt, but there must be the additional circumstance of the loan remaining undischarged. Thus if God should command the life, or property of any one to be taken away, the act would not authorise murder or robbery, words which always include a crime. But that cannot be murder or robbery, which is done by the express command of Him, who is the sovereign Lord of our lives and of all things. There are also some things allowed by the law of nature, not absolutely, but according to a certain state of affairs. Thus, by the law of nature, before property was introduced, every one had a right to the use of whatever he found unoccupied; and, before laws were enacted, to avenge his personal injuries by force.

XI. The distinction found in the books of the Roman Law, assigning one unchangeable right to brutes in common with man, which in a more limited sense they call the law of nature, and appropriating another to men, which they frequently call the Law of

Nations, is scarcely of any real use. For no beings, except those that can form general maxims, are capable of possessing a right, which Hesiod has placed in a clear point of view, observing "that the supreme Being has appointed laws for men; but permitted wild beasts, fishes, and birds to devour each other for food." For they have nothing like justice, the best gift, bestowed upon men.

Cicero, in his first book of offices, says, we do not talk of the justice of horses or lions. In conformity to which, Plutarch, in the life of Cato the elder, observes, that we are formed by nature to use law and justice towards men only. In addition to the above, Lactantius may be cited, who, in his fifth book, says that in all animals devoid of reason we see a natural bias of self-love. For they hurt others to benefit themselves; because they do not know the evil of doing willful hurt. But it is not so with man, who, possessing the knowledge of good and evil, refrains, even with inconvenience to himself, from doing hurt. Polybius, relating the manner in which men first entered into society, concludes, that the injuries done to parents or benefactors inevitably provoke the indignation of mankind, giving an additional reason, that as understanding and reflection form the great difference between men and other animals, it is evident they cannot transgress the bounds of that difference like other animals, without exciting universal abhorrence of their conduct. But if ever justice is attributed to brutes, it is done improperly, from some shadow and trace of reason they may possess. But it is not material to the nature of right, whether the actions appointed by the law of nature, such as the care of our offspring, are common to us with other animals or not, or, like the worship of God, are peculiar to man.

XII. The existence of the Law of Nature is proved by two kinds of argument, *a priori*, and *a posteriori*, the former a more abstruse, and the latter a more popular method of proof. We are said to reason *a priori*, when we show the agreement or disagreement of any thing with a reasonable and social nature; but *a posteriori*, when without absolute proof, but only upon probability, any thing is inferred to accord with the law of nature, because it is received as such among all, or at least the more civilized nations. For a general effect can only arise from a general cause. Now scarce any other cause can be assigned for so general an opinion, but the common sense, as it is called, of mankind. There is a sentence of Hesiod that has been much praised, that opinions which have prevailed amongst many nations, must have some foundation. Heraclitus, establishing common reason as the best criterion of truth, says, those things are certain which generally appear so. Among other authorities, we may quote Aristotle, who says it is a strong proof in our favour, when all appear to agree with what we say, and Cicero maintains that the con. sent of all nations in any case is to be admitted for the law of nature. Seneca is of the same opinion, any thing, says he, appearing the same to all men is a proof of its truth. Quintilian says, we hold those things to be true, in which all men agree. We have called them the more civilized nations, and not without reason. For, as Porphyry well observes, some nations are so strange that no fair judgment of human nature can be formed from them, for it would be erroneous. Andronicus, the Rhodian says, that with men of a right and sound understanding, natural justice is unchangeable. Nor does it alter the case, though men of disordered and perverted minds think otherwise. For he who should deny that honey is sweet, because it appears not so to men of a distempered taste, would be wrong. Plutarch too agrees entirely with what has been said, as appears from a passage in his life of Pompey, affirming that man neither was, nor is, by nature, a wild unsociable creature. But it is the corruption of his nature which makes him so: yet by acquiring new habits, by changing his place, and way of living, he may be reclaimed to his original gentleness. Aristotle, taking a description of man from his peculiar qualities, makes him an animal of a gentle nature, and in another part of his works, he observes, that in considering the nature of man, we are to take our likeness from nature in its pure, and not in its corrupt state.

XIII. It has been already remarked, that there is another kind of right, which is the voluntary right, deriving its origin from the will, and is either human or divine.

XIV. We will begin with the human as more generally known. Now this is either a civil right, or a right more or less extensive than the civil right. The civil right is that which is derived from the civil power. The civil power is the sovereign power of the state. A state is a perfect body of free men, united together in order to enjoy common rights and advantages. The less extensive right, and not derived from the civil power itself, although subject to it, is various, comprehending the authority of parents over children, masters over servants, and the like. But the law of nations is a more extensive right, deriving its authority from the consent of all, or at least of many nations.

It was proper to add MANY, because scarce any right can be found common to all nations, except the law of nature, which itself too is generally called the law of nations. Nay, frequently in one part of the world, that is held for the law of nations, which is not so in another. Now this law of nations is proved in the same manner as the unwritten civil law, and that is by the continual experience and testimony of the Sages of the Law. For this law, as Dio Chrysostom well observes, is the discoveries made by experience and time. And in this we derive great advantage from the writings of eminent historians.

XV. The very meaning of the words divine voluntary right, shows that it springs from the divine will, by which it is distinguished from natural law, which, it has already been observed, is called divine also. This law admits of what Anaxarchus said, as Plutarch relates in the life of Alexander, though without sufficient accuracy, that God does not will a thing, because it is just, but that it is just, or binding, because God wills it. Now this law was given either to mankind in general, or to one particular people. We find three periods, at which it was given by God to the human race, the first of which was immediately after the creation of man, the second upon the restoration of mankind after the flood, and the third upon that more glorious restoration through Jesus Christ. These three laws undoubtedly bind all men, as soon as they come to a sufficient knowledge of them.

2.3.5 Samuel von Pufendorf
De Officio Hominis et Civis Juxta Legem Naturalem Libri Duo

Chapter III On Natural Law

1. What is the character of the natural law, what its necessity, and of what precepts it consists in the present state of mankind, are most clearly seen, after one has thoroughly examined the nature and disposition of man. For, just as for an accurate knowledge of civil laws, it is very important to have a clear understanding of the condition of the state, and of the habits and interests of its citizens, so if we have examined the common disposition of men and their condition, it will be readily apparent upon what laws their welfare depends.

2. Now man shares with all the animals that have consciousness the fact that he holds nothing dearer than himself, and is eager in every way to preserve himself; that he strives to gain what seem to him good things, and to reject the evil. This feeling is regularly so strong that all the others give way to it. And one cannot but resent it, if any man make an attack upon one's life, so much so that, even after the threatened danger has been averted, hatred usually still remains, and a desire for vengeance.

3. But in one respect man seems to be in a worse state even than the brutes, – that scarcely any other animal is attended from birth by such weakness. Hence it would be a miracle, if anyone reached mature years, if he have not the aid of other men, since, as it is, among all the helps which have been invented for human needs, careful training for a number of years is required, to enable a man to gain his food and clothing by his own efforts. Let us imagine a man brought to maturity without any care and training bestowed upon him by others, having no knowledge except what sprang up of itself in his own mind, and in a desert, deprived of all help and society of other men. Certainly a more miserable animal it will be hard to find. Speechless and naked, he has nothing left him but to pluck herbs and roots, or gather wild fruits, to slake his thirst from spring or river, or the first marsh he encountered, to seek shelter in a cave from the violence of the weather, or to cover his body somehow

Samuel von Pufendorf, *De Officio Hominis et Civis Juxta Legem Naturalem Libri Duo*, Volume Two: *The Translation* by Frank Gardner Moore (Oxford: Oxford University Press, 1927). Reprinted with permission of Oxford University Press.

with moss or grass, to pass his time most tediously in idleness, to shudder at any noise or the encounter with another creature, finally to perish by hunger or cold or some wild beast. On the other hand, whatever advantages now attend human life have flowed entirely from the mutual help of men. It follows that, after God, there is nothing in this world from which greater advantage can come to man than from man himself.

4. Yet this animal, though so useful to his kind, suffers from not a few faults, and is endowed with no less power to injure; which facts make contact with him rather uncertain, and call for great caution, that one may not receive evil from him instead of good. First of all, there is generally a greater tendency to injure found in man than in any of the brutes. For the brutes are usually excited by the desire for food and for love, both of which, however, they can themselves easily satisfy. But having stilled that craving, they are not readily roused to anger or to injure people, unless someone provokes them. But man is an animal at no time disinclined to lust, and by its goad he is excited much more frequently than would seem necessary for the conservation of the race. And his belly desires not merely to be satisfied, but also to be tickled, and often craves more than nature is able to digest. That the brutes should not need clothing nature has provided. But man delights to clothe himself, not for necessity only, but also for display. Many more passions and desires unknown to the brutes are found in man, as the desire to have superfluities, avarice, the love of glory and eminence, envy, emulation, and rivalry of wits. Witness the fact that most wars, in which men clash with men, are waged for reasons unknown to the brutes. And all these things can, and usually do, incite men to desire to injure one another. Then too there is in many a notable insolence and passion for insulting their fellows, at which the rest, modest though they be by nature, cannot fail to take offense, and gird themselves to resist, from the desire to maintain and defend themselves and their freedom. At times also men are driven to mutual injury by want, and the fact that their present resources are insufficient for their desires or their need.

5. Moreover men have in them great power for the infliction of mutual injuries. For though not formidable because of teeth or claws or horns, as are many of the brutes, still manual dexterity can prove a most effective means of injury; and shrewdness gives a man the opportunity to attack by cunning and in ambush, where the enemy cannot be reached by open force. Hence it is very easy for man to inflict upon man the worst of natural evils, namely death.

6. Finally, we must also consider in mankind such a remarkable variety of gifts as is not observed in single species of animals, which, in fact, generally have like inclinations, and are led by the same passion and desire. But among men there are as many emotions as there are heads, and each has his own idea of the attractive. Nor are all stirred by a single and uniform desire, but by one that is manifold and variously intermixed. Even one and the same man often appears unlike himself, and if he has eagerly sought a thing at one time, at another he is very averse to it. And there is no less variety in the tastes and habits, the inclinations to exert mental powers, – a variety which we see now in the almost countless modes of life. That men may not thus be brought into collision, there is need of careful regulation and control.

7.   Thus then man is indeed an animal most bent upon self-preservation, helpless in himself, unable to save himself without the aid of his fellows, highly adapted to promote mutual interests; but on the other hand no less malicious, insolent, and easily provoked, also as able as he is prone to inflict injury upon another. Whence it follows that, in order to be safe, he must be sociable, that is, must be united with men like himself, and so conduct himself toward them that they may have no good cause to injure him, but rather may be ready to maintain and promote his interests.

8.   The laws then of this sociability, or those which teach how a man should conduct himself, to become a good member of human society, are called natural laws.

9.   So much settled, it is clear that the fundamental natural law is this: that every man must cherish and maintain sociability, so far as in him lies. From this it follows that, as he who wishes an end, wishes also the means, without which the end cannot be obtained, all things which necessarily and universally make for that sociability are understood to be ordained by natural law, and all that confuse or destroy it forbidden. The remaining precepts are mere corollaries, so to speak, under this general law, and the natural light given to mankind declares that they are evident.

10. Again, although those precepts have manifest utility, still, if they are to have the force of law, it is necessary to presuppose that God exists, and by His providence rules all things; also that He has enjoined upon the human race that they observe those dictates of the reason, as laws promulgated by Himself by means of our natural light. For otherwise they might, to be sure, be observed perhaps, in view of their utility, like the prescriptions of physicians for the regimen of health, but not as laws; since these of necessity presuppose a superior, and in fact one who has actually undertaken the direction of another.

11. But that God is the author of the natural law, is proved by the natural reason, if only we limit ourselves strictly to the present condition of humanity, disregarding the question whether his primitive condition was different from the present, or whence that change has come about. The nature of man is so constituted that the race cannot be preserved without the social life, and man's mind is found to be capable of all the notions which serve that end. And it is in fact clear, not only that the human race owes its origin, as do the other creatures, to God, but also that, whatever be its present state, God includes the race in the government of His providence. It follows from these arguments that God wills that man use for the conservation of his own nature those special powers which he knows are peculiarly his own, as compared with the brutes, and thus that man's life be distinguished from the lawless life of the brutes. And as this cannot be secured except by observing the natural law, we understand too that man has been obliged by God to keep the same, as a means not devised by will of man, and changeable at their discretion, but expressly ordained by God Himself, in order to insure this end. For whoever binds a man to an end, is considered to have bound him also to employ the means necessary to that end. And besides, we have evidence that the social life has been enjoined upon men by God's authority, in the fact that in no other creature do we find the religious sentiment or fear of the Deity, – a feeling which seems inconceivable in a lawless animal. Hence in the minds of men not entirely corrupt a very delicate sense is born, which convinces them that by sin against the natural law they offend Him who holds sway over the minds of men, and is to be feared even when the fear of men does not impend.

12. The common saying that that law is known by nature, should not be understood, it seems, as though actual and distinct propositions concerning things to be done or to be avoided were inherent in men's minds at the hour of their birth. But it means in part that the law can be investigated by the light of reason, in part that at least the common and important provisions of the natural law are so plain and clear that they at once find assent, and grow up in our minds, so that they can never again be destroyed, no matter how the impious man, in order to still the twinges of conscience, may endeavor to blot out the consciousness of those precepts. For this reason in Scripture too the law is said to be "written in the hearts" of men. Hence, since we are imbued from childhood with a consciousness of those maxims, in accordance with our social training, and cannot remember the time when we first imbibed them, we think of this knowledge exactly as if we had had it already at birth. Everyone has the same experience with his mother tongue.

13. Of the duties incumbent upon man in accordance with natural law the most convenient division seems to be according to the objects in regard to which they are to be practiced. From this standpoint they are classified under three main heads: the first of which instructs us how, according to the dictate of sound reason alone a man should conduct himself toward God, the second, how toward himself, the third, how toward other men. Although those precepts of natural law which concern other men may be derived primarily and directly from sociability, which we have laid down as a foundation, indirectly also the duties of man to God as creator can be derived from the same, since the ultimate confirmation of duties toward other men comes from religion and fear of the Deity, so that man would not be sociable either, if not imbued with religion; and since reason alone cannot go further in religion than in so far as the latter subserves the promotion of peace and sociability in this life. For, in so far as religion promotes the salvation of souls, it proceeds from a special divine revelation. But duties of man to himself spring from religion and sociability conjointly. For the reason why he cannot determine certain acts concerning himself in accordance with his own free will, is partly that he may be a fit worshiper of the Deity, and partly that he may be a good and useful member of human society.

[handwritten: totalitarian in its approach]

[handwritten: - "father" of liberalism]
[handwritten: - European nations transitioning from monarchies → democracy]
[handwritten: - how do they ground this philosophically?]

2.3.6 John Locke
Second Treatise of Government

[handwritten: - Rights are a new thing]
[handwritten: - Law of nature - law of reason ⟩ hobbes]
[handwritten: - rights are relinquished when ⟩ (deception + selfishness) you group together]
[handwritten: - market logic]
[handwritten: - contract: mutual transferring of rights]

*[handwritten: * sovereign - idea of hierarchy - benevolent, loving god orders these things]*

Chapter II. of the State of Nature.

Sect. 4. TO understand political power right, and derive it from its original, we must con-*[handwritten: all men are naturally free]* sider, what state all men are naturally in, and that is, a state of perfect freedom to order their actions, and dispose of their possessions and persons, as they think fit, within the bounds of the law of nature, without asking leave, or depending upon the will of any other man.

[handwritten: private property is basic + natural to humanity - complete 180 from hobbes]

A state also of equality, wherein all the power and jurisdiction is reciprocal, no one having more than another; there being nothing more evident, than that creatures of the same species and rank, promiscuously born to all the same advantages of nature, and the use of the same faculties, should also be equal one amongst another without sub-ordination or subjection, unless the lord and master of them all should, by any manifest declaration of his will, set one above another, and confer on him, by an evident and clear appointment, an undoubted right to dominion and sovereignty. *[handwritten: introduces the sovereign *]*

[handwritten: however, natural law still takes effect]

Sect. 5. This equality of men by nature, the judicious Hooker looks upon as so evident in itself, and beyond all question, that he makes it the foundation of that obligation to mutual love amongst men, on which he builds the duties they owe one another, and from whence he derives the great maxims of justice and charity. His words are,

[handwritten: humans are empathetic]

[handwritten left margin: Justice]

The like natural inducement hath brought men to know that it is no less their duty, to love others than themselves; for seeing those things which are equal, must needs all have one measure; if I cannot but wish to receive good, even as much at every man's hands, as any man can wish unto his own soul, how should I look to have any part of my desire herein satisfied, unless myself be careful to satisfy the like desire, which is undoubtedly in other men, being of one and the same nature? To have any thing offered them repug-nant to this desire, must needs in all respects grieve them as much as me; so that if I do harm, I must look to suffer, there being no reason that others should shew greater mea-sure of love to me, than they have by me shewed unto them: my desire therefore to be loved of my equals in nature as much as possible may be, imposeth upon me a natural duty of bearing to them-ward fully the like affection; from which relation of equality between ourselves and them that are as ourselves, what several rules and canons natural reason hath drawn, for direction of life, no man is ignorant, Eccl. Pol. Lib. 1.

Originally published in 1690. Digitized by Dave Gowan, http://www.gutenberg.org/files/7370/7370-h/7370-h.htm.

[handwritten: ⚡ Fundamentally, the love + respect people have for each other goes towards justice + charity.]

Sect. 6. But though this be a state of liberty, yet it is not a state of licence: though man in that state have an uncontroulable liberty to dispose of his person or possessions, yet he has not liberty to destroy himself, or so much as any creature in his possession, but where some nobler use than its bare preservation calls for it. The state of nature has a law of nature to govern it, which obliges every one: and reason, which is that law, teaches all mankind, who will but consult it, that being all equal and independent, no one ought to harm another in his life, health, liberty, or possessions: for men being all the workmanship of one omnipotent, and infinitely wise maker; all the servants of one sovereign master, sent into the world by his order, and about his business; they are his property, whose workmanship they are, made to last during his, not one another's pleasure: and being furnished with like faculties, sharing all in one community of nature, there cannot be supposed any such subordination among us, that may authorize us to destroy one another, as if we were made for one another's uses, as the inferior ranks of creatures are for our's. Every one, as he is bound to preserve himself, and not to quit his station wilfully, so by the like reason, when his own preservation comes not in competition, ought he, as much as he can, to preserve the rest of mankind, and may not, unless it be to do justice on an offender, take away, or impair the life, or what tends to the preservation of the life, the liberty, health, limb, or goods of another.

Sect. 7. And that all men may be restrained from invading others rights, and from doing hurt to one another, and the law of nature be observed, which willeth the peace and preservation of all mankind, the execution of the law of nature is, in that state, put into every man's hands, whereby every one has a right to punish the transgressors of that law to such a degree, as may hinder its violation: for the law of nature would, as all other laws that concern men in this world be in vain, if there were no body that in the state of nature had a power to execute that law, and thereby preserve the innocent and restrain offenders. And if any one in the state of nature may punish another for any evil he has done, every one may do so: for in that state of perfect equality, where naturally there is no superiority or jurisdiction of one over another, what any may do in prosecution of that law, every one must needs have a right to do.

Sect. 8. And thus, in the state of nature, one man comes by a power over another; but yet no absolute or arbitrary power, to use a criminal, when he has got him in his hands, according to the passionate heats, or boundless extravagancy of his own will; but only to retribute to him, so far as calm reason and conscience dictate, what is proportionate to his transgression, which is so much as may serve for reparation and restraint: for these two are the only reasons, why one man may lawfully do harm to another, which is that we call punishment. In transgressing the law of nature, the offender declares himself to live by another rule than that of reason and common equity, which is that measure God has set to the actions of men, for their mutual security; and so he becomes dangerous to mankind, the tye, which is to secure them from injury and violence, being slighted and broken by him. Which being a trespass against the whole species, and the peace and safety of it, provided for by the law of nature, every man upon this score, by the right he hath to preserve mankind in general, may restrain, or where it is necessary, destroy things noxious to them, and so may bring such evil on any one, who hath transgressed that law, as may make him repent the doing of it, and thereby deter him, and by his example others, from doing the like mischief. And in the case, and upon this ground, EVERY MAN HATH A RIGHT TO PUNISH THE OFFENDER, AND BE EXECUTIONER OF THE LAW OF NATURE.

Sect. 9. I doubt not but this will seem a very strange doctrine to some men: but before they condemn it, I desire them to resolve me, by what right any prince or state can put to death, or punish an alien, for any crime he commits in their country. It is certain their laws, by virtue of any sanction they receive from the promulgated will of the legislative, reach not a stranger: they speak not to him, nor, if they did, is he bound to hearken to them. The legislative authority, by which they are in force over the subjects of that commonwealth, hath no power over him. Those who have the supreme power of making laws in England, France or Holland, are to an Indian, but like the rest of the world, men without authority: and therefore, if by the law of nature every man hath not a power to punish offences against it, as he soberly judges the case to require, I see not how the magistrates of any community can punish an alien of another country; since, in reference to him, they can have no more power than what every man naturally may have over another.

Sect. 10. Besides the crime which consists in violating the law, and varying from the right rule of reason, whereby a man so far becomes degenerate, and declares himself to quit the principles of human nature, and to be a noxious creature, there is commonly injury done to some person or other, and some other man receives damage by his transgression: in which case he who hath received any damage, has, besides the right of punishment common to him with other men, a particular right to seek reparation from him that has done it: and any other person, who finds it just, may also join with him that is injured, and assist him in recovering from the offender so much as may make satisfaction for the harm he has suffered.

Sect. 11. From these two distinct rights, the one of punishing the crime for restraint, and preventing the like offence, which right of punishing is in every body; the other of taking reparation, which belongs only to the injured party, comes it to pass that the magistrate, who by being magistrate hath the common right of punishing put into his hands, can often, where the public good demands not the execution of the law, remit the punishment of criminal offences by his own authority, but yet cannot remit the satisfaction due to any private man for the damage he has received. That, he who has suffered the damage has a right to demand in his own name, and he alone can remit: the damnified person has this power of appropriating to himself the goods or service of the offender, by right of self-preservation, as every man has a power to punish the crime, to prevent its being committed again, by the right he has of preserving all mankind, and doing all reasonable things he can in order to that end: and thus it is, that every man, in the state of nature, has a power to kill a murderer, both to deter others from doing the like injury, which no reparation can compensate, by the example of the punishment that attends it from every body, and also to secure men from the attempts of a criminal, who having renounced reason, the common rule and measure God hath given to mankind, hath, by the unjust violence and slaughter he hath committed upon one, declared war against all mankind, and therefore may be destroyed as a lion or a tyger, one of those wild savage beasts, with whom men can have no society nor security: and upon this is grounded that great law of nature, Whoso sheddeth man's blood, by man shall his blood be shed. And Cain was so fully convinced, that every one had a right to destroy such a criminal, that after the murder of his brother, he cries out, Every one that findeth me, shall slay me; so plain was it writ in the hearts of all mankind.

Sect. 12. By the same reason may a man in the state of nature punish the lesser breaches of that law. It will perhaps be demanded, with death? I answer, each transgression may be punished to that degree, and with so much severity, as will suffice to make it an ill bargain to the offender, give him cause to repent, and terrify others from doing the like. Every offence, that can be committed in the state of nature, may in the state of nature be also punished equally, and as far forth as it may, in a commonwealth: for though it would be besides my present purpose, to enter here into the particulars of the law of nature, or its measures of punishment; yet, it is certain there is such a law, and that too, as intelligible and plain to a rational creature, and a studier of that law, as the positive laws of common-wealths; nay, possibly plainer; as much as reason is easier to be understood, than the fancies and intricate contrivances of men, following contrary and hidden interests put into words; for so truly are a great part of the municipal laws of countries, which are only so far right, as they are founded on the law of nature, by which they are to be regulated and interpreted.

Sect. 13. To this strange doctrine, viz. That in the state of nature every one has the executive power of the law of nature, I doubt not but it will be objected, that it is unrea-sonable for men to be judges in their own cases, that self-love will make men partial to themselves and their friends: and on the other side, that ill nature, passion and revenge will carry them too far in punishing others; and hence nothing but confusion and dis-order will follow, and that therefore God hath certainly appointed government to restrain the partiality and violence of men. I easily grant, that civil government is the proper remedy for the inconveniencies of the state of nature, which must certainly be great, where men may be judges in their own case, since it is easy to be imagined, that he who was so unjust as to do his brother an injury, will scarce be so just as to condemn himself for it: but I shall desire those who make this objection, to remember, that absolute mon-archs are but men; and if government is to be the remedy of those evils, which neces-sarily follow from men's being judges in their own cases, and the state of nature is therefore not to how much better it is than the state of nature, where one man, commanding a multitude, has the liberty to be judge in his own case, and may do to all his subjects what-ever he pleases, without the least liberty to any one to question or controul those who execute his pleasure? and in whatsoever he cloth, whether led by reason, mistake or pas-sion, must be submitted to? much better it is in the state of nature, wherein men are not bound to submit to the unjust will of another: and if he that judges, judges amiss in his own, or any other case, he is answerable for it to the rest of mankind.

Sect. 14. It is often asked as a mighty objection, where are, or ever were there any men in such a state of nature? To which it may suffice as an answer at present, that since all princes and rulers of independent governments all through the world, are in a state of nature, it is plain the world never was, nor ever will be, without numbers of men in that state. I have named all governors of independent communities, whether they are, or are not, in league with others: for it is not every compact that puts an end to the state of nature between men, but only this one of agreeing together mutually to enter into one community, and make one body politic; other promises, and compacts, men may make one with another, and yet still be in the state of nature. The promises and bargains for truck, &c. between the two men in the desert island, mentioned by Garcilasso de la Vega, in his history of Peru; or between a Swiss and an Indian, in the woods of America, are binding to them, though they are perfectly in a state of nature, in reference to one another: for truth and keeping of faith belongs to men, as men, and not as members of society.

Sect. 15. To those that say, there were never any men in the state of nature, I will not only oppose the authority of the judicious Hooker, Eccl. Pol. lib. i. sect. 10, where he says,

The laws which have been hitherto mentioned, i.e. the laws of nature, do bind men absolutely, even as they are men, although they have never any settled fellowship, never any solemn agreement amongst themselves what to do, or not to do: but forasmuch as we are not by ourselves sufficient to furnish ourselves with competent store of things, needful for such a life as our nature doth desire, a life fit for the dignity of man; therefore to supply those defects and imperfections which are in us, as living single and solely by ourselves, we are naturally induced to seek communion and fellowship with others: this was the cause of men's uniting themselves at first in politic societies.

But I moreover affirm, that all men are naturally in that state, and remain so, till by their own consents they make themselves members of some politic society; and I doubt not in the sequel of this discourse, to make it very clear.

2.3.7 Sir William Blackstone
Commentaries on the Laws of England in Four Books

Volume 1 [1753]

Section I. On the Study of the Law

Man, considered as a creature, must necessarily be subject to the laws of his Creator, for he is entirely a dependent being. A being, independent of any other, has no rule to pursue, but such as he prescribes to himself; but a state of dependence will inevitably oblige the inferior to take the will of him on whom he depends as the rule of his conduct; not, indeed, in every particular, but in all those points wherein his dependence consists. This principle, therefore, has more or less extent and effect, in proportion as the superiority of the one and the dependence of the other is greater or less, absolute or limited. And consequently, as man depends absolutely upon his Maker for every thing, it is necessary that he should, in all points, conform to his Maker's will.

This will of his Maker is called the law of nature. For as God, when he created matter, and endued it with a principle of mobility, established certain rules for the perpetual direction of that motion, so, when he created man, and endued him with free-will to conduct himself in all parts of life, he laid down certain immutable laws of human nature, whereby that free-will is in some degree regulated and restrained, and gave him also the faculty of reason to discover the purport of those laws.

Considering the Creator only as a being of infinite *power*, he was able unquestionably to have prescribed whatever laws he pleased to his creature, man, however unjust or severe. But, as he is also a being of infinite *wisdom*, he has laid down only such laws as were founded in those relations of justice that existed in the nature of things antecedent to any positive precept. These are the eternal immutable laws of good and evil, to which the Creator himself, in all his dispensations, conforms; and which he has enabled human reason to discover, so far as they are necessary for the conduct of human actions. Such, among others, are these principles: that we should live honestly, should hurt nobody, and should render to every one his due; to which three general precepts Justinian has reduced the whole doctrine of law.

Sir William Blackstone, *Commentaries on the Laws of England in Four Books*. Notes selected from the editions of Archibold, Christian, Coleridge, Chitty, Stewart, Kerr, and others, Barron Field's Analysis, and Additional Notes, and a Life of the Author by George Sharswood. In Two Volumes (Philadelphia: J.B. Lippincott Co., 1893).

But if the discovery of these first principles of the law of nature depended only upon the due exertion of right reason, and could not otherwise be obtained than by a chain of metaphysical disquisitions, mankind would have wanted some inducement to have quickened their inquiries, and the greater part of the world would have rested content in mental indolence, and ignorance its inseparable companion. As, therefore, the Creator is a being not only of infinite *power*, and *wisdom*, but also of infinite *goodness*, he has been pleased so to contrive the constitution and frame of humanity, that we should want no other prompter to inquire after and pursue the rule of right, but only our own self-love, that universal principle of action. For he has so intimately connected, so inseparably interwoven the laws of eternal justice with the happiness of each individual, that the latter cannot be attained but by observing the former; and, if the former be punctually obeyed, it cannot but induce the latter. In consequence of which mutual connection of justice and human felicity, he has not perplexed the law of nature with a multitude of abstracted rules and precepts, referring merely to the fitness or unfitness of things, as some have vainly surmised, but has graciously reduced the rule of obedience to this one paternal precept, "that man should pursue his own true and substantial happiness." This is the foundation of what we call ethics, or natural law; for the several articles into which it is branched in our systems, amount to no more than demonstrating that this or that action tends to man's real happiness, and therefore very justly concluding that the performance of it is a part of the law of nature; or, on the other hand, that this or that action is destructive of man's real happiness, and therefore that the law of nature forbids it.

This law of nature, being coeval with mankind, and dictated by God himself, is of course superior in obligation to any other. It is binding over all the globe in all countries, and at all times: no human laws are of any validity, if contrary to this; and such of them as are valid derive all their force and all their authority, mediately or immediately, from this original.

2.4 Modern

Introduction

Having set out classical, early Christian, medieval, and early modern writings within the central tradition of natural law thinking, the present section opens with a number of selections from the period immediately after World War II. These are representative of a considerable revival of interest in the central natural law tradition at that time, drawing upon an explosion of neo-Thomist scholarship in the nineteenth and early twentieth centuries,[1] which was given considerable focus by the abject failure of legal positivism in 1930s Germany to stem the tide of formally sanctioned evil.

The first selection is taken from a work – *The Natural Law: A Study in Legal and Social History and Philosophy* – by the German jurist and scholar Heinrich Rommen, who had witnessed first-hand the weaknesses of the Weimar judiciary in resisting the onslaught of Nazi ideology.[2] In this work he draws upon a discourse, popular among neo-Scholastics, rooting the rise of modern philosophy in the late medieval trend towards nominalism, giving it a particular jurisprudential focus, whereby the will escaped from under the control of the intellect to become an ever more arbitrary and self-destructive force. In this way, he sought to trace the deeper origins of the type of voluntaristic positivism which lay at the heart of what he termed "Adolf legalite." The extract reproduced here is an account of what was for Rommen perhaps the crucial moment in this wider story, namely William of Ockham's challenge to the synthetic balance reached during the high Middle Ages in the work of Thomas Aquinas. It is the outworking of this challenge in Renaissance and

[1] This is usually traced to the encyclical of Leo XIII, *Aeterni Patris* (1879), but it was also rooted in the work of a number of thinkers active before that time. For the broader developmental context see, among others: R. Cessario, *A Short History of Thomism* (Washington, DC: Catholic University of America Press, 2005); F. Kerr, *After Aquinas: Versions of Thomism* (Oxford: Blackwell, 2002); G. McCool, *From Unity to Pluralism: The Internal Evolution of Thomism* (New York: Fordham University Press, 1999); and A. MacIntyre, *Three Rival Versions of Moral Enquiry: Encyclopedia, Genealogy and Tradition* (South Bend, IN: University of Notre Dame Press, 1991).
[2] H. Rommen, *The Natural Law: A Study in Legal and Social History and Philosophy* (Indianapolis: Liberty Fund, 1998).

The Natural Law Reader, First Edition. Edited by Jacqueline A. Laing and Russell Wilcox.
© 2014 Blackwell Publishing Ltd. Published 2014 by Blackwell Publishing Ltd.

subsequent early modern writings, according to Rommen, that lies at the very heart of the modern project and the fundamental instabilities by which it is beset.

Rommen was one of a group of European émigrés, including Eric Voegelin, Leo Strauss, and Hannah Arendt, arriving in the United States in the late 1930s and early 1940s, and united in its determination to highlight the close association between modern totalitarianism and the project of disembodied, Enlightenment reason. Beyond sharing in the common emphases of this group on the inadequacy of the Romantic reaction as a basis for sustainable resistance to the Enlightenment project and its highlighting of the contrasts between ancient and modern philosophy, Rommen's brand of analysis was distinguished by its rootedness in scholastic (specifically Thomistic) thought, by its belief in the fecundity of the central natural law tradition, and by a willingness to employ the categories of that tradition in a constructive and speculative manner.

Two other émigré thinkers who did follow, even exceed, Rommen in each of these respects were Jacques Maritain and Yves Simon, the authors of the following two extracts. In the first, taken from Maritain's famous work *Man and State*, Maritain offers a summary of traditional natural law thinking in terms comprehensible to the modern reader.[3] Dividing his reflections between a consideration of its ontological and gnoseological or epistemological elements, Maritain characterizes natural law at its base as the "normality of functioning of the human form."[4] In so doing, Maritain represents a wider attempt to demonstrate the relevance of classical categories to contemporary political debate and, specifically, the requirement that post-war democracy be grounded upon a philosophically robust conception of the person.

The second extract, taken from an early lecture by Yves Simon, details an important component of his own attempt to show the relevance of these categories to the modern world: an attempt which eventually found its fullest expression in his work *The Philosophy of Democratic Government*.[5] Simon argued more generally on a non-liberal, natural law, basis to the conclusion that representative democracy most effectively actualizes the properly *political* nature of a given regime, first, because it grounds the most effective institutional means for resisting bad government, and secondly, because it helps realize a natural human tendency to self-government by allowing the governed to remain actively engaged in political decision-making to the widest possible degree. In the particular extract reproduced here, Simon argues against the view that political authority and personal autonomy are in perennial conflict. Rather, he argues that they complement one another since the quest for genuine autonomy, owing to the nature of the human person and the moral law that protects it, must always be sought in community, never in isolation. For Simon, then, it will be the task of some organ of the community, exercising political authority, to choose the means to the common good, but always and only in accordance with respect for the principle of autonomy or subsidiarity. In this way, the principles of authority and autonomy represent mutually constituting limitations one upon the other.

If the United States benefited in the immediate post-war period from the wave of emigration from Nazi occupation, it was accompanied by an altogether more sympathetic

---

[3]   J. Maritain, *Man and State* (Chicago: University of Chicago Press, 1950), Chap. IV.

[4]   Ibid.

[5]   Y. Simon, *The Philosophy of Democratic Government* (South Bend, IN: University of Notre Dame Press, 1993).

treatment of the central natural law tradition in theory and practice among the post-war European states themselves. In scholarship, this is represented here in a brief extract from a well-known work by the influential and distinguished Italian historian of medieval political philosophy, Passerin D'Entreves,[6] and, perhaps a little more ambiguously, in the 1945 piece, "Five Minutes of Legal Philosophy," by neo-Kantian and former Weimar minister of justice Gustav Radbruch.[7] In practice, it was represented by the striking post-war development of a form of natural law jurisprudence by Germany's federal constitutional court.[8] It was also a trend reflected in the flourishing of the Christian Democratic movement – inspired particularly by natural law-based Catholic social teaching – under such figures as Konrad Adenauer, Alcide de Gasperi, and Robert Schuman, whose moral vision formed the basis of their commitment to reconstructing the European mainland on principles of subsidiarity and human dignity so lacking in the totalitarian experiments of the earlier parts of the century.[9] Their achievements, however, were soon dissipated or distorted beyond recognition by subsequent generations.

Outside of the political establishment, even in its reconstituted form, the ongoing and radically critical potential of the idea that there exists a standard of right reason by which to judge the expedient present is amply demonstrated in the next three selections. The first of these is taken from Elizabeth Anscombe's 1956 leaflet, "Mr Truman's Degree," in which she explains her objection to the proposal that Harry S. Truman should receive an honorary degree from the University of Oxford. Anscombe was of the view that Truman's decision to drop atomic bombs on Hiroshima and Nagasaki as a means of terrorizing Japan into submission could not be justified, was an instance of mass murder, and therefore disqualified him from receiving such an honor. For Anscombe, "[c]hoosing to kill the innocent as a means to your ends is always murder,"[10] and this was precisely what the atomic bombings amounted to. Applying something like the principle of double effect, she contrasts this instance of killing as a means to one's end with that of causing death as a side-effect of a licit act of self-defense.

The second selection comprises a set of brief extracts taken from the writings of Mohandas Karamchand Gandhi. Gandhi is principally known as the leader of the movement for Indian independence. His approach to life, to achieving Indian independence, and many of his words and deeds, however, all suggest his place as a teacher and a great exponent of tenets identical to those espoused in the central natural law tradition. Not only is Gandhi committed to a higher law, moral objectivity, and moral truth, his *satyagraha* or truth-force movement gave rise to his method of non-violent resistance. His understanding

[6]   A. D'Entreves, "A Rational Foundation of Ethics," Chap. II in *Natural Law: An Introduction to Legal Philosophy* (London: Hutchinson University Library Series, 1951), pp. 33–47.

[7]   G. Radbruch, "Five Minutes of Legal Philosophy," trans. J. King (2011). Gustav Radbruch, *Fünf Minuten Rechtsphilosophie* first published in RheinNeckarZeitung, 12th September 1945, reprinted in Gustav Radbruch, *Gesamtausgabe* (*Collected Works*), 20 Volumes, Arthur Kaufmann (ed.), vol 3: Winifried Hasemer (ed.) Heidelberg: C. F. Müller, 1990, 78–9. Tr.Julia C. King

[8]   See E. Von Hippel, "The Role of Natural Law in the Legal Decisions of the German Federal Republic," *4 Natural Law Forum*, 106 (1959).

[9]   See A. Fimister, *Robert Schuman: Neo-Scholastic Humanism and the Reunification of Europe* (New York: Peter Lang, gand 2008).

[10]   G.E.M. Anscombe, "Mr Truman' Degree," pamphlet published by the author (Oxford, 1956).

of *satyagraha* springs out of a belief that the cosmos is created by a supreme intelligence and that injustice does not bind the human conscience. *Satyagraha* bears on one's very soul. Because it is not permissible to do evil that good may come, *satyagraha*, and with it the way of non-violent resistance, is his licit way of challenging unjust law. "An unjust law is itself a species of violence. Arrest for its breach is more so."[11]

Like Gandhi, Martin Luther King, Jr., as the leading voice of the American civil rights movement, has become something of a totemic figure in the struggle for racial and political equality. Yet, if Gandhi can be said to have forwarded something substantially the same as a natural law position in the central tradition, the extract reproduced here from King's famous "Letter from a Birmingham Jail" demonstrates that his adherence to that tradition was explicit. In this letter King formulates his response to a statement made by Alabama clerics in April 1963 entitled "A Call for Unity," in which they argued that the social injustices that existed should be fought in the courts and not in the streets. Relying on Aquinas' dictum, taken over from Augustine, that an unjust law is no law at all, King argues that there comes a point when injustice is so great that the only appropriate course is civil disobedience.

The final two selections bring the central tradition of natural law thinking into the contemporary era. The first is a summary statement of what has come to be known as "New Natural Law theory" by one of its principal architects, John Finnis, and upon the basis of which a good deal of more applied contemporary natural law theorizing has taken place. Although brief, the piece reproduced here gives a good sense of the New Natural Law position. Supplementing a little, however, the distinguishing features of that position may be stated, following Christopher Tollefsen,[12] in three central theses: first, practical or action-orientated reason grasps a number of basic goods which give it irreducible or foundational reasons of action, are constitutive of genuine human flourishing for all human agents, are self-evidently desirable, and are not epistemologically dependent upon theoretical reason about the nature of the human being. Various catalogues of these basic goods have been given, and they seem to have undergone some sort of evolution in the works of most of the theory's principal proponents.

Secondly, these basic goods are said to be incommensurable; there is held to be no natural hierarchy of basic human goods such that one basic good can be sacrificed for the sake of another or that one such good "may be said to offer all the good of another plus more."[13] Each basic good is uniquely beneficial and desirable: "each offers something that the other goods do not."[14] Finally, the judgments of practical reason in their recognition of the basic goods, although a condition of morally charged human action, are not, in themselves, moral. Rather, "[m]orality enters in only at the level of deliberation and choice as regards which goods, or which instantiations of goods, to pursue when faced with the less desirable options for choice,"[15] and it is in the context of this sort of

---

[11] Thomas Merton (ed.), *Gandhi on Non-Violence: Selected Texts from Mohandas K. Gandhi, Non-Violence in Peace and War* (New York: New Direction Books, 1967, 2007), p. 88.

[12] C. Tollefsen, "The New Natural Law Theory," *Lyceum* 10, 1, http://lyceumphilosophy.com/?q=node/97, accessed March 27, 2013.

[13] Ibid., p. 2.

[14] Ibid., p. 3.

[15] Ibid.

deliberation that a first principle of morality – here formulated as "integral human fulfillment" – is laid down by the New Naturalists to capture "a reasonable openness to all goods across all persons."[16]

As will be seen in subsequent sections, all of these theses have been subject to criticism by thinkers within the central tradition and, then, from quite different directions and perspectives. Yet, it seems that whatever its inherent merits, New Natural Law theory has provoked something of an upsurge of interest even in the more conventional formulations of the central natural law position, such that these also have been subject to a number of imaginative recoveries and re-engagements. It is appropriate, then, that the present section closes with a selection from one of the most celebrated of these recoveries; that found in the work of Servais Pinckaers.[17] Occasion will be had to return to Pinckaers, but here the extract chosen focuses upon his contention that a proper conception of natural law morality is rooted not just in the metaphysics of the human person as disclosed by three sets of inclinations ordered in hierarchical but mutually inclusive fashion operating at different levels of its being, but also in a correct, metaphysically robust, understanding of the good itself. The enormous historical scholarship in which Pinckaers grounds all his discussions is only hinted at in the present selection, but it is one of the factors which makes him an ideal interlocutor for the New Naturalists and suggests the potential for an ever-richer internal dialogue in the decades to come.

---

[16] Ibid.
[17] S. Pinckaers, *The Sources of Christian Ethics*, tr. M. Noble (Washington, DC: Catholic University of America Press, 1995), pp. 400–423.

2.4.1 Heinrich Rommen
The Natural Law: A Study in Legal and Social History and Philosophy

[…] Good is to be done: such is the supreme commandment of the natural moral law. The highest and basic norm of the natural law in the narrow sense, then, may be stated thus: Justice is to be done. Yet this principle is altogether general. It needs still to be determined to what extent the object striven for by means of a concrete action is a true good. This is done more or less with the aid of a syllogism (which, of course, is not worked out in every case by concrete reasoning): Good is to be done; this action is good, it strives after a good; it is therefore to be performed. Good is that which corresponds to the essential nature. The being of a thing also reveals its purpose in the order of creation, and in its perfect fulfillment it is likewise the end or goal of its growth and development. The essential nature is thus the measure. What corresponds to it is good; what is contrary to it is bad. The measure of goodness, consequently, is the essential idea of a thing and the proportionateness thereto of actions and of other things. That is, "Good is to be done" means the same as "Realize your essential nature." Moreover, since this essential nature issued from God's creative will and wisdom in both its existence and its quiddity, the principle continues: "You thereby realize the will of God, which is truly manifested to you in the knowledge of your essential nature." The same being is truth to the theoretical reason, and goodness to the practical reason.

The train of thought thereupon widens. It follows that there are some actions which, because they correspond to the essential nature and its end, are in themselves good, moral, just; and that there are others which, because they are at variance therewith, are in themselves bad, immoral, unjust. At any rate, this is true on the assumption that both in God and in man the intellect, not the will, holds the primacy. For a natural moral law as an immutable basic norm, and the essential nature as a valid measure of what is moral and just, are possible only when this essence is itself unalterable. This presupposes, however, that the essential nature owes its idea, its quiddity, and its existence to the unchangeable essence of God Himself, of which they are reflections. "If, too, human nature is the immediate measure of moral goodness, it can be the norm of unalterable moral judgments only insofar as it itself embodies the idea of man as this rests from all eternity in the divine mind. But the ideas of things in the divine mind are, in their content, nothing

H. Rommen, *The Natural Law: A Study in Legal and Social History and Philosophy*, tr. Thomas R. Hanley. Introduction and Bibliography by Russell Hittinger (Indianapolis: Liberty Fund, 1998).

else than the images through which God knows His own essence as imitable. This is true also of the idea of man."[1]

The divine essence and, in one and the same act, the divine knowledge thereof and the creative will of God, likewise thereby informed in one and the same act, are (or rather, is) the basis for the essential nature and its immutability. "That God of necessity enacts and cannot alter that law which we call the natural law comes merely from the fact that His will cannot do away with His most perfect essence, that God cannot be at variance with Himself and cannot, as the Apostle says, deny Himself" (Kleutgen). This is the fundamental reason for rejecting moral and legal positivism. The will is not the law; on the contrary, it can only be right law when it is guided even in God by reason and intellect. "But to say that justice depends upon mere will is to say that the divine will does not proceed according to the order of wisdom, which is blasphemy."[2]

[…] With Duns Scotus (d. *cir.* 1308), and with the principle of the primacy of the will over the intellect so much emphasized by him, there began inside moral philosophy a train of thought which in later centuries would recur in secularized form in the domain of legal philosophy. The principle that law is will would be referred in legal positivism, as well as in the theory of will in jurisprudence, to the earthly lawmaker (self-obligation).

For Duns Scotus morality depends on the will of God. A thing is good not because it corresponds to the nature of God or, analogically, to the nature of man, but because God so wills. Hence the *lex naturalis* could be other than it is even materially or as to content, because it has no intrinsic connection with God's essence, which is self-conscious in His intellect. For Scotus, therefore, the laws of the second table of the Decalogue were no longer unalterable. The crux of theology, namely, the problem of the apparent dispensations from the natural law mentioned in the Old Testament and thus seemingly granted by God (the command to sacrifice Isaac, Raphael's apparent lie, Osee's alleged adultery, the polygamy of the patriarchs, and so on), was now readily solved. Yet St. Thomas, too, had been able to solve such cases. Now, however, an evolution set in which, in the doctrine of William of Occam (d. *cir.* 1349) on the natural moral law, would lead to pure moral positivism, indeed to nihilism.

The will is the nobler faculty; the intellect is but the ministering torch-bearer of the will, which is the master. Between God's essence and that of man there exists, apart from the fact of creation, no inherent connection, no analogy of being. Hence, too, there exists no unchangeable moral order grounded in the nature of things, in the ordered universe of being and value. As all being is founded on the mere absolute will of God without participation in His essence, so all oughtness or obligation rests solely on the same absolute will. Oughtness is without foundation in reality, just as the universals are merely vocal utterances (*flatus vocis*) and not mental images of the necessary being of the ideas in God. In this way Occam arrived at a heightened supernaturalism, but only to deprive almost completely the natural order of its value.

For Occam the natural moral law is positive law, divine will. An action is not good because of its suitableness to the essential nature of man, wherein God's archetypal idea of man is represented according to being and oughtness, but because God so wills. God's will could also have willed and decreed the precise opposite, which would then possess the same binding force as that which is now valid – which, indeed, has validity only as long as God's absolute will so determines. Law is will, pure will without any foundation in reality, without foundation in the essential nature of things. Thus, too, sin no longer contains any intrinsic element of immorality, or what is unjust, any inner element of injustice; it is an external offense against the will of God.

As a result, Occam, who sees only individual phenomena, not universals, the concepts of essences, can likewise admit no teleological orientation toward God is inherent in all creation and especially in man; or at least he cannot grant that it can be known. The unity of being, truth, and goodness does not exist for him. Moral goodness consists in mere external agreement with God's absolute will, which, subject only to His arbitrary decree, can always change. To such an extent were God's omnipotence and free will extolled that much subtle speculation was devoted to the question of whether God can, through His absolute power, will hatred of Himself; a question which Occam and many of his disciples answered in the affirmative. Man sins, therefore, because and only so far as a positive law, by which he is bound, stands over him. God, on the other hand, cannot sin because no law stands above Him, not because it is repugnant to His holiness. Hence there exists no unchangeable *lex naturalis*, no natural law that inwardly governs the positive law. Positive law and natural law, which indeed is also positive law, stand likewise in no inner relation to each other. The identity of this thought structure with *The Prince* of Machiavelli, with the *Leviathan* of Hobbes, and with the theory of will of modern positivism (the will of the absolute sovereign is law, because no higher norm stands above him) is here quite obvious.

Notes

1   Viktor Cathrein, S.J., *Moralphilosophie* (2 vols., 4th ed., Freiburg im Breisgau: Herdersche Verlag-shandlung, 1904), I, 185 f. All this, too, should enable one to appreciate the profound statement of St. Thomas: "We do not wrong God unless we wrong our own good" (*Summa contra Gentiles*, Bk. III, chap. 122).

2   St. Thomas, *De veritate*, q.23, a.6.

2.4.2 Jacques Maritain
Man and State

Shall we try to reestablish our faith in human rights on the basis of a true philosophy? This true philosophy of the rights of the human person is based upon the true idea of natural law, as looked upon in an ontological perspective and as conveying through the essential structures and requirements of created nature the wisdom of the Author of Being.

The genuine idea of natural law is a heritage of Greek and Christian thought. It goes back not only to Grotius, who indeed began deforming it, but, before him to Suarez and Francisco de Vitoria; and further back to St. Thomas Aquinas (he alone grasped the matter in a wholly consistent doctrine, which unfortunately was expressed in an insufficiently clarified vocabulary,[1] so that its deepest features were soon overlooked and disregarded); and still further back to St. Augustine and the Church Fathers and St. Paul (we remember St. Paul's saying: "When the Gentiles who have not the Law, *do by nature* the things contained in the Law, these, having not the Law, are a law unto themselves...");[2] and even further back to Cicero, to the Stoics, to the great moralists of antiquity and its great poets, particularly Sophocles. Antigone, who was aware that in transgressing the human law and being crushed by it she was obeying a better commandment, the *unwritten and unchangeable laws*, is the eternal heroine of natural law: for, as she puts it, they were not, those unwritten laws, born out of today's or yesterday's sweet will, "but they live always and forever, and no man knows from where they have arisen."[3]

The First Element (Ontological) in Natural Law

Since I have not time here to discuss nonsense (we can always find very intelligent philosophers, not to quote Mr. Bertrand Russell, to defend it most brilliantly) I am taking it for granted that we admit that there is a human nature, and this human nature is the same in all men. I am taking it for granted that we also admit that man is a being gifted with intelligence, and who, as such, acts with an understanding of what he is doing, and therefore with the power to determine for himself the ends which he pursues. On the other hand, possessed of a nature, or an ontologic structure which is a locus of intelligible

Jacques Maritain, *Man and State* (Chicago: University of Chicago Press, 1950), Chap. IV. Reprinted with permission of University of Chicago Press.

necessities, man possesses ends which necessarily correspond to his essential constitution and which are the same for all – as all pianos, for instance, whatever their particular type and in whatever spot they may be, have as their end the production of certain attuned sounds. If they do not produce these sounds they must be tuned, or discarded as worthless. But since man is endowed with intelligence and determines his own ends, it is up to him to put himself in tune with the ends necessarily demanded by his nature. This means that there is, by the very virtue of human nature, an order or a disposition which human reason can discover and according to which the human will must act in order to attune itself to the essential and necessary ends of the human being. The unwritten law, or natural law, is nothing more than that.

The example that I just used – taken from the world of human workmanship – was purposely crude and provocative; yet did not Plato himself have recourse to the idea of any work of human art whatever, the idea of the Bed, the idea of the Table, in order to make clear his theory (which I do not share) of eternal Ideas? What I mean is that every being has its own natural law, as well as it has its own essence. Any kind of thing produced by human industry has, like the stringed instrument that I brought up a moment ago, its own natural law, that is, the *normality of its functioning*, the proper way in which, by reason of its specific construction, it demands to be put into action, it "*should*" be used. Confronted with any supposedly unknown gadget, be it a corkscrew or a peg-top or a calculating machine or an atom bomb, children or scientists, in their eagerness to discover how to use it, will not question the existence of that inner typical law.

Any kind of thing existing in nature, a plant, a dog, a horse, has its own natural law, that is, the *normality of its functioning*, the proper way in which, by reason of its specific structure and specific ends, it "*should*" achieve fulness of being either in its growth or in its behavior. Washington Carver, when he was a child and healed sick flowers in his garden, had an obscure knowledge, both by intelligence and congeniality, of that vegetative law of theirs. Horse-breeders have an experiential knowledge, both by intelligence and congeniality, of the natural law of horses, a natural law with respect to which a horse's behavior makes him a *good horse* or a *vicious horse* in the herd. Well, horses do not enjoy free will, their natural law is but a part of the immense network of essential tendencies and regulations involved in the movement of the cosmos, and the individual horse who fails in that equine law only obeys the universal order of nature on which the deficiencies of his individual nature depend. If horses were free, there would be an ethical way of conforming to the specific natural law of horses, but that horsy morality is a dream because horses are not free.

When I said a moment ago that the natural law of all beings existing in nature is the proper way in which, by reason of the specific\nature and specific ends, they *should* achieve fulness of being in their behavior, this very word *should* had only a metaphysical meaning (as we say that a good or a normal eye "should" be able to read letters on a blackboard from a given distance). The same word *should* starts to have a *moral* meaning, that is, to imply moral obligation, when we pass the threshold of the world of free agents. Natural law for man is *moral* law, because man obeys or disobeys it freely, not necessarily, and because human behavior pertains to a particular, privileged order which is irreducible to the general order of the cosmos and tends to a final and superior to the immanent common good of the cosmos.

What I am emphasizing is the first basic element to be recognized in natural law, namely the *ontological* element, I mean the *normality of functioning* which is grounded on the essence of that being: man. Natural law in general, as we have just seen, is the ideal formula of development of a given being; it might be compared with an algebraical equation to which a curve develops in space, yet with man the curve has freely to conform to the equation. Let us say, then, that in its ontological aspect, natural law is an *ideal order* relating to human actions, a *divide* between the suitable and the unsuitable, the proper and the improper, which depends on human nature or essence and the unchangeable necessities rooted in it. I do not mean that the proper regulation for each possible human situation is contained in the human essence, as Leibniz believed that every event in the life of Caesar was contained beforehand in the idea of Caesar. Human situations are something existential. Neither they nor their appropriate regulations are contained of that essence. Any given situation, for instance the situation of Cain with regard to Abel, implies a relation to the essence of man, and the possible murder of the one by the other is incompatible with the general ends and innermost dynamic structure of that rational essence. It is rejected by it. Hence the prohibition of murder is grounded on or required by the essence of man. The precept thou shalt do no murder, is a precept of natural law. Because a primordial and most general end of human nature is to preserve being – the being of that existent who is a person, and a universe unto himself; and because man insofar as he is man has a right to live.

Suppose a completely new case or situation, unheard of in human history: suppose, for instance, that what we now call *genocide* were as new as that very name. In the fashion that I just explained, that possible behavior will face the human essence as incompatible with its general ends and innermost dynamic structure: that is to say, as prohibited by natural law. The condemnation of genocide by the General Assembly of the United Nations has sanctioned the prohibition of the crime in question by natural law – which does not mean that that prohibition was part of the essence of man as I know not what metaphysical feature eternally inscribed in it – nor that it was a notion recognized from the start by the conscience of humanity.

To sum up, let us say that natural law is something both *ontological* and *ideal*. It is something *ideal*, because it is grounded on the human essence and its unchangeable structure and the intelligible necessities it involves. Natural law is something *ontological*, because the human essence is an ontological reality, which moreover does not exist separately, but in every human being, so that by the same taken natural law dwells as an ideal order in the very being of all existing men.

In that first consideration, or with regard to the basic *ontological* element it implies, natural law is coextensive with the whole field of natural moral regulations, the whole field of natural morality. Not only the primary and fundamental regulations but the slightest regulations of natural ethics mean conformity to natural law – say, natural obligations or rights of which we perhaps have now no idea, and of which men will become aware in a distant future.

An angel who knew the human essence in his angelic manner and all the possible existential situations of man would know natural law in the infinity of its extension. But we do not. Though the Eighteenth Century theoreticians believed they did.

The Second Element (Gnoseological) in Natural Law

Thus we arrive at the *second* basic element to be recognized in natural law, namely natural law *as known*, and thus as measuring in actual fact human practical reason, which is the measure of human acts.

Natural law is not a written law. Men know it with greater or less difficulty, and in different degrees, running the risk of error here as elsewhere. The only practical knowledge all men have naturally and infallibly in common as a self-evident principle, intellectually perceived by virtue of the concepts involved, is that we must do good and avoid evil. This is the preamble and the principle of natural law; it is not the law itself. Natural law is the ensemble of things to do and not to do which follow therefrom in *necessary* fashion. That every sort of error and deviation is possible in the determination of these things merely proves that our sight is weak, our nature coarse, and that innumerable accidents can corrupt our judgment. Montaigne maliciously remarked that, among certain peoples, incest and thievery were considered virtuous acts. Pascal was scandalized by this. All this proves nothing against natural law, any more than a mistake in addition proves anything against arithmetic, or the mistakes of certain primitive peoples, for whom the stars were holes in the tent which covered the world, prove anything against astronomy.

Natural law is an unwritten law. Man's knowledge of it has increased little by little as man's moral conscience has developed. The latter was at first in a twilight state. Anthropologists have taught us within what structures of tribal life and in the midst of what half-awakened magic it was primitively formed. This proves merely that the knowledge men have had of the unwritten law has passed through more diverse forms and stages than certain philosophers or theologians have believed. The knowledge which our own moral conscience has of this law is doubtless still imperfect, and very likely it will continue to develop and to become more refined as long as humanity exists. Only when the Gospel has penetrated to the very depth of human substance will natural law appear in its flower and its perfection.

So the law and the knowledge of the law are two different things. Yet the law has force of law only when it is promulgated. It is only insofar as it is known and expressed in assertions of practical reason that natural law has force of law.

At this point let us stress that human reason does not discover the regulations of natural law in an abstract and theoretical manner, as a series of geometrical theorems. Nay more, it does not discover them through the conceptual exercise of the intellect, or by way of rational knowledge. I think that Thomas Aquinas's teaching, here, should be understood in a much deeper and more precise fashion than is usual. When he said that human reason discovers the regulations of natural law through the guidance of the *inclinations* of human nature, he means that the very mode or manner in which human reason knows natural law is not rational knowledge, but knowledge *through inclination*.[4] That kind of knowledge is not clear knowledge through concepts and conceptual judgments; it is obscure, unsystematic, vital knowledge by connaturality or congeniality, in which the intellect, in order to bear judgment, consults and listens to the inner melody that the vibrating strings of abiding tendencies make present in the subject.[5]

When one has clearly seen this basic fact, and when, moreover, one has realized that St. Thomas's views on the matter call for an historical approach and a philosophical enforcement of the idea of development that the Middle Ages were not equipped to carry into effect, then at last one is enabled to get a completely comprehensive concept of Natural Law. And one understands that the human knowledge of natural law has been progressively shaped and molded by the inclinations of human nature, starting from the most basic ones. Do not expect me to offer an a priori picture of those genuine inclinations which are rooted in man's being as vitally permeated with the preconscious life of the mind, and which either developed or were released as the movement of mankind went on. They are evinced by the very history of human conscience. Those inclinations *were really genuine* which in the immensity of the human past have guided reason in becoming aware, little by little, of the regulations that have been most definitely and most generally recognized by the human race, starting from the most ancient social communities. For the knowledge of the primordial aspects of natural law was first expressed in social patterns rather than in personal judgments: so that we might say that our knowledge has developed within the double protecting tissue of human inclinations and human society.

With regard to the second basic element, the element of knowledge which natural law implies in order to have force of law, it thus can be said that natural law – that is, natural law *naturally known*, or, more exactly, natural law *the knowledge of which is embodied in the most general and most ancient heritage* of mankind – covers only the field of ethical regulations of which men have become aware by virtue of knowledge *through inclination*, and which are *basic principles* in moral life – progressively recognized from the most common principles to the more and more specific ones.

Let us now discuss further some problems which deal with human rights in general. My first point will relate to the distinction between Natural Law and Positive Law. One of the main errors of the rationalist philosophy of human rights has been to regard positive law as a mere transcript traced off from natural law, which would supposedly prescribe in the name of Nature all that which positive law prescribes in the name of society. They forgot the immense field of human things which depend on the variable conditions of social life and on the free initiative of human reason, and which natural law leaves undertermined.

As I have pointed out, *natural law* deals with the rights and the duties which are connected in a *necessary* manner with the first principle: "Do good and avoid evil." This is why the precepts of the unwritten law are in themselves or in the nature of things (I am not saying in man's knowledge of them) universal and invariable.

Jus gentium, or the *Law of Nations*, is difficult to define exactly, because it is intermediary between natural law and positive law. Let us say that in its deepest and most genuine meaning, such as put forward by Thomas Aquinas, the law of nations, or better to say, the common law of civilization, differs from natural law because it is *known*, not through inclination, but through the *conceptual exercise of reason*, or through rational knowledge,[6] in this sense it pertains to positive law, and formally constitutes a juridical order (though not necessarily written in a code). But as concerns its content, *jus gentium* comprises both things which belong also to natural law (insofar as they are not only known as rationally inferred, but also known through inclination) and things which –though obligatory in a universal manner, since concluded from a principle of natural law – are beyond the content of natural law (because they are *only* rationally inferred, and not known through inclination). In both cases *jus gentium* or the common law of civilization deals, like natural law, with rights and duties which are connected with the first principle in a necessary manner. And precisely because it is known through rational knowledge, and is itself a work of reason, it is more especially concerned with such rights and duties as exist in the realm of the basic natural work achieved by human reason, that is, the state of civil life.

Positive Law, or the body of laws (either customary law or statute law) in force in a given social group, deals with the rights and the duties which are connected with the first principle, but in a *contingent* manner, by virtue of the determinate ways of conduct set down by the reason and the will of man when they institute the laws or give birth to the customs of a particular society, thus stating of themselves that in the particular group in question certain things will be good and permissible, certain other things bad and not permissible.

But it is by virtue of natural law that the Law of Nations and positive law take on the force of law, and impose themselves upon the conscience. They are a prolongation or an extension of natural law, passing into objective zones which can less and less be sufficiently determined by the essential inclinations of human nature. For it is *natural law itself which requires that whatever it leaves undetermined shall subsequently be determined*, either as a right or a duty existing for all men, and of which they are made aware, not by knowledge through inclination, but by conceptual reason – that's for *jus gentium* – or – this is for positive law – as a right or a duty existing for certain men by reason of the human and contingent regulations proper to the social group of which they are a part.

Notes

1   Especially because the vocabulary of the *Commentary on the Sentences*, as concerns the "primary" and "secondary" precepts of Natural Law, is at variance with the vocabulary of the *Summa Theologica*, I–II, qu. 94. Thomas's respect for the stock phrases of the jurists also causes some trouble, particularly when it comes to Ulpian.
2   Paul, Romans, 2:14.
3   "Nor did I deem Your ordinance of so much binding force, As that a mortal man could over-bear The unchangeable unwritten code of Heaven; This is not of today and yesterday, But lives forever, having origin.

    Whence no man knows; whose sanctions I were loath
    In Heaven' sight to provoke, fearing the will Of any man."
                           (Sophocles *Antigone* II, 452–60, George Young's translation)

4   This is, in my opinion, the real meaning implied by St. Thomas, even though he did not use the very expression when treating of Natural Law. Knowledge through inclination is generally understood in all his doctrine on Natural Law. It alone makes this doctrine perfectly consistent. It alone squares with such statements as the following ones: "Omnia illa ad quae homo *habet naturalem incliationem. ratio naturaliter apprehendit ut bona*, et per consequens ut opere prosequenda; et contraria corum. ut mala et vitanda" (S.T., I–II, qu. 94, a. 2); "Ad legem naturae pertinet omne illud ad quod homo inclinatur secundum naturam…. Sed, si loquamur de actibus virtuosis secundum seipsos, prout scilicet in propriis speciebus considerantur, sic *non* omnes actus virtuosi sunt de lege naturae. Multa enirn secundum virtutem fiunt *ad quae natura non priano inclinat; sed per rationis inquisitionem ca homines adinvenerunt*, quasi utilia ad bene vivendum" (S.T., I–II, qu. 94, a. 3). The matter has been somewhat obscured because of the perpetual comparison that St. Thomas uses in these articles between the speculative and the practical intellect, and by reason of which he speaks of the *propria principia* of Natural Law as "*quasi conclusiones principiorum communium*" (I–II, qu. 94, a. 4). As a matter of fact, those *propria principia* or specific precepts of Natural Law are in no way conclusions rationally deduced; they play in the practical realm a part *similar* to that of conclusions in the speculative realm. (And they appear as inferred conclusions to the "after-knowledge" of the philosophers who have to reflect upon and explain the precepts of Natural Law).

5   According to St. Thomas (S.T., I–II, qu. 95, a. 4) *jus gentium* – which he sharply distinguishes
     from natural law and connects rather with positive law – is concerned with all things that
     derive from natural law as *conclusions* from principles.

     Yet he also teaches that the *propria principia* of Natural Law are like conclusions derived
     from *principia communia* (S.T., I–II, qu. 94, a. 4–6). And assuredly the *propria principia* of
     natural law belong to Natural Law, not to *jus gentium!* Well, in qu. 95, a. 2, St. Thomas gives the
     prohibition of murder as an example of a conclusion derived from a principle of natural law
     ("do nobody evil"), and pertaining to what is defined as *jus gentium* in art. 4. It is obvious,
     however, that the prohibition of murder, which is inscribed in the Decalogue, is a precept of
     natural law. What then?

     The only way to realize the inner consistency of all that, and correctly to grasp the Thomis-
     tic distinction between Natural Law and *jus gentium*, is to understand that a precept which *is
     like* a conclusion derived from a principle of natural law but which in actual fact is *known
     through inclination, not through rational deduction*, is part of *natural law*; but that a precept
     which *is known through rational deduction*, and as a *conclusion conceptually inferred* from a
     principle of natural law, is part of *jus gentium*. The latter pertains to positive law more than to
     natural law precisely by virtue of the manner in which it is known and because of the interven-
     tion of human reason in the establishment of the precepts conceptually concluded (whereas
     the *only* reason on which natural law depends is divine Reason). The prohibition of murder, in
     so far as this precept is *known by inclination*, belongs to natural law. The same prohibition of
     murder, if this precept is known as a conclusion *nationally* inferred from a principle of natural
     law, pertains to *jus gentium*.

2.4.3 Yves Simon
Nature and Functions of Authority

[…] Among the various meanings of the notion of liberty, we have to distinguish, fundamentally, an *initial* liberty and a *terminal* liberty. Initial liberty is the sheer power of choosing, I mean the power of choosing the good and the evil as well. This liberty, which immediately flows from our rational nature, this liberty that we are provided with by the very fact that we are given our rational nature, can be used rightly as well as wrongly, and has the value of a means rather than that of an end. Now, at the term of our endeavor to improve our nature by supplementing it with virtues, another liberty appears, which is a power of choosing the good alone. The process through which this terminal liberty is secured consists in an interiorization of the law. The virtuous man is no longer subjected to the law, since the law has become interior to him and rules him from within. The prescriptions of the law are truly identical with the dynamism of the virtuous nature. Terminal liberty does not mean only freedom of choice, but also autonomy.

Now, while initial freedom is but a mixed perfection, a *perfectio mixta* in the precise meaning this expression has in metaphysical language, terminal liberty is an absolute perfection, a *perfectio simpliciter simplex*, a perfection whose concept does not involve any kind of imperfection and which must be attributed to God in a formal sense. So defined, liberty is a divine name. I would even say that it occupies a singular position among the absolute perfections. Consider, indeed, that every being, inasmuch as it *is*, enjoys some amount of autonomy. The basic statement that every nature is the realization of an idea implies that every nature has within itself a law of activity which is its own law. Let us recall the thomistic definition of nature, *ratio artis divinae, indita rebus, qua moventur ad fines*, an idea of the divine art, which is incorporated into things and by which things are directed to their ends. The more a being is elevated in the hierarchy of things, that is, the more perfectly it participates in the idea of being, the greater is the amount of autonomy it enjoys. Autonomy, on the one hand, immediately springs from the perfections of being and, on the other hand, makes those perfections evident, conspicuous and admirable. Autonomy is the glory, the splendor of being. Now, terminal freedom, since it is both freedom of choice and autonomy, is the kind of autonomy which properly fits the rational nature as such. Terminal liberty is the glory of the rational nature.

From these metaphysical considerations, the obvious conclusion is that the progress of liberty is rightly identified with the very progress of man and society, provided we have in mind terminal liberty. As to whether the progress of liberty implies the decay of authority, this is a question that we shall try to answer by considering the forms, functions and instruments of authority in reference to the idea of liberty as meaning autonomy.

Let us do away, first, with the dominion of servitude. It is exceedingly clear that the exploitation of man by man, even when possibly legitimate, is opposed to the require-ments of autonomy. Thus, *the progress of liberty implies the decay of authority insofar as authority takes the form of a dominion of servitude.*

As regards the instruments of authority, it is no less clear that a leadership exercised through persuasion agrees better with the autonomy of those who are lead, then a lead-ership exercised through coercion. *Thus, the progress of liberty implies the substitution of persuasion for coercion wherever this substitution can be reasonably realized.*

Third: the substitutional functions which authority exercises within the practical order are justified, as we have seen, only because of the inability of some persons, or some groups, for self-government. Accordingly, *the progress of liberty implies the decay of authority insofar as authority assumes substitutional functions.*

On the contrary, *the progress of liberty does not imply the decay of authority insofar as the essential function of authority is concerned.* The more effectively a society be united in its common action, the more perfect, happy, and free this society will be.

Thus, as we suggested at the beginning of this paper, the antinomy between authority and liberty is no absolute one. Viewed in the purity of their metaphysical goodness, authority and liberty fully agree with one another and their complementary character definitely prevails over their opposition.

To conclude: it seems that we are now able to set forth, according to our initial wish, principles of a nature to guide us in our endeavor to proportion exactly the forces of authority and those of liberty. Let us call these principles the *principle of authority* and the *principle of autonomy*. They can be formulated as follows: Principle of Authority. *Wherever the welfare of a community requires a common action, the unity of that common action must be assured by the higher organs of that community.* Principle of Autonomy. *Wherever a task can be satisfactorily achieved by the initiative of the individual or that of small social units, the fulfillment of that task must be left to the initiative of the individual or to that of small social units.*

2.4.4 A. D'Entreves
"A Rational Foundation of Ethics"

This is the essential qualification of the Thomist conception of natural law, and we must always keep it in mind lest we entirely misconstrue St. Thomas's endeavour to base a natural system of ethics on it. Natural law is the token of the fundamental harmony between human and Christian values, the expression of the perfectibility of man and of the power and dignity of his reason. But the system of ethics which is based on these assumptions cannot properly be called a rationalist system. The proud spirit of modern rationalism is lacking. There is no assertion of man's self-sufficiency and inherent perfection. There is no vindication of abstract "rights", nor of the autonomy of the individual as the ultimate source of all laws and of all standards.

No doubt a system such as this can be said to contain a recognition, and indeed a defence, of human personality. It can be developed, as has been done by some modern Thomists,[1] into a codified system of human rights based on the Christian view of the supreme value of the individual soul, the goal of Redemption. But on closer inspection it is only too evident that the "rights of the human person" of the Thomist are something entirely different from the "rights of man" which will be examined in the following chapter. The assertion of those rights is always based on the existence of an objective standard of justice. The emphasis is on natural law, not on natural rights. What is stressed is the duty of the State rather than the rights of the individual, the restoration of the right order of things rather than the perilous experiment of revolution. In fact, it is not from the individual that we are asked to start, but from the Cosmos, from the notion of a world well ordered and graded, of which natural law is the expression.

The modern Thomist will insist that the proper foundation of natural law is a metaphysical foundation. But the metaphysics which he has in mind is the Christian, or rather the Thomist. His starting point is that of St. Thomas : "supposing the world to be governed by divine Providence". The theorists of natural rights also had their metaphysics. They also had their providence. But it was no longer the Thomist, perhaps it was not even the Christian providence.

A. D'Entreves, "A Rational Foundation of Ethics." Chap. II in *Natural Law: An Introduction to Legal Philosophy* (London: Hutchinson University Library Series, 1951), pp. 33–47. Reprinted with permission of Taylor & Francis UK Books.

Thus once again the real significance of the notion of natural law seems to lie more in its function than in the doctrine itself. The stroke of genius of medieval writers was to have grasped its importance for the foundation of a natural system of ethics, distinct thought not separate from Christian or revealed ethics. Natural law was the instrument for solving a problem which, from the Christian standpoint, might otherwise seem insoluble or non-existent. Augustinianism and Thomism are often said to constitute the two correlative though not necessarily contradictory poles, so to speak, of Christian thought. The Thomist interpretation of Christianity is unthinkable without the notion of natural law.

That notion has remained a lasting inheritance of legal and moral philosophy. Its importance, one might say transcends the setting of circumstance and time which explain it historically. It represents a fundamental attitude of the Christian towards the problem of life and society. It has outlived St. Thomas as well as medieval Catholicism. The Protestant Hooker made full use of it against the intransigent Augustinianism of the Puritans. It is more than a paradox that this notion should have provided the basis for a defence of the Church of England and indeed of what would nowadays be called the English way of life. The best appreciation of the medieval notion of natural law can be given in Hooker's own words: "these School-implements are acknowledged by grave and wise men not unprofitable to have been invented".

Note

1   Maritain, *The Rights of Man and Natural Law* (1944).

2.4.5 Gustav Radbruch
"Five Minutes of Legal Philosophy"

The First Minute

Orders are orders, for the soldier. The law is the law, says the jurist. Whilst the soldier, however, is required neither by duty nor law to be obedient to an order that he knows to be a felony or misdemeanor, the jurist – because the last natural lawyer became extinct over a hundred years ago – admits no such exception to either the validity of the law or to the obedience demanded of its subjects. Law is valid because it is law, and it is law, generally, if it has the power to prevail.

This conception of law and its validity (we call it a positivistic thesis) has rendered jurists as defenseless as the people to some of the most arbitrary, cruel, and criminal of laws. In the final analysis, the positivistic thesis identifies law with power: there is law only where there is power.

The Second Minute

One might want to augment or replace this thesis with another: law is what is in the public interest.

That means that arbitrariness, breach of contract, and illegality are, insofar as they are socially useful, law. In practice, what the holder of state authority deems to be in the public interest, every whim and conceit of the despot, all unlawful punishment without trial or lawless murder of the weak, is, on this account, law. This *can* come to mean that the utility of those in power is identified with the public interest. It was this identification of law with the supposed public interest which transformed a *Rechtsstaat* into an unjust state.

So this thesis does not mean that everything that is in the public interest is law, but rather the contrary: only what constitutes law is in the public interest.

Gustav Radbruch, *Fünf Minuten Rechtsphilosophie, Gesamtausgabe (Collected Works), Rechts Philosophie III* first published in: RheinNeckarZeitung, 12th September 1945, reprinted in Gustav Radbruch, 20 Volumes, Arthur Kaufmann (ed.), vol 3: Winifried Hasemer (ed.) Heidelberg: C. F. Müller, 1990, 78–9. Translated into English by Julia C King.

The Third Minute

Law is the will to justice. Justice involves judging the individual without bias and measuring each person by the same standard.

If one deems the assassination of the political opponent to be honorable and the murder of other races to be necessary whilst at the same time administering the most barbarous and dishonorable of punishments to those proposing the same for one's own, this is neither justice nor law.

If laws consciously repudiate the will to justice, for example by arbitrarily granting and withdrawing the people's human rights, then they lack validity. The people owe them no obedience and jurists too are called to find the courage to deny their status as laws.

The Fourth Minute

To be sure, another aim of the law, apart from justice, is the public interest. And certainly law as such, even immoral law, has value in that it supplies security against uncertainty. Moreover, it is certain that human imperfection prevents the three values of the law (namely public interest, legal certainty, and justice) from being harmoniously combined. One is left to weigh up whether bad, harmful, or unjust laws should be considered valid for the sake of legal certainty or whether they should be considered invalid because of their injustice or social harm. One thing, however, must be embedded deep within the consciousness of both the people and the jurists: there *can* be laws with such abundance of injustice and social detriment that their validity and legal status must be denied.

The Fifth Minute

Therefore there are fundamental principles of law that are greater than any legal dictate so that any law that defies these fundamental principles loses its validity. We call these fundamental principles the Natural Law or the Law of Reason. Certainly its particulars are surrounded by some doubt, but the labor of centuries has carved out a solid stock of them and it has aggregated a broad consensus in the so-called declarations of human and civil rights. Only the most dedicated skeptic could continue to doubt their existence.

In the language of faith, the same ideas are set down in two Bible verses. On the one hand, it is written: obey them that have the rule over you (Hebrews 13:17). However it is also said: obey God rather than men (Acts 5:29) – this is not a mere pious reflection but a valid legal proposition. The differences between these two statements cannot be resolved by appealing to a third: render unto Caesar the things that are Caesar's, and to God the things that are God's (Mark 12:17), since this statement also leaves the boundary in doubt. In fact it cedes the solution to the voice of God, which speaks to the individual conscience only in the particular case.

2.4.6 G.E.M. Anscombe
"Mr Truman's Degree"

For men to choose to kill the innocent as a means to their ends is always murder, and murder is one of the worst of human actions. So the prohibition on deliberately killing prisoners of war or the civilian population is not like the Queensbury Rules: its force does not depend on its promulgation as part of positive law, written down, agreed upon, and adhered to by the parties concerned.

When I say that to choose to kill the innocent as a means to one's ends is murder, I am saying what would generally be accepted as correct. But I shall be asked for my definition of "the innocent." I will give it, but later. Here, it is not necessary; for with Hiroshima and Nagasaki we are not confronted with a borderline case. In the bombing of these cities it was certainly decided to kill the innocent as a means to an end. And a very large number of them, all at once, without warning, without the interstices of escape or the chance to take shelter, which existed even in the "area bombing" of the German cities.

G.E.M. Anscombe, "Mr Truman's Degree" (1956). Pamphlet published by the author. Oxford. © M.C. Gormally. Reprinted with permission.

2.4.7 M.K. Gandhi, selected excerpts on the existence of a superior law

When we do not like certain laws, we do not break the heads of the law-givers but we suffer and do not submit to the laws. That we should obey laws whether good or bad is a new-fangled notion. There was no such thing in former days. The people disregarded those laws they did not like and suffered the penalties for their breach. It is contrary to our manhood if we obey laws repugnant to our conscience.

If our rulers are doing what in their opinion is wrong, and we feel it is our duty to let them hear our advice even though it may be considered sedition, I urge you to speak sedition – but at your peril, you must be prepared to suffer the consequences. And, when you are ready to suffer the consequences and not hit below the belt, then I think you will have made good your right to have your advice heard even by the Government.

Only he who has mastered the art of obedience to law knows the art of disobedience to law. Those only can take up civil disobedience who believe in willing obedience even to irksome laws imposed by the State so long as they do not hurt their conscience or religion, and are prepared equally willingly to suffer the penalty of civil disobedience. Complete civil disobedience is rebellion without the element of violence in it. An out-and-out civil resister simply ignores the authority of the State. He never uses force and never resists force when it is used against him. In fact, he invites imprisonment and other uses of force against himself.... Submission to the State law is the price a citizen pays for his personal liberty. Submission, therefore, to a State law wholly or largely unjust is an immoral barter for liberty. A citizen who thus realizes the evil nature of a State is not satisfied to live on its sufferance, and therefore appears to others who do not share his belief to be a nuisance to society whilst he is endeavoring to compel the State, without committing a moral breach to arrest him. A body of civil resisters is like an army subject to all the discipline of a soldier's life. One perfect civil resister is enough to win the battle of right against wrong.

M.K. Gandhi, "Hind Swaraj or Indian Home Rule," in *On Violence: A Reader*, ed. Bruce B. Lawrence and Aisha Karim (Durham, NC: Duke University Press, 2007), pp. 110–127, at p. 122.

We thus see that, independent of and apart from men's wishes and opinions, there is something like a moral standard which we may call moral law. If there are laws of the State, why may not there be a moral law too? It does not matter if that law is not committed to writing by man, and indeed it need not be. If we grant or hold that the moral law exists, it is incumbent on us to obey it, just as we ought to obey the laws of the state. A moral law is distinct from and better than the laws of the state or those of business. One may ask, "How does it matter if I do not obey the laws of business and remain poor? Or if I disobey the laws of the State and incur the ruler's displeasure?" But it will never do – either for me or anyone else – to say, "What does it matter whether I tell a lie or tell the truth?"

There is thus a great difference between moral laws and temporal laws. For morality dwells in our hearts. Even a man practicing immorality would admit that he has been immoral. A wrong can never become a right. Even where a people is vile, though men may not observe the moral law, they would make a pretence of doing so; they thus are obliged to admit that moral laws ought to be observed. Such is the greatness of morality. It cares not for custom nor for public opinion. To a moral man, public opinion or custom is binding only so long as it is in harmony with the moral law.

Where does this moral law come from? This law is not laid down by the State, for different laws are found in different States. Many men were opposed to the morality which Socrates observed in his day. Even so the world admits that the morality he observed has remained, and shall remain, morality for ever.

I have disregarded the order served upon me, not for want to respect lawful authority, but in obedience of the higher law of our being – the voice of conscience.

An unjust law is itself a species of violence. Arrest for its breach is more so.

The dignity of man requires obedience to a higher law, to the strength of the spirit.

Mahatma Gandhi, *The Selected Works of Mahatma Gandhi: The Basic Works* (Navajivan Pub. House, 1968), p. 16.

Rajmohan Gandhi, *Gandhi: The Man, His People, and the Empire* (Berkeley: University of California Press, 2007), p. 192.

Gandhi on Non-Violence: Selected Texts from Mohandas K. Gandhi, Non-Violence in Peace and War, ed. Thomas Merton (New York: New Direction Books, 1967, 2007), p. 88.

Liberating Faith: Religious Voices for Justice, Peace, and Ecological Wisdom, ed. Roger S. Gottlieb (Lanham, MD: Rowman and Littlefield, 2003), p. 88.

2.4.8 Martin Luther King Jr., Letter from the Birmingham City Jail (first version)

Martin Luther King, Jr., Birmingham City Jail, April 16, 1963.

[…] I hope, sirs, you can understand our legitimate and unavoidable impatience. You express a great deal of anxiety over our willingness to break laws. This is certainly a legitimate concern. Since we so diligently urge people to obey the Supreme Court's decision of 1954 outlawing segregation in the public schools, it is rather strange and paradoxical to find us consciously breaking laws. One may well ask: "How can you advocate breaking some laws and obeying others?" The answer is found in the fact that there are two types of laws: There are just laws and there are unjust laws. I would be the first to advocate obeying just laws. One has not only a legal but moral responsibility to obey just laws. Conversely, one has a moral responsibility to disobey unjust laws. I would agree with Saint Augustine that "An unjust law is no law at all."

Now what is the difference between the two? How does one determine when a law is just or unjust? A just law is a man-made code that squares with the moral law or the law of God. An unjust law is a code that is out of harmony with the moral law. To put it in the terms of Saint Thomas Aquinas, an unjust law is a human law that is not rooted in eternal and natural law. Any law that uplifts human personality is just. Any law that degrades human personality is unjust. All segregation statutes are unjust because segregation distorts the soul and damages the personality. It gives the segregator a false sense of superiority and the segregated a false sense of inferiority. To use the words of Martin Buber, the great Jewish philosopher, segregation substitutes an "I–it" relationship for an "I–thou" relationship, and ends up relegating persons to the status of things. So segregation is not only politically, economically, and sociologically unsound, but it is morally wrong and sinful. Paul Tillich has said that sin is separation. Isn't segregation an existential expression of man's tragic separation, an expression of his awful estrangement, his terrible sinfulness? So I can urge men to obey the 1954 decision of the Supreme Court because it is morally right, and I can urge them to disobey segregation ordinances because they are morally wrong.

Text taken from the public domain publication listed at http://www.afsc.org/ht/d/ContentDetails/i/4019.

2.4.9 John Finnis
"Natural Law"

'NATURAL LAW'*
Why Called 'Natural'? Why Called 'Law'?

In the discourse of ethics, political theory, or *philosophie de droit* (philosophy of law), the claim that there is a natural law is an offer to explain and defend the substance of certain assertions often made in different terms in pre theoretical discourse (moral argument, politics, and/or law). Pre-theoretically (so to speak), choices, actions, and/or dispositions may be said to be 'inhuman', 'unnaturallycruel', 'perverse', or 'morally unreasonable'; proposals, policies, or conduct may be described as violations of 'human rights'; actions of states, groups, or individuals may be described as 'crimes against humanity' and citizens may claim immunity from legal liability or obligations by appealing to a 'higher law'. A natural law theory offers to explain why such assertions can be rationally warranted and true. It offers to do so by locating these assertions in the context of a general theory of good and evil in human life so far as human life is shaped by deliberation and choice.

Such a theory of good and evil can also be called a general theory of right and wrong in human choices and actions. It will contain both (i) normative propositions identifying types of choice, action, or disposition as right or wrong, permissible, obligatory, etc., and (ii) non-normative propositions about the objectivity and epistemological warrant of the normative propositions.

Theorists who describe their account of good and evil, right and wrong, as a 'natural law theory' are not committed to asserting that the normative propositions they defend are 'derived from Nature' or 'read off' or 'inspected in' 'the nature of things'. Indeed, it is rare for a natural law theory to make such assertions, for their sense is deeply obscure; it is difficult, if not impossible, to understand what epistemic or rational processes would be involved in such 'derivation' or 'reading off' or 'inspection in'.

Still less are natural law theorists committed to claiming that the normative propositions they defend stand in some definite relationship to, or are warranted by, the 'laws of nature'

John Finnis, "Natural Law," in *Reason in Action: Collected Essays*, Volume 1 (Oxford: Oxford University Press, 2011), pp. 199–211. Reprinted with permission of Oxford University Press.
*[1996e] ('Loi naturelle' in Canto-Sperber ed., *Dictionnaire de Philosophie Morale*); an earlier version is 1986a.

in the sense of the regularities observed, and explanatory factors adduced, by the 'natural sciences' (physics, biology, 'experimental psychology', ecology, etc.). Thomas Aquinas, a leading natural law theorist, sharply differentiates the propositions of moral and political philosophy (in which the principles and norms of natural law are identified and elaborated) from (1) the propositions which constitute the natural sciences, (2) the principles and norms of logic, and what others have called the 'laws of thought', and (3) the principles and norms of any and every human technique of manipulating matter which is subject to our will.[1]

Nor is the typical natural law theory (classical, mediaeval, or contemporary) concerned with any alleged 'state of nature', in the sense of some golden age or state of affairs prior to human wrongdoing or to the formation of human societies or of states or political communities.

As for the term 'law', as understood in the phrase 'natural law', it does not connote that the relevant principles and norms have their directive force precisely as the commands, imperatives, or dictates of a superior will. Even those natural law theorists who argue (as most do) that the most ultimate explanation of those principles and norms (as of all other realities) is a transcendent, creative, divine source of existence, meaning, and value, will also argue that the principles and norms are inherently fitting and obligatory (not fitting or obligatory because commanded), or that the source of their obligation is rather divine wisdom than divine will.

Instead, the term 'law' in the phrase 'natural law' refers to standards of right choosing, standards which are normative (that is, rationally directive and 'obligatory') because they are true and choosing otherwise than in accordance with them is unreasonable.

And the term 'natural' (and related uses of 'by nature', 'in accordance with nature', and 'of nature') in this context signifies any one or more of the following: (a) that the relevant standards (principles and norms) are not 'positive', that is, are directive prior to any positing by individual decision or group choice or convention; (b) that the relevant standards are 'higher' than positive laws, conventions, and practices, that is, provide the premises for critical evaluation and endorsement or justified rejection of or disobedience to such laws, conventions, or practices; (c) that the relevant standards conform to the most demanding requirements of critical reason and are objective, in the sense that a person who fails to accept them as standards for judgment is in error; (d) that adherence to the relevant standards tends systematically to promote human flourishing, the fulfilment of human individuals and communities.

Critique of Scepticism and Dogmatism

Historically, natural law theories have been articulated as part or product of a philosophical critique of ethical scepticisms (whether nihilism, relativism, subjectivism, or hedonism). Since the sceptical views thus criticized and rejected by theorists of natural law (e.g. Plato) or natural right/justice (e.g. Aristotle) were themselves articulated in reaction to uncritically accepted conventions or religiously promoted norms, the philosophical critique of scepticism included a differentiation of the rationally grounded norms of natural law (or natural right) from moral dogmatism or conventionalism.

In contemporary thought, scepticism about natural law (and about other moral theories claiming to be objective or true) is very often based upon a logically illicit and rationally

unwarranted inference from certain propositions about what 'is' the case to certain propositions about what is good or obligatory. This particular form of invalid reasoning was
assiduously employed in the ancient manuals of scepticism, reintroduced into European
discourse in the sixteenth century (see e.g. Sextus Empiricus, *Pyrrhonean Hypotyposes*
III, xxiv, 198–238; Sextus Empiricus uses the term 'dogmatism' to insinuate that all
non-sceptical ethical theories, such as natural law theory, are uncritical; but this charge
is not well grounded, and the term is used in this essay to refer to moral positions held
without openness to critical questions).

Examples of the invalid reasoning commonly encountered today include the following:

- X is not universally regarded as good/obligatory; therefore X is not good/obligatory.
- In modern thought ('modernity') X is widely regarded as not good/obligatory; therefore X is not good/obligatory.
- In contemporary society X is widely regarded as good/obligatory; therefore X is
  good/obligatory.
- I have a sentiment of approval of X; therefore X is good (or worthwhile … or obligatory …), at least for me.
- I have opted for or decided upon or am committed to the practical principle that X
  ought to be done; therefore X ought to be done, at least by me.

As this list of *non sequiturs* suggests, there is a link between ethical scepticism (at least in its
popular forms) and ethical conventionalism. There are many natural law theories, on the
other hand, which are not guilty of these or other fallacies, fallacies which consist in concluding to a normative judgement from premises which include no normative proposition.

David Hume suggests that 'every system of morality' prior to his critique illogically
purports to infer *ought* or *ought not* from *is* or *is not*.[2] The suggestion is ungrounded, though
the illicit inference may perhaps be detected in certain eighteenth-century rationalists
(especially Samuel Clarke) whom Hume seems to have had prominently in mind when
writing this part of his *Treatise*. Insofar as Hume's predominant view (among four or five
inconsistent views which he seems to have entertained) concerning the nature and basis
of moral judgements was that they are judgments about what characteristics and actions
arouse approval or disapproval, Hume was himself plainly guilty of this kind of illegitimate
inference. The same cannot be said of Plato, Aristotle, and Aquinas, for example.

The modern form of 'fact-value distinction' and denial of the 'objectivity of value judgments' may be found clearly articulated in Max Weber's methodological writings, which
conclude that any meaning or value must be imposed upon the world by an act of will.
(The question how an act of will could create or impose value remains unanswered.)
Weber's primary argument for his denial of ethical objectivity seems to have been simply
that people, or educated people, in fact disagree with each other about values. But this
has no more validity than the popular arguments listed above; the fact of disagreement
no more disproves a proposition than the fact of agreement proves it. Weber had three
other lines of argument. The first was a neo-Kantian argument that all judgments must
rest upon pre-suppositions, and that selection among competing pre-suppositions must
be non-rational. This argument is self-refuting in its general form, and there is no way to
limit it (as Weber sought to do) to judgments of value. Weber's next argument pointed,
like Sartre after him, to certain supposed political and/or ethical dilemmas before which

reason is supposed to fall silent. Such 'dilemmas', however, seem in truth to be no more than a stimulus to a more nuanced and resourceful practical reasoning, in which one may identify good reasons for preferring one horn of the dilemma, or for settling upon some third course of action, or for narrowing the choice to a small range of reasonable and choiceworthy options (any of which could reasonably be adopted in preference to the indefinitely vast range of irrational or at least unreasonable alternatives). Weber's final argument alleged that there are distinct and incommensurable 'spheres' of practical judgment, such as the political, the erotic, and the ethical, each with its own ultimate values between which reason cannot adjudicate because reason operates only within spheres. This final claim, not defended by Weber, is contradicted by his own acknowledgement that the spheres interpenetrate one another.[3]

As for Weber's direct confrontation with natural law theory, it is abortive. For he asserts that in such theory 'general propositions about regularities of factual occurrences and general norms of conduct are held to coincide ... The ought is identical with the "is", i.e. that which exists in the universal average'.[4] In truth, however, Aristotle explicitly contrasts the natural with the average (*Pol.* IV.1: 1288b10–40 and *NE* V.7: 1135a5), and Aquinas frequently stresses that most people and their actions are foolish and corrupt (*ST* I q.113 a.1; I–II q.9 a.5 ad 3; q.94 a.4; etc.).

Perhaps the most fruitful critique of ethical scepticism is one which takes its cue from Aristotle's critique of general scepticism (*Metaphysics* IV.4: 1005b35–1006a28; IV.8: 1012a29–b18; XI.5: 1062b1–11; XI.6: 1063b30–5). If sceptics are willing to affirm their position as rationally warranted they can be shown to be denying (i) something given, instantiated, in the activity of rationally considering and proposing their or any other position, and/or (ii) some proposition to which their assertion of their position rationally commits them. In the case in hand, the relevant givens include the rationality norms which guide the rational inquiries of those who choose to follow them and to resist temptations to reach conclusions by sub-rational processes; and the propositions to which an argued assertion commits the person asserting it include the proposition that knowledge of truth (at least the truth of such propositions as the one asserted) is a good worth pursuing and instantiating in that argument and assertion, a good worthwhile for its own sake as well as for any instrumental advantage it might yield. An analysis of the activity of inquiring, arguing, and judging can show that it is self-refuting to deny that there are ever free choices,[5] and self-refuting to deny that there are any intrinsic, non-instrumental goods.[6] The proposition, 'Knowledge of truth is a good to be pursued, and ignorance, self-deception, and confusion are to be avoided', is a practical principle which is not grounded on, but is defensible by way of, the analysis of self-referentially inconsistent denials of it.

Cognitivism and Natural Law

Not every non-sceptical ethics is appropriately called a natural law theory. Natural law theories are distinguished from the broader set of cognitivist or objectivist ethical theories in four main ways.

First, they are differentiated from any ethics in a Kantian mould by their willingness to identify certain basic human goods, such as knowledge, life and health, and friendship, as the core of substantive first principles of practical reasoning. Taken together, these basic human goods give shape and content to a conception of human flourishing and thus, too, to a conception of human nature. For: an axiom of Aristotle's method (*De Anima* II. 4: 415a16–21), deployed more generally by Aquinas, shows that while nature is metaphysically (ontologically) fundamental, knowledge of a thing's nature is epistemically derivative: an animate thing's nature is understood by understanding its capacities, its capacities by understanding its activities, and its activities by understanding the objects of those activities. In the case of the human being the 'objects' which must be understood before one can understand and know human nature are the basic goods which are the objects of one's will, i.e. are one's basic reasons for acting and give reason for everything which one can intelligently take an interest in choosing.

Secondly, natural law theories are distinguished from any theory which asserts that moral truths are known essentially by discrete 'intuitions'. Rather, natural law theories contend that specific moral judgments concerning obligation or right are applications or specifications of higher principles. The first principles of the 'system' are known by insight (*nous*: cf. *NE* VI.6: 1141a8 with 5: 1140b17 and 6: 1142a26), without deduction via any middle term (they are *per se nota*: *ST* I–II q.94 a.2). But the insights whose content is the self-evident principles of practical knowledge are not intuitions – 'insights' without data. Rather they are insights whose data are, in the first place, natural and sensory appetites and emotional responses. These data are subsequently enriched by theoretical knowledge or true opinion about possibilities (e.g. about what threatens and enhances health, or about what knowledge is available), and by experience of disharmony (frustrated intentions). It should be added that the classical natural law theorists would reject Maritain's theory that the knowledge of first practical principles is 'connatural' or 'by affinity or congeniality' or 'through inclination' *rather than conceptual*.[7] As Maritain conceded in relation to the expression 'knowledge through inclination', such terms are never used by Aquinas in discussions of the principles of natural law.[8] Nor does Aquinas resort to any sort of non-conceptual knowledge as an intuitionistic source of confessedly inexplicable exceptions to moral norms, as Maritain does.[9] And there seems compelling reason not to accept Maritain's claim that Aquinas must have been referring to such 'knowledge' when saying (in *ST* I–II q.94 a.2) that 'reason naturally understands as good all the objects of man's inclinations'. For Aquinas all knowledge is conceptual (*De Veritate* q.4 a.2 ad 5), and the understanding of basic human goods is quite ordinary, unmysterious, *conceptual* understanding,[10] albeit practical, that is, directive or prescriptive ('is-to-be-done-and-pursued'), rather than purely 'theoretical' or descriptive ('is'). The first principles of natural law are not inclinations, but fundamental human goods understood as reasons for action.

Thirdly, natural law theories are distinguished from any fundamentally aggregative conception of the right and the just. For viable natural law theories postulate no one end to which all human actions might be effective means, no one value in terms of which one might commensurate alternative options as simply better or worse, and no one principle which, without further specification in other principles and norms, should guide deliberation and choice. Rather they claim to identify a number of basic human goods, none of which is simply a means to or simply a part of any other such basic good; they further identify also a number of principles to guide ('morally') the choices necessitated by (i) the variety of basic goods and reasons for action and (ii) the multiple ways of instantiating these goods and acting on these reasons for action by intelligent and creative choice (or indeed by misguided choices whose primary motivation is not reasons but emotion).

Fourthly, natural law theories typically differ from other ethical theories by offering to clarify not only the normative disciplines and bodies of discourse, but also the methods of the descriptive and explanatory social theories (political theory or political science, economics, legal theory…). How best can human societies and their formative concepts be understood, without illusions, but in a general way (as in a project such as Aristotle' *Politics* or Max Weber' *Wirtschaft und Gesellschaft*)? Could such projects be 'value-free'? Or must even descriptive-explanatory theorists, in selecting their concepts, rely upon some definite conceptions of what is important in human existence? Must they not use such conceptions as criteria for selecting topics for study and concepts for describing those topics? Must they not also employ such criteria in judging some types and instantiations of human institutions or practices to be the 'central cases' of such institutions or practices, and also in judging some uses of terms such as 'law' or 'constitution' or 'authority' to be, for critical descriptive theory, the 'focal' uses and senses of those terms? And must not such conceptions and criteria of importance be the subject, not of selection by 'demonic' personal preference (Weber) or silent conformism to academic fashion or political *parti pris*, but rather of an open, public, critical justification? Natural law theories of the classical type, as Aristotle and Aquinas, claim to offer such a justification.[11]

[…]

Derivation of Positive Law

The history of moral and political philosophy, and of natural law theory, is much affected by certain *lacunae* in Aquinas's work. He was the thinker who most clearly articulated and developed the elements of practical philosophy in Aristotle (and thus, in a sense, in Plato), so as to represent them as propositions of or about natural law. Yet he failed to give a clear, full, careful, and consistent statement of the first principles of practical reason, and a satisfying set of illustrations of the way in which first practical principles (such as 'human life is a good to be advanced and respected'), or first moral principles (such as the Golden Rule) are given specificity in less fundamental principles and norms. This failure contributed significantly to the spread of voluntarist and fideistic currents which virtually overwhelmed the tradition of natural law theory, as a living school of thought. It later resulted in neo-Thomistic claims (e.g. those of Maritain and Villey noted above) which are scarcely defensible either as interpretations or as philosophical theses.

Aquinas was the first philosophical thinker to exploit the concept of 'positive law' which emerges in mid-twelfth century theological and juristic speculation. He gave an original and helpful sketch, scarcely surpassed even today, of the differing types of relationship between the high-level principles of natural law and (1) the more specified principles which can be attained by practical reasoning about the implications of those principles in recurrent types of human predicament and opportunity, and (2) norms, rules, precepts, and juridical institutions which cannot be said to be required as the conclusion of any course of practical reasoning, yet which are in some other way rationally connected to, or derived from, principles of the first two sorts, and which are authoritative for upright judges and good citizens if and when chosen and promulgated ('posited') by an appropriate authority. Laws, rights, and institutions derived in the second way are 'positive', yet have moral force in conscience similar to the moral force of the higher level principles of natural law, provided that their positing was by a person or body constitutionally autho-rized to make such decisions and they were made without serious disregard either for other relevant moral principles and rights or for the 'common' (as opposed to partisan) good of all the members of the community subject to their authority.

This second mode of derivation was called by Aquinas *determinatio*, which might be translated 'concretization'. It is best understood by a comparison such as he offered by way of explanation. From his commission ('build a maternity hospital for our town') an architect can deduce various specifications (the building must be more than one metre in height, and must include doors, means of warming the spaces in winter, etc.). But no amount of attention to the commission (the 'principle' of his work) and to the circumstances (including the 'nature of things') will yield a single, rationally required answer to the unavoidable questions. Should the doors be 2.1 or 2.2 metres high? Of this metal or that? Questions of the latter kind must be answered by decisions (*determinationes*) which are rationally under-determined, yet intelligibly related to (and in this weak sense 'derived from') the master principle (the commission taken with its more or less necessary implications).

In this account the sheer positivity of much of a country's legal system is fully acknowl-edged. But at the same time the moral significance of the law' directives and institutions is affirmed and explained. The affirmation is conditional. If the relationship of 'deriva-tion', albeit non-deductive and 'free', is broken by *ultra vires* (lack of legal authority) or unjust discrimination or violation of inviolable rights, the positive' law' proper moral authority is eliminated. From the point of view of the conscientious judge, citizen, or indeed legislator, this lack of the proper ('normal') moral authority was marked by the sayings found in Plato, Cicero, Aquinas, and most of the philosophical, theological, and juridical tradition down to the nineteenth century: an unjust law, albeit valid by the legal system' own criteria of validity (and in this sense properly described as a law), is not really a law, or is not a law *simpliciter*, that is, sans phrase. It can have some collateral obligatoriness, in that it may be unfair to others to disobey it publicly (e.g. because doing so would encourage others to disobey other laws without good reason). This classical thesis, *lex iniusta non est lex* properly interpreted, is fully compatible with the jurist's or historian's wish to employ an amoral criterion of 'legal validity' or historical cognizability.

Notes

1   *In Eth.*, prol.
2   Hume, *A Treatise of Human Nature*, III, i, 1.
3   See Turner and Factor, *Max Weber and the Dispute over Reason and Value*, 31–46.
4   Weber, *Economy and Society*, 869. [See essay IV.9 (1985b), sec. III.]
5   See Boyle, Grisez, and Tollefsen, *Free Choice: A Self-Referential Argument*. [And essays 3–4]
6   See *NLNR* 73–5.
7   Maritain, *Man and the State*, 91–4; *La loi naturelle ou loi non écrite, 30*.
8   *Man and the State*, 91.
9   *La loi naturelle*, 155–6.
10 Grisez, 'The First Principle of Practical Reason' at 172, 196–7.
11 On this issue see *NLNR* 3–22.

2.4.10 Servais Pinckaers
The Sources of Christian Ethics

Natural Inclination and Freedom

It is difficult to speak of natural inclinations today because of the subtle modifications of ideas and associations that have been caused by nominalism. Nominalist categories are so deeply fixed in our minds that they seem self-evident. They influence our reactions to words and ideas. We need therefore to weigh our concepts critically and in depth, so that we may retrieve, at the heart of our experience, the pristine sense of a nature capable of developing in freedom.

Our chief difficulty is caused by our habit of considering nature and freedom as contraries. If we think of freedom as something dependent only on our voluntary decision, and totally indeterminate before we take that decision, then we will be led to think of the natural as something necessarily predetermined. In this view, it is hard to see how we can reconcile the natural and the free. We will see the natural inclinations of both intellect and will as tendencies both blind and coercive.

By way of illustration, here are two quotations from Jacques Leclerq, which describe the situation clearly.

"Natural love, then, is a blind inclination. I repeat that it is regrettable that St. Thomas calls it love, even as he calls the inclination toward the good the natural will; but here again he is following the Greek tradition" (translated from *La philosophie morale de saint Thomas* [Louvain, 1955], 300).

"Metaphysics' affirmation that every being tends toward its own good has little relevance for ethics, for here it is a question of a blind, coercive tendency linked with the idea of goodness and perfection, and the field of ethics deals with free, reflective action. The problem of love is therefore one of intention and thought, a psychological problem. It is not a question of knowing whether man necessarily seeks self-fulfillment or whatever makes him more completely human, but rather of knowing whether he ought to think of himself or of others. These are two different problems, and to confuse them is to understand neither metaphysics nor psychology, and to make any understanding of ethics impossible" (translated from *L'nseignement de la morale* [Paris, 1950], 189).

Servais Pinckaers, *The Sources of Christian Ethics*, tr. M. Noble (Washington, DC: Catholic University of America Press, 1995), pp. 400–407.

Without referring explicitly to St. Thomas, the second quotation also has some bearing upon him. The reflection is based on an a priori category that opposes the natural to the free and determines the relations among metaphysics, psychology, and ethics. This last is the domain of freedom and consequently eludes the power of nature. But how, then, are we to interpret St. Thomas, who bases his moral theory on natural inclinations? The reference to Greek influence is merely an excuse, not an explanation. Moreover, it only shifts the problem to a new setting. For how could Aristotle and so many Greek and Latin Fathers, who accepted "nature" as the foundation of morality, all have fallen together into so grave an error?

Apparently, Jacques Leclerq has not perceived the analogical significance of St. Thomas's use of the terms *nature* and *natural* in passing from the physical or biological level to that of the spiritual. In the physical or animal world, nature, whatever its variations, determines the movements it produces in their entirety. Spiritual nature, on the other hand, is such that the inclinations proceeding from it, far from opposing its freedom by setting limits on it, cause and increase its freedom as a source, providing it with principles of truth and goodness. As we have shown, we are free not in spite of our natural inclinations but because of them.

The following quotation from the treatise on the passions shows clearly the analogical use of the term *natural*. It is about the pleasure or "delight" that serves to define beatitude.

Nature in man can be understood in two ways. First, insofar as intellect and will are the chief constituents of human nature, for it is by reason of them that man is constituted as a species. From this point of view, the pleasures man experiences in regard to his intellect can be called natural: thus it is natural for a man to delight in the contemplation of truth and in the practice of virtue.

In another sense, nature in man can be understood as what differs from reason, that is, what he has in common with other beings and above all what is not subject to reason. In this way, those things relating to the preservation of the body, such as food, drink and sleep, and those related to the preservation of the species, such as sexual activity, may be said to give a man natural pleasure. (IaIIae, q 3 r a 7)

We should note that this distinction in no way sets up an opposition. In fact, the subject matter of the virtue of temperance, for example, consists in natural pleasures inferior to reason, and it moderates them so as to subject them to reason.

Our problem goes beyond the textual interpretation of St. Thomas. It involves the rediscovery of a spiritual nature, which does not oppose human freedom but lies at its origin and forms it. Of such a nature, clearly, are the human inclinations to truth and goodness.

The natural inclination to truth, which is at the source of the contemplative life, of philosophy and the sciences, obviously cannot be a blind tendency, for darkness does not engender light. Because it exists at the origin of the intellect's life and provides it with its first principles, it should rather be called a radiant splendor, a sort of alpha ray of the mind allowing us to share in the divine Light. It is in itself so dazzling that our reason cannot contemplate it directly. It is as though it were always behind us, as in the Platonic myth of the cave. Do we say the sun is blind because we cannot look straight at it without being blinded?

Similarly, our natural inclination to the good is not a compulsive tendency preceding the moral order or being structured within it. It is in reality the deepest source of that spontaneity which shapes our willing a primitive élan and attraction that carries us toward the good and empowers us to choose among lesser and greater goods. Here we are at the very origin and principle of morality; this inclination should be described as higher than morality and supremely free, even a sharing in the freedom, goodness, and spontaneity of God.

Verifying This in the Language of Today

Current language can be of great help here. When we speak of a thirst for truth or happiness we are spontaneously using an analogy that describes spiritual desire in terms borrowed from a biological desire. The latter can certainly become an obstacle to freedom by its heaviness and excess, but we are quite aware that this does not apply to the desire for truth. The better we know the truth, the more capable we are of parrying physical constraints and acting freely. As St. Thomas said, man is distinguished from animals precisely in his knowledge of how his actions are formed; this is what enables him to act freely.

Similarly, no one would imagine that an artist's natural gifts were an obstacle to his freedom or that they set limits to it. Rather, the ideal, in the arts, is to achieve the natural. We do not appreciate a work that seems contrived and artificial and is not inspired by a natural sense of beauty. Condillac wrote, "The natural ... is art become habitual. The poet and dancer are each natural when they achieve that degree of perfection where their conformity to the rules of art appears effortless." And again, "Natural means everything that is not inhibited, strained, artificial, pretentious." Stephen Zweig, speaking of Romain Rolland, remarked, "Nature is art's only rule."

This was the "natural" that the ancients saw as the source of morality and of the arts, and that they proposed to the wise as an ideal. Cicero said that "since all our 'duties' proceed from natural principles, so too should wisdom." To demonstrate this he used the comparison of medicine and dancing, while bringing out the difference: only wisdom exists wholly in each of its acts (*De finibus bonorum et malorum*, x.3,7).[1]

We must therefore regain at any cost the sense of this spiritual "naturalness" inherent in our earliest inclinations. Our entire conception of morality depends on this question.

"Inclination" and "Determination"

The term *inclination* also needs to be clarified. It contains a certain orientation that seems contrary to the indetermination of freedom, or its "indifference." Here, once again, an analogy is at work. A biological inclination such as hunger or thirst directs the appetite in a determined and compelling way. Yet we would hesitate to say that it is contrary to freedom, since by eating we are achieving the physical strength needed for action. Spiritual inclinations in no way limit freedom but rather incite and develop it. Anyone drawn to a person, a virtue, a science, or an art realizes that his freedom increases through the love he feels and is not diminished by its determination.

As for the inclination to truth and happiness, this empowers us to surmount all limitations and directs us to complete freedom. Spiritual inclinations are intimate determinations that liberate us. The term *determination* we have just used is also analogous, depending on whether the will is determined by something exterior or interior. The will's interior determination shows its power, its ability to impose itself and to endure. It is a sign of great freedom.

We can see from the foregoing how delicate is the use of words when we are dealing with freedom. Our concept, whether of freedom of indifference or of freedom for excellence, imperceptibly modifies the meaning of all the other terms we use in discussing it.

Natural inclinations, which we are about to study, constitute the human person's spiritual spontaneity. They are at the source of voluntary free action and, consequently, of morality. They form what St. Thomas occasionally referred to as the *instinctus rationes*, the rational instinct, which, with Aristotle, he likened to the higher instinct, inspired genius. Here the action of the Holy Spirit intervenes with his gifts, which St. Thomas did not hesitate to call the instinct of the Holy Spirit, *instinctus Spiritus Sancti* (IaIIae, q 68 a 1). Our instinct for truth and goodness, which is at bottom an instinct for God, thus enjoys a relationship with freedom quite different from the animal instinct that first comes to mind. It creates freedom, which can neither exist nor develop without it.

Natural Inclinations and Natural Law

We also have difficulty in forming an idea of the relation between natural inclinations and natural law, because we are used to seeing opposition between law, an external principle, and inclinations, which are interior. Can inclination and law harmonize? Does this not run counter to the requirements of law and morality? How, then, can we claim to base moral law on inclinations, natural though they may be?

Yet this is what St. Thomas did, and apparently he found it no great problem. For him, natural law was the expression, in the form of precepts, of our natural inclinations, which were guided by our inclinations to goodness and truth. Thus natural law, imposed externally when taught, was in reality written in the human heart – that is, in the very nature of our human faculties of reason and will, at the root of free action. This teaching on natural inclinations was fundamental for St. Thomas. It established natural law and provided the basis for morality. Inclinations developed into virtues, which received their beginnings from them and would provide morality with its main categories.

We should add that, in St. Thomas's view, inclinations, like the natural law, were God's most precious work in the human person, a direct, unique participation in his own wisdom, goodness, and freedom and the emanation of the eternal law. St. Thomas's entire moral theology was based largely on his teaching on natural inclinations and on the freedom for the good that activated them.

In separating freedom from natural inclinations and in creating opposition between them with his concept of freedom of indifference, Ockham demolished what we might call the capstone of St. Thomas's doctrinal edifice and completely overturned the structure of moral theology. The demolition extended to the relations and proportions of its elements, and even to the basic concept of what they were. According to Ockham, freedom stood alone in opposition to nature, while law and inclinations were separated and left the virtues marginalized and lifeless. All had to be reconstructed anew.

Table of Natural Inclinations

In the *prima secundae* there is a remarkable synthesis of the first principles of natural law, beginning with natural inclinations and based on the essential components of human nature (at q 92, a 2). I know of no other work on the subject, either in St. Thomas himself or in contemporary studies, that can parallel the table of inclinations found there. This is not to say that the teaching was innovative; St. Thomas's table adopts and arranges elements provided by Aristotelian and Stoic traditions. Its origin merits a special historical study. Suffice it to say here that it had already been proposed by Cicero in his *De officiis* (1.4), and so clearly that St. Thomas's work might have been an adaptation of it, although he made no mention of the Latin philosopher. The passage is well worth re-reading, for it shows the antiquity and permanence of the teaching proposed by St. Thomas.

Cicero began with the natural tendency to self-preservation found in every living being, the tendency to avoid the harmful and seek all that was needed for life: food, shelter, and so forth. Next came the inclination common to men and animals, leading to sexual union in view of generation and the rearing of offspring. But Cicero immediately pointed out the difference between men and animals. Man, possessing reason, had a sense of past and future; he could use foresight to establish relations between causes. Thus he was better able to provide for the needs, not only of his own family, but of the wider community of language and life formed with others. This was the natural inclination to life in society, of which Cicero was to speak at greater length, and magnificently, in his *De finibus bonorum et malorum* (3.19): "Thus we are disposed by nature to form groups, assemblies, cities. The world ... is somewhat like a city or commonwealth shared by men and gods, and each one of us is a part of this world."[2]

Another basic inclination was the search for truth, without which there could be no happy life. So truthfulness, simplicity, and sincerity were particularly appropriate to man. Finally, reason conferred upon man the privilege of a sense of order, of fitness, of measure in action and speech, and of beauty. These things together formed *honestas*, the moral quality whose range was divided into four parts: prudence, justice, courage, and temperance. Clearly, this text of Cicero provides the best possible introduction to the teaching of the Angelic Doctor on natural inclinations.

In setting out to describe the precepts of the natural law, St. Thomas was well aware that he was laying the very foundations of moral theory. This was for him the first, and at the same time the most difficult, task of the ethicist. He was at pains therefore to relate these precepts to the first principles of the life of the spirit. As the life of the mind was ruled by its grasp of being, expressed in the speculative intellect by the basic principle that a thing could not simultaneously be affirmed and denied, or even be and not be, so the life of the will was ruled by its perception of the good, which was its end, and was expressed in the principle of the practical reason: "The good is to be done and sought; evil is to be avoided" (Bonum est faciendum et prosequendum, et malum virandum). This was the foundational principle of natural law, at the base of all other laws. The latter would determine and spell out the specific human good, according to the intrinsic qualities of human nature and the inclinations they engendered.

First came an inclination common to man and to all beings insofar as they were substances: the inclination to self-preservation according to each one's nature, that is, to preserve life and avoid death.

In the second place was a more particular inclination, common to men and animals: that of sexual union between male and female and the rearing of offspring.

Thirdly, man possessed two inclinations proper to his rational nature: the inclination to know the truth about God and the inclination to live in society.

To sum up, we can distinguish five natural inclinations:

1. The inclination to the good
2. The inclination to self-preservation
3. The inclination to sexual union and the rearing of offspring
4. The inclination to the knowledge of truth
5. The inclination to live in society.

These inclinations, serving as principles for the practical reason, were comparable to the first principles of speculative reason. According to St. Thomas they were self-evident to all human beings, before any research and formulation had taken place; they were known intuitively, as it were. They served as premises, on which all reasonings and questionings about human good were based. Doubtless not everyone managed to formulate these principles explicitly; some might even deny the propositions they expressed. Nonetheless, the inclinations existed and were active even when denied, for their profound influence was unaffected by the surface agitation of ideas.

Notes

1   "Cum autem omnia officia a principiis naturae profiscantur, ab iisdem necesse est proficisci ipsam sapientiam. … Sola sapientia in se tota conversa est, quod idem in ceteris artibus non fit."

2   "Ita que natura sumus apti ad coetus, concilia, civitates. Mundum autem censent … esse quasi communem urbem et civitatem hominum et deorum, et unumquenque nostrum eius mundi esse partern."

3

Contemporary Natural Law

3.1 Ethical

Introduction

The revival of the central natural law tradition is related to, some might say is even a basic aspect of, a wider interest in virtue-based approaches to ethical inquiry. This revival is almost universally traced back to the appearance in 1953 of an article by the inimitable Elizabeth Anscombe entitled "Modern Moral Philosophy."[1] In this article, the first of the readings included in this section, Anscombe launched a swingeing attack on the then dominant form of ethical discourse centering around differing, more or less sophisticated, forms of deontology and utilitarianism, and famously called for a suspension of moral philosophy until such time as a sufficiently robust philosophical psychology had been developed that could sustain a convincing account of virtue acquisition and human flourishing. In so doing, she was of course harking back to the ethics of Aristotle and the tradition of philosophical reflection it had spawned. Yet, despite that fact, and although her attack had a huge impact upon subsequent ethical inquiry, to claim, as we do, that it was an inspiration for the revival of natural law thinking requires some qualification given the fact that it was linked to a warning that legalistic notions such as 'obligation' are incoherent in a context in which few people believe in a divine lawgiver.

This penetrated to the heart of later debates over the extent to which classical natural law presupposed a wider religious or metaphysical framework of understanding and, if so, in precisely what that might consist. Importantly, Anscombe does not offer a view on the necessity of such comprehensive underpinnings for a fully adequate moral theory. It may be surmised from positions she adopted elsewhere that she did indeed think them indispensable. Her point in "Modern Moral Philosophy," however, was a more narrowly diagnostic one whereby she found a state of intellectual confusion – indeed she would say corruption – so advanced that it was, as a matter of plain feasibility, possible to lay down only much less ambitious goals.

[1]   G.E.M. Anscombe, "Modern Moral Philosophy," *Philosophy* 33, 124 (January, 1958).

The Natural Law Reader, First Edition. Edited by Jacqueline A. Laing and Russell Wilcox.
© 2014 Blackwell Publishing Ltd. Published 2014 by Blackwell Publishing Ltd.

Continuing in the diagnostic vein, the second selection is taken from a central chapter of Alasdair MacIntyre's now classic work *After Virtue* that opened with a similarly coruscating attack on contemporary ethical discussion, expanding into a more comprehensive indictment of the foundations of the modern world.[2] These he sees as conceptual shards wrenched out of the traditions from which they emerged and which made them comprehensible, thereby rendering them apt for ideological appropriation by deeper, more sinister forces as tools of a sort of false consciousness. In pursuing, in the extract reprinted here, a provisional definition of virtue, he canvasses the considerable diversity that has existed amongst its different conceptualizations, but ultimately suggests a tripartite formulation that brings out what is common to them all. First, an account of the notion of practice. Secondly, an account of the narrative unity of a human life. And, thirdly, an account of what constitutes a moral tradition. In his eventual advocacy of a Thomistic virtue ethics, this was to play an important role, as we shall see, both in extending his critique of modernity and in grounding an understanding of collective assent to and dissent from the precepts of natural law in social practice.

In "Irreducibly Social Goods" – the third extract – that other great philosopher of modernity, Charles Taylor, continues the attack on modern modes of thought, this time as manifest in the presumptions of economic science, most specifically of that branch known as welfare economics.[3] Extending a critique begun by Amartya Sen, he sees the utilitarian assumptions which Sen finds so problematic as rooted in a deeper commitment to an essentially atomic view of human beings which characterizes society as merely the sum total of individual decisions and the "interests" to which they attach: one which excludes a robust belief in the existence of irreducibly social goods. It is with defending just such a notion of irreducibly social goods – common goods – that the balance of this piece concerns itself.

Some years before Anscombe's celebrated attack in "Modern Moral Philosophy," her husband, Peter Geach, had already anticipated in his short article, "Good and Evil," what was to become an increasingly important theme in subsequent ethical reflection.[4] In "Good and Evil," reproduced here, Geach argued that the terms good and bad are attributive rather than predicative adjectives, and that it is precisely in failing to recognize this fact, in treating them as predicative, that the dominant schools of modern philosophy have erred. Thus, not only was he concerned to attack as facile the intuitionism of G.E. Moore, but also to meet the perhaps more sinister threat he saw coming from those he termed the "Oxford moralists," who treated "good" as nothing more than a term of commendation. Overall, what Geach was trying to clear the way for was a more plainly descriptivist, not to mention functionalist, account of the good, such that answering the question as to whether or not a thing was good necessarily presupposed answering the prior question of what it was for.

The final three selections in this section offer expansions upon and developments of Geach's theme, drawing with ever-greater confidence upon the Aristotelian patrimony. The first piece is by Philippa Foot, a long-time friend and collaborator of Anscombe.

---

[2]   A. MacIntyre, *After Virtue* (London: Duckworth, 1981), pp. 169–189.

[3]   C. Taylor, "Irreducibly Social Goods," in C. Taylor, *Philosophical Arguments* (Cambridge, MA: Harvard University Press, 1995), pp. 127–145.

[4]   P. T. Geach, "Good and Evil," *Analysis* 17 (1956), pp. 33–42.

Like her, Foot has been a pertinacious critic of consequentialist and deontological ethical thinking, arguing with sustained subtlety and sophistication over her long career for a type of neo-Aristotelian virtue ethics. The extract here is from her most recent book, *Natural Goodness*, in which she argues that good reasons for action are intimately linked to the type of being – the type of animal species – one is talking of, such that natural kinds are seen to have an implicit and irreducibly evaluative content.[5] In the case of human beings, what makes for well-constructed practical reason is characterized by the possibilities and requirements of the human form. Here she can be seen grappling with what makes human goodness, though embedded within wider contexts, to be goodness of a peculiar sort. Her answer is that it concerns itself with the proper functioning of the rational will. Drawing heavily on the battery of distinctions made by Aquinas, she seeks to demonstrate the radical continuity between judgments "usually considered to be the special subject of moral philosophy" with a "wider class of evaluation of conduct with which they share a common conceptual scheme."[6]

The second piece is taken from an article by Michael Thompson, perhaps the central representative of a new generation of Anglo-Saxon moral philosophers taking forward the neo-Aristotelian banner.[7] Making many of the same arguments as Foot, this extract provides a clearer sense of the way in which, by embedding moral philosophy within a broader account of how normative judgments are made about life-forms in the non-human world, it becomes possible to explain how "our fundamental moral and practical knowledge … is at the same time knowledge implicitly about the specifically human form, knowledge of how the well-working human practical reason reasons."[8] The third and final selection, an article by a Spanish philosopher as yet little known in the Anglo-Saxon world, demonstrates remarkable and quite independent mirroring of many of the themes touched upon by Foot and Thompson, though this time rooted in the conceptual soil of continental philosophy.[9] Also drawing heavily on Aristotle and Aquinas, Murillo finds useful insights in the work of Hans Jonas and in that stream of the philosophy of biology into which his work fits. Overall great credence is given in each of these extracts to the analogical connection between the human and the sub-human, which enables them to speak intelligibly and in a systematic manner of continuity in difference.

---

[5]   P. Foot, "Human Goodness," Chap. 5 in *Natural Goodness* (Oxford: Clarendon Press, 2001), pp. 66–80.

[6]   Ibid., pp. 66–67.

[7]   M. Thompson, "Apprehending Human Form," in *Modern Moral Philosophy*, ed. A. O'Hear (Cambridge: Cambridge University Press, 2004), pp. 47–74.

[8]   Ibid., p. 72.

[9]   J. Murillo, "Health as a Norm and Principle of Intelligibility," in *Natural Law: Historical, Systematic and Juridical Approaches*, ed. A.N. Garcia et al. (Newcastle: Cambridge Scholars Publishing, 2008).

3.1.1 G.E.M. Anscombe
"Modern Moral Philosophy"

I will begin by stating three theses which I present in this paper. The first is that it is not profitable for us at present to do moral philosophy; that should be laid aside at any rate until we have an adequate philosophy of psychology, in which we are conspicuously lacking. The second is that the concepts of obligation, and duty – *moral* obligation and *moral* duty, that is to say – and of what is *morally* right and wrong, and of the *moral* sense of 'ought', ought to be jettisoned if this is psychologically possible; because they are survivals, or derivatives from survivals, from an earlier conception of ethics which no longer generally survives, and are only harmful without it. My third thesis is that the differences between the well-known English writers on moral philosophy from Sidgwick to the present day are of little importance.

[…]

It might remain to look for 'norms' in human virtues: just as *man* has so many teeth, which is certainly not the average number of teeth men have, but is the number of teeth for the species, so perhaps the species *man*, regarded not just biologically, but from the point of view of the activity of thought and choice in regard to the various departments of life – powers and faculties and use of things needed – 'has' such-and-such virtues: and this 'man' with the complete set of virtues is the 'norm', as 'man' with, e.g., a complete set of teeth is a norm. But in *this* sense 'norm' has ceased to be roughly equivalent to 'law'. In *this* sense the notion of a 'norm' brings us nearer to an Aristotelian than a law conception of ethics. There is, I think, no harm in that; but if someone looked in this direction to give 'norm' a sense, then he ought to recognize what has happened to the term 'norm', which he wanted to mean 'law – without bringing God in': it has ceased to mean 'law' at all; and *so* the expressions 'moral obligation', 'the moral ought', and 'duty' are best put on the Index, if he can manage it.

But meanwhile – is it not clear that there are several concepts that need investigating simply as part of the philosophy of psychology and – as I should recommend – *banishing ethics totally* from our minds? Namely – to begin with: 'action', 'intention', 'pleasure', 'wanting'. More will probably turn up if we start with these. Eventually it might be possible to advance to considering the concept of a virtue; with which, I suppose, we should be beginning some sort of a study of ethics.

G.E.M. Anscombe, "Modern Moral Philosophy," *Philosophy* 33, 124 (January, 1958), pp. 1–19. Copyright © Royal Institute of Philosophy, published by Cambridge University Press. Reprinted with permission.

I will end by describing the advantages of using the word 'ought' in a non-emphatic fashion, and not in a special 'moral' sense; of discarding the term 'wrong' in a 'moral' sense, and using such notions as 'unjust'.

It is possible, if one is allowed to proceed just by giving examples, to distinguish between the intrinsically unjust, and what is unjust given the circumstances. Seriously to get a man judicially punished for something which it can be clearly seen he has not done is intrinsically unjust. This might be done, of course, and often has been done, in all sorts of ways; by suborning false witnesses, by a rule of law by which something is 'deemed' to be the case which is admittedly not the case as a matter of fact, and by open insolence on the part of the judges and powerful people when they more or less openly say: 'A fig for the fact that you did not do it; we mean to sentence you for it all the same.' What is unjust given, e.g., normal circumstances is to deprive people of their ostensible property without legal procedure, not to pay debts, not to keep contracts, and a host of other things of the kind. Now, the circumstances can clearly make a great deal of difference in estimating the justice or injustice of such procedures as these; and these circumstances may *sometimes* include expected consequences; for example, a man's claim to a bit of property can become a nullity when its seizure and use can avert some obvious disaster: as, e.g., if you could use a machine of his to produce an explosion in which it would be destroyed, but by means of which you could divert a flood or make a gap which a fire could not jump. Now this certainly does not mean that what would ordinarily be an act of injustice, but is not intrinsically unjust, can always be rendered just by a reasonable calculation of better consequences; far from it; but the problems that would be raised in an attempt to draw a boundary line (or boundary area) here are obviously complicated. And while there are certainly some general remarks which ought to be made here, and some boundaries that can be drawn, the decision on particular cases would for the most part be determined κατὰ τὸν ὀϱθὸν λόγον – 'according to what's reasonable' – e.g. that *such-and-such* a delay of payment of a *such-and-such* debt to a person *so* circumstanced, on the part of a person *so* circumstanced, would or would not be unjust, is really only to be decided 'according to what's reasonable'; and for this there can *in principle* be no canon other than giving a few examples. That is to say, while it is because of a big gap in philosophy that we can give no general account of the concept of virtue and of the concept of justice, but have to proceed, using the concepts, only by giving examples; still there is an area where it is not because of any gap, but is in principle the case, that there is no account except by way of examples: and that is where the canon is 'what's reasonable': which of course is *not* a canon.

That is all I wish to say about what is just in some circumstances, unjust in others; and about the way in which expected consequences can play a part in determining what is just. Returning to my example of the intrinsically unjust: if a procedure *is* one of judicially punishing a man for what he is clearly understood not to have done, there can be absolutely no argument about the description of this as unjust. No circumstances, and no expected consequences, which do *not* modify the description of the procedure as one of judicially punishing a man for what he is known not to have done can modify the description of it as unjust. Someone who attempted to dispute this would only be pretending not to know what 'unjust' means: for this is a paradigm case of injustice.

And here we see the superiority of the term 'unjust' over the terms 'morally right' and 'morally wrong'. For in the context of English moral philosophy since Sidgwick it appears legitimate to discuss whether it *might* be 'morally right' in some circumstances to adopt that procedure; but it cannot be argued that the procedure would in any circumstances be just.

Now I am not able to do the philosophy involved – and I think that no one in the present situation of English philosophy *can* do the philosophy involved – but it is clear that a good man is a just man; and a just man is a man who habitually refuses to commit or participate in any unjust actions for fear of any consequences, or to obtain any advantage, for himself or anyone else. Perhaps no one will disagree. But, it will be said, what *is* unjust is sometimes determined by expected consequences; and certainly that is true. But there are cases where it is not: now if someone says, 'I agree, but all this wants a lot of explaining,' then he is right, and, what is more, the situation at present is that we can't do the explaining; we lack the philosophic equipment. But if someone really thinks, *in advance*,[1] that it is open to question whether such an action as procuring the judicial execution of the innocent should be quite excluded from consideration – I do not want to argue with him; he shows a corrupt mind.

In such cases our moral philosophers seek to impose a dilemma upon us. 'If we have a case where the term "unjust" applies purely in virtue of a factual description, can't one raise the question whether one sometimes conceivably ought to do injustice? If "what is unjust" is determined by consideration of whether it is *right* to do so-and-so in such-and-such circumstances, then the question whether it is "right" to commit injustice can't arise, just because "wrong" has been built into the definition of injustice. But if we have a case where the description "unjust" applies purely in virtue of the facts, without bringing "wrong" in, then the question can arise whether one "ought" perhaps to commit an injustice, whether it might not be "right" to. And of course "ought" and "right" are being used in their *moral* senses here. Now either you must decide what is "morally right" in the light of certain *other* "principle", or you make a "principle" about *this* and decide that an injustice is never "right"; but even if you do the latter you are going beyond the facts; you are making a decision that you will not, or that it is wrong to, commit injustice. But in either case, *if* the term "unjust" is determined simply by the facts, it is not the term "unjust" that determines that the term "wrong" applies, but a decision that injustice is *wrong*, together with the diagnosis of the "factual" description as entailing injustice. But the man who makes an absolute decision that injustice is "wrong" has no footing on which to criticize someone who does *not* make that decision as judging falsely.'

In this argument 'wrong' of course is explained as meaning 'morally wrong', and all the atmosphere of the term is retained while its substance is guaranteed quite null. Now let us remember that 'morally wrong' is the term which is the heir of the notion 'illicit', or 'what there is an obligation *not* to do'; which belongs in a divine-law theory of ethics. Here it really does add something to the description 'unjust' to say there is an obligation not to do it; for what obliges is the divine law – as rules oblige in a game. So if the divine law obliges not to commit injustice by forbidding injustice, it really does add something to the description 'unjust' to say there is an obligation not to do it. And it is because 'morally wrong' is the heir of this concept, but an heir that is cut off from the family of concepts from which it sprang, that 'morally wrong' *both* goes beyond the mere factual description 'unjust' *and* seems to have no discernible content except a certain compelling force, which I should call purely psychological. And such is the force of the term that philosophers actually suppose that the divine law notion can be dismissed as making no essential difference even if it is held – *because* they think that a 'practical principle' running 'I *ought* (i.e. am morally obliged) to obey divine laws' is required for the man who believes in divine laws. But actually *this* notion of obligation is a notion which only operates in the context of law. And I should be inclined to congratulate the present-day moral philosophers on depriving 'morally ought' of its now delusive appearance of content, if only they did not manifest a detestable desire to retain the atmosphere of the term.

It may be possible, if we are resolute, to discard the term 'morally ought', and simply return to the ordinary 'ought', which, we ought to notice, is such an extremely frequent term of human language that it is difficult to imagine getting on without it. Now if we do return to it, can't it reasonably be asked whether one might ever need to commit injustice, or whether it won't be the best thing to do? Of course it can. And the answers will be various. One man – a philosopher – may say that since justice is a virtue, and injustice a vice, and virtues and vices are built up by the performance of the actions in which they are instanced, an act of injustice will tend to make a man bad; and essentially the flourishing of a man *qua* man consists in his being good (e.g. in virtues); but for any *X* to which such terms apply, *X* needs what makes it flourish, so a man needs, or ought to perform, only virtuous actions; and even if, as it must be admitted may happen, he flourishes less, or not at all, in inessentials, by avoiding injustice, his life is spoiled in essentials by not avoiding injustice – so he still needs to perform only just actions. That is roughly how Plato and Aristotle talk; but it can be seen that philosophically there is a huge gap, at present unfillable as far as we are concerned, which needs to be filled by an account of human nature, human action, the type of characteristic a virtue is, and above all of human 'flourishing'. And it is the last concept that appears the most doubtful. For it is a bit much to swallow that a man in pain and hunger and poor and friendless is flourishing, as Aristotle himself admitted. Further, someone might say that one at least needed to stay alive to flourish. Another man unimpressed by all that will say in a hard case 'What we need is such-and-such, which we won't get without doing this (which is unjust) – so this is what we ought to do.' Another man, who does not follow the rather elaborate reasoning of the philosophers, simply says 'I know it is in any case a disgraceful thing to say that one had better commit this unjust action.' The man who believes in divine laws will say perhaps 'It is forbidden, and however it looks, it cannot be to anyone's profit to commit injustice'; he like the Greek philosophers can think in terms of flourishing. If he is a Stoic, he is apt to have a decidedly strained notion of what flourishing consists in; if he is a Jew or Christian, he need not have any very distinct notion: the way it will profit him to abstain from injustice is something that he leaves it to God to determine, himself only saying 'It can't do me any good to go against his law.' (He also hopes for a great reward in a new life later on, e.g. at the coming of Messiah; but in this he is relying on special promises.)

It is left to modern moral philosophy – the moral philosophy of all the well-known English ethicists since Sidgwick – to construct systems according to which the man who says 'We need such-and-such, and will only get it this way' *may* be a virtuous character: that is to say, it is left open to debate whether such a procedure as the judicial punishment of the innocent may not in some circumstances be the 'right' one to adopt; and though the present Oxford moral philosophers would accord a man *permission* to 'make it his principle' not to do such a thing, they teach a philosophy according to which the particular consequences of such an action *could* 'morally' be taken into account by a man who was debating what to do; and if they were such as to accord with his ends, it might be a step in his moral education to frame a moral principle under which he 'managed' (to use Mr Nowell-Smith's phrase[2])' to bring the action; or it might be a new 'decision of principle', making which was an advance in the formation of his moral thinking (to adopt Mr Hare's conception), to decide: in such-and-such circumstances one ought to procure the judicial condemnation of the innocent. And that is my complaint.

Notes

1   If he thinks it in the concrete situation, he is of course merely a normally tempted human being. In discussion when this paper was read, as was perhaps to be expected, this case was produced: a government is required to have an innocent man tried, sentenced and executed under threat of a 'hydrogen bomb war'. It would seem strange to me to have much hope of so averting a war threatened by such men as made this demand. But the most important thing about the way in which cases like this are invented in discussions, is the assumption that only two courses are open: here, complaince and open defiance. No one can say in advance of such a situation what the possibilities are going to be – e.g. that there is none of stalling by a feigned willingness to comply, accompanied by a skilfully arranged 'escape' of the victim.

2   P.H. Nowell-Smith, *Ethics* (Harmondsworth, 1954), 308.

3.1.2 Alasdair MacIntyre
After Virtue

The question can therefore now be posed directly: are we or are we not able to disentangle from these rival and various claims a unitary core concept of the virtues of which we can give a more compelling account than any of the other accounts so far? I am going to argue that we can in fact discover such a core concept and that it turns out to provide the tradition of which I have written the history with its conceptual unity. It will indeed enable us to distinguish in a clear way those beliefs about the virtues which genuinely belong to the tradition from those which do not. Unsurprisingly perhaps it is a complex concept, different parts of which derive from different stages in the development of the tradition. Thus the concept itself in some sense embodies the history of which it is the outcome.

One of the features of the concept of a virtue which has emerged with some clarity from the argument so far is that it always requires for its application the acceptance of some prior account of certain features of social and moral life in terms of which it has to be defined and explained. So in the Homeric account the concept of a virtue is secondary to that of *a social role*, in Aristotle's account it is secondary to that of *the good life for man* conceived as the *telos* of human action and in Franklin's much later account it is secondary to that of utility. What is it in the account which I am about to give which provides in a similar way the necessary background against which the concept of a virtue has to be made intelligible? It is in answering this question that the complex, historical, multilayered character of the core concept of virtue becomes clear. For there are no less than three stages in the logical development of the concept which have to be identified in order, if the core conception of a virtue is to be understood, and each of these stages has its own conceptual background. The first stage requires a background account of what I shall call a practice, the second an account of the narrative order of a single human life, and the third an account of what constitutes a moral tradition. Each later stage presupposes the earlier, but not *vice versa*. Each earlier stage is both modified by and reinterpreted in the light of, but also provides an essential constituent of each later stage. The progress in the development of the concept is closely related to, although it does not recapitulate in any straightforward way, the history of the tradition of which it forms the core.

In the Homeric account of the virtues – and in heroic societies more generally – the exercise of a virtue exhibits qualities which are required for sustaining a social role and

Alasdair MacIntyre, *After Virtue* (London: Duckworth, 1981), pp. 123–128.

for exhibiting excellence in some well-marked area of social practice: to excel is to excel at war or in the games, as Achilles does, in sustaining a household, as Penelope does, in giving counsel in the assembly, as Nestor does, in the telling of a tale, as Homer himself does. When Aristotle speaks of excellence in human activity, he sometimes, though not always, refers to some well-defined type of human practice: flute-playing, or war, or geometry. I am going to suggest that this notion of a particular type of practice as providing the arena in which the virtues are exhibited and in terms of which they are to receive their primary, if incomplete, definition is crucial to the whole enterprise of identifying a core concept of the virtues. I hasten to add two *caveats* however.

The first is to point out that my argument will not in any way imply that virtues are *only* exercised in the course of what I am calling practices. The second is to warn that I shall be using the word 'practice' in a specially defined way which does not completely agree with current ordinary usage, including my own previous use of that word. What am I going to mean by it?

By a 'practice' I am going to mean any coherent and complex form of socially established cooperative human activity through which goods internal to that form of activity are realized in the course of trying to achieve those standards of excellence which are appropriate to, and partially definitive of that form of activity, with the result that human powers to achieve excellence, and human conceptions of the ends and goods involved, are systematically extended. Tic-tac-toe is not an example of a practice in this sense, nor is throwing a football with skill; but the game of football is, and so is chess. Bricklaying is not a practice; architecture is. Planting turnips is not a practice; farming is. So are the enquiries of physics, chemistry, and biology, and so is the work of the historian, and so are painting and music. In the ancient and medieval worlds the creation and sustaining of human communities – of households, cities, nations – are generally taken to be a practice in the sense in which I have defined it. Thus the range of practices is wide: arts, sciences, games, politics in the Aristotelian sense, the making and sustaining of family life, all fall under the concept. But the question of the precise range of practices is not at this stage of the first importance. Instead let me explain some of the key terms involved in my definition, beginning with the notion of goods internal to a practice.

Consider the example of a highly intelligent 7-year-old child whom I wish to teach to play chess, although the child has no particular desire to learn the game. The child does, however, have a very strong desire for candy and little chance of obtaining it. I therefore tell the child that if the child will play chess with me once a week I will give the child 50¢ worth of candy; moreover I tell the child that I will always play in such a way that it will be difficult, but not impossible, for the child to win and that, if the child wins, the child will receive an extra 50¢ worth of candy. Thus motivated the child plays and plays to win. Notice, however, that, so long as it is the candy alone which provides the child with a good reason for playing chess, the child has no reason not to cheat and every reason to cheat, provided he or she can do so successfully. But, so we may hope, there will come a time when the child will find in those goods specific to chess, in the achievement of a certain highly particular kind of analytical skill, strategic imagination and competitive intensity, a new set of reasons, reasons now not just for winning on a particular occasion, but for trying to excel in whatever way the game of chess demands. Now if the child cheats, he or she will be defeating not me, but himself or herself.

There are thus two kinds of good possibly to be gained by playing chess. On the one hand there are those goods externally and contingently attached to chess-playing and to other practices by the accidents of social circumstance – in the case of the imaginary child candy, in the case of real adults such goods as prestige, status, and money. There are always alternative ways for achieving such goods, and their achievement is never to be had *only* by engaging in some particular kind of practice. On the other hand there are the goods internal to the practice of chess which cannot be had in any way but by playing chess or some other game of that specific kind. We call them internal for two reasons: first, as I have already suggested, because we can only specify them in terms of chess or some other game of that specific kind and by means of examples from such games (otherwise the meagreness of our vocabulary for speaking of such goods forces us into such devices as my own resort to writing of 'a certain highly particular king of'); and secondly because they can only be identified and recognized by the experience of participating in the practice in question. Those who lack the relevant experience are incompetent thereby as judges of internal goods.

This is clearly the case with all the major examples of practices: consider for example – even if briefly and inadequately – the practice of portrait-painting as it developed in Western Europe from the late middle ages to the eighteenth century. The successful portrait painter is able to achieve many goods which are in the sense just defined external to the practice of portrait-painting – fame, wealth, social status, even a measure of power and influence at courts upon occasion. But those external goods are not to be confused with the goods which are internal to the practice. The internal goods are those which result from an extended attempt to show how Wittgenstein's dictum 'The human body is the best picture of the human soul' (*Investigations*, 178e) might be made to become true by teaching us 'to regard … the picture on our wall as the object itself (the men, landscape and so on) depicted there' (p. 205e) in a quite new way. What is misleading about Wittgenstein's dictum as it stands is its neglect of the truth in George Orwell's thesis 'At 50 everyone has the face he deserves'. What painters from Giotto to Rembrandt learnt to show was how the face at any age may be revealed as the face that the subject of a portrait deserves.

Originally in medieval paintings of the saints the face was an icon; the question of a resemblance between the depicted face of Christ or St Peter and the face that Jesus or Peter actually possessed at some particular age did not even arise. The antithesis to this iconography was the relative naturalism of certain fifteenth-century Flemish and German painting. The heavy eyelids, the coifed hair, the lines around the mouth undeniably represent some particular woman, either actual or envisaged. Resemblance has usurped the iconic relationship. But with Rembrandt there is, so to speak, synthesis: the naturalistic portrait is now rendered as an icon, but an icon of a new and hitherto inconceivable kind. Similarly in a very different kind of sequence mythological faces in a certain kind of seventeenth-century French painting become aristocratic faces in the eighteenth century. Within each of these sequences at least two different kinds of good internal to the painting of human faces and bodies are achieved.

There is first of all the excellence of the products, both the excellence in performance by the painters and that of each portrait itself. This excellence – the very verb 'excel' suggests it – has to be understood historically. The sequences of development find their point and purpose in a progress towards and beyond a variety of types and modes of excellence. There are of course sequences of decline as well as of progress, and progress is rarely to be understood as straightforwardly linear. But it is in participation in the attempts to sustain progress and to respond creatively to moments that the second kind of good internal to the practices of portrait-painting is to be found. For what the artist discovers within the pursuit of excellence in portrait-painting – and what is true of portrait-painting is true of the practice of the fine arts in general – is the good of a certain kind of life. That life may not constitute the whole of life for someone who is a painter by a very long way or it may at least for a period, Gauguin-like, absorb him or her at the expense of almost everything else. But it is the painter's living out of a greater or lesser part of his or her life *as a painter* that is the second kind of good internal to painting. And judgement upon these goods requires at the very least the kind of competence that is only to be acquired either as a painter or as someone willing to learn systematically what the portrait painter has to teach.

A practice involves standards of excellence and obedience to rules as well as the achievement of goods. To enter into a practice is to accept the authority of those standards and the inadequacy of my own performance as judged by them. It is to subject my own attitudes, choices, preferences, and tastes to the standards which currently and partially define the practice. Practices of course, as I have just noticed, have a history: games, sciences, and arts all have histories. Thus the standards are not themselves immune from criticism, but none the less we cannot be initiated into a practice without accepting the authority of the best standards realized so far. If, on starting to listen to music, I do not accept my own incapacity to judge correctly, I will never learn to hear, let alone to appreciate, Bartok's last quartets. If, on starting to play baseball, I do not accept that others know better than I when to throw a fast ball and when not, I will never learn to appreciate good pitching let alone to pitch. In the realm of practices the authority of both goods and standards operates in such a way as to rule out all subjectivist and emotivist analyses of judgement. De gustibus est disputandum.

We are now in a position to notice an important difference between what I have called internal and what I have called external goods. It is characteristic of what I have called external goods that when achieved they are always some individual's property and possession. Moreover, characteristically they are such that the more someone has of them, the less there is for other people. This is sometimes necessarily the case, as with power and fame, and sometimes the case by reason of contingent circumstance as with money. External goods are therefore characteristically objects of competition in which there must be losers as well as winners. Internal goods are indeed the outcome of competition to excel, but it is characteristic of them that their achievement is a good for the whole community who participate in the practice. So when Turner transformed the seascape in painting or W. G. Grace advanced the art of batting in cricket in a quite new way their achievement enriched the whole relevant community.

But what does all or any of this have to do with the concept of the virtues? It turns out that we are now in a position to formulate a first, even if partial and tentative definition of a virtue: *A virtue is an acquired human quality the possession and exercise of which tends to enable us to achieve those goods which are internal to practices and the lack of which effectively prevents us from achieving any such goods.* Later this definition will need amplification and amendment. But as a first approximation to an adequate definition it already illuminates the place of the virtues in human life. For it is not difficult to show for a whole range of key virtues that without them the goods internal to practices are barred to us. but not just barred to us generally, barred in a very particular way.

3.1.3 Charles Taylor
"Irreducibly Social Goods"

So we see two ways of defining irreducibly common goods: (1) the goods of a culture that makes conceivable actions, feelings, valued ways of life, and (2) goods that essentially incorporate common understandings of their value. There is obviously a substantial overlap between the two, in that a cultural good may also exist only to the extent that it is commonly prized. Indeed, the last example seems to have a foot in both categories: that our culture offers the possibility of public relations of frankness and equality shades over into our actually standing in such relations. Neither can perhaps long survive the demise of the other.

So what? Perhaps I'm right here, as a matter of philosophical analysis. But we may want to ask what follows for our social and political life. Is this just an academic dispute?

The answer ought to be already showing through. It can be gleaned from the examples I used that the conception of irreducibly social goods is bound up with some important stands of modern politics. So in articulating this kind of good I am spelling out the philosophical presuppositions of some political positions that are widely held.

Almost the first example that springs to mind is modern linguistic or cultural nationalism. Perhaps this springs first to my mind because I live in Montreal, and have been trying to make sense of what goes on here for the last half-century. It is clear that all stripes of nationalist sentiment in this province concur in seeing the culture of Quebec, and that means in practice the French language, at least as a common good in sense 1, the presupposition of the life they value; and sometimes as a good in sense 2 as well. What has emerged is a politics of defending the language as a common good, considered an important enough goal to take priority in some cases over individual goals that would otherwise have been considered as beyond legitimate constraint. Thus there have been restrictions on where parents could send their children to state-supported schools (totally private schools are unregulated): that is, on the language of schooling they could choose for their children. In response to pleas for freedom of parents' choice as a right,

Charles Taylor, "Irreducibly Social Goods," originally published in *Rationality, Individualism and Public Policy*, ed. Geoffrey Brennan and Clif Walsh (Centre for Research on Federal Financial Relations, 1990); reprinted in *Philosophical Arguments* (Cambridge, MA: Harvard University Press, 1995). © Charles Taylor. Reprinted with kind permission of the author.

nationalist theorists have developed theories of "collective" rights, which are alleged to take precedence in certain cases over individual rights.

I'm not making a judgement here, just reporting a bit of contemporary politics based on concepts that would have to be philosophically explicated in something like the manner I have just outlined. But let me turn to another, perhaps (to some of you) less morally dubious example.

This is one of the central stands of modern democratic culture. I'm talking about the politics that takes participatory self-rule as a good in itself – not simply as something instrumental to other goals, like justice or peace or stability, but as something valued for its own sake. This has a long history in our culture. It connects to the tradition of thought in the modern West which has been called "civic humanist," and which took the ancient polis or republic as a model. Its major thinkers include Machiavelli (an idiosyncratic case, but he built on an influential stand in the Renaissance), Montesquieu, Rousseau, Tocqueville, and in our day Arendt. Its moments of decisive political impact, after the Italian Renaissance, are the civil-war period in England; the American revolution and constitution building; the French revolution; after which it has become a major strand in the self-understanding of western liberal democracies.

It takes the life of the citizen, of a person who is not simply subjected to power but participates in his/her own rule, as an essential component of human dignity. And it contrasts the life in which the citizen turns toward the great issues, where the fate of peoples and cultures hangs in the balance, to the narrow confines of a life focused only on self-enrichment or private pleasures. Civic humanism coins a special sense of the term "freedom" (or borrows it from the ancients), distinct from the common sense of "negative" freedom, to describe this political condition. Tocqueville eloquently described the attractions of this kind of liberty:

> Ce qui, dans tous les temps lui a attaché si fortement le coeur de certains hommes, ce sont ses attraits mêmes, son charme propre, indépendant de ses bienfaits; c'est le plaisir de pouvoir parler, agir, respirer sans contrainte, sous le seul gouvernement de Dieu et des lois. Qui cherche dans la liberté autre chose qu'elle-même est fait pour servir.

And Tocqueville finishes the passage grandly by saying that you either understand this taste for liberty or you don't "On doit renoncer à le faire comprendre aux âmes médiocres qui ne l'ont jarnais ressenti."

But shorn of Tocqueville's aristocratic sensibility, we recognize a widespread aspiration and political value of our time. Now a regime in which people govern themselves as equal citizens is a common good in sense 2 above. It can't exist without some common understanding that this is the basis on which we stand with each other, and the common understanding must englobe the rightness of this basis. Of course this insight goes far back into the civic-humanist tradition of thought about republican rule, right back to the ancients. This kind of regime absolutely requires that we share a love for the "laws," what Montesquieu defined as "vertu."

But the outlook I'm describing here, following Sen, as "welfarist" can't assimilate this kind of good; it can't allow for an undistorted description of it. The politics of nationalism, or republican rule, emerge in its language as the cherishing of some instrumental public good. Or else their status as goods is understood in a purely subjectivist fashion:

they are goods to the extent that people desire them. A certain proportion of Quebeckers have a "taste" for the preservation of the French language, and so this is a good, just like chocolate-chip ice cream and transistor radios.

But both views grievously distort the nature of the good sought, particularly the last. The spokesmen for nationalism, or republican rule, don't see its value as contingent on its popularity. They think that these are goods whether we recognize them or not, goods we ought to recognize. This stance sometimes goes unrecognized because it is somehow morally reprehensible: what right do these people have to tell us that we ought to give our national culture a higher priority in our lives? Or that we ought to participate in our own rule? Are they going to force us to be free? There seems to be something undemocratic in this attitude.

But this is a confusion. Democracy concerns our collective decision-making procedures. A proponent of nationalism or citizen rule can be a democrat as well as anyone else, in the sense of respecting these procedures (and there is a paradox in a proponent of republican rule failing to respect them, as has been tragically enough ilustrated over and over again in modern history). But one doesn't have to tailor opinions about the good to the tastes of the majority. What an individual *advocates* must surely be independent of majority taste. The temptation to think otherwise comes from the rampant subjectivism in so much modern philosophy.

Now for the purposes of this discussion, I take no stand in favor of nationalism and citizen rule. Indeed, I could hardly do so because there are many stands of modern nationalism, and some of them are visibly evil. As a matter of fact, I've spent much of my political life combatting certain strands I dislike. I do confess to being a strong partisan of citizen self-rule, but all this is meant to be beside the point. What I want to bring out here is the way in which an important set of issues that figure in modern politics shows up distortively in the perspective of welfarism. Some alternatives can't be undistortively formulated in this perspective. If these were intellectually incoherent, then it would be entirely to the credit of welfarism to have shown them up as such. But since I argue that this kind of common good is perfectly coherent, I draw the opposite conclusion. The view that all social goods are decomposable is a view we have to scrap, and not just for reasons of intellectual rigor, because it's wrong – but also because it prevents us from adequately understanding important aspects of modern social and political life.

But I haven't yet finished my attack. The welfarist outlook doesn't only distort the political aspirations to common goods; it occludes to some extent the opposition to these aspirations, because this philosophy is not neutral. The utilitarian view is aligned with one of the contestants in the modern struggle to define liberal democracy.

In fact, there are several strands of thought and political aspiration which have gone into making contemporary western societies. The civic-humanist stand is just one, and perhaps not the most powerful. Also of great importance have been the understanding of society as an association of bearers of rights; and the picture of society as an association of bearers of interests, either groups or individuals. The rights perspective goes back to the great seventeenth-century natural rights theories, and even beyond if we trace it out properly. The picture of society as set up to serve the interests of its members also goes back to foundational writers in the seventeenth century. Locke is an important figure for both strands. But the full development of the interest strand comes only in the eighteenth century, with the utilitarian Enlightenment. Today this picture of society as a common instrument for diverse group interests is visible in, for instance, the theories of interest-group pluralism or the "economic" or elite theories of democracy.

This interest strand has been in tension with the republican strand almost since the beginning of the modern representative liberal state. J. G. Pocock has traced the intellectual conflict in eighteenth-century England. The tension can be seen in the work of the writers of the American constitution. And it is evident today.

In our day it turns on our attitude to centralization and bureaucracy. From one perspective these can be positively valued, since they seem to be the conditions of more effective production of goods that people (individually) want. Moreover, greater production can be thought to be the condition of fairer distribution, since it's easier to give to those who have less if you don't have to take away from those who have more. Rapid growth can make social redistribution less of a zero-sum game. And fairness in distribution has always been a central concern of the interest perspective.

On the other side, concentration and bureaucratic organization are seen as the greatest adversaries of self-rule, gradually stifling it or rendering it irrelevant, and producing despair and cynicism in an age of giant, irresponsible agglomerations of power.

Now one of these strands of thought wants to think in terms of individual goods; it wants to see society merely in instrumental terms. It wants to be clear about who is getting what good, because it is concerned about "delivering the goods" maximally and (usually also) equally. The welfarist perspective is a good one to adopt in order to deliberate about alternatives, *granted the goods in which it is interested*. Welfarism is as congenial to this strand of thinking as it is inhospitable to the republican one.

Now if challenged to defend itself as a moral position, this strand would have something to say, because it comes from a moral tradition of some depth. There is an important line of modern moral thinking that I have called elsewhere the "affirmation of ordinary life," which starts with the Reformation and is secularized in the Enlightenment. By "ordinary life" I mean the life of production and reproduction, of work and the family. The central idea is that the good life for human beings is not to be found in some higher activity, beyond ordinary life – be it contemplation or religious asceticism or even citizen rule. It is to be found at the very center of everyday existence, in the acquisition through labor of the means to live and the reproduction of life in the family. This idea perhaps starts with the Puritan stress on the "calling," and then it mutates into the Enlightenment conception of human happiness in a life according to nature. Rousseau too made it central, trying to combine it, paradoxically and perhaps impossibly, with an ethic of citizen rule. And it is visible in the exaltation of man the producer in the work of Marx.

Polemically, thinkers in this strand have directed their attacks on what they saw as the false prestige of the "higher" goods, which often served as a cover to justify the privileged status of a "higher" class properly dedicated to these goods – be it those with leisure to contemplate; or those who have dedicated themselves to religious askesis; or those who seek honor and fame in public life. In this context it is worth remembering that the ethic of republican rule was in a very real sense an aristocratic one for most of human history. Even ancient democracies were far from comprehensive, and they existed on the backs of an underclass of slaves, not to mention the exclusion of metics and the lower status of women. The ethic of ordinary life has always been hostile to that of honor and fame.

So the proponents of welfarism, a politics of instrumental reason aimed at the production of individual happiness, have an answer to the haughty claim of Tocqueville. They can plead that they are not interested in the illusion of supposedly higher concerns; that too much has already been sacrificed of human happiness on such altars; that what they are after is concrete, tangible human welfare; that theirs is the politics of real philanthropy, altruism, and concern for the human good.

A full-scale moral argument is about to break out here, one of some depth and passion, one that could illuminate our current predicament if we carried it forward. And that is what's wrong with welfarism. It prevents this argument from happening. For it not only distorts its opponent's position, but occludes its own. As long as you think that all goods must be individual, and that any other construal is incoherent, you can't see that there is a *moral* argument here. The burden of advocacy of the welfarist stance to policy seems entirely borne by *logical* arguments. The issue seems one of thinking straight, rather than one of acting well. Welfarism, as a doctrine about the nature of the good, has to be dispelled before the really interesting argument, between welfarism as a theory of *what things are good* and its opponents, can swim into focus.

As a philosophical doctrine, welfarism is acting as a screen, which prevents us from seeing our actual moral predicament and from identifying the real alternatives. It pretends to a neutrality it doesn't really enjoy. The result is that it distorts its opponent and, perhaps even more fatefully, hides from itself the rich moral outlook that motivates it. To set it aside is more than a demand of intellectual rigor. It is also a requirement of political and moral lucidity.

And this is why it is worth showing to all sides in the debate that there are, indeed, irreducibly social goods.

3.1.4 P.T. Geach
"Good and Evil"

MY FIRST TASK will be to draw a logical distinction between two sorts of adjectives, suggested by the distinction between *attributive* adjectives (e.g. 'a red book') and *predicative* adjectives (e.g. 'this book is red'); I shall borrow this terminology from the grammars. I shall say that in a phrase 'an A B' ('A' being an adjective and 'B' being a noun) ('A' is a (logically) predicative adjective if the predication 'is an A B' splits up logically into a pair of predications 'is a B' and 'is A'; otherwise I shall say that 'A' is a (logically) attributive adjective. Henceforth I shall use the terms 'predicative adjective' and 'attributive adjective' always in my special logical sense, unless the contrary is shown by my inserting the adverb 'grammatically'.

There are familiar examples of what I call attributive adjectives. 'Big' and 'small' are attributive; 'x is a big flea' does not split up into 'x is a flea' and 'x is big', nor 'x is a small elephant' into 'x is an elephant' and 'x is small'; for if these analyses were legitimate, a simple argument would show that a big flea is a big animal and a small elephant a small animal. Again, the sort of adjective that the mediaevals called *alienans* is attributive; 'x is a forged banknote' does not split up into 'x is a banknote' and 'x is forged', nor 'x is the putative father of y' into 'x is the father of y' and 'x is putative'. On the other hand, in the phrase 'a red book' 'red' is a predicative adjective in my sense, although not grammatically so, for 'is a red book' logically splits up into 'is a book' and 'is red'.

I can now state my first thesis about good and evil: 'good' and 'bad' are always attributive, not predicative, adjectives. This is fairly clear about 'bad' because 'bad' is something like an *alienans* adjective; we cannot safely predicate of a bad A what we predicate of an A, any more than we can predicate of a forged banknote or a putative father what we predicate of a banknote or a father. We actually call forged money 'bad'; and we cannot infer e.g. that because food supports life bad food supports life. For 'good' the point is not so clear at first sight, since 'good' is not *alienans* – whatever holds true of an A as such holds true of a good A. But consider the contrast in such a pair of phrases as 'red car' and 'good car'. I could ascertain that a distant object is a red car because I can see it is red and a keener sighted but colour-blind friend can see it is a car; there is no such possibility of ascertaining that a thing is a good car by pooling independent information that it is good and that it is a car. This sort of example shows that 'good' like 'bad' is essentially an

P.T. Geach, "Good and Evil," *Analysis* 17 (1956), pp. 33–42.

attributive adjective. Even when 'good' or 'bad' stands by itself as a predicate, and is thus grammatically predicative, some substantive has to be understood; there is no such thing as being just good or bad, there is only being a good or bad so-and-so. (If I say that something is a good or bad *thing*, either 'thing' is a mere proxy for a more descriptive noun to be supplied from the context; or else I am trying to use 'good' or 'bad' predicatively, and its being grammatically attributive is a mere disguise. The latter attempt is, on my thesis, illegitimate.)

We can indeed say *simpliciter* 'A is good' or 'A is bad', where 'A' is a proper name; but this is an exception that proves the rule. For Locke was certainly wrong in holding that there is no nominal essence of individuals; the continued use of a proper name 'A' always presupposes a continued reference to an individual as being the same X, where 'X' is some common noun; and the 'X' expresses the nominal essence of the individual called 'A'. Thus use of the proper name 'Peter Geach' presupposes a continuing reference to the same *man*; use of 'the Thames' a continuing reference to the same *river*; and so on. In modern logic books you often read that proper names have no meaning, in the sense of 'meaning' in which common nouns are said to have meaning; or (more obscurely) that they have no 'connotation'. But consider the difference between the understanding that a man has of a conversation overheard in a country house when he knows that 'Seggie' stands for a man, and what he has if he is uncertain whether 'Seggie' stands for a man, a Highland stream, a village, or a dog. In the one case he knows *what* 'Seggie' means, though not *whom*; in the other case he does not know *what* 'Seggie' means and cannot follow the drift of the conversation. Well, then if the common noun 'X' expresses the nominal essence of the individual called 'A'; if *being the same* X is a condition whose fulfilment is presupposed by our still calling an individual 'A'; then the meaning of 'A is good/bad' said *simpliciter*, will be 'A is a good/bad X'. E.g. if 'Seggie' stands for a man, 'Seggie is good' said *simpliciter* will mean 'Seggie is a good man', though context might make it mean 'Seggie is a good deer-stalker', or the like.

The moral philosophers known as Objectivists[1] would admit all that I have said as regards the ordinary uses of the terms 'good' and 'bad'; but they allege that there is an essentially different, predicative, use of the terms in such utterances as 'pleasure is good' and 'preferring inclination to duty is bad', and that this use alone is of philosophical importance. The ordinary uses of 'good' and 'bad' are for Objectivists just a complex tangle of ambiguities. I read an article once by an Objectivist exposing these ambiguities and the baneful effects they have on philosophers not forewarned of them. One philosopher who was so misled was Aristotle. Aristotle, indeed, did not talk English, but by a remarkable coincidence ἀγαθός had ambiguities quite parallel to those of 'good'. Such coincidences are, of course, possible; puns are sometimes translatable. But it is also possible that the uses of ἀγαθός and 'good' run parallel because they express one and the same concept; that this is a philosophically important concept, in which Aristotle did well to be interested; and that the apparent dissolution of this concept into a mass of ambiguities results from trying to assimilate it to the concepts expressed by ordinary predicative adjectives. It is mere prejudice to think that either all things called 'good' must satisfy some one condition, or the term 'good' is hopelessly ambiguous. A philosopher who writes off most of the uses of 'good' as trivial facts about the English language can, of course, with some plausibility, represent the remaining uses of 'good' as all expressing some definite condition fulfilled by good things – e.g. that they either contain, or are conducive to, pleasure; or again that they satisfy desire. Such theories of goodness are, however, open to well-known objections; they are cases of the Naturalistic Fallacy, as Objectivists say. The Objectivists' own theory is that 'good' in the selected uses they leave to the word does not supply an ordinary, 'natural', description of things, but ascribes to them a simple and indefinable *non*-natural attribute. But nobody has ever given a coherent and understandable account of what it is for an attribute to be non-natural. I am very much afraid that the Objectivists are just playing fast and loose with the term 'attribute'. In order to assimilate 'good' to ordinary predicative adjectives like 'red' and 'sweet' they call goodness an attribute; to escape undesired consequences drawn from the assimilation, they can always protest, 'Oh no, not like that. Goodness isn't a *natural* attribute like redness and sweetness, it's a non-natural attribute'. It is just as though somebody thought to escape the force of Frege's arguments that the number 7 is not a figure, by saying that it is a figure, only a non-natural figure, and that this is a possibility Frege failed to consider.

Moreover, can a philosopher offer philosophical utterances like 'pleasure is good' as an *explanation* of how he means 'good' to be taken in his discussions? 'Forget the uses of "good" in ordinary language' says the Objectivist; 'in our discussion it shall mean what I mean by it in such typical remarks as "pleasure is good". You, of course, know just how I want you to take these. No, of course I cannot explain further: don't you know that "good" in my sense is a simple and undefinable term?' But how can we be asked to take for granted at the outset that a peculiarly philosophical use of words necessarily means anything at all? Still less can we be expected at the outset to know what this use means.

I conclude that Objectivism is only the pretence of a way out of the Naturalistic Fallacy: it does not really give an account of how 'good' differs in its logic from other terms, but only darkens counsel by words without knowledge.

What I have said so far would meet with general approval by contemporary ethical writers at Oxford (whom I shall hence forth call the Oxford Moralists); and I now have to consider their positive account of 'good'. They hold that the features of the term's use which I have described derive from its function's being primarily not descriptive at all but commendatory. 'That is a good book' means something like 'I recommend that book' or 'choose that book'. They hold, however, that although the primary force of 'good' is commendation there are many cases where its force is purely descriptive – 'Hutton was batting on a good wicket', in a newspaper report, would not mean 'What a wonderful wicket Hutton was batting on. May you have such a wicket when you bat'.[2] The Oxford Moralists account for such cases by saying that here 'good' is, so to say, in quotation marks; Hutton was batting on a 'good' wicket, i.e. a wicket such as cricket fans would call 'good', i.e. would commend and choose.

I totally reject this view that 'good' has not a primarily descriptive force. Somebody who did not care two pins about cricket, but fully understood how the game worked (not an impossible supposition), could supply a purely descriptive sense for the phrase 'good batting wicket' regardless of the tastes of cricket fans. Again if I call a man a good burglar or a good cut-throat I am certainly not commending him myself; one can imagine circumstances in which these descriptions would serve to guide another man's choice (e.g. if a commando leader were choosing burglars and cut-throats for a special job), but such circumstances are rare and cannot give the primary sense of the descriptions. It ought to be clear that calling a thing a good A does not influence choice unless the one who is choosing happens to want an A; and this influence on action is not the logically primary force of the word 'good'. 'You have ants in your pants', which obviously has a primarily descriptive force, is far closer to affecting action than many uses of the term 'good'. And many uses of the word 'good' have no reference to the tastes of a panel of experts or anything of the sort; if I say that a man has a good eye or a good stomach my remark has a very clear descriptive force and has no reference to any panel of eye or stomach fanciers.

So far as I can gather from their writings, the Oxford Moralists would develop two lines of objection against the view that 'good' has a primarily descriptive force. First, if we avoid the twin errors of the Naturalistic Fallacy and of Objectivism we shall see that there is no one description, 'natural' or 'non-natural', to which all good things answer. The traits for which a thing is called 'good' are different according to the kind of thing in question; a knife is called 'good' if it is UVW, a stomach if it is XYZ, and so on. So, if 'good' did have a properly descriptive force this would vary from case to case: 'good' applied to knives would express the attributes UVW, 'good' as applied to stomachs would express the attributes XYZ, and so on. If 'good' is not to be merely ambiguous its primary force must be taken to be the unvarying commendatory force, not the indefinitely varying descriptive force.

This argument is a mere fallacy; it is another example of assimilating 'good' to ordinary predicative adjectives, or rather it assumes that this assimilation would have to be all right if the force of 'good' were descriptive. It would not in fact follow, even if 'good' were an ordinary predicative adjective, that if 'good knife' means the same as 'knife that is UVW', 'good' means the same as 'UVW'. 'Triangle with all its sides equal' means the same as 'triangle with three sides equal', but you cannot cancel out 'triangle' and say that 'with all its sides equal' means the same as 'with three sides equal'. In the case of 'good' the fallacy is even grosser; it is like thinking that 'square of' means the same as 'double of' because 'the square of 2' means the same as 'the double of 2'. This mathematical analogy may help to get our heads clear. There is no one number by which you can always multiply a number to get its square: but it does not follow either that 'square of' is an ambiguous expression meaning sometimes 'double of', sometimes 'treble of', etc., or that you have to do something other than multiplying to find the square of a number; and, given a number, its square is determinate. Similarly, there is no one description to which all things called 'good so-and-so's' answer; but it does not follow either that 'good' is a very ambiguous expression or that calling a thing good is something different from describing it; and given the descriptive force of 'A', the descriptive force of 'a good A' does not depend upon people's tastes.

'But I could know what "good hygrometer" meant without knowing what hygrometers were for; I could not, however, in that case be giving a definite descriptive force to "good hygrometer" as opposed to "hygrometer"; so "good" must have commendatory not descriptive force.' The reply to this objection (imitated from actual arguments of the Oxford Moralists) is that if I do not know what hygrometers are for, I do not really know what 'hygrometer' means, and *therefore* do not really know what 'good hygrometer' means; I merely know that I could find out its meaning by finding out what hygrometers were for – just as I know how I could find out the value of the square of the number of the people in Sark if I knew the number of people, and *so far* may be said to understand the phrase, 'the square of the number of the people in Sark'.

The Oxford Moralists' second line of objection consists in first asking whether the connexion between calling a thing 'a good A' and advising a man who wants an A to choose this one is analytic or empirical, and then developing a dilemma. It sounds clearly wrong to make the connexion a mere empirical fact; but if we make it analytic, then 'good' cannot have descriptive force, for from a mere description advice cannot be logically inferred.

I should indeed say that the connexion is not merely empirical; but neither is it analytic. It belongs to the *ratio* of 'want', 'choose', 'good', and 'bad', that, normally, and other things being equal, a man who wants an A will choose a good A and will not choose a bad A – or rather will choose an A that he thinks good and will not choose an A that he thinks bad. This holds good whether the A's we are choosing between are knives, horses, or thieves; *quidquid appetitur, appetitur sub specie boni*. Since the qualifying phrase, 'normally and other things being equal', is necessary for the truth of this statement, it is not an analytic statement. But the presence of these phrases does *not* reduce the statement to a mere rough empirical generalization: to think this would be to commit a crude empiricist fallacy, exposed once for all by Wittgenstein. Even if not all A's are B's, the statement that A's are normally B's may belong to the *ratio* of an A. Most chess moves are valid, most intentions are carried out, most statements are veracious; none of these statements is just a rough generalization, for if we tried to describe how it would be for most chess moves to be invalid, most intentions not to be carried out, most statements to be lies, we should soon find ourselves talking nonsense. We shall equally find ourselves talking nonsense if we try to describe a people whose custom it was, when they wanted A's, to choose A's they thought bad and reject A's they thought good. (And this goes for *all* interpretations of 'A'.)

There is, I admit, much more difficulty in passing from 'man' to 'good/bad/man', or from 'human act' to 'good/bad/human act', if these phrases are to be taken as purely descriptive and in senses determined simply by those of 'man' and 'human act'. I think this difficulty could be overcome; but even so the Oxford Moralists could now deploy a powerful weapon of argument. Let us suppose that we have found a clear descriptive meaning for 'good human act' and for 'bad human act', and have shown that adultery answers to the description 'bad human act'. Why should this consideration deter an intending adulterer? By what logical step can we pass from the supposedly descriptive sentence 'adultery is a bad human act' to the imperative 'you must not commit adultery'? It is useless to say 'It is your duty to do good and avoid doing evil'; either this is much the same as the unhelpful remark 'It is good to do good and avoid doing evil', or else 'It is your duty' is a smuggling in of an imperative force not conveyed by the terms 'good' and 'evil' which are *ex hypothesi* purely descriptive.

We must allow in the first place that the question, 'Why should I?' or 'Why shouldn't I?' is a reasonable question, which calls for an answer, not for abusive remarks about the wickedness of asking; and I think that the only relevant answer is an appeal to something the questioner *wants*. Since Kant's time people have supposed that there is another sort of relevant reply – an appeal not to inclination but to the Sense of Duty. Now indeed a man may be got by training into a state of mind in which 'You *must* not' is a sufficient answer to 'Why shouldn't I?'; in which, giving this answer to himself, or hearing it given by others, strikes him with a quite peculiar awe; in which, perhaps, he even thinks he 'must not' ask why he 'must not'. (Cf. Lewis Carroll's juvenile poem 'My Fairy', with its devastating 'Moral: You mustn't.') Moral philosophers of the Objectivist school, like Sir David Ross, would call this 'apprehension of one's obligations'; it does not worry them that, but for God's grace, this sort of training can make a man 'apprehend' practically anything as his 'obligations'. (Indeed, they admire a man who does what he thinks he *must* do regardless of what he actually does; is he not acting from the Sense of Duty which is the highest motive?) But even if *ad hominem* 'You mustn't' is a final answer to 'Why shouldn't I?', it is no rational answer at all.

It can, I think, be shown that an action's being a good or bad human action is of itself something that touches the agent's desires. Although calling a thing 'a good A' or 'a bad A' does not of itself work upon the hearer's desires, it may be expected to do so if the hearer happens to be choosing an A. Now what a man cannot fail to be choosing is his manner of acting; so to call a manner of acting good or bad cannot but serve to guide action. As Aristotle says, acting well, εὐπραξία, is a man's aim *simpliciter*, ἁπλῶς, and *qua* man; other objects of choice are so only relatively, πρός τι, or are the objects of a particular man, τινός³; but *any* man has to choose how to act, so calling an action good or bad does not depend for its effect as a suasion upon any individual peculiarities of desire.

I shall not here attempt to explicate the descriptive force of 'good (bad) human action': but some remarks upon the logic of the phrase seem to be called for. In the first place, a tennis stroke or chess move is a human act. Are we to say, then, that the description 'good tennis stroke' or 'good chess move' is of itself something that must appeal to the agent's desire? Plainly not; but this is no difficulty. Although a tennis stroke or a chess move is a human act, it does not follow that a good tennis stroke or a good chess move is a good human act, because of the peculiar logic of the term 'good'; so calling a tennis stroke or a chess move good is not *eo ipso* an appeal to what an agent must be wanting.

Secondly, though we can sensibly speak of a good or bad human act, we cannot sensibly speak of a good or bad event, a good or bad thing to happen. 'Event', like 'thing', is too empty a word to convey either a criterion of identity or a standard of goodness; to ask 'Is this a good or bad thing (to happen)?' is as useless as to ask 'Is this the same thing that I saw yesterday?' or 'Is the same event still going on?', unless the emptiness of 'thing' or 'event' is filled up by a special context of utterance. Caesar's murder was a bad thing to happen to a living organism, a good fate for a man who wanted divine worship for himself, and again a good or bad act on the part of his murderers; to ask whether it was a good or bad event would be senseless.

Thirdly, I am deliberately ignoring the supposed distinction between the Right and the Good. In Aquinas there is no such distinction. He finds it sufficient to talk of good and bad human acts. When Ross would say that there is a morally good action but not a right act, Aquinas would say that a good human intention had issued in what was, in fact, a bad action; and when Ross would say that there was a right act but not a morally good action, Aquinas would say that there was a bad human act performed in circumstances in which a similar act with a different intention would have been a good one (e.g. giving money to a beggar for the praise of men rather than for the relief of his misery).

Since the English word 'right' has an idiomatic predilection for the definite article – we speak of *a* good chess move but of *the* right move – people who think that doing right is something other than doing good will regard virtuous behaviour as consisting, not just in doing good and eschewing evil, but in doing, on every occasion, *the* right act for the occasion. This speciously strict doctrine leads in fact to quite laxist consequences. A man who just keeps on doing good and eschewing evil, if he knows that adultery is an evil act, will decide that (as Aristotle says) there can be no deliberating when or how or with whom to commit adultery.[4] But a man who believes in discerning, on each occasion, *the* right act for the occasion, may well decide that on this occasion, all things considered, adultery is *the* right action. Sir David Ross explicitly tells us that on occasion *the* right act may be the judicial punishment of an innocent man 'that the whole nation perish not': for in this case 'the *prima facie* duty of consulting the general interest has proved more obligatory than the perfectly distinct *prima facie* duty of respecting the rights of those who have respected the rights of others'.[5] (We must charitably hope that for him the words of Caiaphas that he quotes just had the vaguely hallowed associations of a Bible text, and that he did not remember whose judicial murder was being counselled.)[6]

I am well aware that much of this discussion is unsatisfying; some points on which I think I do see clear I have not been able to develop at proper length; on many points (e.g. the relation between desire and good, and the precise *ratio* of evil in evil acts), I certainly do not see clear. Moreover, though I have argued that the characteristic of being a good or bad human action is of itself bound to influence the agent's desires, I have not discussed whether an action of its nature bad is always and on all accounts to be avoided, as Aristotle thought. But perhaps, though I have not made everything clear, I have made some things clearer.

Notes

1   [Geach seems to have had Moore and Ross in mind; perhaps also Prichard. Ed.]
2   [The text is here slightly altered to remove a misunderstanding that arose over the first version. Ed.]
3   E. N. 1139*b* 2–4.
4   E. N. 1107*a* 16.
5   *The Right and the Good*, p. 61.
6   Holding this notion of *the* right act, people have even held that some creative act would be *the* right act for a God – e.g. that a God would be obliged to create the best of all possible worlds, so that either this world of ours is the best possible or there is no good God. I shall not go further into this; it will be enough to say that what is to be expected of a good Creator is *a* good world, not *the* right world.

3.1.5 Philippa Foot
"Human Goodness"

In earlier chapters I described a logical structure that belongs to the evaluation of all living things 'in their own right', or 'autonomously'; that is, where 'natural' goodness or defect is in view. I said something about differences as well as similarities in the evaluation of plants, animals, and human beings. But now, as we move in towards the subject of 'moral goodness', new specialities appear, and we see that we have a way of speaking of goodness in human beings not corresponding to anything in the other cases. I am thinking now of the thoughts expressed by sentences in which the word 'good' is joined to the name of the species itself, as when we speak of 'a good human being' or, more colloquially, 'a good person'. There is no equivalent to this in the language in which we evaluate plants and animals. Firstly, in so far as we do speak of 'a good S' in these other cases (where, incidentally, we tend rather to say 'a healthy S' or 'a good specimen of an S'), we are thinking about the plant or the animal as a whole; whereas to call someone a good human being is to evaluate him or her only in a certain respect. And as suggested in the previous chapter, this particular evaluation can only be of human beings. For to speak of a good person is to speak of an individual not in respect of his body, or of faculties such as sight and memory, but as concerns his rational will.[1]

In the present chapter I want to consider this particular case of evaluation in more detail, and it may seem that I have now reached the subject of 'moral evaluation'. But I want to show that the judgements usually considered to be the special subject of moral philosophy should really be seen as belonging to a wider class of evaluations of conduct with which they share a common conceptual structure. It is worth remarking that in considering *reasons for action* in the earlier chapters we seemed to move quite naturally between the example of someone kept in bed by flu and that of the explorer Maklay bound by his promise to his servant. Various observations were made about the relation between the concepts of *goodness* and *reasons* with no distinction of 'non-moral' and 'moral' examples. Was this a mistake? I shall try to show that it was not.

My own view is that it is right to see moral judgements as belonging with other evaluations that may perhaps appear not weighty enough to merit such proximity. Thinking about reasons for action, we saw that there is a use of the word 'should' (a practical 'should')

Philippa Foot, "Human Goodness," Chap 5. in *Natural Goodness* (Oxford: Clarendon Press, 2001), pp. 66–80. Reprinted with permission of Oxford University Press.

that implies a reason, and even an 'a.t.c.' reason for action.[2] And we noticed that a certain kind of human goodness – call it practical rationality – hung on the doing of that which *should* be done. But as Elizabeth Anscombe pointed out, 'should' is 'a rather light word with unlimited contexts of application'.

> We say that 'athletes should keep in training, pregnant women watch their weight, film stars their publicity, that one should brush one's teeth, that one should (not) be fastidious about one's pleasures, that one should (not) tell "necessary" lies …'[3]

The use of 'should' in such practical contexts tells us of a possible defect in action, but does not itself tell us whether or not anything of importance is involved. Anscombe shows in other places that she regards lying as often a very serious transgression, but this could not be said of other items in her list. A 'should not' or 'should' may mark something very important, but often an action that it would be merely silly to do or not to do.

How is it then that moral evaluation seems to most philosophers nowadays to be a very special subject, that may have to be understood in terms of the expression of special mental states such as approval, or mental acts such as endorsing? This must have something to do with the fact that these philosophers are focusing on evaluations which are often used in a special context, as when members of society are expressing disapproval of something others have done, and especially where the public good or the rights of a third party are involved. Use in such contexts should not, however, be taken to imply a special logical grammar. Whether or not there is one is the subject next to be explored.

Many if not most moral philosophers in modern times see their subject as having to do exclusively with relations between individuals or between an individual and society, and so with such things as obligations, duties, and charitable acts. It is for this reason that, of the four ancient cardinal virtues of justice, courage, temperance, and wisdom, only the first now seems to belong wholly to 'morality'. The other three virtues are recognized as necessary for the practice of 'morality' but are now thought of as having part of their exercise 'outside morality' in 'self-regarding' pursuits, 'moral' and 'prudential' considerations being *contrasted* in a way that was alien to Plato or Aristotle.[4] J. S. Mill, for instance, expresses this modern point of view quite explicitly, saying in his essay *On Liberty* that 'A person who shows rashness, obstinacy, self-conceit … who cannot restrain himself from harmful indulgences' shows faults (Mill calls them 'self-regarding faults') which 'are not properly immoralities' and while they 'may be proofs of any amount of folly … are only a subject of moral reprobation when they involve a breach of duty to others, for whose sake the individual is bound to have care for himself'.[5]

There is of course nothing wrong with using the word 'moral' as Mill does. It fits in with much of our everyday usage, and I do not want to involve myself in a discussion of the variations in usage found even today.[6] What concerns me is not the exact meaning of 'moral' when used as Mill used it but rather the substance, if there is any substance, of a distinction between 'moral' evaluation and the other evaluations of which he wrote in the passage just quoted. Perhaps it will seem strange even to raise the question of substance, because there is after all a special lexicon for Mill's 'sphere of morality'. Words such as 'wicked' and 'evil' are applied to a deed such as murder but not to even the greatest act of self-destructive folly as such. Even to call an action 'wrong' outside some technical context is to imply that it is unjust, or perhaps uncharitable; that it has to do with conduct whose defect lies in what is done against other individuals or against the public good. Indeed, parts of this special 'moral' vocabulary serve the purpose of picking out special relationships in which individuals stand to other individuals or to society, as, for example, that of having rights, obligations, or duties. And some of these words such as 'wicked' and 'evil' also mark the seriousness of the subject, and the extreme reactions evoked by horrifying and revolting actions of murderers, child abusers, or torturers. The social and emotional surroundings of our use of the vocabulary of moral censure are very different from those settings in which we speak of rashness, obstinacy, imprudence, and folly. But I shall argue that there are features common to all these evaluations that may be labelled 'evaluations of the rational human will'.

What, then, are the features that such evaluations share? In the first place, they all have as their subject not physical or mental abilities, but voluntary action and purpose. This is something that is generally recognized where 'moral' evaluation is concerned. For it is obvious that not everything that humans *do* counts for or against moral goodness. No one is called a murderer because in slipping and falling on a mountainside he has killed someone. What is done involuntarily does not feature, and force, too, can take away voluntariness of movement, as in one who is blown along by the wind or carried away by strong men.[7] Moreover, we must surely count not perhaps as involuntary but as less than voluntary what is done under torture that no one could be expected to withstand.

A more difficult part of this subject opens up, however, when acting with knowledge is added to the conditions of an action's voluntariness.[8] Some examples of excuse in this area are evident enough. For a doctor might kill a patient she was treating in emergency conditions (as, for instance, when the victim was trapped halfway up a cliff), but do this only through ignorance of the patient's allergy to a standard drug. This doctor might say that sadly she had done the wrong thing; but she had perhaps acted heroically in climbing up to give help. Here we must agree with Kant that the unfortunate outcome is irrelevant to goodness of the will, and blame 'step-motherly Nature' instead.[9]

The action of the doctor in this example, though it was intentional under the description 'giving treatment', was of course not intentional under the description 'killing' – under which it could otherwise have been an immediate subject of adverse moral judgement. The example was, however, carefully chosen. For not every case of acting in ignorance is excusable in this way. Our doctor acted in an emergency, so that discovery of the allergy was ruled out. And it was implied that she gave the standard treatment, as any conscientious medic would have done.

This last remark points to the fact that lack of knowledge of what one is doing, though it 'takes away something of voluntariness', does not always excuse. For ignorance itself may be voluntary, as when, in present-day Britain, an arms dealer takes care not to enquire whether the weapons that he is shipping to one country will not be shipped on to a repressive regime. Or if he 'enquires', his conclusion may be guided by self-interest rather than by the evidence at hand: he holds a convenient opinion that does not absolve him, because it is not held, as we say, in good faith.[10] Furthermore, an agent's ignorance may be imputed to his will if, through negligence, he has not taken the trouble to find out facts that he could, and should, have known. This is a particularly interesting case, as well as one that is of everyday practical importance. There may be no moment at which this person decided not to discover the facts, or made it impossible to do so. The fault may be one of pure omission; but omission in action is a common fault, and omitting to find out what one

could and should have found out is only a special case of this. The omission may be culpable on account of some special position of responsibility held by the agent, but the
practical importance of the subject of culpable ignorance does not come only from special positions of responsibility. For are there not things that most adults in countries such
as Britain not only could but should know? I am thinking, for instance, of the basic principles of first aid, and procedures such as cardiac pulmonary resuscitation. To say this may
seem to be going too far, given that no one can be expected to know everything that he or
she might need to know in order to save a life. But such examples give a clue to the criteria
by which it can be judged that most of us here not only can but also should learn about
first aid. That there must be a 'should' as well as a 'could' for culpable ignorance is seen by
contrasting this example with one that I remember Elizabeth Anscombe giving to illustrate the point. Suppose, she said, that an infant had been left on the doorstep of her house
and had perished during the night because she had not known that it was there. It is not
that she could not have known, because had it been her practice to check her doorstep
every hour upon the hour through every night this child would have been saved. But of
course it cannot be said that she should have done this. Nor is it difficult to see the factors
that distinguish this example from that of failure to learn elementary first aid. In both
cases, as it happens, the evil that could come about through ignorance is very great, and
this is relevant. On the other hand, the likelihood of such knowledge being needed is very
different, and so too is the cost to the agent of getting it.[11]

With these observations we have been tracing logical limits to evaluations whose subject is goodness and defect of human action considered as such. The discussion may
have seemed to have to do in particular with what is nowadays called 'moral judgement'
and was explicitly distinguished as such by Mill. Yet 'self-regarding' failings come under
the heading of lack of wisdom, and the corresponding descriptions are conceptually
constrained by conditions of voluntariness, as are 'moral' descriptions such as 'wicked'.
No one is said to do something foolish when what he does is involuntary, as, for instance,
if he falls into the sea when hit by a giant wave. And here, too, ignorance may absolve, as
it absolves of imprudence those who took up smoking in the years before the link between smoking and cancer was known. But, as before, ignorance has this logical force
only when it was itself not ignorance of what the agent could and should have known.
An illiterate in our society who could learn to read, but does not take the trouble to do
so, shows lack of wisdom. And *wisdom* is a telling concept from just this point of view
because it itself implies no more knowledge and understanding than anyone of normal
capacity can and should acquire in the course of an ordinary life.

A special connection with the voluntary is, then, the first of the conceptual marks of
the special evaluations, picked out from others (such as speech defects) which have to do
with goodnesses and defects *in* human beings but are not of the kind that I have indicated by saying that they are about goodness and defect *of the rational will*. And my present point is that their subject matter is more extensive than that picked out by Mill when
he spoke of 'morality'. So there is this first reason for treating the subject of the virtues as
a whole, as the ancients did.

There is, moreover, a second important feature of Mill's 'moral' evaluations that can be
shown to belong to this wider class. It can be summarily described by saying that
goodness or badness can come from different formal features of a single action, which
may be distinguished as follows.

Firstly, goodness can come from the nature of the action itself – from what it is that is done. So, in general, an act of saving life is good in this respect, while an act of killing is bad.[12]

Secondly, the end for which an action is done is an independent source of goodness or badness in it. A good (even obligatory) action may be bad in that it is done for a bad end, as a blackmailer may save the life of his victim in order to continue his extortion. Or, again, a bad action may be done for a good end but one that does not justify it; as when an executor destroys a will in order to see that money goes to a poor person rather than a rich legatee. Contrast an end that does justify, like the need to destroy someone's property to stop the spread of a fire.

A third source of goodness or badness in an action lies in its relation to the agent's judgement of whether he or she is acting badly or well. Here, too, goodness or badness may be combined with either goodness or badness in either act or end. It is often supposed that the fact that someone is doing what he *thinks* right is a circumstance that annuls actual badness of act or purpose; but Aquinas (whose discussion of this topic is a wonderful piece of moral philosophy) insists that erring conscience does not excuse.[13] What Aquinas says is illustrated by a sad story of the fate of a Jewish child sent to a family in Norway in hope of safety when Prague was overrun by the Nazis. She died in Auschwitz because, after the invasion of Norway, the Norwegian family who loved the child thought that it was their duty to hand her over to the Gestapo when ordered to do so. They believed, no doubt through some sympathy with the Nazis, that this was 'the right thing to do'. The erring conscience, or as Aquinas always says, 'reason or conscience' (*ratio vel conscientia*), does not excuse.

Nevertheless, according to Aquinas, to go against one's conscience is itself a source of badness in an action, even when it tells one to do what in fact one should not do. Even an erring conscience binds, he says, because in going against conscience the will tends to an action as something evil in that reason has proposed it as evil. And surely this is right. For acting as one thinks one should not is a very radical form of badness in the will. How could a human being be acting well in doing what he or she saw as evil? Is that not as if an archer should not even aim his arrow at where the target seemed to him to be?

What, then, should the Norwegian couple have done? On Aquinas's reckoning they would have acted badly whether they had or had not given up the Jewish child. The point is that in such a situation there is no way for people *of such views* to act well, and in this example it is not unreasonable to say that they were at fault in this. They already knew that the child needed shelter from the Nazis, and that the Nazi policies were wicked was something that they could and should have recognized. It is hard, however, to believe as Aristotle and Aquinas both suggest, that errors of *principle* are never excusable. There are, after all, famously disputable matters of right and wrong.[14]

I have gone into the question of different sources of badness in action because it seems to me that the subject is seldom well treated in modern moral philosophy. So far, my examples in this section have been from the area that Mill assigned to morality. But these faults have their parallels in those that he excluded, in which self-destructiveness takes the place of curelty to others, and indifference to one's own good that of indifference to theirs. Thus, firstly, there are generally bad acts, such as self-mutilation or suicide, whose badness need not depend on harm likely to come to anyone else.[15] Secondly, no one can act well in seeking, or carelessly incurring, even a lesser harm to himself through self-hatred or the kind of spitefulness to oneself that Dostoevsky unforgettably described in *Notes from the Underground*. Finally, here again one cannot act well in doing what, rightly *or even wrongly*, one seriously thinks that one should not do.

So far, therefore, we have seen no reason to think that Mill's 'moral' evaluations should be treated differently from other evaluations concerning the human will. Nor does one appear if we continue the investigation by asking about the overall judgement in cases where there is a mixture of good and bad in cases such as those described in the previous paragraph, and where there may of course also be goodness *and* badness from 'inside' and 'outside' of Mill's specially distinguished area of morality. In our much earlier example of the foolish burglar whose action was defective in one way in that he was plying his dishonest trade and in another in that he was tarrying in front of the television set (Chapter 1), we have a double dose of badness. So we may mix and match ad lib and then ask about the result. What if different elements point evaluation in different directions? When can an action be called good in such a case? Will it, for instance, be enough for goodness that what is done is (intentionally) to save a life or bring some other kind of help to a person, who needs it? This seems plausible until we think of a blackmailer saving someone from drowning only so as to be able to go on with his extortion. And what again of an action with a good end but carried out by immoral or by foolish means; or of an action that in itself perhaps *should* be done but is *thought* to be foolish or 'wrong' by the doer? Can any of these actions, containing both good and bad elements, be called good? Aquinas, whose distinctions we followed earlier, says firmly that in every one of them the actions are bad, invoking the principle that a single defect is enough for badness, while goodness must be goodness in all respects.[16]

Aquinas here sees asymmetry in the concepts of badness and goodness, which may strike one at first sight as simply wrong. Yet on reflection we observe that this is indeed part of our way of thinking. It is enough to make a house a bad house that it is either badly designed or damp, whereas neither the fact that a house is well designed nor the fact that it is dry is sufficient to make it good. Small faults are not always counted in, but a consideration of major faults and excellences works in this asymmetrical way.

It seems, then, that an action is bad if it has badness from its kind, its end, or its contrariety to the agent's beliefs about what it is good or bad to do. So much for the negative side: we now know what is, formally speaking, sufficient for volitional defect. But what of goodness? What is sufficient for that? Again Aquinas says something that may surprise us. For he says of any individual action (that is, one individuated by the fact that it is done by a particular person at a particular date and time) that *if it is no way bad then it is good*.[17] This has also seemed evident to Anscombe.[18] I remember protest at a convivial philosophical gathering when I remarked as someone started to drink a glass of wine that he was acting well. Yet the principle 'good if not bad' is one that should be seen as unexciting and unexceptional when applied to an operation of a living thing. A plant, after all, is growing well if there is nothing wrong with its development. And we would naturally think in the same way of, for example, the movements of a human hand. If a hand is either weak or spastic, its movements are, in one or the other of these ways, defective. In the absence of any defect it will, however, be said to be good in its operation, just as a normal, healthy child will come to have what we call good balance, to walk well, to talk well, and to relate well to other children.

It may be said that we think differently about human action, and it is true that we sometimes do when it comes to picking out certain actions for special praise. But then it is important to remember that no special praise is due when a rich person contributes to charity a sum of money that he or she would not even miss; while a simple action like telling the truth in a law court, or giving honest opinion on a candidate for an academic position, may merit special praise when performed in especially difficult circumstances.[19] Under Hitler's regime, as under Stalin's, the temptation to prevaricate must have been very great indeed. And extra special goodness does not belong only to what is generally thought of as belonging to the sphere of morality. For clearly it can be an exercise of the virtues of hope and of courage simply to struggle on rather than commit suicide in the face of great adversity. To behave with wisdom in fortunate circumstances may be nothing special, but for a single mother with small children in cramped bed and breakfast accommodation it must be very hard indeed. As a certain doctor put it,

> it is easy to eat healthily … and to address your addiction to cigarettes *if you are not having to deal with conditions that challenge your capacity to get, intact, from one end of the day to the other.*[20]

If acting wisely rather than self-destructively in such circumstances were said to be the kind of action that should be picked out as especially good, one could go along with that.

So far, then, our conceptual analysis has seemed to favour a comparison rather than a contrast between the two classes of evaluations that I see as belonging together. One who objects to this has, however, another card to play. For he or she may insist that there is nevertheless a *logical difference* between 'moral' and 'non-moral' evaluations because, in a clash of reasons for action based on requirements of justice or charity and reasons having to do with one's own needs or desires, the former always trump the latter and take the trick. We saw in discussing Maklay's promise (Chapter 3) the kind of example that may be in mind.

This belief in the general overridingness of Millian 'moral' considerations does not, however, seem to me defensible, and one may wonder why it is held. That it is may have something to do with the special position of certain prohibitions that as a matter of fact all have to do with what Mill counted as morality. For a good case can be made out for a limited moral absolutism by which certain such actions are held to be such as to rule out circumstances in which it could ever be right to perform them. Adultery and lying have been suggested as having this character, though I myself would not agree with Aristotle, Aquinas, or Anscombe about either. I think it especially ludicrous to suggest, for instance, that those fighting with the Resistance against the Nazis should not if necessary have lied through their teeth to protect themselves or their comrades. An absolute moral ban on torture seems, however, to be another matter. If the frequently unchallengeable description 'torture' applies to an action, then, whatever the circumstances, it is in my firm opinion morally 'out'.[21] But 'moral absolutism' of this ilk does not support any general theory of the overridingness of those reasons for action that could be called 'moral reasons' in Mill's lexicon. Nor is it pertinent here to recall a number of descriptions of action that are what I should like to call 'conceptually verdictive' from a practical point of view, in that they entail a 'final' 'should' or 'should not'. 'Unjust' is, for instance, such a description, as is 'cruel'.

If and when it is unjust or cruel to withhold from someone something one owes that person, then one necessarily acts badly in doing so. It may be hard to know whether in a particular case withholding the money really is cruel or unjust: perhaps a debtor's children will go hungry if he discharges the debt – a dilemma that must only too often face a borrower in the Third World. But one who decides that the debt must in justice or charity be paid cannot, at the same time, deny that he will be acting wrongly if he does not pay it. Perhaps it, will be thought that all such verdictives give judgement in favour of a consideration that has to do with the rights or needs of others, or with public morality. But this, even if so, would be of little consequence; and in any case it is not so, as we see if we consider words such as 'imprudent' or 'foolish'. For these too are verdictive, contrasting in this respect with expressions such as 'dangerous' and 'self-regarding'; The latter descriptions can be applied to an action without implying that it should not be done, whereas this is not true of words such as 'imprudent' and 'foolish'.

Nor is it difficult to find examples where, in a clash of reasons for and against an action, it is not the 'other-related' consideration that should have the final vote. There are of course many situations in which one obligation overrides another; but as Bernard Williams has memorably put it, not all overridings of presumptive moral obligations work on the principle 'Obligation out – obligation in'.[22] To see this we have only to go back to our example of the person in bed with flu. Suppose this patient had promised to go to help a friend on the day on which he is ill. Unless the promise were a very solemn promise, or the breaking of it very serious for the promisee, he will be able to say in exoneration, 'I am sorry, but I was not able to get out that day.' It is not that his legs would have failed him, but rather that there was something else that he should, all things considered, have done, that is, to keep to his bed. In fact it is often reasonable for agents to give themselves (never mind their families) preference over others. As John Taurek pointed out some time ago in an excellent article, it is not at all generally believed that, for example, one should incur the certainty of losing a limb even to save another from injury more serious than that.[23] The slogan 'Moral considerations are overriding considerations' expresses not a truth of moral philosophy but an implausible doctrine about what should be done.

My opponent in the main line of our controversy may protest that my attention to a wide class of evaluations has, in taking us outside the realm of obligation and duty, also taken us outside moral philosophy. One might say, 'So much the worse for moral philosophy!' I do not, as I have said, much care how the word 'moral' is used. But it seems important to recognize as virtues of the will (as volitional excellences) a readiness to accept good things for oneself, and to see the great importance for life of the self-regarding aspect of virtues such as hope and a readiness to accept good things.[24] And on the negative side, we might want to use the description 'moral fault' in thinking of the kind of timidity, conventionality, and wilful self-abnegation that may spoil no one's life but one's own. That we tend to speak in moral philosophy only of volitional faults that impinge particularly on others gives the whole subject an objectionably rigoristic, prissy, moralistic tone that we would hardly care to take up in everyday life. It also tends to cloud understanding by suggesting that there is a special meaning for words such as 'ought' in such contexts. In fact 'ought' is very close to 'should', and if we speak of 'a moral context' this usually simply indicates the presence of a reason for acting that has to do with others rather than oneself.

Notes

1   As an approximation, we may say 'will as controllable by reason'.
2   This is the only case that I shall consider from now on.
3   Anscombe, *Intention*, section 35.
4   Gavin Lawrence is a notable exception to the generalization I have just made. See Lawrence, 'The Rationality of Morality', 106.
5   Mill, *On Liberty*, chapter IV, 134–5.
6   I would remark, however, that Isaiah Berlin spoke in a lecture of the 'moral impact' of the Busch Quartet's recording of late Beethoven quartets.
7   Cp. Aristotle, *Nicomachean Ethics*, Book III, chapter 1, 1110al–34.
8   Ibid. 1110b18–1111a20.
9   Kant, *Foundations of the Metaphysics of Morals*, section 1.
10 Many of the beliefs of slave owners, and of white people under South Africa's apartheid regime, must have been of this kind.
11 The case of acting in ignorance through failure to find out what one could and should have found out is particularly interesting from the point of view of philosophy of mind. For this voluntariness is attributed to the action on account of what should have been known, and so to the agent's will *in a way that depends on evaluation itself*. The idea that voluntariness is discovered by a *causal* investigation of the operation of a faculty is hereby shown as a mistake.
12 I am in general following Aquinas in making these distinctions; but what he says about species and circumstances of an action is complex, and I am not trying exactly to represent his view about this. It is natural to say that circumstances often affect the goodness or badness of an action, as the circumstance that the subject has been convicted of a crime by due process of law changes what is done in depriving him or her of liberty. And an end can also operate in this way as a circumstance, though this is not, of course, to say that even a good end will always do so. See the discussion of 'absolutism' on pp. 77–80, 114–115.
13 See Aquinas, *Summa Theologica*, First Part of the Second Part, Question XIX, articles 5 and 6.
14 See Anscombe, 'The Two Kinds of Error in Action'.
15 Except in certain fairly rare cases, for instance of great suffering in a terminal illness, suicide is contrary to the virtue of hope. It may surprise some people that I call hope a virtue, but of course it is; in part because we are often tempted to think that all is lost when *we cannot really know that it is so*. In view of the appalling number of young suicides in our present society, I suggest that hope should be among the first of a fairy godmother's gifts at the cradle of a child.
16 Aquinas, *Summa Theologica*, First Part of the Second Part, Question XVIII, article 4.
17 Ibid. article 9.
18 Anscombe, 'Practical Inference', 34.
19 It is important, of course, to distinguish difficult *circumstances* from the kind of difficulty that comes from lack of virtue itself.
20 P. F. Naish, Chairman, Prevention of Heart Attacks and Strokes Enterprise, North Staffordshire Royal Infirmary: letter in the *Independent*, 17 Aug. 1991 (italics mine).
21 I was glad to see an article by Ronald Dworkin that supports this opinion ('Report from Hell', *New York Review of Books*, 17 July 1986). He sees the ban on torture as a barrier to the power of a tyrannical ruler. One might also see torture as the ultimate negation of the impulse humans have to come to each other's aid.
22 Williams, *Ethics and the Limits of Philosophy*, 180.
23 Taurek, 'Should the Numbers Count?'.
24 A graduate student once said that my lectures had first made him see 'that to be anti-sex could be immoral'. I liked that.

3.1.6 Michael Thompson
"Apprehending Human Form"

These three sorts of judgment about the umbrella jelly and umbrella jellies might be compared to three parallel forms of judgment about human speech – an analogy Darwin himself draws.[1] As we distinguish various species, or natural forms of life, so also we distinguish various languages, or customary forms of discursive interaction. We classify individual organisms as *bearers* of particular life forms; and so also we classify people as *speakers* of particular languages (type A). A naturalist like you, we saw, will make numerous general and atemporal judgments about any given life form under investigation, and will attempt to join them into a system. And so also a linguist will make numerous general atemporal judgments about a given language she is studying, attempting to join *them* into a (quite different) sort of system (type B). She will characterize its lexicon for example, and assign particular meanings to particular words – words which admit indefinitely many individual 'tokenings', as *tentacle 137 of the umbrella jelly* admits indefinitely many instantiations. Finally, a naturalist like you will engage in much vital description of given organisms here and now, framing judgments about what they are up to and what parts these are and so forth. And so also our linguist will be positioned to say what words this person is now using, what sentence he is now asserting, and what, in fact, he is now telling his interlocutor (type C).

But note again the element of reciprocal dependence: once our linguist gets into the system, many of her tensed remarks about individuals will presuppose generic atemporal thoughts about the language in question. For example, any description of a given speaker *hic et nunc* as telling another *that snow is falling* or *that snow fell yesterday* will presuppose a general assignment of meanings to words. Here too, then, there is a sort of dependence of tensed judgments about individuals on untensed general judgments. In each case, vital and linguistic, the connection between the given individual (or pair) and the property ascribed to it is mediated by the presence in it (or them) of a determinate *form*.

We might say, then, if we care to push the linguistic analogy off a cliff, that a life form is like a language that physical matter can speak. It is in the light of judgments about the life form that I assign meaning and significance and point and position to the parts and

Michael Thompson, "Apprehending Human Form," in *Modern Moral Philosophy*. ed. A. O'Hear (Cambridge: Cambridge University Press, 2004), pp. 52–53, 57–62, 72–74 with cuts. © Royal Institute of Philosophy 2004, published by Cambridge University Press. Reproduced with permission.

operations of individual organisms that present themselves to me. As *French* or *English* are to the people and brains of which they take possession, so are things like *umbrella jelly* and *cross jelly* to the physical particles of which *they* take possession. And just as there is no speech – no discourse, no telling and believing people, no knowledge by testimony – without a language that is spoken, which is to say, without a framework for interpreting what is going on between the speakers, so there is no life without a life form, which is to say, without a framework for interpreting the goings-on in the individual organism.

Judgments of natural goodness and standard

But let us move to two further forms of judgment we frame about living things. Note that you will as time goes on be in a position to make judgments of defect and deformity in individual umbrella jellies. Having given names to all one hundred and forty four tentacles of the umbrella jelly in your monograph, you will be able, e.g., to say when an individual jelly is missing a tentacle, or when a tentacle is present but broken. You will be able to say when one of the many mouths is malfunctioning, when contractions of the umbrella-like bell are well or badly effected, and so forth. We might call these judgments *judgments of natural goodness and badness*, judgments of type D. Their canonical form would be something like this: *this S is defective/sound, as an S, in that it is/has/does H*. If some forms of defect or deformity are frequently seen, you might invent special concepts to capture them, as we speak of *lameness* and *blindness* in human beings and *etiolation* in green plants.

Note that what sorts of things are aptly judged good or bad, defective or sound, in the parts and operations of a given umbrella jelly will differ, in detail at least, from what counts as good or bad in jellies of other kinds – still more from what counts as good or bad in the workings of oak trees, bacteria or squid. When you thought, of the first specimen you sighted, that it was a cross jelly, you thought it was woefully deformed. And if it had been a cross jelly, it would have been woefully deformed. But now, with further observation, you can see that that original specimen was quite sound, except perhaps for a few broken tentacles. It is just that it belonged to a *different kind*, and was thus subject to a different standard.

In speaking of 'different standards for different species or kinds or forms', I have implicitly suggested that you will by degrees also come to form *general* judgments with evaluative content, a fifth form of judgment, type E. You will be positioned to say when in *general* an umbrella jelly is formed well or badly or operating well or badly, in respect of some part or capacity. We might call such general judgments *judgments of natural standard*. Their general form would be something like this: *an S is defective/sound in a certain respect if it is/has/does G*. The system of general judgments of natural standard about umbrella jellies will closely track the system of atemporal natural historical judgments about the same kind or form. Indeed, judgments of natural standard might be said simply to transpose our natural historical judgments into an evaluative key: the monograph you have been composing might be viewed as indirectly articulating the ideal, standard or perfect operation of a bearer of this kind of life. A natural history, as we saw, does not describe what happens on average or mostly; its relation to facts about individuals is evidently much more complex.

Your observations, which are at bottom always observations of individual organisms, will thus lead in the end to a possible *critique* or *evaluation* of individual organisms and their parts and operations. And they will lead to the articulation of general *standards of critique* applying to organisms of the kind in question. This sort of critique of the individual is everywhere mediated by the attribution to it of a specific form; to bring an individual under a life form is, we might say, at the same time to bring it under a certain sort of standard. It goes without saying that this sort of critique or evaluation of an individual is not the only sort possible: a dog might be profoundly deformed as a dog, but prize-winning at a general congress of St. Bernards; a tree might be woefully deformed as a Japanese black pine, but prize-winning at a bonsai exhibition.

Note that here again your position is much like that of our imagined linguist. With time she too will take on a critical role. She will be able to declare whether particular statements made by her informants are true or false, if it happens that she knows about the matter under discussion (type D). And if she arrives at the point of a so-called truth theory for her object language, she will be able to say when *in general* a sentence of the language is true or false (type E).

The role of observation in the framing of judgments falling under these diverse types

[…]

Let us apply these thoughts to our real topic, which is the specifically human form, a product of evolutionary history quite as strange in its way as the umbrella jelly. And it seems plain that this empiricist or observationalist picture of things holds for much of what is known about things specifically human. We certainly deploy our five forms of judgment in this connection: 'human' can be put in place of 'S'; your name can replace 'X'. And we happily fill in the other blanks in these judgment-forms on the same sort of ground we met with in the case of the umbrella jelly: we do it, that is, on the basis of observation, or intelligent experience with individual members of the kind. It is clear that the ordinary operations of a doctor or a dentist, for example, will involve implicit or explicit deployment of all five forms of judgment. And it is equally clear that the distinctive knowledge of a doctor or a dentist is purely empirical, or founded on observation, formally no different from your knowledge of the umbrella jellies.

The empiricist propositions

If we take the cases so far canvassed as typical, the overwhelming role of observation in supplying our abstract forms with determinate content might lead us to accept the following propositions. I will call them *the empiricist propositions*:

The concept *species* or *life form* is itself an empirical concept. Concepts of particular life forms (*cross jelly, umbrella jelly, white oak, horseshoe crab, human*) are invariably empirical, or observation-dependent, concepts.

Singular representations of individual organisms are invariably empirical representations.

Substantive knowledge of any given individual organism (propositions of types A, C and D) can only arise from observation.

Substantive knowledge of the character of a given species or life form (propositions of types B and E) can only arise from observation.

The empiricist propositions might be opposed in a number of ways, but my purpose is to oppose them with something like the following *anti-empiricist propositions*:

The concept *life form* is a pure or a priori, perhaps a logical, concept.

The concept *human*, as we human beings have it, is an a priori concept attaching to a particular life form.

A mature human being is typically in possession of a non-empirical singular representation of one individual organism.

Individual human beings are sometimes in possession of non-observational knowledge of contingent facts about one individual organism.

Human beings are characteristically in possession of some general substantive knowledge of the human life form which is not founded empirically on observation of members of their kind, and thus not 'biological'.

The empiricist propositions are rarely affirmed explicitly, but I think they are – or many of them are – implicit in much of our thinking about life and human life. A comparative survey of opposing pairs of propositions from the two lists will show that each disputed point raises potentially absorbing metaphysical and epistemological issues, just by itself. But, as I have said, I am moved to consider the merits of the empiricist propositions by the place that some of them occupy in ethical theory.

Normative naturalism

More particularly I want to consider the place the empiricist propositions implicitly occupy in much of the received criticism of ethical doctrines which appeal to notions of *natural normativity* or *natural goodness*.

By such a doctrine I mean, in the first instance, a theory of the type sketched in the concluding paragraphs of Elizabeth Anscombe's 'Modern Moral Philosophy' and lately developed in the last part of Rosalind Hursthouse's book *On Virtue Ethics*, and still more recently in Philippa Foot's book *Natural Goodness*.[2] These works are of course united in a number of ways, for example in the use they make of the concept of virtue. I will focus, though, on the special significance they attach, within ethical theory, to the idea of the *human* – that is, to the concepts of a *human being* and of the specifically human life form and of so-called human nature.

The idea of the human that these writers propose to make central to ethical theory is not the abstract idea of a rational being or a person [...]

The concept *human* as our naturalist employs it is a concept that attaches to a definite product of nature, one which has arisen on this planet, quite contingently, in the course of evolutionary history. For our naturalist, this product of nature is in some sense the theme of ethical theory as we humans would write it. But there is in the larger literature a kind of fear or dread of any appeal to this sort of concept in ethical theory, and this is what I want to address. The contemporary moralist is anxious to leave this concept behind, and to develop his theory in terms of 'persons' and 'rational beings', but if the naturalist is right the concept in question is everywhere nipping at his heels. There is in practical philosophy a kind of alienation from the concept *human* and the sort of unity of agents it expresses.

A typical difficulty that the normative naturalist means to resolve is this: how are we to account for the intuitive difference between considerations of justice and prudence, on the one hand, and those of etiquette and femininity, on the other? If I criticize an action as unfeminine or as a violation of etiquette – as 'not done' or not *comme il faut* – my appeal is at best, it seems, to convention only; in so speaking I am acting precisely as an arm of convention. If now I criticize an action as unjust or imprudent, or if I praise it has just or prudent, custom or convention may well be part of the story. But I seem to be aiming at something more. My evaluation purports to have what philosophers some-times call 'normative authority'; it purports to speak directly to the genuine 'reasons' that the agent 'has'. It has been a puzzle how we are to understand what these phrases mean, what this further purport is. For our naturalist this further purport is a matter of the supposed goodness and badness of the operations of will and practical reason that would be exhibited in the action judged of. And goodness or badness in the operation of these powers is to be understood, in point of logical position, on the model of goodness or badness of sight, or the well-formedness or ill-formedness of an umbrella jelly's tentacle. Unlike judgments of etiquette or femininity, judgments of prudence and justice claim a place on our five-fold chart. The judgments in which I criticize the actions of individual persons as unjust or imprudent, or criticize the people themselves as unjust or impru-dent people, will thus be *special forms* of what I called judgments of natural goodness or badness, type D on our list, as judgments of blindness and etiolation are. A formulation of general normative principle, or of a basic general form of reason for action, where such a thing is formulable, will be a specific type of judgment of natural standard, a specific form of a type E judgment. The reasons that we 'have' are the ones we take account of when we are *reasoning well*.

That these evaluative judgments pertain to intellectual powers like will and practical reason must introduce numerous peculiarities into their description. But, on naturalist hypotheses, they nevertheless fall onto the same plane in logical space as claims about what makes for good sight. That there is a specific difference could hardly argue against the presence of a common genus.

Life form relativity

Consider, though, that no one thinks that the fact that an individual organism does or doesn't make certain colour-discriminations, just by itself, shows that its visual capacity is defective or sound. In different sighted species, different discriminatory powers count as good sight. In the life of the umbrella jelly no sight is necessary at all. Similarly, what would seem lame in a hare is sound movement in a tortoise. Knowledge of what counts as good sight, or as a sound capacity to move, is thus *substantive knowledge of the specific life form in question*.

For a normative naturalist our fundamental practical evaluative knowledge is, as we have seen, substantive knowledge of what makes for a good will and a good practical reason in a specifically *human being*. What would be virtue in the bearers of another intelligent form of life we don't know. We have no more insight into what would count as a 'reason for action' among Martians, for example, than we have into what would make for good eyesight among them, supposing they have eyes. The mind goes blank at the approach of the question. Thrasymachus and Callicles, in Plato's dialogues, argued in different ways that justice as we ordinarily understand it is mere convention only, and that to take its considerations seriously is a vice in human beings. The so-called just agent is a human bonsai, or worse. Anscombe, Hursthouse and Foot all earnestly deny this, insisting that it is the unjust agent who is twisted and unsound. But I think they should grant that those immoralist teachings might be exactly right for our imagined Martians. Perhaps, that is, our writers should confess to *immoralism about the Martians*. Can't we suppose a sufficiently alien life form to exhibit some quite other way of getting on – that the practical life that is characteristic of their kind has some fundamentally different structure, even though it is mediated by objective judgment and conceptual representation, as ours is? The peculiar structuring imposed by considerations of justice will have no place in it.[3] *Our* practical knowledge, though it is general, is not so general as to rule this out. In this respect normative naturalism breaks with the received Kantian and Humean conceptions of practical rationality, each of which appears to claim possession of a table of principles of sound practical reasoning that would apply indifferently to humans, twin earthers and Martians alike.

These points bring out that any given normative naturalist theory will have two levels, one formal, as we might put it, and the other substantive. Critiques of normative naturalism often leave it unclear to which level their arguments are pitched. Only the first level is at issue here. This formal aspect of the theory might be accepted as much by an 'immoralist' like Callicles or Gide as by an orthodox Aristotelian – namely the naturalist interpretation of the content of judgments of goodness and badness in practical thought as coming under our fourth and fifth headings as more determinate forms. Callicles, in the play he makes with, the opposition between what belongs to *nomos* only and what belongs properly to *phusis*, would seem to be explicitly a normative naturalist in this sense. Or, to put the point another way, the *formal* aspect of the theory could be accepted without alteration by bearers of radically alien forms of 'intelligent life'; it is after all essentially a matter of logical analysis. The *substantive* part of the theory, by contrast, would be addressed to human beings in the first instance, fellow bearers of the form our writers bear, and would amount to the isolation of a table of virtues or basic types of reason for action appropriate to human beings. It is an attempt to make articulate an aspect of something that is present equally in writer and reader, namely what I am calling the specifically human life form. It is here that the struggle with the naturalist immoralist will be pursued: this is a struggle, as we might say, over different conceptions of specifically human life; or, to approach the matter from another direction, it is a dispute over which forms of upbringing damage the human individual – casting a spell on him as Callicles puts it and putting him into mental shackles and so forth – and which upbringings rather yield a sound human practical understanding.

Often in writings on practical philosophy, we find moral principles developed, or substantive formulations of reasons adopted: 'It is impermissible to do A', we read, or

'One has reason to do B'. The question of the scope of this generality, or of the form of generality contained in such judgments, is rarely posed. Suppose, for example, that our writer is rendering verdicts on sundry variants of Philippa Foot's 'trolley problem'. Is she developing the normative consequences of the particular local ensemble of practices under which we bearers of Western modernity live? Or is she proposing a cosmic scope for her propositions, speaking to Martians as well as to me? Doctrines of natural normativity may be understood as holding that the *highest* form of generality that can attach to such claims is the form of generality that is also found in our natural historical judgments or judgments of natural standard.

[…]

Conclusion

[…] We have provided an opening, that is, for the view that our fundamental moral and practical knowledge – our knowledge of good and evil and of what is rational and irrational in human action – is at the same time knowledge implicity about the specifically human form, knowledge of how the well-working human practical reason reasons, yet in no way a biological or empirical knowledge or any sort of knowledge that derives from observation. For it seems that the character of knowledge as *knowledge of a substantive general proposition about a life form* does nothing to settle its character as empirical or biological – no more, as the case of intentional action shows, than the character of knowledge as *knowledge of a process unfolding in the world* does anything to settle *its* character as observational or otherwise empirical.

We have non-observational knowledge in self-consciousness of certain of our inner states, and a special practical knowledge of certain of the processes of which we are the subject, and moreover a knowledge by reflection of some of the powers characteristic of the form we bear; what is to be said against the idea that we might have another kind of practical knowledge – *ethical* knowledge, if you like – of certain norms that attach to us as bearers of a particular life form characterized by practical reason? As my thinking representation of what I am doing intentionally is an *aspect* of what this representation itself is about, so this latter cognition will be an aspect of the life characteristic of the developed human subject and will characteristically mediate her practical operations. Such cognition goes to constitute the form of life in question as one in which the things cognized are true. I speak, as usual, of what is 'characteristic': in individual bearers of the human form, some of this knowledge will often enough go missing, of course, as often some teeth are missing; or the knowledge will be present but nevertheless fail to make it into the determination of action.

In representing my propositions as possessing so-called normative authority, or as expressing something more than private taste or local custom – in reaching, that is, for the concepts *good* and *well* in this connection – I implicitly represent my propositions, the naturalist will say, as possessing the status just described. I represent them not simply as manifestations of the form I bear, as all my thoughts (and heartbeats) are, but as characteristic of the form I bear. I thus represent myself as in this respect in possession of a sound practical understanding *qua* bearer of this form. If all has gone well in the development of my understanding – improbably enough – then my propositions will in fact have this status. And, moreover, I will not be damaging my daughter, or casting spells on her, or binding her feet spiritually speaking, or turning her into a practical bonsai, if I coax *her* into accrediting them as well, by example and precept; for this, on any view, is part of how an organism of this type is brought into apprehension of practical truth. Of course we have no way of judging what practical thoughts and what range of upbringings might be characteristic of the human, and sound in a human, except through application of our fundamental practical judgments – judgments about what makes sense and what might count as a reason and so forth. And these are judgments each of us must recognize to be the result of his own upbringing and reflection.

As these very preliminary remarks suggest, a developed normative naturalism will no doubt assign our general practical knowledge a precise epistemological position that differs from any we contemplated above. It would take another essay, or a treatise, to develop the matter properly – in particular to resolve the very difficult problem of the mediation of a human's apprehension of fundamental practical truth by his induction into more local, specific, determinate so-called social practices, or shapes of *Bildung* or 'second nature'. My present point is only this, that the idea that recognition of the human form is everywhere empirical cannot be permitted smugly to operate as an a priori impediment to the development of a naturalist account.[4]

The specifically human form does not come into our thoughts and intelligences as something alien, from without, through the medium of the senses, but as the form these things themselves manifest it is utterly transparent to them.[5]

Notes

1 Charles Darwin, *The Origin of Species* (1876), P. H. Barrett and R. B. Freeman (eds.) (New York: New York University Press, 1988), 386. He is discussing the principles of hierarchical classification, defending a genealogical or historical conception as ideal.

2 *On Virtue Ethics* (Oxford: Oxford University Press, 1998); *Natural Goodness* (Oxford: Oxford University Press, 2000).

3 The special logical character of 'considerations of justice' is addressed in my essay 'What Is It to Wrong Someone?' in *Practical Reason and Value*, R. J. Wallace, P. Pettit, S. Scheffler and M. Smith (eds.) (Oxford: Oxford University Press, forthcoming.).

4 Very much less, of course, can a manly wisdom about the bloody course of human history be set against the claim that, say, justice belongs 'according to nature' to the human practical understanding; no more than knowledge of the bloody – well, not exactly *bloody* – course of umbrella jelly history considered *in extenso* – in which what happens in your natural history has so rarely happened, almost everything having been thrown against rocks, starved, or eaten by predators – be brought as proof of Pollyannaism against your monograph. This point does not turn on epistemological subtleties, but on the logical form of the propositions in question.

5 To paraphrase Gottlob Frege's summary remark about our apprehension of the numbers, *The Foundations of Arithmetic*, trans. J. L. Austin (Oxford: Blackwells, 1974), 115.

3.1.7 J. Murillo
"Health as a Norm and Principle of Intelligibility"

Health, Happiness and Anthropology

For Aristotle, man's success or failure is linked to the idea of happiness. To speak of happiness in relation to non-human animals is difficult. The correct term might be satisfaction: given that happiness encompasses an understanding of one's life as a whole,[1] of which animals are incapable, happiness cannot be used to describe their state.

The notion of health is connected to the notion of happiness because the latter also connotes perfection, although it adds to it the conscious enjoyment of one's own possibilities and possession of goods without which nature may be healthy and complete but frustrated. The happy man is one who can attain all the goods due to him, and has in fact done so, at least to a certain extent; his life may be said to be fully developed.

The distinction between the notion of health and that of happiness consists in the fact that the healthy man is not necessarily in possession of every good that he desires. Being healthy is not necessarily the same as feeling at ease; one can be healthy in a situation of anxiety or frustration due to external causes. In such cases, health involves, among other things, the capacity to perceive the situation correctly, even if it is painful or distressing, and to react in an adequate way. However, although health is not the same as happiness, perfect happiness encompasses health and does not gainsay it; as the disposition which allows for man's specific activity in accordance with his nature, health is the condition by which the goods that man obtains may be enjoyed. Not only is health a good in itself, it is also a prerequisite for unobstructed action and full enjoyment of what is good. Nobody may be regarded as happy simply because he enjoys good health, but total and perfect happiness includes health.

Fullness of life cannot be equated with health in the case of animals. The idea of fullness of life cannot have practical meaning in the life of an animal; an animal is incapable of acting in the light of an understanding of its own life as a whole. In any case, health is presupposed by any definition of fullness of life that might be applied to an animal. It appears that there is no need to define what fullness of life for a dog might be – difficult task in itself – in order to understand the dog for what it is; however, there can be no understanding of the dog as it is without some knowledge of what a healthy dog is.

J. Murillo, "Health as a Norm and Principle of Intelligibility," in *Natural Law: Historical, Systematic and Juridical Approaches*, ed. A.N. Garcia et al. (Newcastle: Cambridge Scholars Publishing, 2008), pp. 358–361. Reprinted with permission of Cambridge Scholars Publishing.

Thus, the idea that most closely parallels the notion of health in the spiritual order is "virtue". Virtue is not natural in the same way as health. One may be virtuous or not – and that depends mainly on the way one behaves –. Nevertheless, virtue is natural in the sense that it is the fulfilment of natural possibilities. In fact, nature is to a certain extent a norm for virtue, because the real good of a natural being cannot be attained at the expense of its own destruction, but only by encompassing its aspirations and fulfilling them intrinsically. This is, moreover, the classical definition of virtue.[2]

Another difference between virtue and health lies in the fact that, while biological health appears to be limited, there are conceptions of virtue, such as that in the Christian tradition, which affirm that it is always possible to be more virtuous and deny that man may arrive at definitive fulfilment of virtue in his temporal and mortal state.

In any case, and returning to the argument outlined above, if man cannot be understood without reference to his perfection, and it is agreed that there is a more important and decisive type of health than the merely biological, it follows that no anthropology may be developed independently of an idea of fullness of life.

However, these observations prompt further questions. Biology draws on its analysis of healthy specimens: is it possible to carry out the study of anthropology without making reference to virtuous men? This question, in turn, prompts another, classical concern: can anthropology and ethics be separated? There is a further concern in this regard, above all for the purposes of the objective and supposedly neutral project of modern science: where is the healthy man in this second and more inner way, and what qualities may he have? Moreover, is a hypothetical or ideal model of life sufficient to ground anthropological study, or must such study be based on real life?

Saint Augustine takes as read the existence of a certain previous knowledge about the moral perfection of man in his claim that the mind is understood not by the examination of many minds, but by considering the mind in the light of eternal reasons.[3] If everything that is experienced is imperfect, it is difficult to establish in a clear and meaningful way what perfection is; above all, it would be impossible to know whether such perfection may really exist or not.

However, the possibility of achieving such perfection is called into question if this normative knowledge is nothing more than an ideal. It is difficult to accept that a totally unattainable model could move one to aspire to it, even more so given that the attempt to do so might require considerable effort. The conviction that moral goodness is desirable and attainable would appear to be in some way a property of the character of the good man; however, the moral failures of many human beings may cast doubt on this position.

Perhaps this is the reason why anthropology and ethics emerged as scientific (i.e. philosophical) disciplines at the same time, and, from the beginning, drew on the conviction that there is a human model which has real basis.[4] That the schools of thought in anthropology and ethics in ancient times hinge on the work of a number of key figures, especially Socrates, should be noted; but others have followed in their footsteps, with the intention of building on past achievements in this field.[5]

In Christian thought, the notion of personal health is understood in a similar way, although a more nuanced approach is taken. Balanced perfection cannot be fully reached in this life, there can be no complete integration of animal and spiritual health in man, because human nature, affected by sin, is condemned to death, and this mortality, which will not be overcome until the resurrection of the body, entails a degree of incoherence between the two dimensions of man. Nevertheless, Christian anthropology is based on a human model: not only that of Adam, which is beyond us (and relatively unknown), but that of Christ, without whom it is impossible to understand the Christian view of man. In addition, the lives of the saints provide public example of the attempt to put the ideal into practice.

It is clear that the problem of moral health as a guide for action raises new questions that should be dealt with in a considered way. The aim of this paper is not to resolve all the difficulties that arise in the context of the problem it describes, but to point to the fact that the problem must be addressed. The best way to conclude, then, might be offer an overview of the argument that has led to this conclusion in order to frame further discussion. As has been noted, the clear distinction between the scientific description of reality and moral obligation, proposed by Hume and accepted by later thinkers, cannot be applied to knowledge of life. To understand a living being as such, its nature, the criterion of good and evil in its regard, must be acknowledged. Thus, animals are to be understood on the basis of what is known of healthy or fully developed specimens. The problem of defining what constitutes a 'healthy individual' arises in relation to man as a living being, a problem that encompasses moral as well as biological concerns because human perfection connotes man's freedom. In any case, if perfection is a necessary criterion for understanding man as a living being, genuine anthropology must be underwritten by some reference to an exemplary moral norm.

The old conception of natural law, therefore, might also be said to depend on the position adopted in light of what is regarded as the nature and the good of man, and in what way the notion of health may be applied to him.

Notes

1   Aristotle. *Nicomachean Ethics.*, I, 10, 1101a14–21.

2   Ibid., I, 12, 1102a4ff.

3   "Neque enim oculis corporeis multas mentes videndo, per similitudinem colligimus generalem vel specialem mentis humanae notitiam; sed intuemur inviolabilem veritatem, ex qua perfecte, quantum possumus, definiamus, non qualis sit uniuscuiusque hominis mens, sed qualis esse sempiternis rationibus debeat". *De Trinitate*, IX, 6, 9.

4   Aristotle is not slow to propose the good man as a criterion of moral goodness: "If this view is right, as it seems to be, and virtue – that is, the good person in so far as he is good – is the measure of each thing, then pleasures will be what appear so to him, and pleasant things will be what he enjoys". Aristotle, *Nicomachean Ethics.*, X, cap. 5 (1176 a 3-1176 a 30), 192. Thus, for Aristotle, the good is more intelligible in the life of the good man than in its reflection in the conscience of one who aspires to goodness.

5   Ctr. Pierre Hadot, *Qu'est-ce que la philosophie antique?* (Paris: Gallimard, 1996).

Works Cited

Aristotle. *Nicomachean Ethics.* Cambridge: Cambridge University Press, 2000.

Hadot, Pierre. *Qu'est-Ce Que La Philosophie Antique?* Paris: Gallimard, 1996.

Hume, David, *A Treatise of Human Nature.* Aalen: Scientia Verlag, 1964.

Jonas, Hans. *El principio vida. Hacia una biología filosófica.* Madrid: Trotta, 2000.

Kant, I. *Critique of the Power of Judgment.* Cambridge: Cambridge University Press, 2000.

Ricoeur, Paul. "The Problem of the Foundation of Moral Philosophy." *Philosophy today*, no. 22 (1978): 175–92.

3.2 Jurisprudence

Introduction

The present section contains selections of a more obviously jurisprudential nature, though it must be stressed that it is a peculiar feature of the central natural law tradition that it tends to emphasize the overlap, indeed, interpenetration, between the ethical and the juridical. The section is divided into two parts. The first part contains extracts that seek to unpick some of the misattributions and misunderstandings surrounding the central tradition. The first extract in this part, taken from Robert George's *Making Men Moral*,[1] is a detailed review of the famous Hart–Devlin debate, which took place in the middle part of the twentieth century, and was occasioned by the publication of the recommendations of the Wolfenden Commission that the law then prohibiting homosexual intercourse should be abolished. In the course of that protracted exchange, Hart argued the positivist line that the law had no business enforcing private morality; whilst Devlin argued that government had a legitimate interest in enforcing the moral consensus of a society as a way of preserving social cohesion and stability, and that a failure to do so could result in a dangerous disjunction between the law and its necessary sources of popular legitimacy. George is critical not just of the positivist position adopted by Hart, but also of the consensualist-cum-traditionalist approach defended by Devlin which, he regrets, is often taken to be based upon a natural law understanding. As such, George makes the obvious point that Devlin's arguments could be used to justify the enforcement of substantially unjust laws so long as those laws were supported by the weight of accepted opinion. This, George emphasizes, is something that a natural lawyer adhering to the central tradition could never endorse. It is also a position that would distort the natural law by neutralizing any potential it might possess in certain circumstances to ground a radical, even revolutionary, social critique. The second extract is a sophisticated piece by one of the principal representatives – Norman Kretzmann – of a group of scholars of the very highest caliber, who have led a revival of interest in the secular academy in the philosophy of Aquinas, a revival extending

[1]   R.P. George, *Making Men Moral* (Oxford: Oxford University Press, 1995).

The Natural Law Reader, First Edition. Edited by Jacqueline A. Laing and Russell Wilcox.
© 2014 Blackwell Publishing Ltd. Published 2014 by Blackwell Publishing Ltd.

well beyond, though not excluding, his ethical and political writings.[2] Kretzmann seeks conclusively to answer what he quickly exposes as the rather superficial though popular criticism of Aquinas' famous principle that an unjust law is no law at all. In so doing, he points to the sophisticated set of inclusion conditions with which Aquinas is working, which simply render most of the criticisms leveled against him at best otiose and at worst laced with profound philosophical naivety.

The second part of this section deals with a vigorous debate occurring largely amongst those claiming to uphold a theory of natural law fully in line with the central tradition and, more particularly, with the thought of Thomas Aquinas. This has focused upon, but not been confined to, an evaluation of what has come to be termed the "New Natural Law theory," put forward in its most celebrated form by John Finnis in his work *Natural Law and Natural Rights*,[3] but elaborated over several decades in close collaboration with Germain Grisez and Joseph Boyle. Amongst its defenders, it has been variously characterized as an accurate representation of the views of Aquinas himself and as an independent theory in its own right that merely draws upon his work for inspiration. Yet, however so characterized from the hermeneutical point of view, it has also been universally proposed as a theory deserving to be evaluated upon its own philosophical merits. Through the insistent efforts and singularly systematic intelligence of John Finnis it is, as a matter of fact, to be credited with thrusting traditional natural law thinking back into the heart of contemporary Anglo-American jurisprudential discourse.

The first extract here is taken from the second half of an article-length review by Robert George,[4] one of Finnis' most prominent disciples, of an early attack on the Finnis–Grisez position. In his book *A Critique of the New Natural Law Theory*,[5] Russell Hittinger took up the initial misgivings neo-Scholastic and neo-Thomist philosophers Henry Babcock Veatch and Ralph McInerny had expressed over the supposed epistemological foundations of the natural law as presented in the Finnis–Grisez theory. In essence this turned on whether or not, and if so, to what extent, the first principles of practical reason – the basic precepts of the natural law – are speculatively derived and therefore dependent upon a metaphysical understanding of human nature, or whether they enjoy a certain epistemological autonomy. Finnis and Grisez hold to the latter view, and it is in defending them against Hittinger's perceived misunderstandings that the substance of George's review consists.

Taking up these questions in one of the most philosophically and hermeneutically sophisticated treatments to have appeared so far, the next selection by Stephen Brock involves a close reading, in line with an analysis previously canvassed by distinguished Thomist Lawrence Dewan, of what he sees as the central text in Aquinas' treatment of law (*ST* IaIIae. 94. 2) around which controversy swirls.[6] In the course of so doing he pro-

---

[2]   N. Kretzmann, "Lex Iniusta Non est Lex: Laws on Trial in Aquinas' Court of Conscience," *American Journal of Jurisprudence* 33 (1988), pp. 99–122.

[3]   J. Finnis, *Natural Law and Natural Rights*, 2nd edition (Oxford: Oxford University Press, 2011). See also the important early article: G. Grisez, J. Boyle, and J. Finnis, "Practical Principles, Moral Truth and Ultimate Ends," *American Journal of Jurisprudence* 32 (1987).

[4]   R.P. George, "Recent Criticism of the Natural Law Theory," *University of Chicago Law Review* (Fall, 1988).

[5]   R. Hittinger, *A Critique of the New Natural Law Theory* (South Bend, IN: University of Notre Dame Press, 1989).

[6]   S. Brock, "Natural Inclination and the Intelligibility of the Good in Thomistic Natural Law," *Vera Lex* VI.1–2 (Winter 2005), pp. 57–78.

vides a concise resume of the various interpretative positions taken over the past half century and then goes on to argue that most of these interpretations have erred in understanding the inclinations in connection with which the basic precepts of the natural law emerge as being pre-rational. In the alternative, Brock argues that not only the apprehension of what is good but also the inclinations of which Aquinas speaks are rational. Thus for Brock, "[r]eason's natural understanding of human good does not follow the natural inclinations to them. The inclinations follow the understanding."[7]

Moving on from this pivotal controversy, the next selection by Daniel McInerny reflects critically on another aspect of the "New Natural Law theory," namely, the thesis that basic goods are incommensurable;[8] a thesis which states, in the words of Robert George, "that basic values and their particular instantiations as they figure in options for choice cannot be weighed and measured in accordance with an objective standard of comparison."[9] Against this position, McInerny argues that, in fact, it is indeed possible to make "non-arbitrary choices between contending substantial, or intrinsically valuable, goods," but only "when one of the goods is seen either as a necessary or expedient means for the attainment of another and intrinsically more valuable good."[10] Thus he makes reference to a duplex – or twofold – order of human goods both to one another and to the ultimate end, such that even intrinsic goods can appropriately be possessed of a special form of instrumentality in certain circumstances. McInerny argues that a hierarchical understanding of substantial or inherent human goods is necessary not only to make possible non-arbitrary choices on those occasions when they conflict, but also to preserve the overall unity (and therefore integrity) of the human good *per se*. Of course this immediately presages a connection with the debate over epistemological warrant outlined above, since it begs the question as to how the hierarchy of basic goods is to be recognized – a question which McInerny would, no doubt, have little hesitation in answering metaphysically.

The final selection in this section, which is extracted from a review essay by Steven D. Smith, seeks to sidestep the details of many of the criticisms of the New Naturalist project so far canvassed.[11] Instead, Smith, who describes himself as an "outsider" to the major natural law traditions but one who has "watched with sympathetic interest in the revival of natural law thinking,"[12] seeks to analyze the New Natural Law accounts in terms of rhetorical efficacy. Prior to the section extracted here, Smith examines an entirely secular proposal from the jurist Michael Moore, one of a number of self-identified natural law thinkers who show some discomfort with, and maintain a certain distance from, the

---

[7] Ibid., p. 61.

[8] D. McInerny, "Hierarchy and Direction for Choice," in *Virtue's End: God in the Moral Philosophy of Aristotle and Aquinas*, ed. F. Di Blassi, J.P. Hochschild, and J. Langan (South Bend, IN: St. Augustine's Press, 2008), pp. 124–138.

[9] R.P. George, *In Defence of the Natural Law* (Oxford: Oxford University Press, 1999), p. 83; quoted in ibid., p. 125.

[10] Ibid., p. 125.

[11] S.D. Smith, "Natural Law and Contemporary Moral Thought: A Guide from the Perplexed," *American Journal of Jurisprudence* 42 (1997), pp. 299–330. The review is of *Natural Law, Liberalism and Morality: Contemporary Essays*, ed. R.P. George (Oxford: Oxford University Press, 1996).

[12] Ibid., p. 300.

central tradition, and yet who still find liberal neutralism and anti-realist moral theories utterly unconvincing.[13] In this context Moore seeks to exclude all talk of a religious basis for moral theory, finding it a positive hindrance to the task of meeting the attacks on the moral realist position he wants to defend. As an alternative he attempts to put forward an impersonal theory of value that postulates objective reasons for acting which do not consist in satisfying the needs of anyone in particular. After echoing the criticisms of Moore's approach as articulated by his fellow essayist Jorge Garcia[14] and pointing out the complete implausibility of conducting persuasive moral discourse on a basis divorced from the concerns and experiences of everyday life, Smith moves on to a consideration of the arguments put forward by John Finnis in the highly contentious area of sexual relations within homosexual unions.[15] In dealing with such a conflicted area of discourse, where the weight of contemporary "Western" opinion is so clearly against the substantive conclusions to which Finnis argues, his subject could not have been better chosen as a proving ground for the overall argument Smith is seeking to make. Indeed, it is here, if anywhere, that the effectiveness of an argument will consist in more than mere formal consistency if it is not, in practice, to be dismissed as being utterly unworthy of consideration. As such, whilst Smith recognizes that Finnis avoids some of the more serious philosophical problems faced by Moore's impersonal theory of value, he goes on to claim that in the end Finnis "implicitly depends on something that in at least one crucial respect is not so different from Moore's notion: he is committed to an order of goods whose goodness is to some extent independent of human experiencing of them as desirable."[16] For Smith, this seriously undercuts the persuasiveness of Finnis' arguments. The fact that Smith has a good deal more respect for both the moral and intellectual coherence of Finnis and the New Naturalist position in general than he has for that of Moore may be seen from the remainder of the piece where he tries to show the greater richness of an account that does not eschew the invocation of more comprehensive worldviews – worldviews which he terms religious, but which may just as easily be termed metaphysical – in substantive ethical discourse. By questioning Finnis and those who adopt his position on rhetorical rather than mainly philosophical bases, Smith offers an original and possibly more constructive critique than have some others.

---

[13]   M. Moore, "Good Without God," in *Natural Law, Liberalism and Morality*. See also M. Moore, "Law as a Functional Kind," in *Natural Law Theory: Contemporary Essays*, ed. R.P. George (Oxford: Oxford University Press, 1992); M. Moore, "Moral Reality," *Wisconsin Law Review* 6 (1982), pp. 1061–1156; and M. Moore, "A Natural Law Theory of Interpretation," *South California Law Review* 58 (1985), p. 277.

[14]   J. Garcia, "'Deus Sive Natura': Must Natural Lawyers Choose?" in *Natural Law, Liberalism and Morality*.

[15]   J. Finnis, "Is Natural Law Theory Compatible with Limited Government?" in *Natural Law, Liberalism and Morality*. See also S. Macedo, "Against the Old Sexual Morality of the New Natural Law," in *Natural Law, Liberalism and Morality*.

[16]   Smith, "Natural Law and Contemporary Moral Thought," p. 316.

3.2.1 Debates and Clarifications

3.2.1.1 R.P. George
Making Men Moral

The Central Tradition versus Devlinism

I shall defend the proposition that the classic central tradition's defense of morals legislation was sound in insisting that the truth of the morality a society would enforce, whether for the sake of preserving social cohesion or for the sake of promoting virtue and discouraging vice, is a necessary condition for the legitimacy of its enforcement. My claim against Devlin is that morals laws cannot be justified on *any* ground that dispenses with the requirement that the morality enforced under such laws must be *true*. Thus it will be necessary for me to meet the arguments by which Devlin sought to establish that there is something illegitimate about appealing to the moral truth of the obligations enforced under morals laws.

I do not deny that the maintenance of social cohesion and the avoidance of social disintegration are legitimate public interests; nor do I doubt Devlin's claim that these interests are adversely affected by acts of immorality regardless of whether they cause direct, palpable harm to non-consenting parties. Devlin was right to question the notion of purely private immoralities. I shall argue, however, that even in circumstances in which social cohesion is imperiled, as Devlin correctly supposed it could be, by the erosion of a hitherto dominant morality, a concern for social cohesion *per se* is not a sufficient ground

R.P. George, "Social Cohesion and the Legal Enforcement of Morals," in *Making Men Moral*, ed. R.P. George (Oxford: Oxford University Press, 1995), pp. 48–80. Reprinted with permission of Oxford University Press.

for enforcing moral obligations. The justification of morals laws cannot prescind, as Devlin supposed it could, from the question of the moral truth of the obligations they enforce. A concern for social cohesion around a shared morality can justify some instances of the enforcement of morals, but only if that morality is true.

Devlin's rejection of the putative distinction between private and public immoralities was anything but novel. Supporters of morals laws, jurists and laymen alike, have long held that allegedly private immoralities damage the public welfare. Under what I have been calling the 'traditional' view, the public welfare is conceived as the interest shared by all members of the community in, among other things, a cultural milieu free from the corrupting influences of vice.

The tradition holds that the criminal law can, and often should, prohibit at least 'the grosser forms of vice',[1] to encourage people to achieve, and help them to maintain, the good of a morally upright character. Such a character is, according to the tradition, a benefit *primarily* to the individual who possesses it. Still, it is a *common* good, and thus an aspect of *the* common good (for which public authorities have special, albeit non-exclusive, responsibility), in a double sense: (1) it is a good for each and every member of the community (even, indeed especially, those prone to vice); and (2) it is a good that may be maintained and advanced by public efforts, especially efforts to ensure that the cultural milieu in which people make the choices that form their characters is kept free from frequent, powerful inducements to vice.

According to the tradition, statecraft really is, in part, soulcraft. The fundamental distinction relevant to a legislator considering a proposed law aimed at upholding public morals is not the alleged distinction between private and public immorality; rather, the relevant distinction is between immoral acts and acts that are morally acceptable.[2] The job of the legislator, in the first instance, is to ascertain whether the action sought to be banned on the basis of its immorality is in truth – and not merely in common opinion – immoral. If, though unpopular or even widely condemned, the action is in his judgment morally acceptable, then he must consider the proposed law unjustified. If, on the other hand, he agrees on reflection that the action is immoral, he may support the legislation without injustice. (Of course, he may decide that practical considerations – for example those having to do with the difficulty of the law's fair enforcement or its financial or other costs – tip the balance against enacting the law.)

Devlin's position resembles the tradition's in denying that a distinction between private and public (im)morality is serviceable as a principle for deciding where the coercive force of the criminal law may legitimately be brought to bear. The resemblance ends there, however; for Devlin's rationale for denying this distinction (and thus his defense of morals laws) is radically unlike the tradition's rationale. The tradition ultimately is concerned with the *moral character* of members of the community, believing that a cultural milieu that permits vice to flourish presents a grave threat to *this* common good. Devlin ultimately is concerned with the common good of *social cohesion*, believing that social bonds constituted by shared moral beliefs are placed in peril when the law tolerates actions that are generally considered to be wicked.

As we have seen, Devlin's revisionist understanding of the good at stake in matters of public morality leads him to conclude that *no* potentially controversial act is in principle 'private', because *any* act committed in violation of widely and strongly held moral opinions is capable of eroding the common morality that binds together members of a society.

The failure of the law to proscribe such acts places at risk the common morality without which people would 'drift apart'. Morals laws, by upholding and reinforcing *whatever* morality happens to be dominant in a society, uphold one of the *de facto* necessary conditions for avoiding the evil of social disintegration.[3]

Under Devlin's view, the tradition's distinction between immoral acts and morally acceptable acts is as irrelevant to the consideration of a conscientious legislator as the Wolfenden Report's distinction between public and private immorality. What matters is not whether an action is immoral, but only whether a substantial majority strongly *believes* it to be (gravely)[4] so. The legislator must ascertain whether the action in question *is according to his society's dominant morality* so abominable that its toleration will imperil that morality, thereby 'threatening the existence of society'.[5]

According to Devlin, acts that would, in the absence of condemnation under a dominant morality, be harmless (even acts that are, in truth, morally acceptable or indeed laudable) are nevertheless capable of doing grave harm – even threatening the existence of society – in circumstances where, for no good reason, they happen to be condemned by a dominant morality. Therefore a society may ban such acts for the sake of its own preservation.

In a lecture published a few years after his Maccabaean Lecture, Devlin defended his refusal to embrace the tradition's idea (he called it the 'Platonic ideal') that the virtue of the citizenry should be among the goods served by the law:

> If that is [the law's] function, then whatever power is sovereign in the state – an autocrat if there be one, or in a democracy the majority – must have the right and duty to declare what standards of morality are to be observed as virtuous and must ascertain them as it thinks best. This is not acceptable to Anglo-American thought. It invests the State with the power of determination between good and evil, destroys freedom of conscience and is the paved road to tyranny.[6]

Devlin offered these remarks as part of a critique of the majority's reasoning in *Shaw* v. *Director of Public Prosecutions* (1962) AC 200, a then-recent case in which the House of Lords held that the offense of conspiracy to corrupt public morals, under which the unfortunate Mr Shaw had been successfully prosecuted, was indeed known to the common law. Devlin rightly perceived in Viscount Simonds's claim that 'among the supreme and fundamental purpose[s] of the law [are] not only the safety and order but also the moral welfare of the state',[7] a rejection of 'the teaching of John Stuart Mill'.[8] But Devlin's identification of 'Anglo-American thought' with Mill's teaching is baffling – and not only because of the obvious tensions between that teaching and Devlin's own legal moralism. By the time Devlin took up the question of the legitimacy of morals legislation, the spirit of Mill's philosophy had, perhaps, acquired the status of orthodoxy among an academic élite, but views contrary to Mill's libertarianism were not then, nor are they now, alien to 'Anglo-American thought'.

Of course, Devlin's claim that the tradition's view is unorthodox – that it is *not* the tradition's view – is peripheral to the case he makes against it. Even if he could establish that it is 'unacceptable to Anglo-American thought' (something he makes no effort to do) it would strengthen his case only marginally. The philosophically interesting features of Devlin's rejection of the tradition's defense of morals legislation are his claims that the use of the law to promote virtue 'destroys freedom of conscience' and 'is the paved road to tyranny'. I shall consider these claims in turn.

The former claim rests upon the false supposition that the tradition's view must compel not merely conduct, but belief. Since the *compulsion* of belief is possible, if at all, only by brainwashing or some other method of thought control, and since brainwashing indeed destroys freedom of conscience, this supposition, if true, would establish Devlin's claim. Anyone who believes in freedom of conscience would have to reject the traditional defense of morals legislation. This supposition, however, is false. While the tradition envisages the compulsion (in the sense of legal prohibition) of *conduct* both to prevent immoral acts which in themselves (further) corrupt the actor's character and to encourage in him and others the adoption of sound beliefs about morality, the tradition does not seek to *compel belief*. It supports laws that forbid people from *performing* certain immoral acts; it does not support laws that forbid people from *believing* that certain illegal acts are in fact moral.

In this respect, as in so many others, morals laws are no different from other duty-imposing legal norms. Laws against homicide, for example, do not forbid people from *believing* that the sorts of homicides proscribed by the law are in fact morally permissible or even laudable; they forbid people from carrying out those homicides. Even in the case of 'inchoate' crimes, what the law forbids is conduct, not beliefs. Consider, for example, laws against conspiracy. One may be prosecuted for participating in *planning* the violent overthrow of the government; one may not lawfully be prosecuted, however, for *believing* that the government should be violently overthrown. The same is true for crimes of incitement. In certain jurisdictions one may be prosecuted for *inciting* others to treason, for example, or to racial hatred; one may not be lawfully prosecuted, however, for *holding the beliefs* about politics or race expressed in one's illegal communication or advocacy. No doubt the purposes of laws against murder, conspiracy, and incitement include the encouragement of certain beliefs (e.g. reverence for human life, respect for just institutions of government, belief in racial equality). Forbidding wrongful conduct, however, even with a view to encouraging upright belief, leaves people free to judge the acts proscribed by the law, and even the law itself, according to their own consciences.

The tradition recognizes that the law is among the factors that help to shape people's moral opinions. It holds that there is nothing wrong in principle with legally prohibiting immoral behavior for the sake of influencing people to form and retain sound opinions about the immorality of wrongful acts that some may be tempted to commit. It does not authorize the compulsion of opinion, however. To be sure, the morals laws that have been part of the tradition limit liberty of behavior (as do all duty-imposing laws); they do not, however, destroy freedom of conscience. Morals laws may sometimes forbid people from acting on their *conscientious* beliefs. Here again, however, many laws enacted and enforced for reasons having nothing to do with protecting public morals forbid people from acting on conscientious beliefs without 'destroying freedom of conscience'. Nothing changes when the legislative motivation for the law is a concern for public morality.

Let us turn now to Devlin's claim that the tradition's view 'is the paved road to tyranny'. Unlike the former claim, he put this assertion forward not, I think, as a piece of conceptual analysis (e.g. to compel belief is to destroy freedom of conscience), but rather as an ominous prediction of the consequences of adopting the tradition's view. Devlin predicted that using the law to discourage vice for the sake of virtue would lead to the destruction of most meaningful liberty. A claim of this sort requires evidence, and Devlin does not supply any. Arguably, any credibility the claim possesses derives from, and therefore falls with, Devlin's claim that the tradition's view 'destroys freedom of conscience'. Still, the proposition that morals laws lead to tyranny is widely believed. For that reason, if no other, it is worth considering.

Perhaps Devlin believed that the traditional defense of morals laws virtually invites fanatics and rigorists to seize control of the state apparatus to prosecute their moralistic agendas. We have been reminded recently that such people exist; the adoption of the tradition's view by people who are neither fanatical nor rigorist, however, is (1) possible, and (2) unlikely to have much of an impact on the desire of fanatics and rigorists for political power or their ability to attain it. It seems equally plausible to suppose that permissiveness, to the extent that moral laxity follows in its train, encourages fanaticism and rigorism as a backlash.

Devlin, however, may have been making a somewhat different prediction about the consequences of adopting the tradition's position. Perhaps he was claiming that power to enforce one's own conception of the requirements of, say, sexual morality is likely to induce fanaticism or rigorism in those who happen to come into possession of it. This prediction, however, seems even more dubious. Just as the power to deregulate does not seem to induce people of a libertarian bent to become anarchists, the power to enforce public morals for the sake of virtue is unlikely to induce people who subscribe to the tradition to become moral extremists.

Whether or not there is anything worth taking seriously in Devlin's claim that the tradition's ground for enacting morals laws imperils most meaningful liberty, it is worth observing the irony in his asserting it. The legislator acting on the tradition's premises may, of course, make mistakes. For example, he may ban an innocent form of behavior based on the erroneous judgment that it is wicked. He may fall victim to his own peculiar prejudices or to prejudices widely shared in his culture. The premiss he accepts, however, requires him to *reason* about the morality of the behavior in question. Whether he manages, or even tries, to live up to this requirement, the requirement itself demands that he let no prejudice, or partiality, or other non-rational factor, whether his own or others', affect his decision to limit liberty for the sake of public morals. He is committed to the proposition that, in truth, there is a broad class of acts that are perfectly acceptable from the moral point of view and are therefore immune in principle from laws meant to uphold public morals.

Now contrast the understanding of a legislator committed to the tradition's view with that of a Devlinite legislator. The Devlinite may consider an act to be perfectly upright. Still, if he perceives that the morality dominant in his community vigorously condemns it – albeit on the basis of sheer prejudice – he must ban that act for the sake of social cohesion. He must ban the act even if he judges that it is morally acceptable and even holds important benefits for those wishing to perform it. Unlike the legislator who holds to the central tradition, the Devlinite is required to sacrifice the genuine interests of the minority who wish to perform the act for the sake of what Devlinism supposes to be the greater good of social cohesion.

Once we contrast the reasoning of a legislator committed to the tradition with that of a Devlinite legislator, it becomes apparent, I think, that Devlin's version of legal moralism presents the real threat of tyranny. The tradition affords some protection to individuals and minorities by requiring that public authorities *reason* (and, in democracies, publicly *give* reasons) about the human good and the true norms of morality. It does not authorize, much less require, legislators to limit liberty on the basis of mere prejudice. Devlin's willingness to permit – indeed to *require* – the suppression of innocent or even honorable liberties (on the basis that mere prejudices are strongly held) means, by contrast, that no civil liberty is safe from infringement nor is any individual or minority protected from oppression.

According to Devlin, what justifies limitations of liberty is not reason but *feeling* and thus, potentially, mere prejudice. Regardless of whether his disintegration thesis is sound, this aspect of his position lays his defense of morals laws open to the charge of imperiling every civil liberty. To say that the law may forbid genuine immorality – even any form of genuine immorality – is to imply a limit: the law cannot legitimately legislate on moral grounds against acts that are not truly immoral. To say that the law may forbid anything a large majority strongly believes is gravely immoral – even if for no very good reason – is to allow that there is no *limit* to the reach of the law. It is to say that the genuine welfare of individuals and minorities *legitimately* may be sacrificed for the sake of something considered an unconditionally greater good, that is, social cohesion. Having accepted a wide relativity in moral judgments, Devlin's position must appeal in the end to a utilitarian principle by which the 'morality' of enforcing morals is eked out the greatest good of the greatest number.

The central tradition rejects Devlin's relativism and non-cognitivism together with the utilitarian principle appeal to which they render necessary to his defense of morals laws. The public interest served by morals laws, according to the tradition, consists in the maintenance of a cultural context conducive to *genuine* virtue and inhospitable to *genuine* vice. The intelligibility that grounds the public interest thus conceived is primarily that of moral uprightness (as something desirable for its own sake). A secondary ground of that interest is the intelligible good of social cohesion. An implication of the primary intelligibility, however, is that social cohesion may not legitimately be pursued unconditionally. A cultural context conducive to genuine virtue and inhospitable to genuine vice is intelligibly valuable, not only because it helps people to achieve and maintain the good of a morally upright character, but also because it may facilitate a *desirable* integration of human beings around *true* principles held in common. Whatever weakens, or *a fortiori* whatever destroys, such a context may by the same token produce an *undesirable* social disintegration. Under a non-relativist (and non-utilitarian) conception of the public interest, however, social cohesion is not always or unconditionally desirable. The integration of human beings around shared principles of *injustice* or other forms of wickedness is an *undesirable* integration.[9] The cultural context established and maintained by social integration of this sort is conducive to *injustice* or other vices. Social disintegration in these circumstances may be desirable.[10]

Devlin's rejection of the tradition (and his fear of its consequences) appears to have been driven by his moral non-cognitivism. Although non-cognitivist claims do not figure directly in his formal case against the 'Platonic ideal', his Maccabaean Lecture explicitly rejected the tradition's cognitivist premises. The most basic of these premises is the belief that it is possible for human beings to *reason* about the fundamental principles of the human good and the requirements of morality. This premiss in turn supports the tradition's belief in a principled distinction between authentic moral judgments (moral knowledge) and mere prejudices.

If, with Devlin, we assume the truth of non-cognitivism in relation to the acts of individuals, then no legislator can have a *reason* to think that acts commonly supposed to be immoral really do, by virtue of their immorality, *harm* (by corrupting the character of) those individuals who commit them and others who might be induced by their example to do so. All that rational inquiry can reveal about pornography, for example, is that the majority who subscribe to the dominant morality in a community 'feel' it to be wrong and that their feeling is more or less intense. Whether or not legislators share that feeling or its intensity, they cannot *rationally* conclude that, *qua* immoral, pornography damages a true human interest, that is, the genuine good of an upright moral character, by its tendency to corrupt and deprave.

Of course, if there are rational grounds for accepting Devlin's position on the limits of moral reasoning, then reason itself would require us to accept his non-cognitivism. I shall now argue, however, that Devlin has given us no good reason to accept even a limited non-cognitivism. Let us consider the ground he adduced.

Devlin argued not only that 'Morals and religion are inextricably joined', but also that '[no] moral code can claim any validity except by virtue of the religion on which it is based'.[11] As he depicted the situation, basic moral beliefs are derived from the teachings of religions, and religious teachings are based purely on faith, not reason. Moral beliefs are non-cognitive because the religious beliefs from which they derive are non-cognitive. Thus, Devlin reasoned, it is 'illogical' for any state that permits religious liberty to 'concern itself with morals as such'.[12]

> If this view is sound, it means that the criminal law cannot justify any of its provisions by reference to the moral law. It cannot say, for example, that murder and theft are prohibited because they are immoral. The State must justify in some other way the punishments which it imposes on wrongdoers and a function for the criminal law independent of morals must be found.[13]

It is true that most religions have something – often quite a great deal – to say about how human beings ought to behave. They propose teachings about right and wrong. In this respect religion and morality are indeed linked. It is also true that many of the world's positive moralities are associated with religions, though not all of these religions propose their moral teachings exclusively as matters of divine revelation. Some religions propose a set of moral norms not (or not only) as matters of divine revelation, but (also) as available to unaided reason. And some positive moralities are not linked to anything we ordinarily think of as a religion. There are people, indeed whole cultures, who subscribe to these moralities, but not on the basis of anything we ordinarily think of as religious faith.

The point I wish to make against Devlin's argument is that it is a *non sequitur*. From the proposition that people commonly affirm whatever putative moral norms they do affirm as part and parcel of their religious belief and practice, one cannot validly conclude that those norms, or alternatives to them, cannot be affirmed rationally independently of an affirmation of the authority of some religion to propose them. Stripped of the argument involving this fallacy, Devlin's assertion that reason is ultimately impotent in moral matters is gratuitous and begs the question.

It is also worth noting that Devlin wrongly assumes that the case for religious freedom must rest upon some form of religious non-cognitivism. He seems to suppose that the reason the law may not enforce religious beliefs is that such beliefs cannot be reasoned. Someone who believes that reason can judge in (at least some) matters of religion may, however, rationally, and without self-contradiction, oppose the enforcement of religious belief or practice. If someone considers the value of religion to be available only in the free assent of the believer to religious truths, then he might support principles of religious

liberty, not on non-cognitivist grounds, but precisely for the sake of the authentic appropriation by citizens of those religious truths accessible to reason.

Devlin has given us no reason to suppose that moral norms cannot be reasoned (and,
thus, reasonable). Of course, as the religious cognitivist's argument for religious liberty
shows, the sheer fact that reason dictates a certain course of action is not always a
sufficient ground for requiring that action by law. Reason may require precisely that
people be left free to act on their conscientious beliefs with respect to the matter in
question, even if those beliefs are unsound. Cognitivism, whether in religion or morals,
need not be an enemy of honorable liberties; indeed, it can be their greatest friend.

Notes

1   James Fitzjames Stephen, *Liberty, Equality, Fraternity* (2nd edn., London, 1874), 162. This
    phrase seems to have impressed Professor Hart, who, in *Law, Liberty, and Morality*, quotes it
    three times – once in each of the lectures which comprise the book (at 16, 36, 61).
2   'Morally acceptable' acts are those which violate no moral norms. For example, going for a
    pleasant walk in the woods on a day when one has no other responsibilities is neither required
    nor forbidden by a moral norm. It is morally acceptable. Morally acceptable acts really are
    'private' in the Wolfenden Committee's sense, that is, they damage no legitimate public interest.
    Indeed, according to the tradition, it is *in* the public interest, properly conceived, for people to
    be free to choose for themselves from among the vast range of morally acceptable acts.
3   For traditionalists, by contrast, morals laws, by upholding and reinforcing a public morality
    desirable precisely (and only) in so far as it is *true*, encourage people to form (and help them
    to maintain) a virtuous character. The fact that an act is unpopular or condemned by a dom-
    inant morality does not make it a threat to the good at stake in matters of public morality,
    namely, virtue. Only real vices may be banned, because only inducements to genuine wicked-
    ness can present a threat to virtue.
4   Devlin did not maintain that every act popularly believed to be immoral ought to be banned: There
    must be toleration of the maximum individual freedom that is consistent with the integrity of
    society. ... Nothing should be punished by the law that does not lie beyond the limits of tolerance'
    (*The Enforcement of Morals*, 16, 17). Vices that are, from the point of view of those subscribing
    to the dominant morality, comparatively minor may be legally tolerated: 'It is not nearly enough
    to say that a majority dislike a practice; there must be a real feeling of reprobation' (ibid. 17).
5   Ibid. 13 n. 1.
6   Ibid. 89.
7   *Shaw* v. *DPP* at 267. (Quoted in *The Enforcement of Morals*, 88.)
8   *The Enforcement of Morals*, 88.
9   The founders of the central tradition held that wickedness is incompatible with stable, genu-
    ine integration. See, for example, Plato, *The Republic*, ix. 571–80; and Aristotle, *Nicomachean
    Ethics*, ix. 4.
10 Thus a traditionalist defender of morals laws would agree with Hart's criticism of Devlin's
    apparent claim that *any* society may do whatever is required to prevent its own disintegra-
    tion: 'whether or not a society is justified in taking steps to preserve itself must depend both
    on what sort of society it is and what the steps to be taken are' (*Law, Liberty, and Morality*, 19;
    emphasis added).
11 *The Enforcement of Morals*, 4.
12 Ibid. 5.
13 Ibid.

3.2.1.2 Norman Kretzmann
"Lex Iniusta Non est Lex: Laws on Trial in Aquinas' Court of Conscience"

Definition and evaluation in Aquinas' Treatise on Law

A philosopher who, like Aquinas, seriously invokes anything like *non est lex* in assessing a law must be basing his assessment on a putatively complete list of inclusion conditions for law. Aquinas develops such a list in his "Treatise on Law," which occupies Questions 90–108 of *Summa theologiae* IaIIae. [...] Nowhere in the Treatise do we get a unified, complete list of inclusion conditions, however. We have to assemble such a list ourselves out of conditions Aquinas lists in various definitional passages or appeals to in evaluative passages.

Inclusion conditions for law

At the end of the Question on the essence of law, Aquinas announces that from the four articles of the Question we can put together "a definition of law: *Law is nothing other than an ordinance of reason directed toward the common good, promulgated by one who has responsibility for the community*."[1] Near the beginning of the next Question, on the kinds of law, he invokes that definition in these words: "*Law is nothing other than a dictate of practical reason in a sovereign (princeps) who governs a complete community*."[2] Although the phrase "nothing other than" in both of these definitional passages appears to guarantee completeness, each of them contains at least one inclusion condition the other omits.[3] Drawing on both of them, we can extract the following inclusion conditions for law:

- (A) a directive of reason,
- (B) aimed at the common good,
- (C) promulgated by the government,
- (D) pertaining to a complete community.

Norman Kretzmann, "Lex Iniusta Non est Lex: Laws on Trial in Aquinas' Court of Conscience," *American Journal of Jurisprudence* 33 (1988), pp. 110–122. Reprinted with kind permission of Mrs. Kretzmann.

These four conditions did get mentioned in the four articles of Question 90,[4] but so did at least two others, which were not included in either of the definitional passages:

(E)   leading people to or restraining them from certain actions,[5]
(F)   having coercive power.[6]

[…]

A seventh inclusion condition is employed more than once after those two definitional passages and should probably be added to the list at once:

(G)   intended to be obeyed.[7]

Characteristic (G) is obviously closely related to (F), but it seems clearly distinguishable from (F) since a law might fulfill (G) without fulfilling (F), although presumably not (F) without (G). (There is at least one more interesting candidate for inclusion among the essential characteristics, but it raises problems that aren't relevant to our present concerns, and so I'm leaving it out of account.[8]) We now have a list that is at least nearly complete and certainly full enough to support some general observations about the conditions and some investigation of the ways Aquinas uses them in evaluating laws.

Non-evaluative and evaluative conditions

Conditions (A) and (B) are fundamentally different from conditions (C)–(G), although Aquinas' initial presentation of these conditions obscures the difference. (A) and (B) are evaluative (moral) conditions of inclusion among full-fledged laws; (C)–(G), on the other hand, set out non-evaluative (formal) conditions that must be met by anything that is to count as a law at all. To take one of Aquinas' examples of a failure to satisfy a formal condition, the head of a household may make rules that fulfill conditions (A)–(C) and (E)–(G), but because a household is not a complete community (a political unit with some degree of sovereignty) those rules do not satisfy condition (D). In failing to meet one of the formal conditions, those household rules fail to count as laws even technically. If they were put forward as laws, they would be to laws as counterfeit dollars are to dollars: "A person who governs a family can of course make rules or regulations, but not such as have the nature of law strictly speaking."[9] A so-called law that failed to meet any one of the formal conditions would simply be a non-starter in the process of assessment that interests me now. It seems clear that conditions (A) and (B) are at issue only in case conditions (C)–(G) have been met. Aquinas indicates as much when he says that the derivability of a human law from a precept of natural law (or at least its compatibility with those precepts) becomes crucial to its status "*provided that* the *other* [i.e., the formal] conditions that pertain to the essence of law *have been met.*" The status of a law that meets those formal conditions and fails to meet either of the moral conditions remains to be seen, but it should already be clear that Aquinas will not declare it to be no law *at all*.

Aquinas' discussion of law is an extension of his moral philosophy, in which conformity to reason is the principal moral criterion; and so it comes as no surprise to find that his first inclusion condition for law [condition (A)] is that it be a directive of reason. As for condition (B), it can hardly be surprising to find *any* writer on jurisprudence maintaining that being aimed at the common good is an evaluative inclusion condition of law. On the basis of (A) and (B) we expect to find Aquinas dismissing irrational laws or laws that run contrary to the common good, and we won't be disappointed.

But in view of my having begun this investigation by focusing on the slogan "An *unjust* law is not a law" and listing Aquinas as a subscriber to it, it might well be surprising that the *justness* of a law is not explicitly cited among these evaluative conditions. And the surprise would only be heightened by finding out that one of the definitions of law propounded by Aquinas' respected predecessor, Isidore of Seville (ca. 560–636), began with the words: "A law will be virtuous, *just*, naturally possible, ..."[10] But the reason Aquinas doesn't explicitly include justness among the evaluative inclusion conditions of laws is that he takes it to be involved in both (A) and (B) in different ways.[11] In commenting on Isidore's definition, he says "Human discipline of course gives primary consideration to the order of *reason*, and that order is implied in Isidore's using the word 'just'".[12] Likewise, in one of Aquinas' evaluations of laws he says that "in order for [some-one's] willing of things that are commanded [by that person] to have the nature of law, they must be regulated by some reason. That is how we understand the claim that the sovereign's will has the force of law; otherwise the sovereign's will would be *injustice* (*iniquitas*) rather than law."[13] In other words, justness as a moral condition of laws is implicit in rationality as a condition.

That he considers it to be implicit also in the notion of the common good is apparent when he says, drawing on Aristotle, that "justice is counted as a virtue, whether it is particular justice, which directs a person's action rightly relative to another individual human being, or legal justice, which directs a person's action rightly *relative to the common good of society*."[14] In the same vein he says that "the acts of all the virtues can pertain to justice in the sense in which it directs a person to the common good. ... And since it pertains to law to direct people to the common good (as was maintained above), justice of that sort ... is called *legal justice*, because through it a person comes to agree with the law directing the acts of all the virtues toward the common good."[15] So when Aquinas dismisses a law as lacking either of the explicit moral conditions, (A) or (B), he can also be understood to be dismissing it as unjust.

Aquinas' assessments of laws

Aquinas' assessment of certain actual laws as unjust is not always merely implicit. More importantly (in view of the controversy over the *non-est-lex* slogan), not even an explicit assessment of that sort is always explicitly dismissive, as in this remark of his, which simply acknowledges the existence of unjust laws: "some lawgivers have made statutes contrary to secondary precepts of natural law, statutes which are unjust (*iniqua*)."[16]

But what happens when he does offer the kind of dismissive judgment the *non-est-lex* slogan leads us to expect? Not what its critics lead us to expect. Here is the first full-fledged instance of that sort in the Treatise on Law: "A tyrannical law, since it is not in accord with reason," – i.e., since it fails to meet condition (A) – "is *not unconditionally* a law but is, rather, a *perversion* of law. And yet, insofar as it *does have something of the nature of law*, it aims at the citizens' being good. For it has the nature of law only in the sense that it is a dictate of someone who presides over subjects" – condition (C) – "and that it aims at the subjects' being properly obedient to the law" – condition (G). "Their being properly obedient *is* their being good – not unconditionally, but in relation to such a government."[17] Two of the five formal conditions we have identified are expressly mentioned here, and they are said to be the only respects in which a tyrannical law is law, but there is every reason to suppose that the other three formal conditions – (D), (E), and (F) – would also apply to such a case. At least one of the two moral conditions – rationality – is said to be unfulfilled and, as a consequence, Aquinas says (in effect), "An irrational law is not a law." But in this passage he has spelled out what he means by the dismissive judgment. An irrational law is not a law unconditionally because it falls short of at least one of the moral conditions essential to full-fledged law, but it is a law in a certain respect because it satisfies the formal conditions sufficient to establish it technically as a law. It is not a counterfeit but, like the plagiarized paper, a perversion. No "dictum" that "there *cannot be* an unjust law," such as Danto thought he had identified, could stem from this dismissive judgment regarding tyrannical law, a judgment which also contains *the contrary* of what Hart called "a refusal … to recognize evil laws as valid for any purpose."

A second example of a dismissive judgment, this one more emphatic than the first, should help to confirm the impression that the critics of the *non-est-lex* slogan have misinterpreted it. "A human law has the nature of law to the extent to which it is in accord with right reason, and it is clear that in that respect it derives from the eternal law. But to the extent to which it falls short of reason, it is called an unjust law. In that case it does not have the nature of law but, rather, of a kind of violence. And yet, an unjust law itself also derives from the eternal law to the extent to which something of the image of law is preserved in it because the power belonging to the one who administers the law has an ordered relationship [to other power]; for all power is from the Lord God, as is said in Romans 13:1."[18] The same lessons are to be learned from this second example, I think, but I want especially to call attention to the fact that while it expressly says that an unjust law "does *not* have the nature of law," it also labors to bring out a respect in which it *is* law, emphasizing with its recurrent use of "to the extent to which" (*inquantum*) that the dismissive judgment admits of degrees. […]

Laws on trial in the court of conscience

We have now seen something of Aquinas' conception and classification of law, of the evaluative and non-evaluative conditions he considers essential to genuine law, and of the way he applies those conditions as criteria in dismissing unjust laws. Against that background we can understand and evaluate his answers to the questions with which I began. First, is an individual citizen entitled or obliged to decide whether a law of the state is unjust? Second, if so, on what grounds is he or she supposed to make the decision? And third, if an individual citizen has decided on appropriate grounds that a law of the state is unjust, what is he or she entitled or obliged to do about it?

By far the most important source for Aquinas' answers to such questions is his reply to Question 96, article 4, "Does human law impose necessity on a person in the court of conscience?"

> Laws laid down by human beings are either just or unjust. If they are *just*, they do of course have the force of obligating a person in the court of conscience, [a force they acquire] from the eternal law, from which they derive (in accordance with Proverbs 8:15: "Through me

kings reign and lawgivers decree just things"). Now laws are said to be just [1] on the basis of their *end* – i.e., when they are directed toward the common good; [2] on the basis on their *source or authority* – i.e., when the law that is decreed does not exceed the power of the one who decrees it; and [3] on the basis of their *form* – i.e., when burdens for the sake of the common good are imposed on those subject to them in accord with proportional equality. … Laws of that sort, which impose burdens proportionally, are just, they do obligate a person in the court of conscience, and they are legal laws.

On the other hand, laws are *unjust* (*iniustae*) in two ways. In the first way [I], by being *contrary to human good* because of opposition to the conditions mentioned above. Either [I.1] with reference to the *end* – e.g., when someone in authority imposes on people subject to his authority burdensome laws that pertain not to the common good but, rather, to his own greed or glorification; or [I.2] with reference to the *source or authority* – e.g., when someone decrees a law that goes beyond the power entrusted to him; or [I.3] with reference to the *form* – e.g., when burdens are unequally distributed in the community, even if they are directed toward the common good. Occurrences of that sort are instances of violence rather than laws; for, as Augustine says, "that which is not just does not seem to be a law." Therefore, *such laws do not obligate a person in the court of conscience, except, perhaps, for the sake of avoiding a scandal or disruption, for which a person should even give up his right* (in accordance with Matthew 4:40-41: "If someone compels you to go a mile, go with him another two miles; and if someone takes away your coat, give him your shirt as well"[19]).

Laws can be unjust in a second way [II] by being *contrary to divine good* – e.g., tyrants' laws leading people to idolatry or to anything else that is contrary to the divine law. *Such laws must not be observed in any way* because, as is said in Acts 5:29, "We ought to obey God rather than men."

Aquinas' reply offers answers to all three of my questions, but it can be understood and evaluated only in the light of the question it explicitly addresses. If that question had been merely "Does human law impose necessity on a person?," John Austin's line regarding the probable fate of the conscientious objector to a law of the state would constitute an appropriate answer after all. The fact that the question is about the effect of human laws only *in the court of conscience* (*in foro conscientiae*) shows that the primary interest is not in what the community should do about laws of one sort or another, but in what the individual should think about them (and, secondarily, in what the individual should do on the basis of those thoughts). And the fact that the question is whether they impose necessity *in the court of conscience* shows that the primary concern is not whether they create *legal* obligations – we should assume they do – but whether they create *moral* obligations. Finally, although the question itself does not show this, Aquinas' citations of Scriptural authority indicate that in his view it is pre-eminently the conscience of the morally upright, Christian citizen in which these laws are on trial.

Since every citizen, Christian or not, is a rational creature, every citizen has a conscience and, as we have seen, a conscience is at least potentially furnished with the precepts of natural law, morality's innate Constitution, against which every human law is measurable – somewhat as laws promulgated in this country are measurable against its Constitution. With just these observations my first question can already be answered affirmatively: Every individual citizen is at least entitled to decide in the court of conscience whether a law of the state is unjust.

But *three* verdicts are available. A law of the state may be judged just, unjust-I, or unjust-II. Beginning with the third and easiest of them, we can see that the grounds on which to hand down the verdict "unjust-II" is that the law on trial is contrary to some precept of *divine* law, which is taken to be publicly accessible (in Scripture), and which the Christian citizen is obliged to employ in the court of conscience as a criterion of human law. That answers my second question, about the grounds on which the decision that the law is unjust-II is to be made. And the answer to my third question is plain in this case, too. If an individual Christian has decided on those divinely established, objectively accessible grounds that a law of the state is unjust-II, then he or she is *obliged not to obey it*: such "human laws are directed against a commandment of God, which is outside the range of the power of those laws; and so in such cases the human law must not be obeyed."[20] The reliance on divine law rather than unaided natural law for the verdict "unjust-II" seems to indicate that only a Christian's conscience could render that verdict, but I think that a secular version of "unjust-II" is and ought to be available for any conscience confronted with a law that is blatantly and grossly – i.e., intolerably – unjust.

The verdict "just" is not hard to understand, especially given Aquinas' three explicit criteria for it, evidently intended to be separately necessary and jointly sufficient. (Notice that criterion [1] – "when they are directed toward the common good" – is identical with condition (B), and that condition (A) seems implicit in criteria [2] and [3].) It is also easy to see the answer to my third question in this case: just laws do obligate a person in the court of conscience. In a sense the answer to my second question is easy as well: the grounds for the decision are spelled out in the three conditions. But there is a subsidiary empirical question that is not easy to answer: How can a person be sure that the three criteria have been met? Naturally there can be no standard, universally applicable answer to that question, but the guiding principle in the court of conscience must be "just unless proven unjust." The likelihood of subjective error is one pragmatic consideration supporting that principle, but not the only one, as we'll see.

Obviously, the most interesting and difficult cases are those for which the verdict "unjust-I" is appropriate. Since the three criteria for the justness of a law are separately necessary, the failure of any one of them is sufficient to render a law unjust-I; but the disjunction of I.1, I.2, or I.3 is only a superficial complication. And it is easy to think of laws of each of those three varieties which would be assessed as unjust by any disinterested person. The difficulty in answering my second question regarding cases of this sort is only the unavoidable empirical difficulty we already noticed in connection with handing down the verdict "just."[21] It is Aquinas' answer to my third question that is interestingly difficult, and apparently worrisome.

His answer comes in two parts. First, "such laws *do not obligate* a person in the court of conscience" – i.e., if an individual has decided on appropriate grounds that a law of the state is unjust-I, he or she is not morally obliged to obey that law – i.e., he or she *has a moral right not to obey* that law – and is *not* morally *obliged* not to obey that law (as in the case of a law that is unjust-II). If I am right in my reading of this first part, it strikes me as eminently sensible. It is the second part that looks worrisome, claiming that one might after all *be* obliged by such a law in the court of conscience "for the sake of *avoiding a scandal or disruption*, for which a person should even *give up his right*."

Of course the suggestion that we should not exercise a moral right we have often turns out to be wise and not worrisome; but it is seldom a suggestion to be taken lightly. And when the reason provided for our giving up our moral right is the avoidance of scandal or disruption, we should of course suspect that we are being offered a counsel of moral cowardice. On the plausible hypothesis that Aquinas is not suggesting moral cowardice as a morally allowable and sometimes obligatory alternative to civil disobedience, what are we to make of this part of his answer?[22]

The first thing to notice is that this alternative, whatever it turns out to be, is mentioned only in connection with laws that are unjust-I. Laws that are unjust-II *must not* be obeyed, whether or not scandal and disruption ensue. A law that sanctions the abuse of children, for example, *must* be disobeyed. So part of what makes the alternative of giving up one's right appropriate in the case of laws that are unjust-I is, presumably, that the stakes are lower in that case. The good to which *those* unjust laws are contrary is human only, not also divine.

A second bit of help is available further on in this same article, where Aquinas in replying to an objection says that a person is not obliged to obey a law that inflicts unjust oppression on those subject to it "*if* he can resist it without [causing] a scandal or *a greater harm*."[23] Aquinas confronting a law that is unjust-I would clearly not countenance the bravado of the sixteenth-century maxim "*Fiat iustitia, et ruant coeli*."[24] He takes the cautious approach of weighing the potential harm of resisting an unjust law against the potential harm the law is likely to cause if left unchallenged. In another context he offers an illuminating example from the history of the conflict between Church and State: "At that time, the Church in its infancy did not yet have the power of restraining earthly sovereigns, and so it permitted the faithful to obey [the emperor] Julian the Apostate in matters that were not contrary to the faith *in order to avoid a greater danger* to the faith."[25] But in every case of comparing particular potential harms to provide a basis for deciding whether or not to engage in civil disobedience – even a case as dramatically clear as Aquinas' example – there would or should remain the worry that moral cowardice would be a covert make-weight on the side of doing nothing.

I think there is good evidence, however, that for *all* cases of this sort Aquinas had a single sort of scandal or disruption in mind, one the consideration of which should take precedence over all others. I also think that he fosters a responsible moral decision-procedure in cases of this sort by prescribing a remedy for the unavoidable and most important sort of harm caused by civil disobedience. For a person engaging in disobeying a law for the purpose of proclaiming his or her conscientious objection to it is thereby indicating that the law ought to be changed – repealed or amended. But, as Aquinas observes in reply to the question "Should human law be changed whenever something better comes along?",[26] "The mere change of law, considered just in itself, *involves a kind of harm to the common good*; for custom contributes a great deal to the observance of laws, so that things that are done contrary to custom are seen as serious even if they are slight in themselves. For that reason, whenever a law is changed, *the binding power of law is weakened* to the extent to which custom is violated. And so human law ought never to be changed *unless the common good is compensated in some way to the extent to which it was weakened in that respect*."[27]

On the basis of his recognition of the fragility of the fabric of law Aquinas may be seen as advocating *conscientious* conscientious objection. Of course every rebel with a cause could heartily agree that the harm inflicted on the common good as a consequence of his or her morally motivated unlawful act must and will be compensated for – *eventually*:

once the revolution has succeeded, or apartheid has been abolished, or the university has provided enough parking spaces for the faculty. If Aquinas had insisted on *immediate* compensation, his policy would have a tendency to stifle dissent. I think he would see the conscientious objector's deficit as having a time-limit on it, however, and would insist on *prompt* compensation, at the earliest possible opportunity.[28] He seems to have understood that moral people do occasionally need to operate under a long-term debt to the common good, to have been, like thoughtful people in any age, concerned about the concomitant threat to the fabric of law, and consequently to have tried to provide a rational formula of compensation acceptable in the court of conscience.[29]

Notes

1   Q. 90, a. 4.
2   Q. 91, a. 1.
3   The facts that there are discrepancies between these two occurrences of the "definition" and that some inclusion conditions frequently employed by Aquinas are entirely omitted from the "definition" suggest that it is only a loose summation. His applications of the inclusion conditions, both before and after the introduction of the "definition," give us a much more reliable understanding of his concept of law than we can get from the "definition."
4   For (A), see q. 90, a. 1, ad 2; ad 3; a. 2, ad 3. For (B), see q. 90, a. 2c; ad 3. For (C), see q. 90, a. 3; a. 4. For (D), see q. 90, a. 3, ad 3.
5   Q. 90, a. 1.
6   Q. 90, a. 3, ad 2.
7   Q. 91, a. 5; q. 92, a. 1c; ad 4.
8   Aquinas sometimes writes as if it were an essential characteristic of law to contribute to an individual's achieving of his ultimate end – perfect happiness in the beatific vision. See, e.g., q. 91, a. 4: "By law a human being is directed to actions that are appropriate in connection with his ordered relationship toward his ultimate end." But an individual's ultimate end can't be included in the *common* good (except accidentally), and Aquinas surely does not think that any law other than the divine law can make a direct contribution to an individual's destiny. Elsewhere in the *Treatise* Aquinas writes in a way that heightens the impression that the suggestion in q. 91, a. 4, is unintentional. See esp. q. 96, a. 1: "Now the end of law is the *common* good, because, as Isidore says (*Etymologiae* II, 10; V, 21), 'A law must be framed for *no private advantage* but for the common benefit of the citizens.' That is why human laws must be adapted to the common good."
9   The head-of-the-household example is discussed in q. 90, a. 3, obj. 3 and ad 3.
10   *Etymologiae* V, 21; quoted in the introduction to g. 95, a. 3.
11   In at least one passage in the *Treatise on Law* he does come very close to making justness an explicit criterion, however, apart from any consideration of Isidore's definition: "it pertains to law to direct human actions in accord with the order of justice" (q. 91, a. 5).
12   Q. 95, a. 3.
13   Q. 90, a. 1, ad 3.
14   ST IaIIae q. 113, a. 1; cf. q. 100, a. 2, and q. 96, a. 3.
15   ST IIaIIae q. 58, a. 5; cf. q. 58 *passim*.
16   ST IaIIae q. 94, a. 6, ad 3.
17   Q. 92, a. 1, ad 4.
18   Q. 93, a. 3, ad 2.
19   Aquinas is obviously quoting (paraphrasing) from memory here.

20 Q. 96, a. 4, ad 2.

21 In ST IIaIIae q. 147, a. 4, Aquinas offers practical advice relevant to the quandary of the individual faced with difficulties formally similar to these.

22 As John Boler pointed out to me, Aquinas' detailed discussion of scandal should be taken into account here (ST IIaIIae q. 43). Scandal as Aquinas conceives of it has two components. It is something said or done with less than perfect moral justification (*dictum vel factum minus rectum*), and it provides an occasion for someone's spiritual downfall (*praebens occasionem ruinae*). If the avoidance of scandal in this technical sense were the only reason Aquinas gave for giving up one's moral right, my discussion of this issue in the remainder of the paper would be simpler and would draw heavily on IIaIIae g. 43, a. 7, "Should temporal [goods] be given up for the sake of [avoiding] scandal?" But the fact that Aquinas here speaks of the avoidance of "scandal *or disruption*" calls for a broader treatment.

23 Q. 96, a. 4, ad 3.

24 *The Oxford Dictionary of Quotations* attributes the maxim to the Emperor Ferdinand I (1503–1564) in the form "*Fiat iustitia, et pereat mundus*," and to William Watson (1559?–1603) in the more familiar form in which I quote it here.

25 ST IIaIIae q. 12, a. 2, ad 1.

26 Q. 97, a. 2.

27 Cf. Aristotle, *Politics* II 5, 1268b23–1269a28.

28 ST IIaIIae q. 62 has to do with restitution, and although it is concerned primarily with restitution by one individual to another, I think it can be applied, cautiously, to cases of the sort at issue here. Q. 63, a. 8, asks whether a person "is bound to make restitution immediately or can legitimately defer it." The heart of Aquinas's position is that "everyone is bound to make restitution immediately *or to request a postponement from the person who can grant him the use of the thing*" that does not rightfully belong to him. And in his rejoinder to the objection that "sometimes a person *cannot* make restitution immediately" (obj. 2) Aquinas says, "When someone cannot make restitution immediately, that inability itself excuses him from making *instant* restitution (just as a person who is entirely unable to make restitution is entirely excused from it). *He is, however, obliged to request forgiveness or postponement, either in his own right or through someone else, from the person to whom he owes it.*"

29 For comments and criticisms I'm indebted to the members of my Aquinas seminar at Cornell in the spring term of 1986, to philosophical audiences at several institutions, to Barbara Ensign Kretzmann, to John Bennett, to John Boler, and especially to Eleonore Stump. But the largest debt of gratitude by far I owe to David Lyons, who wrote three extremely helpful sets of comments on various drafts and who was, as always, unfailingly generous in his advice and counsel.

3.2.2 "New" and "Old" Natural Law Debate

3.2.2.1 R.P. George "Recent Criticism of the Natural Law Theory"

Practical Reason as Autonomous

Hittinger's book brings together a range of criticisms of the Grisez-Finnis theory marshaled over the years by neo-scholastic and neo-Aristotelian commentators, including Ralph McInerny, Vernon Bourke and Henry Veatch. The chief criticism, perhaps, is the charge that relates to the proposition that practical reason operates autonomously. In other words, Grisez and Finnis contend that practical reason operates on its own first principles without dependence upon methodologically antecedent knowledge drawn from speculative disciplines such as anthropology, metaphysics or theology. Critics contend that this theory embraces Kantian deontologism and borrows all of its problems. As Veatch has put it, 'though the hands are those of Germain Grisez, the voice is that of Immanuel Kant.'[1] Hittinger, it seems, agrees.

The fundamental problem with Kantian moral theory, according to neo-scholastics (and others), is that, in refusing to ground morality in a concern for human well-being, it renders moral rules ultimately pointless. But if human well-being is identified as, in some sense, the ultimate ground of the intelligibility of moral norms, then some substantial knowledge of 'the (human) good' becomes necessary if we are to discern 'the (morally) right.' Yet, the glaring teleological dimension of the Grisez-Finnis theory marks an obvious difference with Kantian ethics. As we have seen, the first practical principles and the basic precepts of natural law refer, under the Grisez-Finnis theory, to basic human goods. In this respect, at

R.P. George, "Recent Criticism of the Natural Law Theory," *University of Chicago Law Review* (Fall, 1988).

least, the theory is radically unlike Kantian deontology. So, we must ask, in what sense do neo-scholastic critics of the Grisez-Finnis theory suppose that theory to be Kantian?

Hittinger suggests the answer. In maintaining that the axiological knowledge needed to get moral theory off the ground comes as the product of practical reflection, rather than a speculative inquiry into human nature, Grisez and Finnis, in effect, accept Kant's supposition that ethics can dispense with the philosophy of nature. The Grisez-Finnis theory resembles Kantianism above all in its declaration of the methodological independence of ethics from metaphysics (or ontology). In Weinreb's pithy formulation, it represents a theory of 'natural law without nature.' Such an approach, in Hittinger's judgment, attempts 'to recover natural law theory by way of shortcuts.'[2] And, for him, no less than for Weinreb (although for a different reason), shortcuts will not do.

Hittinger's critique of the Grisez-Finnis theory begins with a set of arguments purporting to show that the attempt to identify human goods without appeal to a speculative philosophy of nature falls into a sort of intuitionism that leaves the basic goods vulnerable to skeptical attacks. Indeed, he implies that Grisez and Finnis themselves seem to perceive this inasmuch as they regularly marshal evidence acquired by various sorts of speculative inquiry (e.g., anthropological data) in support of the putatively self-evident basic goods. Arguments based on evidence of this sort ought to be unnecessary, Hittinger suggests, if the practical intellect can grasp the first principles that refer to basic goods without inferring anything from speculative knowledge of the goods as natural human ends.[3]

In criticizing Weinreb's account of Finnis's appeals to self-evidence, I discussed the familiar charge that the Grisez-Finnis theory of first practical principles is based on intuitions. Here I wish to say a word about the use of dialectical arguments in defense of propositions claimed to be self-evident. Dialectical argumentation focuses on the relationships between propositions (including putatively self-evident propositions) to be defended and other knowledge. The point of such argumentation is to highlight the unacceptable implications of denying the propositions to be defended, or the inappropriateness of relying on certain evidence (shown to be inapt or defective) to deny or cast doubt on those propositions.

Now, speculative arguments can be useful in casting doubt upon propositions alleged to be self-evident practical truths. For example, the presentation of anthropological evidence tending to show that no form of friendship existed in certain non-Western cultures prior to their contact with the West, while not itself a disproof of the self-evident value of friendship, would cast substantial doubt on the proposition that friendship is intrinsically valuable. It would provide an occasion for anyone who judged friendship to be objectively good to at least rethink the matter. One would be surprised to learn that a self-evidently worthwhile human end was unknown (or known but unvalued) by a substantial part of mankind.

In carefully rethinking the matter, perhaps one would discover a mistake in one's practical judgment about friendship. Perhaps it would transpire that, while friendship is not intrinsically valuable, its historically contingent, but very close, links with certain more fundamental goods in one's own culture deflected one's understanding of the matter, leading one falsely to conclude that the value of friendship is intrinsic (rather than, say, merely instrumental). On the other hand, perhaps, even after a searching reconsideration, one's judgment of the intrinsic worth of friendship would not change. In this event, one would likely find the anthropological evidence perplexing in light of one's considered practical judgment. The phenomenon of a widespread failure to grasp what one judges to be a self-evident practical truth would itself demand an explanation; it would set a substantial question for further speculative inquiry.

Just as speculative arguments can cast doubt on propositions claimed to be self-evident practical truths, speculative arguments can be effective in rebuttal. An effective speculative argument of this sort does not establish the self-evidence of a self-evident practical truth. It simply removes a particular doubt about that truth. For example, an argument that established that the apparent non-existence of friendships in certain non-Western cultures can be accounted for by the failure of Western anthropologists to appreciate the distinctive forms and expressions of friendship in such cultures, would itself remove the doubts raised by the disturbing anthropological evidence. But, one might ask, can there be doubts about self-evident truths? Yes – precisely because such truths are not mere intuitions or innate ideas. They are grasped by intelligent reflection on data presented by experience (e.g., one's own direct or indirect experiences of friendships). And any such grasp involves an act of understanding. Many factors capable of derailing understanding respecting non-self-evident propositions, whether practical or speculative, are equally capable of impeding sound judgment in respect of self-evident propositions. Thus, we would do well to follow Aquinas in distinguishing propositions that are self-evident to everyone, from propositions that are self-evident only to the wise.[4] It is possible for anyone to fail to grasp a self-evident truth; just as it is possible for anyone to mistakenly suppose that what is in reality a derived proposition (or even a false proposition) is a self-evident truth.

Dialectical arguments are, I think, especially powerful in rebuttal. However, they may be employed affirmatively in support of a self-evident practical truth, often with persuasive force. For example, the considerable anthropological evidence tending to show that various form of friendship, knowledge and religion are to be found in virtually all cultures, while not evidence of the self-evidence of the value of these realities (for there can be no 'evidence' of 'self-evidence'), does show that a practical judgment of their intrinsic worth comports well with the data. It places something of a burden on anyone who would deny the proposition stating this practical judgment to account for the universality of phenomena such as friendship, intellectual inquiry and worship. Any theory that proffers an explanation proposing a sociologically deterministic or psychologically reductionistic account will be subject to the increasingly familiar criticisms of all forms of determinism and reductionism. Perhaps someone skeptical about basic goods could meet these criticisms. But here the skeptic would, in any event, be the party attempting to rebut dialectical arguments supporting self-evident practical truths (but not, of course, establishing their self-evidence).

In view of the foregoing analysis, I see no warrant for Hittinger's suspicion of Grisez's or Finnis's use of evidence procured by way of speculative inquiry in support of propositions they hold to be self-evident practical truths. But Hittinger has another, more substantial, argument against the proposal that first practical principles are not derived from speculative knowledge. He argues that there are respects in which at least a certain minimum amount of speculative knowledge is indispensable to our practical judgments. For example, a basic understanding of the integral organic functioning of the human body (i.e., of being alive) is a condition of any judgment, including any practical judgment, about the status of life and health as basic goods. Grisez himself has implicitly acknowledged this, as Hittinger points out, especially in his early work on contraception.[5] There, as Hittinger reports, Grisez argued, for example:

That the good of life must be judged as a whole rather than in relation to the end of each faculty or physiological power. Accordingly, respiration and nutrition cannot be said to be basic human goods. However, from a biological point of view, the 'work of reproduction is the fullest organic realization of the living substance.' [Citation omitted.]

In other words, it differs from respiration in the sense that it bestows the good of life as a whole, and therefore ought to be included within the basic good of life.[6]

Hittinger assumes that Grisez's use of this sort of argument shows that he 'does in fact directly rely upon anthropological, if not metaphysical, evidence for including procreation in the list of basic goods.'[7] Grisez indeed judges that the generation of a new human life is not merely an instrumental end, but is intelligibly worthwhile just for the sake of the new life generated. Hittinger's claim is that the above-quoted passage shows that Grisez himself relies 'upon a theoretical [i.e., speculative] argument concerning what is essential or accidental to human organicity'[8] in reaching this judgment. As Hittinger sees it, then, Grisez's own analysis of at least one basic human good is 'not consistent with his understanding of the inferential and deductive underivability of the basic practical principles.'[9]

Is Hittinger's allegation of inconsistency telling? No. His argument rests on a misunderstanding of what Grisez expects to get out of arguments like the one Hittinger cites. Grisez need not, and, in fact, does not, deny that a certain minimum amount of speculative knowledge is needed as a condition of practical judgment. (Nor does he deny that additional speculative knowledge has any place in moral reasoning.) While practical knowledge is not derived from propositions about the realities judged to be intelligibly choiceworthy, practical judgments (i.e., that something is a 'good to be done and pursued') are not, according to Grisez, made in the complete absence of data for reflection. Without a basic understanding of the realities one is supposed to be making practical judgments about (e.g., life, friendship, religion), one simply could not judge. In the complete absence of speculative knowledge of what Hittinger calls human organicity, for example, no practical judgment of the intelligibility of life or health as an ultimate reason for action would be possible. Can we make sense of someone's choice to act just for the sake of preserving, or protecting, or transmitting human life? It will be impossible to answer that question unless we first have some basic idea of what 'human life' is; thus, some speculative (i.e., biological) knowledge is a condition of our practical knowledge of the goods of life and health. But to acknowledge the need for a minimum of biological knowledge as a condition for reaching axiological judgments of this sort is not to imply that such judgments are inferred, deduced or otherwise derived from the biological knowledge.

Even perfect knowledge of human organicity, including perfect knowledge of what is essential and what is merely accidental to it, could not provide a warrant for judgments about the intelligibility of choosing life or health as ends in themselves (although such knowledge would profoundly enhance our capacity to preserve and promote these goods). The intelligibility of such choices, to the extent that they are intelligible, will be picked out of the data by insights that, while not unconditioned by speculative knowledge, are not logically entailed by it. Any such insight will therefore be not only fundamental, but fundamentally practical.

In arguing that Grisez smuggles speculative knowledge illicitly (on his own terms) into judgments about basic goods, Hittinger claims that among the terms Grisez variously employs 'for the "goods" ... [are] "tendencies" [and] "basic inclinations."'[10] This report comes after, and seems to support, Hittinger's claim that '[a]ll of Grisez's goods have content derived from inclination.'[11] Now, the fact that something is a 'tendency' or 'basic inclination' is straightforwardly an item of speculative knowledge. To treat the fact that humans 'tend' or are 'basically inclined' toward something as a logical warrant for a judgment of the intrinsic value of whatever the tendency or inclination is toward, is to suppose that knowledge of basic practical principles can be derived from speculative knowledge. Were Hittinger's report accurate, Grisez would be guilty of an inconsistency in his treatment of first practical principles. But Grisez never implies, much less says, that basic goods are 'tendencies' or 'basic inclinations.' Hittinger's claim that Grisez 'employs' these terms for the goods has no basis in anything Grisez has written.

Hittinger's misunderstanding of Grisez's theory of basic goods is further evident in his assertion (again without citation) that, for Grisez, 'goods are defined as actions which are attractive to the agent.'[12] Not only does Grisez carefully distinguish goods from the actions by which persons may participate in goods, he never defines the goods by reference to their attractiveness to the persons who participate in them. Any theory of value that does define 'good' as what is 'attractive to the agent' flirts (at a minimum) with subjectivism. But Hittinger does the Grisez-Finnis theory an injustice by implying that a derivation of value from a speculative philosophy of nature is necessary to rescue that theory from subjectivism. Nowhere in the theory is the intelligibility of first practical principles made to depend upon the attractiveness of the basic goods to the acting person (which is to deny neither that basic goods can be attractive nor that their attractiveness can motivate action).

At one point, Hittinger accuses Grisez of holding an axiology in which the basic goods 'are curiously Platonic-like forms.'[13] The charge is untenable. Repeatedly, and in virtually all of their works on ethics, Grisez and Finnis make the point that goods do not exist in some transcendent realm, but are constitutive aspects of persons. To cite perhaps the most forceful statement, Finnis says in *Natural Law and Natural Rights* that 'the basic aspects of human well-being are … not abstract forms, they are analytically distinguishable aspects of the well-being, actual or possible, of you and me – of flesh-and-blood individuals.'[14]

Hittinger seems to assume that the Grisez-Finnis theory must rely on some mysterious Platonic notion of the good because it does not propose to derive basic goods from speculative knowledge of human nature. But, as a critique of the Grisez-Finnis theory of practical knowledge, this assumption simply begs the question. Grisez and Finnis claim that first practical principles are self-evident truths grasped in non-inferential acts of understanding. It is this claim that Hittinger set out to prove false. But this proof cannot be accomplished by a gratuitous assertion – directly contrary to what Grisez and Finnis actually say – that basic goods are 'curiously Platonic-like forms.'

Notes

1   Henry B. Veatch, *Human Rights: Fact or Fancy?* (Baton Rouge, La: Lousiana State University Press, 1985), 98.
2   Hittinger, *A Critique*, 198.
3   Ibid., 44–5.
4   Aquinas, *Summa Theologiae*, 1–2, q. 94, a. 2.
5   Germain Grisez, *Contraception and the Natural Law* (Milwaukee, Wis.: Bruce, 1964).
6   Hittinger, *A Critique*, 62.
7   Ibid.
8   Ibid., 63.
9   Ibid.
10   Ibid., 40.
11   Ibid., 28.
12   Ibid., 55.
13   Ibid., 187.
14   Finnis, J., *Natural Law and Natural Rights*, Oxford: Clarendon Law Series, 1980, 371–2.

3.2.2.2 Stephen L. Brock
"Natural Inclination and the Intelligibility of the Good in Thomistic Natural Law"

[…] The issue that I propose to address here centers on a single clause from the *Summa theologiae*. But it goes nearly to the heart of St Thomas's teaching on natural law. It concerns the way in which Thomas thinks the human mind comes to understand good and evil. The specific question raised by the clause is the role played in this process by what Thomas calls "natural inclination." This question leads to an even more basic one: what it is, for Thomas, that constitutes a truly intellectual grasp of the good.
[…]

The Text and Its Interpretations

The article in which our clause appears is I–II, q. 94, a. 2. The clause is the central portion of the following sentence.

> Since good has the *ratio* of end, and bad the *ratio* of the contrary, hence it is that *all those things to which man has natural inclination, reason naturally apprehends as good*, and consequently as to be pursued by action; and their contraries as bad, and to be avoided.[1]

In the vast literature produced over the past few decades on natural law in St Thomas, this article of the *Summa* has received a great deal of attention. Interpreters often feel a need to offer some explanation for the passage that I have singled out. It is not surprising. Thomas simply lays it down that the objects of natural human inclination are things that reason naturally apprehends as good. One may well wonder why this is so, and here he does not say. The variety of answers that have been offered is astonishing. Here is a brief sketch of what I think are the most prominent positions on the question.

On some readings, what Thomas has in mind in the passage is what he elsewhere speaks of as judgment "by connaturality" or "through inclination." Reason's grasp of an object of natural inclination as good would be an act moved directly by the inclination itself. It is not that reason consciously reflects upon the inclination and then goes on to

Stephen L. Brock, "Natural Inclination and the Intelligibility of the Good in Thomistic Natural Law," *Vera Lex* VI.1–2 (Winter 2005), pp 57–78. Reprinted with permission of Pace University Press and the author.

judge its object good. Rather, the very presence of the inclination casts a kind of light upon the object, and reason spontaneously judges the object in this light. The most famous proponent of this view, Jacques Maritain, holds that such judgments do not even involve rational formulation or conceptualization.[2]

This seems to be a minority position. More interpreters take Thomas to be talking about a kind of knowledge that is more properly rational, involving some conscious reflection and conceptualization. Still, on some accounts, the connection between knowledge and inclination remains very tight. Reason's natural grasp of human goods, though not knowledge "through" inclination, would consist simply in the apprehension "of" natural inclinations and of their objects.[3] Knowing an object of natural inclination as good would be nothing other than knowing it to be such an object.

Others, however, judge it necessary to assign a somewhat less immediate role to natural inclination in the formation of reason's apprehension of the human good. Here there is an even greater insistence on the rationality of the apprehension. The thought would be more or less as follows. That something is the object of natural inclination only means that desire for it naturally exists. But truly rational knowledge that something is good, genuine understanding of its goodness, does not consist in merely registering the existence of desire for it, even desire that exists naturally. Rather, such knowledge serves to make the desire itself intelligible. It shows the desire to be "right" or to "make sense." It consists in seeing the object as something intrinsically desirable, "fit" to be desired. In other words, the mere "fact" of being desired does not show a thing to be *truly* good. Surely, in our passage, Thomas is speaking about apprehending things as true human goods. Seeing them as objects of natural inclination cannot suffice for this. It must only be some kind of preliminary.

What else is required? For some, what is needed is reason's penetration to the root source of the natural inclinations, which is human nature. To understand something as a true human good is to see it as an end toward which man is aimed by nature, a purpose of his being human.[4] For others, the decisive factor in practical reason's natural apprehension of a human reality as a true human good is not the determination of its relation to human nature. It is rather the sheer understanding of the good in general – the basis of the first precept of natural law – and the consideration of the reality in light of it. The latter view is the one initially proposed by Germain Grisez and subsequently adopted by John Finnis.[5]

Finnis and Grisez do however still acknowledge a preliminary role for natural inclinations in the genesis of practical reason's natural understanding of human goods. Experience of the inclinations would be what provides the data in which the goods are first grasped. They point us to the goods, though they are not the criteria by which we judge them good.[6]

Now, despite the serious differences among the positions so far considered, there is one assumption that they all share. I have presented them so summarily because what really interests me here is this assumption. It is that the natural inclinations in question are pre-rational. That is, they would exist independently of reason's apprehension of their objects as good, and the apprehension would somehow follow on them.[7] The differences that I have signaled only regard how it follows.

The assumption is seldom even stated explicitly. However, in Finnis's recent book on Thomas, there is a very interesting and well documented set of observations which I think show him to be uneasy with some of its implications.[8] He is clearly worried about what sort of inclination it is that Thomas could have in mind in our passage. As he explains in considerable detail, there are several types of human inclination that are in some sense "natural" for Thomas, and that cannot possibly fit the bill.

In any case, the assumption that the inclinations are pre-rational has not in fact gone entirely unremarked in the literature, nor unchallenged. I am referring to the interpretation offered by Lawrence Dewan in two very important articles.[9] It seems to me that Dewan's work in this area has received far too little attention. Elsewhere I have expressed my adherence to his view and added a few considerations regarding Thomas's intention in I–II, q. 94, a. 2.[10] What I want to do here is to confirm the position and develop it a little further.

The Inclinations As Results of the Understanding

My basic thesis, then, is that not only the apprehension that Thomas is talking about in our passage, but also the inclination, is rational. Reason's natural understanding of human goods does not follow the natural inclinations to them. The inclinations follow the understanding. I think this is a much more plausible reading of our passage, for several reasons. (These partly overlap with the observations by Finnis that I mentioned a moment ago.)

First, this reading explains easily why Thomas can simply lay it down, as though obvious, that reason naturally apprehends as good all the things to which man is naturally inclined. If he were talking about non-rational inclinations, inclinations that do not follow from reason's own apprehension, it would be a very dubious assertion. There are many non-rational inclinations existing in us by nature whose objects do not become known to us except after much investigation, if at all – certainly not "naturally." Think of some strictly physiological inclination, such as the natural tendency for our brain synapses to fire. Their firing is certainly a good thing. But it is hardly something that we are naturally aware of. Thomas did not even know that brains have synapses. If however he is talking about inclinations that follow upon the natural apprehension of their objects as good, his assertion is self-evident.

Another point is the caliber of the inclinations that he must be talking about. They are right inclinations. Their objects are true human goods. Otherwise they could hardly correspond to precepts of natural law.[11] But Thomas is quite explicit about the fact that sometimes the non-rational inclinations existing naturally in a human being are not right.[12] This is particularly clear in the case of the sensitive appetite.[13] Unreasoned feeling may be right or wrong. The rectitude of a person's feeling is guaranteed only when it is directed by (right) reason. In the very article to which our passage belongs, Thomas says that "the inclinations of the parts of human nature, such as the concupiscible and irascible appetites, pertain to natural law insofar as they are regulated by reason."[14]

Should we see the inclinations as contained in man's very essence, prior even to his physical dispositions and feelings? Thomas does teach that the elements of a subject's essence – its substantial form and matter – are already a sort of inclination (I, q. 59, a. 2). And no doubt he thinks such inclination always right. However, as he explains in the same place, its range is rather limited. It is only toward what is included within the subject's own substantial being.[15] Any inclinations toward objects that extend outside the subject's being must be distinct from its essence. Many of the objects of inclination mentioned in I–II, q. 94, a. 2 are clearly not included in man's substantial being.

If the inclinations are neither physical dispositions, nor spontaneous feelings, nor elements of man's very essence, then in Thomas's conception of human nature, only one possibility remains. They must be movements of man's rational appetite, inclinations of the human will. But if so, they must be inclinations that derive from reason's apprehension of their objects as good. The will is not moved toward anything except what reason – practical reason – apprehends as good and desirable.[16]

I think this is the correct view. If we suppose that Thomas is speaking of inclinations of the will in the corpus of I–II, q. 94, a. 2, none of the aforementioned difficulties arises.

First, these inclinations cannot exist in such a way that any of their objects, or the goodness thereof, escape reason's apprehension. This is obvious, since the inclinations of the will always follow upon such apprehension.

Thomas also teaches that the will's natural inclinations are always right – just as intellect's natural understanding is always true.[17] This in fact is why they are always right. In voluntary matters, he says, even if the rectitude of reasoning about the things that are for an end depends on the rectitude of the appetite of the end, nevertheless the rectitude of the appetite of the end itself depends upon the right apprehension of the end, which is through reason.[18] Here we are surely talking about the right apprehension of the end.[19] "Good has the *ratio* of end."

Finally, the natural inclinations of the will are by no means limited to the goods contained in a man's substantial being. In fact they extend to the whole range of goods cited in I–II, q. 94, a. 2. They include "universally all the things that befit the willing subject according to his nature." And so, "man naturally wants not only the object of the will [the good in general], but also other things that befit other powers, such as knowledge of the true, which suits the intellect; and to be and to live, and other such things as regard natural continuance."[20]

Besides skirting the various difficulties, taking the inclinations to be rational rather than pre-rational also gives our passage a much clearer connection with the truly fundamental article on natural law in the *Summa*, the one concerned with its very existence: I–II, q. 91, a. 2.

Thomas begins the corpus of this article by observing that all creatures have their natural inclinations from some impression of the eternal law of divine providence. He then argues that the rational creature is subject to providence in a higher way than the rest, since he himself "becomes a sharer in providence, providing for himself and others." This in turn shows that he shares in "the eternal reason (*ratio*) through which he has natural inclination toward due act and end." Note the "through which." Man partakes in the *ratio*, the intelligible conception, that is the very source of natural inclination in him. Thomas goes on to trace this share in the eternal reason to the light of man's own natural reason, "by which we discern what good is and what evil is."

Moreover, the article's second objection and reply refer explicitly to the will. The objection argues that there is no natural law in man, because the ordination of human acts to their end is not through "nature," but through reason and will. The objector is taking 'nature' in the sense of something "pre-rational." But Thomas's reply makes no appeal to anything in us that is "natural" in this sense. Instead, he simply reminds us that reason and will themselves have a natural dimension. "All reasoning derives from principles naturally known, and all appetite of things that are for the end derive from the natural appetite of the last end. And so likewise, the first direction of our acts toward the end must come about through a natural law." Thus, to adopt the usual reading of the 94,2 clause is to slip back into the wrong sense of 'natural.' The inclinations that it is referring to are natural effects of reason and will, i.e., of the principles by which man acts *humanly*.[21] They are inclinations of man *as man*.[22]

There is however at least one obvious objection to this reading of the 94,2 clause. This is that the conclusion which Thomas draws from it is that "the order of the precepts of natural law is according to the order of the natural inclinations." He then uses this rule to lay out the order of the precepts. So it may seem that the inclinations are prior to the apprehension, not its result.

[…] [T]o answer this objection, I think it suffices to draw a distinction.

Earlier in the article, we are told that the very first precept of natural law, "good is to be done and pursued, and bad avoided," is "founded upon the *ratio* of good." But we should note that the precept is not simply identical with the *ratio* of good, any more than the absolutely first principle of reasoning, the principle of non-contradiction, is simply identical with the *ratio* of being. One thing is the very discernment of what good is, and another is the judgment that it is to be pursued through action. And likewise, I believe, while the other precepts of natural law present the objects of man's natural inclinations as things "to be done and pursued," they are founded upon the prior apprehension of the objects simply as good. Thus, what Thomas says is that "all those things for which man has a natural inclination, reason naturally apprehends as good, and *consequently* as things to be pursued by action."

In other words, *both* the inclinations and the precepts follow upon the understanding of the objects as good. And if anything, the inclinations follow even more immediately than do the precepts. For the inclinations require nothing but the consideration of the objects as good, desirable. But the precepts require a consideration of the objects not only as good, but also as matters of action, doable or pursuable.

Notes

1   Translations throughout this paper are mine. For the most part I leave *ratio* untranslated.

2   Jacques Maritain, *Man and the State* (Chicago: University of Chicago Press, 1951), 92; "On Knowledge through Connaturality," *The Review of Metaphysics* 4.4 (June 1951): 473–481 (esp. 477–480); "Du savoir moral," *Revue Thomiste* 82 (1982): 533–549. See also Yves R. Simon, *Practical Knowledge* (New York: Fordham University Press, 1991), 33.

3   For example, Paul-M. van Overbeke, O.P., "La loi naturelle et le droit naturel selon S. Thomas," *Revue Thomiste* 57 (1957): 65 ff.; Leo Elders, "Nature as the Basis of Moral Actions," *Jacques Maritain Center, Thomistic Institute*, 2001, http://www.nd.edu/Departments/Maritain/ti01/elders.htm, section III, ¶1 & ¶3; John C. Cahalan, "Natural Obligation: How Rationally Known Truth Determines Ethical Good and Evil," *The Thomist* 66 (2002): 126.

4   See Douglas Flippen, "Natural Law and Natural Inclinations," *The New Scholasticism* 60.3 (Summer 1986): 290–1, 306.

5   To cite only the initial works: Germain Grisez, "The First Principle of Practical Reason: a Commentary on the *Summa theologiae*, I–II Question 94, a. 2," *Natural Law Forum* 10 (1965): 168–201; John Finnis, *Natural Law and Natural Rights* (Oxford: Clarendon Law Series, 1980), esp. 33–36.

6   See Grisez, "The First Principle of Practical Reason," 357-358; Finnis, *Natural Law and Natural Rights*, 34, 402. A similar line, giving a somewhat stronger role to the inclinations, is found Martin Rhonheimer, *Natural Law and Practical Reason: A Thomist View of Moral Autonomy* (New York: Fordham University Press, 2000); see my review in *The Thomist* 66.2 (April 2002); 311–315.

7   In her recent *Nature as Reason. A Thomistic Theory of the Natural Law* (Grand Rapids: Eerdmans, 2005), Jean Porter dwells at some length on the role of the natural inclinations. Her account is complex, but I think it is clear that she too treats them as prior to reason's grasp of their objects as good; see 68–82, 116–39 (esp. 127), 189–90. Of the positions that I have sketched, perhaps the closest to hers would be that of Flippen.

8   John Finnis, *Aquinas. Moral, Political, and Legal Theory* (New York: Oxford University Press, 1998), 92–93.

9   Lawrence Dewan, O.P., "Jacques Maritain and the Philosophy of Co-operation," in M. Gourgues and G.-D. Mailhiot (ed.), *Alterité. Vivre ensemble differents* (Montréal and Paris: Bellarmin/Cerf, 1986), 109–117; "St. Thomas, Our Natural Lights, and the Moral Order," *Angelicum* 67 (1990): 285–307 [originally published in *Maritain Studies/Études maritainiennes* 2 (1986): 59–92]. Also quite pertinent is his "The Real Distinction between Intellect and Will," *Angelicum* 57 (1980): 557–593.

10   Stephen L. Brock, *The Legal Character of Natural Law according to St Thomas Aquinas*, Ph.D. dissertation (University of Toronto, 1988), 143–166.

11   See I–II, q. 93, a. 6: he speaks generally of "inclination to what is consonant with the eternal law."

12   See Finnis, *Aquinas*, 93, n. 150. He also points out that Thomas must be talking about inclinations that everyone has. This too suggests that they cannot be natural bodily or sensitive inclinations, since these vary among individuals; see I–II, q. 51, a. I, near the end of the corpus.

13   See especially I–II, q. 71, a. 2, ad 3; I–II, q. 78, a. 3. Also I, q. 81, a. 3, ad 1 & ad 2; I–II, q. 91, a. 6; I–II, q. 94, a. 4; *In VI Eth.*, lect. xi, §1278; *In XII Meta*, lect. vii, §2522; *De malo* q. 16, a. 2.

14   I–II, q. 94, a. 2, ad 2. See I–II, q. 94, a. 4, ad 3.

15   Compare Anthony Lisska, *Aquinas's Theory of Natural Law. An Analytical Reconstruction* (Oxford: Oxford University Press, 1996), 96-100.

16   I–II, q. 9, a. 1, ad 2. Compare Clifford G. Kossel, S.J., "Natural Law and Human Law (Ia IIae qq. 90–97)," in Stephen J. Pope (ed.), *The Ethics of Aquinas* (Washington, D.C.: Georgetown University Press, 2002, 174.)

17   I, q. 60, a. 1, ad 3; see I, q. 17, a. 3, ad 2.

18   I–II, q. 19, a. 3, ad 2; I–II, q. 58, a. 5, ad 1.

19   Even as regards the last end considered merely formally or abstractly – *beatitudo in communi* – the desire of it depends on the apprehension of it; see I–II, q. 5, a. 8, c. & ad 1; I–II, q. 10, a. 2.

20   I–II, q. 10, a. 1. I use "natural continuance" to translate *naturalem consistentiam*. An indication of what this covers is found in I–II, q. 60, a. 5, where he speaks of the "*bonum … ad consistentiam humanae vitae pertinens in individuo vel in specie, sicut sunt delectabilia ciborum et venereorum.*"

21   I–II, q. 1, a. 1. It is no accident, I think, that earlier in the corpus of I–II, q. 94, a. 2, Thomas remarks that *qui dicit hominem, dicit rationale*.

22   Very pertinent here is III, q. 19, a. 2.

3.2.2.3 Daniel McInerny
"Hierarchy and Direction for Choice"

A Threshold Challenge

In his recent book, *Natural Law and Practical Rationality*, a natural law defense which, like George's, reposes upon the incommensurability thesis, Mark Murphy reads both George and John Finnis as issuing the following threshold challenge to any defender of hierarchy. Any defender of hierarchy must show first either that the incommensurability thesis applied to the basic goods is false, or that incommensurability is consistent with hierarchy.[1]

So to take up the first part of the disjunction: is it the case that the defender of hierarchy must reject the incommensurability thesis as false? The answer, perhaps surprisingly, is no. The incommensurability thesis is, in fact, not false if by incommensurability we mean that intrinsically valuable goods, at least, cannot be reduced to a single genus. This is one of the points pressed by Aristotle against Plato's Form of the Good in the sixth chapter of Book I of the *Nicomachean Ethics*. The Platonists themselves, Aristotle says, do not postulate a single form for classes of things in which prior and posterior are found, as is the case with numbers. While there are forms for individual numbers, there is no form of number itself, because the class of numbers is comprised of various natures ordered to each other and to a first. And so it is with the good. Goodness manifests itself across the categories: there are good substances, good qualities, good relations, and so on. And these various manifestations of good, as with numbers, enjoy an order of prior and posterior. That which has goodness in itself, substance, is prior to all those other goods that manifest their goodness only in relation to substance. From these observations Aristotle concludes that just as there can be no common form of number, so there can be no common form of good.[2]

Thus it is perfectly appropriate to speak of intrinsically valuable (as opposed to instrumental) human goods as incommensurable. For human goods are not commensurable in the sense that they are merely different manifestations of a single kind of good. In this respect, they have no shared *mensura*. Accordingly, the hierarchical understanding of good I am defending has no truck with a commensurability thesis, or with those quasi-mathematical, maximizing strategies of practical rationality that trade on such a thesis, and which natural law theorists like George are absolutely right to condemn.

Daniel McInerny, "Hierarchy and Direction for Choice," in *Virtue's End: God in the Moral Philosophy of Aristotle and Aquinas*, ed. F. Di Blassi, J.P. Hochschild, and J. Langan (South Bend, IN: St. Augustine's Press, 2008), pp. 124–138.

So, if the incommensurability thesis is not to be rejected, then we must affirm the other side of the disjunction, namely, that incommensurability is compatible with a hierarchical understanding of the good. Both Russell Pannier and Mark Murphy have noted that this compatibility has been implicitly recognized by theorists such as George. As Murphy puts it, there is a *tu quoque* rebuff to George's objection to hierarchy, for George himself holds "that each person is under a practical requirement to form a life plan that includes a subjective prioritization of the basic goods in his or her life."[3] But if the basic goods are such that they are amenable to subjective prioritization, then in principle, at least, there is nothing inconsistent in thinking that the basic goods can enjoy objective prioritization. "And if George asks," Murphy writes, "what particular requirements on choice are generated by the goods' naturally forming a hierarchy, the defender of that view can respond that it is the requirements on choice that would be generated by the goods' forming a structurally identical hierarchy through the agent's commitment."[4]

But what reasons are there for thinking that intrinsically valuable human goods actually do form a natural hierarchy? I would like to address that question now, as the next stage in showing how hierarchy works in providing real direction for choice.

The "For-The-Sake-Of" Relation

Earlier I referred to Aquinas's description of the human good as a *duplex ordo*, a twofold order of goods both to one another and to the absolutely ultimate end. As Aquinas also says in this *lectio* of his Commentary, the order of goods to one another is made possible by their order to the absolutely ultimate end.[5] So in setting up the scaffolding of an objective hierarchy of goods, the existence and nature of an absolutely ultimate end must be established, as well as the ligatures that bind other less-than-ultimate ends both to it and to each other. Following both Aristotle's and Aquinas's procedure, I want to consider the ligatures first, the basic means-end structures that characterize the hierarchy of our objectives.

Permit me, first, some rather rudimentary distinctions that are nonetheless absolutely necessary for the argument to follow. Say that I have volunteered to play in a charity golf tournament. The actions that I take in preparation for my play – practicing for the tournament, driving to the site, the play itself – are all ends that I pursue for the sake of my overall end of benefiting some needy children. The benefit of the children serves as the final end, the term, of my action, while the ends subordinate to it serve as means to this final end. We already see that "means" and "ends" are relative terms. What makes the benefit of the children the final end of this train of action is that I would desire this end even if nothing else ever followed from it: such as public recognition of my action. All the other ends, however, at least within this train of activity, would not be pursued unless they were somehow productive of the end of helping the children. I might play golf for other reasons on other days, but I would not tune up to play in a charity tournament unless I was convinced that my participation would truly help the charity. Thus of any end we can ask whether we would pursue that end even if nothing resulted from it but the attainment of the end in question. Would I floss my teeth if that activity had no effect on dental hygiene? For most of us, I hope, the answer is no, and so we identify flossing teeth as a merely instrumental activity. Would we want to play golf apart from any usefulness it may serve? Of course we would. Playing golf is intrinsically valuable, a final end.[6] This example helps clarify that certain ends can be both instrumentally and intrinsically valuable, depending on the context in which they are pursued.

The "for-the-sake-of" relationships that hold between goods exhibit what Richard Kraut has called asymmetrical causal relations.[7] In Aristotle's well-known example, bridle-making is for the sake of riding, meaning that bridle-making helps bring riding into being and thus that riding is more desirable than bridle-making – hence the asymmetry in the relation. Moreover, because bridle-making is for the sake of riding, riding provides the standard or norm against which bridle-making is regulated. Bridle-making takes the form it does because the art of riding, the craft to which it is subordinated, takes the form it does. This is the meaning behind Aristotle's use in this context of the word *architektonikê*, "master-craft." The Greek term connotes a craft that is superior, of course, but superior insofar as it is an *archê*, a ruler, over the others. Politics, Aristotle's *politikê technê*, is the master-craft of master-crafts because it dictates to all other sciences and crafts both what is to be done in these crafts and how they are to be employed for the end of politics: the common good.

We are beginning to see how hierarchy provides direction for choice, insofar as the good for the sake of which another good is pursued regulates the pursuit of the subordinate good. A clarification on this point. A higher good regulates a lower good in more than one way. Commenting on the passage from Aristotle just mentioned, Aquinas claims that politics regulates practical activities both as to *whether* they should be pursued and *how* they should be pursued. But politics regulates speculative activities only as to whether they should be pursued, either at all or by a particular person. Politics does not dictate how a speculative science should be pursued – how in geometry, for example, conclusions should be drawn from premises. For this depends on the very nature of the subject matter of geometry.[8] So in the order of practice, at least, what Aquinas has to say about the relationship between politics and other activities seems to hold generally: lower goods are for the sake of higher goods, which in turn dictate whether and how the lower goods are to be pursued.

It is a good question whether the asymmetry in the for-the-sake-of relationship must always run in the same direction. Can x be for the sake of y, which in turn is for the sake of x? The goods of family life, in any Thomistic view, are ordered for the sake of practicing philosophy. But as a working philosopher, do I not also pursue philosophy for the sake of the goods of family life? This example quickly clarifies the point that goods are not ordered for the sake of each other in the same respect, thus ensuring that there is no true circularity in for-the-sake-of relationships. For while it is true that the goods of family life are ordered to philosophical wisdom, it is not true that philosophical wisdom is ordered, as a subordinate good, to the goods of family life. Philosophy understood *as employment* may be so ordered, but this is just to change the respect in which we consider philosophy. Employment understood as a mere means is always subordinated to the goods of family life, which in turn are always subordinated to the philosophical pursuit of truth.

For Aquinas, all intrinsically valuable goods exist in *per se*, that is necessary, relationships of the prior and posterior. Prudence is a superior virtue to fortitude, according to Aquinas, principally because it perfects that power of the soul concerned with the overall good of the agent. The hierarchy among these virtues is a *necessary* feature of the human good, such that a conception of fortitude not put in the service of and regulated by prudence would not be the genuine article at all. In the film *The Perfect Storm* the members of a fishing crew lose their lives pursuing a catch straight into the teeth of the storm of the century. True, they are down-on-their-luck fishermen, desperately in need of a good catch. But clearly it was not worth risking their lives to catch even more fish than they had already caught. The daring quality they exhibit in battling the storm is in some sense impressive, the film's marketing company may describe it as "courageous," but in the absence of prudence we can't admit that it's anything other than recklessness.[9]

We may conclude from this that the very character of intrinsically valuable goods depends upon how they are subordinated to and regulated by goods superior in the hierarchy. This is why to speak of "basic goods" – even in their instantiations – as discrete, incommensurable items (George employs the unfortunate metaphor of 'quanta'[10]) is not to speak of real goods at all, but only of generic, ghostly entities incapable of directing choice. Once again, it is a feature of intrinsically valuable goods (at least, of all but one of them) that they are instrumental to higher goods, and that the whether and how of their pursuit are guided by these higher goods. We simply don't fully understand the good of "life," for example, until we understand that in certain circumstances it must be sacrificed, subordinated to, the familial or political common good.

Of course, George and others attempt to get around this difficulty by invoking the notion of "integral human fulfillment," an appeal to an ultimate end that brings some definition to the basic goods and provides the ultimate direction for, and justification of, human choice. Hence it is opportune at this juncture of the argument to consider the role of the ultimate end in serving as the *principium* of the hierarchy of goods.

Before that, however, a brief digest of points made so far.

First, the Thomistic understanding of hierarchy affirms that *intrinsically valuable human goods are heterogeneous in character*. These goods are thus not commensurable, such that the many goods we perceive are *merely* instantiations of, or instrumentally useful for, the absolutely ultimate end, the one and only intrinsically valuable human good and the single measure of goodness. This kind of commensuration has been roundly repudiated by contemporary writers and rightly so.

Second, *the incommensurability or heterogeneity of the human good, its resistance to any form of commensuration, does not preclude its being ordered according to priority and posteriority*. All of being is ordered to substance, an order which is manifest in the moral sphere in the way that the different substantial human goods are ordered to that which is the substance of the human good in the most perfect sense: the absolutely ultimate end.

Third, *within this hierarchical ordering of goods there are many different goods which are ultimate or final, though in a qualified sense*. But the fact that they are ultimate in any sense means that they are desirable for their own sake. We don't just desire them because they help us achieve the absolutely ultimate end (though they do that, too); we don't wholly reduce them to instrumental goods simply because they have an instrumental aspect to them.

The Hierarchy of Happinesses

It is a commonplace of much contemporary Aristotelian scholarship and even some Thomistic that the for-the-sake-of relationship that I have been arguing is essential to an understanding of the human good cannot be applied to the ultimate end itself. In his book on *Aquinas*, for example, John Finnis speaks of *beatitudo* as a basic good. "But this turns out to be," he writes, "not so much an item to be added to the list of basic human goods, as rather a kind of synthesis of them: [namely] satisfaction of all intelligent desires and participation in all the basic human goods…and thus a fulfillment which is complete and integral."[11] Elsewhere Finnis describes imperfect beatitude, at least, as "the good of complete reasonableness in one's willing of human goods."[12]

Roughly, then, we might summarize this view of the ultimate end as the activity of pursuing the basic goods in as unified a manner as possible, according to the hierarchy we have constructed for ourselves, without in any way disrespecting the intrinsic value of any of the goods by manipulating it as a mere means. To act in this way is to act both from reason and from virtue – and, apparently, "for the sake of" the ultimate end of imperfect happiness.

But it is important not to confuse the "for-the-sake-of" relationship with this inclusive relationship described by Finnis. By an inclusive relationship I mean a formal relationship of part to whole, as when we say putting is a part of golf, or the pursuit of play is a part of imperfect happiness. To say that putting is "for the sake of" golf makes hash out of the phrase "for the sake of," if all that is meant is that putting is a constituent part of golf. True enough, putting is a part of golf if we are considering the constituent items and activities that go to make up a game of golf, like driving, chipping and cursing. This kind of consideration is formal in character. But within this formal consideration putting is in no meaningful sense "for the sake of" golf; for putting in this sense *simply* is golf. So, the only meaningful use of the phrase "for the sake of" is when the phrase is meant to say that one thing helps bring some other thing extrinsic to it into being and is regulated by it. Therefore, my two-putt on 17 is good insofar as it serves as the end of my desire to play golf on a Saturday morning; "putting" in this sense is the goal of an entire train of instrumental activities "for the sake of" landing me on the golf course. My two-putt on 17 is also good in an instrumental sense, insofar as it brings about, is "for the sake of," my continued play on 18 and my over-arching goal of finishing my round in the lowest possible number of strokes. "Putting" has an instrumental relationship to the good of "golf," if by "golf" we mean the completion of my round, not the game formally considered.[13]

My point here is not to deny that it's meaningful to say, "Happiness for me is my family, my friends, my work, my recreational activities, my devotion to God, etc." We speak in this way all the time. My point, rather, is that this way of speaking does not refer to the primary sense of happiness, the sense which *establishes* the *per se* order of multiple goods according to prior and posterior – and this sense, of course, is founded upon God. Without this sense of happiness, no other sense of happiness (including the reference to a set of constituents thereof), and more importantly, no direction for choice, is possible.

I have no intention of canvassing here Aquinas's arguments for the very existence of an ultimate end, for why the ultimate end must be one and not many, and the dialectical arguments he uses to manifest the nature of both imperfect and perfect happiness. Instead, I simply want to highlight some features of the arguments Aquinas develops in pursuing these questions.

First, when Aquinas argues in article 4, question 1 of the *Prima secundae* that there must be an ultimate end of human life, he stakes his claim on the fact that for human action even to get up and running, whether in the order of intention or of execution, there must be a *per se* order of ends culminating in an absolutely first, absolutely ultimate, end. And when in the next article Aquinas proves that the absolutely ultimate end must be single, he tells us that the hierarchy of "for-the-sake-of" relationships must culminate in a final end that is never for the sake of some other good, and thus serves to regulate every other good in the hierarchy which is, in some respect (though not in every respect) instrumental to it. In the *sed contra* of article 5 Aquinas glosses Matthew 6:24 ("No man can serve two masters") as a way of saying that no one can pursue two final ends *not ordered to one another*; that is, not situated within a network of "for-the-sake-of" relationships.

Apropos of this latter text Germain Grisez has argued that "[o]f course, in choosing, one seeks a good loved for itself. In this sense, one always acts for an ultimate end – that is, an end not pursued as a means to some ulterior end. But an ultimate end in this sense need not be the complete good of the human person, as Thomas assumed when he tried to prove that one's will cannot be directed simultaneously to two or more ultimate ends" [Grisez's citation is then to *ST* I–II, q. 1, a. 5].[14] But it is not the case that Aquinas didn't understand that there could be many final ends, each one imperfectly fulfilling of the human person. It is rather that he understood these less-than-absolutely final ends as existing in a *duplex ordo* to one another and to an absolutely ultimate end, in the absence of which no pursuit of any final end would ever occur. For what gets human action up and going is the pursuit of complete fulfillment of desire.

Human happiness is thus best defined as a unity in multiplicity, and this in more than one sense. As governed by the precepts of the natural law, our pursuit of happiness is always for something that is, in some sense, common. But as there are degrees of finality or perfection in goods in general, so there will be degrees of perfection in common good. There is only one common good that most perfectly satisfies the criteria of human happiness, and that is, strictly speaking, God himself. Accordingly, in the most perfect sense happiness is union with God in the next life; far less perfectly, it is contemplation of God in this life. But because we are not angels but embodied souls, this latter, mundane happiness must include the exercise of the moral and artistic virtues *as ordered to* the happiness of contemplation. This brings out the fact that a more perfect sense of happiness always subsumes that below it: all the happiness we seek in natural goods is taken up into and perfected in God,[15] while all the happiness we seek in the practice of moral and artistic virtue is taken up into and perfected in the life of contemplation.

Observations such as these customarily elicit two objections. The first objection I shall call, borrowing a phrase from Russell Pannier, the "personal destinies" objection. Does this objective hierarchy of goods leave any place for personal predilection and native talent in determining one's happiness?

What the good obliges me to do is structure my commitments according to the hierarchical framework of goods, rules and virtues. However, the basic framework can be instantiated, can be *determined* by the judgment of prudence, in myriad ways. I may possess neither the desire, talent nor opportunity to be a statesman, but justice will still be a good that I am bound to pursue. I may have neither the talent nor opportunity to study philosophy in a rigorous way, but I can still make contemplative activity the highest and best good that I pursue, perhaps by reflection on works of art, or conversations with friends, or by prayer. This solution to the problem does not deny – indeed, it does everything to affirm – a hierarchy of offices and duties that is not the production of individual choice. The wider a common good a particular office or duty looks after, the more divine-like and honorable it is.[16] Yet again, this does not mean that the lives of those who occupy lower offices are diminished. They are perfect in their own order, and in their perfection make a necessary contribution to the common good of the whole.

But what then of the related, "domination" objection? If contemplation and religious observance are the best goods, why shouldn't I spend all my time with them? To answer this we need to recall that higher goods in a hierarchy do not undermine the intrinsic goodness of the goods subordinate to them. My obligation to honor my parents, for instance, binds me to the goods of family life in a way that is constitutive of my happiness. My other obligation to honor God in the practice of the virtue of religion is not a rival to this obligation, even while it remains the more important obligation. The natural law in no way requires that I pursue religious acts to the exclusion of all other obligations. The natural law only demands that the religious obligation is given foremost respect in the tailoring of the hierarchy to my individual circumstances. In fact, it would be contrary to the proper understanding of my religious obligation if I did not understand the way in which it depends upon my lower obligations. The honoring of parents and the enjoyment of the goods of family life not only have their own requirements, but the intellectual and moral education one receives in participating in these goods is required if the religious good is to be fully achieved.

Notes

1 [Mark C.] Murphy, *Natural Law and Practical Rationality* [(Cambridge University Press, 2001)], p. 192.
2 *EN* I.6 1096a17–23. Cf. *In I Ethicorum*, lectio 6, nn. 79–80. On this point I have learned from Kevin L. Flannery, S.J., *Acts Amid Precepts* (Washington D.C.: The Catholic University of America Press, 2001), Chapter 4. It is interesting to relate Aristotle's argument to Aquinas's analysis of the goodness of the human act. The species, or substance, of a human act, according to Aquinas, is a form/matter composite. This composite is considered formally in terms of the end (the object of the interior act of the will), but materially in terms of the object of the exterior act. The circumstances of the act accrue to the substance of the act as accidents of it. Thus in the human act there is an order of priority and posteriority, the substance of the act being prior. See *ST* I–II, q. 18, a. 6 and q. 7, a. 3.,
3 Murphy, *Natural Law and Practical Rationality*, p. 192. Here Murphy also references John Finnis, *Natural Law and Natural Rights*, pp. 100–105. See also Russell Pannier, "Finnis and the Commensurability of Goods," *The New Scholasticism* 61 (1987): 440–61, esp. 443. Unlike Pannier, and for the reasons already given, I do not think it accurate to refer to a hierarchical ordering of goods as a *commensuration* of those goods, except perhaps in a very loose sense.
4 Ibid.
5 *In I Ethicorum*, lectio 1, no. 1.
6 Henry S. Richardson has a nice discussion of the way Aristotle uses counterfactuals in distinguishing final ends from instrumental ends, as well as from final ends that are also instrumental ends. See his *Practical Reasoning About Final Ends* (Cambridge University Press, 1997), pp. 53–57.
7 Richard Kraut, *Aristotle on the Human Good* (Princeton University Press, 1989), Chapter 4.
8 *In I Ethicorum*, lectio 1, no. 27.
9 This kind of argument is developed in Alasdair MacIntyre's defense of a teleological, as opposed to a functionalist, account of virtue in his "Sōphrosunē': How a Virtue Can Become Socially Disruptive," in *Midwest Studies in Philosophy* XIII (1988): pp. 1–11.
10 George, *In Defense of the Natural Law*, p. 96. See also Russell Hittinger, "After MacIntyre: Natural Law Theory, Virtue Ethics, and Eudaimonia," *International Philosophical Quarterly* (December 1989): pp. 449–61.
11 John Finnis, *Aquinas: Moral, Political and Legal Theory* (Oxford University Press, 1998), pp. 85–86.
12 Ibid., p. 108.
13 These remarks can also be taken as a partial rebuttal of J. L. Ackrill's inclusivist understanding of Aristotle's view of the good. See Ackrill's "Aristotle on *Eudaimonia*," reprinted in Amélie Rorty, ed., *Essays on Aristotle's Ethics* (Los Angeles, CA: University of California Press, 1980).
14 Germain Grisez, *The Way of the Lord Jesus, vol. I, Christian Moral Principles* (Chicago: Franciscan Herald Press, 1983), pp. 809–10, quoted and discussed in Ashley, "What is the End of the Human Person? The Vision of God and Integral Human Fulfillment," pp. 68–69, especially.
15 It is interesting to note in this regard that for Aquinas even the moral virtues endure after this life, albert in their formal, rather than material nature. See *ST* I–II, q. 67, a. I. Something analogous holds with the intellectual virtues, including, I assume, the virtues of art (*ST* I–II, q. 67, a. 2).
16 Cf. *In I Ethicorum*, lectio 2, no. 30.

3.2.2.4 Steven D. Smith
"Natural Law and Contemporary Moral Thought: A Guide from the Perplexed"

Natural Law as (Strained) Translation

This diagnosis points to what is so sorely missing in much modern moral discourse. The problem, it turns out, is not the "subjective" account of "goods" given by theories like utilitarianism – indeed, as we have seen, theories that try to solve the modern problem by positing goods that are something other than "subjective" in this sense risk lapsing into unintelligibility – but rather that we lack the background stories needed to give sense to our moral reflections. In a changing or perhaps decaying culture, traditional roles (whether that of mother, father, teacher, or lawyer) that might have guided moral deliberations have lost much of their force. And the notion of a natural or preordained pattern into which we should try to fit our choices and actions seems alien in today's world.[1] Indeed, it is said to be a defining feature of a "postmodern" climate of opinion that it no longer knows or accepts any such "metanarrative."[2]

These difficulties can be overstated, to be sure. Traditional roles, though threatened, have not disappeared. And religious faith continues to supply a pattern of life for many people. Still, for purposes of public debate there is little *shared* sense of any overall pattern or structure for human life. Without such a sense it is understandable that public debate would exude futility.

So can natural law remedy this deficiency? It might seem so. Hauerwas and Burrell note the connection: "[T]he moral life must be grounded in the 'nature' of man. However, that 'nature' is not 'rationality' itself, but the necessity of having a narrative to give our life coherence."[3] In this volume, J. L. A. Garcia refers to "the sort of *story* about God and about God's relationship to humanity which most of the great natural law thinkers have accepted, *the Biblical story*."[4] And Daniel N. Robinson may have something similar in mind when he asserts that "what all theories warranting the label 'Natural Law' have in common is the assumption that there is *a point to life* apart from the physical fact of it. ..."[5]

Despite these promising hints, the narrative dimension of the moral life is a theme that contemporary natural law theory thus far has left largely undeveloped. The reason, I suspect, is that natural lawyers have to a large degree accepted the restrictions on discourse

Steven D. Smith, "Natural Law and Contemporary Moral Thought: A Guide from the Perplexed," *American Journal of Jurisprudence* 42 (1997), pp. 32v6–330. Reprinted with kind permission of the author.

adopted by liberal theorists. As noted, liberals are loath to talk about "the good." Natural lawyers are less reticent on that score, but they draw the line at relying on religious faith. Their project has sought to show that we can have all of the blessings of liberalism – and have them more securely – without breaching the liberal taboo against invoking beliefs grounded in religious faith. For a natural lawyer like Moore, this entails no sacrifice, since he does not accept traditional religion anyway. For someone like Finnis the matter is more delicate. While not apologizing for his religious commitments, Finnis also wants to insist that his "natural law" arguments do not require reliance on religious authority. As one commentator has observed, Finnis "believes that a major contribution of his account of ethics is its demonstration of clear and reliable truths about moral actions that protect *everyone's* flourishing at the same time that they appeal to all rational persons independent of their religious beliefs."[6]

As noted above, though, our narratives – or at least our metanarratives – are likely to be religious in nature. "Narratives" are stories, and stories imply a storyteller. And authoritative metanarrative implies a more than human author. So it is difficult to convey this essential dimension of morality without somehow importing religion.

Precluded by their own commitments from invoking religious authority, modern natural lawyers are forced to translate this concern into secular language. Not surprisingly, the translation often seems strained. One possibility is to somehow squeeze the narrative element into the "goods" to be pursued. Thus, Finnis's current list of goods includes the good of "*harmony* with the widest reaches and *ultimate source* of all reality, including meaning and value."[7] This good might well be a link to the considerations of "fittingness" and "narrative structure" mentioned earlier. But the good of "harmony" is not elaborated in Finnis's essay or applied to the question of sexual morality. Nor is the essay's silence in this respect surprising: the elaboration of what "harmony" entails – and of the more ultimate reality with which our lives ought to "harmonize" – would surely call for the development of a vocabulary that would go well beyond that of a goods-based ethics, and would very likely breach any commitment to avoiding reliance on religious faith or authority.

A different translating strategy would build the narrative dimension of morality into the methods of reason by which we are to know and pursue the basic goods. Thus, Finnis's first requirement of practical reason asserts that we must pursue the basic goods not willy-nilly, but rather according to a "coherent plan of life."[8] Quoting Rawls, Finnis says we should "see our life as one whole, the activities of one rational subject spread out in time."[9] This comes close to saying that we ought to pursue goods *as if* our lives constituted a narrative, not just a series of isolated good-realizing experiences.

But this translation still is a defective and unattractive rendering of the narrative dimension of morality. Unless our lives somehow *are* lived within a natural narrative structure, after all, it is not clear why reason requires us to act *as if* they were. Why not live for the moment, pursuing goods opportunistically as they present themselves, or whimsically as our moods dictate (or as the Spirit directs)? "Take no thought for the morrow."[10] Of course, *some* goods could not be achieved in this way – the aesthetic good of musical virtuosity, for instance – but then not everyone pursues those particular goods anyway. Some might worry that the willy-nilly approach would lead to a lower aggregate total of goods over a lifetime than a more systematic investment strategy would produce. But this can hardly be Finnis's objection, given his opposition to such aggregative calculations.[11] So within his own ethical framework (or rather within the framework that he acknowledges for purposes of doing "natural law"), the admonition to follow a coherent life plan seems arbitrary. And that arbitrariness is simply one manifestation of the difficulty of translating the narrative dimension of morality into the non-narrative and secular vocabulary of "rationality," "basic goods," and "objective reasons for acting."

Conclusion

The discussion, I think, can be summed up simply: theories of "rights" make no sense without reference to understandings about human "goods," but moral theories based on human "goods" are inadequate and unmoored without reference to some overarching pattern into which these goods appropriately fit. Unlike many liberals, natural lawyers understand the first point; that is their valuable contribution. But contemporary natural law seems not to appreciate the second point. Or perhaps we simply lack the cultural conditions or the metaphysical resources needed to act upon the second point, so that natural lawyers feel condemned to translate this consideration, however awkwardly, into a more strained and obscure vocabulary about "objective" goods. Either way, we can infer what it is that our moral and political discourse so desperately needs – and that current versions of natural law seem unable or unwilling to supply. And we can perhaps understand why "goods," however essential, just cannot do all the work that modern theories have burdened them with.

This assessment suggests the nearly insuperable obstacle that confronts any attempt to revive Thomistic natural law ethics for public use under current conditions. It may be that for Thomas, natural law referred to that portion of the eternal law that was accessible to human reason without the aid of revelation; hence it encompassed "goods" that could be known by reason alone. But it is one thing to make such assertions against the implicit backdrop of a Christian culture in which the salvation history and destiny of humanity is taken for granted. (And it is significant that even then, Thomas's proofs of the existence of God, unlike Finnis's, *precede* the discussion of law and ethics.) It is quite another thing to make similar claims about what natural reason teaches in a culture that as a public matter does not recognize the existence of God or of any providential order or divine destiny for humankind.

In this more secularized and divided culture, of course, the *need* for a morality accessible to reason alone may be even more acute. But the assertions about natural reason and what it shows, even though they may *sound* almost identical to assertions made earlier in a different context, just will not mean the same things; and they will not have the same effects.[12] So it should not be surprising if natural law claims that are entirely cogent to scholars who still happen to hold many of the background beliefs more characteristic of a different historical period seem less than compelling, and sometimes quite bizarre,[13] to others for whom those background beliefs probably never entered the field of view.

From a more distant perspective, contemporary natural law theory can be seen as another in a series of efforts to rescue moral reflection from the collapse of what Louis Dupre has called the classical and medieval "ontotheological synthesis" within which nature was understood not merely as matter in motion, but rather as an "ordered totality" with normative as well as physical dimensions.[14] Dupre's study assesses a variety of modern responses to this breakdown – from early Protestantism and the "devout humanism" of Ignatius's *Spiritual Exercises* to baroque drama. He argues that although often brilliant, these responses have also ultimately proven ineffectual insofar as they have remained within the impoverished modern conception of nature. Whether a new synthesis will emerge is uncertain; but if it does, its account of morality will need to earn the title of "*natural* law." That is, it will need to address the question that current natural law theorists only coyly allude to: what does it mean to live "in some sort of harmony" with a "transcendent other and its lasting order"?[15]

Notes

1   For a lengthier discussion, *see* Steven D. Smith, *The Constitution and the Pride of Reason*, ch. 5.

2   *See* David Harvey, *The Condition of Postmodernity* (1990), pp. 44–45.

3   "From System to Story: An Alternative Pattern for Rationality in Ethics," in *Why Narrative? Readings in Narrative Theology*, p. 177.

4   "'Deus sive Natura': Must Natural Lawyers Choose?" in *Natural Law, Liberalism, and Morality* [emphasis added].

5   Daniel N. Robinson, "Lloyd Weinreb's Problems with Natural Law," in *Natural Law, Liberalism, and Morality*, pp. 213, 216 [emphasis added], As its title indicates, Robinson's essay is a critique of an essay by Lloyd Weinreb, "The Moral Point of View," which I have not discussed in this review. Weinreb's animating concern is with moral questions arising out what is often called the problem of free will and determinism. This is a difficult and important problem, obviously, but so far as I can tell it is not the problem that natural law theories and theorists seek to address. Consequently, there is something askew about Weinreb's discussion; he often seems as if he is saying profound things about a conversation going on in the next room.

6   Thomas W. Smith, "Finnis' Questions and Answers: An Ethics of Hope or Fear?" p. 29. Lloyd Weinreb asserts that "in fact, the whole edifice of Finnis's argument seems to be constructed in order to show that by relying on our reason alone – being 'simply reasonable' – we can recognize objective moral truths." *Natural Law, Liberalism, and Morality*, pp. 195, 198–99.

7   "Is Natural Law Theory Compatible with Limited Government?" in *Natural Law, Liberalism, and Morality*, p. 4. In a similar spirit, Charles Taliaferro describes the "good of Divine-human accord." Charles Taliaferro, "God's Natural Lawyers," in *Natural Law, Liberalism, and Morality*, pp. 283, 294. *See also* Finnis, *Natural Law and Natural Rights*, pp. 89–90 (listing "religion" as one of the basic goods). *See ibid.*, p. 90 (observing that if there is a transcendent basis of life "then one's life and actions are in fundamental disorder if they are not brought, as best one can, into some sort of harmony with whatever can be known or surmised about that transcendent other and its lasting order").

8   *Ibid.*, pp. 103–05.

9   *Ibid.*, p. 104.

10 *Matt.* 6:34.

11 *See* "The Natural Law Tradition."

12 Wayne Meeks, arguing for a "holistic" approach to understanding Christian morality, observes that

we must be aware that the culture of any particular society or group, however complex, is so internally interconnected that if we pull out any one of its components – its ideas, its myths, its rules, its logical structures, its material supports – and disregard that element's embeddedness in the whole, we will fail to understand it.

The Origins of Christian Morality, pp. 10–11.

13 *See, e.g.*, Thomas C. Grey, "*Bowers v. Hardwick* Diminished," 68 *U Colo. L. Rev.* (1997), pp. 373, 385, n. 47 (observing that "I find [Finnis's] reasoning impossible to follow" and that "[t]he indefensibility of this accomplished philosopher's best effort to justify in secular terms the traditional condemnation of homosexuality surely strengthens the case against *Hardwick*").

14 Louis Dupre, *Passage to Modernity: An Essay in the Hermeneutics of Nature and Culture* (1993), pp. 11, 17.

15 *Natural Law and Natural Rights*, p. 90.

3.3 Metaphysical, Social, and Critical

Introduction

One of the editors' main concerns in compiling the present volume has been to draw out the interdependencies presupposed by the central natural law tradition with other fields of philosophical and empirical inquiry. In doing so, it is important to recognize that the soundness of this endeavor in no way entails a particular answer to the philosophical controversies swirling around New Natural Law theory hitherto detailed, since even the most ardent "New Naturalist" is at pains to draw a distinction between the epistemological and metaphysical foundations of the natural law, confining his or her claims to the former. The first selection reprinted here, by David Oderberg, is taken from a collection of essays on personal identity.[1] Owing to constraints of space it has been possible to reproduce only a very short extract of this richly rewarding piece by a contemporary analytic philosopher of great acuity. What we have here, then, is a statement of the theses he defends and a summary conclusion of the points he makes in the course of arguing that many of the so-called "hard problems" in contemporary debates surrounding personal identity simply dissolve – or, at the very least, are rendered considerably more tractable – when approached from the perspective of a certain type of pre-Cartesian personal ontology. It is the continuing relevance of this ontology, under the heading "hylemorphic dualism," that it is Oderberg's purpose to vindicate. "Hylemorphic dualism" is, in a sense, a theory combining the Aristotelian categories of form and matter, which provides a more general explanation of the entire physical world. Since the time of Aquinas, this general framework has been joined to a more specialized explanation of its particular application to the human being and almost invariably provided the philosophical context within which the central natural law tradition has been developed. Oderberg argues in this essay not only for the indispensability of the categories of "matter" and "form," but also for the Boethian definition of the human person as an individual substance of a rational nature, and, in line with

---

[1] D. Oderberg, "Hylemorphic Dualism," in *Personal Identity*, ed. E. Paul, F. Miller, and J. Paul (Cambridge: Cambridge University Press, 2005), pp. 70–99.

The Natural Law Reader, First Edition. Edited by Jacqueline A. Laing and Russell Wilcox.
© 2014 Blackwell Publishing Ltd. Published 2014 by Blackwell Publishing Ltd.

Aquinas, that this, given the fact that the exercise of rationality is an essentially immaterial operation, establishes the immaterial nature of the human form even if it remains one simultaneously ordered to embodiment.

In a somewhat different fashion, the second extract, by Anthony Lisska, attempts to defend the metaphysical underpinnings of Aquinas' theory of natural law by assimilating it to, and explaining it in terms of, the modern philosophical debate surrounding natural kinds.[2] Representing a summary of his earlier well-known work, *Aquinas's Theory of Natural Law: An Analytical Reconstruction*,[3] Lisska argues both for the necessity of understanding natural law in terms of an account of human essence as a natural kind and, at the same time, that this does not require any appeal to, or presupposition of, a divine being. This latter contention raises many difficult and controversial issues with respect to the whole field of natural theology and its proper scope. In particular, whilst it may be possible to talk with a relative coherence in terms of contingent human essences independent of non-contingent, real being, it would be disputed by many that there is, in fact, no ontological presupposition of the latter by the former. For present purposes, it is sufficient to note the contrast between Lisska's arguments and those made by Steven Smith in the previous section.

The next selection is taken from a recent article by Russell Wilcox in which it is argued that an adherence to the basic precepts of the natural law is a pre-requisite for the maintenance of maximal social and cultural diversity.[4] This may seem somewhat surprising given the fact that it is of the essence of central natural law thinking that it makes strong universalist claims by postulating a common human nature in all persons and across all societies. Yet although there has been a pervasive tendency in post-Enlightenment thought to view universality and particularity as mutually incompatible categories, it is argued here that the central tradition supports a uniquely sophisticated method of interrelating these two great aspects of reality in a fashion which is mutually reinforcing. As such, not only do the basic precepts of the natural law express and regulate the deep operational structures of the will as it is rooted in a common human nature, but they are also the conditions precedent for the full range of embodiments (individual and collective) in which human nature is apt to find expression. An account is given of how these various embodiments are made possible and how they manifest the observance of common principles in quite different habitual, institutional, and normative settings. In the course of so arguing, a proper understanding of the category of human law is shown to be compatible with considerable normative pluralism and variation in the levels of its formality.

In the final selection extracted here – "Theories of Natural Law in the Culture of Advanced Modernity"[5] – Alasdair MacIntyre points out that, despite the undoubted corroborative support that can be obtained from the empirical and philosophical

---

[2]   A. Lisska, "The Metaphysical Presuppositions of Natural Law in Thomas Aquinas: A New Look at Some Old Questions," in *Virtue's End: God in the Moral Philosophy of Aristotle and Aquinas*, ed. F. Di Blassi, J.P. Hochschild, and J. Langan (South Bend, IN: St. Augustine's Press, 2008), pp. 67–83.

[3]   A. Lisska, *Aquinas's Theory of Natural Law: An Analytical Reconstruction* (Oxford: Oxford University Press, 1998).

[4]   R. Wilcox, "Natural Law as the Basis of Socio-Cultural Diversity."

[5]   A. MacIntyre, "Theories of Natural Law in the Culture of Advanced Modernity," in *Common Truths: New Perspectives on Natural Law*, ed. E.B. McLean (Wilmington, DE: ISI Books, 2004), pp. 91–115.

sciences, if something like the central tradition's description of human nature is, in fact, true, the basic action guiding precepts it purports to sustain should, in important respects, be accessible to all plain persons. In arguing that they are so accessible, MacIntyre sets himself the task of tackling head-on the paradox with which such a position seems to be confronted; namely, its apparent falsification by pervasive contemporary disagreement concerning in what the good life substantively consists. Yet, it is precisely at this, its point of greatest apparent weakness, suggests MacIntyre, that the central natural law, that is, specifically the Thomistic, tradition of moral reflection vindicates its claim to analytical superiority. Since, if true, it is, in fact, only to be expected that, in certain cultural milieus, cultural milieus of which that of advanced modernity is perhaps the most comprehensive and systematic example so far to emerge, the basic precepts of the natural law would be, and in fact are, comprehensively rejected. An "Aristotelian Thomism," in other words, "has implicit within it a theory of moral and legal error."[6] It shows its superiority to rival accounts of moral theory by explaining better than they, not only why they fail to receive sustained, uncontested, support in the current climate, but also why it too fails, indeed, fails altogether more comprehensively than those same competitors, the more the analysis it sustains approximates to the truth.

6   Ibid., p. 108.

3.3.1 David S. Oderberg
"Hylemorphic Dualism"

[…] (1) All substances, in other words all self-subsisting entities that are the bearers of properties and attributes but are not themselves properties or attributes of anything, are compounds of matter (*hylē*) and form (*morphē*). (2) The form is *substantial* since it actualizes matter and gives the substance its very essence and identity. (3) The human person, being a substance, is also a compound of matter and substantial form. (4) Since a person is defined as an individual substance of a rational nature, the substantial form of the person is the rational nature of the person. (5) The exercise of rationality, however, is an essentially immaterial operation. (6) Hence, human nature itself is essentially immaterial. (7) But since it is immaterial, it does not depend for its existence on being united to matter. (8) So a person is capable of existing, by means of his rational nature, which is traditionally called the soul, independently of the existence of his body. (9) Hence, human beings are immortal; but their identity and individuality does require that they be united to a body at some time in their existence.

[…]

My aim in this essay has been to set out the main lines of the much-neglected hylemorphic theory of the person, and of the dualism that is at its heart. It has not been possible to canvass the many questions and objections that may be raised. If the essay shows nothing more than that the theory is worthy of far more serious attention than it has commonly been given, that will be enough. I do, however, want to conclude with a general observation. The theory that I am not strictly identical with my soul, hence that soul and person are distinct, the person having an essential connection to its body as well as its soul, seems more strange to dualist ears than it should. The "problem of personal identity," as it has come to be known, has a relatively recent currency (due to Locke) and is more fitted to a metaphysical viewpoint that at the very least takes the

David S. Oderberg, "Hylemorphic Dualism," in *Personal Identity*, ed. E. Paul, Miller, and J. Paul (Cambridge: Cambridge University Press, 2005), Volume 22, Part 2. Copyright © Social Philosophy and Policy Foundation, published by Cambridge University Press. Reproduced with permission. See also David S Oderberg, 'The Metaphysical Foundations of Natural Law', in H. Zaborowski (ed.) *Natural Moral Law in Contemporary Society* (Washington, DC: Catholic University of America Press, 2010): 4475; *Real Essentialism* (London: Routledge, 2007) *Applied Ethics: A NonConsequentialist Approach* (Oxford: Blackwell, 2000); *Moral Theory: A NonConsequentialist Approach* (Oxford: Blackwell, 2000).

ideas of disembodied existence and of the immateriality of the soul to be at best highly problematic, at worst not even worth a place in the conceptual landscape on which the problem is grappled with. More strongly, I would venture to say that the problem of personal identity is a problem made for materialists – at least those materialists who take seriously the peculiar ontological status of the mental, the existence of free will and rational agency, and perhaps even the possibility of a future life. The contemporary dualist reaction to materialism, however, has tended to be one of recoiling from the idea of any essential connection between body and soul, and hence between person and both. This has led, in turn, to making the apparently "obvious" move (for the dualist) of identifying person with soul, or at least of regarding person and soul as having an exclusive essential relationship.

For the hylemorphic dualist, on the other hand, the acceptance of a genuinely immaterial element in human nature means a greater flexibility in trying to comprehend just how human persons persist. The concept of form can be pushed heavily into service, as can the idea of the person as a compound substance, in this respect just like a material substance – namely, a substance composed of matter and form. Nevertheless, the hylemorphic dualist must avoid the disastrous fall into Cartesianism or Platonism, both of which diminish the role of the body in personhood. Once the soul is united to a body, it is the form of that body for all time, even after that body has ceased to exist. Its identity after death – and hence the identity of the person that is reduced to it – depends on its having once informed certain matter. The soul must always have a retrospective character, one that looks back on what choices it made when it actualized that matter, and hence on what the person did of which it was once the chief part. (Again, think of the chief executive who, long after his corporation's demise, is forever tarred with the brush of responsibility for those decisions *he* made – and hence his corporation made – when he was its chief constituent.) The soul has, as an actualizing principle of matter it has an essential tendency or direction toward the full flowering of its capacities in matter. Whether it may also look forward to a reuniting of itself with matter is, however, beyond the scope of philosophy to answer.

3.3.2 Anthony J. Lisska
"The Metaphysical Presuppositions of Natural Law in Thomas Aquinas: A New Look at Some Old Questions"

The Role of Metaphysics

In discussing the role of metaphysics in Aquinas and in natural law theory, several distinctions must be discussed. The foil is the denial of the necessity of a philosophical anthropology as a necessary condition for explicating Aquinas on natural law. Some Thomist critics of the New Natural Law approach of Finnis/Grisez adopt a particular metaphysical/theological paradigm and argue that this scheme is a necessary condition for underpinning natural law theory in Aquinas. Others deny this entailment of a proposition requiring God's existence. Hence, in considering metaphysics as necessary for natural law in Aquinas – and thus offering a critical response to Finnis/Grisez – at least two versions of metaphysical inquiry require discussion.

a. *"Theological" Metaphysics* (for want of a better term):
Some Thomist critics of Finnis/Grisez like Steven Long and Fulvio Di Blasi, among others, wish to defend the position that the only type of metaphysics found in Aquinas concludes to the position that God is a necessary condition for understanding natural law.[1] It may be the case that one is forced into a position of natural theology after considering the finite character of human beings. However, this theological/metaphysical position concludes to a stronger position. Without God, this position affirms, a consistent account of the metaphysical and moral foundation of natural law in Aquinas is impossible.

b. *Natural Kind Metaphysics*:
An alternative metaphysical theory argues that the existence of natural kinds – essences in Thomas – is a self-sufficient ontological inquiry. Aquinas is at least doing this in his metaphysical discussions. In other words, what is necessary for an adequate metaphysical underpinning for natural law in Aquinas is a theory of natural kinds. The question regarding a dependency-relation to God is a second order question, which follows only after the question of natural kinds has been resolved.

Anthony J. Lisska, "The Metaphysical Presuppositions of Natural Law in Thomas Aquinas: A New Look at Some Old Questions," in *Virtue's End: God in the Moral Philosophy of Aristotle and Aquinas*, ed. F. Di Blassi, J.P. Hochschild, and J. Langan (South Bend, IN: St. Augustine's Press, 2008), pp. 68–79.

This distinction of two versions of a metaphysical theory and its consequences in Aquinas is necessary for this analysis. In responding to Position (a) above, one might argue that the theological/metaphysical critics have begged the question on the nature of metaphysical inquiry. Thomist critics of the new natural law theory need to recall that a natural law philosopher like Henry Veatch argued that a self-sufficient ontological position on human nature was sufficient for articulating a theory of natural law. Veatch elucidated a consistent theory of natural law using properties of human nature as the foundation for this theory. In his *Rational Man*, Veatch wrote: "I wish to set forth a book on ethics, ethics without religion, if you will."[2] Veatch occupies a middle ground between the Finnis/Grisez "New Natural Law" position and the Thomist metaphysical/theological position defended by Long and Di Blasi. Hence, the ontological work of Veatch is important in these discussions.[3] Articulating the role of ethical naturalism derived from human nature itself is in itself a valuable philosophical investigation; moreover, it is compatible with the moral philosophy of Thomas.

Burnyeat on Incomprehensibility of Form in Aquinas: A Problem

For St. Thomas, a theory of essence depends on a theory of substantial form. Among several recent critiques of the concept of form in Aristotelian philosophy, one of the more widely read is Myles Burnyeat's "Is An Aristotelian Philosophy of Mind Still Credible?" in which Burnyeat argued that Aristotelian ontology is not credible, and moreover "ought to be junked."[4] This wholesale "junking" applies equally to Aquinas's moral theory insofar as natural law depends on a theory of essence that is based on substantial form. Burnyeat bases his conclusions on modern philosophy's dismissal of Aristotelian hylomorphism. According to Burnyeat, modern philosophy, riding on the coattails of the rise of the new science with its theory of corpuscular matter, rejected unequivocally any theoretical significance for matter and form put forward in medieval philosophy. Matter was no longer the "enformed" matter characteristic of medieval Aristotelianism. The demise of matter/form ontology entails the rejection of ethical naturalism in Thomas, since ethical naturalism depends foundationally on some acceptance of matter and form as necessary for an Aristotelian essence. Simply put, Burnyeat argued that a theory of ontological hylomorphism is neither acceptable nor understandable by contemporary philosophers.[5]

One might offer two rejoinders to what Burnyeat affirmed concerning the rejection of a philosophical theory of form in analytic philosophy. Both rejoinders suggest that contemporary ontology must consider the issue of the formal structures of reality. The first response to Burnyeat, developed in some detail below, is drawn from the writings of Everett J. Nelson, with special emphasis on his "The Metaphysical Presuppositions of Induction."[6] Nelson argues that scientific laws require synthetic necessary (*a priori*) categories of causality and substance. What Nelson proposes is similar structurally to the Aristotelian concepts of formal cause and primary substance found in the writings of Aquinas. Hence, matter is "structured" in a formal way.

The second response, only briefly sketched here because of space limitations, comes from the recent work of Hilary Putnam[7] and John Haldane.[8] Both Putnam and Haldane suggest that the model of efficient causality prominent in early modern philosophy – and adopted in principle by Burnyeat with his rejection of matter/form ontology – fails to provide an adequate foundation for perception theory in the philosophy of mind. Haldane argues that what contemporary philosophy of mind requires is a return to the Aristotelian hylomorphism found in the writings of Thomas. Haldane writes: "I will proceed boldly and suggest that progress (in the philosophy of mind) may be achieved by making use of the ancient doctrine of hylomorphism."[9] Haldane argues that "formal identity" between mind and thing is a necessary condition in order for awareness to be "veridical" in any significant sense of the term. Therefore, the philosophical dialectic Haldane proposes requires some account of form in order for a theory of perception to cohere theoretically. A discussion of matter/form ontology articulated in the writings of Aquinas, therefore, offers important insights for several issues discussed in contemporary analytic philosophy.

Burnyeat's rejection of Aristotelian ontology theory based on his analysis that modern theories of matter entail the rejection of form will not pass muster in either contemporary metaphysics or philosophy of mind. Insofar as Nelson and Putnam/Haldane argue for the necessity of "enformed" matter, both offer rejoinders to Burnyeat's thesis. Therefore, since substantial form is a necessary condition for developing a theory of natural kinds, and since Thomas's ethical naturalism in his natural law theory is dependent upon a concept of natural kinds, it follows that the establishment of the ontological necessity for form is a necessary condition for undertaking a justification of ethical naturalism.

Everett J. Nelson and Synthetic Necessary Properties: A Realist Ontology

One way of reestablishing the importance of substantial form in contemporary metaphysical discussions is through an analysis of Nelson's arguments postulating the necessity of synthetic necessary causal properties. This work is propaedeutic towards establishing a theory of natural kinds.

In opposition to the prevalent "event ontologies" proposed in early analytic philosophy by Russell and Ayer, among others, Nelson argued for an ontology rooted in substance. These substances, moreover, had synthetic necessary causal connections between them that justified inductive knowledge. In his "The Relation of Logic to Metaphysics," Nelson argued that "…a function of philosophy is to reveal the presuppositions of our beliefs about the world and to construct a hypothesis which satisfies these presuppositions and interrelates those to all fields of knowledge."[10] In his American Philosophical Association Presidential address, Nelson asked the following question important for any realist ontology: "Just what must the principle of induction assert about *the formal structure of the world* in order that it and the empirical data, taken together, would entail the likelihood of the conclusion?"[11] Nelson argued that a justified principle of induction requires as a necessary condition "…the truth of some non-empirical principle that entails that the world or course of events embodies a type of unity that can ground laws and such that instances of them are evidence for them."[12] The realist thrust of Nelson's ontology is readily apparent. He proposed formal structures to reality, a metaphysical claim denied by Burnyeat.

Nomic and Accidental Universal Propositions

Nelson postulated real connections of causality in order to justify what he took to be the real distinction between "nomic universal propositions" and "accidental universal propositions." A nomic universal proposition would be a genuine law-like statement. An accidental universal proposition would be a general statement based on a property that does not generate a law-like proposition.

Examples of nomic universal propositions would be the following:

a. "An acid and a base yield a soluble salt and water."
b. "All humans are mortal."
c. "All crows are black."

Examples of accidental universal statements would be the following:

a. "All the new buildings on the Notre Dame campus are beige brick."
b. "All the chairs in this room are blue."
c. "All Yuppies drive Sport Utility Vehicles and talk incessantly on cell phones while driving."

According to Nelson, only a nomic universal proposition will hold under the scrutiny of a "contrary to fact" or "subjunctive conditional" statement. For instance, one might state categorically: "*Were* this an acid and a base, it *would* yield a soluble salt and water." Under normal conditions, one cannot imagine an instance in chemistry when an acid and a base would not yield a soluble salt and water. An acid and a base are connected causally in virtue of what their predicates signify *in rerum natura*.

Conversely, the same contrary to fact or subjunctive conditional will *not* hold for an accidental universal proposition: "Were there a chair in this room, it would necessarily be blue." The subjunctive conditional does not hold in this case because there is nothing about being a chair in this room that necessitates that it be blue. It might be brown, purple, red, green, or whatever. A Franciscan Missionary of Mary in Northern Alaska might own a SUV and use a cell phone in order to make her ministry rounds in the winter season over the frozen tundra; one would hardly call her a "Yuppie"! One can disconfirm easily any accidental universal proposition. A contrary to fact conditional, however, will hold for nomic universal propositions. Nelson argued that this real, categorical distinction and ontological difference must be justified.[13]

Synthetic Necessary Connections in the World

Nelson proposed that the distinction between nomic and accidental universal propositions can be affirmed only if some ontological categories are true of the world. The connection between an acid and a base, for instance, is more than an accidental grouping of properties. It is not, so Nelson argues, merely a randomly assembled class of properties or a "heap" of qualities. The connection, moreover, is not reducible to an analytic proposition, because the causal connection between an acid and a base does not depend on the use of language. The category of cause is not reducible to a linguistic or conceptual connection. Nelson's account is similar to what Saul Kripke, in *Naming and Necessity*, among other places, once called the "metaphysically necessary."[14] Kripke calls the "metaphysically necessary" a truth that is dependent on reality. This concept is not a mere convention of human language. Hence, the "metaphysically necessary" is not coextensive with the semantic notion of "analytic necessity" common in English speaking philosophy since Hume. Kripke suggests that the proposition, "Water is H_2O," is a metaphysically necessary truth because something would not be water if it were not H_2O. This is the essence, or what Kripke calls the "natural kind" of water. This structure is the nature of the kind of thing water is, and it is, Kripke argues, true in all possible worlds. Kripke's concept of the metaphysically necessary is commensurate with what Aquinas holds for a substantial form. For Aquinas, like Aristotle, an account of an essence is more than a modal necessity. Aquinas intends a *de re* (about things) necessity and not a *de dicto* (about language) necessity. This *de re* necessity entails a synthetic necessary claim about the nature of reality. There are real, causal connections in the world, which causal connections Aquinas grounds in his concept of substantial form.

If the causal connection is not analytic, then it must be synthetic. Furthermore, since it is necessary, it cannot be *a posteriori*. Nelson argues, therefore, that this connection is synthetic *a priori* or synthetic necessary. It is a necessary connection, but one which is true of the world. Nelson suggests that his theory of causal necessities "…asserts that there is something that transcends what a phenomenalist, positivist, or strict empiricist would be willing to admit." The realist overtones of Nelson's ontology are apparent; he adopts a form of ontological realism.

The absence of causal connections in a metaphysical system, Nelson argues, entails the following philosophical paradoxes:

> In fact, the assumption that there are only factual uniformities leaves us with a chaos:
> (a) *ontological* because everything would be completely independent of everything else;
> (b) *epistemological* because no inferential knowledge beyond the immediately given would be possible.[15]

Nelson concludes his analysis with the following remarks: "If the theory of the presuppositions of induction… is at least in principle sound, the only alternative to scepticism is the acknowledgment that some non-empirical metaphysics is true."[16] Commenting on the structure of Nelson's argument, Morris Weitz once wrote that each ontological category Nelson presented "… is presupposed as part of a network of ontological features without which our ordering of experience is incoherent…; they … are the very ontological features and structures which make knowledge possible."[17] This demonstrates that Nelson adopts both "ontological realism" and "epistemological realism."

Nomic universal propositions require the category of real causal connections, which are sortal properties. Furthermore, these causal relations, which are synthetic *a priori* connections in the world, are rooted in a substance. Nomic universal propositions presuppose an ontology of causal entities, which are the formal causal structures of the world. This is, in turn, what Aquinas meant by a *forma substantialis*. Nelson argues that a presupposition of mere uniformities alone is never sufficient to account for inductive knowledge. In his "A Defense of Substance," Nelson once wrote that the category of substance provides "... the connection presupposed by the *stable* compresence of qualities and... of dispositional properties (as well as) to connect the successive states of a series exemplifying a law."[18]

Weitz suggested that the theme running through Nelson's ontological studies was the search for what Weitz called "the grounds of sense."[19] In other words, how do philosophers go about making sense knowledge hang together in a consistent and thoughtful manner? For Nelson, the ultimate ontological category is substance. Like a primary substance in Aristotle and Aquinas, substance for Nelson is "...the ground of power, stability, order and causality in the world."[20] This is, it would appear, coextensive with an Aristotelian primary substance.

Therefore, what Nelson calls a synthetic necessary causal connection is similar structurally to what Aquinas means by a substantial form. A substantial form in Aquinas's metaphysics ties together the real connections in the world of sense. Without a substantial form, Aquinas could not argue for the difference between essential and accidental predications, or for a difference in properties upon which the predications are asserted. Nelson suggests that analytic philosophy, finely wrought, cannot sustain itself without metaphysical presuppositions. Aquinas would say the same about medieval Aristotelian philosophy. For Nelson, the two fundamental ontological categories are causality and substance. For Aquinas, the two categories are substantial form and primary substance. Weitz rendered the following summary statement on Nelson's ontology:

> Now since induction presupposes cause and cause presupposes substance, ... (Nelson's) solution for the validity of induction is a world that, whatever else it may have, contains synthetic causal connections among certain events that are unified in a substantive manner.[21]

Hence, if nomic universal propositions hold, it follows that reality must be structured by an ontological category of form. This analysis of induction put forward by Nelson offers one refutation to the Burnyeat thesis. This is, therefore, a dialectic that establishes the ontological necessity for the existence of natural kinds. This natural kind metaphysics is a necessary condition for ethical naturalism in Aquinas.[22]

Thomas Aquinas and the *Summa Theologiae*

Given the recent renaissance of natural law, one needs to consider briefly the old questions of natural law and how these questions relate to the new look of contemporary philosophy rooted in a theory of natural kinds.[23] The classical canon of natural law theory is the set of relevant passages in Questions 90–97 from the *Prima Secundae* of the Aquinas's *Summa Theologiae*. In addition, a structurally similar account is found in Thomas's *Commentary on the Nicomachean Ethics*.

Two principal points need addressing in Aquinas's account of ethical naturalism rooted in the works of Aristotle: (a) the foundation of a theory of the human person and (b) the requirement of reason as opposed to voluntarism.

The Human Person and the Requirements of Reason

Aquinas bases his moral theory, and *a fortiori* his theory of human or positive law and a derivative but not an explicit theory of human rights, on the foundation of the human person as an instance of a natural kind. Aquinas argues that a human person is, by definition, a substantial unity grounding a set of potentialities, capacities, or dispositions. The substantial form is the ontological ground for this set of dispositional properties. Aquinas divides these capacities into three generic headings, which serve as the basis of this theory of natural kinds for human persons. This is Aquinas's account of human nature – the human natural kind – which is based upon the insights of Aristotle's *Nicomachean Ethics*:[24]

1.   The set of Living Dispositions (what humans share with plants);
2.   The set of Sensitive Dispositions (what humans share with animals);
3.   The set of Rational Dispositions (what renders humans unique in the material realm).

Thomas's ethical naturalism provides for the moral protection that prevents, in principle, the hindering of the development of the basic human dispositions. Considered schematically, a living disposition is the capacity or drive all living beings have to continue in existence. In human persons, this capacity is to be protected.[25] Had humans been created or evolved (e.g., evolution through the *rationes seminales* of Augustine) differently, a different set of proscriptions would hold. A protection is what it is because human nature is what it is. This analysis is similar structurally to what H. L. A. Hart in his discussion of the "natural necessities" in the *Concept of Law* called the human right to the protection against violence.[26]

In a similar fashion, one of the rational dispositions Aquinas considered is the drive human beings have to know – our innate curiosity to know and to understand. Aquinas suggests that this disposition is only developed when human persons know propositions that are true. Hence, human persons have a "moral claim" to the truth. Again, these basic claims protect what human persons are as human beings. Finnis once argued, for instance, that college faculty have an obligation not to teach that which is known to be false, because this fractures the right to true propositions, which right students as human persons possess intrinsically. Finnis offered the same principle for political, academic, and religious leaders. This is based upon the classic position of "a conception of human dignity and worth, precisely as it bears on the interpersonal act of communication."[27]

The English Dominican, Columba Ryan, once wrote that these three general aspects of human nature are "the good of the individual survival, biological good, and the good of human communication."[28] In his *The Morality of Law*,[29] Lon Fuller argued for communication as a necessary condition for what he referred to as substantive theory of natural law. Martin Golding referred to the living dispositions as the "basic requirements of human life," the sensitive dispositions as the "basic requirements for the furtherance of the human species," and the rational dispositions as "the basic requirements for the promotion of [a human person's] good as a rational and social being."[30] In his *Aquinas*, Finnis writes as follows:

> The order Aquinas has in mind is a metaphysical stratification: [1] what we have in common with all substances, [2] what, more specifically, we have in common with other animals, and [3] what is peculiar to us as human beings.[31]

Martha Nussbaum once suggested eight fundamental properties: "we can nonetheless identify (as) certain features of our common humanity, closely related to Aristotle's original list." Nussbaum's eight characteristics are mortality, the body, pleasure and pain, cognitive capability, practical reason, early infant development, affiliation or a sense of fellowship with other human beings, and humor.[32] In his *Natural Law and Natural Rights*, Finnis puts forward what he takes to be a list of basic human goods: life, knowledge, play, aesthetic experience, friendship, practical reasonableness, and religion.[33] The point here is that these theories of ethical naturalism depend upon the concept of the human person and require the "functioning well" of that person – all of which are rooted in Aristotle's concept of *eudaimonia* or "happiness." Furthermore, except for Finnis, *eudaimonia* is rooted in the natural kind of the human person, which is the metaphysical foundation necessary for moral theory in natural law theory. Moreover, the necessity of reason as opposed to will is emphasized continually in the writings of Thomas. Throughout his discussion of law-making and moral theory, Aquinas argues that reason is to be employed with vigor. Law is, as Aquinas emphatically states, "an ordinance of reason." A purely voluntarist account of either moral theory or jurisprudence, according to Aquinas, is incorrect.[34]

The Naturalistic Fallacy and a Theory of Obligation

When considering natural law theory as a form of ethical naturalism, two important philosophical questions remain that need to be addressed:

1. The issue of the "naturalistic fallacy."
2. The derivation of a theory of obligation.

Briefly, a dispositional account of human essence enables Aquinas to transcend the naturalistic fallacy. The "good" is the end to be attained, which is the development of the dispositional property. Hence, a "value" is not added onto a fact; rather, a value is the further development of a dispositional fact. Disposition and end are in the same ontological category of natural properties, the former the formal cause and the latter the final cause. Neither Hume nor Moore considered the possibility of developmental or dispositional properties. In fact, the concept of a mathematical class dominates the discussion of essence in modern philosophy. Descartes dismissed the Aristotelian position on dispositional properties, and this dismissal has remained regnant through most modern and contemporary philosophical discussions of essence or class defining properties. Nothing is more opposed to a dispositional analysis than a mathematical concept of class.

Aquinas, next, adopts what might be called a "metaphysics of finality." Veatch uses this concept in several of his works, which is gleaned from the insights of R.-A. Gauthier, who first addressed the issues of the metaphysics of finality.[35] The ends to be attained are determined by the content of the natural kind of the human person; this differs radically from ordinary teleological theories like utilitarianism. Therefore, the dispositional view of human nature enables Aquinas's version of natural law theory not to succumb to the charges of the naturalistic fallacy and provides a justification for a theory of obligation. In other words, these ends ought to be obtained because of the very dispositional structure of human nature. The ends are not arbitrary because they are determined by the natural kind of human nature itself. Obligation is rooted in the ends themselves.

An important jurisprudential corollary follows from this analysis. The role that this theory of ethical naturalism contributes to successful law making should be apparent. Any law, which, all things being equal, hinders the development of a natural disposition in a human person, is inherently unjust. Aquinas provides a set of criteria by means of which a theory of natural rights could be developed, and from that, a justified theory of law. This jurisprudence derivation is, however, beyond the limits of this analysis.

Notes

1   Steven Long, "Natural Law or Autonomous Practical Reason: Problems for the New Natural Law Theory," in John Goyette, Mark S. Latkovic, and Richard S. Myers: *St. Thomas Aquinas and the Natural Law Tradition: Contemporary Philosophical and Theological Perspectives* (Washington, DC: Catholic University of America Press, 2004); Fulvio Di Blasi. *God and the Natural Law: A Rereading of Thomas Aquinas* (Notre Dame, IN: St. Augustine Press, 2006).

2   Henry Veatch, *Rational Man* (Indianapolis, IN: The Liberty Fund, 2003), p. xxvii.

3   Additional works of Henry Veatch include *For an Ontology of Morals* (Evanston, IL: Northwestern University Press, 1973) and *Human Rights: Fact or Fancy?* (Baton Rouge, LA: Louisiana State University Press, 1985), among others.

4   M. F. Burnyeat, "Is an Aristotelian Theory of Mind Still Credible?" in Martha Nussbaum and Amelie Rorty: *Essays on Aristotle's* De Anima Oxford: OUP, 1995.

5   Burnyeat's philosophy of mind also appears to argue against what he took to be the materialist/physicalist account of Aristotle put forward by Richard Sorabji in "Intentionality and Physiological Processes: Aristotle's Theory of Sense-Perception," in Nussbaum and Rorty, pp. 195–225. Martha Nussbaum and Hilary Putnam wrote an extensive response to the Burnyeat challenge to Aristotle's philosophy of mind. In essence, they refute the materialist account put forward by Sorabji and offer a modified functionalist account of Aristotle. In this author's judgment, all three philosophers neglected a theory of intentionality. It is by intentionality theory that Aristotle and Aquinas find a middle ground between Cartesian dualism on the one hand and the physicalism of many contemporary studies in the philosophy of mind on the other. These issues in the philosophy of mind and intentionality theory, however, are beyond this discussion of ethical naturalism in Thomas Aquinas.

6   Presidential address delivered at the Sixty-fifth Annual Meeting of the Western Division of the American Philosophical Association, and printed in the *Proceedings and Addresses of the American Philosophical Association: 1996–1968* (Yellow Springs, OH., 1967), pp. 19–33; reprinted in Anthony J. Lisska, *Philosophy Matters* (Columbus: Merrill, 1977), pp. 249–60.

7   Hilary Putnam, "Aristotle's Mind and the Contemporary Mind;" p. 29. John Haldane kindly shared an unpublished manuscript. The essay has since appeared in *Aristotle and Contemporary Science*, eds. Demetra Sfendoni-Mentzou, Jagdish Hattiangadi, and David M. Johnson (New York: Peter Lang, 2000), vol. 1, pp. 7–28.

8   John Haldane, "A Return to Form in the Philosophy of Mind," in *Form and Matter: Themes in Contemporary Metaphysics*, edited by David S. Oderberg (Oxford: Blackwell Publishers, 1999), p. 54.

9   Haldane, *op. cit.*, p. 41.

10   *The Philosophical Review*, Vol. LVIII, # 1 (January, 1949), p. 1.

11   Nelson, "The Metaphysical Presuppositions of Induction," found in Lisska, p. 256 (italics not in the original).

12   Nelson, *Ibid.*

13   Nelson reminds one of Aristotle's *Categories* [lb] where Aristotle affirms the distinction between properties "said of" and properties "found in" primary substances. Properties "said of" are reducible to nomic universal statements; these are the sets of essential or sortal properties that

determine a natural kind. On the other hand, properties "found in" are reducible to accidental universal properties. These accidental properties do not determine the essence of the thing but are related, as Aquinas would say, in a *per accidens* manner to the individual.

14   Saul Kripke, "Identity and Necessity," in *Identity and Individuation*, edited by Milton K. Muniz (New York: New York University Press. 1971). pp. 144–46.

15   *Ibid.*, p. 258 (italics not in the original).

16   *Ibid.*, p. 260.

17   Morris Weitz, "The Grounds of Sense," *Philosophy and Phenomenological Research*, Vol. 33. # 4 (June, 1973). p. 460. This is the best overall account of Nelson's ontological commitments found in the literature.

18   *The Philosophical Review*, Vol. LVI, # 5 (September, 1947), p. 499. This is the printed version of Nelson's Pacific Division American Philosophical Association Presidential Address. Nelson was at that time a member of the faculty at the University of Washington before joining the faculty at The Ohio State University as Chair.

19   Weitz, *op cit*.

20   *Ibid.*, p. 466.

21   *Ibid.*

22   A parallel way of approaching the need for form in contemporary philosophical discussions is in the area of philosophy of mind. This has been pursued by John Haldane. Taking his cues from philosophers who recently have defended some version of direct realism (Donald Davidson, John McDowell, Hilary Putnam, and Wilfred Sellars), Haldane has pointed to formal causality as the ontological basis of epistemology. See Haldane, "A Return to Form in the Philosophy of Mind," *op. cit.*, pp. 40–64, as well as "Insight, Inference and Intellection," in *Proceedings of the American Catholic Philosophical Association*, "Insight and Inference," Vol. 75, 1999 (Bronx, NY: Fordham University, 2000).

23   Those interested in this recent revival of natural law theory might consult the author's review essay on eight books in the *American Catholic Philosophical Quarterly*, forthcoming.

24   Thomas Aquinas. *Summa Theologiae*, I–II, Q. 94, a. 2.

25   While both Finnis and Veatch, among others, have developed a theory of human rights from the writings of Aquinas, nonetheless there is not developed explicitly in Aquinas a theory of rights. The work of Brian Tierney might be consulted on these issues. However, a right is determined on the foundation of protecting the basic human dispositional properties.

26   H. L. A. Hart, *The Concept of Law* (Oxford: Oxford University Press, 1961), pp. 194 ff.

27   Finnis, *Aquinas: Moral, Political and Legal Theory* (Oxford: Oxford University Press, 1998), p. 160.

28   Columba Ryan, O.P., "The Traditional Concept of Natural Law: An Interpretation," in *Light on the Natural Law*, edited by Iltud Evans, O.P. (Baltimore: Helicon Press, Inc., 1965), p. 28.

29   Lon Fuller, *The Morality of Law* (New Haven, CT: Yale University Press, 1964).

30   Martin Golding, "Aquinas and Some Contemporary Natural Law Theories," *Proceedings of the American Catholic Philosophical Association (1974)*, pp. 242–43.

31   Finnis, *Aquinas, op. cit.*, p. 81.

32   Nussbaum, "Non-Relative Virtues," in Martha Nussbaum and Amartya Sen (eds.), *The Quality of Life* (Oxford: Clarendon Press, 1993), pp. 263–64.

33   Finnis, *Natural Law and Natural Rights* (corr. ed.) (Oxford: Clarendon Press, 1982), pp. 85–92. Finnis argues that this set of basic goods is known by practical reason and not grounded in a philosophical anthropology. Haldane and this author have suggested that this awareness appears reducible to intuition as elucidated by Sir David Ross in *The Right and the Good*.

34   In contemporary jurisprudence, both Fuller and Golding defend versions of reason in opposition to voluntarism.

35   Veatch, *Swimming Against the Current in Contemporary Philosophy* (Washington, DC: Catholic University of America Press, 1990), p. 116; Veatch acknowledges his debt to Gauthier.

3.3.3 Russell Wilcox
"Natural Law and the Foundations of Social Theory"

A Crucial Distinction

Now, speaking of such a range in this way is to speak in the abstract about the pre-conditions of particular embodiments, it is not yet to attend to those embodiments themselves, nor to the habitual mechanisms which ensure those embodiments a more than merely transitory existence. In order to bring in this aspect of the story, it is necessary to explore a distinction both Aristotle and Aquinas make: namely, that between the possession of a capacity to act, on the one hand, and the employment or use of that a capacity, on the other. Each of these dimensions of human action they see as being the concern of a particular subset of habits or acquired action potentials. Hence the related distinction they draw between the intellectual virtues and the moral or appetitive virtues, virtue being understood as an acquired operative disposition toward the good or proper functioning of its possessor. This distinction they take to be between 'virtue' in the full and complete sense of that term, and 'virtue' in only a derived sense.[1] If the definition of virtue connects it to the proper functioning of its possessor, it must constitute a disposition to act well with respect to the human being as a whole, not just with respect to one or a few of his/her characteristic activities. Virtue in the fullest sense is thus said to confer on its possessor, beyond a mere "aptness to act," also a propensity toward the "right use of that aptness."[2] It is this disposition to act well with respect to the human being as a whole that the moral or appetitive virtues do seem to confer, and it is, in consequence, to these types of disposition that the term virtue is capable of being applied in its fullest sense. At the same time, it is also true that developed capacities to perform particular activities or accomplishments, mere 'aptnesses to act', do indeed contribute to the overall good of their possessors, provided that they are employed in an appropriate manner. The fact that these developed capacities, those conferred by the habit of art in the practical intellect and various habits of the theoretical intellect, are capable of being employed either well or badly means that they can be termed virtues in only a relative or analogical sense. They relate to the development and perfection of particular powers, but they do not – at least intrinsically – relate to the good of their possessor as a whole.

A consequence of this distinction is that there is to every action both a technical and a moral aspect. These aspects are, of course, inextricably bound together in the unity of the particular act. Nevertheless, they admit of appraisals which remain analytically distinct.[3] Moreover, the fact that each aspect is related to a different type of habit indicates that they are lodged in different parts of the overall human *habitus*. Not only does this point to the peculiar unity-in-diversity that each human action represents, it also highlights the fact that different habits and sets of habits are capable of developing in relative independence of each other. For reasons, we do not have the space to enter into here, this is true in a much more limited sense with respect to the virtues of the appetite, since they are braced together in a relatively tight form of co-implication. It is much more true of the various virtues of the theoretical intellect and of art. More relevantly for present purposes, it points to the fact that whilst both appetitive and intellectual virtues are functionality facilitative of human action, they are facilitative in different ways.

This difference relates precisely to the fact pointed to above that the moral virtues – defined and structured as virtues by the same principles underlying the precepts of the natural law – hold the human action system in a functionally optimal state in terms of its overall or generalized character as human, being concerned as they are with the good of the whole person. The intellectual virtues and art, in contrast, are concerned with the development of the particular habits of thought and skilled accomplishments which are ordered towards, and thus enable, the production of particular goods. These goods result either from the production of particular items or networks of knowledge in the human mind, or from the embodying production of particular works of art in the external world. Importantly, since appetitive virtues are concerned with keeping to a mean, that mean necessarily sets a limit to their potential expansion. Once the mean has been achieved, the concern is that it should be maintained in all subsequent action. Such is not the case with the virtues of the intellect and art. In contrast to the appetitive virtues, the virtues of the intellect and art are capable, at least in principle, of infinite expansion.[4] It is precisely the intellectual virtues, then, which enable us to *realize* new possibilities, and to do so without limit,[5] in multiple individual and collective contexts.

Just as it is the diverse habits associated with the intellectual virtues and with art that make possible the production of particular goods, so too it is they which make possible, and indeed come to embody, the production of particular cultural forms, as well accounting for the huge variety that these forms are apt to display. Differing cultures, then, can be understood as embodying in multiple and complex ways, distinctive sets or stocks both of speculative and of practical knowledge, as well as the conditioning attitudes to a whole range of subjects that can only be accounted for as developing out of the particular experiences of particular peoples. When these stocks are fully placed within the inherently inter-personal contexts within which they emerge, this diversity is hugely intensified. They come to include the complexes of interactions, organizations and institutionalized practices connected to the production, use and transmission of symbols and other cultural 'artefacts' or 'products' over time. Indeed, as they attain durability and relative autonomy, these complexes themselves become part of both the artefactual and habitual complement of each culture, and thus become, in their turn, intimately involved in the active development and successive reconfiguration of human consciousness and of the material world that the construction of each culture involves.

All of this makes clear that it is the potential for infinite expansion of the intellectual virtues and art which ultimately makes real human societal growth and development possible, and that it is an inherent part of that growth that it will be signed by a deep-seated diversity. Owing to the unity of the human action system as a whole, however, it is necessary that the development of these intellectual virtues and habits of art always take place in a ways which are congruent with the virtues of the appetite and thus with the precepts of the natural law, if growth is not to be replaced, instead, with decay. Thus the new possibilities opened up by the skills and habits embodied in the virtues of the intellect and art, require that we discern at each instance of their potential realization, whether or not the proposed course of action to be undertaken is, or is not, in accord with the appetitive mean of the moral virtues and the natural law,[6] and this need for discernment applies as much to actions of a collective nature as it does to those of an individual nature.

There exists, then, an enormous realm of legitimate individual and collective human choice and the making of such choice leaves an inevitable habitual trace, in ways that condition and give character to the individual and the culture of which he or she is part. What determines that realm of legitimacy is whether or not the types of action undertaken are respectful of the overall integrity of the human action system as a whole. If they are not, they serve to undermine that system and thereby to restrict the scope and number of truly human possibilities it serves to furnish. It is only possible that an act falls within this realm of legitimate choice if it is chosen with the correct set of appetitive (moral) dispositions, and thus in a way which is compliant with the basic precepts of the natural law. In this sense, the precepts of the natural law can be seen as laying down a set of parameters specifying what is, and what is not, in accord with the full flourishing of the human form. There are many such choices which can be made and activities undertaken with the correct appetitive dispositions and thus in a way which falls within the parameters of legitimacy specified by the natural law. Although, these actions will not actually be required by the natural law, they can still be spoken of as being part of it, since "nature does not bring in their contrary," and they are thus undertaken, if they are undertaken, in full compliance with it.[7] Even if they are undertaken, however, it will not be sufficient for their performance merely that the correct appetitive dispositions be present, they also need to be supplemented by the development of more or less sophisti-cated, technical, competences. It is only when both of these are present that there arise the particular activities of a particular skillful individual or group of individuals. It is only at this point that that unity implied by compliance with the common functional requirements of the human form, is joined to the particular [diversely manifest] skills and habits developed by individuals and their communities in their particular habits of individual and collective behavior.

Human Law

In speaking above of the manner in which human beings habitually embody different cultural forms through the individual and collective choices they make, we have simul-taneously been emphasizing the extent to which it is part of man's very nature to be a conventional animal, and of how the building of these various social conventions plays an indispensable role in the actualization of his natural potentialities. Now just, as we saw earlier, there exists – in the natural law – a preceptual complement to the virtues of the appetite, so also there exists a preceptual complement to the virtues of the intellect and to art. This corresponds, in part, to Aquinas' category of human law: that is, to the third type of law in his famous four-fold legal typology. Overall, human law is presented by Aquinas as a sort of determining embodiment of the universal precepts of the natural law in a particular political and/or socio-cultural context. As such, he tells us, there exists in all human law at least some degree of human artistry or creativity in the precise formulation of laws in which the precepts of the natural law are to find expression:

> …it is from the precepts of the natural law, as from general and indemonstrable principles, that the human reason needs to proceed to certain particular determinations of the laws. These particular determinations, devised by human reason, are called human laws.[8]

Within this broader category, however, it is possible to distinguish two sub-types: human or positive law which, when instituted, represents in its substance, the embodiment of mere *deductions* from the precepts of the natural law, and, on the other hand, human or positive law which, when instituted, represents a *determination* or *specification* of the natural law. As Aquinas puts it:

> But it must be noted that something may be derived from the natural law in two ways: first, as a conclusion from premises, secondly, by way of determination of certain generalities. The first way is like to that by which, in sciences, demonstrated conclusions are drawn from the principles: while the second mode is likened to that whereby, in the arts, general forms are particularized as to details: thus the craftsman needs to determine the general form of a house to some particular shape.[9]

He goes on to explain:

> Some things are therefore derived from the general principles of the natural law, by way of conclusions; e.g., that "one must not kill" may be derived as a conclusion from the principle that "one should do harm to no man": while some are derived therefrom by way of determination; e.g., the law of nature has it that the evil-doer should be punished; but that he be punished in this or that way, is a determination of the law of nature.[10]

The point here is that, whilst there may indeed be some minimal creativity as to *form* involved in instituting the first type of human law – human law by *deduction* – when instituting the second type of human law – human law by *determination* – creativity extends also to *content*. Consequently, whilst it can be said, with only slight qualification, that the content of the first type of human law is required to be embodied or mandated, at least in terms of not being contradicted, in any legal system worth the name, such is not the case with respect to the content of the second type of human law. Indeed, since this second type of human law involves determination of both form *and* content, its institution remains almost entirely at the discretion of the legislator.

The analogy between the two types of virtue here – at least when considering the *content* of the two types of human law – is a strong and obvious one. Whilst the first type of human law – human law by *deduction* – in embodying the basic precepts of the natural law, sets down a series of outer-limits within the confines of which legislators can exercise their free, contentful, creativity, that creativity is only actually exercised in the institution of the second type of human law – human law by *determination*. Thus the first type of human law, when instituted, will embody the same norms of optimality as do the appetitive virtues, whereas the second type of human law will embody a range of properly human artifacts, involving the type of artistry made possible by the virtues of the intellect and art. Likewise, whilst both types of human law can be said to *belong* to the natural law, the first type will belong to it in a positive and direct sense, whereas the second type will belong to it only indirectly.[11] What remains clear is that classical natural law theory allows that there can be many, many different determinations, embodied in human law, which are consistent with the natural law, and that these determinations only create legal/moral obligation once they have actually been enacted. What should also be clear, however, is that if attempts are made to institute human laws which contradict the basic precepts of the natural law, that is, which fall *outside* the series of outer-limits referred to above, they will serve, like vices, to institute the types of action which actually cut against and undermine the systemic integrity of human action, and thus of the legislative capacities of the which they purport to be an expression. They will, in other words, amount to a deeply corrosive form of performative self-contradiction. It is for this reason that Aquinas famously denies them the character of law, stating that they are, in fact, merely "a perversion of law."[12] The further implication here, of course, is that, just as the greatest potential variety of cultural forms are made possible only by compliance with the precepts of the natural law as embodied habitually in the moral or appetitive virtues, so too, the greatest potential plurality of properly legal forms are made possible only by a similar such compliance as embodied in the range of humanly posited norm.

The considerable potential relevance of all this to contemporary debates in comparative law should be clear. It is rooted in the fact that we have here a series of mechanisms and distinctions by which to explain, at least in principle, the emergence of an almost infinite series of legal forms and groupings. In teasing this relevance out, however, it needs properly to be appreciated quite how capacious the category of human law is capable of being made. In particular, it is crucial not to conceive of it in overly formalistic terms. The danger of doing so is to render it discordant as a comparative category with much recent work in the field. This has drawn upon schools of jurisprudential reflection – particularly in the areas of legal anthropology, legal pluralism, the sociology of law, and critical legal studies – which have long been concerned to expand the category of legality away from an emphasis upon explicitly articulated norms, especially those associated with the coercive and regulatory apparatus of the nation-state or other associated state-like structures. Instead, they have sought to give full-weight to norms of an altogether more implicit, frequently only partially articulated, nature. This, it has rightly been concluded, is much truer to the full history and range of human experience, since it recognizes that for the longest periods of time, and in the largest number of human societies, the primary means of intra-communal legal regulation has taken place outside of the state, or of structures approximating to the state, and has been of a largely tacit or customary nature. It is also to recognize that even where there does exist an apparent preponderance of explicitly articulated legal norm, this inevitably presupposes a vast deposit of tacit, habitually co-ordinate, understanding and practice upon which such explicit articulation necessarily rests and through which it is able to function.

The fact that classical natural law theory is fully compatible with such an approach, with taking account, that is, of the full range of differing types of legal norm identified and highlighted by these various schools, is shown by the role that Aquinas himself envisages for custom in the institution, alteration and interpretation of human law. Whilst, it is true that he mentions the role of custom in the *Treatise on Law* only very briefly, what he does say is both dense and highly suggestive:

> All law proceeds from the reason and will of the legislator … The reason and the will are manifested in action through words and deeds, for the way one acts shows what he considers to be good. It is clear that human words can change. So also a law can be changed and developed by the repeated actions that comprise custom. In addition something can be established by custom that obtains the force of law because such repeated external actions effectively reveal internal motives of the will and concepts of the reason, since if something is done a number of times it seems to be the result of a deliberate rational decision. In this sense custom has the power of law, it abolishes law, and it acts as the interpreter of law.[13]

At the heart of this passage is an account of how it is possible for habitual action to carry with it preceptual/action-guiding force in the absence of direct command or intended communication. Thus, it is also contains an understanding of the inherently communicative potential of all human action. It is possible, so Aquinas seems to be suggesting, to read off from the behavior of an individual or group of individuals what they value as good as well as to discern the concrete strategies for attaining that/those good(s) they have opted for. In so far as this action becomes habitual and truly collective, it suggests itself in the manner of a practice into which an individual is capable of being initiated either by imitation or by other, more sophisticated, forms of compliance with its underlying operational logic. From this it would also seem to follow that there is some inherently legislative quality in each human action as well as every cultural product that results from it. Surprisingly, such a conclusion would bring natural law thinking into line with proponents of the strong thesis that, at least in some societies, the categories of law and culture can be treated as co-extensive, though it does not, of course, follow from this that such thinking is hostile to those voices which have recently sought to distinguish more clearly different orders and classes of social and legal normativity. The simple and fundamental point, however, is that the framework of which we have been speaking is able both to take account of the full variety of phenomena to which socio-legal scholars have long pointed, and yet also to offer a more comprehensive and coherent explanation of how, in their diversity, these phenomena were/are capable of arising in the first place.

Notes

1   Aristotle, *Eth. Nic.* 2.6 (1106a 22–23) and *ST* Ia IIae, q. 56, a. 3, c., quoted in G. Reichberg, "The Intellectual Virtues," in *The Ethics of Aquinas*, ed. S. Pope (Washington: Georgetown University Press, 2002), p. 141. See also B. Kent, "Habits and Virtues," in the same volume, p. 121.
2   "Only habits that dispose appetite give both capacity and the bent to use that capacity well." R. McInerney, "Ethics," in *The Cambridge Companion to Aquinas*, ed. N. Kretzmann and E. Stump (Cambridge: Cambridge University Press, 1993), p. 204.

3   In particular, whereas moral appraisal relates to the good of the whole person, technical appraisal relates only to the good of the particular work done. As Maritain puts it: "Making is ordered to such-and-such a definite end, separate and self-sufficient, not to the common end of human life; and it relates to the peculiar good or perfection not of the man making, but of the work made." J. Maritain, *Art and Scholasticism*, tr. J. Scanlon (London: Sheed & Ward, 1947), p. 6.

4   *ST* I–II, q. 66. a. 1.

5   This is seen most clearly with respect to the growth of the habits connected to the acquisition of speculative or theoretical knowledge. No matter how much a person knows it is always possible to know something more, and the more knowledge is acquired the more further insight is made possible in the future. This capacity for unlimited expansion is equally characteristic of practical knowledge since, in the case of art, for example, it is always possible to make new things and thus to develop the practical skills and knowledge associated with such making.

6   In other words, these new possibilities need always to be filtered through the virtue of prudence, whose function it is such discernments to make.

7   *ST* I–II, q. 94, a. 5 ad 3. See also *ST* I–II, q. 94, a. 3.

8   *ST* I–II, q. 91, a. 3.

9   *ST* I–II, q. 95, a. 2.

10   Ibid.

11   In the sense that "nature [does] … not bring in the contrary." *ST* I–II, q. 94, a. 5 ad 3.

12   *ST* I–II, q. 95, a. 2. See also *ST* I–II, q. 96, a. 4.

13   *ST* I–II, q. 97, a. 3.

3.3.4 Alasdair MacIntyre
"Theories of Natural Law in the Culture of Advanced Modernity"

But of what advantage is it to Thomists that they are able to invoke a revised Aristotelian conception of human nature in support of their natural law claims?

One answer likely to be suggested is that it can be of no advantage at all but only a source of disadvantage. Since this particular conception of human nature is widely rejected in modem culture, to annex to a set of already controversial theses about natural law an even more controversial claim – that human nature is very much what Aristotle and Aquinas said that it is – may seem to make the cause of commending and justifying the Thomist's view of natural law an even more hopeless one. But this pessimistic response ignores one crucial resource that the Thomist's account of human nature provides. What that account does enable us to understand is why, if the Thomist's view of natural law is true, we should expect that under certain types of circumstance it will be widely rejected. An Aristotelian Thomism has implicit within it a theory of moral and legal error, a theory that explains why what is at one level evident to every plain person may nonetheless be expected to be ignored or flouted by significant numbers of those same plain persons, let alone by legal theorists and moral philosophers.

What then is the Thomistic account of the natural law and how, in a Thomistic view, is that law grounded in human nature? I follow Jacques Maritain's exposition of it in *Man and the State*[1] and *La personne et le bien commun*.[2] Two ideas are central to that exposition. The first is that the precepts of the natural law are those rules of reason which a human being obeys, characteristically without explicitly formulating them, when that human being is functioning normally. Natural law, says Maritain, "is the ideal formula of development of a given being."[3] When we are functioning normally, we find ourselves inclined in certain directions and toward certain ends. The precepts of the natural law tell us what are or would be deviations from those directions.

The second central idea – like the first, it is primarily Aquinas's and only secondarily Maritain's – is that human beings are essentially sociable, that I achieve whatever I achieve as an individual by being and acting as an individual who is bound to others

Alasdair MacIntyre, "Theories of Natural Law in the Culture of Advanced Modernity," in *Common Truths: New Perspectives on Natural Law*, ed. E.B. McLean (Wilmington, DE: ISI Books, 2004), pp. 123–128. Reprinted with permission of ISI Books.

through a variety of familial, social, and political relationships expressed in joint activity aimed at achieving our common good. My good therefore is the good of someone who is a part of an ordered set of social wholes. My own good can only be achieved in and through the achievement of the common good. And the common good is that toward which we are inclined when we are functioning normally and developing as we should be. The precepts of the natural law thus direct us toward the common good.

What then is it to know the natural law, if we are functioning normally and are developing in a way that at least approximates our ideal development? Here I go beyond Maritain, although remaining close to Aquinas, by replying that it is to inquire of ourselves and of each other "What is my good? What is our common good?" and to answer these questions by our actions and our practices as much as by our judgments. The life that expresses our shared human nature is a life of practical inquiry and practical reasoning, and we cannot but presuppose the precepts of the natural law in asking and answering those fundamental questions through our everyday activities and practices. Generally and characteristically, the social relationships through which we are able to learn how to identify our individual and common goods correctly and adequately are those relationships governed and defined by the precepts of the natural law. I have to learn about my good and about the common good from family and friends, but also from others within my own community, from the members of other communities, and from strangers; from those much older than I and from those much younger. But how can I have relationships of adequate cooperative inquiry and learning except with those whom I can trust without qualification? And how can I trust without qualification, unless I recognize myself and others as mutually bound by such precepts as those that enjoin that we *never* do violence of any sort to innocent human life, that *we always* refrain from theft and fraud, that *always* tell each other the truth, and that *we always* uphold justice in all our relationships. Throughout a life spent asking and attempting to answer questions about our own good, usually practically, but sometimes theoretically, we are recurrently vulnerable to a variety of harms and dangers from other human beings as well as from the vagaries of our natural environment. It is this vulnerability that makes obedience to the natural law necessary for the normal and right functioning of human nature.

Yet what often does and always can function well is always liable to function badly on occasion. Just as functioning well for human beings partially consists in individuals understanding themselves in a particular way, as engaged together with family, friends, and others in a shared discovery of what their individual goods and their common good are, so the malfunctioning of human nature is characteristically expressed in some kind of systematic misunderstanding. In the cultures of advanced modernity, and most notably in contemporary North America, the form often taken by this misunderstanding is one in which the individual is misconceived as someone who has to *choose* for himself what his good is to be. This conception of the sovereignty and central importance of individual choice is generated by several different but mutually reinforcing features of our dominant contemporary social and moral modes. Consider just one of these.

During our upbringing, morality is commonly presented to us in terms of two distinct sets of principles, self-regarding principles and other-regarding principles. The individual is therefore commonly taught to ask not, "How should we in our familial and communal relationships act together?" but "How far should I regard only the promotion of my own happiness and the protection of my own rights, and how far should I also have regard for the happiness of others and the rights of others?" Underlying this latter question is a conception of society as primarily constituted, not as a web of familial and communal relationships, but as a set of individuals to each of whom everyone else is an 'other'. Once social life is thus conceived, individuals are bound to pose the question of how they are to decide between the competing claims of the self and of others. But there is in fact no rational way to make that decision, as we should have learned from Henry Sidgwick long since. There are only sets of competing principles between whose rival claims individuals each have to make their own choice. So individual choice itself becomes morally sovereign.

On a Thomistic view, this is not surprising. On that view, individuals who have not or not yet developed an adequate conception of the good, perhaps because through social mischance they have had no opportunity to do so, and who, perhaps because of miseducation, have not or not yet recognized themselves as engaged in a cooperative attempt to discover the human good, can be expected to find themselves confronted by the competing claims of a variety of passions and appetites, claims that, lacking an adequate conception of the good, they do not and cannot as yet know how to order. If they then try to decide between those competing claims, without joining in action and inquiry with others, in a way that would require them to attend practically to the injunctions of the natural law – that is, if they try to decide between those competing claims from the standpoint of an isolated nonsocial individual for whom there can be no such thing as the common good – then they will find themselves with no resource for decision, beyond their own individual choices. On a Thomistic view, it is to be expected that under certain social conditions in which adequate moral education is unavailable, the place of individual choice in the moral life will be misunderstood in precisely the way it has been misunderstood in the dominant cultures of advanced modernity.

The exercise of individual choice thus understood, that is, not choice as governed by principles but choice as prior to and determining our principles, is often identified in the contemporary world with the exercise of liberty. Liberty is therefore thought to be threatened whenever it is suggested that the principles that ought to govern over our actions are not in fact principles that are up to us to choose, but principles that we need to discover; But since a Thomistic understanding of natural law commits those who possess it to asserting that human nature is such that rational practical principles are antecedent to and govern choice in rational well-functioning human beings, and that therefore those principles have to be discovered, not chosen, any defense of a Thomistic understanding of natural law is very easily construed as a threat to liberty.

While the Senate was engaged in considering the nomination of Clarence Thomas to the Supreme Court, a rumor circulated that Thomas held something dose to a Thomistic view of natural law – a rumor for which there was and is no foundation whatsoever in any judgments of Justice Thomas – and Senator Joseph Biden at once expressed the fear "that natural law dictates morality to us, instead of leaving matters to individual choice."[4] Senator Biden's instantaneous reaction, presupposing as it did widespread agreement among the general public with his own view, was a symptom of just that kind of social and moral attitude that needs to be understood in Thomistic terms.

Senator Biden, of course, was correct in supposing that he was articulating what would be felt – and 'felt' is the right word – by a very large number of North Americans.

Such modern persons are all too likely to reject any Thomistic understanding of natural law, and most of all what that understanding, or more fundamentally the account of human nature upon which it relies, says to them about their own condition, as one giving expression to a distorted view of the moral life. It therefore turns out to be the case, as I wrote earlier, that if my arguments are sound and my conclusions are true, then many people will reject them. Notice, however, that for so doing you will pay a certain price.

What these people will have deprived themselves of is the only account of natural law that not only is able to explain its own rejection, but also justifies plain persons in regarding themselves as already having within themselves the resources afforded by a knowledge of fundamental law, resources by means of which they can judge the claims to jurisdiction over them of any system of positive law. In the United States today, we inhabit a society in which a system of positive law with two salient characteristics has been developed. At a variety of points, it invades the lives of plain persons, and its tangled complexities axe such that it often leaves those plain persons no alternative but to put themselves into the hands of lawyers. It is notorious that ours has become a society of incessant litigation, in which plain persons can all too rarely hope to resolve matters of dispute by appeal among themselves to evident and agreed moral principles – for the loss of an adequate understanding of the natural law has resulted in a widespread belief that there are no such principles – but instead must resort to the courts and therefore to lawyers. Of course, in any society, there cannot but be some need for positive law and for litigation as a last resort. But it is an index of great moral deprivation in a culture when litigation so often becomes a first resort. Perhaps it has done so because the dominant culture of North American modernity is inimical to any adequate conception of the natural law.[5]

Notes

1   Jacques Maritain, *Man and the State* (Chicago: University of Chicago Press, 1951), 84–94.
2   Maritain, *La personne et le bien commun* (Paris: Brouwer, 1947), 44–56.
3   Maritain, *Man and the State*, 88.
4   *Washington Post*, 8 September 1991.
5   I am indebted to Martin B Golding and Paul Weithman for constructive criticisms of earlier drafts of this essay.

4

Applied Natural Law

4.1 Procreation and the Family

Introduction

Contemporary defenders of the central natural law tradition have provoked a barrage of especially vehement criticism for their continued defense of a particular understanding of sexuality, marriage, and the family. This understanding is that sexual activity is properly confined within a monogamous, non-contracepted, heterosexual marital relationship. The reason for the hostility with which such a view is now received seems to be rooted in the fact that it has become, particularly since the sexual revolution of the 1960s, profoundly counter-cultural. Whilst such generalized hostility is of fairly recent provenance, however, sociologists such as Christopher Lasch have been at pains to point out the extent to which it is rooted in longer-term trajectories, and particularly in the dislocations precipitated by industrialization.[1] As such, it is perhaps only the most noticeable expression of MacIntyre's narrative of discursive ethical dislocation contained in *After Virtue*.

Now, just as it has been felt important to mount a defense of the continued relevance of traditional natural law theory to more foundational philosophical debates, such an enterprise has no doubt been driven, at least in part, by a concern to meet the challenges, and what are seen as the real dangers, of the sexual revolution in an altogether more profound manner. The first piece extracted here is taken once more from the work of Servais Pinckaers,[2] in which he situates the developed natural law teachings of Aquinas on sexuality and marriage in their historical context. In doing so, he pays particular attention to the way in which Aquinas sought to show that the natural inclination towards sexual congress, when correctly understood and integrated within the context of the distinctively rational ends of the human being, could "provide a solid bedrock for the formation

[1]   See especially C. Lasch, *Haven in a Heartless World: The Family Besieged* (New York: W.W. Norton, 1977); *The Minimal Self: Psychic Survival in Troubled Times* (New York: W.W. Norton, 1985); and *The Culture of Narcissism: American Life in an Age of Diminishing Expectation* (New York: W.W. Norton, 1991).
[2]   S. Pinckaers, "Inclination to Sexuality," in *The Sources of Christian Ethics*, tr. M. Noble (Washington, DC: Catholic University of America Press, 1995), pp. 437–456.

The Natural Law Reader, First Edition. Edited by Jacqueline A. Laing and Russell Wilcox.

of virtue," bringing with it a battery of distinctively personal and inter-personal goods which, in the family, issue forth in society's foundational cell. By emphasizing as the ends of conjugality *both* procreation and mutual support, and by showing how the special form of friendship to be had between man and wife is the natural complement, indeed prerequisite, of the special kind of friendship to be had between parent and child, Pinckaers highlights the indispensable contribution that virtues of conjugality make to the fulfillment of the other inclinations of the human person. He also strongly empha-sizes the contrast such an understanding registers with the dualistic understanding of human being – severing, as it does, the physical and the biological from "reason and the moral order" – inaugurated in the writings of Descartes, and lying at the heart of the modern project.

Building on this basis, the second extract is Elizabeth Anscombe's highly controversial defense of Pope Paul VI's renewed condemnation of the immorality of contraception in his 1968 encyclical letter *Humanae Vitae*.[3] With characteristic briskness and drawing upon some of the earlier distinctions she had made in her famous work *Intention*,[4] Anscombe was at pains to explain, amongst other things, why Pope Paul had allowed for the permissibility of natural methods of family planning (what often and incorrectly are still referred to generically as the rhythm method) whilst not that of artificial methods. Many had argued that here was a distinction without a difference since both methods were directed towards the avoidance of conception. Anscombe shows that whilst the remote intention in both may indeed be the same, the direct intention is clearly different and that what Pope Paul was maintaining was illicit was not the avoidance of conception *per se* but, rather, the deliberate rendering of an otherwise fertile act infertile. To adopt this line of argument is of course to place great store by the physical integrity of the sexual act, but to do otherwise is to suggest by implication that the physicality of such an act is somehow in this context sub- or non-personal. It is, in other words, to fall into pre-cisely the sort of dualist ontology highlighted by Pinckaers.

The final extract in this section, "Law, Liberalism and the Common Good," by Jacqueline Laing, highlights the pervasive failure of modern liberalism to account for the demands of the common good and of intergenerational justice.[5] Laing is particularly concerned to criticize the idea that family is socially constructed and thus properly answerable to the demands of unrestrained individual autonomy. Such an idea leads to the family being treated as a set of purely legal and social relationships freed from the link with biology and torn from the needs of future generations. Relying once more on the Aristotelian idea of ends and purposes in life and of genuine human flourishing, she suggests there are universal and timeless human needs that are conceptually absent from the modern liberal account of the family. An industry in biotechnology answering to here-and-now consumer and industry demands cannot account for the needs of future generations. Undermining both present and future individuals, their needs and relation-ships, and future societies as coherent and well-functioning entities able to survive

---

[3]   G.E.M. Anscombe, *Contraception and Chastity* (London: Catholic Truth Society, 1975).
[4]   G.E.M. Anscombe, *Intention*, 2nd edition (Cambridge, MA: Harvard University Press, 2000).
[5]   J. Laing, "Law, Liberalism and the Common Good," in *Human Values*, ed. D. Oderberg and T. Chappell (Basingstoke: Palgrave Macmillan, 2004).

through time, modern liberalism is at a loss to supply the conceptual apparatus with which to ensure intergenerational justice and, indeed, conceptually speaking, its very own survival. She argues that modern liberal accounts are inherently self-destructive because they suffer from a defective account of individual human flourishing and of intergenerational justice.

4.1.1 Servais Pinckaers
"Inclination to Sexuality"

The Dualist Interpretation

In connection with this teaching on sexuality and marriage, we need to be on our guard against a dualist concept of the human person. This originated in the rationalism of recent centuries far more than in Platonism, as is often thought. Dualism was radical in Descartes, who defined man as pure thought and who considered animals, and therefore sensibility and the body, simply as mechanisms. Thus the physical and biological were completely separated from reason and the moral order. Descartes was the interpreter of the mentality of an era in which the exaltation of reason led to contempt for the body as bestial. The temptation then was to reduce sexuality to animality, to treat it as a biological function.

Such a reduction comes about in ethics when the use of sexuality within marriage is seen as an essentially biological process having its own proper laws. If these are observed, the moral quality of this activity is assured. This point of view does indeed take into account a certain fundamental aspect of sexuality, but it is defective because it ignores the fact that in the human person the biological dimension is vitally integrated in a spiritual nature.

We come across a similar tendency to reduction, perhaps in a still stronger form, in the practice of the sciences, where biology, physiology, and psychology are rigorously distinguished, and where the yen for specialization often outweighs a concern for synthesis. Attention will focus on the biological processes of sexuality, allowing for the elaboration of techniques to improve this activity and its results. The predominant criterion for judging sexual behavior will then be health, which remains chiefly in the biological order.

Not only is this perspective false, but it is too restricted to take sufficient account of sexuality as a part of the human person, an activity that ought to serve moral progress. Sexuality should be subject to properly moral criteria, all the more since it normally involves relationships between persons and profoundly affects society.

In order to establish a moral teaching on marriage, it is indispensable to rediscover a sense of the profound unity that joins the biological, psychological, moral, and spiritual

Servais Pinckaers, "Inclination to Sexuality," in *The Sources of Christian Ethics*, tr. M. Noble (Washington, DC: Catholic University of America Press, 1995), pp. 440–447.

dimensions within the human person, and establishes communication among these dimensions without confusing them. Human sexuality has a psychological, moral, and even spiritual aspect. [...] At the same time, the life of the spirit permeates sexuality in order to regulate it. We could even say that without the participation of the body, the human spirit could never find complete fulfillment. We could then show how the natural processes of sexuality (yet to be clarified) have a vital connection with the deep relationships between man and woman, and how the orientation of sexuality to fruitfulness is intimately connected with the demand for fruitfulness which precedes what we might call the law of giving, written at the heart of every love. If it does not know how to give, if it is not fruitful, love will sooner or later die. It is therefore because of the interior demand of love that marriage tends toward physical and spiritual fruitfulness in generation and education.

We are not far now from the problem of freedom. Sexuality cannot be given a real rootedness in the human personality unless we accept the fact that natural inclinations penetrate to the heart of our free will and stand at the origin of our actions. Only freedom for excellence proves to us that we are free not in spite of our sexuality but because of it, since through sexuality the inclination toward the other, which provides the human and moral dimension of sexuality, is exercised in a special way. Thus sexuality can constitute the primary cell of human society. Here the commandment of love of neighbor is fulfilled in a unique way, that commandment which expresses one of the principles of our free, spiritual fruitfulness.

Our Other Natural Inclinations Converge with the Inclination to Marriage

The richness of human sexuality is revealed when we consider how our other natural inclinations find their fulfillment in marriage. I shall indicate this briefly from the point of view of the partners and of the children.

The inclination to the good is fulfilled specifically in conjugal love, which finds in the person of the beloved, and in the lifelong union of bodies and souls, the greatest possible human good and happiness. [...]

The inclination to self-preservation is reinforced in marriage, for the spouses become "two in one flesh" – one being, if you will, in the words of Genesis. In this union they experience a strengthening of their essential nature and of their confidence in facing life's challenges. They realize that together they are enabled to give existence to other beings like themselves, and through mutual support their capacity for action and their concern for self-defense grow and intensify.

The inclination to truth receives a special dimension within marriage through the wholly personal knowledge that is gained. Through love, each partner's knowledge of the other renews and deepens self-knowledge and is fulfilled in a unique way because of the difference and complementarity of the sexes and their psychology.

The inclination to life in society finds its first, most natural, and in a sense most complete realization in marriage. In the mutual relationship of the spouses and the bonds between parents and children we can discern the primitive types of relationships formed within society, and various types of government. According to Aristotle monarchy corresponded to the relationship of father to children, aristocracy to that of husband and wife, and democracy to that between siblings. These correspondences are so profound that we can see in them true paradigms.

From the point of view of the children, it is in the home that they first experience existence, basic to all the later experiences of life. The security of home gives them that personal self-assurance which will vitalize and support their activities in society. By the same token, insecurity bred in childhood by division within the family can have serious repercussions and prevent children from developing a courageous attitude toward life, so necessary for the forming of personality.

Children gain their first experience of love and happiness at home, together with the different kinds of affection they have for father, mother, brothers, and sisters. Home is where they learn, first and foremost. In the heart of the family, children come to know the difference between good and evil and receive their first moral and religious formation. Here, too, they may encounter suffering, dissension, and unhappiness at an extremely intimate level.

In the family, children acquire their earliest knowledge at a particularly impressionable age. They learn their mother tongue, become familiar with concrete objects, they are taught the truths of religion, form their first ideas, and learn how to use them. Their earliest teaching, especially regarding morals, comes from their parents, and that formation in virtue which we have seen to be so necessary for the development of freedom for excellence. Because of this, deficiencies in home education can be particularly damaging.

In the family, children have their original experience of social relationships and they apprehend the diversity of those relationships as they learn to differentiate between their rapport with parents and with other family members. They bring these first relationships with them as they enter into the wider social setting [...] [I]t is at home that children first become aware of authority, and learn to relate to it through personal obedience. [...]

The Two Ends of Marriage

The interpretation of the teaching on the two ends of marriage has been profoundly affected by the nominalist conception of freedom and relationship to others. Within the problematic, these ends – procreation and mutual support – have become rivals, the problem being to determine which is stronger. One stands for nature, with its biological force and the moral obligations it imposes. The other is on the side of the person's freedom and sentiment of love, and also on the side of reason, which claims to rule nature through knowledge. Until recent times, ethicists have maintained the classical position, which taught that procreation was the primary end of marriage. This provided them with a solid, objective basis for establishing the obligations of marriage. Currently, a widespread reversal has been initiated in favor of mutual support – of love and its expression – as an autonomous if not overriding end. This calls into question the very institution of marriage, because of the subjective, individual nature of the emotion of love.

In St. Thomas as in Aristotle, the teaching on the two ends of marriage comes through in a very different thought context, where the ends are seen not as conflicting but rather as converging.

Aristotle discusses the relationship of man and woman in marriage in his study on friendship.[1] He sees conjugal affection as a special form of friendship. It is based on nature, that is, the inclination to reproduction found in all animals, but is realized in a higher way, for it includes all the tasks of family life which the man and woman share together. The conjugal relationship may also be based on virtue and become friendship in the full sense of the word. Aristotle also observes that children are a bond uniting the spouses and that they render the marriage more solid. Finally, the community established by marriage, being the source of a natural relationship, is prior to the political society, in which the natural human inclination to societal life is fulfilled. Clearly, his context is in no wise predominantly "biological" but profoundly human, owing to the theme of friendship. Procreation and mutual support, which manifest the friendship of the spouses, correspond to one another.

St. Thomas speaks out of the same perspective.[2] Taking up the question of marriage as a natural institution, he begins by clarifying the sense in which it is called natural: not in the sense of a compelling force, but rather in the sense of an inclination realized with the help of free will. Already we are beyond the biological and moving into the human and moral plane, which includes the biological. St. Thomas then discusses the two natural ends of marriage, insisting on what is properly human in them. Beyond the generation of children, the end will be their instruction and education until adulthood, and their acquisition of virtues. Here again the parents collaborate in their complementary tasks, in friendship and conjugal love.

St. Thomas does not explain why procreation is the principal end of marriage, but he clarifies its formula: we are dealing with the *bonum prolis*, the good of the child, with all that this includes, especially education, not merely the *generatio prolis*, or generation. That children are the direct and primary end of the union of man and woman was a classical teaching. To question it would be unimaginable. Did not physiology itself testify on its behalf? It was so natural that even the word *nature* came from it, for in both Greek and Latin the primary meaning of the word was "to be born."

We note that the development of the thought, in Aristotle and Cicero as in St. Thomas, took the form of an addition and clarification of what properly pertained to human generation: the education of the children and the mutual support of the spouses, the latter being so important as to constitute a distinct end of marriage, second but in no sense secondary. This end is also natural, consonant with the integral human person, body and soul. Its purpose is to form between the husband and wife a friendship or affection of a unique kind, which has full moral value when it is based on the qualities or virtues of each.

To build a moral theory of marriage, therefore, we need not oppose the two ends to each other, nor set them up as rivals. They should be joined and bonded. The principal end, especially the education of the children, cannot be attained without the mutual collaboration of the spouses, their friendship and affection. Here it is seen as a natural requirement for familial education.

On the other hand, the denial of the first end of marriage leads almost necessarily to the failure of the second. The child is the proper, natural fruit of conjugal love. Spouses who refuse to have children condemn their love to sterility, even on the affective level, and pave the way for its eventual extinction. At every level, love tends naturally to fruitfulness. It is, as it were, a law of generosity inscribed on the soul as well as the body of every man and woman. To infringe upon this law is to compromise the very life of love in its truth and depth.

It is therefore extremely important, in teaching about marriage, to take into account the interdependence and interaction of the two ends of marriage, for they are inseparable. This is the logic of the human reality, deeper and more powerful than all ideas, opinions, feelings, and passions.

We should also note the influence of individualism on the relationship between man and woman. The propensity for defending individual freedom (understood as freedom of indifference) leads to viewing woman's natural destiny to motherhood and her specific share in education as constraints, rather than qualities designed to complement the gifts of the man. In this view the distinction between the sexes engenders rivalry, as well as the hopeless pursuit of the suppression of all differences, which is equally damaging to both. Only the frank, positive acceptance of these differences as complementary aptitudes will allow the reestablishment of collaboration between man and woman. This will result in a balance based on each's recognition of the other, and through their mutual support it will favor the flowering of freedom for excellence. Obviously there will be variations in these natural differences, according to social and cultural backgrounds and conditions. They will lead to dynamic, personal equality, always developing like life itself, and not to be confused with a materialistic, defensive equality.

Notes

1   *Nicomachean Ethics*, 8.12, 1162a 6–8; St. Thomas, *In VIII Eth.*, lect. 12, nn. 1719–1725. Friendship is understood in a broader sense than ours. Its extension equals that of love, of which it is a higher form.
2   Supplement, q 41 a1.

4.1.2 G.E.M. Anscombe
Contraception and Chastity

[…] [I]t was obvious that if a woman just happened to be in the physical state which such a contraceptive brings her into by art no theologian would have thought the fact, or the knowledge of it, or the use of the knowledge of it, straightaway made intercourse bad. Or, again, if a woman took an anovulant pill for a while to check dysmenorrhoea no one would have thought this prohibited intercourse. So, clearly; it was the contraceptive intention that was bad, if contraceptive *intercourse* was: it is not that the sexual act in these circumstances is physically distorted. This had to be thought out, and it was thought out in the encyclical *Humanae Vitae*.

Here, however, people still feel intensely confused. Because the intention where oral contraceptives are taken seems to be just the same as when intercourse is deliberately restricted to infertile periods. In one way this is true[.] […] But in another way it's not true.

The reason why people are confused about intention, and why they sometimes think there is no difference between contraceptive intercourse and the use of infertile times to avoid conception, is this: they don't notice the difference between 'intention' when it means the intentionalness of the thing you're doing – that you're doing *this* on purpose – and when it means a *further* or *accompanying* intention *with* which you are doing the thing. For example, I make a table: that's an intentional action because I am doing just *that* on purpose. I have the *further* intention of, say, earning my living, doing my job *by* making the table. Contraceptive intercourse and intercourse using infertile times may be alike in respect of further intention, and these further intentions may be good, justified, excellent. This the Pope has noted. He sketched such a situation and said: 'It cannot be denied that in both cases the married couple, for acceptable reasons,' (for that's how he imagined the case) 'are perfectly clear in their intention to avoid children and mean to secure that none will be born.'* This is a comment on the two things: contraceptive intercourse on the one hand and intercourse using infertile times on the other, for the sake of the limitation of the family.

---

*   *Humanac Vitae* §16.

G.E.M. Anscombe, *Contraception and Chastity* (London: Catholic Truth Society, 1975), pp. 182–183. Reprinted with permission of Catholic Truth Society.

But contraceptive intercourse is faulted, not on account of this further intention, but because of the kind of intentional action you are doing. The action is not left by you as the kind of act by which life is transmitted, but is purposely rendered infertile, and so changed to another sort of act altogether.

In considering an action, we need always to judge several things about ourselves. First: is the *sort* of act we contemplate doing something that it's all right to do? Second: are our further or surrounding intentions all right? Third: is the spirit in which we do it all right? Contraceptive intercourse fails on the first count; and to intend such an act is not to intend a marriage act at all, whether or not we're married. An act of ordinary intercourse in marriage at an infertile time, though, is a perfectly ordinary act of marital intercourse, and it will be bad, if it is bad, only on the second or third counts.

It may help you to see that the intentional act itself counts, as well as the further or accompanying intentions, if you think of an obvious example like forging a cheque to steal from somebody in order to get funds for a good purpose. The intentional action, presenting a cheque we've forged, is on the face of it a dishonest action, not to be vindicated by the good further intention.

If contraceptive intercourse is permissible, then what objection could there be after all to mutual masturbation, or copulation *in vase indebito*, sodomy, buggery,[1] when normal copulation is impossible or inadvisable (or in any case, according to taste)? It can't be the mere pattern of bodily behaviour in which the stimulation is procured that makes all the difference! But if such things are all right, it becomes perfectly impossible to see anything wrong with homosexual intercourse, for example. I am not saying: if you think contraception is all right you will do these other things; not at all. The habit of respectability persists and old prejudices die hard. But I am saying: you will have no solid reason against these things. You will have no answer to someone who proclaims, as many do, that they are good too.

---

[1]   I should perhaps remark that I am using a *legal* term here – not indulging in bad language.

4.1.3 Jacqueline A. Laing
"Law, Liberalism and the Common Good"

Introduction

There is a tendency in contemporary jurisprudence to regard political authority and, more particularly, legal intervention in human affairs as having no justification unless it can be defended by what I shall call the principle of modern liberal autonomy (MLA). According to this principle, if consenting adults want to do something, unless it does specific harm to others here and now, the law has no business intervening. Harm to the self and general harm to society can constitute no justification for legal regulation or prohibition. So pervasive is this understanding of legal intervention in human affairs, that it is common now to encounter arguments in favour of permissive laws on, for example, private drug use, pornography, sexual and reproductive choice, based on the idea that to intervene in these areas would constitute a breach of the liberal ideal.

The only alternative to modern liberal autonomy is assumed to be radical oppression, in which the State intervenes in the individual's life to impose unwarranted measures designed to further its own ends. The legacy of Stalin, Hitler and other modern tyrants has undermined conceptual appeals to the common good. So widespread is this liberal assumption in the Western, English-speaking world that critics of the outlook embodied by MLA are customarily regarded with suspicion and charged with paternalism, narrow-mindedness and intolerance. Given those unbecoming epithets, one will probably be reluctant to identify oneself as a critic of the prevailing ethos. Nonetheless, highlighting contradictions inherent in the modern liberal tradition is precisely the kind of thing I want to do here. I will be arguing that there is a certain reliance on the notion of the common good within the natural law tradition that may be instructive. According to this view, the common good constitutes a mean between two extremes: on the one hand, contemporary liberalism's over-insistence on radical individual autonomy and, on the other hand, totalitarianism's over-emphasis on collective social benefit. There is, I will argue, substantial terrain between the conceptual excesses of modern liberalism and oppressive tyranny that needs to be acknowledged and discussed.

Jacqueline A. Laing, "Law, Liberalism and the Common Good," in *Human Values*, ed. D. Oderberg and T. Chappell (Basingstoke: Palgrave Macmillan, 2004).

Although there are numerous examples of legal prohibition that (at least implicitly) challenge MLA, such as laws imposing taxation, or prohibiting incest and bigamy between consenting adults, or laws prohibiting drug use and controlling pornography, this essay will concentrate for the purposes of simplicity on matters surrounding sex, family, and reproduction. I will be arguing that moral and political debates surrounding the family throw up the sorts of question that challenge the very foundations of modern liberalism.

[We] consider the implications of prohibitions on mass human cloning, incest, bestiality, necrophilia, drug possession, and a number of other activities. An important dilemma facing defenders of MLA is laid bare. Either our commitment to modern liberal versions of individual autonomy will drive us to deny the legitimacy of laws even the fiercest defender of MLA accepts, or we drop our commitment to a modern liberal outlook and admit that modern liberalism, at least in its most widely accepted form, fails. It is [...] an unsustainable doctrine, if not actually incoherent.

Historical Foundations of Modern Liberal Autonomy

The father of modern liberalism is generally thought to be John Stuart Mill. In his essay *On Liberty*, Mill formulates what is generally known as the Harm Principle thus:

> The only purpose for which power can be rightfully exercised over any member of a civilised community, against his will, is to prevent harm to others. His own good, either physical or moral, is not a sufficient warrant. He cannot rightfully be compelled to do or forebear because it will be better for him to do so, because it will make him happier, because in the opinion of others, to do so would be wise, or even right.[1]

Liberalism has, in modern times, come to construe harm and, with it, the role for legal prohibition and regulation, narrowly.

Professor Herbert Hart's reply in *Law, Liberty and Morality*[2] argued that '[r]ecognition of individual liberty as a value involves, as a minimum, acceptance of the principle that the individual may do what he wants, even if others are distressed when they discover what it is that he does – unless, of course, there are other good grounds for forbidding it.'[3] Hart also suggested that Devlin's argument that maintaining moral bonds is essential to preserving society itself rests on an undiscussed assumption 'that all morality – sexual morality together with the morality that forbids acts injurious to others such as killing, stealing, and dishonesty – forms a single seamless web...'[4]

But let us return now to Hart's point about sexual morality. Hart distinguishes between 'sexual morality' and the 'morality that forbids acts injurious to others.'

[Hart's] technique [...] of separating sexual matters from matters in which the State has an interest, can and has been extended to the reproductive realm. Accordingly, the notion of reproductive (as distinct from sexual) privacy has been used to defend a raft of activities now regarded as standard, for example donor insemination, surrogacy, the freezing of gametes and embryos, and so on. [...] Indeed, the concept of sexual and reproductive autonomy is now one of the central and defining features of modern Western liberal society. Moreover, modern liberal autonomy with respect to the sexual and reproductive is a philosophy that fits neatly with a consumer mentality, if for no other reason than that if it does make someone happy there is usually substantial business in it. Whether the industry is in pornography, sex itself, abortion, or fertility, there is usually no small financial incentive involved as well.

That it has come to be widely thought that issues regarding family life, sex, and reproduction are wholly private matters in which the State has no business, cannot be doubted. Attempts at legal regulation of these areas of human activity are thought to be aimed at regulating private morality in the same objectionable way as penalising thoughts would be. Accordingly, it is supposed that these areas remain largely within the realm of the self-regarding and so implicitly non-harmful, rather than the other-regarding and therefore potentially harmful. This domain of human behaviour is generally thought to be properly immune from any legal regulation and prohibition deriving from consideration of the common good.

Because taboos surrounding sex, family, and reproduction are regarded as without rational foundation, a host of laws once thought justifiable, and indeed a necessary feature of the law's communicative function, are now thought to be wholly unjustifiable. Laws upholding monogamy and preventing polygamy or punishing bigamy are now beginning to be thought to impinge unnecessarily upon the private. Indeed Hart himself noted that opponents of the bigamy law might 'plausibly urge, in an age of waning faith, that the religious sentiments likely to be offended by the public celebration of a bigamous marriage are no longer widespread or very deep and it is enough that such marriages are held legally invalid.'[5] Further, it might now be argued that because in other societies polygamy is permitted, only outmoded Christian taboos, insupportable by liberal values, could explain traditional Western practice. Reproductive and sexual liberty, as we have said, is thought to be an essential feature of MLA. Indeed the prospect of multiple-party same-sex civil partnership arrangements might well constitute the future of the new family. In this intellectual climate so imbued with the assumptions of MLA, only the demand for incest between consenting adults gives the modern liberal pause.

Before concluding this section on the historical foundations of MLA, it is worth remembering that in most other societies now and in the past, it would have seemed most peculiar to assume that the mere characterisation of an activity as one that relates to the sexual or reproductive, would be sufficient to take it outside the public sphere and into the domain of the purely private, there to be regarded as an inappropriate subject of restrictions or regulations. Behaviour in this realm would have been regarded, on the contrary, as the right and proper subject of restriction if only because the interests of the next generation, of children, of family, and of the tribe were at stake. The very character and spirit of the group or society would have been thought to be involved. Accordingly it would have been unthinkable to hive off the sexual and the reproductive from other areas of legitimate social or political intervention.

It is also worth remembering that, on any view of the matter, beyond the familial, there are vast numbers of laws, even now, that interfere with the activities of consenting adults. These laws appear to exist irrespective of whether they are undertaken in private, and irrespective of whether they are thought to involve any direct harm to others here and now. Accordingly, any cursory examination of current English law will yield up offences of incest, bestiality, necrophilia, grave robbery, non-dangerous road traffic offences, non-dangerous forgery and counterfeiting, customs and excise offences as well as a host of non-dangerous offences against public justice such as making false statements as to births and deaths, and so on. These offences appear to exist despite what consenting adults might want to do in private and despite the fact that no harm can be discerned immediately, here and now. We discuss some of these matters in the next section.

The Natural Law Tradition and the Common Good

The classical natural law tradition has had little difficulty with the anxieties of modern liberalism. This is so for a variety of reasons. Modern liberalism stresses the propensity of individuals to value different things differently, and often aligns itself with both individual and social relativism. The classical natural law tradition generally rejects this understanding of the world. Humans, by use of their reason, are able to understand the natural order inherent in the universe. The natural law tradition also stresses that there is a law that is the same for all people, i.e. at a certain level of generality, and that can be discerned by proper understanding of our nature. This is so even if there is a substantial portion of human law that is quite properly regarded as different for different peoples and at different times, such laws governing the side of the road on which citizens might travel, laws governing, corporations, taxation, planning, and so on.

A second important reason why the natural law tradition does not share the worries of the modern liberal is because, in the main, it is a tradition that has a developed sense of the common good. The writings of Plato, Aristotle, Cicero, Augustine, and Aquinas bear this out. [...] The common good, then, is conceived in eternal terms, not solely in terms of what might produce most satisfaction either to those who would rule or to those who would be ruled. The common good is conceived in terms of the fellowship of heavens and earth, of God and men.

For Aristotle, the political community and public authority are based on human nature and likewise belong to an order established by God. The understanding of this order is to be gleaned from the nature of things, the kinds or species to which individuals belong and the ends proper to them. As Aristotle's well-known proposition at the beginning of the *Nicomachean Ethics* has it, 'every art and every inquiry, and similarly every action and pursuit, is thought to aim at some good; and for this reason the good has rightly been declared to be that at which all things aim.'[6] All things aim at the good but the good of the community is regarded as the more godlike to attain. This is because 'even if the end is the same for a single man and for a state, that of the state seems at all events something greater and more complete whether to attain or to preserve; though it is worth while to attain the end merely for one man, it is finer and more godlike to attain it for a nation or for city-states. These, then, are the ends at which our inquiry aims, since it is political science, in one sense of that term.'[7]

But for Aristotle, the art of politics does not rule over the gods any more than virtue presides over philosophic wisdom. This is because politics derives from the gods and virtue derives from philosophic wisdom:

> But again [virtue] is not supreme over philosophic wisdom, i.e. over the superior part of us, any more than the art of medicine is over health; ... [f]urther, to maintain its supremacy would be like saying that the art of politics rules the gods because it issues orders about all the affairs of the state.[8]

And good government is neither tyranny, nor oligarchy, nor democracy, as Aristotle conceives it, because this would amount to corruption of the common good.[9] Furthermore, the common good is for Aristotle, as for Plato, a matter of friendship between men and God (or the gods) and not confined merely to the transient world of human convention. For Aristotle, the friendship of children to parents, and of men to God, is a relation to them as to something good and superior, 'for they have conferred the greatest benefits, since they are the causes of their being and of their nourishment, and of their education from their birth; and this kind of friendship possesses pleasantness and utility also, more than that of strangers, inasmuch as their life is lived more in common.'[10]

For Aquinas, the common good is that for which human society exists, it is the purpose of the human community.[11] Aquinas believes that human society, like every-thing else, exists to glorify God. Relative to the members of human society, it exists for the sake of the full flourishing of all of those members. That flourishing, the good of each individual, is dictated by the natural law. It is dictated by what reason determines to be the end or ends toward which God has determined every human to be directed according to his or her rational nature.

[...]

The classical natural law tradition appears, then, to reject some of the central driving forces behind MLA. It does not regard value as entirely a matter of individual or socially relative preference. On the contrary, it regards value as a mind-independent reality. A substantial part of human law may indeed be different for different people at different times (road rules, planning laws, etc.). But that part does not exhaust the totality of human law. This is so because there is a part of the law that is the same for all people at all times. This part is eternal and unchanging and is closely related to reason and truth. Examples of laws that are eternal and unchanging are those which prohibit the persecution, violation, or destruction of the innocent, and those principles within human law that demand proportionality and equity. For Plato and others in the classical natural law tradition, the common good is conceived in eternal terms, not solely in terms of what brings about, say, the greatest sensory satisfaction either for the ruler or those ruled. The common good is conceived in terms of the fellowship of the heavens and the earth, of gods and men.

[...]

What, it might be asked, have asexual reproduction and the biotechnological reproductive revolution got to do with the Hart-Devlin debate? [...] Huxley's vision challenges the assumption that sex and reproduction are and ought to be somehow immune from public scrutiny because these are purely private matters between commissioning parties or sole reproducers,[12] as they are now called, and service providers. We cannot regard sex, family, and reproduction as purely private matters when they are entered into by consenting adults, and therefore as being immune from questions relating to the common good.

A man may indeed wish to clone himself one thousand times over. Or he may want to create a group of animal–human hybrids for useful service. Or he may be a doctor motivated by charity and so, pleased also to create hundreds of children for consenting, infertile women – using his own sperm. MLA gives us no way of explaining why these desires ought not to be accommodated. If we are to say these kinds of acts are impermissible we need to go beyond the MLA and reach out for other general principles. [...]

The point to be understood from the use of the example of mass human cloning is this. If we are to hold on to the idea that the law ought to intervene to prevent this kind of abuse, we will need to jettison MLA. It is hard to see what version of MLA could perform the conceptual work necessary to demonstrate why legal intervention is desirable. After all, there appears to be no immediate harm or offence done 'here and now' by permitting a man to clone himself a hundred times over where he is able to find consenting parties to assist him in his plan. Whatever conceptual apparatus we use to conclude that legal prohibition is appropriate will, I would argue, need to be derived from a moral world well beyond MLA.

Likewise, if we are to understand why we might balk at the prospect of routine creation of animal–human hybrids, we are going to need to appeal to moral generalities surrounding the interests of the class of children so created, their health, identity, family and kinship. These generalities will emerge from a moral hinterland well beyond that traversed by MLA.

These paradigm cases of identity fragmentation place in sharp focus the issues concerning people conceived by donor gamete and other artificial reproductive techniques. Although not suffering the same number and kinds of loss as those suffered by clones, there are certain similar questions that arise for children born of both kinds of procedure. Very often, modern intuitions are so affected by notions of reproductive liberty that there is an unwillingness to hear of the concerns, loss, and grief of people conceived by the fertility industry. Their outrage is discounted as unwarranted and unjustifiable. It is often assumed that their sense of loss is best suppressed. So pervasive in contemporary Western society are the dogmas of MLA, that they seem to obliterate ordinary human sympathy.

In fact there are, even in Western nations, familiar limits on both sexual and reproductive liberty. There are offences of bigamy[13] and incest even where the parties to the offence are consenting adults.[14] There are offences of bestiality (whether or not this causes immediate offence to anyone)[15] and there are offences of sexually interfering with a corpse, again whether or not the dead person would have agreed in life to such interference and whether or not the act causes offence to anyone.[16] The point of these examples is to challenge the notion adopted by Hart, and developed further in recent times, that sexual morality does not raise matters that imply harm to others in which the law has any business interfering, where the individuals involved are consenting adults.

If there is to be any recognition of the above examples as genuine offences, there will need to be an admission that MLA does not supply the necessary conceptual foundation for legal intervention in these areas. Whatever else is true, MLA cannot be the sole operative principle in determining the proper limits of the law in relation to sex and reproduction. We cannot assume that matters relating to sex and reproduction are intrinsically private, self-regarding matters that are 'not the law's business'. Nor can we assume that in such matters, the desires of consenting adults, here and now, are the only relevant factors to be taken into consideration. There are societal interests, of which Devlin spoke so eloquently, and there are the interests of the next generation to be considered.

It is perhaps a little easier, then, to see why other cultures and other peoples have found strange the view that there should be no taboos or legal restrictions surrounding sex and reproduction: these involve the well-being and capacity to flourish of the people or culture, as well as, potentially, its very survival. This touches on Devlin's statement, so jarring to the modern ear, that the 'suppression of vice is as much the law's business as the suppression of subversive activities'. The statement sounds crude to us now, but states a fundamental truth about the need to consider both the common good and the interests of the next generation in public matters surrounding sex and reproduction. If we are to be able to explain why we need to restrict the desires of the multiple cloner, we need to jettison our commitment to MLA. If we cling to MLA, we have no way of explaining what is wrong with mass human cloning and other abusive ways of creating people, such as incestuous reproduction.

The sexual and reproductive realms are not, however, the only ones that challenge MLA. It is worth remembering that there are a great many other areas of law which appear to contravene the principle. There are offences prohibiting the possession of controlled drugs (such as heroin, cocaine, and a multitude of other substances) whether or not the parties in possession are consenting adults, whether or not the harm caused by their use is solely done to the self, and whether or not this possession would allow the adult involved greater freedom to express himself in the manner he, as an individual, thinks fit. The rationale behind criminalising possession of drugs will be framed, if at all, in terms of the common good and the interests of society. Rational debate about whether a substance ought to be regarded as 'controlled', and how it should be classified, must revolve around the immediacy and scope of the impact of the substance, the propensity of the substance to cause long-term illness whether mental or physical, the likelihood that widespread availability of the substance will interfere with the ordinary life of fellow citizens, as well as the cost to the nation of long-term, freely available use. All of these questions presuppose a realm of rational discussion that is well beyond the scope envisaged by MLA.

Again, a large part of criminal law is dedicated to non-dangerous road traffic offences. Not only are there offences that do not immediately raise the spectre of danger or harm, such as parking offences, but there are also offences that prohibit driving without a seatbelt or riding a motorbike without a helmet. There might well be rational debate about whether these regulations intrude too deeply into the individual's life in defence of the common good. But such debate, insofar as it accepts the in principle legitimacy of such laws and regulations, takes it for granted that *some* intervention is warranted to promote the common good, whether or not such intervention limits the individual's freedom to express himself.

There are, in addition, offences against public justice, whether or not these offences cause any actual harm or affront to others, and irrespective of whether the offender's interest in freedom of expression is thereby limited. False statutory declarations,[17] concealment of evidence,[18] contempt of court,[19] false statements about births, marriages, and deaths, and perjury[20] are offences whether or not there is any third-party victim. It is generally assumed that there is a legitimate category of offence dedicated to the defence of the common good of public justice.

Indeed there are a great many offences relating to the vice of dishonesty which do not depend on the existence of any victim before they take effect. Certain kinds of fraud, counterfeiting, tax offences, forgery: none of these depend essentially on the notion of a victim of harm, whether actual or threatened.

In English law, at least, there is also the contentious offence of assisting suicide whether or not the victim consented.[21] Likewise, a German court recently convicted self-confessed cannibal Armin Meiwes of manslaughter, sentencing him to eight-and-a-half-years in prison.[22] [...] The conviction and punishment of a defendant accused of killing his albeit willing victim, demonstrates that violation of a person's consent is not the only rationale for the prohibition on killing.

[...]

The Self-Destructive and Totalitarian Aspects
of Liberalism

The preservation or ruin of society depends on this more than on anything else. Where the law is overruled or obsolete, I see destruction hanging over the community; where it is sovereign over the authorities and they its humble servants, I discern the presence of salvation and every blessing heaven sends on a society.

In the course of his discussion, Lord Devlin argued that there must be 'toleration of the maximum individual freedom that is consistent with the integrity of society', and that 'tolerance should cease where ... the practice is injurious to society'. [...]

There is, however, one matter which neither Devlin nor Hart expressly considered in their respective essays on liberalism, perhaps because the problem did not present itself as starkly in those days as it does now, and perhaps too because they were not concerned with matters of fertility and reproduction.

Hart's liberalism is now establishment ideology but there are grounds for suspecting that this once unconventional perspective is running into difficulty. One interesting feature of liberalism is that it appears to go hand in hand with native populations' decline. This may be the result of the fragmentation of what is left of the tribe, viz. the nuclear family, as well as of widespread contraception, abortion, infertility, and the greater atomisation of individuals. Whichever way we look at it, Western liberal societies appear not to be in the business of replacing themselves. One obvious problem with any prevailing ideology in a society that fails to replace itself, is that the society may well be replaced by people who do not adopt the same ideology as those establishmentarians, liberal or otherwise, within it.

That native population decline is a feature of modern Western liberal society cannot be doubted. [...] The United Nations method of choice for addressing the declining population and creating the numbers necessary for economic survival is replacement migration.[23] It recommends one million replacement immigrants a year to make up the shortfall in the skilled workforce of the UK and to pay the pensions of an ageing population. Hart spoke with equanimity of changing morality, never explicitly recognising that a potential volte face in the outlook of Western countries' inhabitants might be entirely at odds with his own liberal ideals. Not all ideologies are logically compatible with liberalism. It cannot be assumed that replacement societies will adopt modern liberalism as their preferred ideology. It is in this environment that the oppressiveness of liberalism is bound to become manifest.

[...]

Conclusion

We have seen a number of ways in which the principle of modern liberal autonomy is challenged by existing English law. Drug possession and traffic laws, laws protecting public justice and government are examples of laws that protect the public interest irrespective of whether these acts do harm to others here and now. Likewise laws preventing human cloning and animal–human hybrids demonstrate that there are undoubtedly limits on reproductive liberty in the interests of generations to come. Laws punishing incest, bestiality and necrophilia (never mind more contentious laws entrenching Christian values like monogamy) whether or not undertaken behind closed doors, challenge the principle of sexual liberty. All threaten MLA. We have observed that many of these laws, in different ways, seek to protect the interests of the vulnerable, the next generation and the very fabric of society (implicit in institutions such as that of the family, public justice, or government itself).

Modern liberalism prides itself on having secured certain rights and freedoms – to destroy one's self, one's offspring, and collectively to destroy one's culture. Built on the empty rhetoric of relativism and blind to its own *de facto* subservience to illicit industries, MLA promises the good life and then drives us to individual and collective self-destruction. […]

By contrast, certain strands of thought within the classical natural law tradition, the earliest articulation of which can be found in the thought of Plato and Aristotle, supply the conceptual mechanism that enables us to discover a place of equilibrium between the dual excesses of liberalism and totalitarianism. It is here that a proper understanding of both common and individual flourishing is to be discovered. It is from within the natural law perspective that the self-destructiveness of liberalism and the injustice of totalitarianism may be discerned. As we move into an era of mass human cloning, animal–human hybrids, routine freezing of young human life and children conceived asexually or of parents long dead, it will be vital to turn to the wealth of understanding contained in the classical natural law tradition.

Notes

1   J.S. Mill, *On Liberty* (London: Penguin, 1974), pp. 68–69. For an opposing view, see Sir James Fitzjames Stephen, *Liberty, Equality, Fraternity and Three Brief Essays* (Chicago: University of Chicago Press, 1991 [1873]).

2   H.L.A. Hart, *Law, Liberty and Morality* (Oxford: Oxford University Press, 1963). Quotations from 1975 edition.

3   *Law*: 47.

4   *Law*: 50–51.

5   *Law*: 43.

6   Aristotle, *Nicomachean Ethics* I.1, 1094a, trans. W.D. Ross: *The Works of Aristotle* vol. IX, ed. Ross (Oxford: Clarendon Press, 1925).

7   *Ethics* I.2, 1094b.

8   *Ethics* VI.13, 1145a.

9   Aristotle, *Politics* III.7, 1279b, trans. Jowett: *The Works of Aristotle* vol. X, ed. Ross (Oxford: Clarendon Press, 1921): 'Of the above-mentioned forms, the perversions are as follows: – of royalty, tyranny; of aristocracy, oligarchy; of constitutional government, democracy. For tyranny is a kind of monarchy which has in view the interest of the monarch only; oligarchy has in view the interest of the wealthy; democracy, of the needy: none of them the common good of all.'

10   *Ethics* VIII.12, 1162a.

11   St Thomas Aquinas, *Summa Theologica* I–II, q.92 a.1 ad 3: 'The goodness of any part is considered in comparison with the whole; hence Augustine says (*Confess*. iii) that "unseemly is the part that harmonizes not with the whole." Since then every man is a part of the state, it is impossible that a man be good, unless he be well proportionate to the common good: nor can

the whole be well consistent unless its parts be proportionate to it.' (Trans. Fathers of the English Dominican Province; London: Burns, Oates and Washbourne, 1927 (2nd ed.), vol. 8.)

12   Julian Savulescu, 'Procreative Beneficence: Why We Should Select the Best Children', *Bioethics* 15 (2002): 413–26. See also John Harris, 'Rights and Reproductive Choice', in John Harris and Soren Holm (eds), *The Future of Human Reproduction: Choice and Regulation* (Oxford: Oxford University Press, 1998): 5–37.

13   Offences Against the Person Act 1961, s.57.

14   Sexual Offences Act 2003, s.64.

15   Sexual Offences Act 2003, s.69.

16   Sexual Offences Act 2003, s.70.

17   Perjury Act 1911, s.5.

18   Criminal Law Act 1967, s.5.

19   Contempt of Court Act 1981.

20   Perjury Act 1911.

21   Suicide Act 1961, s.2.

22   See global press, 30 January 2004.

23   'Immigrants Needed to Save West from Crisis', *The Guardian* 22 March 2000. See also: *Expert Group Meeting on Policy Responses to Population Ageing and Population Decline*, Population Division, Department of Economic and Social Affairs, United Nations Secretariat, New York, 16–18 October 2000.

4.2 Medical Ethics and Biotechnology

Introduction

Laing's piece marks a convenient transition to another highly contentious area in which contemporary defenders of the central natural law tradition have been increasingly active, namely that of medical ethics and biotechnology. The context in which their arguments here have been forged, of course, has been that of the gradual extension of those technological developments that have underpinned the modern, industrial, and post-industrial world, from a primary focus upon the external environment towards a focus upon the perceived deficiencies of the human form itself. Once again, the root cause of the technologization of attitudes towards the human body to which this trend is connected, is the very dualistic anthropology Servais Pinckaers made reference to in his extract at the beginning of the previous section. Thus, in direct proportion as the human mind has been defined as in radical discontinuity with the material world, the better to render the latter subject to unlimited exploitation, to that extent it has also ended up emphasizing the discontinuity of the mental and physical aspects of the human form in a way that presents the body as a site of infinite malleability.

For this reason, the first selection in the current section is an abbreviated version of the New Natural Law argument against this attitude,[1] as set out by Patrick Lee and Robert George in their recent book-length treatment of the same issue, unfolded in dialectical tension with the dominant, utilitarian, forms of bioethical analysis to which such a dualistic anthropology has given rise.[2] In the extract reproduced here, they argue that the only proper criterion for a person's moral worth is his/her nature as a rational substance. Crucially, whilst an individual's ability to shape his/her own life through the exercise of rational thought, deliberation, and free choice is certainly conclusive evidence of the possession of such a nature, it is not the only such evidence. Since the person possessing

---

[1] P. Lee and R.P. George, "The Nature and Basis of Human Dignity," *Ratio Juris* 21, 2 (June 2008), pp. 173–193.
[2] P. Lee and R.P. George, *Body–Self Dualism in Contemporary Ethics and Politics* (Cambridge: Cambridge University Press, 2009).

The Natural Law Reader, First Edition. Edited by Jacqueline A. Laing and Russell Wilcox.
© 2014 Blackwell Publishing Ltd. Published 2014 by Blackwell Publishing Ltd.

such a nature is a radical material/immaterial unity, his/her living body will amount to similarly conclusive proof. Whilst, then, these capacities may be the specific distinguishing attributes of a rational substance, it does not follow that they need always, or indeed ever, be actually exercised in practice. It follows that it is in the *existence* of a rational nature that moral worth consists, rather than the *exercise* of the distinctively rational capacities which normally, though not always, flow from it. Alternative views, argue Lee and George, such as those put forward by the well-known thinker Peter Singer, that moral worth is grounded in the capacity for suffering or enjoyment, "all follow from the fact that ... the proposed criterion ... [relate] to the possession of an accidental attribute that varies in degrees."[3] And they go on to demonstrate how, if applied consistently, this can lead to the most terrifying of consequences.

In the course of their discussion, Lee and George relate what they say to a whole raft of specific bioethical issues. It is not possible to reproduce separate pieces concerning each one of these "hot-button" topics, but, in this mold, the editors felt the need to include at least one representative piece. Their choice is a reflection by Daniel Callahan – long-time director of the Hastings Center – on the subject of euthanasia.[4] The particular focus of Callahan's piece is on questions of self-determination and patient autonomy. He argues that euthanasia cannot be confined to the private choice of an individual since it involves the active complicity of at least one other person; that it is wrong-headed to deny, as many pro-euthanasia advocates do, the crucial distinction between killing and letting die; that there is, in fact, and despite claims to the contrary, a great deal of evidence as to the dire social consequences of loosening legal restrictions on so-called "assisted dying"; and, finally, that it is a practice which profoundly distorts the sacred relationship between doctor and patient. Each of these arguments makes use of philosophical resources identifiably falling within the central tradition of the natural law.

The final two pieces in this section deal in a broad-ranging manner with the challenges posed by new technologies. In the first piece, former chairman of the US President's Commission on Bioethics, Leon Kass, "prescinding from particular ethical questions," reflects upon the "moral meaning of genetic technology" for humanity in general.[5] In so doing, Kass, who, in the tradition of Paul Ramsey and Hans Jonas, is a consistent, profound, and, for that reason, much vilified voice of caution in the headlong rush towards ever-greater scientific and technological novelty, draws upon his own scientific training to explain the unique nature of genetic technology. This consists in its potential to affect not just present but also future generations and to create entirely new human capacities. By thereby removing the distinction between therapy and enhancement, it promises a sort of genetic arms race that has as its consequence endless dissatisfaction and redefinition. This raises inevitable questions as to how much genetic self-knowledge is too much, how likely that knowledge will be used for fundamentally coercive purposes, and ultimately how compatible the entire project of genetic manipulation is with basic human dignity. In exploring these questions, Kass frames the rest of his discussion around the implications of "playing God," of treating human beings as the

---

3   Lee and George, "The Nature and Basis of Human Dignity," p. 177.
4   D. Callahan, "When Self-Determination Runs Amok," Hastings Center Report (March–April 1992).
5   L.R. Kass, "Triumph or Tragedy? The Moral Meaning of Genetic Technology," *American Journal of Jurisprudence* 45 (2000), pp. 1–16.

objects of manufacture and commodification, of having no fixed or stable standards against which to measure "improvement," and finally of the literally soul-destroying prospects of actually achieving the genetic utopia so longed for.

Reflecting many of the worries articulated by Kass, the piece by Finn Bowring completes this section with a sustained phenomenological meditation upon the longer-term implications underlying contemporary attitudes to the relationship between technology and the human form.[6] For Bowring as for many of our other authors, these attitudes are rooted in profound reconceptualizations of human being: reconceptualizations Bowring sees as amounting to an "end of metaphysics" or, perhaps more accurately, an end of the belief that there is anything metaphysically distinctive about humanity that would prevent it from becoming the site of unconstrained manipulation. The paradox of asserting the absolute sovereignty of the will whilst simultaneously undermining any foundation upon which to base its claims is a theme we have seen repeated time and again in the foregoing pages. Apart from the general richness of Bowring's analysis, his particular contribution is to situate the discourses engendered by cybernetic, virtual reality and post-humanist enthusiasts in the jaws of this paradox, demonstrating in the process that such discourses, far from being the preserve of the intellectually or socially eccentric, actually represent its ultimate logical outworking.

[6] F. Bowring, "The Cyborg Solution," in F. Bowring, *Science, Seeds and Cyborgs: Biotechnology and the Appropriation of Life* (London: Verso, 2003), pp. 259–277.

4.2.1 Patrick Lee and Robert P. George "The Nature and Basis of Human Dignity"

[…] [A]ll human beings have real dignity simply because they are persons – entities with natural capacities for thought and free choice. *All* human beings have this capacity, so all human beings are persons. Each human being therefore deserves to be treated by all other human beings with respect and consideration. It is precisely this truth that is at stake in the debates about killing human embryos, fetuses, and severely retarded, demented, or debilitated human beings, and many other debates in bioethics.

[…]

The Problem of Moral Status

The general problem regarding the ground of moral status can be expressed as follows. It seems that it is morally permissible to *use* some living things, to consume them, experiment on them for our own benefit (without their consent, or perhaps when they are unable to give or withhold consent), but that it is not morally permissible to treat other beings in this way. The question is: Where do we draw the line between those two sorts of beings? By reference to what criterion do we draw that line? Or perhaps there just is no such line, and we should always seek to preserve *all* beings, of whatever sort.

But we must eat, we must use some entities for food and shelter, and in doing so we inevitably destroy them. When we eat we convert entities of one nature into another and thus destroy them. Moreover, no one claims that we should not try to eradicate harmful bacteria (which are forms of life). That is, we should kill harmful bacteria in order to protect ourselves and our children. And it seems clear that we must harvest wheat and rice for food, and trees for shelter. So, plainly it is permissible to kill and use some living things. Given that it is not morally permissible to kill just any type of being, it follows that a line must be drawn, a line between those entities it is morally permissible to use, consume, and destroy. How can the line be drawn in a non-arbitrary way?

Various criteria for where the line should be drawn have been proposed: sentience, consciousness, self-awareness, rationality, or being a moral agent (the last two come to

Patrick Lee and Robert P. George, "The Nature and Basis of Human Dignity," *Ratio Juris* 21, 2 (June 2008), pp. 175–193. Reprinted with permission of John Wiley & Sons Ltd.

the same thing). We will argue that the criterion is: having a rational nature, that is, having the natural capacity to reason and make free choices, a capacity it ordinarily takes months, or even years, to actualize, and which various impediments might prevent from being brought to full actualization. (Severely retarded human beings have the same nature and thus the same basic rights as other humans: Were a therapy or surgery developed to correct whatever defect causes their mental disability, this would not change their nature. It would not change them into a different kind of being; rather, it would enable them to flourish more fully precisely as the kind of being they are – a human being.) Thus, every human being has full moral worth or dignity, for every human being possesses such a rational nature.

While membership in the species *Homo sapiens* is sufficient for full moral worth, it is not in any direct sense the criterion for moral worth. If we discovered extra-terrestrial beings of a rational nature, or learned that some terrestrial species have a rational nature, then we would owe such beings full moral respect. Still, all members of the human species do have full moral worth because all of them do have a rational nature, though many of them are not able immediately to exercise basic capacities. One could also say that the criterion for full moral worth is *being a person*, since a person is a rational subject.[1]

The other suggestions listed above, we believe, are not tenable as criteria of full moral worth, and, worse yet, often have the practical effect of leading to the denial that human beings have full moral worth, rather than simply adding other beings to the set of beings deserving full moral respect (Teichman 1996). Hence it is vital to explain how being a person, that is, being a distinct substance with the basic natural capacities for conceptual thought and free choice, is a basis for the possession of dignity and basic rights.

The Capacity for Enjoyment or Suffering as a Criterion

Animal welfarists argue that the criterion of moral worth is simply the ability to experience enjoyment and suffering. Peter Singer, for example, quotes Jeremy Bentham (1948, chap. 17): "The question is not, Can they *reason*? nor Can they *talk*? but, Can they *suffer*?" Singer then presents the following argument for this position:

> The capacity for suffering and enjoyment is *a prerequisite for having interests at all*, a condition that must be satisfied before we can speak of interests in a meaningful way. [...] A stone does not have interests because it cannot suffer. Nothing that we can do to it could possibly make any difference to its welfare. The capacity for suffering and enjoyment is, however, not only necessary, but also sufficient for us to say that a being has interests – at an absolute minimum, an interest in not suffering. (Singer 1990, 7)

In short, Singer's argument is: All and only beings that have interests have moral status; but all and only beings that can (now) experience suffering or enjoyment have interests; therefore, all and only beings that can (now) experience suffering or enjoyment have moral status.

The major difficulties with Singer's position all follow from the fact that his proposed criterion for moral status involves the possession of an accidental attribute that varies in degrees. Both the capacity for suffering and the possession of interests are properties which different beings have in different degrees, and the interests themselves are possessed in varying degrees. As we shall show, this feature of Singer's theory leads to untenable conclusions. Here we will mention four.

First, although Singer has made famous the slogan, "All animals are equal," this theory actually leads to *denying* that all animals, including all humans, have equal moral worth or basic rights. Singer means that "All animals are equal" in the sense that all animals are due "equal consideration." Where the interests of two animals *are* similar in quality and magnitude, then those interests should be counted as equal when deciding what to do, both as individuals and in social policies and actions. However, as Singer himself points out, (on this view) some animals can perform actions which others cannot, and thus have interests which those others do not. So the moral status of all animals is not, in fact, equal. One would not be required to extend the right to vote, or to education in reading and arithmetic, to pigs, since they are unable to perform such actions. This point leads to several problems when we attempt to compare interests. According to this view it is the *interests* that matter, not *the kind of being* that is affected by one's actions. So, on this view, it would logically follow that if a human child had a toothache and a juvenile rat had a slightly more severe toothache, then we would be morally required to devote our resources to alleviating the rat's toothache rather than the human's.

Second, a human newborn infant who will die shortly (and so does not appear to have long-term future interests), or a severely cognitively impaired human, will be due *less* consideration than a more mature horse or pig, on the ground that a mature horse or pig will have richer and more developed interests. Since the horse and the pig have higher cognitive and emotional capacities (in the sense of immediately or nearly immediately exercisable capacities) than those newborn infants (that will die shortly) and severely cognitively impaired humans – and it is the interests that directly count morally, not the beings that have those interests – then the interests of the horse and the pig should (on this account) be preferred to the interests of the newborn or the cognitively impaired human.[2]

Third, let us consider the differences between types of interests. Singer's position actually implies an indirect *moral elitism*. It is true that according to this position no animal is greater than another solely on the ground of its species (that is, according to its substantial nature). Still, one animal will be due more consideration – indirectly – if it has capacities for higher or more complex mental functions. As Singer puts it: "Within these limits we could still hold that, for instance, it is worse to kill a *normal* adult human, with a capacity for self-awareness, and the ability to plan for the future and have meaningful relations with others, than it is to kill a mouse, which presumably does not share all of these characteristics [...]" (Singer 1990, 19, emphasis supplied). But this difference between degrees of capacity for suffering and enjoyment, will also apply to individuals within each species. And so, on this view, while a human will normally have a greater capacity for suffering and enjoyment than other animals, and so will have a higher moral status (indirectly), so too, more intelligent and sophisticated human individuals will have a greater capacity for suffering and enjoyment than less intelligent and less sophisticated human individuals, and so the former will have a higher moral status than the latter. As Richard Arneson (1999, 105) expressed this point, "For after all it is just as true that a creative genius has richer and more complex interests than those of an ordinary average Joe as it is true that a human has richer and more complex interests than a baboon."

Finally, there is a fourth difficulty for the animal welfarist position, a difficulty that also clarifies the principal difference between that position and traditional morality. Singer's argument was that moral worth is based on interests, and interests are based on the ability to experience suffering or enjoyment. In other words, a key premise in his argument is that only beings with feelings or some level of consciousness can be reasonably considered to have interests. However, this is simply not true. Rather, all living beings, not just those with consciousness, have interests. It is clear that living beings are fulfilled by certain conditions and damaged by others. As Paul Taylor, who defends a biocentrist view (*all* living beings have moral worth), explains,

> We can think of the good of an individual nonhuman organism as consisting in the full development of its biological powers. Its good is realized to the extent that it is strong and healthy. (Taylor 1984, 488)

One can then say that what promotes the organism's survival and flourishing is *in its interest* and what diminishes its chances of survival or flourishing is *against its interests*. Further, while it may be initially plausible to think that all animals have rights because they have interests, it is considerably less plausible to think that all living beings (which include wheat, corn, and rice, not to mention weeds and bacteria) have rights. But the interest argument would lead to that position.

And this point, we think, clarifies the issue. The arguments advanced by Singer and Taylor do not actually attempt to establish that nonhuman animals and other living things have moral rights in the full sense of the term. We think it is true of *every* living being, in some way, that we should not *wantonly* destroy or damage it.[3] With sentient beings, whether their life goes well or badly for them will significantly include their pleasure, comfort, or lack of suffering. And so their flourishing includes pleasure and lack of pain (though it also includes other things such as their life and their activities). Yet it does not follow from these points that they have full basic and inherent dignity (moral worth) or rights (Lombardi 1983). There simply is no conceptual connection between pleasure and pain (enjoyment and suffering) on the one hand, and full moral worth (including genuine rights), on the other hand (Oderberg 2000a, 101).

However, almost no one actually argues that these beings have basic dignity or full moral rights. Rather, biocentrists argue that all living things merit *some* consideration, but also hold that human beings are due *more* consideration (though not, apparently, a different *kind* of consideration: see, for example, Taylor 1984). In effect, instead of actually holding that all living beings (in the case of biocentrists), or all animals (in the case of animal welfarists) have *rights*, they have simply denied the existence of rights in the full sense of the term.[4] Instead, they hold only that all living beings (or animals or higher mammals) deserve some (varying) degree of respect or consideration. We agree with this point, but we also maintain that every human being is a subject of rights, that is, every human being should be treated according to the golden rule.[5] In other words, we grant that we should take account of the flourishing of living beings, and the pleasures and pains of nonhuman animals. But we are not morally related to them in the same way that we are related to other beings who, like ourselves, have a rational nature – beings whom (out of fairness) we should treat as we would have them treat us.

But one might argue for animal rights starting from our natural empathy or affection for them (though most people's natural empathy or affection, notably, does *not* extend to all animals, for example, to spiders or snakes). If one identifies what is to be protected and pursued with what can be felt, that is, enjoyed or suffered in some way, then one might conclude that every entity that can have pleasure or pain deserves (equal?) consideration. If the only intrinsic good were what can be enjoyed, and the only intrinsic bad were suffering, then it would not be incoherent to hold that sentience is the criterion of moral standing, that is, that every entity with sentience has (some degree of) moral standing. In other words, it seems that one can present an *argument* for animal rights that begins from natural feelings of empathy only by way of a hedonistic value theory. We can think of no other arguments that begin from that natural empathy with, or affection for, other animals.

But hedonism as a general theory of value is mistaken. The central tenet of hedonism – that the good consists in the experiential – is false. Real understanding of the way things are, for example, is pleasurable because it is fulfilling or perfective of us, not vice versa. The same is true of life, health, or skillful performance (one enjoys running a good race because it is a genuine accomplishment, a skillful performance, rather than vice versa). So, as Plato and Aristotle pointed out, hedonism places the cart before the horse.

Clearly, some desires are bad and some are merely whimsical but some desires are neither. So, in many cases, prior to being desired, the object desired has something about it that makes it *fitting*, or *suitable*, to be desired. We are capable of desiring certain things while other things leave us unmoved, uninterested. So, prior to being desired, the object desired must have something about it which makes it *fitting*, or *suitable*, to be desired. What makes it fitting is that it is *fulfilling* or *perfective* of us in some way or other. Thus, what makes a thing good cannot consist in its being enjoyed, or in its satisfying desires or preferences. Rather, desires and preferences are rational only if they are in line with what is genuinely good, that is, genuinely fulfilling.[6] So, hedonism is mistaken. It cannot provide support for the view that sentience (or the capacity for suffering and enjoyment) is the criterion of full moral worth. While we are prepared to grant, at least for the sake of argument, that it is wrong to kill a plant, insect, or other non-rational creature wantonly, still it can be morally right to do so for a good reason.[7]

These difficulties in Singer's position are all due to the selection of a criterion of moral worth that varies in degrees. If the moral status-conferring attribute varies in degrees – whether it be the capacity for enjoyment or suffering, or another attribute that comes in degrees – it will follow that some humans will possess that attribute to a lesser extent than some non-human animals, and so inevitably some interests of some non-human animals will trump the interests of some humans. Also, it will follow that some humans will possess the attribute in question in a higher degree than other humans, with the result that not all humans will be equal in fundamental moral worth, i.e., *dignity*. True, some philosophers bite the bullet on these results. But in our judgment this is too high a price to pay. A sound view of worth and dignity will not entail such difficulties.

Rather, our position is that a rights-bearing subject has rights in virtue of the kind of substantial entity he or she is, not in virtue accidental attributes such as race, sex, ethnicity, age, size, stage of development, or condition of dependency. There are many things to be said in defense of this position, but let us make here just a few brief points. First, this view will explain why it at least seems to most people that our moral concern should be for *persons*, rather than only for their properties or accidental attributes. After all, when dealing with other persons we at least tend to think that the locus of value is the persons themselves. We do not normally view persons as mere vehicles for what is intrinsically valuable: One's child, one's neighbor, or even a stranger, is not valuable only because of the valuable attributes they possess. If persons were valuable as mere vehicles for something else – some other quality that is regarded as what is *really* of value – then it would follow that the basic moral rule would be simply to maximize those valuable attributes. It would not be morally wrong to kill a child, no matter what age, if doing so enabled one to have two children in the future, and thus to bring it about that there were two vehicles for intrinsic value rather than one. So, persons themselves are valuable, rather than mere vehicles for what is really intrinsically valuable.

But if that is so, then it would make sense that what distinguishes those entities that have full moral status (inherent dignity) from those that do not should be the type of substantial entity they are, rather than any accidental attributes they possess. True, it is not self-contradictory to hold that the person himself is valuable, but only in virtue of some accidental attributes he or she possesses. Still, it is more natural, and more theoretically economical, to suppose that *what* has full moral status, and *that in virtue of which* he or she has full moral status, are the same.

Second, this position more closely tracks the characteristics we tend to think are found in genuine care or love. Our genuine love for a person remains, or should remain, for as long as that person continues to exist, and is not dependent on his or her possessing further attributes. That is, it seems to be the nature of care of love that, at least ideally, it should be unconditional, that we should continue to desire the well-being or fulfillment of someone we love for as long as he or she exists. Of course, this still leaves open the question whether continuing to live is always part of a person's well-being or fulfillment; we also maintain that a person's life always *is* in itself a good, but that is a distinct question from the one being considered just now (see Lee and George 2007, chap. 5). The point is that caring for someone is a three-term relation. It consists in actively willing that a good or benefit be instantiated *in* a person, viewed as a subject of existence, in other words, as a substance. And this structure is more consonant with the idea that the basis of dignity or moral worth is being a certain sort of substance, rather than possessing certain attributes or accidental characteristics.

The Difference in Kind between Human Beings and Other Animals

[...]

The capacity for conceptual thought in human beings radically distinguishes them from other animals known to us. This capacity is at the root of most of the other distinguishing features of human beings. Thus, syntactical language, art, architecture, variety in social groupings and in other customs,[8] burying the dead, making tools, religion, fear of death (and elaborate defense mechanisms to ease living with that fear), wearing clothes, true courting of the opposite sex (Scruton 1986), free choice, and morality – all of these and more, stem from the ability to reason and understand. Conceptual thought makes all of these specific acts possible by enabling human beings to escape fundamental limitations of two sorts. First, because of the capacity for conceptual thought, human beings' actions and consciousness are not restricted to the spatio-temporal present. Their awareness and their concern go beyond what can be perceived or imagined as connected immediately with the present (Reichmann 2000, chap. 2; see also Campbell 1994). Second, because of the capacity for conceptual thought, human beings can reflect back upon themselves and their place in reality, that is, they can attain an objective view, and they can attempt to be objective in their assessments and choices. [...]

Marginal Cases

On this position every human being, of whatever age, size, or stage of development, has inherent and equal fundamental dignity and basic rights. If one holds, on the contrary, that full moral worth or dignity is based on some accidental attribute, then, since the attributes that could be considered to ground basic moral worth (developed consciousness, etc.) vary in degree, one will be led to the conclusion that moral worth also varies in degrees.

It might be objected against this argument, that the basic natural capacity for rationality also comes in degrees, and so this position (that full moral worth is based on the possession of the basic natural capacity for rationality), if correct, would also lead to the denial of fundamental personal equality (Stretton 2004). However, the criterion for full moral worth is having a nature that entails the capacity (whether existing in root form or developed to the point at which it is immediately exercisable) for conceptual thought and free choice – not *the development* of that basic natural capacity to some degree or other. The criterion for full moral worth and possession of basic rights is not the possession of a capacity for conscious thought and choice considered as an accidental attribute that inheres in an entity, but being a certain kind of thing, that is, having a specific type of substantial nature. Thus, possession of full moral worth follows upon being a certain type of entity or substance, namely, a substance with a rational nature, despite the fact that some persons (substances with a rational nature) have a greater intelligence, or are morally superior (exercise their power for free choice in an ethically more excellent way) than others. Since basic rights are grounded in being a certain type of substance, it follows that having such a substantial nature qualifies one as having full moral worth, basic rights, and equal personal dignity.

An analogy may clarify our point. Certain properties follow upon being an animal, and so are possessed by every animal, even though in other respects not all animals are equal. For example, every animal has some parts which move other parts, and every animal is subject to death (mortal). Since various animals are equally animals – and since being an animal is a type of substance rather than an accidental attribute – then every animal will equally have *those* properties, even though (for example) not every animal equally possesses the property of being able to blend in well to the wooded background. Similarly, possession of full moral worth follows upon being a person (a distinct substance with a rational nature) even though persons are unequal in many respects (intellectually, morally, etc.).

These points have real and specific implications for the great controversial issues in contemporary ethics and politics. Since human beings are intrinsically valuable as subjects of rights at all times that they exist – that is, they do not come to be at one point, and acquire moral worth or value as a subject of rights only at some later time – it follows that human embryos and fetuses are subjects of rights, deserving full moral respect from individuals and from the political community. It also follows that a human being remains a person, and a being with intrinsic dignity and a subject of rights, for as long as he or she lives: There are no subpersonal human beings. Embryo-destructive research, abortion, and euthanasia involve killing innocent human beings in violation of their moral right to life and to the protection of the laws.

In sum, human beings are animals of a special kind. They differ in kind from other animals because they have a rational nature, a nature characterized by having the basic natural capacities for conceptual thought and deliberation and free choice. In virtue of having such a nature, all human beings are persons; and all persons possess profound, inherent, and equal dignity. Thus, every human being deserves full moral respect.

Notes

1 Boethius's definition, especially as interpreted by St. Thomas Aquinas, is still valid: "An individual substance (that is, a unique substance) of a rational nature." So, neither a nature held in common by many, nor a part is a person. But every whole human being performing its own actions, including actions such as growth toward the mature stage of a human, *is* a person. See Boethius 1891, and St. Thomas Aquinas 1981, Pt. I, q. 29, a. 1.
2 Jeff McMahan (2002, 205–6), whose view is in other respects more complex than Singer's, still holds that only interests are of direct moral concern, and explicitly recognizes, and accepts, this logical consequence.
3 Could it be true of every being, living or not? It is hard to see what the good or fulfillment of a non-living being is, since on that level it is hard to know just what are the basic, substantial entities as opposed to aggregates of entities. Thus, when we breathe we convert oxygen and carbon molecules into carbon dioxide molecules – have we destroyed the oxygen in that process or have we only rearranged the atoms in their constitution? It is hard to say.
4 Peter Singer acknowledges that he is "not convinced that the notion of a moral right is a helpful or meaningful one, except when it is used as a shorthand way of referring to more fundamental considerations."
5 We are laying aside here now the issue of capital punishment.
6 Thus, the pleasures of the sadist or child molester are *in themselves* bad; it is false to say that such pleasures are bad only because of the harm or pain involved in their total contexts. It is false to say: "It was bad for him to cause so much pain, but at least he enjoyed it." Pleasure is secondary, an aspect of a larger situation or condition (such as health, physical, and emotional); what is central is what is really fulfilling. Pleasure is not a good like understanding or health, which are goods or perfections by themselves, that is, are good in themselves even if in a context that is overall bad or if accompanied by many bads. Rather, pleasure is good (desirable, worthwhile, perfective) if and only if attached to a fulfilling or perfective activity or condition. Pleasure *is* a good: A fulfilling activity or condition is better with it than without it. But pleasure is *unlike* full-fledged goods in that it is not a genuine good apart from some other, fulfilling activity or condition. It is a good if and only if attached to another condition or activity that is already good.
7 It is worth noting that nonhuman animals themselves not only regularly engage in killing each other, but many of them (lions and tigers, for example) seem to depend for their whole mode of living (and so their flourishing), on hunting and killing other animals. If nonhuman animals

really did have full moral rights, however, we would have a *prima facie* obligation to stop them from killing each other. Indeed, we would be required to invest resources presumptively protecting zebras and antelopes from lions, sheep and foxes from wolves, and so on.

8   Mortimer Adler (1990) noted that, upon extended observation of other animals and of human beings, what would first strike one is the immense uniformity in mode of living among other animals, in contrast with the immense variety in modes of living and customs among human beings.

References

Adler, Mortimer. 1990. *Intellect: Mind Over Matter*. New York: Macmillan. St. Thomas Aquinas. 1981. *Summa Theologiae*. Westminster, MD: Christian Classics.

Arneson, Richard. 1999. What, If Anything, Renders All Humans Morally Equal? In *Singer and his Critics*. Ed. D. Jamieson, 103–27. Malden, MA: Blackwell.

Bentham, Jeremy. 1948. *Introduction to the Principles of Moral and Legislation*. Oxford: Oxford University Press.

Boethius. 1891. De Duabus Naturis. In *Patrologia Latina*, ed. J.-P. Migne, 1354–412. Paris: Migne, 1891.

Lee, Patrick, and Robert P. George. 2007. *Body-Self Dualism and Contemporary Ethics and Politics*. New York: Cambridge University Press.

Lombardi, Louis G. 1983. Inherent Worth, Respect, and Rights. *Environmental Ethics* 5: 257–70.

McMahan, Jeff. 2002. *The Ethics of Killing, Problems at the Margin of Life*. New York, N.Y.: Oxford University Press.

Oderberg, David S. 2000a. *Applied Ethics: A Non-Consequentialist Approach*. Oxford: Blackwell.

Oderberg, David S. 2000b. *Moral Theory: A Non-Consequentialist Approach*. Oxford: Blackwell.

Reichmann, James B. 2000. *Evolution, Animal "Rights," and the Environment*. Washington, D.C.: Catholic University of America Press.

Scruton, Roger. 1986. *Sexual Desire: A Moral Philosophy of the Erotic*. New York, N.Y.: Free Press.

Singer, Peter. 1990. *Animal Liberation*. 2nd ed. New York, N.Y.: The New York Review of Books.

Stretton, Dean. 2004. Essential Properties and the Right to Life: A Response to Lee. *Bioethics* 18: 264–82.

Taylor, Paul. 1984. The Ethics of Respect for Nature. In *Morality in Practice*. 4th ed. Ed. J. P. Sterba, 487–99. Belmont, Calif.: Wadsworth.

Teichman, Jenny. 1996. *Social Ethics: A Student's Guide*. Oxford: Blackwell.

4.2.2 Daniel Callahan
"When Self-Determination
Runs Amok"

The euthanasia debate is not just another moral debate, one in a long list of arguments in our pluralistic society. It is profoundly emblematic of three important turning points in Western thought. The first is that of the legitimate conditions under which one person can kill another. The acceptance of voluntary active euthanasia would morally sanction what can only be called "consenting adult killing," By that term I mean the killing of one person by another in the name of their mutual right to be killer and killed if they freely agree to play those roles. This turn flies in the face of a longstanding effort to limit the circumstances under which one person can take the life of another, from efforts to control the free flow of guns and arms, to abolish capital punishment, and to more tightly control warfare. Euthanasia would add a whole new category of killing to a society that already has too many excuses to indulge itself in that way.

The second turning point lies in the meaning and limits of self-determination. The acceptance of euthanasia would sanction a view of autonomy holding that individuals may, in the name of their own private, idiosyncratic view of the good life, call upon others, including such institutions as medicine, to help them pursue that life, even at the risk of harm to the common good. This works against the idea that the meaning and scope of our own right to lead our own lives must be conditioned by, and be compatible with, the good of the community, which is more than an aggregate of self-directing individuals.

The third turning point is to be found in the claim being made upon medicine: it should be prepared to make its skills available to individuals to help them achieve their private vision of the good life. This puts medicine in the business of promoting the individualistic pursuit of general human happiness and well-being. It would overturn the traditional belief that medicine should limit its domain to promoting and preserving human health, redirecting it instead to the relief of that suffering which stems from life itself, not merely from a sick body.

I believe that, at each of these three turning points, proponents of enthanasia push us in the wrong direction. Arguments in favor of euthanasia fall into four general categories, which I will take up in turn: (1) the moral claim of individual self-determination and well-being; (2) the moral irrelevance of the difference between killing and allowing

Daniel Callahan, "When Self-Determination Runs Amok," *Hastings Center Report* (March–April 1992). Reprinted with permission of John Wiley & Sons Ltd.

to die; (3) the supposed paucity of evidence to show likely harmful consequences of legalized euthanasia; and (4) the compatibility of euthanasia and medical practice.

Self-Determination

Central to most arguments for euthanasia is the principle of self-determination. People are presumed to have an interest in deciding for themselves, according to their own beliefs about what makes life good, how they will conduct their lives. That is an important value, but the question in the euthanasia context is, What does it mean and how far should it extend? If it were a question of suicide, where a person takes her own life without assistance from another, that principle might be pertinent, at least for debate. But euthanasia is not that limited a matter. The self-determination in that case can only be effected by the moral and physical assistance of another. Euthanasia is thus no longer a matter only of self-determination, but of a mutual, social decision between two people, the one to be killed and the other to do the killing.

How are we to make the moral move from my right of self-determination to some doctor's right to kill me – from *my* right to *his* right? Where does the doctor's moral warrant to kill come from? Ought doctors to be able to kill anyone they want as long as permission is given by competent persons? Is our right to life just like a piece of property, to be given away or alienated if the price (happiness, relief of suffering) is right? And then to be destroyed with our permission once alienated?

In answer to all those questions, I will say this: I have yet to hear a plausible argument why it should be permissible for us to put this kind of power in the hands of another, whether a doctor or anyone else. The idea that we can waive our right to life, and then give to another the power to take that life, requires a justification yet to be provided by anyone.

Slavery was long ago outlawed on the ground that one person should not have the right to own another, even with the other's permission. Why? Because it is a fundamental moral wrong for one person to give over his life and fate to another, whatever the good consequences, and no less a wrong for another person to have that kind of total, final power. Like slavery, dueling was long ago banned on similar grounds; even free, competent individuals should not have the power to kill each other, whatever their motives, whatever the circumstances. Consenting adult killing, like consenting adult slavery or degradation, is a strange route to human dignity.

There is another problem as well. If doctors, once sanctioned to carry out euthanasia, are to be themselves responsible moral agents – not simply hired hands with lethal injections at the ready – then they must have their own *independent* moral grounds to kill those who request such services. What do I mean? As those who favor euthanasia are quick to point out, some people want it because their life has become so burdensome it no longer seems worth living.

The doctor will have a difficulty at this point. The degree and intensity to which people suffer from their diseases and their dying, and whether they find life more of a burden than a benefit, has very little directly to do with the nature or extent of their actual physical condition. Three people can have the same condition, but only one will find the suffering unbearable. People suffer, but suffering is as much a function of the values of individuals as it is of the physical causes of that suffering. Inevitably in that circumstance, the doctor will in effect be treating the patient's values. To be responsible, the doctor would have to share those values. The doctor would have to decide, on her own, whether the patient's life was "no longer worth living."

But how could a doctor possibly know that or make such a judgment? Just because the patient said so? I raise this question because, while in Holland at the euthanasia conference reported by Maurice de Wachter elsewhere in this issue, the doctors present agreed that there is no objective way of measuring or judging the claims of patients that their suffering is unbearable. And if it is difficult to measure suffering, how much more difficult to determine the value of a patient's statement that her life is not worth living?

However one might want to answer such questions, the very need to ask them, to inquire into the physician's responsibility and grounds for medical and moral judgment, points out the social nature of the decision. Euthanasia is not a private matter of self–determination. It is an act that requires two people to make it possible, and a complicit society to make it acceptable.

Killing and Allowing to Die

Against common opinion, the argument is sometimes made that there is no moral difference between stopping life-sustaining treatment and more active forms of killing, such as lethal injection. Instead I would contend that the notion that there is no morally significant difference between omission and commission is just wrong. Consider in its broad implications what the eradication of the distinction implies; that death from disease has been banished, leaving only the actions of physicians in terminating treatment as the cause of death. Biology, which used to bring about death, has apparently been displaced by human agency. Doctors have finally, I suppose, thus genuinely become gods, now doing what nature and the deities once did.

What is the mistake here? It lies in confusing causality and culpability, and in failing to note the way in which human societies have overlaid natural causes with moral rules and interpretations. Causality (by which I mean the direct physical causes of death) and culpability (by which I mean our attribution of moral responsibility to human actions) are confused under three circumstances.

They are confused, first, when the action of a physician in stopping treatment of a patient with an underlying lethal disease is construed as *causing* death. On the contrary, the physician's omission can only bring about death on the condition that the patient's disease will kill him in the absence of treatment. We may hold the physician morally responsible for the death, if we have morally judged such actions wrongful omissions. But it confuses reality and moral judgment to see an omitted action as having the same causal status as one that directly kills. A lethal injection will kill both a healthy person and a sick person. A physician's omitted treatment will have no effect on a healthy person. Turn off the machine on me, a healthy person, and nothing will happen. It will only, in contrast, bring the life of a sick person to an end because of an underlying, fatal disease.

Causality and culpability are confused, second, when we fail to note that judgments of moral responsibility and culpability are human constructs. By that I mean that we human beings, after moral reflection, have decided to call some actions right or wrong, and to devise moral rules to deal with them. When physicians could do nothing to stop death, they were not held responsible for it. When, with medical progress, they began to have some power over death – but only its timing and circumstances, not its ultimate inevitability – moral rules were devised to set forth their obligations. Natural causes of death were not thereby banished. They were, instead, overlaid with a medical ethics designed to determine moral culpability in deploying medical power.

To confuse the judgments of this ethics with the physical causes of death – which is the connotation of the word *kill* – is to confuse nature and human action. People will, one way or another, die of some disease; death will have dominion over all of us. To say that a doctor "kills" a patient by allowing this to happen should only be understood as a moral judgment about the licitness of his omission, nothing more. We can, as a fashion of speech only, talk about a doctor *killing* a patient by omitting treatment he should have provided. It is a fashion of speech precisely because it is the underlying disease that brings death when treatment is omitted; that is its cause, not the physician's omission. It is a misuse of the word *killing* to use it when a doctor stops a treatment he believes will no longer benefit the patient – when, that is, he steps aside to allow an eventually inevitable death to occur now rather than later. The only deaths that human beings invented are those that come from direct killing – when, with a lethal injection, we both cause death and are morally responsible for it. In the case of omissions, we do not cause death even if we may be judged morally responsible for it.

This difference between causality and culpability also helps us see why a doctor who has omitted a treatment he should have provided has "killed" that patient while another doctor – performing precisely the same act of omission on another patient in different circumstances – does not kill her, but only allows her to die. The difference is that we have come, by moral convention and conviction, to classify unauthorized or illegitimate omissions as acts of "killing." We call them "killing" in the expanded sense of the term: a culpable action that permits the real cause of death, the underlying disease, to proceed to its lethal conclusion. By contrast, the doctor who, at the patient's request, omits or terminates unwanted treatment does not kill at all. Her underlying disease, not his action, is the physical cause of death; and we have agreed to consider actions of that kind to be morally licit. He thus can truly be said to have "allowed" her to die.

If we fail to maintain the distinction between killing and allowing to die, moreover, there are some disturbing possibilities. The first would be to confirm many physicians in their already too-powerful belief that, when patients die or when physicians stop treatment because of the futility of continuing it, they are somehow both morally and physically responsible for the deaths that follow. That notion needs to be abolished, not strengthened. It needlessly and wrongly burdens the physician, to whom should not be attributed the powers of the gods. The second possibility would be that, in every case where a doctor judges medical treatment no longer effective in prolonging life, a quick and direct killing of the patient would be seen as the next, most reasonable step, on grounds of both humaneness and economics. I do not see how that logic could easily be rejected.

Calculating the Consequences

When concerns about the adverse social consequences of permitting euthanasia are raised, its advocates tend to dismiss them as unfounded and overly speculative. On the contrary, recent data about the Dutch experience suggests that such concerns are right on target. From my own discussions in Holland, and from the articles on that subject in this issue and elsewhere, I believe we can now fully see most of the *likely* consequences of legal euthanasia.

Three consequences seem almost certain, in this or any other country, the inevitability of some abuse of the law; the difficulty of precisely writing, and then enforcing, the law; and the inherent slipperiness of the moral reasons for legalizing euthanasia in the first place.

Why is abuse inevitable? One reason is that almost all laws on delicate, controversial matters are to some extent abused. This happens because not everyone will agree with the law as written and will bend it, or ignore it, if they can get away with it. From explicit admissions to me by Dutch proponents of euthanasia, and from the corroborating information provided by the Remmelink Report and the outside studies of Carlos Gomez and John Keown, I am convinced that in the Netherlands there are a substantial number of cases of nonvoluntary euthanasia, that is, euthanasia undertaken without the explicit permission of the person being killed. The other reason abuse is inevitable is that the law is likely to have a low enforcement priority in the criminal justice system. Like other laws of similar status, unless there is an unrelenting and harsh willingness to pursue abuse, violations will ordinarily be tolerated. The worst thing to me about my experience in Holland was the casual, seemingly indifferent attitude toward abuse. I think that would happen everywhere.

Why would it be hard to precisely write, and then enforce, the law? The Dutch speak about the requirement of "unbearable" suffering, but admit that such a term is just about indefinable, a highly subjective matter admitting of no objective standards. A requirement for outside opinion is nice, but it is easy to find complaisant colleagues. A requirement that a medical condition be "terminal" will run aground on the notorious difficulties of knowing when an illness is actually terminal.

Apart from those technical problems there is a more profound worry. I see no way, even in principle, to write or enforce a meaningful law that can guarantee effective procedural safeguards. The reason is obvious yet almost always overlooked. The euthanasia transaction will ordinarily take place within the boundaries of the private and confidential doctor–patient relationship. No one can possibly know what takes place in that context unless the doctor chooses to reveal it. In Holland, less than 10 percent of the physicians report their acts of euthanasia and do so with almost complete legal impunity. There is no reason why the situation should be any better elsewhere. Doctors will have their own reasons for keeping euthanasia secret, and some patients will have no less a motive for wanting it concealed.

I would mention, finally, that the moral logic of the motives for euthanasia contain within them the ingredients of abuse. The two standard motives for euthanasia and assisted suicide are said to be our right of self-determination, and our claim upon the mercy of others, especially doctors, to relieve our suffering. These two motives are typically spliced together and presented as a single justification. Yet if they are considered independently – and there is no inherent reason why they must be linked – they reveal serious problems. It is said that a competent, adult person should have a right to euthanasia for the relief of suffering. But why must the person be suffering? Does not that stipulation already compromise the principle of self-determination? How can self-determination have any limits? Whatever the person's motives may be, why are they not sufficient?

Consider next the person who is suffering but not competent, who is perhaps demented or mentally retarded. The standard argument would deny euthanasia to that person. But why? If a person is suffering but not competent, then it would seem grossly unfair to deny relief solely on the grounds of incompetence. Are the incompetent less entitled to relief from suffering than the competent? Will it only be affluent, middle-class people, mentally fit and savvy about working the medical system, who can qualify? Do the incompetent suffer less because of their incompetence?

Considered from these angles, there are no good moral reasons to limit euthanasia once the principle of taking life for that purpose has been legitimated. If we really believe in self-determination, then any competent person should have a right to be killed by a doctor for any reason that suits him. If we believe in the relief of suffering, then it seems cruel and capricious to deny it to the incompetent. There is, in short, no reasonable or logical stopping point once the turn has been made down the road to euthanasia, which could soon turn into a convenient and commodious expressway.

Euthanasia and Medical Practice

A fourth kind of argument one often hears both in the Netherlands and in this country is that euthanasia and assisted suicide are perfectly compatible with the aims of medicine. I would note at the very outset that a physician who participates in another person's suicide already abuses medicine. Apart from depression (the main statistical cause of suicide), people commit suicide because they find life empty, oppressive, or meaningless. Their judgment is a judgment about the value of continued life, not only about health (even if they are sick). Are doctors now to be given the right to make judgments about the kinds of life worth living and to give their blessing to suicide for those they judge wanting? What conceivable competence, technical or moral, could doctors claim to play such a role? Are we to medicalize suicide, turning judgments about its worth and value into one more clinical issue? Yes, those are rhetorical questions.

Yet they bring us to the core of the problem of euthanasia and medicine. The great temptation of modern medicine, not always resisted, is to move beyond the promotion and preservation of health into the boundless realm of general human happiness and well-being. The root problem of illness and mortality is both medical and philosophical or religious, "Why must I die?" can be asked as a technical, biological question or as a question about the meaning of life. When medicine tries to respond to the latter, which it is always under pressure to do, it moves beyond its proper role.

It is not medicine's place to lift from us the burden of that suffering which turns on the meaning we assign to the decay of the body and its eventual death. It is not medicine's place to determine when lives are not worth living or when the burden of life is too great to be borne. Doctors have no conceivable way of evaluating such claims on the part of patients, and they should have no right to act in response to them. Medicine should try to relieve human suffering, but only that suffering which is brought on by illness and dying as biological phenomena, not that suffering which comes from anguish or despair at the human condition.

Doctors ought to relieve those forms of suffering that medically accompany serious illness and the threat of death. They should relieve pain, do what they can to allay anxiety and uncertainty, and be a comforting presence. As sensitive human beings, doctors should be prepared to respond to patients who ask why they must die, or die in pain. But here the doctor and the patient are at the same level. The doctor may have no better an answer to those old questions than anyone else; and certainly no special insight from his training as a physician. It would be terrible for physicians to forget this, and to think that in a swift, lethal injection, medicine has found its own answer to the riddle of life. It would be a false answer, given by the wrong people. It would be no less a false answer for patients. They should neither ask medicine to put its own vocation at risk to serve their private interests, nor think that the answer to suffering is to be killed by another. The problem is precisely that, too often in human history, killing has seemed the quick, efficient way to put aside that which burdens us. It rarely helps, and too often simply adds to one evil still another. That is what I believe euthanasia would accomplish. It is self–determination run amok.

4.2.3 Leon R. Kass
"Triumph or Tragedy? The Moral Meaning of Genetic Technology"

"Playing God"

Curiously, worries about dehumanization are sometimes expressed, paradoxically, in the fear of super-humanization, that is, that man, or rather *some* men, will be "playing God." This complaint is too facilely dismissed by scientists and nonbelievers. The concern has meaning, God or no God. By it is meant one or more of the following: man, or some men, are becoming creators of life, and indeed, of individual living human beings (in vitro fertilization, cloning); not only are they creating life, but they stand in judgment of each being's worthiness to live or die (genetic screening and abortion) – not on moral grounds, as is said of God's judgment, but on somatic and genetic ones; they also hold out the promise of salvation from our genetic sins and defects (gene therapy and genetic engineering).

Never mind the exaggeration that lurks in this conceit of man's playing God: even at his most powerful, after all, man is capable only of *playing* God. Never mind the implicit innuendo that nobody has given to others this creative and judgmental authority, or the implicit retort that there is theological warrant for acting as God's co-creator in overcoming the ills and suffering of the world. Consider only that if scientists are seen in this godlike role of creator, judge, and savior, the rest of us must stand before them as supplicating, tainted creatures. Despite the hyperbolic speech, this worry is not far-fetched.

Practitioners of prenatal diagnosis, working today with but a fraction of the information soon to be available from the Human Genome Project, already screen for a long list of genetic diseases and abnormalities, from Down's Syndrome to dwarfism. Possession of any one of these defects, they believe, renders a prospective child unworthy of life. Persons who happen still to be born with these conditions, having somehow escaped the spreading net of detection and eugenic abortion, are increasingly regarded as "mistakes," as inferior human beings who should not have been born.[1] Not long ago, at my own university, a physician making rounds with medical students stood over the bed of an intelligent, otherwise normal ten-year-old boy with spina bifida. "Were he to have been conceived today," the physician casually informed his entourage, "he would have been aborted."

Leon R. Kass, "Triumph or Tragedy? The Moral Meaning of Genetic Technology," *American Journal of Jurisprudence* 45 (2000), pp. 1–16. Reprinted with kind permission of the author.

Determining who shall live and who shall die – on the basis of genetic merit – is a godlike power already wielded by genetic medicine. This power will only grow.

Manufacture and Commodification

But, one might reply, genetic technology also holds out the promise of redemption, of a *cure* for these life-crippling and life-forfeiting disorders. Very well. But in order truly to practice their salvific power, genetic technologists will have to greatly increase their manipulations and interventions, well beyond merely screening and weeding out. True, in some cases genetic testing and risk management aimed at prevention may actually cut down on the need for high-tech interventions aimed at cure. But in many other cases, ever-greater genetic scrutiny will lead necessarily to ever more extensive manipulation. And, to produce Bentley Glass's healthy and well-endowed babies, let alone babies with the benefits of genetic enhancement, a new scientific obstetrics will be necessary, one that will come very close to turning human procreation into manufacture.

This process has already crudely begun with in vitro fertilization. It will soon take giant steps forward with the ability to screen in vitro embryos before implantation; with cloning; and, eventually, with precise genetic engineering. Just follow the logic and the aspirations of current practice: the road we are travelling leads all the way to the world of designer babies – reached not by dictatorial fiat, but by the march of benevolent humanitarianism, and cheered on by an ambivalent citizenry that also dreads becoming simply the last of man's man-made things.

Make no mistake: the price to be paid for producing optimum or even only genetically sound babies will be the transfer of procreation from the home to the laboratory and its coincident transformation into manufacture. Increasing control over the product can only be purchased by the increasing depersonalization of the entire process. Such an arrangement will be profoundly dehumanizing, no matter how genetically good or healthy the resultant children. And let us not forget the powerful economic interests that will surely operate in this area; with their advent, the commodification of nascent human life will be unstoppable.

Standards, Norms, and Goals

According to Genesis, God, in His creating, looked at His creatures and *saw* that they were *good* – intact, complete, well-working wholes, true to the spoken idea that guided their creation. What standards will guide the genetic engineers?

For the time being, one might answer, the norm of health. But even before the genetic enhancers join the party, the standard of health is being deconstructed. Are you healthy if, although you show no symptoms, you carry genes that will definitely produce Huntington's disease, or that predispose you to diabetes, breast cancer, or coronary artery disease? What if you carry, say, 40 percent of the genetic markers thought to be linked to the appearance of Alzheimer's disease? And what will "healthy" and "normal" mean when we discover your genetic propensities for alcoholism, drug abuse, pederasty, or violence? The idea of health becomes at once both imperial and vague: medicalization of what have hitherto been mental or moral matters paradoxically brings with it the disappearance of any clear standard of health itself.

Once genetic *enhancement* comes on the scene, standards of health, wholeness, and fitness will be needed more than ever, but just then is when all pretense of standards will go out the window. "Enhancement" is, of course, a soft euphemism for "improvement," and the idea of improvement necessarily implies a good, a better, and perhaps even a best. If, however, we can no longer look to our previously unalterable human nature for a standard or norm of what is regarded as good or better, how will anyone know what constitutes an improvement? It will not do to assert that we can extrapolate from what we like about ourselves. Because memory is good, can we say how much more memory would be better? If sexual desire is good, how much more would be better? Life is good; but how much extension of the lifespan would be good for us? Only simplistic thinkers believe they can easily answer such questions.[2]

More modest enhancers, like more modest genetic therapists and technologists, eschew grandiose goals. They are valetudinarians, not eugenicists. They pursue, or think they pursue, not some far away positive good, but the positive elimination of evils: diseases, pain-and-suffering, the likelihood of death. But let us not be deceived. Hidden in all this avoidance of evil is nothing less than the quasi-messianic goal of a painless, suffering-free, and, finally, immortal existence. What's more, though unstated, this implicit goal is in fact held to be uncontroversial and paramount. Only the presence of such a goal justifies the sweeping aside of any opposition to the relentless march of medical science. Only such a goal gives trumping moral power to the principle "cure disease, relieve suffering."

"Cloning human beings is unethical and dehumanizing, you say? Never mind: it will help us treat infertility, avoid genetic disease, and provide perfect materials for organ replacement." Such, indeed, was the tenor of the June 1997 report of the National Bioethics Advisory Commission, *Cloning Human Beings*. Notwithstanding its call for a temporary ban on the practice, the only moral objection the commission could agree upon was that cloning "is not safe to use in humans at this time," because the technique has yet to be perfected.[3] Even this elite ethical body, in other words, was unable to muster any other moral argument sufficient to cause us to forego the possible health benefits of cloning.[4]

The same argument will also justify creating and growing human embryos for experimentation, revising the definition of death to increase the supply of organs for transplantation, growing human body parts in the peritoneal cavities of animals, perfusing newly dead bodies as factories for useful biological substances, or reprogramming the human body and mind with genetic or neurobiological engineering. Who can sustain an objection if these practices will help us live longer and with less overt suffering?

It turns out that even the more modest biogenetic engineers, whether they know it or not, are in the immortality business, proceeding on the basis of a quasi-religious faith that all innovation is by definition progress and that longer life is simply better, no matter what is sacrificed to attain it.

The Tragedy of Success

What the enthusiasts do not see is that their utopian project will not eliminate suffering but merely shift it around. Forgetting that contentment requires that our desires do not outpace our powers, they have not noticed that the enormous medical progress of the last half-century has not left the present generation satisfied. Indeed, we are already witnessing a certain measure of public discontent as a paradoxical result of rising expectations in the healthcare field: although their actual health has improved substantially in recent decades, people's *satisfaction* with their current health status has remained the same or declined. But that is hardly the highest cost of success in the medical/humanitarian project.

As Aldous Huxley made clear in his prophetic *Brave New World*, the conquest of disease, aggression, pain, anxiety, suffering, and grief unavoidably comes at the price of homogenization, mediocrity, pacification, drug-induced contentment, trivialized human attachments, debasement of taste, and souls without love or longing – the inevitable result of making the essence of human nature the final object of the conquest of nature for the relief of man's estate. Like Midas, bioengineered man will be cursed to acquire precisely what he wished for, only to discover – painfully and too late – that what he wished for is not exactly what he wanted. Or, worse than Midas, he may be so dehumanized he will not even recognize that in aspiring to be perfect, he is no longer even truly human.[5]

The main point here is not the rightness or wrongness of this or that imagined scenario – all this is admittedly highly speculative. I surely have no way of knowing whether my worst fears will be realized, but you surely have no way of knowing that they will not.[6] The point is rather the plausibility, even the wisdom, of thinking about genetic technology, like the entire technological venture, under the ancient and profound idea of tragedy, that poignant human adventure of living in grand self-contradiction. In tragedy, the hero's failure is embedded in his very success, his defeats in his victories, his miseries in his glory. What I am suggesting is that the technological way of approaching both the world and human life, a way deeply rooted in the human soul and spurred on by the utopian promises of modern thought and its scientific crusaders, may well turn out to be inevitable, heroic, and doomed.

To say that technology, left to itself as a way of life, is doomed does not yet mean that modern life – our life – *must* be tragic. Everything depends on whether the technological disposition is allowed to proceed to its self-augmenting limits, or whether it can be restricted and brought under intellectual, spiritual, moral, and political rule. But here, I regret to say, the news so far is not encouraging. For the relevant intellectual, spiritual, and moral resources of our society, the legacy of civilizing traditions painfully acquired and long-preserved, are taking a beating – not least because they are being called into question by the findings of modern science itself. The technologies present troublesome ethical dilemmas, but the underlying scientific notions call into question the very foundations of our ethics.

The challenge goes far beyond the notorious case of evolution versus biblical religion. Is there *any* elevated view of human life and human goodness that is proof against the belief, trumpeted by biology's most public and prophetic voices, that man is just a collection of molecules, an accident on the stage of evolution, a freakish speck of mind in a mindless universe, fundamentally no different from other living – or even nonliving – things? What chance have our treasured ideas of freedom and dignity against the teachings of biological determinism in behavior, the reductive notion of "the selfish gene" (or, for that matter, of "genes for altruism"), the belief that DNA is the essence of life, and the credo that the only natural concerns of living beings are survival and reproductive success?

As sociologist Howard Kaye notes:

> For over forty years, we have been living in the midst of a biological and cultural revolution of which innovations such as artificial insemination with donor semen, in vitro fertilization, surrogacy, genetic manipulation, and cloning are merely technological offshoots. In both aim and impact, the end of this revolution is a fundamental transformation in how we conceive of ourselves as human beings and how we understand the nature and purpose of human life rightly lived. Encouraged by bio-prophets like Francis Crick, Jacques Monod, E.O. Wilson, and Richard Dawkins, as well as by humanists and social scientists trumpeting the essential claims of race, gender, and ethnicity, we are in the process of redefining ourselves as biological, rather than cultural and moral beings. Bombarded with white-coated claims that "Genes-R-Us," grateful for the absolution which such claims offer for our shortcomings and sins, and attracted to the promise of using efficient, technological means to fulfill our aspirations, rather than the notoriously unreliable moral or political ones, the idea that we are essentially self-replicating machines, built by the evolutionary process, designed for survival and reproduction, and run by our genes continues to gain. But still the public's ambivalence persists, experienced in the form of anxiety at what such a transformation would mean.[7]

These transformations are, in fact, welcomed by many of our leading scientists and intellectuals. In 1997, the luminaries of the International Academy of Humanism – including biologists Crick, Dawkins, and Wilson and humanists Isaiah Berlin, W. V. Quine, and Kurt Vonnegut – issued a statement in defense of cloning research in higher mammals and human beings. Their reasons were revealing:

> What moral issues would human cloning raise? Some world religions teach that human beings are fundamentally different from other mammals – that humans have been imbued by a deity with immortal souls, giving them a value that cannot be compared to that of other living things. Human nature is held to be unique and sacred. Scientific advances which pose a perceived risk of altering this "nature" are angrily opposed. ... As far as the scientific enterprise can determine, [however] ... [h]uman capabilities appear to differ in degree, not in kind, from those found among the higher animals. Humanity's rich repertoire of thoughts, feelings, aspirations, and hopes seems to arise from electrochemical brain processes, not from an immaterial soul that operates in ways no instrument can discover.... Views of human nature rooted in humanity's tribal past ought not to be our primary criterion for making moral decisions about cloning.... The potential benefits of cloning may be so immense that it would be a tragedy if ancient theological scruples should lead to a Luddite rejection of cloning.[8]

In order to justify ongoing research, these intellectuals were willing to shed not only traditional religious views but *any* view of human distinctiveness and special dignity, their own included. They fail to see that the scientific view of man they celebrate does more than insult our vanity. It undermines our self-conception as free, thoughtful, and responsible beings, worthy of respect because we alone among the animals have minds and hearts that aim far higher than the mere perpetuation of our genes. It undermines, as well, the beliefs that sustain our mores, practices, and institutions – including the practice of science itself. For why, on this radically reductive understanding of "the rich repertoire" of human thought, should anyone choose to accept as true the results of *these* men's "electrochemical brain processes," rather than his own? Thus do truth and error themselves, no less than freedom and dignity, become empty notions when the soul is reduced to chemicals.

The problem may lie not so much with the scientific findings themselves but with the shallow philosophy that recognizes no other truths but these and with the arrogant pronouncements of the bioprophets. For example, in a letter to the editor complaining about a review of his book, *How the Mind Works*, the well-known evolutionary psychologist and popularizer Stephen Pinker rails against any appeal to the human soul:

> Unfortunately for that theory, brain science has shown that the mind is what the brain does. The supposedly immaterial soul can be bisected with a knife, altered by chemicals, turned on or off by electricity, and extinguished by a sharp blow or a lack of oxygen. Centuries ago it was unwise to ground morality on the dogma that the earth sat at the center of the universe. It is just as unwise today to ground it on dogmas about souls endowed by God.[9]

One hardly knows whether to be more impressed with the height of Pinker's arrogance or with the depth of his shallowness. But he speaks with the authority of science, and few are able and willing to dispute him on his own grounds.[10]

There is, of course, nothing novel about reductionism, materialism, and determinism of the kind displayed here; these are doctrines with which Socrates contended long ago. What is new is that, as philosophies, they seem to be vindicated by scientific advance. Here, in consequence, is perhaps the most pernicious result of our technological progress – more dehumanizing than any actual manipulation or technique, present or future: the erosion, perhaps the final erosion, of the idea of man as noble, dignified, precious, or godlike, and its replacement with a view of man, no less than of nature, as mere raw material for manipulation and homogenization.

Hence, our peculiar moral crisis. We are in turbulent seas without a landmark precisely because we adhere more and more to a view of human life that both gives us enormous power and that, *at the same time*, denies every possibility of nonarbitrary standards for guiding its use. Though well equipped, we know not who we are or where we are going. We triumph over nature's unpredictabilities only to subject ourselves, tragically, to the still greater unpredictability of our capricious wills and our fickle opinions. Engineering the engineer as well as the engine, we race our train we know not where. That we do not recognize our predicament is itself a tribute to the depth of our infatuation with scientific progress and our naive faith in the sufficiency of our humanitarian impulses.

Does this mean that I am therefore in favor of ignorance, suffering, and death? Of killing the goose of genetic technology even before she lays her golden eggs? Surely not. But unless we mobilize the courage to look foursquare at the full human meaning of our new enterprise in biogenetic technology and engineering, we are doomed to become its creatures if not its slaves. Important though it is to set a moral boundary here, devise a regulation there, hoping to decrease the damage caused by this or that little rivulet, it is even more important to be sober about the true nature and meaning of the flood itself.

That our exuberant new biologists and their technological minions might be persuaded of this is, to say the least, highly unlikely. For all their ingenuity, they do not even seek the wisdom that just might yield the kind of knowledge that keeps human life human. But it is not too late for the rest of us to become aware of the dangers – not just to privacy or insurability, but to our very humanity. So aware, we might be better able to defend the increasingly beleaguered vestiges and principles of our human dignity, even as we continue to reap the considerable benefits that genetic technology will inevitably provide.

Notes

1   For a discussion of the implications of genetic screening for our belief in human equality, see my essay, "Perfect Babies: Pre-Natal Diagnosis and the Equal Right to Life." Chapter Three in my book, *Toward a More Natural Science: Biology and Human Affairs* (New York: The Free Press, 1985). One of the most worrisome but least appreciated aspects of the godlike power of the new genetics is its tendency to "re-define" a human being in terms of his genes. Once a person is decisively characterized by his genotype, it is but a short step to justifying death solely for genetic sins.

2   This is the real problem with positive eugenics: less the threat of coercion, more the presumption of thinking we are wise enough to engineer "improvements" in the human species.

3   National Bioethics Advisory Commission, *Cloning Human Beings*, 1997, p. iii. For a bolder and more far-reaching assessment of cloning, see Leon R. Kass and James Q. Wilson, *The Ethics of Human Cloning* (Washington, D.C.: AEI Press, 1998).

4   I forbear mentioning what is rapidly becoming another trumping argument: increasing the profits of my biotech company and its shareholders.

5   To paraphrase Bertrand Russell, technological humanitarianism is like a warm bath that heats up so imperceptibly you don't know when to scream.

6   Aldous Huxley's portrait was and still is science fiction, but it is sobering to notice how many possibilities that were dismissed as mere science fiction not twenty years ago are today genuine biological possibilities.

7   Howard Kaye, "Anxiety and Genetic Manipulation: A Sociological View," *Perspectives in Biology and Medicine* 41 (1998), 483, 488. See also Kaye's book, *The Social Meaning of Modern Biology*, second edition (New Brunswick, NJ: Transaction Publishers 1997).

8   International Academy of Humanism, "Statement in Defense of Cloning and the Integrity of Scientific Research," May 16, 1997.

9   Steven Pinker, "A Matter of Soul," Correspondence Section, *The Weekly Standard*, February 2, 1998, p.6.

10   For an attempt to dispute such reductionist claims and to point the way to a more adequate account of living nature (on philosophical, not religious grounds), see my *Toward a More Natural Science: Biology and Human Affairs* (New York: The Free Press, 1985) and *The Hungry Soul: Eating and the Perfecting of Our Nature* (New York: The Free Press, 1994; paperback second edition, Chicago: University of Chicago Press, 1999). See also Hans Jonas, *The Phenomenon of Life: Toward a Philosophical Biology* (New York: Harper & Row, 1966; Chicago: University of Chicago Press, 1982).

4.2.4 Finn Bowring
"The Cyborg Solution"

A Rational Nature

What is the significance of Straus's phenomenological account of the upright posture? First of all, Straus shows that our uniquely human way of being-in-the-world – our rationality and reflectiveness, our humility and sociality, our appreciation of form and of creature comforts, our sense of moral rectitude-cannot be explained as the expression of some large and sophisticated neurological apparatus (whose cognitive powers may be upgraded or replaced), nor of a disembodied spirit or consciousness in fundamental opposition to its animal flesh. We are, rather, *rational thinking bodies –* our humanity is always present in and conveyed by the totality of our physical and animal being:

> The traditional definition of man as a rational animal has frequently been interpreted to mean that one has to conquer the animal in order to be rational – that rationality has to be servered from animal existence. Considering awakeness, one may find that rationality originates in and issues from the animal nature, i.e., from corporeality and motility. While man transcends the boundaries of his here and now, he remains bound to the original situation.[1]

'The "rational" is', as Straus puts it, 'as genuine a part of human nature as the "animal".'[2] We acknowledge this fact, Leon Kass suggests, when we honour – as do all cultures – the lifeless bodies of the dead.[3]

Yet there is another side to our human nature, for our embodiment also makes us vulnerable and suffering creatures. Our rational humanity is a natural possibility but a precarious accomplishment, for it is continually menaced and interrupted by our perishable and needy bodies, by our finitude and mortality, by our material exigencies, appetites and inconveniences. To be a natural body is to be an object of nature. And here indeed lies the ambiguity of the human condition: to exercise our rational nature, we

Finn Bowring, "The Cyborg Solution," in Finn Bowring, *Science, Seeds and Cyborgs: Biotechnology and the Appropriation of Life* (London: Verso, 2003), pp. 259–277. Reprinted with permission of Verso.

must defy nature in a natural way. For just as we owe to gravity the dignity of our upright posture, so we gather against the opposition of nature a ballast of interiority, a refusal of the object – and of being an object in its thrall – which enables us to reapprehend the world in its aesthetic and moral dimensions, and to perpetuate and embolden this awareness through cultural representations. Hence 'man's natural opposition to nature enables him to produce society, history, and conventions'.[4]

The adornment of the body is one such convention. The fig leaf, as Kant rethinks the biblical creation myth, is the means by which the transient natural impulses of sexual attraction 'can be prolonged and even increased by means of the imagination – a power which carries on its business, to be sure, the more moderately, but at once also the more constantly and uniformly, the more its object is removed from the senses'.[5] The concealment of our nakedness is not merely symbolic of our refusal of nature, for it also moderates, rationalises and prolongs the attraction of that nature, removing from sight the object of desire, but simultaneously stimulating the erotic imagination, the arts of love and romance, the thought and anticipation of sexual fulfilment. By clothing our bodies we not only hide our vulnerability, our blemishes and imperfections, our imperious physiological needs and desires. We also cultivate a subjective inwardness – an *awareness* of our physicality, which is often all the more enhanced by garments that must be *mastered* by their wearer, and whose mastery expresses, as itself a magnetic object of attraction, the human qualities of elegance, composure, balance and refinement.

Contrast this, then, with the casual brutality of the cosmetic surgeon, who is paid not to conceal the body's imperfections or to encourage the client's expressive use of his or her body, but rather to make that body into the shameless object of a disembodied desire. The surgically 'enhanced' body loses its affinity with selfhood, ceases to be a medium for the subtle arts of eroticism and intimacy, and instead becomes a form of manipulable and hard-earned property, an object *designed for display*. In the case of the now-growing fashion in the US for female cosmetic genital surgery ('labiaplasty'), we have an extraordinary example of the repressive 'deployment of sexuality' described by Foucault in *The History of Sexuality*.[6] Here the most intimate and unexamined of physical idiosyncrasies, the smallest and most concealed anatomical imperfections, no longer seem worthy of an assertion of privacy, an erotics of modesty, or a defence of undisclosed interiority, but are instead willingly exposed, under the pretext of sexual liberation, to the normalising discipline of the social and technocratic gaze.

Today this social immobilisation of the body, its disconnection from the expressive spirit of the person, is equally apparent in the prolific use of the botulinum toxin to lessen, by paralysing non-essential facial muscles, the decipherable wrinkles of ageing skin, as well as in new keyhole surgery aimed at preventing excessive blushing by severing the relevant nerve chains.[7] The ultimate function of such procedures, by erasing all signs of personal history and character, and by denying the natural form of the body any organic relationship to personhood, seems to be to remove all meaningful criteria for *being oneself*. The result is that satisfaction with one's commodity-enhanced body becomes an ever more elusive possibility, while the body itself ceases to express who one is, but instead conveys how much of who one isn't one can afford.

The transformation of our bodies into inert and imperishable objects of human design is, of course, the mutual concern both of cyborg theorists and of biotech companies like Geron Corporation and Human Genome Sciences – firms that are eagerly searching for genetic means to extend the human life-span.[8] If these efforts are successful, one likely political consequence will be chronic generational conflict, as older people refuse to make way for new social entrants by moving *down* the hierarchy they so painstakingly ascended.[9] Conquering death also has dramatic existential ramifications, for it is the very perishability of human life, and the futility of devoting ourselves exclusively to our own survival, which moves us to human acts of creation and moral judgement. Without the certainty of death, we would have no reason to live life passionately and to the full, for everything would have the status of a rehearsal, would be repeatable or revisable a second time around. Without death, there would be no anguish, no cherishing of the good, no commitment worthy of the name, no meaningful sacrifice, no nobility in the face of non-being. Since an immortal population would have no call to procreate, the abolition of death would also mean the abolition of youth, and with it the wonder and curiosity that rarely survives the passage to adulthood.

Kevin Warwick envisages a human being liberated from the inconvenience of sleep, and whose thoughts can be communicated without the need to struggle with miscommunicating language or speech. Virtual reality enthusiasts like Ray Kurzweil anticipate the artificial stimulation of 'neurological correlates of spiritual experiences', and the generation of pleasurable sensations and feelings independent of the objects of pleasure and the effort to attain them. What applies to the impermanence of human life is equally applicable here: we cannot be upstanding without the interruption of sleep, we cannot be creators of meaning without suffering the inadequacy of language, and we cannot find a home in the world – indeed, there can be no 'world' – unless things first exceed our grasp. Death, sleep, language, things, by removing us from ourselves, allow us to recover our given nature in a human way.

A Fatal Contradiction

The means by which human beings reason and make sense of their world, while often opposed to the forces of nature, are thus fundamentally corporeal in their significance. There is no act of human perception, thought, imagination, calculation or judgement which is not the act of a living, suffering, decaying body. The argument that humans have acquired the knowledge and competence to dictate the path of their own evolution thus founders on the fact that this capacity is itself only meaningful to a corporeal, suffering being. In the post-humanist account offered by Max More,[10] humans are biochemical machines of such sophistication and complexity that they have developed the emergent, non-mechanical properties of consciousness and reason. Yet for More the emancipatory possibilities of consciousness remain shackled by our biological–mechanical heritage, which makes us prisoners of our genes, our mortality, our uncontrollable emotions, hormones, and neural events. "The whole appeal of seeing that we are a complex functionally interrelated collection of mechanical parts is that it opens up an appealing prospect: that technology will allow us to modify our nature, to alter ourselves, to augment and shape ourselves according to our values."[11]

Yet on the basis of what values, what self-evidences, what certainties, is this project of 'transbiomorphosis' to be grounded? Does not the post-humanist programme simply reintroduce the dualism of mind and body which More otherwise takes to be 'scientifically and philosophically indefensible', in which the capacity to reason and choose is uprooted from the world of sentient experience? It is unsurprising that More draws confidence for his vision from Nietzsche's *Übermensch*, proposing that humans become 'artists of the self',[12] and thus making the sheer will to self-transformation, the restless defiance of everything that endures, the constant and uncompromising renunciation of all mores, habits, limitations and conventions, the quintessential expression of freedom.[13]

The contradiction in this post-humanist perspective is noted by Hans Jonas, who points out that the capacity to even contemplate intervening in our evolution is a product of evolution – and a perishable product at that. On what premises, therefore, do today's genetic and cyborg revolutionaries claim the authority to make the human species an object of instrumental manipulation? Unlike Marx's proletarians, they certainly have something to lose other than their chains, for they assume a degree of power and depth of knowledge that is historically unprecedented. Yet if their judgement is that human nature is flawed and inadequate, then so must be their judgement of that inadequacy, as well as the remedy they propose for its failings, for these too are the contingent products of evolution. If, on the other hand, they proclaim the superiority of their wisdom, then in asserting their qualification to change humanity they reaffirm its premise – the adequacy of their inherited natural constitution, which should not therefore be endangered.

> Some kind of authority must be asserted for the determination of models, and unless we subscribe to dualism and say that the cognitive subject is from above the world, this authority can only base itself on an essential sufficiency of our nature such as it has evolved within this world … [T]his innate sufficiency of human nature … we must posit as the enabling premise for any creative steering of destiny … Most evidently, the authority which it imparts can never include the disfiguring, endangering, or refashioning of itself. No gain is worth this price, no hope of gain justifies this risk. And yet, today, this very share of transcendence too is in danger of being thrown into the crucible of bio-technological alchemy – as if the enabling condition for all our freedom to revise the given were itself among the revisables.[14]

Humankind is not, Jonas points out, the object of a programmed schedule of completion running, as in the growth and maturation of the individual, from the unfinished to the finished, from the provisional to the definitive, from the not yet to the true and full being. The human person is an incomplete finality, an imperfect perfection. But humanity, in its incompleteness and imperfection, is always already there, fully and without qualification, and it must therefore be preserved as such. As Paul Virilio cites St. Hildegarde of Bingen: *Homo Est Clausura Mirabilium Dei* – 'Man is the closing point of the marvels of the universe'.[15]

> The basic error of the ontology of 'not yet' and its eschatological hope is repudiated by the plain truth – ground for neither jubilation nor dejection – that genuine man is always already there and was there throughout known history: in his heights and his depths, his greatness and wretchedness, his bliss and torment, his justice and his guilt – in short, in all the *ambiguity* that is inseparable from his humanity. Wishing to abolish this constitutive ambiguity is wishing to abolish man in his unfathomable freedom … The really unambiguous man of utopia can only be the flattened, behaviourally conditioned homunculus of futuristic psychological engineering.[16]

The constitutive ambiguity of the human essence is precisely why the much-lauded 'dignity of man' is always only a potential – a natural capacity for uprightness which must be constantly exercised and reaffirmed – and why the dignified being of Man can only be declared with unpardonable vanity. But the fulfilment of this possibility is every person's responsibility, and one which must, Jonas asserts, never be put at risk: 'the possibility of there being responsibility in the world, which is bound to the existence of men, is of all objects of responsibility the first'.[17]

Needs and Imperatives

So the improvement of the human species is a possibility which no human being is qualified to fulfil, and its pursuit risks the very survival of that possibility itself. But what if the re-engineering of humanity were a *necessity*, rather than a mere possibility, as some of today's cyber-enthusiasts maintain?

In the account offered by Kevin Warwick, humans will in the future be living in a world dominated by intelligent and self-replicating machines, a world 'in which humans, if they still exist, will be subservient'.[18] Theodore Kaczynski, the American 'Unabomber', similarly predicted in his manifesto, 'Industrial Society and its Future', that our tendency to delegate tasks to evermore sophisticated machines may eventually reach a point 'at which the decisions necessary to keep the system running will be so complex that human beings will be incapable of making them intelligently. At that stage the machines will be in effective control.'[19] In his heretical essay, 'Why the Future Doesn't Need Us', the respected computer scientist and co-founder of Sun Microsystems, Bill Joy, became the first prominent figure in the world of information technology to share these concerns, acknowledging 'that I may be working to create tools which will enable the construction of the technology that may replace our species'.[20]

In the view of Hans Moravec, the mismatch between humans' natural and culturally acquired competencies and their technological environments is already apparent. 'The world we inhabit is radically different, culturally and physically, from the one to which we adapted biologically.'

> Today, as our machines approach human competence across the board, our stone-age biology and our information-age lives grow ever more mismatched ... As societal roles become yet more complex, specialised, and far removed from our inborn predispositions, they require increasing years of rehearsal to master, while providing fewer visceral rewards. The essential functioning of a technical society eludes the understanding of an increasing fraction of the population ... The mismatch between instinct and necessity induces alienation in the midst of unprecedented physical plenty.[21]

For cyborg theorists such as Warwick, Kurzweil and Moravec, the solution to humans' dwindling control over their environments and the prospect of eventual extinction is to use the technology we have spawned to enhance our powers of thought, reasoning, memory, longevity and action. As Alvin and Heidi Toffler counsel against the Kaczynski-inspired pessimism of Joy: 'The very technologies they regard as most dangerous – robotics, genetics and nanotech – may very well help us expand the human brain's capabilities and make it possible for us to use those technologies in completely new ways.'[22]

What is desired by the cyborg enthusiasts is, in effect, the elimination or revision of those features of human existence which, being censored, repressed, harmed and alienated by modern social conditions, lead to disempowerment, frustration and suffering. The elimination of our capacity to suffer is not, however, a satisfactory answer to suffering – or at least not a *human* one. The human answer to suffering is *relief from suffering*, which must also suffer the precariousness of this relief and the knowledge of the burden that has been lightened. Because the elimination of human's capacity to suffer would mean the creation of a post-human being, the goal and beneficiary of this solution *cannot be humanity itself*. The need for the cyborg, in other words, is not a *human* need, a need whose satisfaction would reaffirm the essence of humanity. It is, rather, a *technological imperative*, for the true purpose of the re-engineering of the human being is the abolition of the obstacles presented by people to the reproduction of machines. As George Dyson candidly describes it, humans have today become 'bottlenecks' in the circulation and processing of knowledge and information:

> Most of the time, despite the perception of being inundated with information, we will remain out of the loop. Human beings have only limited time and ability to communicate: you can watch television, check your E-mail, and talk on your cellular phone at the same time, but that's the limit. We are now the bottleneck – able to absorb a limited amount of information while producing even less, from the point of view of machines.[23]

From the point of view of machines, the pedestrian individual is a hindrance, an obstructive inconvenience which must be removed, as Virilio describes it, by the total mobilisation and motorisation of the person – by the transformation of the person into a prosthesis of the machine.[24] 'In the second half of the twenty-first century', Kurzweil confidently predicts, 'you'll be able to read a book in a few seconds'.[25] Will this be an ability or an imperative, one wonders; will we be able to choose a more leisurely read (say a few minutes per book)? Kurzweil's promise is in any case meaningless. His prescription for a post-human intelligence has no other aim than that of reconciling individuals to 'the point of view of the machine': reducing the human subject to quantifiable units of memory and processing power which can be speeded up, magnified, rendered more accurate, efficient, predictable and powerful, but which are incapable of furnishing a sense of purpose or meaning to their existence.

Subjectivity and Forgetfulness

The necessity of the cyborg is nothing other than the technological imperative, sometimes resisted but increasingly treated as the acceptable price of progress, that humans be modified to function in a world, imagined, sought-after or anticipated, which is devoid of human references – a world we can no longer call 'home'. We can see this ambition, most pertinently, in the text where the term was originally coined. 'Cyborgs and Space', written by two senior American research scientists and published in *Astronautics* in 1960, was a response to an invitation from NASA to consider ways of modifying human nature 'to permit man's existence in environments which differ radically from those provided by nature as we know it'. In their account of 'self-regulating man-machine systems', Manfred Clynes and Nathan Kline rejected the path of genetic engineering in favour of 'biochemical, physiological, and electronic modifications of man's existing modus vivendi'. They proposed instead psychotropic medicine to keep astronauts awake and alert for 'weeks or even a few months', prophylactic drugs which would be automatically injected in response to detected radiation, induced hypothermia to reduce energy needs during long journeys, the modification of cardiovascular functioning (either by drugs or electrical stimulation) to suit different environments, and the 'sterilisation of the gastrointestinal tract, plus intravenous or direct intragastric feeding', to eliminate faecal waste.

'An inverse fuel cell,' they add, 'capable of reducing CO_2 to its components with removal of the carbon and recirculation of the oxygen, would eliminate the necessity for lung breathing.' 'Solving the many technological problems involved in manned space flight by adapting man to his environment, rather than vice versa,' they concluded, 'will not only mark a significant step forward in man's scientific progress, but may well provide a new and larger dimension for man's spirit as well.'[26]

Can the spirit of humanity be enlarged by its liberation from the natural needs, rhythms and magnitudes of the human body, from its intrinsic vitality, its capacity for self-animation, self-healing and survival? More importantly, what credence can we give to a scientific vision of humankind *which does not understand itself*, which denies its own rootedness in the sensible and ambiguous world, which glorifies the negation of its own conditions of possibility? To reconcile the human being with the imperatives of an inhuman environment is to make that being a functionary of its environment, and of our refusal to change that environment or resist its allure in favour of a familiar, more human world.

This refusal of scientists to return human beings, humble but uplifted, to the experienced world in which they truly dwell, is what aligns modern science with the adversaries of the human condition. The origins of this betrayal lie, as Edmund Husserl wrote in the 1930s, in a scientific project which, by failing to account for its own existence, its groundedness in the vague and fluid typifications of sensory experience, mistakes the results of its formalised method – the idealised reduction of the world to exact, measurable and universally translatable essences – for the world itself:

> In this way, the world of our experience is from the beginning interpreted by recourse to an 'idealisation' – but it is no longer seen that this idealisation, which leads to the exact space of geometry, to the exact time of physics, to exact causal laws, and which makes us see the world of our experience as being thus determined in itself, is itself the result of a function of cognitive methods, a result based on the data of our immediate experience. This experience in its immediacy knows neither exact space nor objective time and causality.[27]

This original experience, though self-evident and indubitable in its substance, is permeated by mystery and uncertainty, by the inexactitude of its object and by the impossibility of illuminating that inexactitude, of recovering lived experience, in a precise and objective way. It is from this metaphysical breach at the heart of human existence that positivist science offers an escape, promising a means of understanding the world that no longer has to understand itself – an experience, exemplified in the being of the cyborg, devoid of the unspeakable doubt, the wonder, the incommunicable convictions, that are definitive of the human subject.

> Mathematical science of nature is a technical marvel for the purpose of accomplishing inductions whose fruitfulness, probability, exactitude, and calculability could previously not even be suspected. As an accomplishment it is a triumph of the human spirit. With regard to the rationality of its methods and theories, however, it is a thoroughly relative science. It presupposes as data principles that are themselves thoroughly lacking in actual rationality. In so far as the intuitive environing world, purely subjective as it is, is forgotten in the scientific thematic, the working subject is also forgotten.[28]

The vision of the cyborg emanates from the belief, apparent as much in the physico-computational accounts of human consciousness as in the reduction of life to a universally translatable language of genes, 'that the infinite totality of what is in general is intrinsically a rational all-encompassing unity that can be mastered, without anything left over, by a corresponding universal science'.[29] Today this orthodoxy not only permits those who aspire to re-engineer the human being to forget the subject who makes that aspiration possible. It also provides a programme, a manifesto, to make this state of amnesia constitutive of the post-human condition. We should therefore heed Merleau-Ponty's warning, made before the biotech revolution had cast its fatal spell:

> Thinking 'operationally' has become a sort of absolute artificialism, such as we see in the ideology of cybernetics, where human creations are derived from a natural information process, itself conceived on the model of human machines. If this kind of thinking were to extend its reign to man and history; if, pretending to ignore what we know of them through our own situations, it were to set out to construct man and history on the basis of a few abstract indices ... then, since man really becomes the *manipulandum* he takes himself to be, we enter into a cultural regimen where there is neither truth nor falsity concerning man and history, into a sleep, or a nightmare, from which there is no awakening.[30]

Notes

1   Erwin W. Straus, 'Awakeness', in *Phenomenological Psychology*. London: Tavistock, 1966, p. 116.
2   Straus, 'The Upright Posture', ibid., p. 165.
3   Leon R. Kass. 'Thinking About the Body', in *Towards a More Natural Science: Biology and Human Affairs*, New York: Free Press, 1985.
4   Straus, 'The Upright Posture', p. 142.
5   Immanuel Kant, 'Conjectural Beginning of Human History', in Lewis White Beck, ed., *Kant On History*, Indianapolis: Bobbs-Merrill, 1963, p. 57.
6   Michel Foucault, *The History of Sexuality: vol. 1*, Harmondsworth: Penguin, 1990.
7   Anthony Browne, 'New surgery may be a sweat but it can save the lady's blushes', *Guardian*, 21 January 2001.
8   Aside from the regenerative potential of stem cells, Geron is also interested in – and indeed has patented – the gene for telomerase, an enzyme which rebuilds the tips of the chromosomes. As the cell divides and ages, the ends of the chromosomes, which are comprised of a single

six-nucleotide sequence repeated thousands of times, get shorter and shorter until, after fifty or more divisions, the cell can divide no further and becomes senescent. Since offspring must of course be born with readily dividing cells, the telomerase gene is activated in the egg and sperm cells, serving to restore the tips of the chromosomes – called telomeres – to their original length. Geron's belief that telomerase offers a means of immortalising human cells must be tempered by the recognition that, because most cancerous cells exhibit an *active* telomerase gene, the natural shortening of the telomeres and resulting finite life-span of cells is a built-in defence against uncontrolled cell growth (cancer). (See Nicholas Wade, *Life Script: The Genome and the New Medicine*, London: Simon and Schuster, 2001, pp. 135–8.)

9   Francis Fukuyama, *Our Posthuman Future: Consequences of the Biotechnology Revolution*, New York: Farrar, Straus and Giroux, 2002, pp. 65–7.

10 Max More is the president of the Californian 'Extropy Institute', which holds conferences and disseminates ideas on future technology and its relevance to human beings. Selling himself as a 'corporate philosopher' (which presumably means 'management consultant'), More has yet to publish his work with a commercial publisher. His lectures and articles are available at <www.maxmore.com> and <www.extropy.org>.

11 Max More, 'Beyond the Machine: Technology and Posthuman Freedom', New York, 1997.

12 As Nietzsche wrote in 1885–6: 'the possibility has been established for the production of international racial unions whose task will be to rear a master race, the future "masters of the earth"; – a new, tremendous aristocracy ... [who will] work as artists upon "man" himself'. (Fricdrich Nietzsche, *The Will to Power*, New York: Vintage, 1968, §960.)

13 Max More, "Technological Self-Transformation: Expanding Personal Extropy', *Extropy*, no. 10, Winter/Spring 1993.

14 Hans Jonas, *The Imperative of Responsibility: In Search of an Ethics for the Technological Age*, Chicago: University of Chicago Press, 1984; p. 33.

15 John Armitage, 'From Modernism to Hypermodernism and Beyond: An Interview with Paul Virilio', in Armitage, ed., *Paul Virilio: From Modernism to Hypermodernism and Beyond*, London: Sage, 2000, p. 30.

16 Jonas, *The Imperative of Responsibility*, pp. 200–1.

17 Jonas, *The Imperative of Responsibility*, p. 99.

18 Kevin Warwick, *In the Mind of the Machine: The Breakthrough in Artificial Intelligence*, London: Arrow, 1998, p. 261.

19 Cited in Kurzweil, R. *The Age of Spiritual Machines*, New York: Viking Press, 1999 p. 225.

20 Bill Joy, 'Why the Future Doesn't Need Us', *Wired*, vol. 8, no. 4, April 2000. <www.wired.com>

21 Moravec, *Robot*, pp. 3, 7.

22 Alvin Toffler and Heidi Toffler, 'More Technology, Not Less', *New Perspectives Quarterly*, vol. 17, no. 3, Summer 2000, p. 8.

23 George Dyson, *Darwin Among the Machines*, Harmondsworth: Penguin, 1997, p. 209.

24 Paul Virilio, *The Art of the Motor*, Minneapolis: University of Minnesota Press, 1995.

25 Kurzweil, *The Age of Spiritual Machines*, p. 123.

26 Manfred E. Clynes and Nathan S. Kline, 'Cyborgs and Space', in Chris Hables Gray, ed., *The Cyborg Handbook*, New York: Routledge, 1995, pp. 29–33.

27 Edmund Husserl, *Experience and Judgement: Investigations in a Genealogy of Logic*, London: Routledge and Kegan Paul, 1973, p. 43.

28 Edmund Husserl, 'Philosophy and the Crisis of European Man', in *Phenomenology and the Crisis of Philosophy*, New York: Harper and Row, 1965, p. 186.

29 Edmund Husserl, *The Crisis of European Sciences and Transcendental Phenomenology: An Introduction to Phenomenological Philosophy*, Evanston, Ill.: Northwestern University Press, 1970, p. 22.

30 Maurice Merleau-Ponty, 'Eye and Mind', in John O'Neill, ed., *Maurice Merleau-Ponty: Phenomenology, Language and Sociology*, London: Heinernarm, 1974, p. 281. 'L'Oeil et l'espirit' was the last work Merleau-Ponty saw published. It appeared in the inaugural issue of *Art de France* in January 1961, and was republished after his death by *Les Temps Modernes* in the same year.

4.3 Human Rights

Introduction

One of the most remarkable chapters in the recent history of natural law thinking was the great revival of interest it underwent in reaction to the atrocities of World War II. An important part of the story of this revival has already been illustrated in earlier selections. These, it will be recalled, placed particular emphasis upon the emergent post-war critique of strict positivism which represented it as allowing for the most monstrous expression of unregulated and ideologically compromised legislative will. At the risk of some oversimplification, this critique may be characterized as the negative expression of the wider post-war response. In contrast, its positive expression was the enthusiastic ground-swell of support for a firm articulation of a basic set of non-gainsayable rights owed to each person merely in virtue of his or her humanity.[1] One of the moving intellects behind the codification of just such a set of fundamental human rights in the Universal Declaration was the French thinker Jacques Maritain, whose work we have already had occasion to encounter. Perhaps unsurprisingly, he was of the view that to be sustainable, such rights need clearly to be grounded in a proper understanding of the basic requirements of human nature, which he saw as needing to be in harmony with the central natural law tradition. A distinguished neo-Thomist whose philosophical acumen ranged his mind across a whole host of subjects, and someone deeply affected by the European conflagration, Maritain was profoundly aware of the power ideas had to affect the course of human history. For this reason he warned of the need to beware of the incompatible philosophies and anthropologies underlying differing interpretative approaches adapted to accepted catalogues of rights: "because here we are no longer dealing with the single recognition of the diverse categories of human rights, but with

[1] See, in general, M. Glendon, *A World Made New: Eleanor Roosevelt and the Universal Declaration of Human Rights* (New York: Random House, 2002).

The Natural Law Reader, First Edition. Edited by Jacqueline A. Laing and Russell Wilcox.
© 2014 Blackwell Publishing Ltd. Published 2014 by Blackwell Publishing Ltd.

the principle of dynamic unification in accordance with which they are carried into effect."[2] Consequently, Maritain goes on, "[e]verything depends upon the supreme values in accordance with which all these rights will be ordered and limit each other."[3] For Maritain and many of the framers of the Universal Declaration this supreme value was "human dignity," but then the question immediately arises: in what does "human dignity" consist and the answer, it would seem, leads straight back to questions of philosophical anthropology.[4]

One of the most influential such attempts to read the commonly accepted catalogues of rights in a manner fully compatible with the anthropology embodied in the central natural law tradition can be traced to John Finnis' now classic study *Natural Law and Natural Rights*.[5] There he outlined how, in his view, "the modern language of rights provides ... a supple and potentially precise instrument for sorting out and expressing the demands of justice."[6] In so doing, he offered a "long but by no means elaborate discussion" of how respect for the most commonly articulated human rights is a "fundamental component of the common good," but also how most are "subject to or limited by each other and by other aspects of the common good,"[7] and he went on to illustrate how the necessary balance might be struck in a way compatible with the true requirements of human nature.[8] The extract reproduced here is from a later article by Finnis which summarizes the position originally set out in *Natural Law and Natural Rights* in a more abbreviated and accessible form without sacrificing any of its central points.[9]

As Mary Ann Glendon notes in the next selection, not everybody within the classical natural law tradition has been as optimistic about pressing the language of rights into the service of real human flourishing.[10] Indeed, some thinkers, such as Michel Villey and Alasdair MacIntyre, have suggested that the whole project embodied in the Universal Declaration is defective at its root, manifesting a hopelessly incoherent array of desires and commitments. Glendon is not quite so dismissive, but, in tracing the history of the drafting of the Declaration, she highlights once again the manner in which its framers were forced to prescind from constructing a fully elaborated underlying philosophy by substituting for it the principle of "human dignity" (in a manner altogether more attenuated than that envisaged by Maritain). As such, although Glendon is keen to give due recognition to the synthetic and comparative achievement of the Universal Declaration so that it cannot, in her view, merely be dismissed as a product, for example, of Western imperialism, she is also clear that the incomplete nature of that achievement has indeed allowed for a form of human rights imperialism,

---

[2]   J. Maritain, "Natural Law and Natural Rights," Chap. 3 in *Natural Law: Reflections on Theory and Practice*, ed. W. Sweet (South Bend, IN: St. Augustine's Press, 2001), pp. 39–74; p. 73.

[3]   Ibid., pp. 73–74.

[4]   For evidence of the malleability this concept has come to obtain in contemporary judicial pronouncements see C. McCrudden, "Human Dignity and Judicial Interpretation of Human Rights," *European Journal of International Law* 19, 4 (2008), pp. 655–724.

[5]   J. Finnis, *Natural Law and Natural Rights* (Oxford: Clarendon Press, 1981).

[6]   Ibid., "Rights," Chap. VIII, pp. 198–226.

[7]   Ibid.

[8]   Ibid.

[9]   J. Finnis, "Natural Law," in *The Collected Essays of John Finnis*, Volume 1: *Reason in Action* (Oxford: Oxford University Press, 2011), pp. 206–211.

[10]   M. Glendon, "Foundations of Human Rights: The Unfinished Business," *American Journal of Jurisprudence* 44 (1999), pp. 1–14.

grounded not in the Declaration itself but in "the efforts of special interest groups to commandeer human rights for their own purposes."[11]

Drawing upon a wealth of historical and contemporary sources, it is the central focus of the final selection in this section – "Human Rights as an Ideological Project" by James Schall – to assess the prospects and difficulties of engaging in the task of completion of the human rights project called for at the end of Glendon's piece.[12] On the whole, it must be said, Schall does not strike a particularly optimistic note. In particular, he is keen to point to the ease with which the idiom of human rights has been hijacked by hostile philosophical forces and used as a rhetorical trope to push for precisely the opposite of what it is claimed is their purpose. It is in the context of this ever-present danger of ideological metastases that Schall seems to feel that the most prudent course with respect to the human rights industry is one of deconstructive critique.

[11] Ibid.
[12] J.V. Schall, "Human Rights as an Ideological Project," *American Journal of Jurisprudence* 32 (1987), pp. 47–61.

4.3.1 John Finnis
"Natural Law"

LOI NATURELLE, DROIT NATUREL,
DROITS NATURELS

Reflection on natural law has in recent time been complicated by the claim of some authors (notably Michel Villey) that there is, in Aquinas and in truth, 'une opposition capitale entre *droit* et *loi*'. Though much insisted upon, it is not easy to understand the alleged 'opposition' or 'radical distinction'. Villey understood *droit* as, centrally, the 'that which is just', the ensemble of right relations between persons and 'things' (in a very broad sense of 'things' which includes freely chosen human actions, e.g. paying compensation); this understanding corresponds to Aquinas's primary definition of *ius* as *id quod iustum est* (that which is just). But Villey insisted that knowledge of this *droit*, even of *droit naturel* as distinct from *droit positif*, comes not from the specification of the higher principles of practical reason which Aquinas called (interchangeably!) *lex naturalis* and *ius naturale*, but from 'l'observation de la nature' (including, of course, 'la nature des hommes' and of 'les sociétés elles-mêmes, données présentes dans la nature'). He drew a sharp distinction between 'la morale individuelle', which he considered could properly be guided by the principles and precepts of natural law, and 'le droit' (juridique), which is guided by the aforesaid 'observation'. No such epistemic distinction can be found in Aquinas, however. More important, the claim that juridical science, law-making, or legal interpretation can be grounded on *observation of facts* must be judged a flight from the rational requirement of pointing to reasons – which in the field of *praxis*, whether individual or social, must be reasons (principles and specifications of principles) that are normative (directive) because pointing to aspects of human fulfilment (individual and social).

There is, of course, a distinction to be made between *loi naturelle* and *droit naturel*, if the latter is understood (as it is sometimes, but not always, in Aquinas) as referring to the Roman law concept of *ius* as the ensemble of morally (or juridically) cognizable relations between say two persons and a subject-matter (e.g. some action of one of them). The distinction is simply that the *loi naturelle* is as such the set of reasons (principles) which

John Finnis, "Natural Law," in *The Collected Essays of John Finnis*, Volume 1: *Reason in Action* (Oxford: Oxford University Press, 2011), pp. 206–211. Reprinted with permission of Oxford University Press.

justify the assertion of the *droit naturel* in question. The latter is the former in its application to a specified class of persons and subject-matter. There is distinction but no question of opposition, still less '*opposition capitale*'.

Villey and many others have also underlined the importance of the shift from the Roman law sense of *ius*, mentioned above, to the modern sense (perhaps beginning to emerge c. 1325 in Ockham's polemics against the Thomist Pope John XXII) of 'my right', '*droits naturels*', subjective right. But while it is clear that this shift is correlated with the emergence of contractualist and voluntarist conceptions of society, authority, law, and obligation, and with modern conceptions or attitudes which can be vaguely called 'individualist', it seems unlikely that the differing semantics and logic of *droit* and *droits* has any truly fundamental importance. Villey was right to call attention to the danger that unilateral claims of right (that is, of rights) would mask sheer unconcern with the interests of others and with the 'whole' which is available for just distribution. But this danger must be confronted not by insisting on semantic distinctions superseded in living usage, but by identifying and insisting upon the rational principles which are available to guide both individual and social judgment and choice and to criticize the unfair (unilateral) demands of individuals or groups and the claims of right which neglect the comparable rights of others. The issue is one of adequately specifying rights, not of seeking to banish talk of them. It is a logical truth that one and the same moral or juridical relationship between, say, two persons and one subject-matter can be spoken of either as an ensemble (a single *ius*) or by articulating its content in terms of the respective benefits which the relationship involves for one or both of the parties to it, benefits which are articulated by statements about the 'subjective' right(s) involved in the relationship.

[...]

INVIOLABLE HUMAN RIGHTS

The collapse of Christianity and other religious cultures, as the matrix for contemporary legal and political orders, has posed a challenge to those who wish to affirm that there is a natural law: to show that, even without the support of a religiously warranted ethic (revealed divine law) having an identical or overlapping content, there are philosophically sound reasons to affirm the truth of non-posited principles or norms which, although not claiming to be authoritative because posited, are sufficiently definite to exclude gross 'crimes against humanity' (Nuremberg, 1945; chattel slavery; abortions of convenience; non-voluntary euthanasia) and to underpin the main institutions of civilized societies (family, property, religious liberty, and so forth). In particular, the challenge is to show that aggregative conceptions of moral and political reasoning, such as classical or contemporary utilitarianism or consequentialism or 'economic analysis of law', are unsound.

Contemporary work in natural law theory therefore includes extensive attempts to criticize aggregative ethics, by showing that their conceptions of value overlook some or all of the basic human goods, and/or that their master principle of maximizing value overlooks the incommensurability not only of one basic human good relative to other such goods, but also of particular instantiations of even one and the same good in alternative options for morally significant choice. The supposition of those undertaking such a critique is that, if the critique is successful, the way will be open to identifying a richer set of moral principles guiding choice. A working postulate has been that any principle which has been the organizing or dominant principle of an entire philosophical ethic (e.g. Kantian universalizability, Epictetan detachment, the principle of commitment expounded by Royce and Marcel) has some place in a developed natural law theory.

But theoretical reflection has yielded a more systematic and unifying 'master principle of morality'. This principle is reached by way of the consideration that, so far as it is in one's power, one should allow nothing but the principles corresponding to the basic human goods to shape one's practical thinking. Aquinas's first principle, 'Good is to be done and pursued and evil avoided', taken as it stands, is not yet moral; it requires only that one not act pointlessly, that is, without reason; it requires only that one take at least one of the principles corresponding to a basic human good and follow through to the point at which one somehow instantiates that good through action. The first *moral* principle makes the stronger demand, not merely that one be reasonable enough to avoid pointlessness, but that one be entirely reasonable in one's practical thinking, choice, and action. It can be formulated: in voluntarily acting for human goods and avoiding what is opposed to them, one ought to choose and otherwise will those and only those possibilities whose willing is compatible with a will toward integral human fulfilment (i.e. the fulfilment of all human persons and communities).

Integral human fulfilment, so defined, is not a goal towards which actions could be organized as means. But it is not empty of critical force, in identifying choices motivated by emotion fettering and deflecting reason. Unfairness, being contrary to the Golden Rule (a principle superior in determinacy to Kant's substitute, universalizability), is one sort of willing that is incompatible with openness to integral human fulfilment. A choice to destroy some instantiation of a basic human good out of hatred is another. A choice precisely to destroy or damage some instantiation of a basic human good as a means to some other end is a third; the exclusion of such choosing is shown to be a demand of reason once the critique of aggregative theories has demonstrated the rational incommensurabilities overlooked by those who think that the goods promised by some envisaged end 'outweigh' the destruction or damage to human personal goods which is intended in a choice of this type.

This third moral principle corresponds not only to the traditional thought, 'the end does not justify these means', but also to the Kantian imperative, 'treat humanity always as an end and never as a means only' – though in recent natural law theory 'humanity' is understood without Kant's dualistic restriction of it to the rational faculties as such. It is a principle specified (made more specific) in the form of the traditional moral norms against murder and fraud. As such it is the backbone, so to speak, of traditional and modern legal systems. Articulated from the viewpoint of the beneficiaries of its moral protection, it is specified in those human rights which are not only inalienable but also, properly speaking, inviolable and absolute. It is the resultant of the classical principle that reason neither need nor should be the slave of the passions, together with (i) a precise understanding of free choice (enabling a firm and definite distinction between what is chosen and what is only accepted as a side effect), and (ii) an understanding, developed in dialectic with Enlightenment and post-Enlightenment aggregative ethics, of the incommensurabilities of the goods, persons, and probabilities at stake in alternative options for choice. In these and related ways, one can think that natural law theory of the classic type is capable of philosophically warranted development.

4.3.2 Mary Ann Glendon
"Foundations of Human Rights: The Unfinished Business"

How Can There be Universal Rights in Diverse Cultures?

Let us now turn to a more sophisticated version of the cultural-relativism critique. Assume that the UNESCO philosophers were right that a few basic norms of decent human behavior are very widely shared. Even if that is so at a general level, different nations and cultures attach quite different weights to these norms. Moreover, different political and economic conditions affect each nation's ability to bring human rights principles to life. That being so, what sense does it make to speak of universality?

That version of the cultural-relativism critique rests on a false premise shared by many rights activists and rights skeptics alike. It is the assumption that universal principles must be implemented in the same way everywhere. The Declaration's framers, however, never envisioned that its "common standard of achievement" would or should produce completely uniform practices.[1] P. C. Chang stressed that point in his 9 December 1948 speech to the General Assembly urging adoption of the Declaration. He deplored that colonial powers had tried to impose on other peoples a standardized way of thinking and a single way of life. That sort of uniformity could only be achieved, he said, by force or at the expense of truth. It could never last.[2] Chang and his colleagues on the Drafting Committee expected the Declaration's rights would be inculturated in various ways, and that over time the corpus of human rights would be enriched by these varied experiences.

The framers of the Universal Declaration also knew it was neither possible nor desirable for the Declaration to be frozen in *time*. They never claimed to have produced the last word on human rights. They expected that new rights would emerge in the future as they had in the past, and that old rights might be reformulated. That did not mean, however, that interpretation was up for grabs. They tried to provide the Declaration with safe passage through such transitions by giving it an interpretive matrix: freedom and solidarity, linked to a thick concept of personhood, and grounded in dignity.

The framers' approach was remembered by at least one distinguished international lawyer on the document's thirty-fifth anniversary in 1983. Philip Alston wrote on that occasion, "The Declaration does not purport to offer a single unified conception of the

Mary Ann Glendon, "Foundations of Human Rights: The Unfinished Business," *American Journal of Jurisprudence* 44 (1999), pp. 7–14. Reprinted with kind permission of the author.

world as it should be nor does it purport to offer some sort of comprehensive recipe for the attainment of an ideal world. Its purpose is rather the more modest one of proclaiming a set of values which are capable of giving some guidance to modern society in choosing among a wide range of alternative policy options."[3] By the 1970s, however, the original understanding of the Declaration was largely forgotten. And what oblivion had not erased, opportunism was eroding. The abstentions by South Africa and Saudi Arabia from the final vote approving the Declaration had been early warnings of more trouble ahead. South Africa had objected, among other things, to the word "dignity," apparently fearing its implications for the apartheid system it was then constructing. And Saudi Arabia had claimed that some of the so-called universal rights, particularly the right to change one's religion, were really just "Western" ideas. In 1948, those were isolated claims. But no sooner was the Declaration adopted than the Cold War antagonists pulled apart and politicized its provisions. That set the stage for further mischief. In 1955, the charge that some rights represented "Western" neo-colonialism resurfaced with particular vehemence at the Bandung conference, where the "nonaligned" nations found unity of a sort in shared resentment of the dominance of a few rich and powerful countries in world affairs.

The Deconstruction Derby

Over the 1960s and 1970s, the Declaration's framers, one by one, were departing from the world stage. The U.N. grew into an elaborate bureaucracy with more than 50,000 employees. Its specialized agencies become closely intertwined with the nongovernmental organizations that proliferated as the international human rights movement gained ground in the 1960s and 1970s. That movement in turn was deeply affected by the ideas about rights that predominated in the United States in those days.[4] The movement, like the Declaration itself, attracted many persons and groups who were more interested in harnessing its moral authority for their own ends than in furthering its original purposes.

Another important development, set in motion by the Cold War antagonists, was the nearly universal habit of reading the Declaration in the way that Americans read the Bill of Rights, that is, as a string of essentially separate guarantees. Its dignity-based language of rights began to be displaced by the more simplistic kinds of rights talk that were then making great inroads on political discourse in the United States. Several features of that new, hyper-individualistic dialect had the potential to wreak havoc with the Declaration: rights envisioned without individual or social responsibilities; one's favorite rights touted as absolute with others ignored; the rights-bearer imagined as radically autonomous and self-sufficient; the trivialization of core freedoms by special interests posing as new rights.[5]

Thus, ironically, the charge of cultural imperialism has more credibility than it had in 1948. The global spread of hyper-libertarian, radically individualistic, sound-bite rights ideas has rendered the contemporary international human rights project more vulnerable to the label of "Western" than the Declaration ever was. Launched as a commitment by the nations to compete in advancing human freedom and dignity, the Declaration is now in danger of becoming what its critics have always accused it of being – an instrument of neo-colonialism!

For decades, the seamlessness of the Declaration has been ignored by its professed supporters as well as by its attackers. By isolating each part from its place in the overall design, the now-common misreading of the Declaration promotes misunderstanding and facilitates misuse. Nations and interest groups ignore the provisions they find inconvenient and treat others as trumps. A major casualty has been the Declaration's insistence on the links between freedom and solidarity, just at a time when affluent nations seem increasingly to be washing their hands of poor countries and peoples.

For examples of deconstruction in operation, one could do no better than to eavesdrop on the rights babble of the big U.N. conferences of the 1990s. At first glance, the U.N. might seem to be an unlikely forum for the pursuit of law reform. But its agencies and conferences have attracted numerous special interest groups whose agendas have trouble passing muster in ordinary domestic political processes. Over the years, lobbyists of various sorts have acquired considerable influence in the U.N. bureaucracy, whose processes are even less transparent than those of U.S. administrative agencies.

Thus was the stage set for the U.N. and its conferences to become offshore manufacturing sites where the least popular (or least avowable) ideas of special interest groups could be converted into "international norms." These norms, though technically lacking the status of fundamental rights, could then be portrayed at home as universal standards, and imposed on poor countries as conditions for the receipt of aid.

At the U.N.'s 1995 Women's Conference in Beijing, for example, strenuous efforts were made to advance a new human rights paradigm – mainly by representatives from affluent countries. In her speech to a plenary session on the second day of the conference, U.S. First Lady Hillary Rodham Clinton gave high visibility to a misleading slogan. "If there is one message that echoes forth from this conference," she asserted, "it is that human rights are women's rights, and women's rights are human rights."[6] The statement was half true, but only half true. Human rights do belong to everyone. But not every right that has been granted to women by a particular nation-state has gained the status of a human right. The slogan was mainly aimed at universalizing extreme, American-style abortion rights in a world where few countries, if any, go as far as the United States and China in permitting abortions of healthy, viable unborn children.

That there might be some such demolition derby in the Declaration's future was foreseen long ago by Richard McKeon. McKeon realized what every lawyer knows: practical agreements such as those reached by the U.N. member states in 1948 are achieved only at the price of a certain ambiguity. The framers knew that the same generality that made agreement possible, rendered the document vulnerable to misunderstanding and manipulation. In his UNESCO report, McKeon pointed out that different understandings of the meanings of rights usually reflect divergent concepts of man and of society which in turn cause the persons who hold those understandings to have different views of reality. Thus, he predicted that "difficulties will be discovered in the suspicions, suggested by these differences, concerning the tangential uses that might be made of a declaration of human rights for the purpose of advancing special interests."[7] That was a philosopher's way of saying, "Watch out, this whole enterprise could be hijacked!"

In sum, the human rights project, launched as a multicultural commitment to compete in advancing freedom and dignity, is now in danger of becoming what its enemies and critics have always accused it of being – an instrument of "Western" cultural imperialism.

That irony did not escape the attention of Calcutta-born, Cambridge economist, Amartya Sen. In 1994, just before the U.N.'s Cairo Conference on Population and Development, Sen warned in the *New York Review of Books* that the developed nations were exhibiting a dangerous tendency to approach population issues with a mentality that "treats the people involved not as reasonable beings, allies faced with a common problem, but as impulsive and uncontrolled sources of great social harm, in need of strong discipline."[8] Sen, who won the Nobel Prize for his works on inequality and world hunger, charged that international policy makers, by giving priority to "family planning arrangements in the Third World countries over other commitments such as education and health care, produce negative effects on people's well-being and reduce their freedoms."[9] In short, the whole range of human rights of poor people is at risk when special interests are dressed up as universal rights.

The good news is that as the U.N. enters a period of austerity, the era of big conferences like Cairo and Beijing is probably drawing to a close. The bad news is that the same economic pressures that are putting a damper on huge international gatherings, however, may aggravate the danger of capture of U.N. agencies by well-financed special interests. A case in point is CNN founder Ted Turner's $1 billion "gift" to the U.N. announced in the fall of 1997. Many who look to the U.N. for leadership in humanitarian aid were overjoyed when Mr. Turner announced that his donation was to help "the poorest of the poor."[10] Paid out in installments of $100 million a year for ten years, this infusion of funds would have ranked behind the annual contributions of only the U.S., Japan, and Germany.

The news seemed too good to be true. It was. It soon appeared that the U.N. would not have control over the funds. Rather, its agencies would be required to submit proposals for approval by a foundation headed by a man Mr. Turner chose because "he thinks as I do."[11] The man designated to have the chief say in allocating the Turner millions is former U.S. State Department official Timothy Wirth, who spearheaded the aggressive U.S. population control agenda at the 1994 Cairo conference. Wirth has been so zealous in advocating population control that he has even praised China, with its coercive one-child-per-family policy, for its "very, very effective high-investment family planning."[12] As for Mr. Turner, he told a California audience in 1998 that in the post-Cold War world, "The real threat is no longer an army marching on us, it's people infiltrating us, you know, people that are starving."[13]

As its details have unfolded, Mr. Turner's gesture looks less like a gift and more like a take-over bid aimed at U.N. agencies with privileged access to vulnerable populations. The next few years are thus likely to be a time of testing for the U.N. if its prestige and organizational resources are not to be, literally, for sale.

As memories fade about why the nations of the world determined after World War II to affirm certain basic rights as universal, efforts to deconstruct the Universal Declaration and remake it nearer to the heart's desire of this or that special interest group will continue. Whether the relatively rich and complex vision of human rights in the Universal Declaration can withstand the combined stresses of aggressive lobbying, heightened national and ethnic assertiveness, and the powerful, ambiguous forces of globalization, is impossible to foresee. Not only U.N. agencies, but the governments of several liberal democracies have become implicated in breaking down the connections among its indivisible rights and deconstructing its core principle, human dignity.

The Challenge Of Human Rights

The contest for control of the meaning of the Declaration forcefully reminds us that the framers of the Universal Declaration left the human rights movement with a problem. As John Paul II put it in his Address to the Vatican Diplomatic Corps in January 1989, "[T]he 1948 Declaration does not contain the anthropological and moral bases for the human rights that it proclaims." How, then, can one handle the problem of reconciling tensions among the various rights, or the related problem of integrating new rights from time to time?

Those problems are serious, and have led some thoughtful persons to conclude that the Declaration is hopelessly incoherent. The late Michel Villey, for example, maintained that, "Each of the so-called human rights is the negation of other human rights, and when practiced separately generates *injustices*."[14] Alasdair MacIntyre argues that different rights, borrowed from different traditions, often rest on different, and incommensurable, moral premises.[15]

These problems were not overlooked by Maritain and his colleagues. Maritain noted that, "Where difficulties and arguments begin is in the determination of the scale of values governing the exercise and concrete integration of these various rights."[16] The Declaration, he went on, would need some "ultimate value whereon those rights depend and in terms of which they are integrated by mutual limitations." That value, explicitly set forth in the Declaration, is human dignity. But as time went on, it has become painfully apparent that dignity possesses no more immunity to hijacking than any other concept. One need only think of current defenses of active euthanasia in terms of "the right to die with dignity." (There is no end, it seems, of pseudo-rights that the stronger are eager to confer upon the weaker whether the latter are willing or not.)

The shift from nature to dignity in modern thinking about the foundations of human rights thus entails a host of difficulties. The common secular understandings are that human beings have dignity because they are autonomous beings capable of making choices (Kant), or because of the sense of empathy that most human beings feel for other sentient creatures (Rousseau). But the former understanding has alarming implications for persons of diminished capacity, and the latter places all morality on the fragile basis of a transient feeling. Most believers, for their part, would say that dignity is grounded in the fact that human beings are made in the image and likeness of God, but that proposition is unintelligible to nonbelievers.

Moreover, the path from dignity to rights is not clear and straight, even for believers. Brian Benestad has pointed out that the term "dignity of the human person" has two different connotations in Christian teaching – "[it] is *both* a given and an *achievement* or an end to be gradually realized."[17] The Catholic Catechism, he notes, begins its discussion of morality with this quotation from Pope Leo the Great: "Christian, recognize your dignity, and now that you share in God's own nature, do not return by sin to your former base condition." But if dignity is a quality to be achieved by strenuous effort to overcome sin and practice virtue, then it is not altogether clear that the dignity of the rights claimant is an adequate basis for human rights. Not every rights claimant, obviously, has made strenuous effort to overcome sin. From a Christian point of view, the resolution of this dilemma may be that human rights are grounded in the obligation of everyone to perfect one's own dignity which in turn obliges one to respect the "given" spark of dignity of others whatever they may have done with it. In other words, it may be our own quest for dignity (individually and as a society) that requires us to refrain from inflicting cruel punishments on criminals, or from terminating the lives of the unborn and others whose faculties are undeveloped or dormant.

In that light, the drafters of the U.N. Charter were prudent to say that human rights rest upon a "faith" in human dignity. It would be a mistake, however, to leap from that proposition to the notion that this faith is merely an act of will, an arbitrary choice. All in all, one may say of "dignity" in the Universal Declaration what Abraham Lincoln once said about "equality" in the Declaration of Independence: it is a hard nut to crack. The framers of the Universal Declaration were far from naive about the difficulties that lay ahead. That is evident from many statements in which they acknowledged the priority of culture over law. Though Maritain was not, strictly speaking, a framer, he said it best. Whether the music played on the Declaration's thirty strings will be "in tune with, or harmful to, human dignity," he wrote, will depend primarily on the extent to which a "culture of human dignity develops."[18]

If Maritain, Eleanor Roosevelt, Charles Malik, René Cassin and others who held this view were right, then a great challenge faces the world's religions, for religion is at the heart of culture. Ultimately it will be up to the religions to demonstrate whether they are capable of motivating their followers to fulfill their own calling to perfect their own dignity, and in so doing to respect the dignity of fellow members of the human family.[19]

Notes

1   Jacques Maritain, "Introduction" in *Human Rights: Comments and Interpretations*, UNESCO ed. (New York: Wingate, 1949), 16.

2   P. C. Chang's speech may be found in U.N. General Assembly, 182d Plenary Session, December 10, 1948, Summary Records, p. 895.

3   Philip Alston, "The Universal Declaration at 35," 60, 69.

4   See generally, Mary Ann Glendon, *Rights Talk: The Impoverishment of Political Discourse* (New York: Free Press, 1991) (especially Chapter 6); Anthony Lester, "The Overseas Trade in the American Bill of Rights," *Columbia Law Review* 88 (1988) 537.

5   See generally, Glendon, *Rights Talk*. On the need for care in accepting new rights, see Philip Alston, "Conjuring up New Rights: A Proposal for Quality Control," *American Journal of International Law* 78 (1984) 607.

6   Steven Mufson, "First Lady Critical of China, Others on Women's Rights," *Washington Post*, September 6, 1995, p. A1.

7   Richard McKeon, "The Philosophic Bases and Material Circumstances of the Rights of Man," in *Human Rights: Comments and Interpretations* (New York: Columbia University Press, 1949), 35, 36.

8   Amartya Sen, "Population: Delusion and Reality," *New York Review of Books*, September 22, 1994, 62.

9   Ibid., 71; see also, Reed Boland, "The Environment, Population, and Women's Human Rights," *Environmental Law* 27 (1997) 1137.

10   Betsy Pisik, "Gift Keeps on Giving," *Washington Times*, January 19, 1998, p. A1.

11   Barbara Crossette, "Turner Picks State Dept. Official to Allocate UN Fund," *International Herald Tribune*, November 21, 1997, 4; Colin Woodard, "Ted Turner Gift Poised to Boost UN," *Christian Science Monitor*, April 22, 1998, 1.

12   Quoted in Jeffrey Gedmin, "Clinton's Touchy-Feely Foreign Policy," *Weekly Standard*, May 13, 1996, 19, 22.

13   Ann Bardach, "Turner in 2000?," *New Yorker*, November 23, 1998, 36, 37.

14   Michel Villey, *Le droit et les droits de l'homme* (Paris: Presses Universitaires de France, 1983), 13.

15   Alasdair MacIntyre, *After Virtue*, 2d ed. (Notre Dame, Ind.: University of Notre Dame Press, 1981).

16   Jacques Maritain, "Introduction" in *Human Rights: Comments and Interpretations*, UNESCO ed. (London & New York: Wingate, 1949), 9, 15–16.

17   Brian Benestad, "What Do Catholics Know about Catholic Social Thought?" in *Festschrift for George Kelly* (Christendom Press, forthcoming).

18   Jacques Maritain, "Introduction" at 16.

19   Giorgio Filibeck, "Universal Religions and the Universality of Human Rights," Presentation at the Harvard Law School World Alumni Congress Panel on "Religion and Human Rights," held at the Islamic Center of Rome, Italy, June 11, 1998.

4.3.3 James V. Schall
"Human Rights as an
Ideological Project"

Voegelin [...] argued that the origin of ideology consisted in the combination of the classical sense of nature *and* the Judaeo-Christian concept of the content of this elevated nature. In *The Republic*, Socrates always had denied that the city that he was building could exist anywhere else but in speech. This, of course, need not, in itself, have meant anything more than that there was a natural incompleteness in the heart of finite reality, though this would seem to argue that nature did indeed produce something properly "in vain." What seemed to be required was a way to protect the finite order from any merely human effort to complete it, by its own means or powers, in a manner different from the end or intention that was already found intelligible in nature by the human intellect. All of this needed, further, to be argued within a tradition which, as Aristotle had held, admitted that man's actions in the polity were good and worthwhile, without being the highest ones that were open to man.

In the revelational tradition, this completion of what nature seemed to proffer but lack in terms of means to accomplish it was supplied by faith. Augustine was probably the best expositor of the notion of the "two cities," which was a direct response to the location of the Platonic city. Augustine indicated that the Platonic questions were, in fact, legitimate, but ultimately incapable of solution by political or other worldly or human means. However, as Voegelin also remarked, this same solution had the paradoxical result of almost encouraging alternate conceptions of ultimate explanation. The very tenuousness of faith seemed to encourage non-faith, more visible answers.[1] Yet, the ones who took up this endeavor most enthusiastically were almost always intellectuals who had been exposed to the vision but who had lost faith. Thus, there would be efforts to solve these problems by imposing solutions formulated theoretically from within the human intellect as such.

Voegelin's analysis of this approach is most insightful:

> In the first place, all ideology came out of the classic and Christian background (beginning with the Enlightenment) – so one element always is the survival of apocalypse, the idea that this present imperfect world is to be followed by a more perfect phase. A second element is gnostic, that is, knowledge of the recipe for bringing about a more perfect realm. (That is

James V. Schall, "Human Rights as an Ideological Project," *American Journal of Jurisprudence* 32 (1987), pp. 52–61. Reprinted with kind permission of the author.

gnostic: the recipe). Third, immanentization, as distinguished from older apocalypses. In the older apocalypse, the new realm … is brought about by the intervention of God. In modern immanentist ideologies, it is always brought about by human action.[2]

Thus, when I speak of human rights as an ideological project, I mean it in this sense, that the struggle over human rights is not a neutral one, but one that endeavors often to impose what is in effect a "man-made" view of man onto the public order with the promise, in the process, of locating its evils. This effort to eliminate evils involves replacing what the outline of man in the natural law tradition held to be most normative. What man "should be" is promised as a project of effecting human rights, as a feasible project, to be brought about by human means. The three notes which Voegelin saw in ideology are found in the newer human rights traditions, the complete improvement of the world by a formula derived from exclusively human speculation.

Why is this particular ideological struggle over, specifically, "human rights?" We have become used to the fact that the term "human rights," with its adjuncts, "social" and "economic" rights, has replaced the earlier term "natural right." Natural right was itself a term that had replaced the Christian and Roman notion of "natural law." And this in turn was a further reflection on the Greek concept of natural right. In context, these are by no means equivalent terms. Their differences need to be spelled out.

Alexander Passerin d'Entreves, in his book, *The Natural Law*, wrote:

> The modern theory of natural law was not, properly speaking, a theory of law at all. It was a theory of rights. A momentous change has taken place under the cover of the same verbal expressions. The *jus naturale* of the modern political philosopher is no longer the *lex naturalis* of the medieval moralist nor the *just naturale* of the Roman lawyer.[3]

The essence of this difference was most clearly manifested in Hobbes, but, as John Finnis pointed out, it was prepared for by the theories of Occam and Suarez, in their notion of law as command.

The idea of law as command, in essence, meant that right was not so much a norm of action but the power of acting as such. By shifting the meaning of law to right, the force of the idea was on a being endowed with "powers" or "rights," not on a being with intelligence, for whom right action depended on its prior discovery of an order it did not make. The human function in this latter sense was to create an order in which human "powers" or "rights" could be exercised. The latter notion presupposes the nature of man as a rational being; the former sees him as a mere source of action, presupposed only to himself, a source of action to do what he wills, with his "rights" unlimited except by other wills.

This is why, as Josef Pieper hinted, the "Leviathan" of Hobbes and the "Deity" of Occam were in a sense the same being – that is, a sovereign power whose act it was to do what it willed, with not even contradictions able to limit it.[4] "Right" became what is willed. In the classical view, the question could be at least posed whether what was willed was "right," because the standard was found in something already made. "To will" meant "to will something," not just "to will." But if right and will were identified, then the function of political philosophy in particular is merely to spell out how we can have what we will, not whether what we will is right to have or what it is we ought to have based on the reality of what we are and *what is*. Politics in the classical sense is a free endeavor to allow and encourage us to be what we ought to be, whereas in the modern sense, it was designed to allow us to be whatever it is we willed to be, wherein what we want to be is to have all our rights guaranteed to us at first by ourselves, then by society. The omnipotence of polity, then, could replace the omnipotence of God. Hobbes was perfectly logical.

Rights have had a peculiar way of undermining themselves. Bennett Cerf told the story of a crotchety old bachelor who heard of a parrot up at a local auction. He figured it would be good company for him, so he went to cast a bid for what he thought would be a cheap bird. However, the bidding was intense and the gentleman, caught in the action, found himself bidding, $100, then $125, then $175, then $250. At last, he got the parrot for $450 and took it home to have his first conversation with it. He tried a couple of lines, the usual "Polly want a cracker?" "What's your name?" but nothing worked. The bachelor grew increasingly exasperated and finally shouted, "My heavens, do you mean I spent $450 for this darn parrot, and it can't even talk?" At this, the parrot yelled back, "Can't even talk? Who the hell do you think it was that bid you up to $450?" Our sense of justice and right, in other words, comes back to haunt us if we do not have it straight.

What we are trying to understand here, then, is the intellectual structure of argument that enabled the notion of human rights to become autonomous and revolutionary against the meaning of man found in the classical natural law tradition. This led us to ask how natural law became natural right. Now we ask how natural right in turn divided itself into a positive and negative form, so that the question is not what it is our duty to do because of what we are, but what it is we are owed because of what we are.

In 1921, G. K. Chesterton visited the United States, after which tour, he wrote his *What I Saw in America*. He had many provocative things to say about this land, among which, I recall, was his observation that the United States was the last of the medieval monarchies, because it gives its king both honor and power, while limiting him with all sorts of representative institutions. But Chesterton also soberly judged that for this favored land, someday an "ultimate test" would come. This test, he thought, would be centered, at its roots, over the question of whether its democracy could remain itself without a faith to keep what its people wanted sane and healthy. But there was a dire side of this if this did not occur. Chesterton saw two likely alternatives. One would be a return to a sort of wage slavery, not unlike antiquity, while the other, and this is remarkable in the light of Voegelin, was that Americans would

> seek relief in theories that are destructive not merely in method but in aim; since they are but the negatives of human appetite for property and personality. … Men will more and more realize that there is no meaning in a democracy if there is no meaning in anything; and that there is no meaning in anything if the universe has not a center of significance and an authority that is the author of our rights.[5]

If we can assume that the great public issues are but the workings out of obscure philosophical battles fought out long ago, these are indeed almost prophetic words.

What are theories like that are destructive not merely in method but in aim? And what are these "negatives" of the human appetites for property and personality? A theory destructive in aim would be one that directly endeavored to replace or radically alter the being of man as he exists in history or nature because he is evil. And would not the negative of property be communal property and of personality some sort of group replacement of the unique individual with a transcendent destiny? This would presuppose a "theory" which had eliminated any "absolute natural law" which could guarantee the structure of man, body and soul. This would require a theory that would leave man malleable in principle. Such a metaphysics would leave open the being of man as intrinsically "aimless" so that he could be properly "formulated" into some being greater than that given to him in nature or revelation. He would, however, have to give this to himself.

The immediate background to this transformed possibility in early modern times, as Charles N. R. McCoy recognized, was Grotius and his famous affirmation that even if God did not exist, the natural law would be the natural law. "All the political philosophers of note will revive a theory of human nature and society whose cardinal principle is the autarky of human reason founded on an autonomous nature whose 'reasons' are perfectly accessible to human reason."[6] In the classical Thomist position, this was not the case. The being of man was itself ordered to his action, and among these actions, he was ordered to his highest ones, to an objective good which was not directly himself. Nature itself, though it revealed an order, did not yield the full destiny or meaning of particular men, since they were called beyond nature to the end of the universe itself.

This meant, then, in relation to Grotius and the sort of modern natural right which he founded, that a natural "law" presupposed to full comprehension by human reason became, in effect, a natural "right," which itself yielded no theoretic reason for being what it was, no "author" of its right. The autonomous reason and factual nature were thus theoretically left open to be radically altered so that the optimum configuration of nature would itself depend on a political will which conceived itself capable of determining *what man is*. This is the "revolutionary" source of modern natural right, the turn that Burke was sensitive to in his opposition to "the rights of man."

To natural right, natural law, natural rights, and human rights must be added the notion of divine law and civil law, with the transformation of the latter into the idea of "civil rights." The notion of civil law in Aquinas, for example, as the notion of divine law or revelation, meant a particular ordinance, over and above natural reasonableness, one posited or put into the world by God, the other by legitimate political authority acting properly. The civil or human law was held to be variable in its particulars but was required to exist for man's fullness as a social being. Thus, the civil order enabled man to be actually what he was only potentially, but with a potency man did not give himself. As Aristotle remarked, the polity allowed man to live well, not just to live or survive.

In the course of time, civil law and ecclesiastical law existed side by side as systems devoted to the same men but concerned with differing ends of the same human being. The doctrine that an unjust law was no law presupposed the fact that civil law or even positive ecclesiastical law were not justified merely by themselves. Were unjust laws precisely "laws?" Obviously, in the positivist sense, they were laws, since they had been put there by the proper authority following legitimate procedures. And what was to happen when these two conflicted? Who was to say? And what was to be done about it? One solution, of course, the modern Hobbesian or Rousseauian one, was to subsume all law, including natural and divine law, into the sovereign itself, so that there could be no conflict between law and duty. Everyone gives himself the law. The older solution, that of a Socrates, was to obey the positive law but in the act of obeying it, to affirm a higher law than that of the polity.

But by human rights as an ideological project, I mean something more ambitious. I mean this first of all as a logical aspect of the modern project of the full autonomy of man, not merely the Lockean idea of the state as the protector of my "rights" which I have from nature, but the state as the primary contractor not only to "protect" my civil rights – the problem of negative rights – but the state as the promoter and distributor of all that is good, but this in a world where the theoretic definition of good has no metaphysical content or stability.

In his review of Harold Berman's important book, *Law and Revolution: The Formation of the Western Legal Tradition*, Ellis Sandoz pointed out that for Berman, paradoxically, through the work of the medieval popes and canonists, "the Roman Catholic Church is transformed into the first true state and turns its attention for the first time to a concerted reform of the world, even as it continues the vocation of saving souls for eternity."[7] Berman went on to argue that the theological doctrines of purgatory and the Incarnation in particular were the ones which served to transform religious chiliasm into political expectations, a thesis that was elaborated by Carl Becker in his famous *Heavenly City of the Eighteenth Century Philosophers*.[8] Why I bring this up here is not only because, in the view of many contemporary critics, religion itself has lost its other-wordly orientation to become frequently an agent to implement the modern ideologies, but also because the immanentist project came to mean the political program of guaranteeing to everyone his full "human rights." This implied a completeness, in the innerworldly sense, one whose whole causality was due to man. Dante had held that the purpose of civilization was to actualize all the potential of the possible intellect. Stripped of its Averroistic overtones, this shifted the origin of man from some separate active intellect to the race as such as the cause or carrier of this wholeness.

Here, human rights did not mean the civil liberties against the state or others, but the guarantee that, since this is all there was, everyone would have everything he would have a "right" to. This would not include, of course, any destiny beyond man as such. The classical limits of politics arising from nature, finiteness, or evil, were to be confronted directly. Yet, the content of these new rights – moral, social, political, or economic – at several basic points was conceived to mean exactly the opposite of the natural law tradition. This meant implicitly the legal construction of the new man by the power of the state or public opinion resulted in a situation wherein rights equalled being, and rights were the product of power.

In his trenchant essay, *What Are Human Rights?*, Maurice Cranston sensed the nature of the problem:

> The traditional human rights are political and civil rights such as the right to life, liberty, and a fair trial. What are now being put forward as universal human rights are economic and social rights, such as the rights to unemployment insurance, old-age pensions, medical services, and holidays with pay....
>
> To speak of a universal right is to speak of a universal duty; to say that all men have a right to life is to impose on all men the duty of respecting human life, to put all men under the same prohibition against attacking, injuring, or endangering the life of any other human being. Indeed, if this universal duty were not imposed, what sense could be made of the concept of a universal right?
>
> The so-called economic and social rights, insofar as they are intelligible at all, impose no such universal duty. They are rights to be given things, things such as a decent income, schools, and social services. But who is called upon to do the giving?[9]

To this latter question, of course, there is an ideological answer – the state or society or mankind. What I have called the "all-caring state" thus can arise easily out of a theory of human rights, compassion, and concern. And this, in turn, is based on a revolutionary theory of property and personality which grounds the "giving" agent.[10]

Henry Veatch, in his penetrating study on human rights, took great care to attend to this difference between negative and positive rights. He was rightly concerned about the danger of positing some sort of "hyper-organism" which would be the distributor of such given rights in their essential formulations. Veatch saw here too another issue of great importance, that is, the protection of a higher area that is not defined by or covered wholly by a theory of rights. To put it another way with Aquinas, the world is not conceived ultimately in justice, even though there is a place for justice in the world. Veatch doubted the very existence of any so-called positive rights because rights in any defensible sense depend upon the autonomy, freedom, and will of each person to be and to develop what he already is from his being. We do not have to show ourselves that we "deserve" them. Positive rights ought to be considered rather a matter of policy, of results of choice, work, and enterprise.[11]

Veatch stated the problem in this way:

> ... Far from possessing positive rights to food, clothing, shelter, education, health care, a minimum wage, and so on – as if these things were owing to us as individuals and we had a right to have them handed to us on a silver salver – we are not. No, we are not initially entitled to these things because we are obligated to work for and to provide ourselves with them.[12]

Veatch refused to identify the existence of the needy with the demand that they be taken care of rather than encouraging all men to provide for themselves.[13] At issue, is the original being of each person to act to achieve his own good. This is the defense of personality as Chesterton understood it.

Ernest Fortin has written that "the prevailing view among Catholic scholars is that the modern rights doctrine is simply a perfected version of the old natural law doctrine."[14] Fortin was right to accept this position very cautiously, because he realized the problems connected with the evolution of the modern doctrine of natural and human rights in their various forms and justifications. Harry Jaffa also has noticed this problem:

> A government may not deliberate over whether it will act to secure the lives and liberties of those who have consented to be governed by it. It may only consider how best to do these things. Human rights ... define the ends of government, those things that cannot, as Aristotle says, be otherwise. ... What is wrong about placing desirable means among those things properly regarded as ends? ...
>
> To place vacations with pay, maternity leave, free medical care, permanent full employment, among human rights is therefore to remind mankind of its proper goal: the leap into freedom, at the end of history, after the Revolution. It is to remind mankind that its proper duty – the one duty whose fulfillment marks the end of all possible duties – is Revolution.[15]

Jaffa remarked that this utopian scheme, however dubious, attracts millions, even, he thinks, "great numbers – perhaps a majority – of the Christian Clergy."[16]

Maritain once wrote that the word "sovereignty" is so confusing, so ambiguous, that perhaps we should simply stop using it, since it can do nothing but cause mischief.[17] No doubt, one can similarly wonder about the term human or natural rights. Natural law and natural right may be, as d'Entreves indicated, simply equivocal terms, destined ever to confuse us. But the history of what has gone on under the aegis of these terms can be attended to, understood. What is perhaps more difficult to accept is the ease with which natural rights or human rights become revolutionary principles that undermine any existing polity, even the fairly tolerable, even the best. Here, equivocation only contributes to the problem. As Yves Simon indicated, a pursuit of the idea of equality, by itself, can easily lead to its opposite, to the Platonic project modernized, which ends up with the destruction of the family. Sobran, likewise, noticed how good will and compassion can lead to a similar result with regard to both our families and our property, the two things joined together in the central tradition.

The ideological project that can be found lurking earnestly under the name of human rights, then, is nothing less than the complete transformation of human reality itself as it has been understood from the beginning. That this latter remains much more "human" is the irony of the endeavor to find something more human by ourselves. Thus, the effort to take ideology seriously, to see its origins, is the reverse side of taking being seriously, of, to use Dworkin's phrase, taking rights seriously. The fine art of making poison pleasant, whether it be in the case of whisky or ideas, in the end, is not unrelated to the fine art of choosing our own poison. Ideologies, as Voegelin noted, are chosen, not necessitated. We can easily bid ourselves into them against our own selves when we do not know the natural law against which they define themselves. "*Est etiam necessaria creaturarum consideratio non solum ad veritatis instructionem, sed etiam ad errores excludendos*," Aquinas wrote in the *Contra Gentiles*. (**II, 3**) That is, when we know why "utopian unreality" can be embraced to transform the world, we can retain the world and ourselves. Natural law recognized the need for an author of rights which was not merely ourselves collectively considered. To the degree that human rights cannot recognize this, to that degree they will constantly lend themselves to ideological projects designed to transform our property and our personality, usually the latter by the former.

Notes

1   Eric Voegelin, *Science, Politics, and Gnosticism* (Chicago: Gateway, 1968), p. 109.
2   Voegelin, *Conversations, ibid.*, p. 26.
3   Alexander Passerin d'Entreves, *The Natural Law* (New York: Harper Torchbooks, 1965), p. 59.
4   Josef Pieper, *Scholasticism* (New York: McGraw-Hill), p. 147 ff.
5   G. K. Chesterton, *What I Saw in America, in As I Was Saying: A Chesterton Reader*, Edited by Robert Knille (Grand Rapids: Eerdmans, 1985), p. 40.
6   Charles N. R. McCoy, *The Structure of Political Thought* (New York: McGraw-Hill, 1963), p. 192.
7   Ellis Sandoz, Review of *Law and Revolution: The Formation of Western Legal Thought*, in 45 *Louisiana Law Review* (May, 1985), p. 1113.
8   Carl Becker, *The Heavenly City of the Eighteenth Century Philosophers* (New Haven: Yale, 1932).
9   Maurice Cranston, *What Are Human Rights?* (New York: Taplinger, 1973), pp. 65, 68–69. See also, Iredell Jenkins, *Social Order and the Limits of Law* (Princeton: Princeton University Press, 1980).

10   James V. Schall, "The All-Caring State," *Homiletic and Pastoral Review*, LXXXIII (January, 1983), pp. 25–29; "From *Compassion to Coercion*," *Vital Speeches*, XLVIII (July 15, 1983), pp. 594–99.

11   Veatch, Henry B. *Human Rights: Fact or Fancy?* Baton Rouge: Louisiana State U P, 1985.

12   Veatch, *ibid.*, p. 182.

13   *Ibid.*, pp. 182–83.

14   Ernest L. Fortin, "The New Rights Theory of Natural Law," 44 *Review of Politics* (October, 1982), p. 591.

15   Harry V. Jaffa, "Human Rights and the Crisis of the West," Paper Given at the Tocqueville Forum on Contemporary Public Affairs, Wake Forest University, February 4, 1982, pp. 20, 22.

16   *Ibid.*, p. 22.

17   Jacques Maritain, *Man and the State* (Chicago: University of Chicago Press, 1951), pp. 28–53.